Drugs in Palliative Care

Second Edition

Andrew Dickman MSc MRPharmS

Consultant Pharmacist – Palliative Care
Blackpool Teaching Hospitals NHS Foundation Trust
Whinney Heys Road
Blackpool
Lancashire
UK

and

Marie Curie Palliative Care Institute
Department of Molecular and Clinical Cancer Medicine
University of Liverpool
Cancer Research Centre
Liverpool
UK

OXFORD
UNIVERSITY PRESS

OXFORD
UNIVERSITY PRESS

Great Clarendon Street, Oxford OX2 6DP

Oxford University Press is a department of the University of Oxford.
It furthers the University's objective of excellence in research, scholarship,
and education by publishing worldwide. Oxford is a registered trade mark of
Oxford University Press in the UK and in certain other countries

© Andrew Dickman 2012

The moral rights of the author has been asserted

First Edition published in 2010
Second Edition published in 2012
ProStrakan Edition printed in 2012

Impression: 1

British Library Cataloguing in Publication Data
Data available

Library of Congress Cataloging in Publication Data
Data available

ISBN 978–0–19–967597–5

L.E.G.O. S.p.A.

Oxford University Press makes no representation, express or implied, that the
drug dosages in this book are correct. Readers must therefore always check
the product information and clinical procedures with the most up-to-date
published product information and data sheets provided by the manufacturers
and the most recent codes of conduct and safety regulations. The authors and
the publishers do not accept responsibility or legal liability for any errors in the
text or for the misuse or misapplication of material in this work. Except where
otherwise stated, drug dosages and recommendations are for the non-pregnant
adult who is not breast-feeding.

Some of the medication discussed in this book may not be available through normal
channels and only available by special arrangements. Other examples used in
research studies and recommended in international guidelines are unlicensed or
may be subject to being used outside of their licensed dosage ranges within the UK.
We suggest consulting the BNF and local prescribing guidelines/protocols before
using unfamiliar medication. Some brands are included in the drug monographs,
however these do not constitute recommendations and other brands may be
available. We regret any inconvenience to overseas readers.

Links to third party websites are provided by Oxford in good faith and for
information only. Oxford disclaims any responsibility for the materials contained in
any third party website referenced in this work.

Dedication

I would like to dedicate this book to my wife, Victoria,
for without her continued inexhaustible support,
this work would not have been possible.

Foreword

It is widely recognized that palliative care encompasses the physical, psychological, social, and spiritual needs of patients, together with support for their carers. Fundamental to this is good symptom control—if patients have uncontrolled symptoms then addressing the other domains of care is often unachievable.

The key elements to symptom control include assessment, diagnosis, and treatment. The treatment falls into pharmacological and non-pharmacological modalities. When pharmacological intervention is deemed necessary, the knowledge to choose the most suitable drug and the skill to prescribe appropriately is fundamental to good symptom control.

Drugs in Palliative Care aims to support healthcare professionals, including doctors, nurses, and pharmacists involved in the management of palliative care patients, by providing pertinent information in an easily accessible format about many of the medicines likely to be encountered. The first edition was highly commended at the BMA Book Awards in 2011. Building on this success, the newly revised second edition offers up-to-date information presented in a logical and comprehensive way, from basic clinical pharmacology through to succinct monographs. There is clear indexing to enable readers to access specific drugs and cross-referencing to other relevant areas.

This book has a place in everyday practice in palliative care, both for the specialist and also the generalist in supporting decision-making and prescribing for palliative care patients. It will enable the healthcare professional to make the most appropriate choice of drug at the right dose for the right symptom. Good palliative care is only as good as the healthcare professionals providing it. This book can function as an essential aide-mémoire and support to healthcare professionals in the provision of excellent palliative care for patients and their families.

John E Ellershaw MA FRCP
Professor of Palliative Medicine, University of Liverpool
Director, Marie Curie Palliative Care Institute Liverpool (MCPCIL)

Contents

Detailed contents

Symbols and abbreviations

☹	adverse effects
📖	cross-reference
📖	dose/dose adjustments
⟐	pharmacology
¥	unlicensed indication
5-HT	5-hydroxytryptamine (serotonin)
ACE	angiotensin-converting enzyme
ACEI	angiotensin-converting enzyme inhibitor
ADH	antidiuretic hormone
ALP	alkaline phosphatase
ALT	alanine transaminase
ALT DIE	every other day (*alternus die*)
AST	aspartate transaminase
AV	atrioventricular
BD	twice a day (*bis die*)
BP	blood pressure
BTcP	breakthrough cancer pain
Ca^{2+}	Calcium (ion)
CD1	controlled drug—Schedule 1
CD2	controlled drug—Schedule 2
CD3	controlled drug—Schedule 3
CD4a	controlled drug—Schedule 4 part 1
CD4b	controlled drug—Schedule 4 part 2
CD5	controlled drug—Schedule 5
CHF	congestive heart failure
CNS	central nervous system
COPD	chronic obstructive pulmonary disease
COX-1	cyclo-oxygenase-1
COX-2	cyclo-oxygenase-2
CrCl	creatinine clearance
CSCI	continuous subcutaneous infusion
CTZ	chemoreceptor trigger zone
CV	cardiovascular
CVA	cerebrovascular accident
DVT	deep vein thrombosis
e/c	enteric coated

eGFR	estimated glomerular filtration rate
g	gram(s)
G6PD	glucose 6-phosphate dehydrogenase
GFR	glomerular filtration rate
GGT	gamma glutamyl transpeptidase
GI	gastrointestinal
gp	glycoprotein
GSL	general sales list (medicine)
GTN	glyceryl trinitrate
H+	hydrogen (proton)
HPA	hypothalamic–pituitary–adrenal
IM	intramuscular
INR	international normalized ratio
IV	intravenous
K^+	potassium (ion)
L	litre(s)
LFT	liver function test(s)
LHRH	luteinizing hormone-releasing hormone
LMWH	low-molecular-weight heparin
m/r	modified release
MAOI	monoamine oxidase inhibitor
MHRA	Medicines and Healthcare products Regulatory Agency
mg	milligram(s)
Mg^{2+}	magnesium (ion)
micromol	micromole(s)
min	minute(s)
mL	millilitre(s)
mm	millimetre(s)
mmol	millimole(s)
Na^+	sodium (ion)
NaCl	sodium chloride
NG	nasogastric
NICE	National Institute for Health and Clinical Excellence
NRI	noradrenaline reuptake inhibitor
NRT	nicotine replacement therapy
NSAID	non-steroidal anti-inflammatory drug
NYHA	New York Heart Association
OD	daily (*omni die*)
OM	in the morning (*omni mane*)
ON	in the evening (*omni nocte*)

OTC	over-the-counter
P	pharmacy only (medicine)
PAH	polycyclic aromatic hydrocarbon
PDD	Parkinson's disease dementia
PE	pulmonary embolism
PM	poor metabolizer
PO	orally (*per os*)
POM	prescription-only medicine
PPI	proton pump inhibitor
PR	rectally (*per rectum*)
PRN	when necessary (*pro re nata*)
QDS	four times daily (*quarta die sumendus*)
SC	subcutaneously
SeCr	serum creatinine
SIADH	syndrome of inappropriate anti-diuretic hormone hypersecretion
SL	sublingually
SPC	Summary of Product Characteristics
s/r	standard release
SSRI	selective serotonin reuptake inhibitor
TCA	tricyclic antidepressant
TDS	three times daily (*ter die sumendus*)
U&Es	urea and electrolytes
UGT	uridine diphosphate glucuronosyltransferase
UM	ultrarapid metabolizer
UTI	urinary tract infection
VTE	venous thromboembolism
WFI	Water for Injections
WHO	World Health Organization

Chapter 1

Clinical pharmacology overview

Introduction

Interpatient variation is a substantial clinical problem when considering drug therapy. Examples of variation include failure to respond to treatment, increased incidence of undesirable effects, and increased susceptibility to drug interactions. The concept of 'one dose fits all' is clearly incorrect and is demonstrated by the unacceptable rate of hospital admissions caused by adverse drug reactions (~5% in the UK and ~7% in the US). This variation is hardly surprising, given all the factors that ultimately determine an individual's response to a drug (see Fig. 1.1).

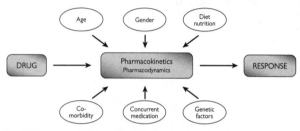

Fig. 1.1 Factors that influence an individual's response to drug therapy.

Pharmacokinetics

The rate and manner that a drug is absorbed, distributed, and eliminated is described by pharmacokinetics. In other words, *what the body does to the drug*.

Absorption

The bioavailability of a drug describes the proportion of a dose of a drug that enters the systemic circulation, e.g. for intravenous (IV) morphine this would be 100% compared to 15–65% for oral morphine.

For drugs taken orally that are intended for systemic action, a significant proportion of a given dose may not even enter the systemic circulation. This may be due to poor absorption from the gastrointestinal (GI) tract, or metabolism in the gut wall or liver (called first-pass metabolism—see Box 1.1).

Box 1.1 First-pass metabolism

First-pass metabolism is a term used to describe the metabolism that occurs between the gut lumen and the systemic circulation. It can reduce the bioavailability of a drug so much so that oral administration is not feasible. Although gastric secretions inactivate certain drugs (e.g. insulin), the main sites of first-pass metabolism are the gut wall and liver.

The cytochrome P450 isoenzyme CYP3A4 (see Box 1.3) is located in the gut wall and liver. It metabolizes many drugs and therefore alterations in CYP3A4 activity can significantly influence bioavailability. It is susceptible to inhibition and induction by a variety of drugs and foods. For example, one glass of grapefruit juice can cause significant inhibition of intestinal CYP3A4 while repeated consumption can interfere with hepatic CYP3A4. The majority of orally administered drugs must pass through the liver before entering the systemic circulation. Some drugs are susceptible to extensive first-pass metabolism such that only a small proportion of the oral dose enters the systemic circulation which renders oral administration impossible (e.g. lidocaine, fentanyl).

First-pass metabolism can be affected by disease, genetic influences, and enzyme inhibition or induction. This helps to explain the wide interpatient variation in drug absorption and hence bioavailability of several drugs (e.g. morphine 15–65%).

Several transporter proteins are present in the intestines which influence the absorption of drugs. P-glycoprotein (P-gp) is an efflux transporter molecule that can affect the bioavailability of many drugs (see Box 1.2). Less well categorized influx transporter proteins are also present and their activity may well be influenced by drugs and food.

Box 1.2 The P-glycoprotein (P-gp) drug transporter

P-gp is one of many protein transporters that can influence the bioavailability, distribution, and elimination of many drugs relevant to palliative care, e.g. P-gp is believed to be a major determinant of the bioavailability of morphine and tramadol. It is found in the GI tract, kidney, liver, and blood–brain barrier. There is wide patient variation because P-gp is genetically encoded and is subject to polymorphism (see 📖 Pharmacogenetics, p.11). Drug interactions can occur through induction or inhibition of P-gp, the clinical significance of which are just being realized.

Distribution

Many drugs, such as albumin, bind to plasma proteins. Bound drug is inactive; only unbound drug is available to bind to receptors or cross cell membranes.

Changes in protein binding can alter a drug's distribution, although this is rarely clinically important (with the exception of phenytoin).

P-gp is involved in the distribution of several drugs across the blood–brain barrier, e.g. P-gp limits the entry of morphine into the brain.

Elimination

Various processes are involved in drug elimination, although hepatic and renal processes are the most important.

Metabolism

The liver is the main organ of drug metabolism. There are generally two types of reaction (Phase I and Phase II) that have two important effects:
• Make the drug more water soluble—to aid excretion by the kidneys.
• Inactivate the drug—in most cases the metabolite is less active than the parent drug, although in some cases the metabolite can be as active, or more so, than the parent. Prodrugs are inactive until metabolized to the active drug (e.g. codeine is metabolized to morphine).

Phase I metabolism involves oxidation, reduction, or hydrolysis reactions. Oxidation reactions are most common and are catalysed by cytochrome P450 isoenzymes (see Box 1.3) located primarily in the liver. The main exception is CYP3A4, which is also located in the GI tract (see 📖 Absorption, p.3).

Phase II metabolism involves conjugation reactions, such as glucuronidation or sulphation, which produce more water-soluble compounds, enabling rapid elimination.

Many drugs are dependent on cytochrome P450 isoenzymes (see 📖 inside back cover) for metabolism and/or elimination. Genetic variations or co-administration of inducers or inhibitors can lead to the development of significant toxicity or lack of effect.

Drug excretion

The main route of excretion of drugs is the kidney. Renal elimination is dependent on multiple factors that include:

- Glomerular filtration rate (GFR)
- Active tubular secretion (may involve P-gp)
- Passive tubular secretion.

If a drug is metabolized to mainly inactive compounds (e.g. fentanyl), renal function will not greatly affect the elimination. If, however, the drug is excreted unchanged (e.g. pregabalin), or an active metabolite is excreted via the kidney (e.g. morphine), changes in renal function will influence the elimination. Dose adjustments may be necessary.

Box 1.3 The cytochrome P450 system

The cytochrome P450 system consists of a large group of >500 isoenzymes that are involved in the metabolism of endogenous (e.g. steroids, eicosanoids) and exogenous (e.g. drugs) compounds. They are grouped according to amino acid sequence; a family is defined by >40% homology and a subfamily is defined by >55% homology. Five subfamilies, CYP1A, CYP2C, CYP2D, CYP2E, and CYP3A have a major role in hepatic drug metabolism, with others having a lesser role. The following list briefly describes the isoenzymes involved. Also see 📖 inside back cover for a list of important substrates, inducers, and inhibitors.

CYP1A subfamily

- CYP1A1: mainly found in lungs and metabolizes tobacco to potentially carcinogenic substances.
- CYP1A2: responsible for metabolism of ~15% of drugs; is induced by tobacco smoke. Also involved in activation of procarcinogens. Polymorphisms exist, but distribution remains undetermined. Important substrates include olanzapine and theophylline.

CYP2A subfamily

- CYP2A6: metabolizes small number of drugs including nicotine and the prodrug tegafur. Also metabolizes tobacco to potentially carcinogenic substances. Polymorphisms exist, with 1% of the Caucasian population being poor metabolizers (PMs).

CYP2B subfamily

- CYP2B6: involved in the metabolism of an increasing number of drugs including ketamine and methadone. Clopidogrel is a potentially potent inhibitor, while rifampicin induces this isoenzyme. Polymorphisms exist, but distribution and consequence remain undetermined.

CYP2C subfamily

- CYP2C8: a major hepatic cytochrome and shares substrates with CYP2C9. Polymorphisms exist, but distribution and consequence remain undetermined.

Box 1.3 (cont.)

- CYP2C9: the most important of the CYP2C subfamily. Responsible for the metabolism of many drugs, including warfarin, celecoxib, ibuprofen, diclofenac, and phenytoin. Is inhibited by several drugs including fluconazole; rifampicin induces activity of CYP2C9. Polymorphisms exist; 1–3% of Caucasians have reduced activity and are poor PMs.
- CYP2C19: involved in the metabolism of several drugs, including omeprazole, lansoprazole, diazepam, and citalopram. Inhibitors include modafinil, omeprazole, and fluoxetine. Carbamazepine can induce this isoenzyme. 3–5% of Caucasians lack the enzyme and are PMs.

CYP2D subfamily

- CYP2D6: no known inducer. Responsible for the metabolism of ~25% of drugs, including codeine, tramadol, and tamoxifen. 5–10% of Caucasians lack this enzyme and are termed PMs; 1–5% have multiple copies of the gene and are termed ultrarapid metabolizers (UMs).

CYP2E subfamily

- CYP2E1: has a minor role in drug metabolism. Main importance is paracetamol metabolism and potential toxicity. Polymorphisms exist, but distribution and consequence remain undetermined.

CYP3A subfamily

This subfamily is the most abundant in the liver and is responsible for the metabolism of >50% of drugs, including midazolam and alfentanil. There are 4 CYP3A genes, although only 2 are likely to be of importance in human adults. Nonetheless, these isoenzymes are so closely related that they are often referred to collectively as CYP3A. Polymorphisms exist, but distribution and consequence remain undetermined.

- CYP3A4: most significant isoenzyme involved in drug metabolism and is frequently implicated in drug interactions. It is located mainly in the liver, but significant amounts are present in the GI tract, where it has an important role in first-pass metabolism. There are several inducers (e.g. carbamazepine, rifampicin) and inhibitors (e.g. clarithromycin, grapefruit juice).
- CYP3A5: similar substrate spectrum to CYP3A4, but is possibly less efficient, so is unlikely to have such a dramatic effect on drug metabolism.

Pharmacodynamics

The effect of the drug and how it works in terms of its interaction with a receptor or site of action is described by pharmacodynamics. In other words, *what the drug does to the body*.

Most drugs act upon proteins:

- Receptor (e.g. morphine and μ-opioid receptor)
- Ion channel (e.g. lidocaine and Na^+ channel; capsaicin and TRPV1)
- Enzyme (e.g. non-steroidal anti-inflammatory drug (NSAID) and cyclo-oxygenase)
- Transporter complex (e.g. SSRI0).

The exceptions include antibiotics, cytotoxic drugs, and immunosuppressants. The term 'receptor' is used loosely to describe the earlier listed protein targets.

- *Agonists* bind to and activate receptors to produce an effect.
- *Antagonists* also bind to receptors without causing activation. They may prevent the action of, or displace, an agonist.
- *Partial agonists* activate receptors to a limited extent, but may also interfere with the action of the full agonist. The circumstances in which a partial agonist may act as an antagonist or an agonist depends on both the efficacy (see later in list) of the drug and the pre-existing state of receptor occupation by an agonist, e.g. buprenorphine will generally act as an antagonist if a patient is using excessive doses of morphine. At lower doses of morphine, buprenorphine will act as an agonist.
- *Affinity* is a term used to describe the tendency of a drug to bind to its receptors, e.g. naloxone has higher affinity for opioid receptors than morphine, hence its use in opioid toxicity.
- The *intrinsic activity* of a drug describes its ability to elicit an effect.
- *Efficacy* refers to the potential maximum activation of a receptor and therefore desired response i.e. a full agonist has high efficacy, a partial agonist has medium efficacy, and an antagonist has zero efficacy.
- *Potency* refers to the amount of drug necessary to produce an effect, e.g. fentanyl is more potent than morphine since the same analgesic effect occurs at much lower doses (micrograms vs. milligrams).
- Very few drugs are specific for a particular receptor or site of action and most display a degree of *relative selectivity*. Selectivity refers to the degree by which a drug binds to a receptor relative to other receptors. In general, as doses increase, the relative selectivity reduces such that other pharmacological actions may occur, often manifesting as undesirable effects, e.g. meloxicam at doses of 7.5mg/day is selective for COX-2, but at higher doses it loses this selectivity and also binds to COX-1.
- *Tolerance* is the decrease in therapeutic effect that may occur, over a period of time, by identical doses of a drug. Although often expected, this has yet to be conclusively identified for opioid analgesia
- *Tachyphylaxis* is the rapid development of tolerance. It can occur with salcatonin (calcitonin), leading to a rebound hypercalcaemia.

- *Therapeutic index or margin* is the ratio between the dose producing undesired effects and the dose producing therapeutic effects. Drugs with narrow therapeutic margins are often implicated in drug interactions.
- *Competitive antagonism* describes the situation that occurs when an antagonist competes with the agonist for the binding site of receptors. In such a situation, increasing the concentration of the agonist will favour agonist binding (and vice versa).
- *Irreversible competitive antagonism* can occur when the antagonist disassociates very slowly, or not at all, from receptors. Increasing the dose of the agonist does not reverse the situation.
- *Non-competitive antagonism* occurs when the antagonist blocks the effects of the agonist by interaction at some point other than the receptor binding site of the agonist.

Effect of hepatic impairment

Impaired liver function can affect the pharmacokinetics and pharmacodynamics of many drugs. Reduction in hepatic blood flow and a potential fall in the number and the activity of hepatocytes can alter liver function and impact on drug clearance. A reduced synthesis of albumin can result in reduced drug–protein binding thereby affecting the volume of distribution. Cholestasis can affect the biliary excretion of drugs and metabolites. Patients with impaired hepatic function may also develop a degree of renal impairment due to decreased renal plasma flow and GFR. Use of the Cockcroft and Gault equation (see Box 1.4) can overestimate renal function due to a reduced synthesis of creatinine.

Unlike impaired renal function, there is no simple test that can determine the impact of liver disease on drug handling. A combination of factors needs to be considered before such impact can be assessed, which include liver function tests (LFTs), diagnosis, and physical symptoms.

In general, the metabolism of drugs is unlikely to be affected unless the patient has severe liver disease. Most problems are seen in patients with jaundice, ascites, and hepatic encephalopathy. As such, doses of drugs should be reviewed in the following situations:
- Hepatically metabolized drug with narrow therapeutic index.
- Renally excreted drug with narrow therapeutic index.
- There is a significant involvement of the cytochrome P450 system (CYP3A4/5 is highly susceptible to liver disease, while CYP2D6 appears relatively refractory).
- International normalized ratio (INR) >1.2.
- Bilirubin >100micromol/L.
- Albumin <30g/L.
- Signs of ascites and/or encephalopathy.

Where possible, dosage amendments will be discussed in each monograph.

Effect of renal impairment

The elimination of many drugs and metabolites is dependent upon renal function. Impaired renal function, coupled with rising urea plasma concentrations, induces changes in drug pharmacokinetics and pharmacodynamics. Implications for drug therapy include:

- Increased risk of undesirable effects and toxicity through reduced excretion of the drug and/or metabolite(s), e.g. pregabalin, morphine.
- Increased sensitivity to drug effects, irrespective of route of elimination, e.g. antipsychotics.
- Increased risk of further renal impairment, e.g. NSAIDs.

Many of these problems can be avoided by simple adjustment of daily dose or frequency of administration. In other situations, however, an alternative drug may need to be chosen. It is worth noting that patients with end-stage renal disease may be at risk of increased drug toxicity due to the reduced activity of CYP3A4/5 and CYP2D6.

Estimating renal function

Unlike liver impairment, the impact of declining renal function is quantifiable. Accurate methods of determining renal function, or GFR are unsuitable for routine clinical use. *Serum creatinine* (creatinine is a product of muscle metabolism) has been used as a simple tool to estimate GFR. However, there are serious limitations to this approach:

- As renal function deteriorates, serum creatinine increases. However, many patients may have reduced GFR but serum creatinine concentrations fall inside the conventional laboratory normal ranges, e.g. an increase from 50micromol/L to 100micromol/L is still within normal limits, even though renal function has clearly deteriorated.
- Renal function declines with age, but serum creatinine generally remains stable. Thus a 75-year-old may have the same serum creatinine as a 25-year-old, despite having a reduced renal function.

Creatinine clearance serves as a surrogate for GFR. It can be determined from the Cockcroft and Gault equation (see Box 1.4), which takes weight, age, gender, and serum creatinine into consideration. The majority of dosage adjustment guidelines in the monographs are based upon creatinine clearance. There are limitations, however, with this method as it may report inaccurately for obese and underweight patients.

Box 1.4 Cockcroft and Gault equation for calculating creatinine clearance

CrCl = ([140−'age'] × ['weight (kg)'] × F)/(SeCr ('micromol/L'))

Where F = 1.23 (male)

1.04 (female)

In the UK, renal function is increasingly being reported in terms of *estimated GFR* (eGFR), normalized to a body surface area of 1.73m². The formula used to calculate eGFR was derived from the Modification of Diet in Renal Disease (MDRD) study. eGFR assumes the patient is of average size (assumes an average body surface area of 1.73m²), allowing a figure to be determined using only serum creatinine, age, gender, and ethnic origin. It is primarily a tool for determining renal function, of which 5 categories have been described (see Table 1.1).

eGFR is only an estimate of the GFR and has not been validated for use in the following groups or clinical scenarios:
- Children (<18 years of age)
- Acute renal failure
- Pregnancy
- Oedematous states
- Muscle wasting disease states
- Amputees
- Malnourished patients.

Table 1.1 Stages of renal failure

Stage	eGFR (mL/min/1.73m²)
1 Normal GFR[a]	>90
2 Mild impairment[a]	60–89
3 Moderate impairment	30–59
4 Severe impairment	15–29
5 Established renal failure	<15

[a] The terms stage 1 and stage 2 chronic kidney disease are only applied when there are structural or functional abnormalities. If there are no such abnormalities, an eGFR ≥60 mL/min/1.73m² is regarded as normal.

While eGFR may be used to determine dosage adjustments in place of creatinine clearance for most drugs in patients of average build, application in palliative care patients may produce erroneous results. For example, the eGFR may underestimate the degree of renal impairment in cachectic or oedematous patients resulting in excessive doses. For palliative care patients, providing height and weight are known, it would be prudent to calculate the *absolute GFR* (GFR$_{ABS}$) (see Box 1.5) and use this to determine dosage adjustments.

Box 1.5 Calculating absolute GFR (GFR$_{ABS}$) and body surface area (BSA)

$$GFR_{ABS} = eGFR \times \frac{BSA}{1.73}$$

$$BSA = \sqrt{\frac{(height\ (cm) \times weight\ (kg))}{3600}}$$

Pharmacogenetics

If it were not for the great variability among individuals, medicine might as well be a science and not an art.

Sir William Osler, 1892

Just over 50 years ago, two adverse drug reactions were described as being caused by genetic mechanisms. G6PD deficiency and pseudo-cholinesterase deficiency were shown to be manifestations of specific gene mutations. Two years later, in 1959, the term 'pharmacogenetics' was introduced. It was only towards the end of the last century that significant advances were made. As a result of the Human Genome Project, a broader term, 'pharmacogenomics', was introduced (see Box 1.6).

Box 1.6 Basic genetic concepts

The human genome consists of 23 pairs of chromosomes (or 22 pairs of *autosomes* and 1 pair of sex-linked chromosomes) within which are sequences of DNA that are referred to as *genes*. With the exception of the sex-linked X- and Y-chromosomes, an individual inherits 2 copies of each gene, 1 from each parent. A gene can exist in various forms, or *alleles*. Only 3% of the human genome encodes proteins.

An individual's inherited genetic profile, or *genotype*, may be described as being:

- Homozygous dominant (i.e. a specific gene consists of 2 identical dominant alleles).
- Heterozygous (i.e. a specific gene consists of 2 different alleles, 1 usually being dominant, the other recessive).
- Homozygous recessive (i.e. a specific gene consists of 2 identical recessive alleles).

An individual's *phenotype* describes the observable characteristics that are a result of the genotype and environment. Particular inherited phenotypical traits may be described as being *autosomal dominant* or *recessive*.

Pharmacogenetics is the study of how variation in an individual gene affects the response to drugs which can lead to adverse drug reactions, drug toxicity, therapeutic failure, and drug interactions.

Pharmacogenomics is the study of how variation in the human genome can be used in the development of pharmaceuticals.

Polymorphisms refer to commonly occurring genetic variants (i.e. differences in DNA sequences). In most regions of the genome, a polymorphism is of little clinical consequence. However, a polymorphism in a critical coding or non-coding region can lead to altered protein synthesis with clinical implications such as abnormal drug responses.

Genetic variability can affect an individual's response to drug treatment by influencing pharmacokinetic and pharmacodynamic processes, e.g. variations in genes that encode cytochrome P450 isoenzymes, drug receptors, or transport proteins can determine clinical response. Pharmacogenetics can aid in the optimization of drug therapy through the identification of individuals who are likely to respond to treatment, or those who are most likely at risk of an adverse drug reaction. Although the exact proportion of adverse drug reactions caused by genetic variability is unclear, emerging evidence suggests an increasing role. Pharmacogenetic testing is currently in early development, but current examples include:

- The need for human epidermal growth factor 2 (HER2) testing before initiating trastuzumab (Herceptin®) therapy.
- Genetic testing of Han Chinese is recommended for patients before commencing carbamazepine therapy due to an association between toxic skin reactions and a specific genotype.

Pharmacogenetic testing has the potential to improve the safety and efficacy of several drugs commonly encountered in palliative care, e.g. analgesics, antidepressants, and antipsychotics.

Genetic influences on pharmacokinetics

Variations in genes that encode transport proteins have been implicated in altered therapeutic response, e.g. P-gp polymorphisms have been associated with altered morphine analgesia. However, the characterization and implications of transporter protein variations are less developed when compared to drug metabolism. There is no doubt that polymorphism of metabolic enzymes has a great effect on interpatient variability.

Several polymorphisms that affect drug metabolism have been identified and there is substantial ethnic variation in distribution. Functional changes as a result of a polymorphism can have profound effects:

- Adverse drug reaction
- Toxicity
- Lack of effect
- Drug interaction.

The isoenzymes CYP2C9, CYP2C19, and CYP2D6 are responsible for ~40% of cytochrome P450-mediated drug metabolism. They display high levels of polymorphism which have been shown to affect the response of individuals to many drugs (see Box 1.7). Pharmaceutical manufacturers have realized the importance of pharmacogenetics; fewer drugs will be developed that are affected by pharmacogenetic factors because potential agents will be discarded at an early stage of development.

Box 1.7 Examples of the effect P450 polymorphisms have on selected drugs

Analgesia
- Codeine: needs to be metabolized by CYP2D6 to morphine before analgesia is observed. PMs derive no analgesia from codeine. Drugs that inhibit CYP2D6 will mimic the PM phenotype. UMs are at risk of life-threatening adverse drug reactions as codeine is metabolized at a very high rate.

Box 1.7 (cont.)

- Methadone: shows complex pharmacology. Mainly metabolized by CYP3A, but CYP2B6 and CYP2D6 are also involved. PMs of CYP2B6 and CYP2D6 are at risk of developing toxicity if methadone is titrated too quickly.
- NSAIDs: is a suggestion that specific CYP2C8/9 genotypes can cause increased risk of toxicity to NSAIDs.
- Tamoxifen: the active metabolite, endoxifen, is produced by a reaction involving CYP2D6. Patients with a PM phenotype are at risk of therapeutic failure with tamoxifen. Drugs that inhibit CYP2D6 will also mimic the PM phenotype and should be avoided.
- Theophylline: the metabolism of theophylline is highly dependent on CYP1A2 activity, which varies with specific genotypes.
- Tramadol: is primarily metabolized by CYP2D6 to an active compound, M1, which is a more potent opioid agonist. PMs show a poor response to tramadol. As with codeine, drugs that inhibit CYP2D6 can mimic the PM phenotype.

Genetic polymorphisms of cytochrome P450 isoenzymes (see 📖 Box 1.3, p.5) can be divided into 4 phenotypes:
- *Poor metabolizers* (PM) have 2 non-functional alleles and cannot metabolize substrates.
- *Intermediate metabolizers* (IM) have 1 non-functional allele and 1 low-activity allele, so metabolize substrates at a low rate.
- *Extensive metabolizers* (EM) have 1 or 2 copies of a functional allele and metabolize substrates at a normal rate.
- *Ultrarapid metabolizers* (UM) have 3 or more copies of a functional allele and metabolize substrates at an accelerated rate.

The consequences of a particular phenotype depend upon the activity of the drug. PMs are at an increased risk of therapeutic failure (through poor metabolism to an active compound) or undesirable effects (due to excessive dose). In contrast, UMs are at increased risk of therapeutic failure with conventional doses due to excessive metabolism; in the case of a prodrug, rapid production of the active compound could lead to toxicity. For example, a patient with UM phenotype for CYP2D6 may rapidly convert codeine to morphine, increasing the risk of developing toxicity; a patient with PM status for CYP2D6 will derive little, if any analgesic benefit from codeine.

Genetic influences on pharmacodynamics

Genetic polymorphisms of drug receptors, or disease-related pathways, can influence the pharmacodynamic action of drug. These are generally less well categorized than pharmacokinetic consequences. Nonetheless, genetic variations have been shown to be clinically relevant for morphine analgesia and antidepressant therapy. In the latter case, associations between serotonin transport gene polymorphisms and depression have been demonstrated. It has also been shown that genotyping for polymorphisms of certain serotonin or noradrenaline pathways can inform clinical choice of antidepressant, e.g. a patient that fails to respond to citalopram (selective serotonin reuptake inhibitor (SSRI)) could in fact respond to reboxetine (noradrenaline reuptake inhibitor (NRI)).

Drug interactions

Be alert to the fact that all drugs taken by patients, including over-the-counter medicines, herbal products, and nutritional supplements, have the potential to cause clinically relevant drug interactions. The patient's diet can also affect drug disposition.

The pharmacological actions of a drug can be enhanced or diminished by other drugs, food, herbal products, and nutritional supplements. Clinically relevant and potentially significant drug–drug interactions are included in the monographs.

In terms of a drug–drug interaction, the actions of the *object* drug are altered by the *precipitant* in most cases. Occasionally, the actions of both object and precipitant can be affected.

While it is possible to predict the likelihood of a drug interaction, it is often difficult to predict the clinical relevance. Elderly patients or those with impaired renal and/or hepatic function are more at risk. Drug interactions may be overlooked and explained as poor compliance, or even progressive disease. Knowledge of drug interaction processes can aid in the diagnosis of unexplained or unexpected response to drug therapy.

It is impossible to accurately determine the incidence of drug interactions. Knowledge of many drug–drug interactions comes from isolated case reports and/or small studies in healthy volunteers. It is, however, possible to indirectly assess a patient's risk; there are several factors that predispose patients receiving palliative care to a drug interaction (see Box 1.8).

Box 1.8 Factors that predispose a patient to drug interactions

- Advancing age
- Multiple medications
- Compromised renal/hepatic function
- More than one prescriber
- Comorbidity.

While the majority of risks cannot be reduced, they can be anticipated and managed. For example, a thorough medication history should be taken upon presentation and must include over-the-counter medications, herbal products, or nutritional supplements. In some cases, changes to diet should be enquired about, e.g. the effect of warfarin can be reduced by a diet suddenly rich in leafy, green vegetables (a source of vitamin K).

As part of the multidisciplinary team, the pharmacist is an excellent source of information and is often involved in the recording of drug histories.

There are 2 main mechanisms involved in drug interactions:
- Pharmacokinetic
- Pharmacodynamic.

Pharmacokinetic

The precipitant drug alters the absorption, distribution, metabolism, or excretion of the object drug. Pharmacokinetic drug interactions are likely to be encountered in palliative care since many of the drugs used are substrates or inducers/inhibitors of cytochrome P450 isoenzymes (see 📖 Metabolism, p.4). These interactions are often difficult to predict.

Absorption

> CYP3A4, mainly found in the liver, is also present in the gut wall. It is involved in reducing the absorption of many drugs and is subject to both induction and inhibition (see 📖 Metabolism, p.4). Grapefruit juice inhibits the action of CYP3A4 in the bowel (and liver with repeated consumption) and can lead to significant increases in bioavailability of several drugs, e.g. ciclosporin, diazepam, sertraline, simvastatin. This interaction is highly variable since the active component of the juice cannot be standardized. This interaction can occur even after consuming just 200mL of grapefruit juice and inhibition can persist for up to 72 hours. An interaction may occur, whatever the source, e.g. fresh grapefruit and grapefruit juices including fresh, frozen, or diluted from concentrate. Drugs with a narrow therapeutic index are more likely to be affected.

The rate of absorption or amount of object drug absorbed can be altered by the precipitant. Delayed absorption is rarely of clinical relevance unless the effect of the object drug depends upon high peak plasma concentrations (e.g. the effect of paracetamol can be enhanced by combination with metoclopramide). If the amount of drug absorbed is affected, clinically relevant effects can occur.

Absorption interactions involving simple insoluble complex formation can be easily avoided by changing the administration time of the drugs involved, e.g. ciprofloxacin and antacids.

Some interactions involve the induction or inhibition of P-gp (see 📖 Box 1.2, p.4), although the clinical significance of many such interactions remains unclear. Enhanced activity of P-gp will reduce the absorption and bioavailability of a drug. The effect of drugs and food on influx transporters is currently less well categorized but could well contribute to unexplained and unanticipated drug effects.

Distribution

Such interactions are usually of little clinical relevance and often involve alterations in protein binding.

The distribution of some drugs is dependent on the activity of P-gp, which also appears to act as a component of the blood–brain barrier, e.g. P-gp can limit the entry of hydrophilic opioids into the brain. The clinical significance of induction or inhibition of P-gp is unclear.

Metabolism

Many drugs are metabolized via the hepatic cytochrome P450 system (see 📖 Box 1.3, p.5) which is subject to both inhibition and induction.

CYP3A4 may account for up the metabolism of up to 50% of currently used drugs; CYP2D6 may account for up to 25% (see 📖 inside back cover). The effect that smoking can have on drug therapy should not be overlooked (see Box 1.9).

Box 1.9 Smoking and potential drug interactions

- Tobacco smoke contains several polycyclic aromatic hydrocarbons (PAHs) that are potent inducers of CYP1A1, CYP1A2, and, to a lesser extent, CYP2E1. PAHs can also induce glucuronide conjugation.
- Induction of CYP1A1 in the lungs causes activation of pro-carcinogens from tobacco smoke and is believed to be a major mechanism in the development of lung cancer.
- Although CYP1A1 is not important for drug metabolism, several drugs are substrates of CYP1A2 (see 📖 inside back cover). Metabolism of these drugs can be induced by tobacco smoke, potentially resulting in increased clearance of the drug and consequent clinically significant reductions in effects. Smokers may require higher doses of these drugs.
- Note that exposure to 'second-hand' smoke can produce similar effects.
- The PAHs cause these pharmacokinetic drug interactions, not the nicotine. Thus, nicotine replacement therapy (NRT) will not cause these effects.
- Tobacco smoke and NRT are both implicated in several pharmacodynamic drug interactions. Nicotine can have an alerting effect, thereby countering the action of other drugs.
- The prescriber should consider a dosage reduction of drugs metabolized by CYP1A2 if a patient stops smoking. Similarly, doses of anxiolytics and hypnotics should be reviewed, unless NRT is initiated. If a patient starts smoking, doses of drugs metabolized by CYP1A2 may need increasing whereas doses of anxiolytics and hypnotics may need reviewing.

- Enzyme inhibition is the mechanism most often responsible for life-threatening interactions. It can also result in reduced drug effect where activation of a prodrug is required (e.g. codeine has a reduced analgesic profile when administered with CYP2D6 inhibitors). Inhibition is generally caused by competitive binding for the isoenzyme between object and precipitant. It follows that high doses of the precipitant will cause a greater degree of inhibition. Clinically relevant interactions can be evident within 2 days. The effect of enzyme inhibition generally depends upon the half-life of the precipitating drug and the therapeutic index of the object drug. The effect will decrease as blood levels fall. Note that drugs competing for the same isoenzyme can give rise to competitive inhibition. The more drugs that are co-prescribed, the greater the risk of this occurring.

- Induction can occur when the precipitant stimulates the synthesis of more isoenzyme, increasing metabolic capacity. It can take several days or even weeks to develop and may persist for a similar duration once the precipitant has been withdrawn. Problems with toxicity can occur if doses of the object drug are increased but are not reduced once the precipitant is stopped.
- Many drugs are not always metabolized by one specific pathway and for this reason it is often difficult to precisely predict the outcome of a drug interaction. Nonetheless, although *in vivo* data may not be available for many drugs, *in vitro* evidence of metabolism and specific cytochrome P450 isoenzyme involvement can be used to anticipate and avoid a potentially dangerous drug interaction. The drug monographs (see 📖 Chapter 3) mention actual and potential drug interactions.

Elimination

In palliative care, it is likely that the most common and potentially more clinically relevant elimination drug interactions will involve renal function. For example, with advancing age, renal function declines but compensatory mechanisms are activated that involve the production of vasodilatory prostaglandins. NSAIDs can significantly impair this compensatory measure, such that there is a marked reduction in renal function and consequential risk of drug interactions.

Pharmacodynamic

The pharmacological actions of the object drug are changed by the presence of the precipitant. Pharmacodynamic interactions can be additive or antagonistic in nature.

Additive

When 2 or more drugs with similar pharmacodynamic effects are co-prescribed, the additive results may result in exaggerated response or toxicity. Additive responses can occur with the main therapeutic action of the drug as well as the undesirable effects, e.g. SSRI plus tramadol may give rise to the serotonin syndrome (see Box 1.10).

Antagonistic

When 2 drugs with opposing pharmacodynamic effects are co-prescribed, there may be a net reduction in response to 1 or both drugs, e.g. warfarin and vitamin K, NSAIDs and angiotensin-converting enzyme (ACE) inhibitors, metoclopramide and cyclizine.

Box 1.10 The serotonin syndrome

Serotonin syndrome is a potentially life-threatening condition associated with increased serotonergic activity in the central nervous system (CNS). It can occur as the result of co-administration of drugs that have the net effect of increasing serotonergic neurotransmission. It may also occur after initiation of a single serotonergic drug or by simply increasing the dose of a serotonergic drug.

The syndrome is characterized by a triad of mental, autonomic, and neurological disorders with a sudden onset of <24 hours after the beginning of treatment. Diagnosis is complex, but includes the addition of a serotonergic agent to an already established treatment (or increase in dosage) and manifestation of at least 4 major symptoms or 3 major symptoms plus 2 minor ones:
• Mental (cognitive and behavioural) symptoms:
  • Major symptoms: confusion, elevated mood, coma or semicoma
  • Minor symptoms: agitation and nervousness, insomnia
• Autonomic symptoms:
  • Major symptoms: fever, hyperhidrosis
  • Minor symptoms: tachycardia, tachypnoea and dyspnoea, diarrhoea, low or high blood pressure
• Neurological symptoms:
  • Major symptoms: myoclonus, tremors, chills, rigidity, hyper-reflexia
  • Minor symptoms: impaired coordination, mydriasis, akathisia.

Implicated drugs include:
• Citalopram, fluoxetine, paroxetine
• Trazodone, venlafaxine
• Sumatriptan
• Tramadol
• Ondansetron, granisetron.

Treatment is largely symptomatic and includes the discontinuation of the serotonergic agents; most patients improve completely within 24 hours upon withdrawal. Benzodiazepines may be used for anxiety and although effectiveness has not been demonstrated, cyproheptadine or olanzapine (both 5-HT$_{2A}$ antagonists) may be useful.

Chapter 2

Prescribing guidance

Unlicensed use of medicines

In the UK, the Medicines and Healthcare products Regulatory Agency (MHRA) grants a marketing authorization (previously referred to as product licence) to pharmaceutical companies enabling them to market and supply a product for the specific indication(s) mentioned in the summary of product characteristics. It is also possible for pharmaceutical companies to receive a European wide marketing authorization through the European Medicines Agency.

The Medicines Act 1968 defines the actions of a doctor; this Act ensures a doctor can legally prescribe unlicensed medicines (those without a marketing authorization) or licensed medicines for 'off-label' purposes (e.g. unlicensed dose, route, or indication). Supplementary prescribers can also prescribe licensed medicines for off-label purposes as well as unlicensed medicines provided it is part of a patient's clinical management plan. Independent nurse and pharmacist prescribers can prescribe licensed medicines for off-label purposes (must be accepted practice) and unlicensed medicines.

Although the use of unlicensed medicines in palliative care is rare, the use of licensed medicines for unlicensed indications, i.e. 'off label,' is both common and necessary and is generally encountered on a daily basis. Off-label use of medicines is highlighted in relevant monographs by the symbol ¥.

The patient should be informed that a drug is to be used beyond its marketing authorization and consent should be documented in the patient's case notes. Although some may feel this is impractical, given the widespread use in palliative care, certain inpatient units gain consent during the admission process.

Legal categories of medicines

Medicines for human use are classified in the following way. There are 3 classes of medicine, as defined by the Medicines Act 1968:
- *General Sales List (GSL):* a medicinal product that can be sold or supplied without the supervision of a pharmacist.
- *Pharmacy Medicine (P):* a medicinal product that is available for sale from a pharmacy under the supervision of a pharmacist.
- *Prescription-Only Medicine (POM):* a medicinal product that can be sold or supplied from a pharmacy in accordance with a prescription from an appropriate practitioner.

Controlled drugs (CDs) are further governed by the Misuse of Drugs Regulations 2001, as amended. These drugs are classified into 5 schedules according to different levels of control.
- *Schedule 1 (CD1):* production, possession, and supply of drugs in this Schedule are limited in the public interest to purposes of research or other special purposes. Includes drugs such as cannabis, LSD and ecstasy-type substances which have virtually no therapeutic use.
- *Schedule 2 (CD2):* includes the opioids (e.g. alfentanil, diamorphine, fentanyl, methadone, and morphine) and amphetamine (e.g. methylphenidate). Note that parenteral codeine and dihydrocodeine are classified as Schedule 2 drugs. These drugs are subject to prescription requirements (see Box 2.1), safe custody (i.e. CD cupboard), and the need for drug registers.
- *Schedule 3 (CD3):* includes barbiturates, buprenorphine, midazolam, and temazepam. These drugs are subject to prescription requirements (except temazepam), but not safe custody (except temazepam, buprenorphine, flunitrazepam, and diethylpropion) nor is there a need to keep drug registers (although certain centres may insist upon this as good practice). Note that there is no requirement to store midazolam or phenobarbital in a CD cupboard.
- *Schedule 4 Part 1 (CD4a):* includes the benzodiazepines (except midazolam and temazepam), ketamine, and zolpidem. These drugs are not subject to CD prescription or safe storage requirements and there is no need for a register.
- *Schedule 4 Part 2 (CD4b):* includes androgenic and anabolic steroids. These drugs are not subject to CD prescription or safe storage requirements and there is no need for a register.
- *Schedule 5 (CD5):* includes certain CDs, e.g. codeine, co-phenotrope, pholcodine, and morphine, which are exempt from full control when present in medicinal products of low strength.

The quantity of Schedule 2, 3, or 4 CDs to be prescribed at any one time should not exceed 30 days' supply. This represents good practice rather than a legal requirement as there may be circumstances where there is a genuine need to prescribe more than 30 days' supply. Note, however, that prescriptions for Schedule 2, 3, or 4 CDs are only valid for 28 days.

Box 2.1 Prescription requirements for Schedule 2 and 3 controlled drugs

Prescriptions for CDs must be indelible, be signed by the prescriber, be dated, and specify the prescriber's address. The prescription must always state:

- The name and address of the patient.
- In the case of a preparation, the form, and, where appropriate, the strength of the preparation.
- Either the total quantity (in both words and figures) of the preparation, or the number (in both words and figures) of dosage units to be supplied; in any other case, the total quantity (in both words and figures) of the CD to be supplied.
- The dose.
- The words 'for dental treatment only' if issued by a dentist.

Travelling abroad with medicines

- When planning to travel abroad, patients need to be aware of the laws that govern medicine use in both the UK and their destination(s). It is the patient's responsibility to take the necessary steps to ensure compliance with these laws.
- Note that certain OTC medicines in the UK may be CDs in other countries.
- If *any* medicines are to be taken abroad (including OTC medicines, e.g. co-codamol 8/500), the patient should contact the Embassy, Consulate, or High Commission of the country or countries to be visited regarding local policies on the import of medicines (see Box 2.2).
- UK requirements for export/import depend upon the medicines in question and the duration of travel abroad.

Box 2.2 Useful contact details

Embassy, Consulate, and High Commission
- http://www.homeoffice.gov.uk/publications/alcohol-drugs/drugs/drug-licences/embassy-list

Application form for personal licence
- http://www.homeoffice.gov.uk/drugs/licensing/personal

Home Office
- Home Office
  Drugs Licensing
  Peel Building
  2 Marsham Street
  LONDON
  SW1P 4DF
- Email: licensing_enquiry.aadu@homeoffice.gsi.gov.uk
- Tel: 0207 035 0467

Less than 3 months

- For all POMs, patients are advised to carry a letter from the prescribing doctor that states:
  - patient's name, address, and date of birth
  - outbound and inbound dates of travel
  - destination(s)
  - name, form, dose, and total amount of medicine(s) being carried.
- Certain countries may require additional information, such as details of the illness. This information can be obtained from the Embassy, Consulate, or High Commission.

More than 3 months

- Patients carrying any amount of medicines listed in Schedules 2, 3 or 4 (part 1) of the Misuse of Drugs Regulations 2001 will require a personal export/import licence. The application form can be downloaded from the Home Office website (see Box 2.2).
- The application must be supported by a covering letter from the prescriber, which should state:
  • patient's name and address
  • quantity of medicine(s) to be carried
  • name, strength, and form of medicine(s) to be carried
  • destination(s)
  • outbound and inbound dates of travel.
- The completed form, together with covering letter, should be sent to the Home Office (see Box 2.2).
- Alternatively, the completed form, together with a scanned copy of the covering letter may be emailed to the Home Office (see Box 2.2).
- The patient must be advised that application for a personal licence can take at least 2 weeks.
- Patients taking other POMs abroad are advised to carry a letter from the prescribing doctor that states:
  • patient's name, address, and date of birth
  • outbound and inbound dates of travel
  • destination(s)
  • name, form, dose, and total amount of medicine(s) being carried.
- Certain countries may require additional information, such as details of the illness. This information can be obtained from the Embassy, Consulate, or High Commission.
- When travelling by air, POMs should be carried:
  • in original packaging
  • in hand luggage*
  • with a valid personal licence (if applicable)
  • with a covering letter from the prescriber, unless a personal licence is held.

*Due to liquid restrictions, airport and airline regulations must be checked prior to departure. As of June 2008, medicines essential for the journey may be permitted in quantities >100mL. The patient must have secured the prior agreement of the airline and airport, in addition to having the documentation previously described.

Drugs and driving

It is an offence to drive, attempt to drive, or be in charge of a vehicle when unfit through drugs; the law does not distinguish between illegal drugs and prescribed medication. Patients should be advised that impairment might be present even in the absence of subjective symptoms. The effects may be more pronounced in the elderly.

Some prescription drugs and OTC medicines can impair skills needed for safe driving. Examples of such effects include blurred vision, dizziness, drowsiness, hypotension, and impaired judgement. In many cases, these effects are dose-dependent and may diminish with time. In general, any drug with a prominent CNS effect has the potential to impair an individual's ability to operate a vehicle. The Driver and Vehicle Licensing Agency (DVLA) recommends that healthcare professionals prescribing or dispensing medication should consider the risks associated with each drug, or combination of drugs, and take the opportunity to appropriately advise their patients.

Patients should generally be warned to avoid driving either after commencing or when titrating potentially sedating medication. Driving should not be attempted unless the patient feels safe to do and the undesirable effects of the drug(s) have diminished. This may take up to a week after commencing or increasing doses of certain drugs (e.g. opioids). If a patient uses rescue doses of oral opioids to treat pain flares (whether due to BTcP, or poorly controlled background pain), driving should be avoided for up to 3 hours, or until after any effect subsides. Patients should also be warned that cognitive effects will be exacerbated by the concurrent use of alcohol, or other medication, whether prescribed or bought OTC.

When considering the prescription of new drugs, the patient's existing treatment should be reviewed. Drug interactions may affect drug metabolism and excretion, or could produce additive or synergistic interactions. Refer to the drug monographs in 📖 Chapter 3 for relevant prescribing information, including possible effects on driving and potential drug interactions. A selection of drugs that may cause problems is described as follows.

Anticholinergic drugs
- Examples include amitriptyline, cyclizine, glycopyrronium, hyoscine (butyl- and hydrobromide), levomepromazine, nortriptyline (less than amitriptyline), olanzapine, oxybutynin, paroxetine, and propantheline.
- Anticholinergic effects that can impair driving performance include ataxia, blurred vision, confusion and sedation.

Antidepressants

- Examples include amitriptyline, citalopram, fluoxetine, mirtazapine, nortriptyline, paroxetine, trazodone, and venlafaxine.
- In general, antidepressants that have antihistamine, anticholinergic, or α-adrenergic properties are likely to be problematic. While the undesirable effects of the SSRIs tend to be mild and well-tolerated, patients should be made aware of potential problems that may impair driving, such as sleep disturbances (e.g. insomnia, leading to daytime drowsiness), anxiety, and restlessness.
- Mirtazapine should be given at night to avoid daytime drowsiness, although this should improve as the dose increases.
- It is often unknown whether the risks are associated with the drug, an interaction, or the condition itself. Patients should be advised not to drive during the initial stages of dosage titration if they experience undesirable effects that may impair driving.

Anti-emetics

- Many drugs from different classes are used as anti-emetics, e.g. 5-HT$_3$ antagonists, anticholinergics, antihistamines, antipsychotics, and dopamine antagonists.
- Undesirable effects that may impair driving performance include blurred vision, confusion, dystonias, headache, and sedation.

Anti-epileptic drugs

- Examples include carbamazepine, clonazepam, levetiracetam, and sodium valproate.
- Affected patients should not drive during treatment initiation, withdrawal, or dosage titration due to the risk of potential undesirable effects that may impair driving performance, or precipitate seizures.

Antihistamines

The first-generation antihistamines (e.g. chlorphenamine, cyclizine, cyproheptadine, promethazine) may have pronounced CNS effects and have been shown to impair driving performance, e.g. including the inability to maintain a constant distance from the vehicle in front and remain in lane. Of concern, patients may experience impairment even in the absence of subjective symptoms. Patients who take sedating antihistamines should be advised not to drive. In contrast, most non-sedating antihistamines (e.g. cetirizine, loratadine) cause less sedation and therefore lower risk of driving impairment when used at recommended doses. Despite drowsiness being reported as a rare adverse effect, patients should be advised not to drive if affected.

Antipsychotics

Both typical and atypical antipsychotic medications have a strong potential to impair driving performance through various CNS effects. Some of the older generation of antipsychotics are sedating, and all produce extrapyramidal symptoms (EPS). Although atypical drugs have a lower tendency to cause EPS, many are also sedating. An additional problem with the antipsychotics is the risk of hypotension which may cause light-headedness or fatigue, further impairing driving performance.

Anxiolytics/benzodiazepines

Benzodiazepines impair driving and increase the risk of road traffic accidents. At low doses they cause sedation, while at higher doses the effects are comparable to alcohol intoxication.

Opioid analgesics

- The driving performance of cancer patients receiving long-term opioid treatment at stable doses does not appear to be adversely effected.
- Following dose adjustments, performance may be affected for about 7 days. If rescue doses are used, the patient should be advised not to drive for at least 3 hours afterwards, or until any undesirable effect has resolved.

Management of pain

- The pain experience is a multifaceted process that can be due to a multitude of factors.
- The International Association for the Study of Pain define pain as: 'an unpleasant sensory and emotional experience associated with actual or potential tissue damage, or described in terms of such damage'.
- There are many different ways to classify pain; common terms are shown in Table 2.1.

Table 2.1 A list of common types of pain

Type of pain	Definition
Acute pain	Typically of short duration, arbitrarily taken to be <3 months. It serves as a warning for injury, or potential for further harm. It subsides as healing occurs. Responds well to analgesia
Chronic pain	Chronic pain serves no purpose and generally does not relate to injury (except cancer pain), persisting beyond the usual healing period. Response to analgesia can be unpredictable
Total pain	The total pain that the patient experiences is influenced by emotional, psychological, and spiritual factors, in addition to the physical pain caused by the disease
Nociceptive pain	Caused by noxious stimuli in the periphery. Inflammatory mediators, such as prostaglandins, sensitize nociceptors. Types of nociceptive pain include somatic pain (e.g. skin, bone) and visceral pain (e.g. bowel). Generally responds well to analgesia
Somatic pain	Often described as aching or throbbing, somatic pain is generally localized and constant. Usually responds well to classic analgesics, although occasionally adjuvant analgesics are required, e.g. bone pain (bisphosphonates)
Visceral pain	May be described as a constant, sharp pain (e.g. bowel colic). It is often diffuse and poorly localized and the pain may be referred to other non-visceral areas. Usually responds well to classic analgesics, although occasionally adjuvant analgesics are required e.g. bowel colic (hyoscine butylbromide). Nausea may accompany visceral pain
Neuropathic pain	Caused by damage to, or changes in the central or peripheral nervous system. Typically responds poorly to common analgesics; adjuvant analgesics generally required. Described by a variety of terms, depending upon the nerve affected, e.g. hot/cold, sharp, shooting, stabbing, itch
Breakthrough cancer pain	A transient exacerbation of pain that occurs either spontaneously or in relation to a specific predictable or unpredictable trigger, experienced by patients who have relatively stable and adequately controlled background pain

Management of pain: selection of a NSAID

Summary

- NSAIDs/COX-2 inhibitors are associated with renal undesirable effects in addition to cardiovascular (CV) and/or gastrointestinal (GI) toxicity.
- Diclofenac, in doses available OTC, elevates the risk of CV toxicity.
- Naproxen reportedly has a superior CV safety profile, while celecoxib has a superior GI safety profile.
- Before prescribing a NSAID/COX-2 inhibitor, consider whether alternative treatment would be appropriate.
- Prescribe the lowest effective dose of NSAID/COX-2 inhibitor for the shortest time necessary. Review response to treatment after 14 days. Discontinue if no improvement.
- COX-2 inhibitors are *contraindicated* for use in patients with established ischaemic heart disease and/or cerebrovascular disease and also in patients with peripheral arterial disease (but see the following recommendations). Although NSAIDs are presently licensed for use in these conditions, they should be used with extreme caution.
- Blood pressure and renal function should be assessed prior to and within 7 days of starting a NSAID/COX-2 inhibitor or increasing the dose in patients at risk of CV toxicity.
- All patients receiving long-term treatment with a NSAID/COX-2 inhibitor should receive gastroprotective therapy, i.e. proton pump inhibitor (PPI), misoprostol. Use PPIs with caution in patients receiving clopidogrel.

Table 2.2 suggests a NSAID/COX-2 inhibitor selection strategy, which is discussed as follows:

Is a NSAID/COX-2 necessary?

- Can alternatives be used? For example:
  - Topical NSAID
  - Paracetamol
  - Tramadol or tapentadol
  - Gabapentin or pregabalin.
- The risk of a CV event associated with COX-2 inhibitors is relatively low; the number of additional events *per year* has been shown to be 3 per 1000 patients, but the mortality is unknown. Compare this with 1 in 500 perforations, ulcers, or gastroduodenal bleeds that occur with NSAIDs after just 2 months' treatment. In addition, 1 in 1200 patients may die from gastroduodenal complications of NSAIDs after receiving 2 months' treatment. The choice of treatment will depend upon the prescriber's assessment of the individual's risk factors.

- COX-2 inhibitors (e.g. celecoxib) are *contraindicated* for use in patients with established CV disease (but see following strategy), while the CV safety of conventional NSAIDs remains controversial (e.g. ibuprofen is associated with a high stroke risk; diclofenac has been shown to be similar in terms of CV toxicity as etoricoxib).

Patients at risk of, or with established CV disease with no concurrent risk of GI toxicity

- If NSAID treatment is necessary, consider the following options:
  - *Naproxen* + misoprostol or PPI (NB: caution with PPI if patient on clopidogrel).

Patients at risk of, or with established CV disease with concurrent risk of GI toxicity

- If NSAID treatment is absolutely necessary, consider the following options:
  - *Naproxen* + misoprostol or PPI (NB: caution with PPI if patient on clopidogrel).
  (Note: a multidisciplinary European expert panel[1] suggests celecoxib + PPI as a suitable alternative option for patients with rheumatic disease and both CV and GI risk factors, despite the contraindication.)

Patients at risk of GI toxicity with no concurrent CV risks

- If NSAID treatment is necessary, consider the following options:
  - *COX-2 inhibitor* + misoprostol or PPI
  OR
  - *Nabumetone* + misoprostol or PPI.

Patients not at risk of GI toxicity and no CV risks

- Consider the following approach:
  - *Non-selective NSAID* (e.g. diclofenac, ibuprofen, nabumetone) + misoprostol or PPI.

Table 2.2 Selection of NSAID according to cardiovascular history and gastrointestinal risk factors

Step	No CV or GI risk(s)	CV risk(s) ± GI risk(s)	GI risk(s) No CV risk(s)
1	Alternative analgesia	Alternative analgesia	Alternative analgesia
2	Non-selective NSAID,[a] e.g. diclofenac, ibuprofen, naproxen	Naproxen[a]	COX-2 inhibitor[a]
3	COX-2 inhibitor[a]	(Celecoxib[b])[a]	Nabumetone[a]
4			Non-selective NSAID,[a] e.g. diclofenac/ibuprofen

[a] With PPI or misoprostol. [b] Suggested by multidisciplinary European panel of experts[1]

Reference and further reading

1 Burmester G, Lanas A, Biasucci L, et al. The appropriate use of non-steroidal anti-inflammatory drugs in rheumatic disease: opinions of a multidisciplinary European expert panel. *Ann Rheum Dis* 2011; **70**(5):818–22.

Salvo F, Fourrier-Réglat A, Bazin F, et al. Cardiovascular and gastrointestinal safety of NSAIDs: a systematic review of meta-analyses of randomized clinical trials. *Clin Pharmacol Ther* 2011; **89**(6):855–66.

Trelle S, Reichenbach S, Wandel S, Hildebrand P et al. Cardiovascular safety of non-steroidal anti-inflammatory drugs: network meta-analysis. *Br Med J* 2011; **342**:c7086.

Management of pain: opioid substitution

- Morphine is the strong opioid of choice in palliative care. It may become necessary to switch to another route of administration or indeed opioid due to problems such as:
  - deterioration in condition
  - drug interactions
  - dysphagia
  - intolerable undesirable effects (e.g. nausea, constipation, hallucinations, myoclonus)
  - malabsorption
  - patient request (e.g. reduction of tablet load)
  - poor analgesic response, despite dose titration
  - renal impairment.
- Before considering opioid substitution, consider simple measures such as:
  - adjuvant medications to improve undesirable effects, e.g. haloperidol for hallucinations, methylnaltrexone for constipation
  - check for drug interactions (e.g. erythromycin and fentanyl)
  - dose reduction
  - rehydration.
- When converting from one opioid to another (or route), the suggested equianalgesic dose becomes gradually less precise as the dose increases, even more so if there has been recent rapid dose escalation. If converting from oral morphine to another opioid (or even route), the wide interpatient variability in its pharmacokinetics must be borne in mind (oral bioavailability can range from 10–65%).
- Equianalgesic dose ratios serve as an approximate guide only. There is also some disparity in the literature. Table 2.3 illustrates commonly used ratios, along with manufacturers' recommendations where applicable. Note that the values in Table 2.3 are an approximate guide only since equianalgesic doses are difficult to ascertain due to wide interpatient variations and non-interchangeability of products. The prescriber is ultimately responsible for his/her own actions.
- When switching to a new opioid (or route), initial dose conversions should be conservative. It is considered appropriate in most cases to reduce the equianalgesic dose by 25–50% since it is preferable to underdose the patient and use rescue medication for any shortfalls.
- The prescriber should use clinical judgement when deciding how much to adjust the dose by. There are several factors that must be considered before deciding on an appropriate dose, e.g.:
  - concurrent morbidity (a 50% dose reduction may be appropriate when converting a frail, elderly patient)
  - current dose of opioid to be switched (a 50% dose reduction may be more appropriate when converting at high doses)
  - current pain status (no dose reduction may be appropriate in patients experiencing severe pain at the time of the switch)
  - drug interaction (e.g. converting from morphine to an equianalgesic dose of fentanyl in a patient taking carbamazepine may result in worsening pain; converting a patient from morphine to an equianalgesic dose of oxycodone in a patient taking erythromycin

may actually result in opioid toxicity due to increased production of the more potent active metabolite)
  - hepatic impairment
  - renal impairment.
- Once the dose of the opioid has been decided, the choice of formulation and associated chronological profile need to be considered. For example, consider a patient receiving twice daily, oral modified-release (m/r) morphine preparation who is being converted to a transdermal fentanyl patch. The patch will be applied at the same time as the last oral dose of morphine.
- Ensure appropriate rescue medication is prescribed to ensure titration of background analgesia.

Table 2.3 Equianalgesic ratios

Opioid	Conversion ratio[a] (opioid:oral morphine)	Notes
Alfentanil (SC)	1:30	
Buprenorphine (TD)	1:75 to 1:115	
Codeine (PO)	10:1	
Diamorphine (SC)	1:3	
Dihydrocodeine (PO)	10:1	
Fentanyl (TD)	1:100	Manufacturer recommends 1:150
Hydromorphone (PO)	1:7.5	
Methadone (PO)	Refer to monograph	
Morphine (SC)	1:2	Studies suggest a 1:3 ratio is effective
Oxycodone (PO)	1:1.5	Manufacturer recommends 1:2
Oxycodone (SC)	1:2	PO oxycodone:SC oxycodone is 1.5:1. The manufacture states 2:1
Tapentadol (PO)	2.5:1	
Tramadol	Refer to monograph	

[a] Examples:

Morphine PO 60mg BD = Alfentanil 4mg via CSCI over 24 hours

Morphine PO 60mg BD = Oxycodone PO 40mg BD

Morphine PO 30mg BD = Fentanyl TD 600 micrograms in 24 hours

= 25 micrograms/hour patch

Morphine PO 30mg BD = Buprenorphine TD 840 micrograms in 24 hours

= 35 micrograms/hour patch (based on 75:1 ratio)

Further reading

Knotkova H, Fine PG, Portenoy RK. Opioid rotation: the science and the limitations of the equianalgesic dose table. *J Pain Symptom Manage* 2009; **38**(3):426–39.

Mercadante S, Caraceni A. Conversion ratios for opioid switching in the treatment of cancer pain: a systematic review. *Palliat Med* 2011; **25**(5):504–15.

Management of pain: breakthrough pain

Summary

- Breakthrough pain can be caused by poorly controlled background pain, incident pain, or spontaneous pain.
- Poorly controlled background pain is treated by optimizing background analgesia (e.g. by titrating m/r opioid analgesia, or adding adjuvant analgesia).
- Incident and spontaneous pain are encompassed by the term *breakthrough cancer pain (BTcP)*.
- BTcP episodes can be:
  - unpredictable, e.g. caused by involuntary actions, such as coughing (non-volitional incident pain)
  - predictable, e.g. precipitated by a specific activity like walking (volitional incident pain), or dressing change (procedural pain)
  - idiopathic, with no known precipitant (spontaneous pain).
- BTcP episodes typically reach peak intensity in as little as 3min, with a median duration of 30min, and a mean of 4 episodes per day.
- Opioids are considered the drugs of choice for most episodes of BTcP.
- There is no correlation between background analgesic dose and the rescue dose for BTcP.
- While newer fentanyl-based products are licensed for the treatment of BTcP, oral standard-release opioids may be appropriate for some episodes of BTcP.

Introduction

Pain is a common symptom of cancer with a prevalence of up to 90% in patients with advanced disease. Background pain (also referred to as baseline or persistent pain) can, in most cases, be treated successfully with background analgesia, typically long-acting opioid formulations and adjuvant drugs such as gabapentin, pregabalin, or amitriptyline.

In addition to background pain, cancer patients can experience pain that 'breaks through' background analgesia. This can occur as a result of:
- Poorly controlled background pain (i.e. continued dose titration, or the addition of an adjuvant is warranted).
- Incident pain (precipitated by movement or activity), which can be *volitional* (i.e. predictable pain caused by voluntary event, e.g. walking), *non-volitional* (i.e. unpredictable pain caused by involuntary actions, e.g. coughing, sneezing), or *procedural* (i.e. caused by a particular therapeutic intervention, e.g. wound dressing).
- Spontaneous pain (unpredictable with no identifiable precipitant).

Collectively, these exacerbations of pain have been described as *breakthrough pain*. There is, however, no universally accepted definition of this phenomenon and a lack of consensus unquestionably leads to inadequate assessment and subsequent suboptimal treatment which impacts on the patient's quality of life. Traditionally, treatment of breakthrough pain has been guided by the World Health Organization's (WHO) analgesic ladder, where fixed doses of oral standard-release opioids (usually 1/6 to 1/10 of the background analgesic dose) are administered to treat any exacerbation of pain, irrespective of the cause. Adjustments to the background dose are considered, dependent on the number of doses of standard-release opioid given in the preceding 24 hours, without any regard to the nature of the exacerbation. This approach could lead to rapid development of opioid toxicity.

In an attempt to improve the approach to treatment of pain that 'breaks through' background analgesia, the term *breakthrough cancer pain* (BTcP) has been introduced. This essentially proposes that patients with poorly controlled background pain need different management to those with incident or spontaneous pain.

Definition
The term BTcP has been introduced to describe a transient exacerbation of pain that occurs either spontaneously or in relation to a specific predictable or unpredictable trigger, experienced by patients who have relatively stable and adequately controlled background pain.

Characteristics of BTcP
Clinical features can vary between patients in that some patients may only experience one type of pain, while others may experience several distinct pains. Furthermore, the clinical features can vary within a patient during the course of the disease.

BTcP is usually of moderate to severe intensity and the pathophysiology is often, but not always, the same as background pain; it can be neuropathic, nociceptive, or a combination of both. The reported prevalence of BTcP varies widely (19–95%), mainly due to a lack of accepted definition and different study designs. Nonetheless, it is suggested that BTcP:
- Typically reaches a maximum intensity after 3–5min.
- Has a reported median duration of 30min, with a mean of 4 episodes per day.

Untreated BTcP pain could have a profound impact on quality of life and a number of consequences have been reported:
- Impairment of daily activities, e.g. walking, working
- Anxiety and depression
- Interference with sleep
- Reduced social interaction
- Higher pain severity
- Dissatisfaction with overall pain management
- Greater healthcare costs.

Management
The patient must be accurately assessed in order to differentiate between *incident/spontaneous* pain (i.e. BTcP) and exacerbations of *poorly-controlled background pain* because subsequent treatment modalities are completely different. It is important that BTcP is considered separately from background pain and its treatment must be individualized. The treatment of BTcP primarily involves pharmacotherapy, although consideration should

be given to non-pharmacological interventions such as massage, application of heat or cold, and distraction or relaxation techniques.

Successful management of BTcP includes the following:
- Assessment of the characteristics of both the pain (e.g. temporal profile, aetiology) and patient (e.g. disease, preferences).
- Treatment of the underlying cause (e.g. radiotherapy, chemotherapy, surgery).
- Avoidance of precipitating factors.
- Adjustment of background analgesia (e.g. addition of adjuvant analgesics).
- Re-assessment.

Opioids are considered the drugs of choice for the treatment of BTcP. Note that opioids are unlikely to control all types of BTcP and alternative strategies may need to be adopted. There is no correlation between background analgesic dose and the rescue dose of opioid needed to successfully control BTcP. This must be determined by individual titration.

The choice of opioid and formulation for this condition continues to be a controversial issue, which is undoubtedly a consequence of the lack of a clear definition coupled with the relatively high acquisition costs of the newer, fentanyl-based products. Once the cause of breakthrough pain has been identified as incident or spontaneous pain, rather than poorly controlled background pain (i.e. a diagnosis of BTcP), pharmacological treatment should focus on the temporal characteristics of the pain episode. Oral standard-release opioid formulations are unlikely to be the ideal option for most episodes of BTcP that resolve after 30–60min. The pharmacokinetic profiles of oral opioids (onset of action 20–30min, peak analgesia 60–90min) do not complement the temporal characteristics of these brief episodes of BTcP. There is also the prolonged duration of action to consider (e.g. up to 4 hours with morphine) which can potentially manifest as undesirable effects such as drowsiness. Nonetheless, such an approach would be suitable for BTcP of duration of more than an hour, or in situations where anticipatory treatment of an identifiable cause is both possible and acceptable, e.g. BTcP precipitated after a period of walking may be successfully managed with oral standard-release opioid formulations.

For many brief episodes of BTcP (i.e. lasting less than one hour), the use of a short-acting opioid with quick onset of action may be the most appropriate treatment. There are presently 5 products licensed specifically for the treatment of BTcP (📖 Fentanyl, p.203). In addition, there is an unlicensed alfentanil product available (📖 Alfentanil, p.65).

Non-opioid analgesics (e.g. paracetamol, NSAIDs, ketamine) and non-pharmacological techniques (e.g. massage, heat/cold, and relaxation) have been used to treat BTcP, although there is presently very little evidence to support their use. A variety of interventional techniques can be considered for the treatment of BTcP (e.g. neural blockade, neuroablation).

Further reading

Caraceni A, Hanks G, Kaasa S, Bennett MI et al. Use of opioid analgesics in the treatment of cancer pain: evidence-based recommendations from the EAPC. *Lancet Oncol* 2012; **13**(2):e58–e68.

Zeppetella G. Opioids for the management of breakthrough cancer pain in adults: a systematic review undertaken as part of an EPCRC opioid guidelines project. *Palliat Med* 2011; **25**(5): 516–24.

Management of pain: neuropathic pain

- The WHO analgesic ladder should be followed.
- Contrary to the common belief of poor efficacy in neuropathic pain, opioids have been found useful in several in various neuropathic conditions.
- Strong opioids should be titrated against response. If the patient experiences intolerable undesirable effects or poor efficacy during titration with an opioid:
  - try an alternative opioid (□ Management of pain: opioid substitution, p.32)
  - consider using a psychostimulant (e.g. modafinil, methylphenidate) if excessive fatigue
  - the pain may be opioid-insensitive.
- The National Institute for Health and Clinical Excellence (NICE) issued treatment guidance in 2010, which were viewed by some as controversial. Following a period of consultation on proposed amendments in late 2011, modifications to the guideline (Fig. 2.1) are expected in 2012.

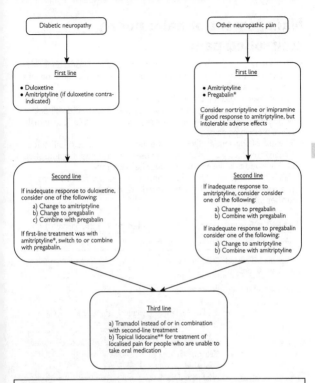

Diabetic neuropathy

First line
- Duloxetine
- Amitriptyline (if duloxetine contra-indicated)

Second line
If inadequate response to duloxetine, consider one of the following:
  a) Change to amitriptyline
  b) Change to pregabalin
  c) Combine with pregabalin

If first-line treatment was with amitriptyline*, switch to or combine with pregabalin.

Other neuropathic pain

First line
- Amitriptyline
- Pregabalin*

Consider nortriptyline or imipramine if good response to amitriptyline, but intolerable adverse effects

Second line
If inadequate response to amitriptyline, consider consider one of the following:
  a) Change to pregabalin
  b) Combine with pregabalin

If inadequate response to pregabalin consider one of the following:
  a) Change to amitriptyline
  b) Combine with amitriptyline

Third line
a) Tramadol instead of or in combination with second-line treatment
b) Topical lidocaine** for treatment of localised pain for people who are unable to take oral medication

Comments
$ There is a risk of serotonin syndrome when tramadol is combined with other serotonergic drugs
**Lidocaine plasters may be a more appropriate first-line option for patients with localised neuropathic pain
* The NICE guideline currently favours pregabalin over gabapentin; some may prefer to use the latter

Other options
Dexamethasone is a suitable option for patients with suspected nerve-compression pain. **Tapentadol** has only recently been launched and may offer an advantage over tramadol. **Clonazepam** and **ketamine** offer additional options for patients with neuropathic pain.

Fig. 2.1 Suggested approach for the use of adjuvant analgesics for neuropathic pain. Source: Data from NICE guidance: National Institute for Health and Clinical Excellence (2010). *Neuropathic pain – pharmacological management (CG96)*. London: National Institute for Health and Clinical Excellence

Management of pain: poorly controlled pain

- There may be occasions encountered whereby traditional approaches to pain relief do not work, or the patient simply derives little benefit from pharmacotherapy.
- Cancer pain is often multimodal (i.e. components of neuropathic and nociceptive pain). Simply increasing the dose of an opioid will not necessarily control a patient's pain; high doses of opioids can actually cause worsening pain.
- The use of adjuvant analgesia will be necessary in cases of difficult pain. When introducing an adjuvant, the dose of concomitant opioid should be reviewed as an dose reduction may be necessary.
- Table 2.4 lists some of the commonly encountered difficult pains and suggested treatments. Refer to the individual drug monographs for further information.

Table 2.4 Suggested treatment for a selection of difficult pain

Pain	Suggested treatment
Headache associated with brain tumour	Dexamethasone
Malignant bone pain	Radiotherapy NSAIDs Bisphosphonate (e.g. pamidronate, zoledronic acid) Gabapentin/pregabalin
Mucositis	Antifungal e.g. fluconazole if oral candidiasis suspected Gelclair® (an oral gel classed as a dressing) Topical (dia)morphine Antacid and oxetacaine oral suspension
Painful wounds	Topical (dia)morphine
Smooth muscle spasm e.g. bowel colic e.g. rectal pain	Glycopyrronium Hyoscine butylbromide Hyoscine hydrobromide GTN, nifedipine
Skeletal muscle spasm	Baclofen Clonazepam Diazepam

Management of nausea and vomiting

- Many patients with advanced cancer (up to 60%) can experience nausea and vomiting. There are many causes, some of which are reversible (see Box 2.3).

Box 2.3 Common causes of nausea and vomiting in advanced cancer

- Anxiety
- Autonomic neuropathy
- Biochemical (e.g. ↑Ca^{2+} ↓Na^+)
- Bowel obstruction
- Constipation
- Cough
- Drugs
- Gastritis
- Gastroparesis
- Infection
- Pain
- Raised intracranial pressure
- Renal failure
- Vestibular disturbance.

- The choice of antiemetic depends on the cause, although many patients may have multiple, irreversible causes. Suggested choices are shown in Table 2.5.

Table 2.5 Suggested drug choices for nausea and vomiting

Cause	First-line drug	Second-line drug[a]	Notes
Unknown	Cyclizine ± haloperidol or levomepromazine	–	–
Gastric stasis	Domperidone or metoclopramide	–	Antimuscarinic drugs and 5-HT3 antagonists may reduce the prokinetic effect
Gastric irritation (e.g. drugs, tumour infiltration)	Domperidone or metoclopramide	Levomepromazine or ondansetron	Consider PPI or ranitidine if NSAID-induced

(Continued)

Table 2.5 (cont.) Suggested drug choices for nausea and vomiting

Cause	First-line drug	Second-line drug[a]	Notes
Total bowel obstruction	Haloperidol ± hyoscine butylbromide or Hyoscine hydrobromide or glycopyrronium	Add cyclizine or Levomepromazine or Add ondansetron	In difficult cases, consider the use of dexamethasone 8–12mg daily (SC) and review after 5 days Octreotide ± glycopyrronium may be beneficial if vomiting large volumes Consider a nasogastric tube or venting gastrostomy
Partial bowel obstruction (without colic)	Domperidone or metoclopramide	Add dexamethasone	Consider faecal softener (e.g. docusate sodium)
Chemoreceptor trigger zone (e.g. drugs, hypercalcaemia)	Haloperidol or metoclopramide	Add cyclizine or levomepromazine	The prokinetic effect of metoclopramide may be inhibited by cyclizine
Raised intracranial pressure	Dexamethasone and cyclizine	Levomepromazine and dexamethasone	Do not administer dexamethasone and levomepromazine together via the same CSCI

[a] Substitute the first-line drug with the second-line agent unless the table states otherwise.

Management of constipation

- Constipation should be defined by the patient, not the practitioner.
- Patients with ECOG1 performance status 3 or 4 are at a high risk of developing constipation (i.e. patients confined to bed or chair for >50% of waking hours or totally confined to bed or chair).
- Patients receiving opioids are at a high risk of developing constipation. Note that the risk is independent of dose.
- Common causes of constipation are shown in Box 2.4. Where possible, address reversible causes.
- Evidence for the optimum treatment of constipation in palliative care is lacking. In 2008, the EAPC issued clinical practice recommendations based largely on expert opinion (Fig. 2.2).
- In patients at risk of complications from opioid-induced constipation (and unable to tolerate oral laxatives), Targinact® (oxycodone/naloxone combination, see page 409) may offer a suitable alternative treatment option.
- The suggested treatment of constipation is shown in Fig. 2.2.

Box 2.4 Common causes of constipation in advanced cancer

- Anal fissure
- Bowel obstruction
- Brain tumour
- Confusion
- Dehydration
- Depression
- Drugs (e.g. anti-cholinergics, 5-HT$_3$ antagonists)
- Environmental
- Haemorrhoids
- Hypercalcaemia
- Immobility
- Poor food intake
- Spinal cord compression
- Weakness.

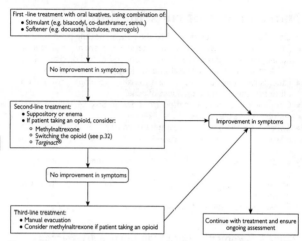

Fig. 2.2 Suggested management of constipation. Source: Data from Larkin PJ, Sykes NP, Centeno C, Ellershaw JE et al. The management of constipation in palliative care: clinical practice recommendations. *Palliat Med* 2008; **22**(7):796–807.

Discontinuing and/or switching antidepressants

Summary

- All antidepressants can cause discontinuation symptoms if stopped abruptly or if doses are missed.
- If antidepressants are taken regularly for 8 weeks or more they should generally be discontinued by tapering the dose over at least 4 weeks.
- Longer-term maintenance therapy may need to be discontinued over a 6-month period.
- Fluoxetine has a long plasma half-life; doses ≤20mg OD may be stopped abruptly without dose tapering, although gradual withdrawal may be necessary at higher doses.
- Care is required when switching between antidepressants.
- When switching between SSRIs, tricyclic antidepressant (TCAs), and related antidepressants, the ideal method would be to incrementally reduce the dose of the first antidepressant and discontinue it before starting the second antidepressant. This is not always possible in the palliative care setting and cross-tapering or immediate switch may need to be considered.
- The potential for medication errors with complicated switching regimens should be considered.

Discontinuation

If a patient has been taking antidepressants for 8 weeks or more the antidepressant should not be stopped abruptly due to the risk of withdrawal symptoms, *unless*:

- The drug has caused a serious undesirable effect, e.g. a cardiac arrhythmia in association with a TCA.
- The patient is entering the terminal phase.

Onset of withdrawal symptoms can occur within a few days, although missing a single dose can precipitate symptoms in susceptible individuals. Problems are more likely with high doses, or long courses. Withdrawal symptoms can usually be avoided by tapering the dose of the antidepressant rather than abruptly stopping it. Symptoms should not usually last longer than 1–2 weeks. The antidepressant can be restarted if the symptoms are severe or prolonged, after which withdrawal symptoms usually resolve within 24 hours. More gradual tapering can then be commenced.

Withdrawal symptoms experienced depend on the type of antidepressant and can vary in form and intensity. For SSRIs the commonest symptoms include flu-like illness, dizziness exacerbated by movement, insomnia, excessive (vivid) dreaming, and irritability. For TCAs, withdrawal symptoms include rebound cholinergic effects such as headache, restlessness, diarrhoea, and nausea or vomiting. Refer to individual monographs for further detail.

In general, when discontinuing an antidepressant, the following should be applied:

- If taken for <8 weeks, dose taper over 1–2 weeks.
- If taken for ≥8 weeks, dose taper over 4 weeks.

One exception is *fluoxetine*. At a dose of 20mg daily this may be stopped abruptly because of the long plasma half-life and active metabolite, but at higher doses gradual withdrawal may be required.

Switching antidepressants

Switching antidepressants can increase the risk of undesirable effects due to the potential for interaction between drugs (e.g. serotonin syndrome); there is also the likelihood of withdrawal symptoms developing due to discontinuation of the first antidepressant.

In the palliative care setting there may be limited time to achieve an improvement in the mood of the patient and hence in their quality of life. A more rapid switch under close medical supervision may be indicated.

Before switching antidepressants, there are several factors that must be considered:

- What is the need and urgency for the switch?
- What is the patient's condition?
- What is the current dose of the antidepressant to be withdrawn?
- What is the duration of treatment of the antidepressant to be withdrawn? If ≤8 weeks, it may be possible to shorten the withdrawal period or stop the drug abruptly.
- Is there a risk of serotonin syndrome? (See 🕮 Box 1.10, p.18.)
- Could the switch result in medication error?

There are several approaches to switching antidepressants that can be considered. Whichever method is used, the patient should be closely monitored.

Method 1: withdrawal and switch

- Involves gradual withdrawal of the first antidepressant over several weeks, followed by initiation (at low doses) of the new antidepressant, with or without a washout period.
- If the first antidepressant has been taken for:
  - ≥8weeks, dose taper over 4 weeks
  - <8weeks, dose taper over 1–2 weeks
- Potential risks of administering two antidepressants together include pharmacokinetic interaction (e.g. increased clomipramine levels with paroxetine due to CYP2D6 inhibition) and pharmacodynamic interactions, such as the serotonin syndrome. This method is suggested for switches where there is considerable risk of serious drug interaction.
- Switching from fluoxetine requires careful consideration. Refer to Table 2.6 for advice and further examples.

Method 2: cross-taper

- The dose of the first antidepressant is gradually reduced while the dose of the second is introduced at a low initial dose and gradually increased. The speed of the cross-taper may need to be adjusted according to how well the patient tolerates the process.
- Be aware of the possibility of drug interactions when cross-tapering.
- Some drugs should never be co-administered due to the risk of serious drug interactions (see Ⓜ Method 1: withdrawal and switch, p.46) and in these cases cross-tapering should be avoided.
- Cross-taper is generally not suitable for fluoxetine due to its long half-life (see Ⓜ Method 3: immediate switch, p.47)
- See Table 2.6 for specific examples.

Method 3: immediate switch

- The current antidepressant is stopped abruptly and the new antidepressant is introduced at a low dose, with or without a washout period.
- Useful if switching between 2 very similar antidepressants, e.g. 2 SSRIs. The first drug should be discontinued and the new drug introduced at a low dose.
- Usual method to adopt when swapping from fluoxetine.
- This process may put a patient at a greater risk of developing withdrawal symptoms.
- See Table 2.6 for specific examples.

Table 2.6 A guide to switching and stopping antidepressants. Adapted from UK Medicines Information (UKMI). Switching between tricyclic, SSRI and related antidepressants, from National Electronic Library for Medicines 2009, with permission of the author Simone Henderson. Available from http://www.nelm.nhs.uk/en/NeLM-Area/Evidence/Medicines-Q~-A/Switching-between-tricyclic-SSRI-and-related-antidepressants/

To From	SSRI (except fluoxetine)	TCA[a]	Venlafaxine	Duloxetine	Mirtazapine	Reboxetine
SSRI (except fluoxetine)	*Method 1* Withdraw old SSRI gradually. Initiate new SSRI at low dose the following day **or** *Method 3* Immediate switch	*Method 1* Withdraw SSRI gradually. Initiate the TCA at a low dose the next day. If the SSRI being stopped is paroxetine or fluvoxamine, ideally have washout period of 2–3 days. **or** *Method 2* Cross-taper cautiously[a]	*Method 2* Cross-taper cautiously starting with venlafaxine 37.5mg daily and increase very slowly **or** *Method 3* Immediate switch	*Method 3* Immediate switch. Withdraw SSRI abruptly and initiate duloxetine 60mg daily	*Method 2* Cross-taper cautiously	*Method 2* Cross-taper cautiously
Fluoxetine 20mg daily[b]	*Method 3* Immediate switch. Stop fluoxetine abruptly. Initiate second SSRI at half the normal starting dose 4–7 days later.	*Method 3* Immediate switch. Stop fluoxetine abruptly. Initiate TCA at low dose 4–7 days later; increase dose very slowly	*Method 3* Immediate switch. Stop fluoxetine abruptly. Initiate venlafaxine 37.5mg daily; increase dose very slowly.	*Method 3* Immediate switch. Stop fluoxetine abruptly. Initiate duloxetine 60mg daily	*Method 3* Immediate switch. Stop fluoxetine abruptly. Initiate mirtazapine 4–7 days later	*Method 3* Immediate switch. Stop fluoxetine abruptly. Initiate reboxetine at 2mg twice daily and increase dose gradually

Table 2.6 (cont.) A guide to switching and stopping antidepressants. Adapted from UK Medicines Information (UKMI). Switching between tricyclic, SSRI and related antidepressants, from National Electronic Library for Medicines 2009, with permission of the author Simone Henderson. Available from http://www.nelm.nhs.uk/en/NeLM-Area/Evidence/Medicines-Q--A/Switching-between-tricyclic-SSRI-and-related-antidepressants/

TCA[a]	*Method 2* Gradually reduce the dose of TCA to 25–50mg daily and then start SSRI at usual dose. Withdraw TCA over next 5–7 days[a]	*Method 2* Cross-taper cautiously	*Method 2* Cross-taper[a] cautiously, starting with venlafaxine 37.5mg daily	*Method 2* Cross-taper using a starting dose of duloxetine 60mg on alternate days and increase dose slowly	*Method 2* Cross-taper cautiously	*Method 2* Cross-taper cautiously
Venlafaxine	*Method 2* Reduce venlafaxine dose *then* cross-taper using SSRI at half normal dose **or** *Method 3* Immediate switch	*Method 2* Cross-taper[a] using a low starting dose of TCA. e.g. amitriptyline 25mg daily	*Method 1* Withdraw venlafaxine gradually. Initiate venlafaxine the following day		*Method 1* Withdraw venlafaxine gradually. Initiate duloxetine 60mg on alternate days the following day and increase dose slowly	*Method 2* Cross-taper cautiously
Duloxetine	*Method 1* Withdraw duloxetine gradually. Initiate SSRI the following day **or** *Method 2* Cross-taper cautiously.	*Method 2* Cross-taper using a low starting dose of TCA	*Method 1* Withdraw duloxetine gradually. Initiate venlafaxine the following day			*Method 1* Withdraw duloxetine gradually. Initiate mirtazapine the following day *Method 2* Cross-taper cautiously

(Continued)

Table 2.6 (cont.) A guide to switching and stopping antidepressants. Adapted from UK Medicines Information (UKMI). Switching between tricyclic, SSRI and related antidepressants, from National Electronic Library for Medicines 2009, with permission of the author Simone Henderson. Available from http://www.nelm.nhs.uk/en/NeLM-Area/Evidence/Medicines-Q--A/Switching-between-tricyclic-SSRI-and-related-antidepressants/

To From	SSRI	TCA[a]	Venlafaxine	Duloxetine	Mirtazapine	Reboxetine
Mirtazapine	*Method 1* Withdraw mirtazapine gradually. Initiate SSRI the following day. **or** *Method 2* Cross-taper cautiously	*Method 1* Withdraw mirtazapine gradually. Initiate TCA the following day. **or** *Method 2* Cross-taper cautiously	*Method 2* Cross-taper cautiously	*Method 1* Withdraw mirtazapine gradually. Initiate duloxetine 60mg on alternate days the following day and increase slowly		*Method 1* Withdraw mirtazapine gradually. Initiate reboxetine the following day.
Reboxetine	*Method 2* Cross-taper cautiously	*Method 2* Cross-taper cautiously	*Method 2* Cross-taper cautiously	*Method 2* Cross-taper cautiously	*Method 2* Cross-taper cautiously	

[a] Cross-tapering clomipramine with venlafaxine or a SSRI is not recommended.

[b] Fluoxetine at doses greater than 20mg may need to be withdrawn gradually rather than stopping abruptly.

Continuous subcutaneous infusions

Important considerations

- There are at least 4 devices available; ensure familiarity with the selected device.
- The MS16A, MS26, and MP Daily all deliver a length of fluid (mm) in a given time period; the T34 syringe pump delivers a volume (mL) in a given time period.
- In general, use a 20mL Luer-Lok® syringe as the minimum size. There are occasions whereby a 10mL syringe may be adequate, but always check local guidelines.
- Mixtures can be diluted with either NaCl 0.9% or water for injections (WFI). Refer to local policies.
- The continuous subcutaneous infusion (CSCI) can be started at the time the next oral m/r opioid dose is due. PRN analgesia may be required to cover the initial stages.

Syringe drivers/pumps

- CSCIs represent an effective method of drug administration and are particularly useful in palliative care, whether for end-of-life care or continued symptom relief earlier in the disease.
- There are presently at least 4 devices that are used to deliver CSCIs in the UK:
  - CME T34
  - Micrel MP Daily
  - Smiths Medical MS26
  - Smiths Medical MS16A

Practical points

- WFI can be used to dilute all mixtures, although this may increase the risk of infusion site reactions. Anecdotally, NaCl 0.9% may reduce the incidence of infusion site reactions; it can be used to dilute most mixtures except those containing:
  - cyclizine (use WFI)
  - diamorphine >40mg/mL (becomes hypertonic; use WFI).
- To reduce the incidence of infusion site reactions, the following is suggested:
  - dilute the solution with NaCl 0.9% using a minimum 20mL Luer-Lok® syringe
  - in the case of cyclizine, consider using a 10mL syringe as this may be more appropriate since dilution with WFI may produce a hypotonic solution (which itself can cause site reactions)
  - rotate the site at least every 72 hours
  - use non-metal cannulae
  - review the drug combination
  - consider the addition of 1mg dexamethasone, after checking compatibility.

- If a patient is being transferred from an oral m/r opioid formulation, for practical purposes the CSCI can be started at the time the next oral dose is due, although PRN analgesia may be necessary during the first few hours. Some centres choose to start the CSCI 4 hours beforehand to maintain adequate analgesia.
- If a CSCI is necessary for a patient using transdermal buprenorphine or fentanyl patches, it is considered best practice to leave these *in situ*; any further analgesic requirements can be added to a CSCI.

Use of drugs in end-of-life care

- Symptoms commonly experienced by patients in the dying phase are:
  - pain
  - nausea and vomiting
  - delirium and terminal restlessness
  - respiratory tract secretions
  - dyspnoea.
- *Anticipatory prescribing* of core drugs is essential for the control of symptoms at the end of life. Typically, these are (dia)morphine, midazolam, levomepromazine, and glycopyrronium.
- All medication should be reviewed and non-essential drugs should be discontinued. Unavoidable sudden discontinuation of certain drugs (e.g. antidepressants, antiparkinsonian medication, baclofen, gabapentin) may lead to the development of withdrawal reactions. These need to be anticipated and treated symptomatically (e.g. with midazolam and/or anti-emetics; in the case of Parkinson's disease, hyoscine hydrobromide has been used).
- In the case of diabetes mellitus, there is a lack of consensus between healthcare practitioners over the choice of treatment during end of life care. For type 1 diabetes, the patient should be maintained on insulin, but at a reduced dose in order to limit the risk of symptomatic ketoacidosis (e.g. reduced by 30–50%). A dose of isophane insulin 10 units SC ON will provide a basal insulin level and can be used if the patient is not eating. An alternative approach would be to administer soluble insulin with glucose monitoring. For type 2 patients, oral hypoglycaemics should be discontinued. Some consider it inappropriate to monitor blood glucose levels in type 2 patients with a life expectancy of a few days.
- Unless corticosteroids are used for symptom management (e.g. pain, headache, seizures) it is usually appropriate for them to be withdrawn.
- An alternative method of drug administration will invariably be required in order to maintain adequate symptom control. The SC route is usually employed and most symptoms experienced at the end of life can be adequately controlled with a small number of drugs. Administration via a CSCI is a safe, practical, and effective solution.

Managing pain

- *Morphine* is generally considered the first-line opioid for subcutaneous administration at the end of life, unless the patient is already established on an alternative opioid. Initial doses depend upon current opioid requirements. A suitable dose of morphine for an opioid naïve patient would be rescue doses of 2.5–5mg SC 2–4-hourly PRN. A CSCI should be initiated should ≥2 rescue doses be required in a 24-hour period.

- Occasionally, *diamorphine* may be used as the opioid of first choice for SC administration if opioid requirements are excessive.
- Patients established on a regular dose of oral opioid should be converted to an appropriate dose for CSCI as follows:

Oral morphine to subcutaneous morphine (2:1)
- Divide the total daily dose of oral morphine by 2 to give the equivalent daily dose of subcutaneous morphine.
- E.g. morphine m/r 90mg PO BD
    = 180mg *oral* morphine daily
    = 90mg *subcutaneous* morphine daily.

Oral morphine to subcutaneous diamorphine (3:1)
- Divide the total daily dose of oral morphine by 3 to give the equivalent daily dose of subcutaneous diamorphine.
- E.g. morphine m/r 90mg PO BD
    = 180mg *oral* morphine daily
    = 60mg *subcutaneous* diamorphine daily.

Oral oxycodone to subcutaneous oxycodone (1.5:1)
- Divide the total daily dose of oral oxycodone by 1.5 to give the equivalent daily dose of subcutaneous oxycodone (NB: manufacturer states divide by 2).
- E.g. oxycodone m/r 45mg PO BD
    = 90mg *oral* oxycodone daily
    = 60mg *subcutaneous* oxycodone daily.

Oral hydromorphone to subcutaneous hydromorphone
- Note that parenteral formulations of hydromorphone are presently unlicensed in the UK.
- Oral bioavailability shows wide interpatient variation and published equianalgesic values range from 2:1 to 5:1. A practical approach would be to choose the lower equianalgesic dose and prepare for upward titration.
- If a patient has been using oral *methadone* and a CSCI is required, halve the oral dose, although some patients may require a fairly rapid dose escalation as for some the ratio approaches 1:1.
- Should it be necessary to change to an alternative opioid, initial dose conversions should be conservative because equianalgesic doses are difficult to determine in practice due to wide interpatient variation. The lowest equianalgesic dose should be chosen if a range is stated. Refer to ⌷ Management of pain: opioid substitution, p.32 for conversion between opioids.
- The use of opioids at the end of life is summarized in Fig. 2.3.
- Morphine and diamorphine should be used cautiously in patients with renal impairment due to accumulation of active metabolites. In patients displaying signs of opioid toxicity, such as myoclonus, agitation, restlessness, and worsening pain, conversion to *alfentanil* for use in a CSCI may be appropriate.

- If a patient is receiving analgesic treatment with a transdermal patch (i.e. buprenorphine or fentanyl), this should remain *in situ* with further analgesic requirements being administered using rescue doses SC morphine (or alternative) and subsequent CSCI. Suitable rescue doses for transdermal buprenorphine and fentanyl patches are shown in Tables 2.7 and 2.8 respectively.
- BTcP should be managed as described in ⌑ Management of pain: breakthrough pain, p.35. The products currently available can be used successfully during end-of-life care.
- Unresolved pain can present problems during end-of-life care. The vast majority of adjuvant analgesics cannot be administered subcutaneously. Some of the adjuvants, such as TCAs will have a relatively long half-life, so their actions may persist for several days after discontinuation. Drugs such as *clonazepam*, *ketamine*, or *ketorolac* can be administered via CSCI and may be considered for the treatment of unresolved pain.

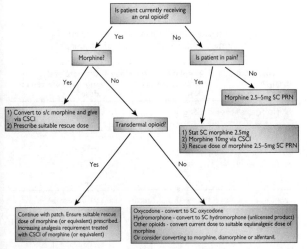

Fig. 2.3 Management of pain with opioids at the end of life.

Table 2.7 Determination of subcutaneous rescue doses of diamorphine, morphine and oxycodone for patients using a transdermal buprenorphine patch

Buprenorphine patch strength	Morphine or oxycodone subcutaneous rescue dose[a]	Diamorphine subcutaneous rescue dose
35 micrograms/hour	5–10mg	2.5–5mg
52.5 micrograms/hour	10mg	5–10mg
70 micrograms/hour	10–15mg	5–10mg
105 micrograms/hour	15–25mg	10–15mg
140 micrograms/hour	20–30mg	15–20mg

[a] Based on a conversion of 1:1 between subcutaneous morphine and oxycodone (see 📖 Management of pain: opioid substitution, p.32)

Table 2.8 Determination of subcutaneous rescue doses of diamorphine, morphine and oxycodone for patients using a transdermal fentanyl patch

Fentanyl patch strength	Morphine or oxycodone subcutaneous rescue dose[a]	Diamorphine subcutaneous rescue dose
12 micrograms/hour	2.5mg	2.5mg
25 micrograms/hour	5mg	2.5–5mg
50 micrograms/hour	10mg	5–10mg
75 micrograms/hour	15mg	10mg
100 micrograms/hour	20mg	15mg

[a] Based on a conversion of 1:1 between subcutaneous morphine and oxycodone (see 📖 Management of pain: opioid substitution, p.32)

Managing nausea and vomiting

- The choice of anti-emetic will depend upon the cause of nausea and vomiting.
- If no identifiable cause, *levomepromazine* 6.25–12.5mg SC OD or via CSCI over 24 hours may be the most appropriate treatment for nausea and vomiting during end-of-life care.
- Alternatively, *cyclizine* 100–150mg and *haloperidol* 3–5mg via CSCI over 24 hours can also be used.
- Note that cyclizine can exacerbate congestive heart failure and should be avoided in patients with such.
- Haloperidol alone may be preferred for patients with chronic renal impairment.
- If large volumes are being vomited, the use of antisecretory drugs such as *octreotide* 500 micrograms ± *glycopyrronium* 1.2mg (or *hyoscine butylbromide* 120mg) via CSCI over 24 hours can be considered.
- The 5-HT$_3$ antagonists (e.g. *granisetron, ondansetron*) are suitable second-line choices if the cause of nausea and vomiting is due to renal failure or damage to GI enterochromaffin cells, i.e. recent radiotherapy/chemotherapy, bowel obstruction, or gastric cancers.
- *Dexamethasone* can be used in resistant cases and often produces an indirect anti-emetic effect, particularly in bowel obstruction.
- *Ranitidine* via CSCI has been used to treat dyspepsia.

Managing delirium and terminal restlessness

- Delirium is one of the most common neurological problems experienced with advanced, or end-stage disease.
- The underlying aetiologies are numerous and include CNS malignancy, drug undesirable effects, infection, liver/renal impairment, and metabolic abnormalities.
- The diagnosis of delirium is made using the DSM-IV criteria. All of the following symptoms should be present:
  - disturbance of consciousness (e.g. reduced ability to maintain focus, or shift attention)
  - altered cognition that represents a change from the patient's usual state, such as memory deficit or disorientation
  - condition develops abruptly (usually hours to days) and can fluctuate throughout the day
  - disturbance is related to a medical condition.
- There are 3 clinical subtypes of delirium:
  - hypoactive: characterized by fatigue, lethargy, and sedation; often mistaken for depression or drug undesirable effects
  - hyperactive: characterized by restlessness, agitation, myoclonus, hallucinations and delusions; can be mistaken for uncontrolled pain
  - mixed.
- Hypoactive delirium is believed to be the more common subtype and is associated with a greater mortality rate.

- Delirium may be a reversible condition (e.g. nicotine withdrawal), or it can signal an irreversible deterioration due to disease progression.
- Numerous 'reversible' precipitating factors have been identified and include:
  - hypoxia, metabolic disturbances, and anticholinergic medications (hypoactive)
  - alcohol and drug withdrawal, drug intoxication, or medication undesirable effects (hyperactive).
- Agitation and delirium contribute to the condition known as 'terminal restlessness.' The treatment of terminal restlessness is defined by the symptoms displayed.
- Reversible causes should be corrected where possible or appropriate:
  - alcohol/nicotine withdrawal
  - biochemical abnormalities (e.g. hypercalcaemia, hypoglycaemia)
  - brain tumour/metastases
  - constipation
  - drugs (e.g. as renal/liver function deteriorate)
  - emotional distress (e.g. fear, anxiety)
  - infection
  - pain
  - urinary retention.
- Non-pharmacological measures may be useful and include a quiet room and the avoidance of isolation or loneliness.
- Benzodiazepines are considered first-line choice for management of agitation. Note that they can exacerbate symptoms associated with delirium. If the patient shows signs of delirium (e.g. paranoia, hallucinations, altered cognition), an antipsychotic may be more appropriate first-line treatment.

Agitation

1. Begin with *midazolam* 2.5–5mg SC PRN.
2. If ≥2 PRN doses are administered in a 24-hour period consider adding to or commencing a CSCI. A suitable dose would be 10mg via CSCI over 24 hours. Continue to administer appropriate PRN doses and review requirements daily.
3. Alternatively, *clonazepam* 0.5mg SC PRN may be used. If ≥2 PRN doses are administered in a 24-hour period consider adding to or commencing a CSCI. A suitable staring dose would be 2mg via CSCI over 24 hours.
4. The dose can be increased as necessary, up to an arbitrary dose of 30mg midazolam or 3–4mg clonazepam via CSCI over 24 hours. Further dose increases should only occur after thorough assessment.
5. If partial response to the benzodiazepine, consider adding *levomepromazine* 25mg to the CSCI (check for compatibility). Increase the dose as necessary in 25–50mg increments up to a max of 200mg over 24 hours. It is a useful adjunct to a benzodiazepine for uncontrolled agitation.

6. If no response to the benzodiazepine, change to *levomepromazine* 25mg via CSCI over 24 hours. In patients with cerebral tumours, midazolam should be continued since levomepromazine may lower the seizure threshold.
7. In refractory cases, *phenobarbital* may be used for the management of agitation at the end of life.

Delirium

1. Begin *haloperidol* 0.5–2.5mg SC PRN.
2. Consider adding to or commencing a CSCI if ≥2 PRN doses administered in a 24-hour period. A suitable staring dose would be 2.5mg via CSCI over 24 hours. Increase the dose as necessary up to a maximum of 10mg over 24 hours.
3. If no, or partial response, *levomepromazine* as detailed previously may used in place of haloperidol.
4. In refractory cases, *phenobarbital* may be used.

Managing respiratory tract secretions

- The management of respiratory tract secretions in the dying patient is primarily aimed at minimizing the distress of relatives or carers, rather than the patient.
- Non-pharmacological measures are an important part of the management of respiratory tract secretions and may include repositioning the patient and suction.
- The main treatment of terminal secretions involves the use of anticholinergic drugs:
  - *hyoscine <u>butylbromide</u>* 20mg SC PRN and 60–180mg via CSCI over 24 hours
  - *glycopyrronium* 0.2mg SC PRN and 0.6–1.2mg via CSCI over 24 hours
  - *hyoscine <u>hydrobromide</u>* 0.4mg SC PRN and 1.2–2.4mg via CSCI over 24 hours.
- There is no evidence to support the superiority of any one drug.
- A PRN dose should be administered as soon as symptoms develop. Anticholinergic drugs do not relieve symptoms from already present secretions. Regular administration or a CSCI should be started as soon as possible.

Managing dyspnoea

- The aim of treatment is to reduce the level of anxiety and alter the perception of breathlessness, ensuring the patient remains comfortable.
- Non-pharmacological measures, such as a fan passing cool air over the face or a calming hand, are important and should not be overlooked.
- Terminal secretions may contribute to the development of terminal dyspnoea and should be treated as described in 📖 Managing respiratory tract secretions, p.59.

- Pharmacological treatment of dyspnoea can involve:
  - *Midazolam* 2.5–5mg SC PRN. If ≥2 PRN doses are administered in a 24-hour period consider adding to or commencing a CSCI.
  - *Morphine* 1.25–2.5 mg SC PRN (for opioid naïve patients). If ≥2 PRN doses are administered in a 24-hour period consider adding to or commencing a CSCI (suitable starting dose 5–10mg via CSCI over 24 hours). For patients established on opioids, use PRN doses initially based on 1/6 of the background dose and amend as necessary.
  - Other options include *levomepromazine*, *promethazine*, and *furosemide*. The evidence for these is weaker.

Chapter 3

Drug monographs A–Z

Monographs

The monographs are divided into sections as described under the following headings. The layout has been designed to provide the healthcare professional with quick access to useful, practical, and relevant information. If more in-depth pharmacological information is required, other reference sources should be consulted.

Products available

- Information about the brand(s) and generic formulations (where applicable), including legal category, available strengths, and the quantity of tablets, capsules, etc. per original pack (where available).
- The legal classification of medicines is shown on 🕮 Legal Categories of medicines, p.21.
- Some brands are included in the drug monographs. These do not constitute recommendations and other brands may be available. It is not practical to include brand names for all countries and we regret any inconvenience to overseas reader.

Indications

Lists the indications for which the drug is used in palliative care. This can include both licensed and unlicensed uses; the latter are clearly marked with a symbol (¥). Note that unlicensed uses may only relate to case reports and inclusion here does not constitute a recommendation to prescribe (see References at the end of each monograph). Readers should also refer to 🕮 Unlicensed use of medicines, p.20 for information on the use of licensed drugs for unlicensed purposes.

Contraindications and precautions

A selection of contraindications and precautions are presented here. The reader should refer to a product's Summary of Product Characteristics (SPC) for a complete list. Note that it assumed that hypersensitivity to the drug is a contraindication and is not included in each monograph.

😣 Adverse effects

- Describes a selection of adverse effects that have been reported.
- The monographs classify adverse effects as per the SPC:
  - very common (≥10%)
  - common (≥1%, <10%)
  - uncommon (≥0.1%, <1%)
  - rare (≥0.01%, <0.1%)
  - very rare (<0.01%)
  - unknown.
- Certain SPCs have not been updated and do not use this system. In such cases, the frequency of adverse effects as described in the SPC has been included.
- The reader is referred to the SPC for a complete list.

Drug interactions

Provides a list of potential and actual pharmacokinetic and pharmacodynamic drug interactions. The reader should read 🕮 Chapter 1 in order to fully appreciate this section. Information relating to cytochrome involvement is provided as this information can be used to anticipate or identify drug interactions. The table on the 📖 inside back cover provides a quick reference guide to cytochrome substrates, inducers, and inhibitors. Be aware that some drugs are metabolized by multiple cytochrome pathways and while one drug interaction may seem unimportant, if additional drugs are co-prescribed that block other metabolic pathways, this interaction may assume greater significance.

🜥 Dose
Information for each indication described in the second section is provided. Unlicensed indications are shown by the symbol (¥).

🜥 Dose adjustments
A quick guide to dosage adjustments that may be required in the elderly, or those with hepatic/renal impairment. For complete information, the reader is referred to the SPC.

Additional information
• Further relevant information about the practical use of the drug is found here.
• Although brief CSCI stability information is also provided here, this does not indicate stability for all ranges of concentrations. For more in depth information, the reader is referred to Dickman A, Schneider J. *The Syringe Driver* (3rd edn). Oxford: Oxford University Press, 2011.

⟳ Pharmacology
A synopsis of the pharmacology is included in the monograph.

Alfentanil

Rapifen® (CD2 POM)
Injection: 500 micrograms/mL (10 × 2mL; 10 × 10mL).

Rapifen Intensive Care® (CD2 POM)
Injection: 5mg/mL (10 × 1mL).

Generic (CD2 POM)
Injection: 500 micrograms/mL (10 × 2mL; 10 × 10mL).

Unlicensed special (CD2 POM)
Nasal spray: 5mg/5mL (5mL; each actuation delivers 0.14mg in 0.14mL; attachment supplied for sublingual or buccal administration).

See additional following information for supply issues.

- Alfentanil is a Schedule 2 CD. Refer to 📖 Legal categories of medicines, p.21 for further information.

Indications
- *Alternative analgesic for subcutaneous administration, especially in renal failure.[1]
- *Management of BTcP[2]. Refer to 📖 Management of pain: breakthrough pain, p.35 for guidance relating to BTcP.

Contraindications and precautions
- Refer to 📖 Use of drugs in end-of-life care, p.53 for end-of-life care issues.
- If the dose of an opioid is titrated correctly, it is generally accepted that there are no absolute contraindications to the use of such drugs in palliative care, although there may be circumstances where one opioid is favoured over another (e.g. renal impairment, constipation).
- Avoid if the patient has received a monoamine oxidase inhibitor (MAOI) within the previous 2 weeks.
- May cause hypotension; use caution if the patient is ambulatory.
- Empirical dose adjustment may be necessary in hepatic impairment (see 📖 Dose adjustments, p.67).
- Is metabolized by CYP3A4 and is susceptible to drug interactions (see 📖 Drug interactions, p.66)
- Alfentanil may modify reactions and patients should be advised not drive (or operate machinery) if affected. Refer to 📖 Drugs and driving, p.25.

😔 Adverse effects
Strong opioids tend to cause similar adverse effects, albeit to varying degrees. See also 📖 Morphine, p.371.

Very common
- Constipation
- Nausea
- Vomiting.

Common
- Bradycardia
- Drowsiness
- Postural hypotension.

Uncommon
- Headache
- Pruritus.

Rare
- Respiratory depression.

Unknown
- Irritation/local reaction (nasal spray).

Drug interactions
Pharmacokinetic
- Alfentanil is metabolized by CYP3A4. Co-administration with drugs that are metabolized by, or affect the activity (induction or inhibition — see 📖 inside back cover) of this pathway may lead to clinically relevant drug interactions and the prescriber should be aware that dosage adjustments may be necessary, particularly of drugs with a narrow therapeutic index.
- *Clarithromycin*—may enhance effect of alfentanil; dose reduction may be necessary.
- *Erythromycin* —may enhance effect of alfentanil; dose reduction may be necessary.
- *Fluconazole* —may inhibit the metabolism of alfentanil (although more likely to occur when fluconazole doses >200mg daily).
- *Midazolam* —effect may be enhanced by alfentanil (competitive inhibition of metabolism).

Pharmacodynamic
- *Antihypertensives* —increased risk of hypotension.
- *CNS depressants*—risk of excessive sedation.
- *Haloperidol* —may be an additive hypotensive effect.
- *Ketamine* —there is a potential opioid-sparing effect with ketamine; the prescriber should be aware of the need to reduce the opioid dose.
- *Levomepromazine*—may be an additive hypotensive effect.

⚖ Dose
The initial dose of alfentanil depends upon the patient's previous opioid requirements. Refer to 📖 Management of pain: opioid substitution, p.32 for information regarding opioid dose equivalences.

¥ Pain
- For opioid naïve patients, typical starting dose 0.5–1mg via CSCI over 24 hours, with 100–250 micrograms SC PRN (hourly if necessary) for breakthrough pain

- Given the short duration of action of alfentanil (<30min), it is unusual to titrate background pain with PRN doses of this opioid. Typically, an equivalent dose of alternative opioid (e.g. oxycodone) is used, based on 1/6 of the 24-hour alfentanil requirements. Note that it may be necessary to make empirical dose adjustments of the alternative opioid in renal impairment. For example:
  - 3mg alfentanil via CSCI = 40mg oxycodone via CSCI
  - 5–10mg oxycodone SC PRN (normal renal function)
  - 2.5–5mg oxycodone SC PRN (impaired renal function).

¥ *BTcP*

- There is no correlation between the dose of opioid used for persistent background pain and the dose needed to treat BTcP.
- The patient must be using opioids for persistent background pain.
- No validated treatment schedule exists. A suggested starting dose is 250–500 micrograms SC or 140–280 micrograms using the nasal spray (equivalent to 1–2 sprays) and increase as necessary.
- In the case of the nasal spray, the prescriber should consider any coexisting oral or nasal condition

₰ Dose adjustments

Elderly

- No specific guidance is available. Dose requirements should be individually titrated.

Hepatic/renal impairment

- No specific guidance available.
- In hepatic impairment, the half-life and free-fraction of alfentanil increase. An empirical dose reduction may be necessary as the effect can be more prolonged and pronounced. This is of particular importance if changing from another opioid using conventional equianalgesic values.
- Alfentanil is the drug of choice in renal disease. Although the clearance is unaltered, the free-fraction of alfentanil is raised in renal impairment. Dose requirements should be individually titrated.

Additional information

- Alfentanil spray is available from the manufacturing unit at Torbay Hospital. Delivery can take up to 5 working days (Tel: 01803 664707; Fax: 01803 664354).
- Via CSCI, alfentanil is reportedly compatible with clonazepam, dexamethasone, glycopyrronium, haloperidol, hyoscine butylbromide, hyoscine hydrobromide, levomepromazine, metoclopramide, midazolam, octreotide, and ondansetron. There is a possible concentration-dependent compatibility issue with cyclizine.

⊙ Pharmacology

Alfentanil is a synthetic opioid, chemically related to fentanyl and is more lipophilic than morphine. It is a suitable alternative to morphine for use in a CSCI, particularly in patients with renal failure. Alfentanil is approximately 10 times as potent as diamorphine (given subcutaneously). It is extensively metabolized in the liver by the CYP3A4 isoenzyme to inactive compounds.

Drugs that inhibit or induce CYP3A4 (see 🕮 inside back cover) could alter responses to alfentanil. Note that although patients requiring a CSCI of alfentanil are unlikely to be using most of these drugs, their effect on alfentanil metabolism may persist for several days even after cessation.

References

1. Murtagh FE, Chai MO, Donohoe P, *et al* The use of opioid analgesia in end-stage renal disease patients managed without dialysis: recommendations for practice. *J Pain Palliat Care Pharmacother* 2007; **21**(2):5–16.
2. Duncan A. The use of fentanyl and alfentanil sprays for episodic pain. *Palliat Med* 2002; **16**(6):550.

Allopurinol

Zyloric® (POM)
Tablet: 100mg (100); 300mg (28).

Generic (POM)
Tablet: 100mg (28); 300mg (28).

Indications

- Prophylaxis of:
  - gout
  - hyperuricaemia associated with cancer chemotherapy
  - renal stones.

Contraindications and precautions

- Allopurinol should be withdrawn immediately if a skin rash or other evidence of sensitivity occurs as this could result in more serious hypersensitivity reactions (e.g. Stevens–Johnson syndrome).
- Allopurinol treatment should not be started until an acute attack of gout has completely resolved.
- Acute attacks of gout may be precipitated during allopurinol use. It is advisable to give prophylaxis treatment during early treatment (e.g. until 1 month after hyperuricaemia corrected) with a NSAID or colchicine. Allopurinol need not be discontinued.
- Patients should be adequately hydrated to prevent xanthine deposition in the urinary tract (of particular importance during chemotherapy).
- Use with caution in patients with hepatic and renal impairment (see ⬚ Dose adjustments, p.70).

Adverse effects

Common
- Rash (withdraw treatment; can re-introduce gradually if mild but withdraw permanently if recurs).

Uncommon
- Altered LFTs
- Hypersensitivity reactions
- Nausea/vomiting (can be avoided by taking after meals).

Rare
- Hepatitis
- Stevens–Johnson syndrome
- Toxic epidermal necrolysis.

Drug interactions

Pharmacokinetic
- Is metabolized by xanthine oxidase (the cytochrome P450 system is not involved).
- *Aspirin/salicylates* —may reduce the effectiveness of allopurinol.
- *Azathioprine/6-mercaptopurine*—azathioprine is a prodrug of 6-mercaptopurine; allopurinol inhibits the metabolism of 6-mercaptopurine.

Doses of both azathioprine and 6-mercaptopurine should be reduced by 75%.
- *Ciclosporin* —plasma concentration of ciclosporin may increase.
- *Theophylline* —plasma levels of theophylline may increase.

Pharmacodynamic
- *Amoxicillin*—possible increase in skin reactions.

🥄 Dose
- Initial dose 100mg PO OD.
- Usual maintenance dose:
  - 100–200mg PO daily (mild conditions)
  - 300–600mg PO daily (moderate conditions)
  - 700–900mg PO daily (severe conditions).
- Doses over 300mg are given in 2 or more divided doses (to reduce GI intolerance).

🥄 Dose adjustments
Elderly
- The lowest effective dose should be used.

Hepatic/renal impairment
- In hepatic impairment, the manufacturer advises that reduced doses should be used. Periodic LFTs should be performed.
- In mild–moderate renal impairment, a maximum dose of 100mg PO OD is recommended and should only increase if response is inadequate. In severe renal impairment, doses should not exceed 100mg PO OD, or the dosing interval should be increased.

Additional information
- Tablets can be dispersed in water immediately prior to administration if necessary.

✪ Pharmacology
Allopurinol (and its main metabolite oxipurinol) inhibits the enzyme xanthine oxidase, blocking the conversion of hypoxanthine and xanthine to uric acid. It is rapidly absorbed from the upper GI tract and the majority of a dose is eliminated through metabolism; <10% is excreted unchanged.

Amitriptyline

Generic (POM)
Tablet: 10mg (28); 25mg (28); 50mg (28).
Oral solution: 25mg/5mL (150mL); 50mg/5mL (150mL).

Indications

- Depression
- Nocturnal enuresis
- Neuropathic pain.[¥]

Contraindications and precautions

- Amitriptyline is contraindicated for use in the following:
  - arrhythmias
  - mania
  - porphyria
  - recent myocardial infarction
  - severe liver disease.
- Do not use with an irreversible MAOI, or within 14 days of stopping one, or at least 24 hours after discontinuation of a reversible MAOI (e.g. moclobemide, linezolid). Note that in exceptional circumstances linezolid may be given with paroxetine, but the patient must be closely monitored for symptoms of serotonin syndrome (see 📖 Box 1.10, p.18).
- Amitriptyline should be used with caution in patients with:
  - cardiovascular disorders
  - epilepsy
  - hepatic impairment
  - hyperthyroid patients or those receiving thyroid medication (enhances response to antidepressant)
  - narrow-angle glaucoma
  - prostatic hypertrophy
  - urinary retention.
- Elderly patients are more susceptible to adverse effects (see 📖 Dose adjustments, p.73). Subtle deficits in attention, memory, and reasoning may occur with therapeutic dosages of anticholinergic drugs without signs of obvious toxicity. These deficits have often been mistaken for symptoms of early dementia in elderly patients.
- Depression is associated with an increased risk of suicidal thoughts, self-harm, and suicide which persists until remission. Note that that the risk of suicide may increase during initial treatment.
- Hyponatraemia should be considered in all patients who develop drowsiness, confusion, or convulsions while taking an antidepressant. Hyponatraemia has been associated with all types of antidepressants, although it is reportedly more common with SSRIs.
- Avoid abrupt withdrawal as symptoms such as nausea, headache, and malaise can occur. Although generally mild, they can be severe in some patients. Withdrawal symptoms usually occur within the first few days of discontinuing treatment and they usually resolve within 2 weeks, though they can persist in some patients for up to 3 months or

longer. See 📖 Discontinuing and/or switching antidepressants, p.45 for information about switching or stopping antidepressants. If withdrawal symptoms emerge during discontinuation, raise the dose to stop symptoms and then restart withdrawal much more gradually.

- Amitriptyline may modify reactions and patients should be advised not drive (or operate machinery) if affected. Refer to 📖 Drugs and driving, p.25.

Adverse effects

The frequency is not defined, but reported adverse effects include:

- Abnormal LFTs
- Arrhythmias
- Blurred vision
- Confusion
- Constipation
- Convulsions
- Delirium (particularly in the elderly)
- Difficulty with micturition
- Dizziness
- Dry mouth
- Galactorrhoea
- Gynaecomastia
- Hallucinations
- Headache
- Hypomania or mania
- Hyponatraemia
- Increased appetite and weight gain
- Movement disorders
- Nausea
- Postural hypotension
- Sedation
- Sexual dysfunction
- Stomatitis
- Sweating
- Tachycardia
- Taste disturbances
- Tinnitus
- Tremor.

Drug interactions

Pharmacokinetic

- Amitriptyline is a substrate of CYP1A2, CYP2C9, CYP2C19, CYP2D6 (major), and CYP3A4. Co-administration with drugs that are metabolized by, or affect the activity (induction or inhibition; see 📖 inside back cover) of these pathways may lead to clinically relevant drug interactions and the prescriber should be aware that dosage adjustments may be necessary, particularly of drugs with a narrow therapeutic index.
- *Fluconazole* —may increase the plasma concentrations of amitriptyline.
- *Methylphenidate* —may inhibit the metabolism of amitriptyline as a degree of competitive inhibition may develop.

Pharmacodynamic

- Amitriptyline may cause prolongation of the QT interval. There is a potential risk that co-administration with other drugs that also prolong the QT interval (e.g. *amiodarone, erythromycin, haloperidol, quinine*) may result in ventricular arrhythmias.
- *Anticholinergics* —increased risk of adverse effects.
- *Anti-epileptics* —amitriptyline antagonizes the effect.
- *Antihypertensives* —possible increased risk of hypotension.
- *β_2-agonists* —combination may predispose patients to cardiac arrhythmias.
- *CNS depressants*—additive sedative effect.
- *Domperidone* —may inhibit prokinetic effect.

- *MAOIs*, including *linezolid*, should be avoided (see 📖 Contraindications and precautions, p.71).
- *Metoclopramide*—may inhibit prokinetic effect.
- *Nefopam*—increased risk of anticholinergic adverse effects.
- *Serotonergic drugs*—caution is advisable if amitriptyline is co-administered with serotonergic drugs (e.g. *methadone, mirtazapine, SSRIs, tramadol, trazodone*) due to the risk of serotonin syndrome (see 📖 Box 1.10, p.18).
- *SSRIs*—increased risk of seizures and serotonin syndrome.
- *Tramadol*—increased risk of seizures and serotonin syndrome.

Dose
- All indications:
  - 10–25mg PO ON, increasing as necessary to a maximum of 150mg PO daily in divided doses.

Dose adjustments
Elderly
- Elderly patients are particularly susceptible to adverse anticholinergic effects, with an increased risk for cognitive decline and dementia. No specific dose reductions are recommended by manufacturers. However, it is suggested that elderly patients are initiated on the lower end of the usual range, i.e. 10mg ON and the dose increased as necessary and as tolerated.

Hepatic/renal impairment
- There are no specific instructions for dose reduction in hepatic impairment. It is contraindicated for use in severe liver disease and should be used with caution in patients with hepatic impairment. If the drug has to be used, the patient should be closely monitored and the lowest effective dose should be prescribed.
- There are no specific instructions for dose adjustment in renal impairment. The lowest effective dose should be prescribed.

Additional information
- May have immediate benefits in treating insomnia or anxiety; antidepressant action may be delayed 2–4 weeks.

Pharmacology
Amitriptyline is a tertiary amine TCA with strong anticholinergic activity. It undergoes first-pass metabolism to the primary active metabolite nortriptyline. Both amitriptyline and its active metabolite block the reuptake of noradrenaline and serotonin. The interference with the reuptake of noradrenaline and serotonin is believed to explain the mechanism of the antidepressant and analgesic activity of amitriptyline.

Reference
1. Saarto T, Wiffen PJ. Antidepressants for neuropathic pain. *Cochrane Database Syst Rev* 2007; **4**.:CD005454.

Amoxicillin

Amoxil® (POM)
Capsule: 250mg (21); 500mg (21).
Sachet (sugar-free): 3g (2).
Injection: 500mg (5; 10); 1g (5; 10).

Generic (POM)
Capsule: 250mg (21); 500mg (21).
Sachet (sugar-free): 3g (2).
Oral suspension (as powder for reconstitution): 125mg/5mL (100mL); 250mg/5mL (100mL).
Note: sugar-free formulations are available.
Injection (as powder for reconstitution): 250mg (10); 500mg (10); 1g (10).

Indications
- Refer to local guidelines.
- Broad-spectrum antibiotic indicated for the treatment of commonly occurring bacterial infections.
- *Helicobacter pylori* eradication.

Contraindications and precautions
- Is contraindicated for use in patients with penicillin hypersensitivity.
- Use with caution in renal impairment (risk of crystalluria). Maintain adequate hydration with high doses.

Adverse effects
Common
- Diarrhoea
- Nausea
- Skin rash.

Uncommon
- Pruritus
- Urticaria
- Vomiting.

Very rare
- Antibiotic associated colitis
- Crystalluria
- Hepatitis
- Interstitial nephritis.

Drug interactions
Pharmacokinetic
- *Oral contraceptives*—reduced efficacy.
- *Warfarin* —possible increase in INR.

Pharmacodynamic
- *Allopurinol*—possible increase in skin reactions.

⚕ Dose
Standard doses are described here. Refer to local guidelines for specific advice.

- 250mg PO TDS, increasing to 500mg PO TDS in severe infections. Higher doses (1g PO TDS) have been used.
- 500mg IV injection or infusion TDS, increasing to 1g IV injection or infusion QDS in severe infections. Higher doses (2g IV injection or infusion 4-hourly have been used for serious infections).

♣ Dose adjustments

Elderly
- No dose adjustment necessary.

Hepatic/renal impairment
- No specific guidance is available for use in hepatic impairment. Use the lowest effective dose.
- Patients in severe renal impairment may need dose adjustments, although no specific guidance is available. Standard adult doses should be tolerated; only the high doses for severe infections may need reducing.

Additional information

- Once reconstituted, the *oral solution* must be discarded after 14 days.
- To reconstitute the *injection*, add 5mL WFI to 250mg vial (final volume 5.2mL), 10mL WFI to 500mg vial (final volume 10.4mL), or 20mL WFI to 1g vial (final volume 20.8mL).
- Administer IV *injection* over 3–4min; administer IV *infusion* in 50–100mL NaCl 0.9% (or glucose 5%) over 30–60min.

♦ Pharmacology

Amoxicillin is a broad-spectrum antibiotic active against a wide range of Gram-positive bacteria, with a limited range of Gram-negative cover. It is well absorbed following oral administration, particularly in comparison with other β-lactam antibiotics. Amoxicillin is bactericidal in that it interferes with the synthesis of the bacterial cell wall. As a result, the cell wall is weakened and the bacterium swells, then ruptures.

Anastrozole

Arimidex® (POM)
Tablet: 1mg (28).

Indications

- Treatment of advanced breast cancer in postmenopausal women.

Contraindications and precautions

- Anastrozole is contraindicated for use in:
  - premenopausal women
  - pregnant or lactating women
  - patients with severe renal impairment (creatinine clearance <20mL/min)
  - patients with moderate or severe hepatic disease.
- Avoid concurrent administration of tamoxifen (see 📖 Drug interactions).
- Asthenia (weakness) and drowsiness have been reported with the use of anastrozole. Caution should be observed when driving or operating machinery while such symptoms persist.

Adverse effects

Very common

- Fatigue
- Headache
- Hot flushes
- Joint pain
- Nausea
- Rash
- Weakness.

Common

- Alopecia
- Anorexia
- Carpal tunnel syndrome
- Diarrhoea
- Drowsiness
- Hypercholesterolaemia
- Vaginal bleeding.

Uncommon

- Altered LFTs (gamma GT and bilirubin)
- Hepatitis
- Urticaria.

Rare

- Erythema multiforme.

Drug interactions

Pharmacokinetic

- Unlikely to be involved in pharmacokinetic interactions.

Pharmacodynamic

- *Oestrogens*—may antagonize the effect of anastrozole.
- *Tamoxifen*—may reduce the beneficial effect of anastrozole.

🎗 Dose

- 1mg PO OD.

♣️ Dose adjustments

Elderly
- No dosage adjustments are necessary.

Hepatic/renal impairment
- No dose change is recommended in patients with mild hepatic disease, but anastrozole is contraindicated for use in patients with moderate or severe hepatic disease.
- No dose change is recommended in patients with mild or moderate renal impairment, but anastrozole is contraindicated for use in patients with severe renal impairment (creatinine clearance <20mL/min).

⋺ Pharmacology

Anastrozole is a potent and selective non-steroidal aromatase inhibitor which does not possess any progestogenic, androgenic or oestrogenic activity. It is believed to work by significantly lowering serum oestradiol concentrations through inhibition of aromatase (converts adrenal androstenedione to oestrone, which is precursor of oestradiol). Many breast cancers have oestrogen receptors and growth of these tumours can be stimulated by oestrogens.

Antacid and oxetacaine

Unlicensed Special (POM)
Oral suspension (sugar-free): each 5mL contains oxetacaine 10mg, aluminium hydroxide 200mg, and magnesium hydroxide 100mg (150mL). See 📚 Additional information, p.79 for supply issues.

Indications
- ⃰Mucositis[1]
- ⃰Painful oral candidiasis.[1]

Contraindications and precautions
- Avoid use in acute GI conditions (e.g. acute inflammatory bowel diseases, abdominal pain of unknown origin, intestinal obstruction).
- Avoid use in patients with hypophosphataemia (aluminium binds phosphate).
- Use with caution in patients with renal impairment, or undergoing haemodialysis (see 📚 Dose adjustments, p.79).
- Do not exceed a daily dose of 60mL, as the risk of adverse effects will increase accordingly.
- The use of antacid and oxetacaine should be viewed as a short treatment for the painful oral condition, while the underlying cause is treated or improves.

☺ Adverse effects
The frequency is not stated, but adverse effects include:
- Constipation
- Diarrhoea
- Hypersensitivity reactions (e.g. angio-oedema, glossitis, pruritus).

At doses >60mL/day
- Dizziness
- Drowsiness
- Faintness
- Hyperaluminaemia (may occur in renal impairment; symptoms include apparent dementia and encephalopathy)
- Hypermagnesaemia (may occur in renal impairment; symptoms include nausea, vomiting, confusion, drowsiness).

Drug interactions
Pharmacokinetic
- Antacid and oxetacaine can influence the rate and extent of absorption of a variety of drugs. It should not be given within 1 hour of the following drugs/formulations:
  - *bisacodyl*—may remove the enteric coat and increase the risk of dyspepsia
  - *demeclocycline*—reduced absorption
  - *diazepam*—absorption may be delayed
  - *digoxin*—possible reduced absorption
  - *enteric coated formulations*
  - *ferrous sulphate* —possible reduced absorption

- *gabapentin*—reduced absorption
- *lansoprazole*—reduced absorption
- *paroxetine*—reduced absorption of suspension
- *rabeprazole*—reduced absorption.

Pharmacodynamic
- *Opioids* —risk of respiratory depression (associated with hypermagnesaemia).

Dose

- 5–10mL PO 15min before meals and at bedtime. A maximum daily dose of 60mL should not be exceeded.
- The dose can be reduced gradually as symptoms improve.

Dose adjustments

Elderly
- No specific guidance is available. Nonetheless, unless the patient has renal impairment, usual adult doses can be used.

Hepatic/renal impairment
- No specific guidance is available for patients with hepatic impairment. Nonetheless, use with caution in patients with severe hepatic impairment due to the possible risk of subsequent renal impairment.
- Hypermagnesaemia and hyperaluminaemia can develop in patients with renal impairment. Use lower doses, or choose an alternative.
- Hyperaluminaemia can also develop in patients undergoing haemodialysis.

Additional information

- Antacid and oxetacaine is an unlicensed product which is available as a special order from Rosemont Pharmaceuticals (0800 919312). Delivery is approximately 2 days from making the order. Advise patients to request a prescription at least 4 days before the supply is needed.
- Review the expiry date of the product; it has a shelf-life of 3 months.

Pharmacology

As the name suggests, this product reduces gastric pH, while forming a gel that coats and protects the damaged mucosa. Partly due to the adherent nature of the aluminium/magnesium vehicle, oxetacaine produces a topical anaesthetic effect that is both more potent and prolonged than lidocaine. Only small amounts of aluminium or magnesium are absorbed from the bowel, while the absorbed oxetacaine undergoes rapid and extensive metabolism.

Reference

1. Barber C, Powell R, Ellis A, *et al.* Comparing pain control and ability to eat and drink with standard therapy vs Gelclair: a preliminary, double centre, randomized controlled trial on patients with radiotherapy-induced oral mucositis. *Support Care Cancer* 2007; **15**(4):427–40.

Azathioprine

Imuran® (POM)
Tablet: 25mg (100); 50mg (100).

Generic (POM)
Tablet: 25mg (28); 50mg (56).

Indications
- Immunosuppression (*not discussed*)
- ¥Pulmonary fibrosis.[1]

Contraindications and precautions
- Full blood counts should be performed weekly (or more frequently if the patient has severe hepatic or renal impairment) during the first 8 weeks of treatment.
- The patient should be warned to report signs or symptoms of bone marrow suppression, such as inexplicable bruising or bleeding, sore throat, fever, and any other sign of infection.
- Use with caution in patients with liver and/or renal impairment (see 📖 Dose adjustments, p.81).
- Warn patients to reduce exposure to UV light as there is a risk of photosensitivity and skin cancer.
- Patients without a definite history of chickenpox should be advised to avoid close personal contact with chickenpox or herpes zoster.
- Hypersensitivity may develop during treatment and can manifest as a variety of symptoms including arthralgia, diarrhoea, dizziness, fever, general malaise, hepatic impairment, hypotension, myalgia, nausea and vomiting, rash, renal impairment, and vasculitis. Withdrawal of azathioprine usually resolves the symptoms.

☹ Adverse effects
Very common
- Bone marrow depression
- Leucopenia.

Common
- Thrombocytopenia.

Uncommon
- Altered LFTs (gamma GT and bilirubin)
- Anaemia
- Cholestasis
- Hypersensitivity reactions (see 📖 Contraindications and precautions)
- Increased susceptibility to infection (bacterial, fungal, or viral)
- Pancreatitis.

Rare
- Alopecia
- Aplastic anaemia
- Megaloblastic anaemia
- Pancytopenia

Drug interactions

Pharmacokinetic

- *Allopurinol*—inhibits xanthine oxidase. Patients receiving azathioprine and allopurinol concomitantly should have the dose of azathioprine reduced by 75%.
- *Furosemide*—*in vitro* tests have shown a reduction in the metabolism of azathioprine; the clinical significance remains unknown.

Pharmacodynamic

- *Corticosteroids*—may increase the immunosuppressive effect.
- *Warfarin*—anticoagulant effect may be reduced.

Dose

¥ Pulmonary fibrosis

- Initial dose of 2–3mg/kg/day PO (maximum 150mg/day). Increase if necessary in 25mg increments every 7–14 days, to a maximum of 150mg daily.
- Has been used in conjunction with prednisolone (see Prednisolone, p.437) and N-acetylcysteine (600mg TDS PO).

Dose adjustments

Elderly

- No specific dose adjustments are required, but lower doses are recommended.

Hepatic/renal impairment

- No specific dose adjustments are suggested for patients with hepatic or renal impairment, although lower doses are recommended and haematological response should be carefully monitored.

Additional information

- Azathioprine is cytotoxic. Tablets must not be crushed, or cut. If necessary, the tablets can be dispersed in water forming a solution that can be administered via enteral tube. Gloves should be worn during preparation and administration.

Pharmacology

Azathioprine is a prodrug that is converted to 6-mercaptopurine (6-MP), which (after additional metabolism) blocks purine synthesis and leads to the incorporation of cytotoxic nucleotides into DNA. Azathioprine is well absorbed following oral administration with maximum plasma concentrations appearing within 2 hours. It is eliminated via metabolism in erythrocytes and the liver, initially forming 6-MP. Metabolism of 6-MP involves a variety of enzymes; hypoxanthine-guanine phosphoribosyltransferase (HGPRT) and subsequent multi-enzymatic processes produce pharmacologically active 6-thioguanine nucleotides; metabolism of 6-MP via xanthine oxidase (XO) and thiopurine S-methyltransferase (TPMT) produce inactive metabolites. Drug interactions (particularly XO) and genetic variability (TPMT) can influence the response to azathioprine.

Reference

1. Bradley B, Branley HM, Egan JJ, *et al.* Interstitial lung disease guideline: the British Thoracic Society in collaboration with the Thoracic Society of Australia and New Zealand and the Irish Thoracic Society. *Thorax* 2008; **63**(Suppl 5):v1–v58

Baclofen

Lioresal® (POM)
Tablet: 10mg (84).
Liquid (sugar-free): 5mg/5mL (300mL).

Generic (POM)
Tablet: 10mg (84).
Liquid*: 5mg/5mL (300mL).
* Check each generic product for sugar content.

Indications
- Relief of spasticity of voluntary muscle
- ¥Hiccup.[1]

Contraindications and precautions
- Avoid in patients with active peptic ulceration.
- Baclofen should be used cautiously in the following conditions since it may lead to exacerbations:
  - confusional states
  - depressive or manic disorders
  - epilepsy
  - Parkinson's disease
  - schizophrenia.
- Baclofen should also be used cautiously in the following conditions:
  - cerebrovascular accident (CVA)
  - diabetes mellitus (baclofen may cause rise in blood glucose)
  - hepatic impairment (baclofen may elevate LFTs)
  - hypertension (see 📖 Drug interactions, p.83)
  - renal impairment (see 📖 Dose adjustments, p.83).
  - respiratory impairment (see 📖 Adverse effects).

- Do not withdraw baclofen abruptly as symptoms such as anxiety, confusions, convulsions, dyskinesia, hallucinations, mania, paranoia, psychosis, and tachycardia can occur. These symptoms may occur within a few hours after discontinuation. In addition, rebound temporary aggravation of spasticity can also occur. Treatment should always be discontinued over a period of about 1–2 weeks by gradual dosage reduction, unless a serious adverse event has occurred. If such symptoms occur, the dose should be increased and a longer withdrawal should be planned. Refer to 📖 Use of drugs in end-of-life care, p.53 for end-of-life care issues.

- Baclofen may modify reactions and patients should be advised not to drive (or operate machinery) if affected. Refer to 📖 Drugs and driving, p.25.

☺ Adverse effects
Very common
- Nausea
- Sedation
- Somnolence.

Common

- Ataxia
- Confusion
- Constipation
- Depression
- Diarrhoea
- Dizziness
- Dry mouth
- Dysuria
- Euphoria
- Fatigue
- Hallucinations
- Headache
- Hypotension
- Insomnia
- Light-headedness
- Muscular weakness
- Myalgia
- Nightmares
- Nystagmus
- Polyuria
- Respiratory depression
- Sweating
- Tremor
- Visual disturbances.

Rare

- Abnormal LFTs
- Abdominal pain
- Paraesthesia
- Urinary retention.

Drug interactions

Pharmacokinetic

- *ACEIs*—may reduce renal excretion of baclofen.
- *NSAIDs*—may reduce renal excretion of baclofen.

Pharmacodynamic

- *Antihypertensives*—additive hypotensive effect.
- *CNS depressants*—increased risk of adverse effects such as sedation and respiratory depression.

⚕ Dose

Muscle spasticity/spasm

- Initial dose 5mg PO TDS, increasing by 5mg PO TDS every 3 days until satisfactory control is achieved, or a dose of 20mg PO TDS is reached. The dose can be increased further under supervision to a maximum daily dose of 100mg.
- Patients may require a slower titrating schedule if adverse effects become problematic.

¥ Hiccup

- Initial dose 5mg PO BD, increasing to 10mg PO BD after 3 days. Further dose increases may be necessary.

⚕ Dose adjustments

Elderly

- No specific dose reductions are necessary but lower initial doses are recommended (e.g. 2.5–5mg PO BD). Further titration should be cautious. Also refer to following renal impairment guidance.

Hepatic/renal impairment

- For liver impairment, no specific guidance is available. Dose requirements should be individually titrated.

- Baclofen is substantially excreted by the kidney and dose reductions will be necessary in those with impaired renal function. The manufacturer recommends that an initial low dose (e.g. 5mg PO OD) should be used and the patient should be observed for signs of toxicity if the dose is increased further. Only use in end-stage renal failure if perceived benefit outweighs the risk.

Additional information

- If the patient develops hypotonia which is considered problematic during the day, increasing the evening dose and reducing the daytime dose(s) may overcome this issue.

✷ Pharmacology

Baclofen is a gamma-aminobutyric acid derivative that is a specific agonist at GABA-B receptors. The precise mechanism of action is not fully understood and there is no conclusive evidence that actions on GABA systems lead to the clinical effects. Nonetheless, it inhibits reflexes at the spinal level and actions at supraspinal sites may also occur. The clinical effect in hiccups may be due to a direct effect on the diaphragm. Baclofen is rapidly and extensively absorbed and is excreted primarily by the kidney in unchanged form (85% of the dose is excreted unchanged).

Reference

1. Seker MM, Aksoy S, Ozdemir NY, *et al.* Successful treatment of chronic hiccup with baclofen in cancer patients. *Med Oncol* 2012; **29**(2): 1369–1370.

Benzydamine

Difflam® (P)
Oral rinse: benzydamine hydrochloride 0.15% w/v (300mL).
Oromucosal spray: benzydamine hydrochloride 0.15% w/v (30mL).

Indications
- Painful inflammatory conditions of the mouth and throat.

Contraindications and precautions
- Difflam® oral rinse should generally be used undiluted. Should stinging occur, it can be diluted with an equal volume of water.
- The use benzydamine should be viewed as a short treatment for the painful oral condition, while the underlying cause is treated or improves.

☺ Adverse effects
- The frequency is not defined, but reported adverse effects include:
  - hypersensitivity (very rarely reported, but include bronchospasm, pruritus, rash, urticaria)
  - numbness (local)
  - stinging (local).

Drug interactions
Pharmacokinetic
- None known.

Pharmacodynamic
- None known.

♣ Dose
Oral rinse
- 15 mL, as an oral rinse or gargle, every 1½–3 hours as required. The patient must not swallow.

Oromucosal spray
- 4–8 sprays to the affected area every 1½–3 hours as required.

♣ Dose adjustments
Elderly
- No adjustments necessary.

Hepatic/renal impairment
- Systemic absorption with correct use is minimal, so dose adjustments are unnecessary for patients with renal or hepatic impairment.

⟴ Pharmacology
Benzydamine is a NSAID, thought to produce an anti-inflammatory and analgesic action by stabilizing the cellular membrane and inhibiting prostaglandin synthesis.

Betahistine

Serc® (POM)
Tablet: 8mg (120); 16mg (scored; 84).

Generic (POM)
Tablet: 8mg (84; 120); 16mg (84).

Indications

- Ménière's syndrome
- Tinnitus
- Vertigo.

Contraindications and precautions

- Contraindicated for use in patients with phaeochromocytoma.
- Use with caution in patients with patients with a history of:
  - asthma
  - peptic ulcer.

Adverse effects

The frequency is not defined, but reported adverse effects include:

- Headache
- Dyspepsia
- Nausea
- Peptic ulcer disease.

Drug interactions

Pharmacokinetic

- None known.

Pharmacodynamic

- *H_1 antihistamines*—theoretical risk of reduction in effect of betahistine.

Dose

- Initial dose 16mg PO TDS. Dose can be increased as necessary to 24–48mg PO daily in divided doses.

Dose adjustments

Elderly

- No specific guidance available.

Hepatic/renal impairment

- No specific guidance available. However, betahistine is excreted unchanged so the prescriber should be aware that dose reductions may be necessary.

Additional information

- Tablets can be crushed and dispersed in water immediately prior to administration if necessary.

Pharmacology

Betahistine is a specific histamine agonist and it appears to act on the precapillary sphincter in the stria vascularis of the inner ear, reducing the pressure in the endolymphatic space.

Bicalutamide

Casodex® (POM)
Tablet: 50mg (28); 150mg (28).

Indications

- Treatment of advanced prostate cancer in combination with luteinizing hormone-releasing hormone (LHRH) analogue therapy or surgical castration (50mg).
- Locally advanced prostate cancer at high risk of disease progression, either alone or as adjuvant treatment to prostatectomy or radiotherapy (150mg).
- Locally advanced, non-metastatic prostate cancer when surgical castration or other medical intervention inappropriate (150mg).

Contraindications and precautions

- Contraindicated for use in women and children.
- Should only be initiated by or under the supervision of a specialist.
- Use with caution in patients with liver disease (see 📖 Dose adjustments, p.88).
- Bicalutamide inhibits CYP3A4; the manufacturer advises caution when co-administered with drugs metabolized predominantly by CYP3A4.

😊 Adverse effects

Very common

- Abdominal pain
- Anaemia
- Breast tenderness
- Constipation
- Dizziness
- Fatigue
- Gynaecomastia
- Haematuria
- Hot flushes
- Nausea
- Oedema.

Common

- Alopecia
- Altered LFTs (manufacturer recommends checking LFTs periodically)
- Chest pain
- Cholestasis
- Decreased libido
- Dry skin
- Dyspepsia
- Impotence
- Jaundice
- Myocardial infarction (apparent increased risk when used in combination with LHRH agonists)
- Pruritus
- Weakness
- Weight gain.

Uncommon

- Depression
- Hypersensitivity reactions.

Drug interactions

Pharmacokinetic

- Bicalutamide is an inhibitor of CYP3A4. Co-administration with drugs that are metabolized by, or affect the activity (induction or inhibition—see 📖 inside back cover) of this pathway may lead to clinically relevant drug interactions and the prescriber should be aware that dosage adjustments may be necessary, particularly of drugs with a narrow therapeutic index.

- *Warfarin* —may be displaced from protein binding sites; check INR if bicalutamide started in patient already on warfarin

Pharmacodynamic

- No clinically important interactions.

♒ Dose

- Treatment of advanced prostate cancer in combination with LHRH analogue therapy or surgical castration:
  - 50mg PO OD.
  - Treatment should be started at least 3 days before commencing treatment with an LHRH analogue, or at the same time as surgical castration.
- Locally advanced prostate cancer:
  - 150mg PO OD.
  - It should be taken for at least 2 years, or until the disease progresses.

♒ Dose adjustments

Elderly

- Dosage adjustments are unnecessary.

Hepatic/renal impairment

- Bicalutamide is extensively metabolized in the liver. However, dosage adjustments are not required for patients with mild hepatic impairment. Increased accumulation may occur in patients with moderate to severe hepatic impairment, although no specific guidance is available. Patients should be closely monitored for signs of deteriorating liver function.
- Dosage adjustments are not required for patients with renal impairment.

Additional information

Although tablets may be crushed and dispersed in water prior to administration, it is not recommended to be performed due to the risk of exposure.

⊸ Pharmacology

Bicalutamide is a non-steroidal anti-androgen that blocks the action of androgens of adrenal and testicular origin which stimulate the growth of normal and malignant prostatic tissue. It is well absorbed following oral administration, is highly protein bound, and is extensively metabolized. The metabolites are eliminated via the kidneys and bile.

Bisacodyl

Generic (P)
Tablet: 5mg (500; 1000).
Suppository: 10mg (12).

Indications
- Treatment of constipation.

Contraindications and precautions
- Contraindicated in:
  - abdominal pain of unknown origin
  - acute inflammatory bowel diseases
  - anal fissure (suppository)
  - ileus
  - intestinal obstruction
  - severe dehydration
  - ulcerative proctitis (suppository).

☺ Adverse effects
Common
- Abdominal cramps and discomfort
- Diarrhoea
- Nausea.

Uncommon
- Vomiting.

Unknown
- Colitis.

Drug interactions
Pharmacokinetic
- *Antacids*—may remove the enteric coat and increase the risk of dyspepsia.

Pharmacodynamic
- *Anticholinergics*—antagonizes the laxative effect.
- *Cyclizine*—antagonizes the laxative effect.
- *Opioids*—antagonizes the laxative effect.
- *5-HT$_3$ antagonists*—antagonizes the laxative effect.
- *TCAs*—antagonizes the laxative effect.

⚖ Dose
- Initial dose 5–10mg PO ON. Dose can be increased as necessary to a maximum of 20mg PO ON.
  - ¥Higher doses may be necessary.
- Alternatively, 10mg PR OM.
  - ¥Additional doses may be needed.

⚖ Dose adjustments
Elderly
- No specific dose adjustments recommended by the manufacturer.

Hepatic/renal impairment
• No specific dose adjustments recommended by the manufacturer.

Additional information
• Suppositories are usually effective in about 20min; tablets take effect between 6–12 hours.
• Tablets must not be crushed due to risk of dyspepsia.

⟳ Pharmacology
Bisacodyl is a locally acting laxative which undergoes bacterial cleavage in the colon to produce stimulation of the both the large intestine and rectum causing peristalsis and a feeling of rectal fullness.

Bisoprolol

Cardicor® (POM)
Tablet: 1.25mg (28); 2.5mg (scored—28); 3.75mg (scored—28); 5mg (scored —28); 7.5mg (scored—28); 10mg (scored—28).

Emcor® (POM)
Tablet: 5mg (scored—28); 10mg (scored—28).

Generic (POM)
Tablet: 1.25mg (28); 2.5mg (28); 5mg (28); 10mg (28).

Indications

- Adjunctive treatment of stable chronic moderate to severe heart failure (Cardicor®).
- Angina.
- Hypertension.

Note: Cardicor® is only licensed for use in the treatment of heart failure.

Contraindications and precautions

- Bisoprolol is contraindicated for use in patients with:
  - acute heart failure
  - atrioventricular (AV) block of second or third degree (without a pacemaker)
  - bradycardia with <60 beats/min before the start of therapy
  - hypotension (systolic blood pressure <100mmHg)
  - late stages of peripheral arterial occlusive disease
  - metabolic acidosis
  - Raynaud's syndrome
  - severe bronchial asthma or severe chronic obstructive pulmonary disease (COPD)
  - sick sinus syndrome
  - sinoatrial block
  - untreated phaeochromocytoma.
- Bisoprolol must be used with caution in:
  - asthma
  - AV block of first degree
  - diabetes mellitus (may mask signs of hypoglycaemia)
  - obstructive airways diseases
  - peripheral arterial occlusive disease
  - Prinzmetal's angina
  - psoriasis (bisoprolol may exacerbate).
- Treatment with bisoprolol should not be stopped abruptly unless clearly indicated, especially in patients with ischaemic heart disease.
- There is a risk that sensitivity to allergens is increased with bisoprolol.

☺ Adverse effects

Common

- Cold/numb extremities
- Constipation
- Diarrhoea
- Dizziness

- Exhaustion
- Headache
- Nausea

- Tiredness
- Vomiting.

Uncommon
- Bradycardia
- Bronchospasm
- Cramps
- Depression

- Muscular weakness
- Sleep disturbances
- Postural hypotension
- Worsening of heart failure.

Drug interactions
Pharmacokinetic
- Bisoprolol is metabolized by CYP3A4. Co-administration with drugs that are metabolized by, or affect the activity (induction or inhibition—see 📖 inside back cover) of this pathway may lead to clinically relevant drug interactions and the prescriber should be aware that dosage adjustments may be necessary, particularly of drugs with a narrow therapeutic index.
- The effect of grapefruit juice on the bioavailability of bisoprolol is unknown, but excessive amounts should be avoided.

Pharmacodynamic
- *Antihypertensives*—increased risk of hypotension.
- *Digoxin*—increased risk of bradycardia.
- *Diltiazem*—increased risk of hypotension and AV block.
- *Haloperidol*—potential increased risk of hypotension.
- *Insulin/oral antidiabetic drugs*—symptoms of hypoglycaemia may be masked.
- *Levomepromazine*—potential increased risk of postural hypotension.
- *NSAIDs*—may reduce hypotensive effect of bisoprolol.
- *Verapamil*—increased risk of hypotension and AV block.

🔳 Dose
Adjunct in stable moderate to severe heart failure
- Initial dose 1.25mg PO OM for 7 days; if necessary increase the dose to 2.5mg PO OM for 7 days then 3.75mg PO OD for 7 days, then 5mg PO OD for 4 weeks, then 7.5mg PO OM for 4 weeks, then 10mg PO OM; maximum dose 10mg PO daily.

Angina and hypertension
- Initial dose 10mg PO OM, increased as necessary to maximum 20mg PO daily.

🔳 Dose adjustments
Elderly
- No dose adjustment necessary, although 5mg daily may be a more suitable starting dose for hypertension/angina.

Liver/renal impairment
- In patients with liver impairment or severe renal impairment (CrCl <20mL/min) the dose should not exceed 10mg daily.

Additional information

• Tablets may be crushed and dispersed in water immediately prior to administration.

⟐ Pharmacology

Bisoprolol is a competitive, highly selective β_1-adrenergic receptor antagonist and is generally not to be expected to influence the airway resistance. This selectivity extends beyond the therapeutic range. It is well absorbed orally with a bioavailability of 90%; excretion is divided evenly between metabolism (mainly by CYP3A4) and renal elimination of unchanged drug. The metabolites are inactive and are also excreted renally.

Buprenorphine

Temgesic® (CD3 POM)
Sublingual tablet: 200 micrograms (50), 400 micrograms (50).

BuTrans® (CD3 POM)
Patch: 5 micrograms/hour for 7 days (2); 10 micrograms/hour for 7 days (2); 20 micrograms/hour for 7 days (2).

Transtec® (CD3 POM)
Patch: 35 micrograms/hour for 96 hours (4); 52.5 micrograms/hour for 96 hours (4); 70 micrograms/hour for 96 hours (4).

Generic (CD3 POM)
Sublingual tablet: 200 micrograms, 400 micrograms.
Injection: 300 microgram/mL (10 × 1mL).

> • Buprenorphine is a Schedule 3 CD. Refer to 🕮 Legal categories of medicines, p.21 for further information.

Indications
• Acute pain (tablets and injection—*not discussed*).
• Treatment of non-malignant pain of moderate intensity unresponsive to non-opioid analgesics (*BuTrans®* patches).
• Management of moderate to severe cancer pain and severe pain unresponsive to non-opioid analgesics (*Transtec®* patches).

Contraindications and precautions

> If the dose of an opioid is titrated correctly, it is generally accepted that there are no absolute contraindications to the use of such drugs in palliative care, although there may be circumstances where one opioid is favoured over another (e.g. renal impairment, constipation).

• Refer to 🕮 Use of drugs in end-of-life care, p.53 for end-of-life care issues.
• Must not be used if the patient has received a MAOI within the previous 2 weeks.
• Transdermal formulations should not be used if the patient has variable analgesic requirements.
• Naloxone can reverse the effects of buprenorphine (usually needing a continuous infusion of high doses).
• Dose adjustments may be necessary in hepatic impairment (see 🕮 Dose adjustments, p.96).
• Should not be used in opioid-naïve patients, or for the treatment of acute or intermittent pain.
• Use with caution in patients with:
  • concurrent CYP3A4 inhibitors (see 🕮 Drug interactions, p.95)
  • hepatic impairment (empirical dose adjustment may be necessary—see 🕮 Dose adjustments, p.96)

- pyrexia (transdermal route only—increased buprenorphine delivery rate)
- severe respiratory disease.
- Patients should be advised to avoid exposing the patch application site to direct heat sources such as hot water bottles, electric blankets, heat lamps, saunas, or baths because of the risk of increased fentanyl absorption.
- Patients who experience serious adverse events should have the patches removed immediately and should be monitored for up to 24 hours after patch removal.
- Buprenorphine may modify reactions and patients should be advised not drive (or operate machinery) if affected. Refer to 📖 Drugs and driving, p.25.

😔 Adverse effects

- Strong opioids tend to cause similar adverse effects, albeit to varying degrees. See also 📖 Morphine, p.371.

Very common

- Application site reaction
- Constipation
- Dizziness
- Drowsiness
- Dry mouth
- Erythema
- Headache
- Nausea
- Pruritus
- Vomiting.

Common

- Anorexia
- Confusion
- Depression
- Dyspnoea
- Insomnia
- Nausea
- Nervousness.

Uncommon

- Postural hypotension
- Sleep disorder
- Tachycardia.

Rare

- Hallucinations
- Respiratory depression
- Visual disturbances.

Drug interactions

Pharmacokinetic

- Buprenorphine undergoes extensive first-pass metabolism via both CYP3A4 and glucuronidation. Inhibition of CYP3A4 alone may have a less than expected effect on buprenorphine clearance, due to the impact of glucuronidation. Co-administration with drugs that are metabolized by, or affect the activity (induction or inhibition) of CYP3A4 or glucuronidation may lead to clinically relevant drug interactions.

Pharmacodynamic

- *Antihypertensives*—increased risk of hypotension.
- *CNS depressants*—risk of excessive sedation.
- *Haloperidol*—may be an additive hypotensive effect.

- *Ketamine*—there is a potential opioid-sparing effect with ketamine; the prescriber should be aware of the need to reduce the opioid dose.
- *Levomepromazine*—may be an additive hypotensive effect.

Dose

- For moderate pain unresponsive to non-opioids, i.e. suitable for opioid naïve patient:
  - Using BuTrans® patches, initial dose 5 micrograms/hour patch for 7 days.
  - The analgesic effect should not be evaluated for at least 72 hours after application in order to allow for gradual increase in plasma-buprenorphine concentration.
  - The dose can be adjusted, if necessary, at 3-day intervals using a patch of the next strength or 2 patches of the same strength (applied at same time to avoid confusion).
  - A maximum of 2 patches can be used at any one time.
- For moderate to severe cancer pain and severe pain unresponsive to non-opioids:
  - Using Transtec® patches, initial dose of buprenorphine is based upon previous opioid requirements. For opioid naïve patients, the manufacturer recommends 35 micrograms/hour for 96 hours.
  - The analgesic effect should not be evaluated for at least 24 hours after application in order to allow for gradual increase in plasma-buprenorphine concentration
  - The dose can be adjusted, if necessary, at intervals of no longer than 96 hours using a patch of the next strength or using 2 patches of the same strength (applied at same time to avoid confusion).
  - A maximum of 2 patches can be used at any one time.
  - Refer to 📖 Management of pain: breakthrough pain, p.35 for guidance relating to BTcP.

Dose adjustments

Elderly
- No dosage adjustments are necessary, although dose requirements should be individually titrated.

Hepatic/renal impairment
- Buprenorphine undergoes extensive metabolism, yet it is well tolerated in liver impairment. Although metabolized via CYP3A4, glucuronidation also occurs and this is generally considered to be less affected by liver impairment. No specific guidance is available, but dose adjustments and close monitoring are advisable in patients with severe liver impairment.
- No dosage adjustments are necessary for patients with renal impairment, although dose requirements should be individually titrated.

Additional information

- Like all opioids, buprenorphine may be of benefit for central neuropathic pain.
- The following is a guide on how to initiate a patch in relation to previous opioid therapy:

- 4-hourly hydromorphone/morphine/oxycodone—give regular 4-hourly doses for the first 12 hours after applying the patch
- 12-hourly hydromorphone/morphine/oxycodone—give the final oral dose at the same time as applying the first patch
- 24-hourly morphine—apply the patch 12 hours after the final oral dose
- CSCI—continue the syringe driver for the first 12 hours after applying the patch.
- When converting from hydromorphone, morphine or oxycodone to buprenorphine, the dose of any laxative may need reducing.
- Patches should be applied to clean, dry, non-irritated skin and sites rotated regularly to reduce the chance of skin reactions. The same site should be avoided for at least 6 days (*Transtec*®) or at least 3 weeks (*BuTrans*®).
- After removal of a buprenorphine patch, significant plasma concentration persists and a substitute background opioid should not be started until 24 hours after patch removal.
- Should the transdermal patch cause application site irritation, avoid using a steroid inhaler or cream; the manufacturer states such actions can effect the rate of absorption. The advice is to change to alternative opioid.
- It is appropriate to use alternative pure opioid agonists as rescue doses for BTcP, or dose titration. At clinical doses, there will be no risk of antagonism.

✦ Pharmacology

Buprenorphine is a semi-synthetic opioid described as being a partial μ-receptor agonist, although at clinical doses, it acts like a full agonist; no analgesic ceiling affect has been described even at doses up to 32mg daily. It is also an opioid-receptor-like (ORL-1) agonist and a β-receptor antagonist. Buprenorphine binds to the μ-receptor with high affinity and prolonged occupancy. Despite this, naloxone can reverse the effects of buprenorphine (usually needing a continuous infusion of high doses) and analgesia can be supplemented with other μ-receptor agonists, such as morphine.

Buprenorphine is highly lipophilic and undergoes extensive first-pass metabolism via CYP3A4 and glucuronidation to form the weakly active metabolite norbuprenorphine (about 40–50 times less active than buprenorphine), buprenorphine glucuronide, and norbuprenorphine glucuronide respectively. Buprenorphine is mainly eliminated through biliary excretion, with up to 30% being excreted in urine. Enterohepatic circulation of buprenorphine occurs through cleavage of the glucuronide by intestinal bacteria which could partly explain the prolonged half-life and pharmacological effects. Since buprenorphine and norbuprenorphine are conjugated and inactivated, liver disease or inhibitors of CYP3A4 may have a less than expected effect on buprenorphine clearance. Nonetheless, in patients with severe liver impairment, or those receiving CYP3A4 inhibitors, close monitoring is recommended. Renal impairment does not affect the elimination of buprenorphine.

Cannabis extract

Sativex® (CD1 POM) (Note - presently CD1, but Home Office currently assessing status. Prescriptions must comply with CD2 requirements)
Oromucosal spray: dronabinol (THC) 27mg and cannabidiol (CBD) 25mg/mL (2.7mg and 2.5mg per spray respectively).

Indications
- Adjunct in moderate to severe spasticity in multiple sclerosis (specialist use only).
- *Intractable cancer pain.[1]

Contraindications and precautions
- Contraindicated for use in patients with:
  - known or suspected history or family history of schizophrenia, or other psychotic illness
  - significant psychiatric disorder.
- *Sativex®* is not recommended for use in patients with serious cardio-vascular disease.
- Use with caution in patients with:
  - epilepsy
  - hepatic impairment
  - renal impairment.
- It may modify reactions and patients should be advised not drive (or operate machinery) if affected. Refer to 📖 Drugs and driving, p.25.

☺ Adverse effects
Very common
- Dizziness
- Fatigue.

Common
- Amnesia
- Anorexia
- Constipation
- Depression
- Diarrhoea
- Dissociation
- Drowsiness
- Dry mouth
- Dysgeusia
- Lethargy
- Malaise
- Memory impairment
- Mouth ulceration
- Nausea and/or vomiting
- Vertigo
- Visual disturbances
- Weakness.

Uncommon
- Hallucinations
- Hypertension
- Oral mucosal discoloration (reported with long-term use)
- Paranoia.
- Pharyngitis
- Suicidal ideation
- Tachycardia
- Tooth discoloration.

Drug interactions
Pharmacokinetic
- *Sativex®* is metabolized by a variety of cytochromes, including CYP1A2, CYP2C9, CYP2C19, CYP2D6, and CYP3A4.

- Although no clinically significant drug interactions have been identified during clinical trials, co-administration with drugs that are metabolized by, or affect the activity (induction or inhibition) of one or more of these pathways may lead to clinically relevant drug interactions.
- Co-administration with *omeprazole* (CYP2C19 inhibitor) did not result in any notable change in parameters.

Pharmacodynamic

- *Baclofen*—theoretical increased potential for reduced muscle tone and power with subsequent risk of falls.
- *CNS depressants*—risk of excessive sedation.

♪ Dose

All indications

- Complex dose titration is necessary, performed over a period of up to 2 weeks. The dose is to be administered buccally. Refer to Table 3.1.

Table 3.1 Dose for cannabis extract

Day	Morning dose (before 2pm)	Evening dose (after 4pm)
1	0	1
2	0	1
3	0	2
4	0	2
5	1	2
6	1	3
7	1	4
8	2	4
9	2	5
10	3	5
11	3	6
12	4	6
13	4	7
14	5	7

- There should be at least a 15min gap between sprays.
- Adverse reactions such as dizziness or other CNS-type reactions may develop at any time. Treatment should be suspended until they resolve. These adverse effects may be overcome by increasing the interval between doses, or reducing the dose. Patients may need re-titrating to achieve a tolerated dosage regimen that gives acceptable pain relief.
- The usual daily dose ranges between 4–8 sprays. Doses in excess of 12 sprays daily, although not recommended, may be used if the perceived benefits outweigh the risks.

⚓ Dose adjustments

Elderly
- No specific dose recommendations are available. Use the lowest effective dose.

Hepatic/renal impairment
- Manufacturer advises *Sativex*® should be used with care in patients with significant hepatic and/or renal dysfunction. The effect of *Sativex*® is expected to be exaggerated and prolonged and patients should be frequently reviewed.

Additional information

- In overdose, symptoms such as delusions, dizziness, hallucinations, paranoia may occur. In addition, tachycardia or bradycardia with hypotension. Treatment is symptomatic.

⚓ Pharmacology

There are at least 2 types of cannabinoid (CB) receptor, CB_1 and CB_2. CB_1 receptors are found on pain pathways in the brain and spinal cord, where they are thought to regulate cannabinoid-induced analgesia by attenuating the effects of excitatory neurotransmitters, e.g. glutamate. CB_1 receptors also affect cognition, memory, and motor function. CB_2 receptors have an effect on immune cells and may cause cannabinoids to display anti-inflammatory effects.

Following buccal administration, maximum plasma concentrations of both THC and CBD typically occur within 2–4 hours. They are both highly lipid soluble and accumulate in fatty tissue, leading to a prolonged half-life. They may be stored in fatty tissues for up to 4 weeks, leaching out at sub-therapeutic levels. Both cannabinoids undergo a degree of first-pass metabolism producing active metabolites; further metabolism occurs in the liver via several cytochromes (CYP1A2, CYP2C9, CYP2C19, CYP2D6, and CYP3A4), although CYP2C9 may have a more predominant role.

Reference

1. Johnson JR, Burnell-Nugent M, Lossignol D, *et al.* Multicenter, double-blind, randomized, placebo-controlled, parallel-group study of the efficacy, safety, and tolerability of THC:CBD extract and THC extract in patients with intractable cancer-related pain. *J Pain Symptom Manage* 2010; **39**(2):167–79.

Carbamazepine

Different preparations may vary in bioavailability. Therefore, it is recommended that patients should remain on the same product once treatment has been stabilized. Inclusion of the brand name on the prescription is suggested.

Standard release

Tegretol® (POM)
Tablet (scored): 100mg (84); 200mg (84); 400mg (56).
Chewtab: 100mg (56); 200mg (56).
Liquid (sugar-free): 100mg/5mL (300mL).
Suppository: 125mg (5); 250mg (5).

Generic (POM)
Tablet: 100mg (28); 200mg (28); 400mg (28).
Includes branded-generics.

Modified release

Tegretol Retard® (POM)
Tablet (scored): 200mg (56); 400mg (56).

Carbagen SR® (POM)
Tablet (scored): 200mg (56); 400mg (56).

Indications

- Generalized tonic–clonic and partial seizures
- Trigeminal neuralgia
- *Neuropathic pain.[1]

Contraindications and precautions

- Refer to 📖 Use of drugs in end-of-life care, p.53 for end-of-life care issues.
- Carbamazepine is contraindicated for use in patients with:
  - acute porphyria
  - AV block
  - history of bone marrow depression.
- Agranulocytosis and aplastic anaemia have been associated with carbamazepine. Ensure patients and/or their carers can recognize signs of blood, liver, or skin disorders, and advise they seek immediate medical attention if symptoms such as fever, sore throat, rash, mouth ulcers, bruising, or bleeding develop.
- Avoid abrupt withdrawal, unless clearly indicated, as seizures may be precipitated.
- Use with caution in the following circumstances:
  - angle-closure glaucoma
  - cardiac disease
  - elderly (see 📖 Dose adjustments, p.104).

- Han Chinese and Thai population (patient should be screened for HLA-B*1502 before initiating treatment due to association with risk of developing Stevens–Johnson syndrome)
  - hepatic impairment
  - renal impairment.
- Manufacturer recommends LFTs should be performed before initiating treatment and periodically thereafter, particularly in patients with a history of liver disease and in elderly patients. Carbamazepine should be withdrawn immediately in cases of aggravated liver dysfunction or acute liver disease.
- It can cause altered LFTs, such as elevations of GGT and ALP. In the absence of other signs or symptoms, carbamazepine does not need withdrawing.
- Carbamazepine has weak anticholinergic activity. It may precipitate confusion or agitation in the elderly, or precipitate glaucoma.
- It may modify reactions and patients should be advised not drive (or operate machinery) if affected. Refer to 🕮 Drugs and driving, p.25.
- Patients should be monitored for signs of suicidal ideation since anti-epileptic drugs have been associated with this behaviour.
- Subtle deficits in attention, memory, and reasoning may occur with therapeutic dosages of anticholinergic drugs without signs of obvious toxicity. These deficits have often been mistaken for symptoms of early dementia in elderly patients.

☺ Adverse effects

Very common
- Altered LFTs (raised GGT/ALP)
- Ataxia
- Dizziness
- Drowsiness
- Fatigue
- Leucopenia
- Nausea, vomiting
- Urticaria.

Common
- Dry mouth
- Eosinophilia
- Headache
- Hyponatraemia (syndrome of inappropriate anti-diuretic hormone hypersecretion—SIADH)
- Oedema
- Thrombocytopenia
- Visual disturbances (e.g. diplopia)
- Weight increase.

Uncommon
- Dystonia
- Exfoliative dermatitis
- Nystagmus
- Tremor.

Rare
- Gynaecomastia
- Systemic lupus erythematosus.

Drug interactions

Pharmacokinetic
- Is metabolized by CYP3A4; it is also a strong inducer of CYP1A2, CYP2B6, CYP2C8/9, CYP2C19, CYP3A4, and UGT enzymes. Co-administration with drugs that are metabolized by, or affect the

activity (induction or inhibition—see 📖 inside back cover) of these pathways may lead to clinically relevant drug interactions and the prescriber should be aware that dosage adjustments may be necessary, particularly of drugs with a narrow therapeutic index. Carbamazepine may lower the plasma concentration, diminish or even abolish the activity of many drugs through enzyme induction. Several interactions are listed as follows, but refer to the table on 📖 inside back cover for a list of drugs that may potentially be affected.

- *Alfentanil*—risk of reduced analgesic benefit.
- *Celecoxib*—effect of celecoxib may be reduced.
- *Clonazepam*—effect of clonazepam may be reduced.
- *Codeine*—possible altered analgesic effect (due to CYP3A4/UGT induction)
- *Corticosteroids*—effect of corticosteroids reduced; higher doses necessary (possibly double or more).
- *Erythromycin*—risk of carbamazepine toxicity (avoid combination or monitor closely).
- *Fentanyl*—risk of reduced analgesic benefit.
- *Fluconazole*—possible risk of carbamazepine toxicity and/or loss of activity of fluconazole.
- *Haloperidol*—effect of haloperidol reduced.
- *Levothyroxine*—increased metabolism may precipitate hypothyroidism.
- *Metoclopramide*—theoretical risk of neurotoxicity due to possible increased rate of absorption of carbamazepine.
- *Mirtazapine*—effect of mirtazapine may be reduced.
- *Modafinil*—effect of modafinil may be reduced.
- *Oxycodone*—possible risk of reduced analgesic benefit.
- *Paracetamol*—may increase the risk of hepatoxicity of paracetamol.
- *Tramadol*—reduced analgesic effect.
- Avoid excessive amounts of grapefruit juice as it may increase the bioavailability of carbamazepine through inhibition of intestinal CYP3A4.

Pharmacodynamic

- *Antipsychotics*—seizure threshold lowered.
- *Antidepressants*—seizure threshold lowered.
- *CNS depressants*—risk of excessive sedation.
- *MAOIs*—avoid concurrent use.
- *Tramadol*—seizure threshold lowered.

♣ Dose

Carbamazepine induces its own metabolism after several days. Always start with a low dose and increase gradually by increments of 100–200mg every 2 weeks.

All indications

- Initial dose 100–200mg PO OD or BD (using standard or modified release formulation).
- Increase dose gradually until response is obtained (usually 400–600mg PO BD).
- Alternatively, 125–250mg PR BD OD or BD. Recommended max. duration of treatment via rectal route is 7 days; recommended max. dose is 250mg PR QDS.

♪ Dose adjustments

Elderly

- No specific guidance available. Use with caution due to the potential risk of drug interactions. Carbamazepine has anticholinergic activity and the elderly have been shown to be at an increased risk for cognitive decline and dementia with such drugs.

Hepatic/renal impairment

- No specific guidance available. Manufacturer advises caution in hepatic impairment; lower doses may be necessary.
- Normal doses can be used in renal impairment.

Additional information

- Standard-release oral formulations can be taken TDS–QDS if necessary to reduce risk of adverse effects. Alternatively, the modified-release formulation can be used.
- Carbamazepine standard-release tablets can be dispersed in water prior to use if necessary.
- Therapeutic plasma concentration range: 4–12 micrograms/mL, or 17–50micromol/L. Plasma samples are taken immediately prior to next dose (at steady state).

♦ Pharmacology

Carbamazepine is structurally related to TCAs. The mechanism of action is believed to be mediated by blockade of use-dependent sodium channels. It has a range of other pharmacological properties, including anticholinergic, antidiuretic, muscle relaxant, and antidepressant actions. Carbamazepine is well absorbed after oral administration (>85%) and is extensively metabolized by CYP3A4; it is a potent inducer of CYP1A2, CYP2B6, CYP2C8/9, CYP2C19 and CYP3A4. Many drugs are affected (see 📖 Drug interactions, p.102).

Reference

1. Wiffen PJ, Derry S, Moore RA, et al. Carbamazepine for acute and chronic pain in adults. *Cochrane Database Syst Rev* 2011; **1**:CD005451.

Carbocisteine

Mucodyne® (POM)
Capsule: 375mg (120).
Oral liquid: 125mg/5mL (300mL); 250mg/5mL (300mL).

Indications
- Reduction of sputum viscosity (e.g. for use in COPD).

Contraindications and precautions
- Contraindicated for use in active peptic ulceration.

☺ Adverse effects
The frequency is not defined, but reported adverse effects include:
- GI bleeding (rare)
- Skin rashes (rare).

Drug interactions
Pharmacokinetic
- None known.

Pharmacodynamic
- None known.

♨ Dose
- Initial dose 750mg PO TDS, reducing to 750mg PO BD when a satisfactory reduction in cough and sputum production is evident.

♨ Dose adjustments
Elderly
- No dose adjustments are necessary.

Hepatic/renal impairment
- No specific guidance available.

♦ Pharmacology
Carbocisteine affects the nature and amount of mucus glycoprotein which is secreted by the respiratory tract, reducing the viscosity and allowing easier expectoration.

Celecoxib

Celebrex® (POM)
Capsule: 100mg (60); 200mg (30).

Indications
- Symptomatic relief of osteoarthritis, rheumatoid arthritis, and ankylosing spondylitis.
- ⨏Pain associated with cancer.[1]

Contraindications and precautions
- Celecoxib is contraindicated for use in patients with:
  - active peptic ulceration or GI bleeding
  - congestive heart failure (CHF) (New York Heart Association (NYHA) class II–IV)
  - established ischaemic heart disease, peripheral arterial disease and/or cerebrovascular disease
  - hypersensitivity reactions to ibuprofen, aspirin or other NSAIDs (e.g. asthma, nasal polyps, rhinitis)
  - hypersensitivity to sulphonamides
  - inflammatory bowel disease
  - severe hepatic dysfunction (serum albumin <25g/L or Child–Pugh score ≥10)
- severe renal impairment (estimated CrCl <30mL/min).
- Use the minimum effective dose for the shortest duration necessary in order to reduce the risk of cardiac and GI events.
- Elderly patients are more at risk of developing adverse effects (see 📖 Dose adjustments, p.108).
- Treatment should be reviewed after 2 weeks. In the absence of benefit, other options should be considered.
- Use with caution in the following circumstances:
  - concurrent use of diuretics, corticosteroids and NSAIDs (see 📖 Drug interactions, p.107)
  - CHF and/or left ventricular dysfunction
  - hepatic impairment
  - hyperlipidaemia
  - hypertension (particularly uncontrolled)
  - recovery from surgery
  - renal impairment
  - smoking
  - type 1 and 2 diabetes (risk factors for cardiovascular events).
- The manufacturer recommends monitoring of blood pressure and renal function in patients at risk of cardiovascular adverse effects during the initiation of therapy.
- Patients known to be CYP2C9 poor metabolizers should be treated with caution; similarly, drugs that inhibit CYP2C9 should be used with caution (see 📖 Drug interactions, p.107).
- Discontinue treatment at the first appearance of skin rash, mucosal lesions, or any other sign of hypersensitivity.

- Celecoxib may prevent the development of signs and symptoms of inflammation/infection (e.g. fever).
- Consider co-prescription of misoprostol or a PPI if:
  - long-term NSAID therapy
  - concurrent use of drugs that increase the risk of GI toxicity (see 📖 Drug interactions)
- Refer to 📖 Selection of a NSAID, p.29 for further information, including selection.

☺ Adverse effects

Very common
- Hypertension (at doses of 400mg daily).

Common
- Abdominal pain
- Cough
- Diarrhoea
- Dizziness
- Insomnia
- Myocardial infarction
- Peripheral oedema
- Pharyngitis
- Rash
- Sinusitis
- Upper respiratory tract infection
- Urinary tract infection (UTI).

Uncommon
- Anaemia
- Anxiety
- Blurred vision
- CVA
- Depression
- Drowsiness
- Gastritis
- Heart failure
- Hyperkalaemia
- Leg cramps
- Stomatitis.

Rare
- Confusion
- Duodenal ulceration
- Gastric ulceration
- Leucopenia
- Melaena
- Oesophagitis
- Oesophageal ulceration
- Thrombocytopenia.

Unknown
- Acute renal failure
- Bronchospasm
- Conjunctivitis
- Headache
- Hepatic failure
- Hyponatraemia
- Stevens–Johnson syndrome
- Toxic epidermal necrolysis.

Drug interactions

Pharmacokinetic
- Celecoxib is a substrate of CYP2C9; it is also a moderate inhibitor of CYP2C19 and CYP2D6. Co-administration with drugs that are metabolized by, or affect the activity (induction or inhibition—see 📖 inside back cover) of this pathway may lead to clinically relevant drug interactions and the prescriber should be aware that dosage adjustments may be necessary, particularly of drugs with a narrow therapeutic index.
- *Carbamazepine*—can reduce the effectiveness of celecoxib.
- *Clopidogrel*—antiplatelet action may be reduced.

- *Codeine*—possibly reduced analgesic benefit.
- *Fluconazole*—use half-recommended doses of celecoxib as plasma concentration increased.
- *Haloperidol*—celecoxib may inhibit metabolism; possible increased risk of adverse effects.
- *Miconazole*—may increase the effectiveness of celecoxib and risk of adverse effects.
- *Rifampicin*—can reduce the effectiveness of celecoxib.
- *Risperidone*—celecoxib may inhibit metabolism; possible increased risk of adverse effects.
- *Tramadol*—possibly reduced analgesic benefit.

Pharmacodynamic
- *Anticoagulants*—increased risk of bleeding.
- *Antihypertensives*—reduced hypotensive effect.
- *Antiplatelet drugs*—increased risk of bleeding.
- *Corticosteroids*—increased risk of GI toxicity.
- *Ciclosporin*—increased risk of nephrotoxicity.
- *Diuretics*—reduced diuretic effect.
- *SSRIs*—increased risk of GI bleeding.

Dose
- Osteoarthritis, rheumatoid arthritis and ankylosing spondylitis:
  - Initial dose 100mg PO BD or 200mg PO OD. Increase if necessary to 200mg PO BD. If no benefit after **2 weeks** discontinue treatment and review.
- *Cancer pain:
  - Initial dose 100mg PO BD or 200mg PO OD. Increase if necessary to 200mg PO BD. If no benefit after **2 weeks** discontinue treatment and review.

Dose adjustments
Elderly
- Usual adult doses recommended. Note that the elderly are particularly susceptible to adverse effects. Use the lowest effective dose and for the shortest duration possible.

Hepatic/renal impairment
- Use of celecoxib in patients with severe hepatic dysfunction is contra-indicated. In patients with established moderate hepatic impairment with a serum albumin of 25–35g/L, an initial dose 100mg PO OM is suggested.
- Use of celecoxib in severe renal impairment is contraindicated. No specific guidance is available for use in mild–moderate renal impairment. The elderly and those with pre-existing impaired renal function, heart failure or liver impairment are at greatest risk for renal toxicity. Use the lowest effective dose and for the shortest duration possible. Close monitoring of renal function is recommended.

Additional information
- Contents of the capsule can be dispersed in water or fruit juice if necessary prior to administration.

- Despite contraindication, several studies have shown that celecoxib can be used safely in patients with aspirin/NSAID sensitivity. There is, however, a risk of cross-sensitivity. If celecoxib is to be used, it should be under close monitoring.

✦ Pharmacology

Like traditional NSAIDs, the mechanism of action of celecoxib is believed to be due to inhibition of prostaglandin synthesis. Unlike most NSAIDs, however, celecoxib is a selective non-competitive inhibitor of COX-2. Celecoxib is mainly eliminated by metabolism, with <1% of the dose being excreted unchanged in urine. Celecoxib metabolism is primarily mediated via CYP2C9 to form 3 inactive metabolites.

Reference

1. McNicol ED, Strassels S, Goudas L, *et al*. NSAIDS or paracetamol, alone or combined with opioids, for cancer pain. *Cochrane Database Syst Rev* 2005; **2**: CD005180.

Ciprofloxacin

Ciproxin® (POM)
Tablet (scored): 250mg (10; 20); 500mg (10; 20); 750mg (10).
Suspension (for reconstitution with provided diluent): 250mg/5mL (100mL).
Injection: 100mg/50mL; 200mg/100mL; 400mg/200mL.

Generic (POM)
Tablet: 250mg (10; 20); 500mg (10; 20); 750mg (10).
Injection: 100mg/50mL; 200mg/100mL; 400mg/200mL.

Indications
- Refer to local guidelines.
- Broad-spectrum antibiotic indicated for the treatment of infections caused by susceptible organisms (mainly Gram-negative).

Contraindications and precautions
- Ciprofloxacin should not be used to treat infections caused by Gram-positive organisms (e.g. *Streptococcus pneumonia*) due to poor activity.
- Concurrent use of *duloxetine* and *tizanidine* is contraindicated.
- Use with caution in the following:
  - concurrent use of CYP1A2 substrates, or drugs that prolong the QT interval (see 🕮 Drug interactions, p.111)
  - epilepsy
  - glucose-6-phosphate dehydrogenase (G6PD) deficiency
  - renal impairment (risk of crystalluria).
- Ciprofloxacin may modify reactions and patients should be advised not drive (or operate machinery) if affected. Refer to 🕮 Drugs and driving, p.25.

☺ Adverse effects
Common

- Diarrhoea
- Nausea.

Uncommon

- Abdominal pains
- Abnormal LFTs (raised bilirubin, AST)
- Anorexia
- Dizziness
- Dyspepsia
- Flatulence
- Headache
- Musculoskeletal pain
- Renal impairment
- Sleep disorders
- Taste disorders
- Vomiting
- Weakness.

Rare

- Anaemia
- Antibiotic associated colitis
- Confusion
- Crystalluria
- Depression
- Hallucinations
- Hyperglycaemia
- Seizures
- Thrombocytopenia
- Tremor.

Drug interactions

Pharmacokinetic

- Ciprofloxacin is an inhibitor of CYP1A2. Co-administration with drugs that are metabolized by, or affect the activity (induction or inhibition—see 📖 inside back cover) of this pathway may lead to clinically relevant drug interactions and the prescriber should be aware that dosage adjustments may be necessary, particularly of drugs with a narrow therapeutic index.
- Concurrent use of *duloxetine* and *tizanidine* is contraindicated (due to CYP1A2 inhibition).
- *Diazepam*—possible increase in effect.
- *Methadone*—effect of methadone may be increased.
- *Ropinirole*—significant increase in effect requiring dose adjustment.
- *Sucralfate*—marked reduction in oral absorption of ciprofloxacin; avoid by 2 hours.
- *Theophylline*—plasma concentrations of theophylline can be markedly increased.
- *Warfarin*—possible increase in INR.

Pharmacodynamic

- Ciprofloxacin can cause dose-related prolongation of the QT interval. There is a potential risk that co-administration with other drugs that also prolong the QT interval (e.g. *amiodarone, erythromycin, haloperidol, quinine*) may result in ventricular arrhythmias.
- *CNS depressants*—additive sedative effect.

🍸 Dose

- Dose dependent upon infection. Refer to local guidelines.
- Typical doses:
  - urinary tract infections: 250–500mg PO BD
  - respiratory tract infections: 250–750mg PO BD
  - by IV infusion, 200–400mg BD.

🍸 Dose adjustments

Elderly

- Dose adjustments are not required.

Hepatic/renal impairment

- Dose adjustments are not required in hepatic impairment.
- For patients with renal impairment, dose adjustments will be necessary (see Table 3.2).

Additional information

- The tablets can be dispersed in water immediately prior to administration if necessary.
- Note that the suspension is unsuitable for administration through a feeding tube (may block).
- Once reconstituted, the oral suspension should be used within 14 days.
- A 200mg IV infusion should be administered over 30–60min; 400mg over 60min.
- Each 100mL of IV infusion contains 15.4mmol of sodium.

Table 3.2 Dose adjustments for ciprofloxacin

Creatinine clearance (mL/min/1.73 m²)	Serum creatinine (micromol/L)	Oral dose (mg)
>60	<124	See usual dosage.
30–60	124–168	250–500mg every 12 hours
<30	>169	250–500mg every 24 hours
Patients on haemodialysis	>169	250–500mg every 24 hours (after dialysis)
Patients on peritoneal dialysis	>169	250–500mg every 24 hours

⊛ Pharmacology

Ciprofloxacin is a broad-spectrum antibiotic active against a wide range of Gram-negative bacteria, with a limited range of Gram-positive cover. It is bactericidal and works by inhibiting bacterial DNA gyrase, an enzyme involved with DNA synthesis. Ciprofloxacin is well absorbed following oral administration and has good penetration into tissues and cells.

Citalopram

Cipramil® *(POM)*
Tablet: 10mg (28); 20mg (28); 40mg (28).
Oral drops (sugar-free): 40mg/mL (15mL).

Generic (POM)
Tablet: 10mg (28); 20mg (28); 40mg (28).

Indications

- Depression
- Panic
- ⚥Delirium/agitation (including that associated with dementia).[1]

Contraindications and precautions

- Do not use with an irreversible MAOI (including *rasagiline* and *selegiline*), or within 14 days of stopping one, or at least 24 hours after discontinuation of a reversible MAOI (e.g. *moclobemide, linezolid*). At least 7 days should elapse after discontinuing citalopram treatment before starting a MAOI or reversible MAOI. Note that in exceptional circumstances *linezolid* may be given with citalopram, but the patient must be closely monitored for symptoms of serotonin syndrome (see 📖 Box 1.10, p.18).
- If citalopram has to be used with a MAOI, doses should not exceed 10mg PO daily.
- There is a risk of QT prolongation/Torsade de pointes:
  - avoid in patients with congenital long QT syndrome
  - correct hypokalaemia or hypomagnesaemia before commencing treatment
  - do not use doses above 40mg unless recommended by a specialist.
- Depression is associated with an increased risk of suicidal thoughts, self-harm, and suicide which persists until remission. Note that that the risk of suicide may increase during initial treatment.
- Hyponatraemia should be considered in all patients who develop drowsiness, confusion, or convulsions while taking an antidepressant. Hyponatraemia has been associated with all types of antidepressants, although it is reportedly more common with SSRIs.
- May precipitate psychomotor restlessness, which usually appears during early treatment.
- Use with caution in:
  - diabetes (alters glycaemic control)
  - elderly (greater risk of hyponatraemia)
  - epilepsy (lowers seizure threshold)
  - hepatic impairment (see 📖 Dose adjustments, p.115).
- Avoid abrupt withdrawal as symptoms such as agitation, anxiety, dizziness, nausea, sleep disturbance (e.g. insomnia, intense dreams) and tremor can occur. Although generally mild, they can be severe in some patients. Withdrawal symptoms usually occur within the first few days of discontinuing treatment and they usually resolve within 2 weeks, though they can persist in some patients for up to 3 months or longer.

See 📖 Discontinuing and/or switching antidepressants, p.45 for information about switching or stopping antidepressants.

- Citalopram may increase the risk of haemorrhage (see 📖 Drug Interactions).
- It may modify reactions and patients should be advised not drive (or operate machinery) if affected. Refer to 📖 Drugs and driving, p.25.

😊 Adverse effects

Very Common

- Drowsiness
- Dry mouth
- Headache
- Insomnia
- Nausea
- Sweating.

Common

- Agitation
- Amnesia
- Anxiety
- Appetite decreased
- Arthralgia
- Confusion
- Constipation
- Diarrhoea
- Dizziness
- Fatigue
- Myalgia
- Paraesthesia
- Pruritus
- Rhinitis
- Sexual dysfunction
- Tinnitus
- Tremor
- Vomiting
- Weight loss
- Yawning.

Uncommon

- Aggression
- Alopecia
- Bradycardia
- Hallucinations
- Menorrhagia
- Mydriasis (may lead to glaucoma)
- Oedema
- Rash
- Syncope
- Tachycardia
- Urticaria.

Rare

- Convulsions
- Hyponatraemia
- Taste disturbance.

Unknown

- Ecchymosis
- Haemorrhage (e.g. epistaxis, gastrointestinal)
- QT prolongation/Torsade de pointes (associated with use in patients with pre-existing cardiac conditions)
- Serotonin syndrome
- SIADH
- Suicidal behaviour
- Thrombocytopenia
- Visual disturbance.

Drug interactions

Pharmacokinetic

- Citalopram is a substrate of CYP2C19 and CYP3A4; it is also a weak inhibitor of CYP2C19 and CYP2D6. Co-administration with drugs that are metabolized by, or affect the activity (induction or inhibition —see 📖 inside back cover) of these pathways may lead to clinically relevant

drug interactions and the prescriber should be aware that dosage adjustments may be necessary.
• *Fluconazole*—serotonin syndrome has been reported with this combination.
• Avoid excessive amounts of grapefruit juice as it may increase the bioavailability of citalopram through inhibition of intestinal CYP3A4.

Pharmacodynamic
• Risk of serotonin syndrome (see 📖 Box 1.10, p.18) with:
  • MAOIs
  • rasagiline
  • selegiline
  • serotonergic drugs—e.g. duloxetine, methadone, mirtazapine, TCAs, tramadol and trazodone.
• *Anticoagulants*—potential increased risk of bleeding.
• *Carbamazepine*—increased risk of hyponatraemia.
• *Cyproheptadine*—may inhibit the effects of serotonin reuptake inhibitors.
• *Diuretics*—increased risk of hyponatraemia.
• *NSAIDs*—increased risk of GI bleeding.

💊 Dose
Note: 8mg (4 drops) Cipramil® oral drops can be considered equivalent in therapeutic effect to 10mg citalopram tablet. The drops should be mixed with water, orange juice, or apple juice before taking.

Depression
• Initial dose:
  • Tablets—20mg PO OD. The dose should be reviewed after 2–3 weeks and increased if necessary to a maximum of 40mg PO OD. Higher doses should only be used on the advice of a specialist (risk of QT prolongation/Torsade de pointes).
  • Oral drops—16mg PO OD (8 drops). The dose should be reviewed after 2–3 weeks and increased if necessary in 16mg increments to a maximum of 32mg PO OD (16 drops). Higher doses should only be used on the advice of a specialist (risk of QT prolongation/Torsade de pointes).

Panic
• Initial dose:
  • Tablets—10mg PO OD. The dose can be increased in 10mg increments to the recommended dose of 20–30mg PO OD. Further dose increases in careful increments up to 40mg PO OD may be necessary. Higher doses should only be used on the advice of a specialist (risk of QT prolongation/Torsade de pointes).
  • Oral drops—8mg PO OD (4 drops). The dose can be increased in 8mg increments to the recommended dose of 16–24mg PO OD (8–12 drops). Further dose increases in careful increments up to 32mg PO OD (16 drops) may be necessary. Higher doses should only be used on the advice of a specialist (risk of QT prolongation/Torsade de pointes).

¥ *Delirium/agitation*
- Initial dose:
  - Tablets—10mg PO OD. The dose can be increased in 10mg increments to a suggested dose of 20–30mg PO OD.
  - Oral drops—8mg PO OD (4 drops). The dose can be increased in 8mg increments to a suggested dose of 16–24mg PO OD (8–12 drops).

♪ Dose adjustments

Elderly
- Initial doses unchanged, but the maximum dose should not exceed 20mg PO OD in patients over 60 years of age (unless on the advice of a specialist—risk of QT prolongation).

Hepatic/renal impairment
- In hepatic impairment, doses should not exceed 20mg PO OD (unless on the advice of a specialist—risk of QT prolongation).
- Mild or moderate renal impairment, no dosage adjustment is necessary. Information is unavailable for severe renal impairment (CrCl <20mL/min).

Additional information
- Response in depression may be evident within the first week of treatment; generally, an effect is seen after at least in the second week of treatment.
- Symptoms of anxiety or panic may worsen on initial therapy. This can be minimized by using lower starting doses.
- If withdrawal symptoms emerge during discontinuation, increase the dose to prevent symptoms and then start to withdrawal more slowly.
- The SSRIs sertraline and citalopram may be of use in the management of agitation and psychosis in patients with dementia.

⟐ Pharmacology
Citalopram is a highly selective inhibitor of neuronal serotonin reuptake, with only very minimal effects on noradrenaline and dopamine neuronal reuptake. It has a weak affinity for muscarinic receptors, but little affinity for α_1, α_2, D_2, 5-HT$_1$, 5-HT$_2$, and H$_1$ receptors. Citalopram is metabolized by primarily by CYP2C19 and CYP3A4 to active metabolites, but they are unlikely to contribute to the overall antidepressant effect. Citalopram is excreted mainly via the liver, with <20% via the kidneys.

Reference
1. Seitz DP, Adunuri N, Gill SS, *et al.* Antidepressants for agitation and psychosis in dementia. *Cochrane Database Syst Rev* 2011; **2**:CD008191.

Clarithromycin

Standard release

Klaricid® (POM)
Tablet: 250mg (14); 500mg (14; 20).
Granules: 250mg (14).
Suspension: 125mg/5mL (70mL; 100mL); 250mg/5mL (70mL).
Injection: 500mg vial.

Generic (POM)
Tablet: 250mg (14); 500mg (14).
Suspension: 125mg/5mL (70mL); 250mg/5mL (70mL).
Injection: 500mg vial.

Modified release

Klaricid XL® (POM)
Tablet: 500mg (7; 14).

Indications

- Refer to local guidelines.
- Broad-spectrum antibiotic indicated for the treatment of infections caused by susceptible organisms.
- *Helicobacter pylori* eradication.

Contraindications and precautions

- Clarithromycin is an inhibitor of CYP3A4 and has the potential to interact with many drugs (see 📖 Drug interactions, p.118).
- Avoid co-administration of clarithromycin and colchicine—deaths have been reported.
- Use with caution in patients with hepatic and/or renal impairment (see 📖 Dose adjustments, p.118).
- Electrolyte disturbances must be corrected (e.g. hypokalaemia) due to the risk of QT prolongation.
- Clarithromycin may result in an overgrowth of non-susceptible bacteria or fungi, leading to secondary infection (e.g. candidiasis).

😣 Adverse effects

The frequency is not defined, but reported adverse effects include:

- Abdominal pain
- Anxiety
- Arthralgia
- Cholestasis
- Confusion
- Diarrhoea
- Dizziness
- Dyspepsia
- Headache
- Hepatic dysfunction
- Hepatitis
- Insomnia
- Myalgia
- Nausea
- Paraesthesia
- QT prolongation
- Stevens–Johnson syndrome
- Stomatitis
- Tooth-enamel discoloration
- Toxic epidermal necrolysis
- Urticaria
- Vertigo
- Vomiting.

Drug interactions

Pharmacokinetic

- Clarithromycin is a substrate of CYP3A4; it is an inhibitor of CYP3A4 and P-gp. Co-administration with drugs that are metabolized by, or affect the activity (induction or inhibition —see 📖 inside back cover) of these pathways may lead to clinically relevant drug interactions and the prescriber should be aware that dosage adjustments may be necessary, particularly of drugs with a narrow therapeutic index.
- Several interactions are listed, but refer to 📖 inside back cover for a list of drugs that may potentially be affected.
- *Alfentanil*—increased risk of alfentanil toxicity; dose reduction may be necessary.
- *Carbamazepine*—risk of carbamazepine toxicity (avoid combination or monitor closely).
- *Colchicine*—risk of colchicine toxicity.
- *Fentanyl*—increased risk of fentanyl toxicity; dose reduction may be necessary.
- *Midazolam*—increased risk of midazolam toxicity; dose adjustments may be necessary if clarithromycin is added or discontinued.
- *Theophylline*—risk of theophylline toxicity; dose reduction may be necessary.
- *Warfarin*—risk of raised INR.
- *Zopiclone*—increased plasma concentration and effects of zopiclone.

Pharmacodynamic

- Clarithromycin has been associated with prolongation of the QT interval. There is a potential risk that co-administration with other drugs that also prolong the QT interval (e.g. *amiodarone, amitriptyline, haloperidol, quinine*) may result in ventricular arrhythmias.

💊 Dose

- Standard doses are described here. Refer to local guidelines for specific advice.
- Usual dose 250mg PO BD (12-hourly) for 7 days, increased in severe infections to 500mg PO BD for up to 14 days.
- *Klaricid XL®*—usual dose 500mg PO OD for 7–14 days, doubled in severe infections.
- Alternatively, 500mg BD (12-hourly) by IV infusion (usually for 2–5 days, then swap to PO).

💊 Dose adjustments

Elderly

- Usual adult doses can be used.

Hepatic/renal impairment

- No specific guidance is available for patients with hepatic impairment, although the manufacturer advises caution because clarithromycin has been associated with hepatic dysfunction.

- In patients with renal impairment who have creatinine clearance <30mL/min, the dose of clarithromycin should be reduced to 50% of the usual adult dose.

Additional information

- Once reconstituted, the *suspension* (or *granules*) must be discarded after 14 days.
- To reconstitute the *injection*, add 10mL WFI to each vial to give a solution of 500mg/10mL. Once reconstituted in 10mL WFI, the *injection* can be stored for 24 hours (5–25°C). This solution must be further diluted prior to administration as follows:
  - dilute 10mL of the reconstituted erythromycin (500mg/10mL) with at least 250mL NaCl 0.9% or glucose 5% and administer into a large peripheral vein over 60min.

⟳ Pharmacology

Clarithromycin is a derivative of erythromycin, with a broad spectrum of activity. It acts by penetrating the bacterial cell membrane and reversibly binding to ribosomes during cell division resulting in suppression of protein synthesis. It is rapidly and well absorbed after oral administration; first-pass metabolism produces an active metabolite. Clarithromycin is excreted both hepatically and renally.

Clonazepam

Rivotril® (CD4a)
Tablet (scored): 500 micrograms (100); 2mg (100).
Injection: 1mg/mL with 1mL WFI (10).

Generic (CD4a)
Liquid: 500 micrograms/5mL; 2mg/5mL.

Indications
- Epilepsy
- Myoclonus
- *Neuropathic pain[1]
- *Restless legs syndrome[2]
- *Terminal restlessness.[3]

Contraindications and precautions
- Refer to 📖 Use of drugs in end-of-life care, p.53 for end-of-life care issues.
- Contraindicated for use in patients with myasthenia gravis or severe hepatic impairment.
- Suicidal ideation and behaviour have been reported with anti-epileptics.
- Clonazepam should be used with caution in patients with chronic respiratory disease, renal impairment or moderate hepatic impairment.
- Dose reductions may be necessary in the elderly (see 📖 Dose adjustments, p.121).
- Avoid abrupt withdrawal, even if short duration treatment. In epileptic patients, status epilepticus may be precipitated. In addition, prolonged use of benzodiazepines may result in the development of dependence with subsequent withdrawal symptoms on cessation of use, e.g. agitation, anxiety, confusion, headaches, restlessness, sleep disturbances, sweating, and tremor. The risk of dependence increases with dose and duration of treatment. Gradual withdrawal is advised.
- Clonazepam may modify reactions and patients should be advised not drive (or operate machinery) if affected. Refer to 📖 Drugs and driving, p.25.

☺ Adverse effects
The frequency is not defined, but commonly reported adverse effects include:

- Ataxia
- Co-ordination disturbances
- Dizziness
- Drowsiness
- Fatigue
- Light-headedness
- Muscle weakness.

Other reported adverse effects include:
- Anterograde amnesia
- Headache
- Sexual dysfunction.

Drug interactions

Pharmacokinetic

- Clonazepam is a major substrate of CYP3A4. Co-administration with drugs that are metabolized by, or affect the activity (induction or inhibition —see 📖 inside back cover) of this pathway may lead to clinically relevant drug interactions and the prescriber should be aware that dosage adjustments may be necessary.
- Avoid excessive amounts of grapefruit juice as it may increase the bioavailability of clonazepam through inhibition of intestinal CYP3A4.

Pharmacodynamic

- *Alcohol*—may precipitate seizures.
- *Antidepressants*—reduced seizure threshold.
- *Antipsychotics*—reduced seizure threshold.
- *CNS depressants*—additive sedative effect.

⚕ Dose

The mean absolute oral bioavailability of clonazepam has been shown to be 90%; for CSCI administration, the same dose as oral is recommended, but the prescriber should be alert for the possibility of a less predictable response due to sorption into PVC infusion sets (see 📖 Additional information, p.122).

Epilepsy/myoclonus

- Initial dose 1mg PO ON, increased as necessary up to 8mg PO in 2–4 divided doses.
- ¥Alternatively, 0.5–4mg via CSCI every 24 hours (but see 📖 Additional information, p.122).

¥ Neuropathic pain

- Initial dose 0.5mg PO ON, increased as necessary up to 8mg PO daily in 2–4 divided doses.
- Alternatively, 0.5–4mg via CSCI every 24 hours (but see 📖 Additional information, p.122).

¥ Restless legs syndrome

- Initial dose 0.5mg PO ON, increased as necessary to 2mg PO ON.

¥ Terminal restlessness

- 1–4mg via CSCI every 24 hours (but see 📖 Additional information, p.122).

⚕ Dose adjustments

Elderly

- No specific dose reductions stated, but initial doses should not exceed 1mg PO daily.

Hepatic/renal impairment

- No specific guidance available. The dosage of clonazepam must be carefully adjusted to individual requirements.

Additional information

- Clonazepam tablets disperse in water after a short period of time. The tablets may be administered sublingually.
- The 1mg/mL injection of clonazepam must be diluted with the supplied WFI prior to parenteral administration. However, if clonazepam is to be administered via CSCI, this is not necessary.
- Clonazepam may adsorb to PVC. The clinical significance remains unknown but the manufacturer recommends the use of non-PVC equipment for infusions.
- The manufacturer states that the stability of diluted parenteral clonazepam is maintained for up to 12 hours. While CSCIs of clonazepam have been administered over 24 hours without apparent unexpected effect, prescribers should consider the use of 12-hourly infusions until further data become available.
- Clonazepam via CSCI is reportedly compatible with alfentanil, cyclizine, dexamethasone, diamorphine, glycopyrronium, haloperidol, hyoscine butylbromide, hyoscine hydrobromide, levomepromazine, metoclopramide, morphine sulphate, midazolam, octreotide, and oxycodone.

◆ Pharmacology

The exact mechanism of action is unknown, but it is believed to act via enhancement of GABA-ergic transmission in the CNS. It is extensively metabolized by CYP3A4 to inactive metabolites.

References

1. Hugel H, Ellershaw JE, Dickman A. Clonazepam as an adjuvant analgesic in patients with cancer-related neuropathic pain. *J Pain Symptom Manage* 2003; **26**(6):1073–4.
2. Trenkwalder C, Hening WA, Montagna P, *et al*. Treatment of restless legs syndrome: an evidence-based review and implications for clinical practice. *Mov Disord* 2008; **23**(16):2267–302.
3. Burke AL. Palliative care: an update on terminal restlessness. *Med J Aust* 1997; **166**:39–42.

Co-amoxiclav

Augmentin® (POM)
Tablet: 375mg (amoxicillin 250mg, clavulanic acid 125mg) (21); 625mg (amoxicillin 500mg, clavulanic acid 125mg) (21).

Augmentin® 125/31 (POM)
Suspension (as powder for reconstitution—sugar-free): co-amoxiclav 125/31 per 5mL (100mL).

Augmentin® 250/62 (POM)
Suspension (as powder for reconstitution—sugar-free): co-amoxiclav 250/62 per 5mL (100mL).

Augmentin-Duo® (POM)
Suspension (as powder for reconstitution—sugar-free): co-amoxiclav 400/57 per 5ml (35mL; 70mL).

Augmentin® Intravenous (POM)
Injection: 600mg (amoxicillin 500mg, clavulanic acid 100mg); 1.2g: (amoxicillin 1000mg, clavulanic acid 200mg).

Generic (POM)
Tablet: 250/125 (21); 500/125 (21).
Suspension (as powder for reconstitution): 125/31 per 5mL (100mL); 250/62 per 5mL (100mL); 400/57 per 5mL (35mL; 70mL)—specify 'sugar-free' on prescription if needed.
Injection (as powder for reconstitution): 500/100; 1000/200.

Indications
- Refer to local guidelines.
- Broad-spectrum antibiotic indicated for the treatment of commonly occurring bacterial infections.

Contraindications and precautions
- Is contraindicated for use in patients with penicillin hypersensitivity.
- Use with caution in renal impairment (risk of crystalloid/seizures). Maintain adequate hydration with high doses (see 📖 Dose adjustments, p.124).
- Monitor hepatic function in patients with hepatic impairment.
- Cholestatic jaundice can occur either during or shortly after the use of co-amoxiclav, the risk being about 6 times more common with co-amoxiclav than amoxicillin. The duration of treatment should normally not exceed 14 days.

☺ Adverse effects
Common
- Diarrhoea
- Mucocutaneous candidosis

Uncommon
- Dizziness
- Headache
- Indigestion
- Nausea
- Pruritus

- Raised liver enzymes
- Rash
- Urticaria
- Vomiting.

Rare
- Erythema multiforme
- Leucopenia
- Thrombocytopenia
- Thrombophlebitis (at injection site).

Drug interactions

Pharmacokinetic
- *Methotrexate*—penicillins may reduce the excretion of methotrexate.
- *Oral contraceptives*—reduced efficacy.
- *Warfarin*—possible increase in INR.

Pharmacodynamic
- *Allopurinol*—possible increase in skin reactions

Dose

Standard doses are described here. Refer to local guidelines for specific advice.
- One 250/125 tablet PO TDS, increased in severe cases to one 500/125 tablet PO TDS. Alternatively, 250/62 suspension PO TDS, increased in severe cases to 500/124 suspension PO TDS.
- *Augmentin-Duo*® is administered twice daily. Usual dose is 400/57 suspension PO BD, increased in severe cases to 800/114 suspension PO BD.
- 1000/200 by IV injection (over 3–4min) or infusion TDS.

Dose adjustments

Elderly
- No dose adjustment necessary.

Hepatic/renal impairment
- Co-amoxiclav should be used cautiously in patients with hepatic impairment; liver function should be monitored at regular intervals.
- Patients with a CrCl >30mL/min will not need a dose adjustment. Dose adjustments will be necessary for patients with a greater degree of renal impairment:
  - CrCl between 10–30mL/min:
    —PO: 500mg PO BD (in terms of amoxicillin content)
    —IV:initial dose 1000mg, then 500mg IV BD (in terms of amoxicillin content)
  - CrCl <10mL/min:
    —PO: 500mg PO OD (in terms of amoxicillin content)
    —IV:initial dose 1000mg IV, then 500mg IV OD (in terms of amoxicillin content)

- Haemodialysis:
  —PO: 500mg PO OD, with 500mg PO during dialysis, repeated at the end of dialysis (in terms of amoxicillin content).
  —IV: initial dose 1000mg IV, followed by 500mg IV OD, plus a dose of 500mg IV at the end of dialysis (in terms of amoxicillin content).

Additional information

- Once reconstituted, the *oral solution* must be stored in a refrigerator and be discarded after 7 days.
- To reconstitute the *injection*, add 10mL WFI to 500/100 vial (final volume 10.5mL), then dilute in 50mL infusion fluid; add 20mL WFI to 1000/200 vial (final volume 20.9mL) and dilute in 100mL infusion fluid.
- Administer IV *injection* over 3-4min; administer IV *infusion* in NaCl 0.9% (or glucose 5%) over 30–40min.

◈ Pharmacology

Co-amoxiclav consists of amoxicillin and clavulanic acid. Amoxicillin is a broad-spectrum antibiotic active against a wide range of Gram-positive bacteria, with a limited range of Gram-negative cover. It is susceptible to degradation by beta-lactamases produced by resistant bacteria. Clavulanic acid is structurally related to penicillins and it inactivates some beta-lactamase enzymes, preventing inactivation of amoxicillin. Clavulanic acid does not have any clinically useful antibacterial effect. The clinical effect of co-amoxiclav is due to the amoxicillin component. It is well absorbed following oral administration, particularly in comparison with other β-lactam antibiotics. Amoxicillin is bactericidal in that it interferes with the synthesis of the bacterial cell wall. As a result, the cell wall is weakened and the bacterium swells, then ruptures.

Co-danthramer

Co-danthramer (POM)
Capsule: 25/200, dantron 25mg + poloxamer '188' 200mg (60).
Suspension: 25/200 in 5mL, dantron 25mg, poloxamer '188' 200mg/5mL (300mL; 1000mL).

Co-danthramer strong (POM)
Capsule: 37.5/500, dantron 37.5mg + poloxamer '188' 500mg (60).
Suspension: 75/1000 in 5mL, dantron 75mg, poloxamer '188' 1 g/5mL (300mL).
Note: co-danthramer suspension 5mL = 1 × co-danthramer capsule; *strong* co-danthramer suspension 5mL = 2 × *strong* co-danthramer capsules.

Indications

- Treatment of constipation in terminally ill patients.

Contraindications and precautions

- Contraindicated in intestinal obstruction.
- Avoid in patients with abdominal pain of unknown origin.
- Use with caution in incontinent patients (both urinary and faecally) due to the risk of superficial sloughing of the skin.

☺ Adverse effects

- Dantron may cause a temporary and harmless pink or red colouring of the urine and perianal skin.
- Prolonged contact with the skin can lead to superficial sloughing of the skin (co-danthramer 'burn'). This should be prevented by application of a barrier cream in susceptible patients.

Drug interactions

Pharmacokinetic
- No known pharmacokinetic interactions.

Pharmacodynamic
- *Anticholinergics*—antagonizes the laxative effect.
- *Cyclizine*—antagonizes the laxative effect.
- *Opioids*—antagonizes the laxative effect.
- *5-HT$_3$ antagonists*—antagonizes the laxative effect.
- *TCAs*—antagonizes the laxative effect.

⨌ Dose (see Table 3.3)

⨌ Dose adjustments

Elderly
- No specific dose adjustments recommended by the manufacturer.

Hepatic/renal impairment
- No specific dose adjustments recommended by the manufacturer.

Table 3.3 Co-danthramer dosage

	Co-danthramer capsules	Co-danthramer suspension	Co-danthramer strong capsules	Co-danthramer strong suspension
Initial dose	1–2 PO ON	5–10mL PO ON	1–2 PO ON	5mL PO ON
Dose adjustment (*following doses are higher than licensed*)	¥ Increase as necessary to max. 2 PO BD. Consider changing to co-danthramer strong if no response	¥ Increase as necessary to max. 10mL PO BD. Consider changing to co-danthramer strong if no response	¥ Increase as necessary to max. 3 PO BD. Review treatment if no response	¥ Increase as necessary to max. 10mL PO BD. Review treatment if no response

Additional information

• Warn patients that urine may be coloured red/orange.

✈ Pharmacology

Co-danthramer consists of dantron poloxamer 188. Dantron is an anthraquinone derivative chemically related to the active principle of cascara and senna. It is believed to stimulate muscles of the large intestine through action on the myenteric plexus. Griping should not occur as the small intestine is not affected. Poloxamer 188 is a surfactant that improves the penetration of water into faecal material and it also has a lubricant effect.

Codeine

Generic (CD5 POM)
Tablet: 15mg (28); 30mg (28); 60mg (28).
Syrup: 25mg/5mL (100mL).
Linctus: 15mg/5mL (100mL).
Note: sugar-free linctus is available.
Injection: 60mg/mL (10) (CD2 POM).

Combination products
Certain products containing <15mg codeine and paracetamol are available OTC (CD5 P).

Several branded formulations are available for the following combination products.

Co-codamol 8/500 (CD5 POM)
Tablet: codeine phosphate 8mg, paracetamol 500mg (30).
Capsule: codeine phosphate 8mg, paracetamol 500mg (10; 20).
Effervescent or dispersible tablet: codeine phosphate 8mg, paracetamol 500mg (100).

Co-codamol 15/500 (CD5 POM)
Caplet: codeine phosphate 15mg, paracetamol 500mg (100).

Co-codamol 30/500 (CD5 POM)
Tablet: codeine phosphate 30mg, paracetamol 500mg (100).
Caplet: codeine phosphate 30mg, paracetamol 500mg (100).
Capsule: codeine phosphate 30mg, paracetamol 500mg (100).
Effervescent or dispersible tablet: codeine phosphate 30mg, paracetamol 500mg (32; 100).

Co-codaprin 8/400 (CD5 POM)
Dispersible tablet: codeine phosphate 8mg, aspirin 400mg (100).

Indications
- Management of mild to moderate pain
- Treatment of diarrhoea
- Cough (linctus).

Contraindications and precautions
- If the dose of an opioid is titrated correctly, it is generally accepted that there are no absolute contraindications to the use of such drugs in palliative care, although there may be circumstances where one opioid is favoured over another (e.g. renal impairment, constipation).
- Use codeine with caution in the following instances:
  - acute alcoholism
  - arrhythmias
  - asthma (can release histamine)
  - bowel obstruction

- concurrent use with CYP2D6 inhibitors (see 📖 Drug interactions)
- diseases of the biliary tract (e.g. gallstones)
- elderly
- head injury
- hepatic impairment
- obstructive airways disease
- pancreatitis
- paralytic ileus
- raised intracranial pressure
- renal impairment
- prostatic hypertrophy
- respiratory depression.
- Effervescent formulations contain up to Na$^+$ 16.9mmol/L (check individual product). Avoid in renal impairment and use with caution in patients with hypertension or CHF.
- Codeine may modify reactions and patients should be advised not drive (or operate machinery) if affected. Refer to 📖 Drugs and driving, p.25.

- Ultrarapid metabolizers convert codeine into its active metabolite, morphine, more rapidly and completely than other people which can result in higher than expected plasma morphine concentrations. Even at usual doses, ultrarapid metabolizers may experience symptoms of overdose, such as extreme sleepiness, confusion, or shallow breathing.
- Poor metabolizers or those taking concurrent CYP2D6 inhibitors (see 📖 Drug interactions) may derive little or no analgesic benefit from codeine. Titration of an alternative opioid is recommended, rather than substitution to an equianalgesic dose.

☺ Adverse effects

The frequency is not defined, but commonly reported adverse effects include:

- Constipation
- Drowsiness
- Headache
- Nausea and/or vomiting
- Pruritus
- Rash.

Less commonly reported adverse effects include:

- Abdominal pain
- Biliary spasm
- Confusion
- Decreased libido
- Dizziness
- Dry mouth
- Flushing
- Hallucinations
- Hypotension
- Paraesthesia
- Paralytic ileus
- Respiratory depression
- Sweating
- Ureteric spasm
- Urinary retention
- Visual disturbances.

Drug interactions

Pharmacokinetic

- Codeine is a pro-drug and is metabolized by CYP2D6 to morphine. A minor pathway involves CYP3A4. Co-administration with drugs that are metabolized by, or affect the activity (induction or inhibition—see 📖 inside back cover) of these pathways may lead to clinically relevant drug interactions and the prescriber should be aware that dosage adjustments may be necessary.

- The efficacy of codeine may be reduced by CYP2D6 inhibitors (such as *duloxetine, fluoxetine, haloperidol, levomepromazine,* and *paroxetine*) or increased by CYP3A4 inducers (e.g. carbamazepine, rifampicin). The clinical implications of co-administration with these drugs are unknown; the prescriber should be aware of the potential for altered response.

Pharmacodynamic

- *Antihypertensives*—increased risk of hypotension.
- *CNS depressants*—risk of excessive sedation.
- *Haloperidol*—may be an additive hypotensive effect.
- *Ketamine*—there is a potential opioid-sparing effect with ketamine and the dose of codeine may need reducing.
- *Levomepromazine*—may be an additive hypotensive effect.

💊 Dose

Pain

- 30–60mg PO or IM every 4 hours when necessary for pain to a maximum of 240mg daily.
- ⁺Alternatively, codeine can be given either 30–60mg SC every 4 hours when necessary, or via CSCI over 24 hours.

Combination products

- Co-codamol 8/500, 15/500, and 30/500; 1–2 tablets PO every 4 hours (maximum 8 daily due to paracetamol).

Diarrhoea

- 30mg PO TDS —QDS. Higher doses have been used (e.g. 30–60mg every 4 hours).

Cough

- 5–10mL (of linctus) PO TDS–QDS.

💊 Dose adjustments

Elderly

- No specific guidance is available, although lower starting doses may be preferable. Dose requirements should be individually titrated.

Hepatic/renal impairment

- No specific guidance is available, although in patients with hepatic impairment, the plasma concentration is expected to be increased. In view of its hepatic metabolism, caution is advised when giving dihydrocodeine to patients with hepatic impairment. Lower starting doses may be preferable and dose requirements should be individually titrated.
- No specific guidance is available for patients with renal impairment. However, in view of the fact that metabolites are renally excreted, lower starting doses may be preferable and dose requirements should be individually titrated.

Additional information

- CYP2D6 poor metabolizers (up to 10% of the Caucasian population) cannot produce the active metabolite of codeine—morphine. Drug interactions can affect the metabolism of codeine via inhibition of CYP2D6. The clinical consequences of genotype and drug interaction are unknown Genetic variations lead to the possibility of a modified adverse effect profile and varied analgesic response with tramadol.
- Codeine is included in a number OTC preparations for coughs, colds, and pain so drug histories must include remedies patients may have self-selected.

✧ **Pharmacology**

Codeine is a naturally occurring weak opioid agonist derived from opium. By mouth, it is of similar potency as dihydrocodeine; parenterally it is considered to be half as potent as dihydrocodeine. Oral codeine is normally regarded as being about 1/10 as potent as oral morphine; it is de-methylated to morphine in the liver by CYP2D6. A percentage of the Caucasian population (5–10%) are poor metabolizers of CYP2D6 so codeine will be less effective or even ineffective in this group. Co-administration of CYP2D6 inhibitors produces similar effects. A minor pathway involving CYP3A4 usually produces an active metabolite in very small amounts. However, this pathway becomes important in poor metabolizers and with CYP2D6 inhibition or CYP3A4 induction. The metabolites are renally excreted.

Cyclizine

Valoid®
Injection (POM): 50mg/mL (5).

Generic
Injection (POM): 50mg/mL (5).
Tablet (P): 50mg (100).

Unlicensed (POM)
Suppositories: 12.5mg; 25mg; 50mg; 100mg.
Available on a named-patient basis as manufactured special.

Indications
- Prevention and treatment of nausea and vomiting.

Contraindications and precautions
- Refer to 📖 Use of drugs in end-of-life care, p.53 for end-of-life care issues.
- Avoid in patients with porphyria.
- Cyclizine should be used with caution in patients with:
  - glaucoma
  - severe CHF
  - prostatic hypertrophy.
- The anticholinergic effect of cyclizine can be additive with other drugs. Subtle deficits in attention, memory, and reasoning may occur with therapeutic dosages of anticholinergic drugs without signs of obvious toxicity. These deficits have often been mistaken for symptoms of early dementia in elderly patients.
- Cyclizine may modify reactions and patients should be advised not drive (or operate machinery) if affected. Refer to 📖 Drugs and driving, p.25.

☺ Adverse effects
The frequency is not defined, but reported adverse effects include:

- Blurred vision
- Confusion
- Constipation
- Delirium
- Drowsiness
- Dry mouth
- Extrapyramidal motor disturbances (rare)
- Hallucinations (especially with higher doses)
- Headache
- Hypersensitivity reactions (rare)
- Nervousness
- Restlessness
- Tachycardia
- Urinary retention.

Drug interactions
Pharmacokinetic
- No recognized pharmacokinetic interactions.

Pharmacodynamic
- *Anticholinergics*—increased risk of adverse effects.
- *CNS depressants*—increased risk of CNS adverse effects.

- *Domperidone*—may inhibit prokinetic effect.
- *Metoclopramide*—may inhibit prokinetic effect.
- *Nefopam*—increased risk of anticholinergic adverse effects.
- *TCAs*—increased risk of anticholinergic adverse effects.

Dose

- Initial dose 50–100mg PO or SC$^¥$ BD-TDS PRN. Alternatively, 100–150mg via CSCI$^¥$ over 24 hours.
- Maximum daily dose 200mg$^¥$ PO or SC.

Dose adjustments

Elderly

- The manufacturer indicates that the normal adult dosage is appropriate. Note that the elderly may be more susceptible to the central and anticholinergic effects of cyclizine (which may be additive with concomitant drugs); there may be an increased risk for cognitive decline and dementia.

Hepatic/renal impairment

- No specific guidance available. Dose requirements should be individually titrated.
- In hepatic impairment, empirical dose adjustments may be necessary since cyclizine is undergoes hepatic clearance.
- The manufacturer states that dose reductions may be necessary in renal impairment.

Additional information

- The antiemetic effect should occur within 2 hours of oral administration and lasts approximately 4 hours. Parenteral administration would be expected to produce a much quicker response.
- Cyclizine should be avoided in severe CHF because it can cause a reduction in cardiac output associated with increases in heart rate, mean arterial pressure, and pulmonary wedge pressure.
- Cyclizine injection must be diluted with WFI. It is incompatible with NaCl 0.9% and in solutions with a pH of 6.8 or more.
- Cyclizine and diamorphine mixtures are chemically and physically stable in WFI up to concentrations of 20mg/mL over 24 hours. If the diamorphine concentration exceeds 20mg/mL, crystallization may occur unless the concentration of cyclizine is no greater than 10mg/mL. Similarly, if the concentration of cyclizine exceeds 20mg/mL, crystallization may occur unless the concentration of diamorphine is no greater than 15mg/mL.
- There are concentration-dependent compatibility issues with alfentanil, dexamethasone, glycopyrronium, hyoscine butylbromide, metoclopramide and oxycodone although the specific details are unknown.
- Cyclizine via CSCI is compatible with clonazepam, diamorphine, dihydrocodeine, haloperidol, hyoscine hydrobromide, levomepromazine, midazolam, morphine, octreotide, and ondansetron.

⟩ **Pharmacology**

Cyclizine is a histamine H_1 receptor antagonist and has a low incidence of drowsiness. It also possesses anticholinergic activity. The exact mechanism by which cyclizine can prevent or suppress nausea and vomiting from various causes is unknown, but it may have an inhibitory action within part of the midbrain referred to as the vomiting centre. Cyclizine also increases lower oesophageal sphincter tone and reduces the sensitivity of the labyrinthine apparatus. It is metabolized in the liver to a relatively inactive metabolite.

Cyproheptadine

Periactin® (POM)
Tablet (scored): 4mg (30).

Indications

- Symptomatic relief of allergy (e.g. hayfever, allergy).
- Vascular headache and migraine.
- ⚥Symptomatic relief of serotonin syndrome.[1]
- ⚥Appetite stimulant (other treatments preferred).[2]
- ⚥Management of diarrhoea associated with Carcinoid syndrome (octreotide generally preferred).[2,3]

Contraindications and precautions

- Contraindicated for use in patients with:
  - glaucoma
  - pyloroduodenal obstruction
  - stenosing peptic ulcer
  - symptomatic prostatic hypertrophy
  - predisposition to urinary retention or bladder neck obstruction.
- Use cautiously in patients with:
  - bronchial asthma
  - increased intraocular pressure
  - hyperthyroidism
  - cardiovascular disease
  - hypertension.
- Avoid concurrent use with MAOIs (see 📖 Drug Interactions).
- Cyproheptadine may modify reactions and patients should be advised not drive (or operate machinery) if affected. Refer to 📖 Drugs and driving, p.25.

☺ Adverse effects

The frequency is not defined, but commonly reported adverse effects include:

- Abdominal pain
- Appetite stimulation
- Diarrhoea
- Dizziness
- Drowsiness (should improve within 1 week of treatment)
- Dry mouth
- Thickening of bronchial secretions
- Fatigue
- Headache
- Nausea
- Nervousness
- Weight gain.

Drug interactions

Pharmacokinetic

- Mechanism of hepatic metabolism unspecified.
- No known pharmacokinetic interactions.

Pharmacodynamic

- SSRIs—antidepressant effect may be reduced by cyproheptadine.
- CNS depressants—risk of excessive sedation.
- MAOIs—may cause hallucinations.

♣ Dose

Symptomatic relief of allergy

- Initial dose 4mg PO TDS. Dose can be increased to a maximum of 32mg PO daily.

Vascular headache and migraine

- Initial dose 4mg PO, repeated if necessary after 30min. Patients who respond usually obtain relief with 8mg, and this dose should not be exceeded within a 4–6-hour period.
- Usual maintenance dose is 4mg PO every 4–6 hours.

¥ Symptomatic relief of serotonin syndrome

- Initial dose 4–8mg PO. Can be repeated in 2 hours. If no response is seen after 16mg it should be discontinued. If there is a response then it may be continued in divided doses up to 32mg/day (e.g. up to 8mg four times daily).

¥ Appetite/¥ carcinoid

- Initial dose 4mg PO TDS. Dose can be to 8mg PO TDS. Further dose increases are unlikely to be of further benefit.

♣ Dose adjustments

Elderly

- Elderly patients are more likely to experience adverse effects such as dizziness, sedation, and hypotension. The UK manufacturer contraindicates the use of cyproheptadine in elderly patients. However, for the treatment of serotonin syndrome, the lowest effective dose should be used.

Hepatic/renal impairment

- No specific guidance available. Dose requirements should be individually titrated.

Additional information

- Tablets can be crushed and dispersed in water prior to administration if necessary.

⊕ Pharmacology

Cyproheptadine is a piperidine antihistamine with weak anticholinergic properties. In addition, it also antagonizes serotonin receptors. This latter effect makes cyproheptadine particularly useful in the symptomatic treatment of serotonin syndrome. The drug is extensively metabolized, with the metabolites being excreted renally. The exact mechanism of metabolism is unknown, but may involve the cytochrome P450 system.

References

1. Gillman PK. Monoamine oxidase inhibitors, opioid analgesics and serotonin toxicity. *Br J Anaesth* 2005; **95**(4):434–41.
2. Kardinal CG, Loprinzi CL, Schaid DJ, *et al*. A controlled trial of cyproheptadine in cancer patients with anorexia and/or cachexia. *Cancer* 1990; **65**(12):2657–62.
3. Moertel CG, Kvols LK, Rubin J. A study of cyproheptadine in the treatment of metastatic carcinoid tumor and the malignant carcinoid syndrome. *Cancer* 1991; **67**(1):33–6.

Cyproterone

Cyprostat® (POM)
Tablet (scored): 50mg (168); 100mg (84).

Generic (POM)
Tablet: 50mg (56); 100mg (84).

Indications

- Prostate cancer:
  - to suppress 'flare' with initial gonadorelin therapy
  - long-term palliative treatment where gonadorelin analogues or orchidectomy contraindicated, not tolerated, or where oral therapy preferred
  - treatment of hot flushes in patients receiving gonadorelin therapy or after orchidectomy.

Contraindications and precautions

- Hepatic toxicity has been reported in patients treated with cyproterone acetate >100mg PO daily, usually after several months. LFTs should be performed before and regularly during treatment. If symptoms of hepatotoxicity occur and are believed to be caused by cyproterone, it should normally be withdrawn.

- Cyproterone must not be used in patients with:
  - existing thromboembolic condition
  - malignant tumours (except prostate)
  - meningioma or a history of meningioma.
- Use with caution in the following:
  - depression (condition may deteriorate)
  - hepatic impairment (see earlier in list)
  - history of thromboembolic disease (may recur with cyproterone)
  - diabetes (cyproterone can affect carbohydrate metabolism; also increased risk of thromboembolic events)
  - sickle cell anaemia.
- Regular blood counts (as well as LFTs) should be performed due to the risk of anaemia.
- Cyproterone may modify reactions and patients should be advised not drive (or operate machinery) if affected. Refer to 📖 Drugs and driving, p.25.

☼ Adverse effects

Very common

- Decreased libido
- Erectile dysfunction
- Reduced sexual drive.

Common

- Depression
- Dyspnoea
- Fatigue
- Gynaecomastia
- Hepatotoxicity (jaundice/hepatitis)

- Hot flushes
- Restlessness (usually short-term)
- Sweating
- Weight gain (long-term treatment).

Uncommon
- Rash.

Rare
- Galactorrhoea.

Very rare
- Benign and malignant liver tumours.

Unknown
- Anaemia (long-term treatment)
- Dry skin
- Meningioma (long-term treatment)
- Osteoporosis
- Thromboembolic events.

Drug interactions

Pharmacokinetic
- Cyproterone is metabolized by CYP3A4; at high doses it may inhibit CYP2C8, CYP2C9, CYP2C19, CYP2D6 and CYP3A4. Co-administration with drugs that are metabolized by, or affect the activity (induction or inhibition—see 📖 inside back cover) of this pathway may lead to clinically relevant drug interactions and the prescriber should be aware that dosage adjustments may be necessary, particularly of drugs with a narrow therapeutic index.

Pharmacodynamic
- None known.

💊 Dose

Suppression of 'flare'
- 300mg PO in 2–3 divided doses after meals for several days before and several weeks after gonadorelin therapy. The dose may be reduced to 200mg PO in 2–3 divided doses if the higher dose is not tolerated.

Long-term palliative treatment
- 200–300mg PO daily in 2-3 divided doses after meals.

Hot flushes
- Initial dose 50mg PO OD, increasing if necessary to 50mg PO BD–TDS.

💊 Dose adjustments

Elderly
- Usual adult doses recommended.

Hepatic/renal impairment
- No specific guidance is available for use in hepatic impairment. The manufacturer advises caution.
- No specific guidance is available for use in renal impairment, although accumulation is unlikely given the hepatic clearance of the drug.

Additional information

- Although tablets may be crushed and dispersed in water prior to administration, it is not recommended to be performed due to the risk of exposure.

Pharmacology

Cyproterone is an anti-androgen that antagonizes the actions of testosterone and its metabolite, dihydrotestosterone. It also has progestogenic activity, which exerts a negative feedback effect on the hypothalamus, causing a reduction in gonadotrophin release, and subsequent diminished production of testicular androgens. It is completely absorbed orally and undergoes extensive metabolism by various pathways. The main metabolite has similar anti-androgen properties but little progestogenic activity.

Dalteparin

Fragmin® *(POM)*
Injection (single-dose syringe for SC use): dalteparin sodium 12,500 units/mL
2500 units (0.2mL syringe); 25,000 units/mL, 5000 units (0.2mL syringe); 7500
units (0.3mL syringe); 10,000 units (0.4mL syringe); 12,500 units (0.5mL syringe)
15,000 units (0.6mL syringe); 18,000 units (0.72mL syringe).

Injection (for SC or IV use): dalteparin sodium 2500 units/mL, 10,000 units
(4mL ampoule); 10,000 units/mL, 10,000 units (1mL ampoule).

Injection (for SC use): 25,000 units/mL, 100,000 units (4mL multi-dose vial).

Injection (graduated syringe for SC use): dalteparin sodium 10,000 units/mL,
10,000 units (1mL syringe).

Indications
- Treatment and prophylaxis of deep vein thrombosis (DVT) and
  pulmonary embolism (PE).
- Extended treatment of symptomatic venous thromboembolism (VTE)
  and prevention of its recurrence in patients with solid tumours.
- Prophylaxis of DVT.
- Other indications apply but are not normally relevant in palliative care.

Contraindications and precautions
- Dalteparin is contraindicated for use in:
  - acute gastroduodenal ulcer
  - body weight <40kg at time of VTE (extended use only, due to lack
    of data)
  - cerebral haemorrhage (within 3 months)
  - known haemorrhagic diathesis
  - septic endocarditis.
- Use with caution in patients with an increased risk of bleeding
  complications:
  - brain tumours (increased risk of intracranial bleeding)
  - concurrent use of anticoagulant/antiplatelet agents/NSAIDs (see
    📖 Drug interactions, p.141)
  - haemorrhagic stroke
  - retinopathy (hypertensive or diabetic)
  - surgery
  - severe hepatic impairment
  - severe renal impairment
  - trauma
  - thrombocytopenia
  - uncontrolled hypertension.
- A baseline platelet count should be taken prior to initiating treatment
  and monitored closely during the first 3 weeks (e.g. every 2–4 days)
  and regularly thereafter.
- Not for IM use.
- Advice should be sought from anaesthetic colleagues if considering an
  epidural intervention in a patient receiving dalteparin due to the risk of
  spinal haematoma.

- LMWH can inhibit aldosterone secretion, which can cause hyperkalaemia. Patients with pre-existing renal impairment are more at risk. Potassium should be measured in patients at risk prior to starting a LMWH and monitored regularly thereafter, especially if treatment is prolonged beyond 7 days.
- *Prophylactic doses of dalteparin are not sufficient to prevent valve thrombosis in patients with prosthetic heart valves.*

☺ Adverse effects

Common
- Bleeding (at any site)
- Haematoma at injection site
- Transient changes to liver transaminase levels—clinical significance unknown
- Thrombocytopenia.

Uncommon
- Hyperkalaemia
- Osteoporosis with long-term treatment
- Pruritus
- Urticaria.

Rare
- Skin necrosis.

Unknown
- Hypoaldosteronism
- Intracranial bleeds
- Prosthetic cardiac valve thrombosis (see 🕮 Contraindications and precautions, p.140)
- Spinal or epidural haematoma.

Drug interactions

Pharmacokinetic
- None recognized.

Pharmacodynamic
- Drugs with anticoagulant or antiplatelet effect may enhance the effect of dalteparin:
  - aspirin
  - clopidogrel
  - dipyridamole
  - NSAIDs.
- *ACEIs*—increased risk of hyperkalaemia
- *Amiloride*—increased risk of hyperkalaemia
- *Antihistamines*—possibly reduce anticoagulant effect
- *Ascorbic acid*—possibly reduces anticoagulant effect
- *Corticosteroids*—increased risk of GI bleeding
- *Spironolactone*—increased risk of hyperkalaemia
- *SSRIs*—increased risk of bleeding

♣ Dose

Treatment of VTE
- The dose is weight-dependent and is administered once daily subcutaneously (see Table 3.4).
- Alternatively, a dose of 200 units/kg (max. 18,000 units) can be given.
- Patients at a high risk of bleeding should have the daily dose divided and administered twice daily.

Table 3.4 Dalteparin dosage for treatment of DVT and PE

Weight (kg)	Dose (units)
<46	7500
46–56	10,000
57–68	12,500
69–82	15,000
83 and over	18,000

- Patients usually start oral anticoagulation at the same time and continue both until the INR is within the target range. This generally takes 5 days. However, cancer patients unsuitable for oral anticoagulation may require long-term treatment with a LMWH. Treatment is occasionally continued indefinitely.

Extended treatment of VTE
- The recommended duration of treatment is 6 months, extended if necessary based on a risk:benefit assessment.
- For the first 30 days of treatment, use the dose schedule as previously described.
- In the case of chemotherapy-induced thrombocytopenia, the following dose adjustments should be made:
  - platelet counts between 50,000 and 100,000/mm^3 reduce daily dose by 2500 units until the count ≥ 100,000mm^3
  - platelet counts <50,000/mm^3, discontinue until the count >50,000/mm^3
- For months 2–6, the dose should be as shown in Table 3.5.
- During the extended phase of treatment (months 2–6), the following dose adjustments should be made in the case of chemotherapy-induced thrombocytopenia:
  - platelet counts <50,000/mm^3, discontinue until the count >50,000/mm^3
  - platelet counts between 50,000 and 100,000/mm^3, reduce the dose as shown in Table 3.6 until the count ≥ 100,000mm^3.

Table 3.5 Extended treatment of VTE

Weight (kg)	Dose (units)
<56	7500
57–68	10,000
69–82	12,500
83–98	15,000
99 and over	18,000

Table 3.6 Dose adjustments for low platelet counts

Weight (kg)	Adjusted dose (units)
<56	5000
57–68	7500
69–82	10,000
83–98	12,500
99 and over	15,000

Prophylaxis of DVT

- For medical prophylaxis (including immobile cancer patients) 5000 units SC OD. The duration of treatment depends upon the risk factors identified (e.g. immobile in-patients may be considered for treatment from admission until discharge). Graduated compression stockings should be considered if LMWH is contraindicated.
- For surgical prophylaxis:
  - moderate risk—2500 units before procedure and each day for 5–7 days or longer (until mobilized)
  - high risk—2500 units before procedure and 8–12 hours later, then 5000 units SC OD for 5–7 days or longer (until mobilized).

Dose adjustments

Elderly

- Usual adult doses recommended.

Hepatic/renal impairment

- No specific guidance is available for patients with hepatic impairment. The manufacturer advices caution due to an increased risk of bleeding.
- In the case of significant renal impairment, defined as a CrCl <30mL/min, the dose of dalteparin should be adjusted based on anti-Factor Xa activity. If the anti-Factor Xa level is less than or greater than the desired range, the dose of dalteparin should be increased or reduced respectively, and the anti-Factor Xa measurement should be repeated after 3–4 doses. This process should be repeated until the desired anti-Factor Xa level is achieved.

Additional information
- The risk of heparin-induced thrombocytopenia is low with LMWH but may occur after 5–10 days. If there is a 50% reduction of the platelet count, LMWH should be stopped.

✥ Pharmacology

Dalteparin is a LMWH produced from porcine-derived sodium heparin It acts mainly through its potentiation of the inhibition of Factor Xa anc thrombin by antithrombin. Dalteparin is eliminated primarily via the kidneys, hence the need for dose adjustments in renal impairment. Loca protocols may help to indicate when treatment of palliative care patients with dalteparin is appropriate.

Demeclocycline

Ledermycin® (POM)
Capsule: 150mg (28).

Indications

- Treatment of chronic syndrome of SIADH.

Contraindications and precautions

- Use with caution in patients with liver or renal impairment, or in patients with concurrent use of potentially hepatotoxic or nephrotoxic drugs.
- Care should be taken in patients with myasthenia gravis due to a potential for weak neuromuscular blockade.
- May cause photosensitive skin reactions—warn the patient to avoid direct exposure to sunlight or sunlamps and to discontinue at the first sign of skin discomfort.

☺ Adverse effects

The frequency is not defined, but reported adverse effects include:

- Blood dyscrasias (e.g. haemolytic anaemia, neutropenia, thrombocytopenia)
- Candidiasis
- Diarrhoea
- Dizziness
- Dysphagia
- Headache
- Hepatitis
- Nausea
- Oesophagitis
- Pancreatitis
- Photosensitivity (avoid direct exposure to sunlight or artificial ultraviolet light)
- Renal impairment
- Visual disturbances
- Vomiting.

Drug interactions

Pharmacokinetic

- *Antacids*—absorption of demeclocycline is impaired by the concomitant administration of preparations containing calcium, magnesium, aluminium, or sodium bicarbonate.

Pharmacodynamic

- *NSAIDs*—increased risk of nephrotoxicity.
- *Penicillins*—bacteriostatic effect of demeclocycline may reduce bactericidal action of penicillins.
- *Warfarin*—plasma prothrombin activity may be depressed needing lower warfarin doses.

♣ Dose

Demeclocycline capsules should be swallowed whole with plenty of fluid while sitting or standing. Doses should be taken an hour before or 2 hours after meals as absorption is impaired by milk and food.

- Initial dose 900–1200mg daily in 3–4 divided doses.
- If poorly tolerated, a lower initial dose may be used (e.g. 150mg BD–TDS), but time to effect may be delayed.
- Usual maintenance dose is 600–900mg daily in 3–4 divided doses.

♣ Dose adjustments

Elderly
- No specific guidance is available. Use the lowest effective dose.

Hepatic/renal impairment
- No specific guidance is available, although the manufacturer recommends that patients with liver disease should not receive more than 1g daily and lower doses are indicated in cases of renal impairment to avoid excessive systemic accumulation.
- In both cases, regular blood tests (LFTs, U&Es) are advisable with prolonged therapy.

Additional information

- The effect in SIADH should be apparent within 3–5 days.
- The capsule should not be opened for oral administration due to the risk of developing oesophagitis or oesophageal ulceration.

♦ Pharmacology

Demeclocycline is a tetracycline antibiotic. The use in SIADH actually relies on the adverse effect of nephrogenic diabetes insipidus through inhibition of antidiuretic hormone (ADH) on renal tubules. It undergoes minor hepatic metabolism; the majority of a dose is excreted renally as unchanged drug.

Dexamethasone

Generic (POM)
Tablet: 0.5mg (28); 2mg (100).
Oral solution (sugar-free): 2mg/5mL (150mL).
Injection: 3.3mg/mL (10); 4mg/mL (10); 6.6mg/mL (10) (See 📖 Additional information, p.151).

Indications[1]

- Suppression of inflammation (including cerebral oedema)
- Immunosuppression (see 📖 Additional information, p.151)
- *Appetite stimulation
- *Bowel obstruction
- *Dyspnoea
- *Nausea and vomiting
- *Pain (e.g. bone pain, nerve compression)
- *Spinal cord compression
- *Superior vena cava obstruction.

Contraindications and precautions

- In general, contraindications are relative in conditions where the use of dexamethasone may be life saving.
- The use of dexamethasone is contraindicated in systemic infection unless specific anti-infective therapy is employed.
- Patients without a definite history of chickenpox should be advised to avoid close personal contact with chickenpox or herpes zoster.
- Refer to 📖 Use of drugs in end-of-life care, p.53 for end-of-life care issues.
- Dexamethasone may prevent the development of signs and symptoms of inflammation/infection (e.g. fever).
- Caution is advised when considering the use of systemic corticosteroids in patients with the following conditions:
  - concurrent use of NSAIDs (see 📖 Drug interactions, p.149)
  - CHF
  - diabetes mellitus (risk of hyperglycaemia—close monitoring of blood glucose recommended)
  - epilepsy (see 📖 Drug interactions, p.149)
  - glaucoma
  - hypertension
  - hypokalaemia (correct before starting dexamethasone)
  - liver or renal impairment (see 📖 Dose adjustments, p.150).
  - osteoporosis
  - recent myocardial infarction (risk of myocardial rupture)
  - peptic ulceration
  - psychotic illness (symptoms can emerge within a few days or weeks of starting the treatment).

Dexamethasone withdrawal

In patients who have received more than physiological doses of systemic corticosteroids (i.e. >1mg dexamethasone) for >3 weeks, withdrawal should be gradual in order to avoid acute adrenal insufficiency. Abrupt withdrawal of doses of up to 6mg daily of dexamethasone for 3 weeks is unlikely to lead to clinically relevant hypothalamic–pituitary–adrenal (HPA)-axis suppression in the majority of patients. In the following cases, withdrawal may need to be more gradual:

- Patients who have had repeated courses of systemic corticosteroids, particularly if taken for >3 weeks.
- Patients receiving doses of systemic corticosteroid >6mg daily of dexamethasone.
- Patients repeatedly taking doses in the evening.

There is no evidence as to the best way to withdraw corticosteroids and it is often performed with close monitoring of the patient's condition. The dose may initially be reduced rapidly (e.g. by halving the dose daily) to physiological doses (~1mg dexamethasone) and then more slowly (e.g. 500 micrograms per week for 1–2 weeks).

A 'withdrawal syndrome' may also occur including fever, myalgia, arthralgia, rhinitis, conjunctivitis, painful itchy skin nodules, and loss of weight.

In dying patients, once the decision is made to withdraw corticosteroids, they can be discontinued abruptly. Patients with brain tumours may require additional analgesia as raised intracranial pressure can develop and may manifest as worsening headache, or terminal restlessness.

☺ Adverse effects

The frequency is not defined. Adverse effects are generally predictable and related to dosage, timing of administration and the duration of treatment. They include:

- Endocrine:
  - hirsutism
  - hyperglycaemia
  - hyperlipidaemia
  - weight gain.
- Fluid and electrolyte disturbances:
  - CHF
  - hypertension
  - hypokalaemia
  - sodium and water retention.
- Gastrointestinal:
  - acute pancreatitis
  - dyspepsia peptic ulceration with perforation
  - haemorrhage
  - hiccups (if problematic, may resolve if alternative corticosteroid used).
- Musculoskeletal:
  - aseptic necrosis of femoral head

- avascular necrosis
  - loss of muscle mass
  - osteoporosis
  - proximal myopathy
  - tendon rupture.
- Neurological:
  - aggravation of epilepsy
  - anxiety
  - confusion
  - depression
  - insomnia
  - mood elevation
  - psychotic reactions.
- Other:
  - glaucoma
  - impaired wound healing
  - increased susceptibility and severity of infections (signs can be masked)
  - sweating.

Corticosteroid-induced osteoporosis

- Patients aged over 65 years and with prior or current exposure to oral corticosteroids are at an increased risk of osteoporosis and bone fracture. Treatment with corticosteroids for periods as short as 3 months may result in increased risk. 3 or more courses of corticosteroids taken in the previous 12 months are considered to be equivalent to at least 3 months of continuous treatment.
- Prophylactic treatment (e.g. bisphosphonate, calcium and vitamin D supplements, hormone replacement therapy) should be considered for all patients who may take an oral corticosteroid for 3 months or longer.

Drug interactions

Pharmacokinetic

- Dexamethasone is a substrate of CYP3A4. It is also a moderate inducer of CYP3A4 at doses ≥16mg/day. Co-administration with drugs that are metabolized by, or affect the activity (induction or inhibition—see 📖 inside back cover) of this pathway may lead to clinically relevant drug interactions and the prescriber should be aware that dosage adjustments may be necessary, particularly of drugs with a narrow therapeutic index.
- Note that low activity of CYP3A4 (e.g. through inhibition) can contribute to the development of osteonecrosis of the femoral head.
- *Carbamazepine*—effect of dexamethasone likely to be reduced; consider doubling the dexamethasone dose and monitor the response.
- *Colestyramine*—may decrease the absorption of dexamethasone.
- *Erythromycin*—may increase the effects of dexamethasone through inhibition of CYP3A4.

- *Phenytoin*—effect of dexamethasone likely to be reduced—consider doubling the dexamethasone dose and monitor the response; phenytoin plasma concentrations may also be affected (increased or decreased).
- Avoid excessive amounts of grapefruit juice as it may increase the bio-availability of dexamethasone through inhibition of intestinal CYP3A4.

Pharmacodynamic

- *Anticoagulants*—increased risk of bleeding.
- Antihypertensives—effect antagonized by dexamethasone.
- Azathioprine—additive immunosuppressive effect.
- Ciclosporin—additive immunosuppressive effect; convulsions reported with combination.
- Diuretics—effect antagonized by dexamethasone; increased risk of hypokalaemia and hyperglycaemia.
- Hypoglycaemic drugs—effect antagonized by dexamethasone.
- NSAIDs—increased risk of GI toxicity.
- SSRIs—increased risk of bleeding.
- Thalidomide—toxic epidermal necrolysis reported with concurrent use.

💊 Dose

Cerebral oedema

- Initial dose (mild symptoms) 4–8mg PO/IV OM; initial dose (moderate–severe symptoms) 8–16mg PO/IV OM (or 8mg PO/IV BD, last dose 2pm). Review after 2–4 days and consider stopping over 5–7 days.
- ¥Alternatively, 8–16mg via CSCI over 24 hours.

¥ Appetite

- Initial dose 2–6mg PO OM. Dose reduction should be guided by symptom response.

¥ Bowel obstruction, spinal cord compression, superior vena cava obstruction

- Initial dose 8–16mg via CSCI over 24 hours or 8–16mg PO/IV/SC OM (or 8mg PO/IV/SC BD, last dose 2pm). Review after 2–4 days. Dose reduction should be guided by symptom response.

¥ Dyspnoea, pain

- Initial dose 4–8mg PO/IV/SC OM. Alternatively, 4–8mg via CSCI over 24 hours. Dose adjustment should be guided by symptom response.

¥ Nausea and vomiting

- Initial dose 4–16mg PO/IV/SC OM. Alternatively, 4–16mg via CSCI over 24 hours. Dose adjustment should be guided by symptom response.

💊 Dose adjustments

Elderly

- No specific dose adjustments are necessary. Use the lowest dose for the shortest duration possible since the elderly are more susceptible to adverse effects.

Hepatic/renal impairment

- No specific guidance available. The lowest effective dose should be used for the shortest duration possible.

Additional information

- The immunosuppressant activity of dexamethasone can be used at the end of life to manage the symptoms associated with transplant rejection (e.g. pain and rejection of a kidney). Seek specialist advice.
- A change in product availability of the parenteral formulation may lead to some confusion. Dexamethasone should always be prescribed in terms of dexamethasone base in order to avoid administration errors.
- Consider oral hygiene with dexamethasone use. The patient may develop oral candidiasis and may need a course of nystatin (or fluconazole).
- Oral anti-inflammatory corticosteroid equivalences are:
  - dexamethasone 750 micrograms = hydrocortisone 20mg = prednisolone 5mg.
- Dexamethasone should be administered alone via CSCI, unless specific compatibility data are available.
- Low-dose (0.5–1mg) dexamethasone is occasionally added to CSCIs in some centres to reduce site reactions. Unless specific compatibility is available, this practice cannot be recommended.
- Betamethasone (as sodium phosphate) via SC injection or CSCI has, anecdotally, been used successfully as a substitute in situations of dexamethasone unavailability (using identical doses).

⋟ Pharmacology

Dexamethasone is a highly potent and long-acting glucocorticoid with negligible mineralocorticoid effects. Like other glucocorticoids, dexamethasone also has anti-allergic, antipyretic, and immunosuppressive properties. It is metabolized mainly in the liver, with some occurring in the kidney. Dexamethasone and its metabolites are excreted in the urine.

Reference

1. Shih A, Jackson KC. Role of corticosteroids in palliative care. *J Pain Palliat Care Pharmacother* 2007; **21**(4):69–76.

Diamorphine

Generic (CD2 POM)
Injection: 5mg (5), 10mg (5), 30mg (5), 100mg (5), 500mg (5).
Tablet: 10mg (rarely used).

Diamorphine is a Schedule 2 controlled drug. Refer to 📖 Legal categories of medicines, p.21 for further information.

Indications
- Relief of severe pain
- ¥Painful skin lesions (topical)[1]
- ¥Mucositis (topical)[1]
- ¥Dyspnoea.[2]

Contraindications and precautions
- Refer to 📖 Use of drugs in end-of-life care, p.53 for end-of-life care issues.
- If the dose of an opioid is titrated correctly, it is generally accepted that there are no absolute contraindications to the use of such drugs in palliative care, although there may be circumstances where one opioid is favoured over another (e.g. renal impairment, constipation). Nonetheless, manufacturers state that diamorphine is contraindicated for use in patients with:
  - biliary colic
  - concurrent administration of MAOIs or within 2 weeks of discontinuation of their use (*NB—initial low doses, careful titration, and close monitoring may permit safe combination*)
  - obstructive airways disease (morphine may release histamine)
  - phaeochromocytoma (due to the risk of pressor response to histamine release)
  - respiratory depression
- Use with caution in the following instances:
  - acute alcoholism
  - Addison's disease (adrenocortical insufficiency)
  - asthma (morphine may release histamine)
  - constipation
  - delirium tremens
  - diarrhoea (may mask underlying severe constipation)
  - diseases of the biliary tract
  - elderly patients
  - head injury
  - hepatic impairment (see earlier in list)
  - history of alcohol and drug abuse
  - hypotension associated with hypovolaemia (diamorphine may result in severe hypotension)
  - hypothyroidism
  - inflammatory bowel disorders

- pancreatitis
- prostatic hypertrophy
- raised intracranial pressure
- significantly impaired hepatic and renal function
- Diamorphine may modify reactions and patients should be advised not drive (or operate machinery) if affected. Refer to 📖 Drugs and driving, p.25.

☺ Adverse effects

Strong opioids tend to cause similar adverse effects, albeit to varying degrees. The frequency is not defined, but reported adverse effects include:

- Anorexia
- Biliary pain
- Confusion
- Constipation
- Drowsiness
- Dry mouth
- Dyspepsia
- Exacerbation of pancreatitis
- Euphoria
- Insomnia
- Headache
- Hyperhidrosis

- Myoclonus
- Nausea
- Pruritus
- Sexual dysfunction (e.g. amenorrhea, decreased libido, erectile dysfunction)
- Urinary retention
- Vertigo
- Visual disturbance
- Vomiting
- Weakness.

The following can occur with excessive dose:

- Agitation
- Exacerbation of pain
- Hallucinations
- Miosis

- Paraesthesia
- Respiratory depression
- Restlessness.

Drug interactions

Pharmacokinetic

- No clinically significant pharmacokinetic interactions reported.

Pharmacodynamic

- *Antihypertensives* —increased risk of hypotension.
- *CNS depressants*—risk of excessive sedation.
- *Haloperidol* —may be an additive hypotensive effect.
- *Ketamine* —there is a potential opioid-sparing effect with ketamine and the dose of morphine may need reducing.
- *Levomepromazine*—may be an additive hypotensive effect

♣ Dose

Pain

- The initial dose of diamorphine depends upon the patient's previous opioid requirements. Refer to 📖 Management of pain: opioid substitution, p.32 for information regarding opioid dose equivalences. Refer to 📖 Breakthrough pain, p.35 for guidance relating to BTcP.
- Initial dose in opioid naïve patients is 2.5mg SC 4-hourly PRN. Alternatively, 10mg via CSCI over 24 hours and increase as necessary.

- Diamorphine is very soluble in water; 1g dissolves in 1.6mL of water, permitting high doses via SC injections.

¥ *Painful skin lesions (topical)*
- As with morphine, often use 0.1% or 0.125% w/w gels initially. These can be prepared immediately prior to administration by adding 10mg diamorphine injection (diluted with 0.5mL WFI) to 8g Intrasite® gel (making a 0.125% w/w gel). Higher strength gels, typically up to 0.5%, can be made if necessary.
- Initial dose: 5–10mg diamorphine in Intrasite® gel to affected area at dressing changes (up to twice daily).
- Use within 1 hour of preparation and discard any remaining product.

¥ *Mucositis*
- As with morphine, often use 0.1% w/v initially. Preparations should be prepared immediately prior to administration by adding 10mg diamorphine injection (diluted with 0.5mL WFI) to 10mL of a suitable carrier (e.g. Gelclair®, OralBalance Gel®).
- Higher strength preparations, up to 0.5% w/v can be used if required.
- Initial dose: 10mg to the affected area BD–TDS.
- Use within 1 hour of preparation and discard any remaining product.

¥ *Dyspnoea*
- For opioid naïve patients, initial dose is 1.25mg SC PRN. If patients require >2 doses daily, use of a CSCI should be considered.
- In patients established on opioids, a dose that is equivalent to 25% of the current PRN rescue analgesic dose may be effective. This can be increased up to 100% of the rescue dose in a graduated fashion.

⚖ Dose adjustments

Elderly
- No specific guidance is available, although lower starting doses in opioid naïve patients may be preferable. Dose requirements should be individually titrated.

Hepatic/renal impairment
- No specific guidance is available, although in patients with hepatic impairment, the plasma concentration is expected to be increased. In view of its eventual hepatic metabolism, caution is advised when giving diamorphine to patients with hepatic impairment. Lower starting doses in opioid naïve patients may be preferable and dose requirements should be individually titrated.
- No specific guidance is available for patients with renal impairment. However, in view of the fact that the active metabolite morphine-6-glucuronide is renally excreted, lower starting doses in opioid naïve patients may be preferable and dose requirements should be individually titrated. Alternatively, a different opioid may be more appropriate (e.g. alfentanil).

Additional information
- The United Kingdom is one of the few places where diamorphine is used medicinally. Its use developed in palliative care mainly because

its high solubility in water enables large doses to be included in the contents of a syringe driver. Many of the listed side effects are normally only seen when the dose of diamorphine is too high. When the dose is titrated accurately to manage pain, many of these should be absent.

- If other analgesic measures are introduced—pharmacological or otherwise, e.g. radiotherapy—the dose of diamorphine may need to be reduced.
- Diamorphine via CSCI is reportedly compatible with clonazepam, dexamethasone, glycopyrronium, haloperidol, hyoscine butylbromide, hyoscine hydrobromide, ketamine, ketorolac, levomepromazine, metoclopramide, midazolam, octreotide, ondansetron, and ranitidine. Refer to Dickman A, Schneider J. *The Syringe Driver* (3rd edn), Oxford University Press, 2011, for further information.
- Diamorphine displays concentration-dependent incompatibility with cyclizine. Mixtures are chemically and physically stable in WFI up to concentrations of 20mg/mL over 24 hours. If the diamorphine concentration exceeds 20mg/mL, crystallization may occur unless the concentration of cyclizine is no greater than 10mg/mL. Similarly, if the concentration of cyclizine exceeds 20mg/mL, crystallization may occur unless the concentration of diamorphine is no greater than 15mg/mL.

⟡ Pharmacology

Diamorphine is a synthetic opioid agonist with about one and a half times the potency of morphine when both are given parenterally. Given orally, both diamorphine and morphine are considered equianalgesic. It interacts predominantly with the μ-opioid receptor. Diamorphine is rapidly de-acetylated to an active metabolite, 6-mono-acetylmorphine (6-MAM), which is also rapidly de-acetylated to morphine. Metabolism is then as for morphine.

References

1. LeBon B, Zeppetella G, Higginson IJ. Effectiveness of topical administration of opioids in palliative care: a systematic review. *J Pain Symptom Manage* 2009; **37**(5):913–17.
2. Viola R, Kiteley C, Lloyd NS, *et al.* The management of dyspnea in cancer patients: a systematic review. *Support Care Cancer* 2008; **16**(4):329–37.

Diazepam

Generic (CD4a)
Tablet: 2mg (28); 5mg (28); 10mg (28).
Oral solution: 2mg/5mL (100mL).
Strong oral solution: 5mg/5mL (100mL).
Injection (emulsion): 5mg/mL (10).
Injection (solution): 5mg/mL (10).
Rectal solution: 2.5mg/1.25mL (2; 5); 5mg/2.5mL (2; 5); 10mg/5ml (2; 5).
Suppository: 10mg (6).

Indications

- Anxiety (short-term use only)
- Insomnia (short-term use only)
- Status epilepticus
- Muscle spasm.

Contraindications and precautions

- Is contraindicated for use in patients with:
  - acute pulmonary insufficiency
  - myasthenia gravis
  - severe hepatic insufficiency
  - sleep apnoea syndrome.
- Diazepam should not be used alone in the treatment of depression or anxiety associated with depression due to the risk of precipitation of suicide.
- Use with caution if there is a history of drug or alcohol abuse.
- Diazepam should be used with caution in patients with chronic respiratory disease, renal impairment or moderate hepatic impairment.
- Dose reductions may be necessary in the elderly (see 📖 Dose adjustment, p.158).
- Avoid abrupt withdrawal, even if short duration treatment. Prolonged use of benzodiazepines may result in the development of dependence with subsequent withdrawal symptoms on cessation of use, e.g. agitation, anxiety, confusion, headaches, restlessness, sleep disturbances, sweating and tremor. The risk of dependence increases with dose and duration of treatment. Gradual withdrawal is advised.
- Diazepam may modify reactions and patients should be advised not drive (or operate machinery) if affected. Refer to 📖 Drugs and driving, p.25.

☺ Adverse effects

The frequency is not defined, but reported adverse effects include:

- Anterograde amnesia
- Ataxia
- Confusion
- Depression
- Dizziness
- Drowsiness
- Fatigue
- Hallucinations

- Headache
- Muscle weakness
- Nightmares
- Paradoxical events such as agitation, irritability, and restlessness
- Respiratory depression
- Sexual dysfunction
- Sleep disturbance
- Visual disturbances.

Drug interactions

Pharmacokinetic

- Diazepam is a major substrate of CYP2C19 and CYP3A4. Unexplained effects may be explained by the fact that up to 5% of the white population are CYP2C19 poor metabolizers. Co-administration with drugs that are metabolized by, or affect the activity (induction or inhibition —see 📖 inside back cover) of these pathways may lead to clinically relevant drug interactions and the prescriber should be aware that dosage adjustments may be necessary, particularly of drugs with a narrow therapeutic index.
- *Antacids*—may delay the absorption of diazepam.
- *Carbamazepine*—may reduce the effect of diazepam.
- *Erythromycin*—may increase the effect of diazepam.
- *Fluconazole*—may increase the effect of diazepam.
- *Omeprazole*—may increase the effect of diazepam (inhibits CYP2C19 and CYP3A4).
- *Phenytoin* —may reduce the effect of diazepam.
- *Sodium valproate* —may increase the effect of diazepam.
- Avoid excessive amounts of grapefruit juice as it may increase the bioavailability of diazepam through inhibition of intestinal CYP3A4.

Pharmacodynamic

- *Alcohol*—may precipitate seizures.
- *Antidepressants*—reduced seizure threshold.
- *Antipsychotics*—reduced seizure threshold.
- *Baclofen*—increased risk of sedation.
- *CNS depressants*—additive sedative effect.

⚖ Dose

Anxiety

- Patients may require lower than licensed doses. Initial dose 2mg PO at bedtime, increasing gradually as required to 2mg TDS. The dose can then be increased as necessary to a maximum of 30mg daily in divided doses.
- Although available, other alternatives such as SC midazolam are preferred to the use of rectal diazepam. Typical dose is 10–30mg PR daily (suppository) or 0.5mg/kg, repeated 12 hourly (rectal solution).

Insomnia

- Patients may require lower than licensed doses. Initial dose 2mg PO at bedtime, increasing gradually as necessary to 15mg PO at bedtime.
- Note that patients with insomnia related to anxiety may benefit from a single dose at bedtime (e.g. 10–15mg PO ON).

Status epilepticus

- 0.5mg/kg PR, repeated after 15min if necessary (rectal solution).
- 10mg IV at a rate of 1mL (5mg) per minute, repeated if necessary after 10min (injection).

Muscle spasm
- Patients may require lower than licensed doses. Initial dose 2mg PO at bedtime, increasing gradually as required to 2mg PO TDS. The dose can then be increased as necessary to a maximum of 30mg PO daily in divided doses.

♨ Dose adjustments
Elderly
- Generally adopt half the normal adult dose.

Hepatic/renal impairment
- No specific guidance available. Patients with liver or renal impairment may be particularly susceptible to adverse effects and lower initial doses should be used.

Additional information
- Diazepam has a long duration of action due to several active metabolites. The formation of these is highly variable and treatment must therefore be individualized. Some patients may be able to take diazepam once daily due to the presence of an active metabolite with a long half-life.
- If there are unexpected responses, such as excessive sedation, consider drug interactions, which could be additive.

♦ Pharmacology
The exact mechanism of action is unknown, but it is believed to act via enhancement of GABA-ergic transmission in the CNS. Diazepam undergoes first-pass metabolism via cytochromes CYP2C19 and CYP3A4. Numerous active metabolites are formed, one of which can have a prolonged half-life.

Diclofenac

Standard release
Diclofenac sodium
Voltarol® (POM)
Tablet (e/c): 25mg (84); 50mg (84).
Dispersible tablet (sugar-free): 50mg (21).
Injection: 75mg/3mL (10).
Suppository: 12.5mg (10); 25mg (10); 50mg (10); 100mg (10).

Generic (POM)
Tablet (e/c): 25mg (84); 50mg (84).
Suppository: 100mg (10).

With misoprostol (see ☐ Misoprostol, p.366).
Arthrotec® 50 (POM)
Tablet: diclofenac sodium 50mg, misoprostol 200 micrograms (60).

Arthrotec® 75 (POM)
Tablet: diclofenac sodium 75mg, misoprostol 200 micrograms (60).

Modified release
Diclomax SR® (POM)
Capsule: 75mg (56).

Voltarol® 75mg SR (POM)
Tablet: 75mg (28; 56).

Diclomax Retard® (POM)
Capsule: 100mg (28).

Voltarol® Retard (POM)
Tablet: 100mg (28).

Motifene® 75mg (POM)
Capsule: 75mg (56).

Generic (POM)
Tablet: 100mg (28).

Diclofenac potassium
Voltarol® Rapid (POM)
Tablet: 25mg (30); 50mg (30)

Note: 12.5mg tablets are available for sale in pharmacies for the treatment of headache, dental pain, period pain, rheumatic and muscular pain, backache and the symptoms of cold and flu (including fever). Patients must be aged over 14 years and the maximum daily dose is 75mg. Treatment should not exceed 3 days.

Indications
- Relief of pain and inflammation in several conditions:
  - acute gout
  - arthritic conditions
  - *cancer pain.[1]
  - musculoskeletal disorders
  - pain resulting from trauma

Contraindications and precautions

- Avoid in patients with a history of, or risk factors for ischaemic heart disease. Diclofenac has been shown to have a small increased risk of cardiovascular toxicity comparable to COX-2 inhibitors. This is not shared by ibuprofen (low dose <1200mg/day) or naproxen (1000mg/day). A National Prescribing Centre key therapeutic topic in 2010/2011 was the review of NSAID prescribing and recommendation to start with either ibuprofen or naproxen. Refer to 📖 Selection of a NSAID, p.29.

- Contraindicated for use in patients with:
  - a history of, or active, peptic ulceration
  - hypersensitivity reactions to ibuprofen, aspirin, or other NSAIDs (e.g. asthma, nasal polyps, rhinitis)
  - severe cardiac, hepatic, or renal impairment.
- Discontinue diclofenac at the first sign of skin rash, mucosal lesions, or any other signs of hypersensitivity.
- Use the minimum effective dose for the shortest duration necessary in order to reduce the risk of cardiac and GI events. Treatment should be reviewed after *2 weeks*. In the absence of benefit, other options should be considered.
- Elderly patients are more at risk of developing adverse effects.
- Use with caution in the following circumstances:
  - concurrent use of diuretics, corticosteroids, and NSAIDs (see 📖 Drug interactions, p.161)
  - CHF and/or left ventricular dysfunction
  - established ischaemic heart disease, peripheral arterial disease, and/ or cerebrovascular disease need careful consideration due to the increased risk of thrombotic events
  - hepatic impairment
  - hyperlipidaemia
  - hypertension (particularly uncontrolled)
  - recovery from surgery
  - renal impairment
  - smoking
  - type 1 or 2 diabetes.
- Patients taking long-term therapy need regular monitoring of renal and liver function.
- Abnormal LFTs can occur; discontinue NSAID if this persists.
- Patients with systemic lupus erythematosus (SLE) and mixed connective tissue disorders may be at risk of developing aseptic meningitis.
- Diclofenac may prevent the development of signs and symptoms of inflammation/infection (e.g. fever).
- Consider co-prescription of misoprostol or a PPI if:
  - long-term NSAID therapy
  - concurrent use of drugs that increase the risk of GI toxicity (see 📖 Drug interactions, p.161).
- Refer to 📖 Selection of a NSAID, p.29 for further information.
- Diclofenac may modify reactions and patients should be advised not drive (or operate machinery) if affected. Refer to 📖 Drugs and driving, p.25.

☺ Adverse effects

Common

- Abdominal cramps
- Anorexia
- Diarrhoea
- Dizziness
- Dyspepsia
- Elevated LFTs (discontinue if this persists)
- Flatulence
- Headache
- Nausea
- Rashes
- Vomiting.

Rare

- Gastritis
- GI bleeding
- GI ulcers
- Drowsiness
- Hepatitis
- Jaundice
- Oedema.

Very rare

- Acute renal insufficiency
- Agranulocytosis
- Anaemia (aplastic; haemolytic)
- CHF
- Erythema multiforme
- Hypertension
- Leucopenia
- Stevens–Johnson syndrome
- Thrombocytopenia.

Drug interactions

Pharmacokinetic

- Diclofenac is a metabolized by CYP1A2, CYP2B6, CYP2C8, CYP2C9 (major), CYP2C19, CYP2D6, and CYP3A4. Diclofenac may have a clinically significant inhibitory action on CYP3A4, CYP1A2, and UDP-glucuronyl-transferases. Co-administration with drugs that are metabolized by, or affect the activity (see 📖 inside back cover) of these pathways may lead to clinically relevant drug interactions and the prescriber should be aware that dosage adjustments may be necessary, particularly of drugs with a narrow therapeutic index. Note that co-administration of an enzyme inhibitor is unlikely to be clinically significant due to metabolism via multiple pathways.
- *Antacids*—avoid giving within 1 hour of enteric coated tablets.
- *Methotrexate*—reduced excretion of methotrexate.

Pharmacodynamic

- *Anticoagulants*—increased risk of bleeding.
- *Antihypertensives*—reduced hypotensive effect.
- *Antiplatelet drugs*—increased risk of bleeding.
- *Corticosteroids*—increased risk of GI toxicity.
- *Ciclosporin*—increased risk of nephrotoxicity.
- *Diuretics*—reduced diuretic effect; nephrotoxicity of diclofenac may be increased.
- *SSRIs*—increased risk of GI bleeding.

♪ Dose

Standard release

- Initial dose 50mg PO BD increasing to 50mg PO TDS as necessary.

- The rectal route is generally avoided in palliative care. Nonetheless, it may be preferable to a CSCI. The usual dose is 75–150mg daily in divided doses.
- ⱡAlternatively, 100–150mg via CSCI over 24 hours. Note diclofenac should not be mixed with other drugs and a separate CSCI will be needed.

Modified release
- Dose 100mg OD, or 75mg BD.

⚗ Dose adjustments

Elderly
- The elderly are at an increased risk of adverse effects. Use the lowest effective dose and for the shortest duration possible.

Hepatic/renal impairment
- Diclofenac is contraindicated for use in patients with severe hepatic or renal impairment.
- In patients with mild–moderate liver impairment, no specific dose recommendations are available and the metabolism of diclofenac is stated to be unaffected. However, the lowest dose possible should be used for the shortest duration possible and the patient should be closely monitored. If abnormal LFTs develop and persist or deteriorate further, diclofenac must be discontinued.
- The use of diclofenac may result in deterioration of renal function. The lowest effective dose should be used and renal function monitored.

Additional information

- If *Arthrotec*® is used, ensure a PPI is not co-prescribed.
- Diclofenac via CSCI is incompatible with the majority of drugs likely to be encountered. As such, it should be administered via separate CSCI.

⊕ Pharmacology

Diclofenac is a NSAID with analgesic, anti-inflammatory, and antipyretic properties. The potassium salt of diclofenac is more rapidly absorbed. The mechanism of action of diclofenac, like that of other NSAIDs, is not completely understood but may be related to inhibition of COX-1 and COX-2. Diclofenac is believed to be more selective for COX-2 and indeed has been shown to have cardiovascular profile similar to the COX-2 inhibitors.

Diclofenac is rapidly and completely absorbed after oral administration, although the bioavailability is slightly less with the dispersible tablets. Oral bioavailability is about half that of an equivalent parenteral dose, presumable as a result of the high first-pass metabolism. It is highly protein bound to albumin (about 99%) and extensively metabolized in the liver by a variety of isoenzymes (including CYP1A2, CYP2B6, CYP2C8, CYP2C9 (major), CYP2C19, CYP2D6, and CYP3A4) to inactive (or weakly active) metabolites; glucuronidation of the parent molecule also occurs to a lesser extent. The metabolites are glucuronidated and excreted via the kidney and faeces.

Reference

1. McNicol ED, Strassels S, Goudas L, Lau J, Carr DB. NSAIDS or paracetamol, alone or combined with opioids, for cancer pain. *Cochrane Database of Syst Rev* 2005; **2**: CD005180.

Diethylstilbestrol

Generic (POM)
Tablet: 1mg (28); 5mg (28).

Indications

- Palliation of prostate cancer.
- Palliation of breast cancer in postmenopausal women (uncommon).

Contraindications and precautions

There is a significant increase in risk of DVT with diethylstilbestrol treatment and patients should be reviewed for the need for concurrent antiplatelet/anticoagulant therapy.

- Diethylstilbestrol is contraindicated for use in patients with:
  - cardiovascular or cerebrovascular disorder or a history of thromboembolism
  - hyperlipoproteinaemia
  - moderate to severe hypertension
  - oestrogen-dependent neoplasms
  - porphyria
  - premenopausal carcinoma of the breast
  - severe or active liver disease
  - undiagnosed vaginal bleeding.
- It should be used with caution in patients with:
  - cardiac failure
  - cholelithiasis
  - cholestatic jaundice (or history of)
  - contact lenses
  - depression
  - diabetes (glucose tolerance may be lowered)
  - epilepsy
  - hepatic impairment
  - hypertension
  - migraine
  - renal impairment.
- Thyroid function tests may be difficult to interpret as diethylstilbestrol may increase thyroid hormone binding globulin leading to increased circulating total thyroid hormone.

☺ Adverse effects

The frequency is not defined, but reported adverse effects include:
- Cholelithiasis
- Cholestatic jaundice
- Corneal discomfort (in contact lens wearers)
- Glucose tolerance reduced
- Gynaecomastia
- Hypercalcaemia and bone pain may occur in breast cancer
- Hypertension
- Impotence

- Nausea
- Sodium and water retention
- Thromboembolism
- Weight gain.

Drug interactions

Pharmacokinetic

- Despite extensive hepatic metabolism, there are no recognized pharmacokinetic interactions.

Pharmacodynamic

- *Antihypertensives*—effect may be antagonized by diethylstilbestrol.
- *Diuretics*—effect may be antagonized by diethylstilbestrol.
- *Tamoxifen*—potential antagonism.

Dose

Prostate cancer

- Initial dose 1mg PO OD. Dose can be increased, as determined by a specialist, to 3mg PO OD.
- Higher doses were previously used, but are no longer recommended.

Breast cancer

- Initial dose 10mg PO OD, increased as determined by a specialist to 20mg PO OD.

Dose adjustments

Elderly

- The recommended adult dose is appropriate.

Hepatic/renal impairment

- Diethylstilbestrol should not be used in patients with active liver disease.
- There are no specific dose recommendations for patients with renal impairment. The lowest effective dose should be used.

Additional information

- Ideally, blood pressure should be checked before initiating diethylstilbestrol and should be monitored at regular intervals. Should hypertension develop, treatment should be stopped.

Pharmacology

Diethylstilbestrol is a synthetic oestrogen and it binds to an intracellular receptor protein within the cytoplasm when it is transported to the nucleus of the cell. It then has an action on mRNA and associated protein synthesis. Its action in palliative treatment is not completely understood.

Diethylstilbestrol is readily absorbed from the GI tract. It is slowly metabolized in the liver to 3 metabolites; CYP2A6 may be involved in this process. Further metabolism to glucuronides occurs. Excretion is mainly via the kidneys and gall bladder (enterohepatic circulation may occur).

Dihydrocodeine

Standard release
DF118 Forte® (CD5 POM)
Tablet: 40mg (100).

Generic (CD5 POM)
Tablet: 30mg (28).
Oral solution: 10mg/5mL (150mL).
Injection: 50mg/mL *(CD2 POM)*.

Modified release
DHC Continus® (CD5 POM)
Tablet: 60mg (56); 90mg (56); 120mg (56).

Combination products
Certain products containing <10mg dihydrocodeine and paracetamol are available OTC (CD5 P).

Remedeine® (CD5 POM)
Tablet: dihydrocodeine 20mg/paracetamol 500mg (112).

Remedeine Forte® (CD5 POM)
Tablet: dihydrocodeine 30mg/paracetamol 500mg (112).

Generic (CD5 POM)
Tablet (scored): co-dydramol 10/500 (dihydrocodeine 10mg/paracetamol 500mg) (30).

Indications
• Management of moderate to severe pain.

Contraindications and precautions
• If the dose of an opioid is titrated correctly, it is generally accepted that there are no absolute contraindications to the use of such drugs in palliative care, although there may be circumstances where one opioid is favoured over another (e.g. renal impairment, constipation).
• Dihydrocodeine is contraindicated for use in:
  • acute alcoholism
  • head injury
  • obstructive airways disease
  • paralytic ileus
  • raised intracranial pressure
  • respiratory depression.
• Use with caution in the following instances:
  • asthma (can release histamine)
  • bowel obstruction

- diseases of the biliary tract
- elderly
- hepatic impairment
- pancreatitis
- prostatic hypertrophy
- renal impairment.
- Dihydrocodeine may modify reactions and patients should be advised not drive (or operate machinery) if affected. Refer to 📖 Drugs and driving, p.25.

☺ Adverse effects

The frequency is not defined, but commonly reported adverse effects include:

- Constipation
- Drowsiness
- Headache
- Nausea and/or vomiting
- Pruritus
- Rash.

Less commonly reported adverse effects include:

- Abdominal pain
- Biliary spasm
- Confusion
- Decreased libido
- Dizziness
- Dry mouth
- Flushing
- Hallucinations
- Hypotension
- Paraesthesia
- Paralytic ileus
- Respiratory depression
- Sweating
- Ureteric spasm
- Urinary retention
- Visual disturbances.

Drug interactions

Pharmacokinetic

- Dihydrocodeine is metabolized by CYP2D6 to an active metabolite. Co-administration with drugs that are metabolized by, or affect the activity (induction or inhibition —see 📖 inside back cover) of this pathway may lead to clinically relevant drug interactions and the prescriber should be aware that dosage adjustments may be necessary, particularly of drugs with a narrow therapeutic index.
- Note that unlike codeine, interactions between CYP2D6 inhibitors and dihydrocodeine do not appear to reduce analgesic benefit significantly.

Pharmacodynamic

- *Antihypertensives*—increased risk of hypotension.
- *CNS depressants*—risk of excessive sedation.
- *Haloperidol*—may be an additive hypotensive effect.
- *Ketamine*—there is a potential opioid-sparing effect with ketamine and the dose of dihydrocodeine may need reducing.
- *Levomepromazine*—may be an additive hypotensive effect.

💊 Dose

Oral

Standard release

- 30–60mg PO every 4–6 hours when required. Maximum daily dose 240mg.
- Using *DF118 Forte*®, 40–80mg PO TDS PRN. Maximum daily dose 240mg.

Modified release
- 60–120mg PO every 12 hours.

Parenteral
- 50mg by SC or deep IM injection repeated every 4–6 hours.
- ¥Alternatively, 100–200mg via CSCI over 24 hours. Higher doses have been used.

⚗ Dose adjustments

Elderly
- No specific guidance is available, although lower starting doses may be preferable. Dose requirements should be individually titrated.

Hepatic/renal impairment
- No specific guidance is available, although in patients with hepatic impairment, the plasma concentration is expected to be increased. In view of its hepatic metabolism, caution is advised when giving dihydrocodeine to patients with hepatic impairment. Lower starting doses may be preferable and dose requirements should be individually titrated.
- No specific guidance is available for patients with renal impairment. However, in view of the fact that metabolites are renally excreted, lower starting doses may be preferable and dose requirements should be individually titrated.

Additional information

- Dihydrocodeine and codeine have traditionally been used instead of morphine (or alternative) for the headache associated with brain metastases. There is no evidence to support this use.
- *DHC Continus*® tablets must be swallowed whole and not be broken, crushed or chewed
- Nausea and vomiting are relatively common, limiting side effects to the use of regular dihydrocodeine alone. This can be overcome by using lower doses more frequently (e.g. 30mg PO 4-hourly), or using a modified-release preparation.
- In the absence of a liquid formulation, oral standard-release tablets can be crushed and dispersed in water immediately prior to use.
- Via CSCI, dihydrocodeine has been shown to be compatible with cyclizine, glycopyrronium, haloperidol, levomepromazine, and midazolam

⊙ Pharmacology

- Dihydrocodeine is a potent synthetic opioid analgesic with a low oral bioavailability, presumably due to first-pass metabolism. By mouth, it is of similar potency as codeine; parenterally it is considered to be twice as potent as codeine. Dihydrocodeine is metabolized in the liver by CYP2D6 to dihydromorphine, which adds to its analgesic effect. Unchanged drug, plus metabolites are renally excreted.

Docusate sodium

Dioctyl® (P)
Capsule: 100mg (30; 100).

Docusol® (P)
Oral solution (sugar-free): 12.5mg/5mL (300mL); 50mg/5mL (300mL).

Norgalax Micro-enema® (P)
Enema: 120mg in 10g (1 × 10g).

Indications
- Chronic constipation.

Contraindications and precautions
- Manufacturer advises that docusate should not be administered to patients with abdominal pain, nausea, vomiting, or intestinal obstruction.

☻ Adverse effects
The frequency is not defined, but reported adverse effects include:
- Abdominal cramps
- Diarrhoea
- Nausea
- Skin rash.

Drug interactions
Pharmacokinetic
- *Mineral oils (e.g. liquid paraffin)*—increased risk of toxicity through enhanced absorption.

Pharmacodynamic
- *Anticholinergics*—antagonizes the laxative effect.
- *Cyclizine*—antagonizes the laxative effect.
- *Opioids*—antagonizes the laxative effect.
- *5-HT$_3$ antagonists*—antagonizes the laxative effect.
- *TCAs*—antagonizes the laxative effect.

⚓ Dose
Oral
- Initial dose 100mg PO BD, increased as necessary according to response, to a usual maximum of 200mg PO TDS.[¥]
- Licensed maximum dose is 500mg/day in divided doses.

Rectal
- Usual dose 120mg OD (one enema). It can be repeated on the same or the next day.

⚓ Dose adjustments
Elderly
- No specific recommendations.

Hepatic/renal impairment
• No specific recommendations

Additional information
• Oral preparation can take up to 72 hours to work; enema usually works within 20min.

⟡ **Pharmacology**

Docusate sodium is a surfactant and used as a faecal softening agent. It works by allowing water to penetrate faeces, allowing then to soften. It is believed to have a mild stimulant action, particularly at the higher doses.

Domperidone

Motilium® (POM)
Tablet: 10mg (30; 100).
Orodispersible tablet: 10mg (10).
Suspension: 5mg/5mL (200mL).
Suppository: 30mg (10).

Generic (POM)
Tablet: 10mg (30; 100)
Note: Motilium® tablets and orodispersible tablets may be sold in pharmacies at a maximum daily dose of 40mg (10mg TDS and bedtime), for the relief of:
- Post-prandial symptoms of excessive fullness, nausea, epigastric bloating and belching, occasionally accompanied by epigastric discomfort and heartburn (for a maximum of 2 weeks).
- Nausea and vomiting (of <48 hours' duration).

Indications
- Nausea and vomiting
- Gastro-oesophageal reflux
- Dyspepsia.

Contraindications and precautions
- Contraindicated for use in patients with:
  - bowel obstruction or perforation
  - GI haemorrhage
  - prolactinoma.
- Certain manufacturers contraindicate the use of domperidone in patients with hepatic and/or renal impairment (see 📖 Dose adjustments, p.171).
- Motilium® orodispersible tablets contain aspartame—avoid in phenylketonuria.
- Avoid concurrent use of CYP3A4 inhibitors (see 📖 Drug interactions, p.170).

☻ Adverse effects
Common
- Dry mouth
- Headache.

Rare
- Hyperprolactinaemia (with associated symptoms e.g. galactorrhoea, gynaecomastia and amenorrhoea)
- Intestinal cramps.

Very rare
- Extrapyramidal effects
- Urticaria.

Drug interactions
Pharmacokinetic
- Domperidone is a substrate of CYP3A4, CYP1A2 and CYP2E1. The main metabolic pathway involves CYP3A4. Co-administration with drugs that are metabolized by, or affect the activity (induction or

inhibition —see 📖 inside back cover) of these pathways may lead to clinically relevant drug interactions and the prescriber should be aware that dosage adjustments may be necessary, particularly of drugs with a narrow therapeutic index.

- Co-administration with CYP3A4 inhibitors (see 📖 inside back cover) can increase peak plasma concentrations of domperidone and can also lead to increases in the QT interval. The clinical significance is unknown, but the prescriber should be aware of the potential for interactions and need to avoid concurrent use (see 📖 Contraindications and precautions, p.170).

Pharmacodynamic
- *Anticholinergics*—may antagonize the prokinetic effect.
- *Cyclizine*—may antagonize the prokinetic effect.
- *Opioids*—antagonize the prokinetic effect.
- *5-HT$_3$ antagonists*—antagonize the prokinetic effect.
- *TCAs*—may antagonize the prokinetic effect.

⚕ Dose
For all indications:
- By mouth, 10–20mg TDS–QDS. Maximum daily dose of 80mg.
- By rectum, 60mg BD.

⚕ Dose adjustments
Elderly
- No specific guidance is available, but the dose should be carefully adjusted to individual requirements.

Hepatic/renal impairment
- The manufacturer recommends domperidone is avoided in patients with liver impairment due to extensive metabolism.
- In patients with severe renal impairment (i.e. SeCr >600micromol/L), the dosing frequency should be reduced to once or twice daily with repeated use. Dose adjustments are unnecessary for single administration.

Additional information
- Domperidone is likely to be better tolerated than metoclopramide (i.e. less frequent and less severe adverse effects).
- It is a suitable first-line choice for the management of nausea/vomiting associated with Parkinson's disease therapy.
- If necessary, the tablets can be crushed before administration if the suspension is unavailable.

⟐ Pharmacology
Domperidone is a peripheral D2-receptor antagonist and does not usually cross the blood–brain barrier. Domperidone undergoes extensive first-pass metabolism (CYP3A4) and metabolites are inactive. Its anti-emetic effect is due to 2 distinct effects: a prokinetic effect and dopamine blockade in the chemoreceptor trigger zone (CTZ), which lies outside the blood–brain barrier.

Donepezil

Aricept® (POM)
Tablet: 5mg (28); 10mg (28).

Aricept Evess® (POM)
Orodispersible tablet: 5mg (28); 10mg (28).

Generic (POM)
Tablet: 5mg; 10mg
Orodispersible tablet: 5mg; 10mg

Indications
- Symptomatic treatment of mild to moderately severe Alzheimer's dementia.
- ¥Cognitive impairment of vascular disease of the brain.[1]
- ¥Parkinson's disease dementia (see 🕮 Additional information, p.173).[2]

Contraindications and precautions
- Donepezil should be used with caution in the following:
  - asthma
  - COPD
  - severe hepatic impairment
  - supraventricular conduction abnormalities (may cause bradycardia)
  - susceptibility to peptic ulcers (increase in gastric acid secretion).
- All patients receiving donepezil should have their ability to continue driving or operating complex machines evaluated. Refer to 🕮 Drugs and driving, p.25.

😐 Adverse effects
Very common
- Diarrhoea
- Headache
- Nausea.

Common
- Agitation
- Dizziness
- Fatigue
- Hallucinations
- Insomnia
- Muscle cramps
- Sweating
- Urinary incontinence.

Uncommon
- Bradycardia
- GI haemorrhage
- Peptic ulcer.

Rare
- Extrapyramidal reactions.

Drug interactions

Pharmacokinetic

- Is metabolized by CYP3A4 and CYP2D6. Co-administration with drugs that are metabolized by, or affect the activity (induction or inhibition —see 🕮 inside back cover) of these pathways may lead to clinically relevant drug interactions and the prescriber should be aware that dosage adjustments may be necessary, particularly of drugs with a narrow therapeutic index.
- Avoid excessive amounts of grapefruit juice as it may increase the bioavailability of donepezil through inhibition of intestinal CYP3A4.

Pharmacodynamic

- *Anticholinergics*—may antagonize the effects.

🛫 Dose

- Initial dose 5mg PO ON, increased if necessary after 1 month to max. 10mg PO ON.

🛫 Dose adjustments

Elderly

- Usual adult doses can be used.

Hepatic/renal impairment

- For patients with mild–moderate hepatic impairment, dose escalation should be performed according to individual tolerability. There is no recommendation for use in severe hepatic disease.
- Usual adult doses can be used in renal impairment.

Additional information

- *Rivastigmine* is licensed for the treatment of Parkinson's disease dementia.
- Tablet can be dispersed in water immediately prior to administration if the orodispersible product is unavailable.

⟳ Pharmacology

Donepezil is a centrally acting specific and reversible inhibitor of acetylcholinesterase. Its therapeutic effect is through enhancement of cholinergic function. It is well absorbed with a relative oral bioavailability of 100%. It is metabolized by CYP3A4 and CYP2D6, as well as undergoing glucuronidation. The main metabolite has similar activity as donepezil. ~17% of the dose is excreted unchanged in the urine.

References

1. Malouf R, Birks J. Donepezil for vascular cognitive impairment. *Cochrane Database Syst Rev* 2004; **1**: CD004395.
2. van Laar T, De Deyn PP, Aarsland D, *et al.* Effects of cholinesterase inhibitors in Parkinson's disease dementia: a review of clinical data. *CNS Neurosci Ther* 2011; **17**(5):428–41.

Doxycycline

Vibramycin-D® (POM)
Dispersible tablet (scored): 100mg (8).

Generic (POM)
Capsule: 50mg (28); 100mg (8).

Indications
- Refer to local guidelines.
- Broad-spectrum antibiotic indicated for the treatment of infections caused by susceptible organisms.

Contraindications and precautions
- Use with caution in patients with hepatic impairment (see 📖 Dose adjustments, p.175).
- May cause photosensitive skin reactions—warn the patient to avoid direct exposure to sunlight or sunlamps and to discontinue at the first sign of skin discomfort.
- Care should be taken in patients with myasthenia gravis due to a potential for weak neuromuscular blockade.
- Capsules should be taken with plenty of fluid while the patient remains sitting upright or standing (risk of oesophagitis).

☻ Adverse effects
The frequency is not defined, but reported adverse effects of tetracyclines include:

- Abdominal pain
- Anorexia
- Anxiety
- Diarrhoea
- Dizziness
- Dry mouth
- Dyspepsia
- Flushing
- Headache
- Hepatitis
- Nausea
- Oesophagitis
- Photosensitivity (avoid direct exposure to sunlight or artificial ultraviolet light)
- Rash
- Renal impairment
- Steven–Johnson syndrome
- Teeth discoloration and enamel hypoplasia (with long-term use)
- Thrombocytopenia
- Tinnitus
- Toxic epidermal necrolysis
- Visual disturbances
- Vomiting.

Drug interactions
Pharmacokinetic
- *Antacids*—absorption of doxycycline is impaired by the concomitant administration of preparations containing aluminium, calcium, magnesium or other preparations containing these, zinc, iron salts, or bismuth; separate administration by at least 2 hours.

Pharmacodynamic
- *NSAIDs*—increased risk of nephrotoxicity.
- *Penicillins*—bacteriostatic effect of doxycycline may reduce bactericidal action of penicillins.
- *Warfarin*—plasma prothrombin activity may be depressed needing lower warfarin doses.

↲ Dose
- Dose depends on indication/infection. Refer to local guidelines.
- Typical dose 200mg on day 1, followed by 100mg PO OD for at least 24–48 hours after symptoms resolve (usually 7–10 days).

↲ Dose adjustments
Elderly
- No dose adjustments are necessary.

Hepatic/renal impairment
- No specific information is available for patients with hepatic impairment. The manufacturer advises that doxycycline should be administered with caution to such patients.
- No dose adjustments are necessary for patients with renal impairment.

Additional information
- If gastric irritation occurs, doxycycline can be given with food or milk without affecting absorption.

↬ Pharmacology
Doxycycline is a bacteriostatic antibiotic and is believed to exert its effect by the inhibition of bacterial protein synthesis. It is active against a wide range of Gram-positive and Gram-negative bacteria. After administration, doxycycline is almost completely absorbed with an oral bioavailability over 90%. It is primarily excreted unchanged in urine and bile, with no significant metabolism occurring.

Duloxetine

Cymbalta® (POM)
Capsule: 30mg (28); 60mg (28).

Yentreve® (POM)
(Licensed for stress incontinence in women and not discussed further.)

Indications
- Major depressive episodes.
- Generalized anxiety disorder.
- Diabetic peripheral neuropathic pain in adults.

Contraindications and precautions
- Duloxetine is contraindicated in the following conditions:
  - uncontrolled hypertension
  - moderate–severe hepatic impairment
  - severe renal impairment (CrCl <30mL/min).
- Co-administration with potent CYP1A2 inhibitors (see 🕮 Drug interactions, p.178) must be avoided.
- Do not use with an irreversible MAOI (including *rasagiline* and *selegiline*), or within 14 days of stopping one; at least 5 days should be allowed after stopping duloxetine before starting an irreversible MAOI.
- The combination with selective reversible MAOIs (e.g. *linezolid*, *moclobemide*) is not recommended and the manufacturer offers no specific advice.
- There is a risk of haemorrhage with duloxetine. Use with caution in patients using anticoagulants and drugs with an antiplatelet action e.g. aspirin, NSAIDs (see 🕮 Drug interactions, p.178).
- Use with caution in:
  - elderly (greater risk of hyponatraemia)
  - epilepsy (lowers seizure threshold)
  - glaucoma (may cause mydriasis)
  - thrombocytopenia (risk of haemorrhage).
- Hyponatraemia should be considered in all patients who develop drowsiness, confusion, or convulsions while taking an antidepressant. Hyponatraemia has been associated with all types of antidepressants, although it is reportedly more common with SSRIs.
- Depression is associated with an increased risk of suicidal thoughts, self-harm, and suicide which persists until remission. Note that that the risk of suicide may increase during initial treatment.
- Abrupt discontinuation should be avoided due to the risk of withdrawal reactions, e.g. agitation, anxiety, diarrhoea, dizziness, drowsiness, fatigue, headache, hyperhidrosis, nausea and/or vomiting, sensory disturbances (including paraesthesia), and sleep disturbances. When stopping treatment, the dose should be reduced gradually over at least 1–2 weeks. See 🕮 Discontinuing and/or switching antidepressants, p.45 for information about switching or stopping antidepressants.
- May precipitate psychomotor restlessness, which usually appears during early treatment. The use of duloxetine should be reviewed.

- Duloxetine may modify reactions and patients should be advised not drive (or operate machinery) if affected. Refer to 📖 Drugs and driving, p.25.

😕 Adverse effects

Very common

- Drowsiness
- Dry mouth
- Headache
- Nausea.

Common

- Abdominal pain
- Agitation
- Anxiety
- Appetite reduced
- Blurred vision
- Constipation
- Diarrhoea
- Dizziness
- Dyspepsia
- Dysuria
- Fatigue
- Flatulence
- Flushing
- Insomnia
- Lethargy
- Musculoskeletal pain
- Palpitations
- Paraesthesia
- Rash (acneiform reported—treat as acne, or withdraw drug)
- Sexual dysfunction (e.g. reduced libido)
- Sleep disturbances (including abnormal dreams)
- Sweats (less commonly night sweats, or cold sweats)
- Tinnitus
- Tremor
- Vomiting
- Weight loss
- Yawning.

Uncommon

- Abnormal bleeding (bruising, epistaxis)
- Altered taste
- Atrial fibrillation
- Bruxism
- Ear pain
- Gastritis
- GI haemorrhage
- Hepatitis
- Hyperglycaemia (especially in diabetic patients)
- Hypertension
- Hypotension (postural hypotension reported during initiation)
- Laryngitis
- Myoclonus
- Restless legs syndrome
- Suicidal ideation
- Tachycardia
- Urinary symptoms (e.g. hesitation, retention)
- Vertigo
- Visual disturbances.

Rare

- Aggression
- Anaphylaxis
- Convulsions
- Extrapyramidal reactions
- Glaucoma
- Hallucinations
- Hepatic impairment (including jaundice)
- Hypertensive crisis
- Psychomotor restlessness
- Serotonin syndrome (see 📖 Drug interactions, p.178)
- SIADH/hyponatraemia
- Stevens–Johnson syndrome
- Stomatitis
- Suicidal behaviour.

Drug interactions

Pharmacokinetic

- Duloxetine is a moderate inhibitor of CYP2D6; it is a substrate of CYP1A2 and CYP2D6. Co-administration with drugs that are metabolized by, or affect the activity (induction or inhibition—see 📖 inside back cover) of these pathways may lead to clinically relevant drug interactions and the prescriber should be aware that dosage adjustments may be necessary, particularly of drugs with a narrow therapeutic index.
- Smokers may have almost 50% lower plasma concentrations of duloxetine (CYP1A2 induction) compared with non-smokers. Dosage adjustments may be necessary upon smoking cessation—see Box 1.9, p.16. Co-administration of CYP1A2 inducers (see 📖 inside back cover) may lead to reduced duloxetine concentrations, although the clinical significance is unknown. The prescriber should be aware of the potential for interactions and that dosage adjustments may be necessary.
- Co-administration of duloxetine with potent inhibitors of CYP1A2 (e.g. *amiodarone, ciprofloxacin, fluvoxamine*—see 📖 inside back cover) is likely to result in higher concentrations of duloxetine (see 📖 Contraindications and precautions, p.176).

Pharmacodynamic

- Risk of serotonin syndrome (see Box 1.10, p.18) with:
  - MAOIs
  - Rasagiline
  - Selegiline
  - Serotonergic drugs—e.g. methadone, mirtazapine, TCAs, tramadol, and trazodone.
- *Anticoagulants*—potential increased risk of bleeding.
- *CNS depressants*—additive sedative effect.
- *Cyproheptadine*—may inhibit the effects of duloxetine.
- *Diuretics*—increased risk of hyponatraemia.
- *NSAIDs*—increased risk of bleeding (potentially worse with aspirin and naproxen).

🔏 Dose

Major depressive episodes

- Initial and maintenance dose 60mg PO OD with or without food. There is no evidence to suggest that 120mg PO daily offers any therapeutic advantage.

Generalized anxiety disorder

- Initial dose 30mg PO OD with or without food. Doses can be increased as necessary to a usual maintenance dose of 60mg PO OD with or without food. Further dose increases up to 90mg or 120mg may be considered, based upon clinical response.

Diabetic peripheral neuropathic pain

- Initial dose 60mg PO OD with or without food. Doses can be increased as necessary to 60mg PO BD.

♣ Dose adjustments

Elderly
- Dosage reductions not necessary.

Hepatic/renal impairment
- Duloxetine is not recommended for use in patients with moderate–severe hepatic impairment.
- No dosage adjustment is necessary for patients with mild or moderate renal impairment (CrCl ≥30mL/min). Duloxetine is contraindicated in patients with severe renal impairment (CrCl <30mL/min).

Additional information

- Antidepressant therapeutic response is usually seen after 2–4 weeks of treatment.
- In the treatment of anxiety, duloxetine should be continued for several months after therapeutic response in order to prevent relapse.
- For neuropathic pain, response to treatment should be evaluated after 2 months. If the patient has not responded after this time, benefit is unlikely and duloxetine should be gradually withdrawn. Patients who respond should be re-assessed regularly, at least every 3 months.

♦ Pharmacology

Although the exact mechanisms of the antidepressant and analgesic actions of duloxetine are unknown, they are believed to be related to its potentiation of serotonergic and noradrenergic activity in the CNS. Duloxetine is a combined serotonin and noradrenaline reuptake inhibitor, with a weak inhibition of dopamine reuptake.

Duloxetine is extensively metabolized by the cytochrome P450 isoenzymes CYP1A2 and CYP2D6; 2 major, but inactive, metabolites are formed which are mainly excreted renally.

Enoxaparin

Clexane® (POM)
Injection (single-dose syringe for SC use): 20mg (0.2mL, 2000 units); 40mg (0.4mL, 4000 units); 60mg (0.6mL, 6000 units); 80mg (0.8mL, 8000 units); 100mg (1mL, 10,000 units).

Clexane® Forte (POM)
Injection (single-dose syringe for SC use): 120mg (0.8mL, 12,000 units); 150mg (1mL, 15,000 units).

Clexane® Multidose (POM)
Injection (multi-dose vial): 300mg (3mL, 30,000 units).

Indications
- Treatment and prophylaxis of DVT and PE.
- Other indications apply but are not normally relevant in palliative care.

Contraindications and precautions
- Enoxaparin is contraindicated for use in patients with:
  - acute bacterial endocarditis
  - recent haemorrhagic stroke
  - thrombocytopenia
  - active gastric or duodenal ulceration
  - spinal anaesthesia.
- Use with caution in patients with an increased risk of bleeding complications:
  - brain tumours (increased risk of intracranial bleeding)
  - concurrent use of anticoagulant/antiplatelet agents/NSAIDs (see 🕮 Drug interactions, p.181)
  - haemorrhagic stroke
  - retinopathy (hypertensive or diabetic)
  - surgery
  - severe hepatic impairment
  - severe renal impairment
  - trauma
  - thrombocytopenia
  - uncontrolled hypertension.
- A baseline platelet count should be taken prior to initiating treatment and monitored closely during the first three weeks (e.g. every 2–4 days) and regularly thereafter.
- Not for IM use.
- Advice should be sought from anaesthetic colleagues if considering an epidural intervention in a patient receiving enoxaparin due to the risk of spinal haematoma.
- LMWH can inhibit aldosterone secretion, which can cause hyperkalaemia. Patients with pre-existing renal impairment are more at risk. Potassium should be measured in patients at risk prior to starting a LMWH and monitored regularly thereafter, especially if treatment is prolonged beyond 7 days.
- *Prophylactic doses of enoxaparin are not sufficient to prevent valve thrombosis in patients with prosthetic heart valves.*

☺ Adverse effects

The frequency is not defined, but reported adverse effects include:

- Bleeding (at any site)
- Haematoma at injection site
- Hyperkalaemia
- Hypoaldosteronism
- Intracranial bleeds
- Osteoporosis with long-term treatment
- Prosthetic cardiac valve thrombosis (see 📖 Contraindications and precautions, p.180)
- Skin necrosis
- Spinal or epidural haematoma
- Transient changes to liver transaminase levels—clinical significance unknown
- Thrombocytopenia.

Drug interactions

Pharmacokinetic

- None recognized.

Pharmacodynamic

- Drugs with anticoagulant or anti-platelet effect may enhance the effect of enoxaparin:
  - aspirin
  - clopidogrel
  - dipyridamole
  - NSAIDs.
- *ACEIs*—increased risk of hyperkalaemia.
- *Amiloride*—increased risk of hyperkalaemia.
- *Antihistamines*—possibly reduce anticoagulant effect.
- *Ascorbic acid*—possibly reduces anticoagulant effect.
- *Corticosteroids*—increased risk of GI bleeding.
- *Spironolactone*—increased risk of hyperkalaemia.
- *SSRIs*—increased risk of bleeding.

⚕ Dose

Treatment of DVT and PE

- Usual dose 1.5mg/kg (or 150 units/kg) daily, administered by subcutaneous injection.
- Patients usually start oral anticoagulation at the same time and continue both until the INR is within the target range. This generally takes 5 days. However, cancer patients unsuitable for oral anticoagulation may require long-term treatment with a LMWH. Treatment is occasionally continued indefinitely.

Prophylaxis of DVT and PE

- For medical prophylaxis (including immobile cancer patients), 40mg (4000 units) SC OD. The duration of treatment depends upon the risk factors identified (e.g. immobile in-patients may be considered for treatment from admission until discharge). Graduated compression stockings should be considered if LMWH is contraindicated.

- For surgical prophylaxis:
  - moderate risk—20mg (2000 units) before procedure and each day for 7–10 days or longer (until mobilized)
  - high risk—40mg (4000 units) before procedure and each day for 7–10 days or longer (until mobilized).

₰ Dose adjustments
Elderly
- Usual adult doses recommended.

Hepatic/renal impairment
- No specific guidance is available for patients with hepatic impairment. The manufacturer advices caution due to an increased risk of bleeding.
- No dosage adjustments are recommended in patients with moderate renal impairment (CrCl 30–50mL/min) or mild renal impairment (CrCl 50–80mL/min), although careful monitoring is recommended. Dosage adjustments are recommended in patients with severe renal impairment (CrCl <30mL/min). In severe renal impairment where 1.5mg/kg is indicated as a treatment dose, this should be reduced to 1mg/kg and in prophylaxis, 40mg once daily should be reduced to 20mg once daily.

Additional information
- The risk of heparin-induced thrombocytopenia is low with LMWH but may occur after 5–10 days. If there is a 50% reduction of the platelet count, LMWH should be stopped.

♦ Pharmacology
Enoxaparin is a LMWH produced from porcine-derived sodium heparin. It acts mainly through its potentiation of the inhibition of Factor Xa and thrombin by antithrombin. Enoxaparin is eliminated primarily via the kidneys, hence the need for dose adjustments in renal impairment. Local protocols may help to indicate when treatment of palliative care patients with enoxaparin is appropriate.

Erlotinib

Tarceva® (POM)
Tablet: 25mg (30); 100mg (30); 150mg (30).

Indications
- Non-small cell lung cancer.
- Pancreatic cancer (in combination with gemcitabine).

Contraindications and precautions
- Avoid erlotinib in patients with severe hepatic and renal impairment (CrCl <15mL/min).
- Avoid concurrent use of the following drugs (see 📖 Drug interactions, p.184):
  - PPIs and H_2 antagonists
  - CYP3A4 inducers/inhibitors.
- There is an increased risk of GI perforation associated with erlotinib. Use with caution in patients with a history of peptic ulcer disease, or concurrent use of NSAIDs or corticosteroids.
- Patients with Gilbert's syndrome (a genetic glucuronidation disorder) may develop increased unconjugated bilirubin plasma concentrations because erlotinib is a potent inhibitor of UGT1A1 (a UDP glucurono-syltransferase isoenzyme).
- Use cautiously in patients with pre-existing liver disease or concomitant hepatotoxic drugs (periodic LFTs recommended).
- Smokers should be encouraged to discontinue smoking since the metabolism of erlotinib is increased (CYP1A2 induction) and plasma concentrations will be reduced.
- If patients develop acute onset of new and/or progressive unexplained pulmonary symptoms such as dyspnoea, cough, and fever, treatment should be interrupted pending diagnostic evaluation.
- Should patients develop symptoms of keratitis, an urgent referral to an ophthalmologist should be arranged.

☺ Adverse effects
Very common
- Abdominal pain
- Abnormal LFTs
- Alopecia
- Anorexia
- Conjunctivitis
- Cough
- Depression
- Diarrhoea
- Dry skin
- Dyspepsia
- Dyspnoea
- Fatigue
- Flatulence
- Headache
- Infection
- Nausea
- Peripheral neuropathy
- Rash
- Stomatitis
- Vomiting.

Common
- Epistaxis
- GI bleeding (often associated with NSAID or warfarin co-administration)
- Keratitis
- Raised LFTs.

Moderate or severe diarrhoea should be treated with loperamide and a dose reduction in steps of 50mg should be considered. Erlotinib treatment should be interrupted if severe or persistent diarrhoea, nausea, anorexia, or vomiting associated with dehydration develops.

Patients who develop a rash should use an emollient regularly. Consider the use of topical hydrocortisone 1% if the rash persists. Patients can develop a pustular rash, but topical antibiotic or acne formulations are not recommended, unless on the advice of a microbiologist. The rash may worsen on exposure to direct sunlight. Patients should use sunscreen or protective clothing in sunny weather. Patients who develop a rash may have a longer overall survival compared to patients who do not develop a rash. Patients who do not develop a rash after 4–8 weeks of treatment should be reviewed.

Drug interactions

Pharmacokinetic
- Erlotinib is metabolized mainly by CYP3A4, although CYP1A2 is also involved. Erlotinib is a moderate inhibitor of CYP3A4 and CYP2C8; it is also a potent inhibitor of UGT1A1 and a substrate of P-gp, although the clinical significance of is unknown.
- *Antacids*—take at least 4 hours before or 2 hours after erlotinib.
- *Ciprofloxacin*—plasma concentration of erlotinib may increase (dose may need reducing if adverse effects develop).
- *H_2 antagonists*—take erlotinib at least 2 hours before or 10 hours after H_2 antagonist.
- *PPIs*—avoid combination as bioavailability of erlotinib can be significantly reduced.
- Concomitant administration of CYP3A4 and CYP2C8 substrates is unlikely to cause significant interactions. However, concomitant administration of other inhibitors will be additive in effect and may cause problems with drugs that have a narrow therapeutic index.
- The clinical significance of co-administration with CYP3A4 inducers or inhibitors (see 🕮 inside back cover) is unknown. The prescriber should be aware of the potential for interactions and that dose adjustments may be necessary.
- Avoid grapefruit juice as it may increase the bioavailability of erlotinib through inhibition of intestinal CYP3A4.

Pharmacodynamic
- None known

⚡ Dose

Non-small cell lung cancer
- 150mg PO OD taken at least 1 hour before, or 2 hours after the ingestion of food.

Pancreatic cancer
- 100mg PO OD taken at least 1 hour before, or 2 hours after the ingestion of food.

Dose adjustments
Elderly
- No dose adjustments necessary.

Liver/renal impairment
- No specific guidance is available. Use with caution in patients with mild–moderate hepatic impairment; avoid in patients with severe hepatic impairment.
- No dose adjustments are necessary for patients with mild–moderate renal impairment; avoid in patients with severe renal impairment (CrCl <15mL/min).

Pharmacology
Erlotinib is a human epidermal growth factor receptor type 1/epidermal growth factor receptor (HER1/EGFR) tyrosine kinase inhibitor. It inhibits the intracellular phosphorylation of tyrosine kinase associated with EGFR which causes cell stasis and/or death. Erlotinib is metabolized mainly by CYP3A4, and to a lesser extent CYP1A2, to several active metabolites and it is predominantly excreted in the faeces.

Erythromycin

Erymax® (POM)
Capsule: 250mg (28; 112).

Erythrocin® (POM)
Tablet: 250mg (28); 500mg (28).

Erythroped® (POM)
Oral suspension (as powder for reconstitution—sugar-free): 125mg/5mL (140mL); 250mg/5mL (140mL); 500mg/5mL (140mL).

Erythroped A® (POM)
Tablet: 500mg (28).

Generic (POM)
Tablet: 250mg (28); 500mg (28).
Capsule: 250mg (28).
Oral suspension (as powder for reconstitution): 125mg/5mL (100mL); 250mg/5mL (100mL); 500mg/5mL (100mL).
Note: sugar-free formulations are available.
Injection: 1g.

Indications

- Refer to local guidelines.
- Broad-spectrum antibiotic indicated for the treatment of commonly occurring bacterial infections.
- ¥Pro-kinetic agent.

Contraindications and precautions

- Due to the risk of QT prolongation and cardiac arrhythmias, concurrent use of the following drugs is contraindicated:
  - amisulpride
  - astemizole
  - ergotamine
  - mizolastine
  - pimozide
  - sertindole
  - simvastatin
  - terfenadine
  - tolterodine.
- Erythromycin should be avoided in patients with acute porphyria.
- Electrolyte disturbances must be corrected (e.g. hypokalaemia) due to the risk of QT prolongation.
- It should be used with caution in patients with hepatic and/or renal impairment (see 📖 Dose adjustments, p.188).
- Erythromycin is an inhibitor of CYP3A4 and has the potential to interact with many drugs (see 📖 Drug interactions, p.187)
- Avoid grapefruit juice as it may increase the bioavailability of erythromycin through inhibition of intestinal CYP3A4.

☺ Adverse effects

The frequency is not defined, but reported adverse effects include:

- Abdominal discomfort
- Abnormal LFTs
- Arrhythmias
- Cholestatic jaundice
- Confusion
- Diarrhoea (antibiotic-associated colitis reported)
- Nausea
- Pancreatitis
- Reversible hearing loss (reported after large doses by IV infusion)
- Urticaria
- Vomiting.

Drug interactions

Pharmacokinetic

- Erythromycin is a substrate of CYP3A4; it is a strong inhibitor of CYP3A4. Co-administration with drugs that are metabolized by, or affect the activity (induction or inhibition—see 📖 inside back cover) of this pathway may lead to clinically relevant drug interactions and the prescriber should be aware that dosage adjustments may be necessary, particularly of drugs with a narrow therapeutic index.
- Several interactions are listed here, but refer to the table on 📖 inside back cover for a list of drugs that may potentially be affected.
- *Alfentanil*—increased risk of alfentanil toxicity; dose reduction may be necessary.
- *Carbamazepine*—risk of carbamazepine toxicity (avoid combination or monitor closely).
- *Fentanyl*—increased risk of fentanyl toxicity; dose reduction may be necessary.
- *Midazolam*—increased risk of midazolam toxicity—use lower initial doses; dose adjustments may be necessary if erythromycin is added or discontinued.
- *Theophylline*—risk of theophylline toxicity; dose reduction may be necessary.
- *Warfarin*—risk of raised INR.
- *Zopiclone*—increased plasma concentration and effects of zopiclone.

Pharmacodynamic

- Erythromycin has been associated with prolongation of the QT interval. There is a potential risk that co-administration with other drugs that also prolong the QT interval (e.g. *amiodarone, amitriptyline, haloperidol, quinine*) may result in ventricular arrhythmias.

⚗ Dose

Antimicrobial

- Standard doses are described here. Refer to local guidelines for specific advice.
- Usual dose 250–500mg PO QDS (6-hourly), or 0.5–1g BD (12-hourly).
- Maximum oral dose is 4g daily in divided doses.

- By continuous IV infusion, 50mg/kg daily, or by intermittent infusion 6-hourly.

¥ *Prokinetic effect*
- Initial dose 250mg PO or IV infusion BD. The dose can be increased if necessary to achieve the desired response.

٫ؤ Dose adjustments

Elderly
- Usual adult doses can be used.

Hepatic/renal impairment
- No specific guidance is available for patients with hepatic impairment, although the manufacturer advises caution since erythromycin has been associated with increased liver enzymes and/or cholestatic hepatitis.
- No specific guidance is available for patients with renal impairment. In severe impairment, it is suggested that a dose reduction of up to 50% should be made.

Additional information

- Once reconstituted, the *oral solution* must be discarded after 7 days.
- To reconstitute the *injection*, add 20mL *WFI* to each 1g vial to give a solution of 50mg/mL. This solution must be further diluted prior to administration as follows:
  - dilute 20mL of the reconstituted erythromycin (50mg/mL) with at least 200mL NaCl 0.9% and administer over 20–60min
  - for the prokinetic effect, dilute 5mL of the reconstituted erythromycin (250mg) to at least 50mL with NaCl 0.9% and infuse over 20min.

⊙ Pharmacology

Erythromycin is a broad-spectrum bacteriostatic macrolide antibiotic. It acts by penetrating the bacterial cell membrane and reversibly binding to ribosomes during cell division resulting in suppression of protein synthesis. It diffuses readily into most body fluids. Erythromycin is extensively metabolized by CYP3A4, with only 5% being excreted in the urine unchanged.

Esomeprazole

Nexium® (POM)
Tablet: 20mg (28); 40mg (28).
IV injection/infusion: 40mg.

Indications

- Gastro-oesophageal reflux disease.
- Treatment and prophylaxis of NSAID-associated peptic ulcer disease.

Contraindications and precautions

- Do not administer with atazanavir or erlotinib.
- Treatment with esomeprazole may lead to a slightly increased risk of developing GI infections (e.g. *Clostridium difficile*). Therefore, avoid unnecessary use or high doses.
- Rebound acid hypersecretion may occur on discontinuation of the patient has received >8 weeks' treatment.
- PPIs are associated with a range of electrolyte disturbances, such as hyponatraemia and hypomagnesaemia (and associated hypocalcaemia and hypokalaemia). Suspect the PPI should unexplainable symptoms present (e.g. confusion, delirium, generalized weakness, nausea). The effect on sodium metabolism is unclear, possibly involving ADH. PPIs may reduce active magnesium absorption in the small intestine by affecting function of a transient receptor protein channel.

☺ Adverse effects

Common

- Abdominal pain
- Constipation
- Diarrhoea
- Flatulence
- Headache
- Nausea/vomiting.

Uncommon

- Dermatitis
- Dizziness
- Drowsiness
- Dry mouth
- Paraesthesia
- Peripheral oedema
- Pruritus
- Raised liver enzymes
- Rash
- Urticaria
- Vertigo.

Rare

- Agitation
- Alopecia
- Arthralgia
- Bronchospasm
- Confusion
- Depression
- Hepatitis with or without jaundice
- Hyponatraemia
- Leucopenia
- Photosensitivity
- Taste disturbance
- Thrombocytopenia.

Drug interactions

Pharmacokinetic

- Esomeprazole is metabolized by CYP2C19 (major) and CYP3A4 (minor); it may inhibit CYP2C19. Co-administration with drugs that are metabolized by, or affect the activity (induction or inhibition—see 📖 inside back cover) of this pathway may lead to clinically relevant drug interactions and the prescriber should be aware that dosage adjustments may be necessary, particularly of drugs with a narrow therapeutic index.
- Drugs with pH dependent absorption can be affected:
    - *atazanavir*—avoid combination due to substantially reduced absorption
    - *digoxin*—increased plasma concentrations possible
    - *erlotinib*—avoid combination as bioavailability of erlotinib can be significantly reduced
    - *ketoconazole/Itraconazole*—risk of sub-therapeutic plasma concentrations
    - *metronidazole suspension*—ranitidine may reduce/prevent the absorption of metronidazole.
- *Azole antifungals*—fluconazole may cause increased esomeprazole concentrations (CYP2C19 inhibition).
- *Citalopram*—esomeprazole can increase the plasma concentration of citalopram through inhibition of CYP2C19.
- *Clarithromycin*—inhibition of CYP3A4 metabolism can lead to increased esomeprazole concentrations.
- *Clopidogrel*—antiplatelet action may be reduced (avoid combination).
- *Diazepam*—plasma concentrations of diazepam can be increased through inhibition of CYP2C19.
- The clinical significance of co-administration with CYP2C19 inducers or inhibitors (📖 inside back cover) is unknown. The prescriber should be aware of the potential for interactions and that dosage adjustments may be necessary.
- The clinical significance of co-administration with CYP3A4 inducers or inhibitors (📖 inside back cover) is unknown. The prescriber should be aware of the potential for interactions and that dosage adjustments may be necessary.
- The clinical significance of co-administration of CYP2C19 substrates (📖 inside back cover) is unknown. Caution is advised if omeprazole is co-administered with drugs that are predominantly metabolized by CYP2C19. The prescriber should be aware of the potential for interactions and that dosage adjustments may be necessary, particularly of drugs with a narrow therapeutic index.

Pharmacodynamic

- No clinically significant interactions noted.

🔬 Dose

Gastro-oesophageal reflux disease

- With oesophagitis, initial dose 40mg PO OD for 4 weeks. Continue for a further 4 weeks if not fully healed or symptoms persist.
- Alternatively, in patients unable to tolerate oral therapy, 40mg IV or IV infusion OD.

- Maintenance dose 20mg PO OD.
- In the absence of oesophagitis, initial dose 20mg PO OD for up to 4 weeks.
- Alternatively, in patients unable to tolerate oral therapy, 20mg IV or IV infusion OD.
- Maintenance dose 20mg PO OD PRN.

Treatment of NSAID-associated gastric ulcer
- Initial dose 20mg PO OD for 4–8 weeks.
- Alternatively, in patients unable to tolerate oral therapy, 20mg IV or IV infusion OD.

Prophylaxis of NSAID-associated peptic ulcer disease
- 20mg PO OD.
- Alternatively, in patients unable to tolerate oral therapy, 20mg IV or IV infusion OD.

Dose adjustments
Elderly
- Dose adjustments are not necessary in the elderly.

Hepatic/renal impairment
- In liver impairment, the dose should not exceed 20mg OD.
- Dosage adjustments are not required for patients with renal impairment.

Additional information
- The tablet can be dispersed in water to form a suspension of enteric-coated granules. The solution can be swallowed, or administered via a feeding tube.
- Injection should be administered over at least 3min.
- Intravenous infusion should be administered over a period of 10–30min.

Pharmacology
Esomeprazole is the S-isomer of omeprazole. It is a PPI that suppresses gastric acid secretion in a dose-related manner by specific inhibition of the H^+/K^+-ATPase in the gastric parietal cell. Esomeprazole is rapidly absorbed orally, with a bioavailability of 89% after repeated dosing. It is completely metabolized by the liver, with CYP2C19 being involved in the major metabolic pathway. CYP3A4 is also involved in the metabolism of esomeprazole, but to a lesser extent. The major metabolites of esomeprazole are inactive.

Etamsylate

Dicynene® (POM)
Tablet: 500mg (100).

Indications

- ¥Prophylaxis and control of haemorrhages from small blood vessels.[1]

Contraindications and precautions

- Is contraindicated for use in patients with porphyria.
- Avoid in patients with wheat allergy (tablet contains wheat starch).
- Discontinue treatment if the patient develops a fever.

☻ Adverse effects

The frequency is not defined, but reported adverse effects include:

- Diarrhoea
- Fever
- Headaches
- Nausea
- Skin rashes
- Vomiting.

Drug interactions

Pharmacokinetic

- No clinically important interactions.

Pharmacodynamic

- No clinically important interactions.

Dose

- 500mg PO QDS.
- Take after food if symptoms such as nausea and vomiting occur.

Dose adjustments

Elderly

- No specific dose reductions stated.

Hepatic/renal impairment

- No specific dose reductions stated.

Additional information

- Tablets can be dispersed in water prior to administration

☀ Pharmacology

Etamsylate is a non-hormonal agent which reduces capillary exudation and blood loss. It does not affect normal coagulation since it has no effect on prothrombin times, fibrinolysis, platelet count or function. Although the exact mechanism is unknown, etamsylate is believed to increase capillary vascular wall resistance, platelet adhesiveness through inhibition of the synthesis and action of prostaglandins that cause platelet disaggregation, vasodilation, and increased capillary permeability. Etamsylate is well absorbed orally and excreted via the kidneys unchanged.

Reference

1. Garay RP, Chiavaroli C, Hannaert P. Therapeutic efficacy and mechanism of action of ethamsylate, a long-standing hemostatic agent. *Am J Ther* 2006; **13**(3):236–47.

Etoricoxib

Arcoxia® (POM)
Tablet: 30mg (28); 60mg (28); 90mg (28); 120mg (7).

Indications

- Pain and inflammation in osteoarthritis, rheumatoid arthritis, and ankylosing spondylitis.
- Acute gout
- ¥Pain associated with cancer.[1]

Contraindications and precautions

- Etoricoxib is contraindicated for use in patients with:
  - active peptic ulceration or active GI bleeding
  - CHF (NYHA II–IV)
  - established ischaemic heart disease, peripheral arterial disease, and/or cerebrovascular disease
  - hypersensitivity reactions to ibuprofen, aspirin or other NSAIDs (e.g. asthma, nasal polyps, rhinitis)
  - hypertension persistently elevated above 140/90mmHg and has not been adequately controlled
  - inflammatory bowel disease
  - severe hepatic dysfunction (serum albumin <25g/L or Child–Pugh score ≥10)
  - severe renal impairment (estimated renal CrCl <30mL/min).
- Use the minimum effective dose for the shortest duration necessary in order to reduce the risk of cardiac and GI events.
- Elderly patients are more at risk of developing adverse effects.
- Treatment should be reviewed after 2 weeks. In the absence of benefit, other options should be considered.
- Use with caution in the following circumstances:
  - concurrent use of diuretics, corticosteroids, and NSAIDs (see 🕮 Drug interactions, p.194)
  - CHF and/or left ventricular dysfunction
  - hepatic impairment
  - hyperlipidaemia
  - hypertension (particularly uncontrolled)
  - prior history of GI disease
  - recovery from surgery
  - renal impairment
  - smoking
  - type 1 and 2 diabetes (risk factors for cardiovascular events).
- Monitor blood pressure and renal function in patients at risk of cardiovascular adverse effects during the initiation of therapy.
- Etoricoxib may prevent the development of signs and symptoms of inflammation/infection (e.g. fever).
- Discontinue treatment at the first appearance of skin rash, mucosal lesions, or any other sign of hypersensitivity.
- Consider co-prescription of misoprostol or a PPI if:
  - long-term NSAID therapy

- concurrent use of drugs that increase the risk of GI toxicity (see 📖 Drug interactions).
- Refer to 📖 Selection of a NSAID, p.29 for further information, including selection.
- Etoricoxib may cause dizziness, drowsiness, or vertigo. Patients should be advised not to drive (or operate machinery) if affected. Refer to 📖 Drugs and driving, p.25.

☺ Adverse effects

Common
- Abdominal pain
- Altered liver enzymes (raised ALT/AST)
- Asthenia
- Diarrhoea
- Dizziness
- Dyspepsia

- Ecchymosis
- Flatulence
- Headache
- Hypertension
- Nausea
- Oedema
- Palpitations.

Uncommon
- Anaemia (usually associated with GI bleeding)
- Angina
- Anxiety
- Atrial fibrillation
- Blurred vision
- CVA
- Cough
- Depression
- Drowsiness
- Dry mouth
- Dysgeusia
- Dyspnoea
- Epistaxis
- Flushing
- Gastritis

- Gastroduodenal ulcer
- Hyperkalaemia
- Infection (e.g. conjunctivitis, gastroenteritis, upper respiratory infection, UTI)
- Insomnia
- Muscle cramp
- Myocardial infarction
- Oesophagitis
- Pruritus
- Rash
- Thrombocytopenia
- Transient ischaemic attack
- Vertigo
- Vomiting
- Weight gain.

Very rare
- Bronchospasm
- Confusion
- Hallucinations
- Hepatitis

- Hypertensive crisis
- Hypersensitivity reaction
- Stevens–Johnson syndrome
- Toxic epidermal necrolysis.

Drug interactions

Pharmacokinetic
- Is metabolized primarily by CYP3A4. Co-administration with drugs that are metabolized by, or affect the activity (induction or inhibition—see 📖 inside back cover) of this pathway may lead to clinically relevant drug interactions and the prescriber should be aware that dosage adjustments may be necessary, particularly of drugs with a narrow therapeutic index.
- Avoid excessive amounts of grapefruit juice as it may increase the bioavailability of etoricoxib through inhibition of intestinal CYP3A4.

Pharmacodynamic
- *Anticoagulants*—increased risk of bleeding.
- *Antihypertensives*—reduced hypotensive effect.
- *Antiplatelet drugs*—increased risk of GI toxicity (no effect on antiplatelet action).
- *Corticosteroids*—increased risk of GI toxicity.
- *Ciclosporin*—increased risk of nephrotoxicity.
- *Diuretics*—reduced diuretic effect.
- *SSRIs*—increased risk of GI bleeding.

Dose

Osteoarthritis
- 30mg PO OD increased to 60mg PO OD as necessary.

Rheumatoid arthritis/ankylosing spondylitis
- 90mg PO OD.

Acute gout
- 120mg PO OD for 8 days.

¥ Pain associated with cancer
- Initial dose 60mg PO OD, increased as necessary to 120mg PO OD (NB risk of serious events increases with dose and duration). If no benefit after 2 weeks discontinue treatment and review.

Dose adjustments

Elderly
- Usual adult doses recommended. Note that the elderly are particularly susceptible to adverse effects. Use the lowest effective dose and for the shortest duration possible.

Hepatic/renal impairment
- In patients with mild hepatic impairment (Child–Pugh score 5–6) 60mg PO OD should not be exceeded. In patients with moderate hepatic impairment (Child–Pugh score 7–9), 60mg on alternate days should not be exceeded; administration of 30mg PO OD can also be considered. Etoricoxib is contraindicated for use in patients with severe hepatic impairment.
- Use of etoricoxib in patients with severe renal impairment is contraindicated. No dosage adjustment is necessary for patients with CrCl ≥30mL/min.

Additional information
- Etoricoxib tablets may be dispersed in water prior to administration.

⊕ Pharmacology
Like traditional NSAIDs, the mechanism of action of etoricoxib is believed to be due to inhibition of prostaglandin synthesis. Unlike most NSAIDs, however, etoricoxib is a selective non-competitive inhibitor of COX-2. It has no effect on platelet aggregation. Etoricoxib is well absorbed orally, with an absolute bioavailability of 100%. It is extensively metabolized, with CYP3A4 being the major isoenzyme involved. Some of the metabolites are weakly active COX-2 inhibitors, the rest have no appreciable action. <1% of the total dose is excreted unchanged in the urine.

Reference
1. McNicol ED, Strassels S, Goudas L, *et al.* NSAIDS or paracetamol, alone or combined with opioids, for cancer pain. *Cochrane Database Syst Rev* 2005; **2**: CD005180.

Exemestane

Aromasin® (POM)
Tablet: 25mg (30; 90).

Generic (POM)
Tablet: 25mg (30).

Indications

- Adjuvant treatment of oestrogen-receptor-positive early breast cancer in postmenopausal women following 2–3 years of tamoxifen therapy.
- Advanced breast cancer in postmenopausal women in whom anti-oestrogen therapy has failed.

Contraindications and precautions

- Not to be used in premenopausal women.
- Use with caution in patients with hepatic or renal impairment.
- May cause reduction in bone mineral density and an increased fracture rate. Women with osteoporosis or at risk of osteoporosis should have their bone mineral density formally assessed and treatment should be initiated in at-risk patients.
- Exemestane may modify reactions and patients should be advised not drive (or operate machinery) if affected. Refer to 📖 Drugs and driving, p.25.

☺ Adverse effects

Very common

- Fatigue
- Headache
- Hot flushes
- Increased sweating
- Insomnia
- Musculoskeletal pain
- Nausea.

Common

- Anorexia
- Carpal tunnel syndrome
- Depression
- Dizziness
- Dyspepsia
- Fracture
- Osteoporosis
- Peripheral oedema.

Uncommon

- Drowsiness
- Weakness.

Drug interactions

Pharmacokinetic

- Is metabolized by CYP3A4. Co-administration with drugs that are metabolized by, or affect the activity (induction or inhibition—see 📖 inside back cover) of this pathway may lead to clinically relevant drug interactions and the prescriber should be aware that dosage adjustments may be necessary, particularly of drugs with a narrow therapeutic index.
- The effect of grapefruit juice on the absorption of exemestane is unknown.

Pharmacodynamic
- *Oestrogens*—may antagonize the effect of exemestane.

💊 Dose
- 25mg PO OD, after food.

💊 Dose adjustments
Elderly
- Dose adjustments are unnecessary.

Hepatic/renal impairment
  No dose adjustments are required for patients with liver or renal impairment.

Additional information
- In patients with early breast cancer, treatment should continue until completion of 5 years of combined sequential adjuvant hormonal therapy (tamoxifen followed by exemestane), or earlier if tumour relapse occurs.
- In patients with advanced breast cancer, treatment should continue until tumour progression is evident.

⧉ Pharmacology
Exemestane is an irreversible, steroidal aromatase inhibitor which does not possess any progestogenic, androgenic or oestrogenic activity. It reduces oestrogen levels by blocking the action of aromatase in the adrenal glands.

Fentanyl (transdermal/parenteral)

It is not possible to ensure the interchangeability of different makes of fentanyl transdermal patches in individual patients. Therefore, in addition to avoiding confusion, it is recommended that patients should remain on the same product once treatment has been stabilized. Inclusion of the brand name on the prescription is suggested.

Transdermal

Durogesic DTrans® (CD2 POM)
Patch (matrix):   12 micrograms/hour (5)
                      25 micrograms/hour (5)
                      50 micrograms/hour (5)
                      75 micrograms/hour (5)
                      100 micrograms/hour (5).

Generic (CD2 POM)
Patch (matrix):   12 micrograms/hour (5)
                      25 micrograms/hour (5)
                      50 micrograms/hour (5)
                      75 micrograms/hour (5)
                      100 micrograms/hour (5).

Brands include: Fencino®, Matrifen®, Mezolar®, Osmanil®, Victanyl®.

Generic (CD2 POM)
Patch (reservoir): 25 micrograms/hour (5)
                      50 micrograms/hour (5)
                      75 micrograms/hour (5)
                      100 micrograms/hour (5).

Brands include: Fentalis®.

Parenteral

Sublimaze® (CD2 POM)
Injection: 100 micrograms/2mL (10)
                      500 micrograms/10mL (5).

- Fentanyl is a Schedule 2 CD. Refer to 📖 Legal categories of medicines, p.21 for further information.

Indications
- Severe chronic pain (*transdermal*).
- ¥Treatment of severe pain via subcutaneous administration (*parenteral*)

Contraindications and precautions
- Refer to 📖 Use of drugs in end-of-life care, p.53 for end-of-life care issues If the dose of an opioid is titrated correctly, it is generally accepted that there are no absolute contraindications to the use of such

drugs in palliative care, although there may be circumstances where one opioid is favoured over another (e.g. renal impairment, constipation). Nonetheless, manufacturers' contraindications and precautions are described in the following lists.

Fentanyl may modify reactions and patients should be advised not drive (or operate machinery) if affected. Refer to 📖 Drugs and driving, p.25.

Transdermal

Transdermal fentanyl should not be used in opioid-naïve patients. Such patients should be titrated with low doses of short-acting opioids initially.

Although not recommended for the treatment of acute or intermittent pain, fentanyl patches have been used successfully for the ⁴management of acute postoperative pain. Refer to local guidelines.

Not recommended for use if the patient has received a MAOI within the previous 2 weeks.

Use with caution in patients with:
• severe respiratory disease
• concurrent CYP3A4 inhibitors (see 📖 Drug interactions, p.200)
• bradyarrhythmias
• hepatic impairment (empirical dose adjustment may be necessary—see 📖 Dose adjustments, p.201)
• pyrexia (increased fentanyl delivery rate).

Patients should be advised to avoid exposing the patch application site to direct heat sources such as hot water bottles, electric blankets, heat lamps, saunas, or baths because of the risk of increased fentanyl absorption.

Patients who experience serious adverse events should have the patches removed immediately and should be monitored for up to 24 hours after patch removal.

Parenteral

No specific contraindications if being used for end-of-life care via CSCI. Dose adjustments may be necessary if CYP3A4 inducers or inhibitors are used concurrently.

Adverse effects

Strong opioids tend to cause similar adverse effects, albeit to varying degrees. See also 📖 Morphine, p.371.

Each product has its own list and frequency of adverse effects. Some are listed here, but readers should refer to the manufacturer's SPC for further details.

Very common

Dizziness
Headache
Insomnia

• Nausea
• Vomiting.

Common

Anorexia
Anxiety
Asthenia
Fatigue

• Hallucinations
• Pruritus
• Sweating
• Tachycardia.

Uncommon

- Agitation
- Amnesia
- Application site reaction
- Bradycardia
- Convulsion
- Disorientation

- Euphoria
- Hypotension
- Ileus
- Myoclonus
- Respiratory depression
- Sexual dysfunction.

Drug interactions

Pharmacokinetic

- Fentanyl is a major substrate of CYP3A4. Co-administration with drugs that are metabolized by, or affect the activity (induction or inhibition —see 📖 inside back cover) of this pathway may lead to clinically relevant drug interactions and the prescriber should be aware that dosage adjustments may be necessary, particularly of drugs with a narrow therapeutic index.
- Fentanyl should be used with caution if CYP3A4 inhibitors are co-prescribed due to the increased risk of extended therapeutic effects and the adverse effects.
- *Carbamazepine*—patient may need higher doses of fentanyl if carbamazepine is introduced to treatment.
- *Fluconazole*—may inhibit the metabolism of fentanyl (although more likely to occur when fluconazole doses >200mg daily).
- *Midazolam*—effect may be enhanced by fentanyl (competitive inhibition of metabolism).

Pharmacodynamic

- *Antihypertensives*—increased risk of hypotension.
- *CNS depressants*—risk of excessive sedation.
- *Haloperidol*—may be an additive hypotensive effect.
- *Ketamine*—there is a potential opioid-sparing effect with ketamine and concurrent transdermal fentanyl use is not recommended; however, an empirical fentanyl dose reduction of 25–50% at least 12 hours before starting ketamine is suggested (additional opioid requirements can be treated using PRN analgesia).
- *Levomepromazine*—may be an additive hypotensive effect.

💊 Dose

Transdermal

- Patches should be worn continuously for 72 hours. Occasionally, certain patients may experience reduced efficacy in the period 48–72 hours after application. Such patients should replace the patch after 48 hours.
- Initial dosage of fentanyl is based upon the previous opioid requirements. Refer to 📖 Management of pain: opioid substitution, p.32 for information regarding opioid dose equivalences. Table 3.7 serves as a suggestion and differs from the guidance advised by the manufacturers.

Table 3.7 Suggested oral opioid dose equivalences

Morphine (mg/day)	Oxycodone (mg/day)	Transdermal fentanyl (micrograms/hour)
30	20	12
60	40	25
120	80	50
180	120	75
240	160	100
300	200	125
360	240	150
400	260	162–175
480	320	200
540	340	225
600	400	250
660	440	275
720	480	300
840	560	350[a]
960	640	400[a]
1080	720	450[a]

[a]Manufacturer recommends that above doses of 300 micrograms/hour, alternative or additional method analgesia should be used.

Parenteral
- *For CSCI, dose is based on previous opioid requirements (refer to 📖 Management of pain: opioid substitution, p.32 for information regarding opioid dose equivalences).
- Given the volume of injection, fentanyl is unlikely to be administered by SC injection and use in a CSCI will be uncommon.

Dose adjustments

Elderly
- No specific guidance available. Dose requirements should be individually titrated.

Hepatic/renal impairment
- No specific guidance available. Dose requirements should be individually titrated.

Additional information
- Opioid withdrawal symptoms (e.g. nausea, vomiting, diarrhoea, sweating, and shivering) can occur in patients after switching from

previously prescribed opioids to a transdermal fentanyl patch. This is because the majority of the opioid dose is entering the CNS, creating a withdrawal situation in the periphery. Rescue doses of morphine or oxycodone can be administered to treat these symptoms if warranted.

Transdermal

- Higher doses may be necessary in cachectic patients due to impaired absorption.
- Evaluation of the analgesic effect should not be made until the patch has been worn for at least 24 hours (to allow for the gradual increase in plasma-fentanyl concentration). Steady-state plasma concentrations of fentanyl are generally achieved in 36–48 hours and the patient should be encouraged to use PRN doses during the initial 72 hours (to ameliorate potential withdrawal symptoms). If necessary, the dose should be adjusted at 72-hour intervals in steps of 12–25 micrograms/hour.
- The following is a guide on how to initiate the patch in relation to previous opioid therapy:
  - 4-hourly hydromorphone/morphine/oxycodone—give regular 4-hourly doses for the first 12 hours after applying the patch
  - 12-hourly hydromorphone/morphine/oxycodone—give the final oral dose at the same time as applying the first patch
  - 24-hourly morphine—apply the patch 12 hours after the final oral dose
  - CSCI—continue the syringe driver for the first 12 hours after applying the patch.
- When converting from hydromorphone, morphine or oxycodone to fentanyl, the dose of any laxative should be halved and subsequently adjusted according to need.
- High quantities of fentanyl remain in the transdermal patches after a 72-hour period. Used transdermal patches should be folded with the adhesive surfaces inwards, covering the release membrane.
- If a CSCI is needed, treatment should continue with the patch and additional analgesic requirements should be managed with suitable doses of rescue medication. Refer to 📖 Management of pain: opioid substitution, p.32 for information regarding opioid dose equivalences.
- Ensure that patients and caregivers are aware of the signs and symptoms of fentanyl overdose—i.e. sedation, confusion, feeling faint, dizzy, or confused. Patients and caregivers should be advised to seek medical attention immediately if overdose is suspected.

Parenteral

- Fentanyl via CSCI is reportedly compatible with dexamethasone, haloperidol, hyoscine hydrobromide, ketorolac, levomepromazine, metoclopramide, midazolam and ondansetron.

⟐ Pharmacology

Fentanyl is a synthetic opioid, chemically related to pethidine, with an action primarily at the μ-receptor. The main route of elimination is hepatic metabolism via CYP3A4 to inactive compounds, which are mainly excreted in the urine. The metabolites of fentanyl are non-toxic and inactive. Fentanyl is a suitable opioid to use in patients with renal failure.

Fentanyl (transmucosal)

Oral transmucosal and nasal formulations are not identical and changing from one product to another will require a new dose titration. Therefore, it is recommended that patients should remain on the same product once treatment has been stabilized. Inclusion of the brand name on the prescription is suggested.

Abstral® (CD2 POM)

Sublingual Tablet: 100 micrograms (10; 30); 200 micrograms (10; 30); 300 micrograms (10; 30); 400 micrograms (10; 30); 600 micrograms (30); 800 micrograms (30).

Actiq® (CD2 POM)

Lozenge: 200 micrograms (3; 30); 400 micrograms (3; 30); 600 micrograms (3; 30); 800 micrograms (3; 30); 1200 micrograms; 1600 micrograms (3; 30).

Effentora® (CD2 POM)

Buccal tablet: 100 micrograms (4); 200 micrograms (4); 400 micrograms (4); 600 micrograms (4); 800 micrograms (4).

Instanyl® (CD2 POM)

Nasal spray: 50 micrograms per spray (10 dose; 20 dose); 100 micrograms per spray (10 dose; 20 dose); 200 micrograms per spray (10 dose; 20 dose).

PecFent® (CD2 POM)

Nasal spray: 100 micrograms per spray (8 dose; 32 dose); 400 micrograms per spray (8 dose; 32 dose).

- Fentanyl is a Schedule 2 CD. Refer to 📖 Legal categories of medicines, p.21 for further information.

Indications

- BTcP. Refer to 📖 Management of pain: breakthrough pain, p.35 for guidance relating to BTcP.

Transmucosal

Contraindicated for use in:
- opioid-naïve patients
- previous facial radiotherapy (*Instanyl®*)
- recurrent episodes of epistaxis (*Instanyl®*)
- severe respiratory disease.
- Not recommended for use if the patient has received a MAOI within the previous 2 weeks.
- Patient's background analgesia must be stabilized before use (otherwise the patient does not have BTcP).

- Avoid concomitant use of a nasal vasoconstrictor with *Instanyl*® and *PecFent*® (see 🕮 Drug interactions, p.205).
- Avoid concomitant use of other nasally administered medicinal products (effect on *Instanyl*® or *PecFent*® unknown).
- Use with caution in the following:
  - concurrent use of CYP3A4 inhibitors (see 🕮 Drug interactions, p.205)
  - diabetic patients (*Actiq*® lozenges contain 1.89g glucose per dose)
  - elderly (see 🕮 Dose adjustments, p.209)
  - head injury and/or raised intracranial pressure
  - hepatic impairment
  - oral lesions (absorption of fentanyl may be affected from oral formulations)
  - recurrent episodes of epistaxis or nasal discomfort (*Instanyl*® or *PecFent*®).
- Ensure good oral hygiene in order to prevent damage to teeth (*Actiq*®).
- *Effentora*® 100-microgram tablets contain 8mg of sodium (0.3mmol); the 200-, 400-, 600-, and 800-microgram tablets each contain 16mg of sodium (0.6mmol).
- Fentanyl may modify reactions and patients should be advised not drive (or operate machinery) if affected. Refer to 🕮 Drugs and driving, p.25.

☺ Adverse effects

- Strong opioids tend to cause similar adverse effects, albeit to varying degrees. See also 🕮 Morphine, p.371.
- Each product has its own list and frequency of adverse effects. Some are listed here, but readers should refer to the manufacturer's SPC for further details.

Very common

- Application site reactions (*Effentora*®)
- Constipation (*Actiq*®)
- Drowsiness (*Abstral*®, *Actiq*®)
- Dizziness (*Abstral*®, *Actiq*®, *Effentora*®)
- Fatigue (*Abstral*®)
- Headache (*Abstral*®, *Effentora*®)
- Insomnia (*transdermal*)
- Nausea (*Abstral*®, *Actiq*®, *Effentora*®)
- Vomiting (*Effentora*®).

Common

- Anorexia (*Abstral*®, *Effentora*®)
- Anxiety (*Actiq*®, *Effentora*®)
- Application site reactions (*Abstral*®, *Actiq*®)
- Asthenia (*Abstral*®, *Actiq*®, *Effentora*®)
- Confusion (*Actiq*®)
- Constipation (*Abstral*®, *Effentora*®, *PecFent*®)
- Depression (*Abstral*®)
- Dizziness (*Instanyl*®, *PecFent*®)
- Drowsiness (*Instanyl*®, *PecFent*®)
- Dry mouth (*Abstral*®, *Actiq*®, *Effentora*®)
- Dysgeusia (*PecFent*®)
- Dyspepsia (*Abstral*®, *Actiq*®, *Effentora*®)
- Epistaxis (*PecFent*®)

- Fatigue (*Effentora*®)
- Flushing (*Abstral*®, *Actiq*®, *Instanyl*®)
- Hallucinations (*Actiq*®)
- Headache (*Actiq*®, *Instanyl*®, *PecFent*®)
- Insomnia (*Effentora*®)
- Myoclonus (*Actiq*®)
- Nausea (*Instanyl*® *PecFent*®)
- Oral candidiasis (*Effentora*®)
- Pruritus (*Abstral*®, *Actiq*®, *Effentora*®, *PecFent*®)
- Rhinitis (*Abstral*®)
- Sweating (*Actiq*®, *Effentora*®, *Instanyl*®)
- Tachycardia (*Effentora*®)
- Vomiting (*Actiq*®, *Instanyl*®, *PecFent*®).

Drug interactions

Pharmacokinetic

- As for fentanyl (see 📖 Fentanyl (transdermal/parenteral), p.198).
- Fentanyl should be used with caution if CYP3A4 inhibitors are co-prescribed due to the increased risk of extended therapeutic effects and the adverse effects. Alterations in intestinal CYP3A4 activity (induction or inhibition) appear to have little influence on *transmucosal* fentanyl absorption, or onset of effect. Nonetheless, since a significant proportion (~75%) is swallowed and its systemic clearance may be decreased by CYP3A4 inhibitors, caution is required with co-administration.

Pharmacodynamic

- As for fentanyl (📖 Fentanyl (transdermal/parenteral), p.198).
- Nasal vasoconstrictors—can reduce effect of *Instanyl*® and *PecFent*®.

Transmucosal

Products are licensed for use in patients taking at least 60mg oral morphine per day, or equivalent (see 📖 Opioid substitution, p.32 for information regarding opioid dose equivalences) for a week or longer. The effective dose of transmucosal formulations for BTcP is not predictable from the daily maintenance dose of opioid and titration to an effective dose is necessary.

Abstral®

- No more than 2 sublingual tablets should be used for a single episode of BTcP.
- During titration, if adequate analgesia is not obtained within 15–30min of using the first sublingual tablet, a second tablet as shown in Table 3.8 may be used.
- Doses above 800 micrograms have not been evaluated.
- Maintain the patient on the dose established during titration. This may be more than one tablet per BTcP incident.
- Abstral® is licensed to be given for **4** episodes of BTcP per day. If more than 4 episodes of BTcP occur in a day for more than 4 consecutive days, review background analgesia and consider re-evaluating the dosing schedule.
- May discontinue abruptly if no longer required and the patient continues to receive chronic opioid treatment.

Table 3.8 Titration schedule for Abstral®

BTcP Episode	Dose of first Abstral® tablet per episode of BTcP (micrograms)	Dose of additional Abstral® tablet to be taken 15–30min after first tablet, if required (micrograms)
1st	100	100
2nd	200	100
3rd	300	100
4th	400	200
5th	600	200
6th	800	–

Actiq®

- During titration, if adequate analgesia is not obtained within 15min of completing consumption of the first lozenge (i.e. 30min after starting the first lozenge), a second lozenge of the same strength may be used.
- If signs of excessive opioid effects appear before the lozenge is fully consumed, it should be immediately removed, and the dose should be reviewed.
- No more than 2 lozenges should be used to treat a single episode of BTcP.
- Refer to Table 3.9 for the titration schedule. At 1600 micrograms, a second dose is only likely to be required by a minority of patients.
- Maintain the patient on the dose established during titration.
- Actiq® is for use in patients who typically experience no more than **4** episodes of breakthrough pain per day. If more than 4 episodes of BTcP occur in a day for more than 4 consecutive days, review background analgesia and consider re-evaluating the dosing schedule.
- May discontinue abruptly if no longer required and the patient continues to receive chronic opioid treatment.

Table 3.9 Titration schedule for Actiq®

BTcP Episode	Dose of first Actiq® lozenge per episode of BTcP (micrograms)	Dose of additional Actiq® lozenge to be taken 30min after starting the first lozenge, if required (micrograms)
1st	200	200
2nd	400	400
3rd	600	600
4th	800	800
5th	1200	1200
6th	1600	1600

Effentora®
- During titration, if adequate analgesia is not obtained within 30min of using the first buccal tablet, a second tablet of the same strength may be used.
- No more than 2 tablets should be used to treat any individual BTcP episode, *except* during titration as described in Table 3.10.
- The manufacturer recommends using up to 4 100- or 200-microgram tablets to treat a single episode of BTcP during titration.
- Refer to Table 3.10 for the titration schedule.
- Doses above 800 micrograms have not been evaluated.
- Effentora® is licensed to be given for 4 episodes of BTcP per day. If more than 4 episodes of BTcP occur in a day for more than 4 consecutive days, review background analgesia and consider re-evaluating the dosing schedule.
- May discontinue abruptly if no longer required and the patient continues to receive chronic opioid treatment.

Table 3.10 Titration schedule for Effentora®

BTcP Episode	Dose of first Effentora® buccal tablet per episode of BTcP (micrograms)	Dose of additional Effentora® buccal tablet to be taken 30min after starting first tablet, if required (micrograms)
1st	100	100
2nd	200	200
3rd	400	400
4th	600	600
5th	800	–

Instanyl®
- During titration, if adequate analgesia is not obtained after 10min, an additional dose of the same strength can be administered.
- No more than 2 doses should be used to treat any individual BTcP episode.
- Patients should wait at least 4 hours before treating another breakthrough pain episode with Instanyl® during both titration and maintenance therapy.
- Refer to Table 3.11 for the titration schedule.
- Instanyl® is licensed to be given for 4 episodes of BTcP per day. If more than 4 episodes of BTcP occur in a day for more than 4 consecutive days, review background analgesia and consider re-evaluating the dosing schedule.
- May discontinue abruptly if no longer required and the patient continues to receive chronic opioid treatment.

Table 3.11 Titration schedule for Instanyl®

BTcP Episode	Dose of first Instanyl® nasal spray per episode of BTcP (micrograms)	Dose of additional Instanyl® nasal spray to be used 10min after first dose, if required (micrograms)
1st	50	50
2nd	100	100
3rd	200	200
4th	400	–

PecFent®
- Titration with PecFent® differs from the other products in that the effective dose is defined as the dose that successfully treats 2 consecutive episodes of BTP. During titration, an additional dose is not indicated.
- No more than 2 doses (one spray in each nostril) should be used to treat any individual BTcP episode.
- Patients should wait at least 4 hours before treating another breakthrough pain episode with PecFent® during both titration and maintenance therapy.
- Refer to Table 3.12 for the titration schedule.
- PecFent® is licensed to be given for 4 episodes of BTcP per day. If more than 4 episodes of BTcP occur in a day for more than 4 consecutive days, review background analgesia and consider re-evaluating the dosing schedule.
- May discontinue abruptly if no longer required and the patient continues to receive chronic opioid treatment.

Table 3.12 Titration schedule for PecFent®

BTcP Episode	Dose of first PecFent® nasal spray per episode of BTcP (micrograms)	Notes
1	100	If effective, *go to 2a* and continue with 100 micrograms to treat the next episode of BTcP. If ineffective, then for next BTcP episode, *go to 2b*
2a	100	If effective, stop titration and continue with 100 micrograms. If ineffective, then at next BTcP episode, *go to 3a*
2b	200 (1 spray both nostrils)	If effective, *go to 3a* and continue with 200 micrograms to treat the next episode of BTcP. If ineffective, then for next BTcP episode, *go to 3b*

(Continued)

Table 3.12 (cont.) Titration schedule for PecFent®

BTcP Episode	Dose of first PecFent® nasal spray per episode of BTcP (micrograms)	Notes
3a	200 (1 spray both nostrils)	If effective, stop titration and continue with 200 micrograms. If ineffective, then at next BTcP episode, go to 4a
3c	400	If effective, go to 4a and continue with 400 micrograms to treat the next episode of BTcP. If ineffective, then at next BTcP episode, go to 4b
4a	400	If effective, stop titration and continue with 400 micrograms. If ineffective, then at next BTcP episode, go to 5
4b	800 (1 spray both nostrils)	If effective, go to 5 and continue with 800 micrograms to treat the next BTcP episode. If ineffective, contact doctor for advice.
5	800 (1 spray both nostrils)	If effective, stop titration and continue with 800 micrograms. If ineffective contact doctor for advice

Dose adjustments

Elderly
• No specific guidance available. Dose requirements should be individually titrated.

Hepatic/renal impairment
• No specific guidance available. Dose requirements should be individually titrated.

Additional information

• *Abstral®* sublingual tablets should be administered directly under the tongue and at the deepest part. The patient must not swallow, suck or chew the tablet, nor should the patient eat or drink anything until the tablet has completely dissolved (happens within <1min). Water may be used to moisten the buccal mucosa in patients with a dry mouth.
• *Actiq®* lozenges should be rubbed against the cheek, or sucked, but not chewed. Water may be used to moisten the buccal mucosa in patients with a dry mouth. The lozenge should be consumed within 15min.
• *Effentora®* buccal tablets should be placed in the upper portion of the buccal cavity (above an upper rear molar between the cheek and gum). The tablet should not be sucked, chewed or swallowed, nor should the patient eat or drink anything while the tablet is in the mouth. The tablet usually disintegrates within 14–25min; after 30min, the mouth can be rinsed to remove the remnants. Water may be used to moisten the buccal mucosa in patients with a dry mouth.

- *Effentora*® buccal tablets can be placed sublingually if necessary.
- Fentanyl exposure from *Instanyl*® is unaffected by the common cold (providing nasal vasoconstrictors are not co-administered).
- Before using *Instanyl*® for the first time, the nasal spray must be primed until a fine mist appears; 3–4 actuations of the nasal spray are usually required. If the product has not been used during a period of >7 days, the nasal spray must be actuated once before the next dose is taken.
- Prior to using *PecFent*®, the bottle must be primed until a green bar appears in the counting window (should occur after 4 sprays). If the product has not been used for >5 days or if it is >14 days since the product was first used, it must be discarded.

❖ **Pharmacology**

Refer to 🕮 Fentanyl (transdermal/parenteral), p.198.

Finasteride

Proscar® *(POM)*
Tablet: 5mg (28).

Generic (POM)
Tablet: 5mg (28).

Indications
- Benign prostatic hyperplasia (BPH).

Contraindications and precautions
- Finasteride causes a decrease in serum prostate-specific antigen concentrations by ~50% in patients with BPH even in the presence of prostate cancer. Reference values may need adjustment.

Adverse effects
The frequency is not defined, but reported adverse effects include:
- Decreased libido
- Dizziness
- Gynaecomastia
- Impotence
- Postural hypotension
- Testicular pain
- Weakness.

Drug interactions
- Is metabolized by CYP3A4, but no clinically important drug interactions have been identified. Nonetheless, co-administration with drugs that are metabolized by, or affect the activity (induction or inhibition —see inside back cover) of this pathway may lead to clinically relevant drug interactions and the prescriber should be aware that dosage adjustments may be necessary, particularly of drugs with a narrow therapeutic index.

Dose
- 5mg PO OD.

Dose adjustments
Elderly
- No dosage adjustments necessary.

Hepatic/renal impairment
- There are no specific dose recommendations for use in liver impairment; the manufacturer states there are no data available in patients with hepatic insufficiency.
- Dosage adjustments are unnecessary in patients with renal impairment.

Additional information
- Although tablets may be crushed and dispersed in water prior to administration, it is not recommended to be performed due to the risk of exposure.

Pharmacology
Finasteride is a competitive and specific inhibitor of 5 α-reductase, an intracellular enzyme that converts testosterone into the more potent dihydrotestosterone (DHT). Inhibition results in significant decreases in serum and tissue DHT concentrations.

Flucloxacillin

Generic (POM)
Capsule: 250mg (28); 500mg (28).
Oral suspension (as powder for reconstitution): 125mg/5mL (100mL)
250mg/5mL (100mL).
Injection (as powder for reconstitution): 250mg (10); 500mg (10); 1g (10).

Indications
- Refer to local guidelines.
- Antibiotic indicated for the treatment of infections due to sensitive Gram-positive organisms.

Contraindications and precautions
- Is contraindicated for use in patients with penicillin hypersensitivity and with a previous history of flucloxacillin-associated jaundice/hepatic dysfunction.
- Use with caution if:
  - hepatic impairment (greater risk of severe hepatic reaction)
  - patients >50 years old
  - renal impairment (see 📖 Dose adjustments, p.213).
- Cholestatic jaundice and hepatitis may occur up to several weeks after treatment with flucloxacillin has been discontinued. Administration for >2 weeks and increasing age are risk factors.
- With prolonged treatment, regular monitoring of hepatic and renal function is recommended.

☻ Adverse effects
Common
- Minor GI disturbances.

Uncommon
- Rash
- Urticaria.

Very rare
- Cholestatic jaundice
- Hepatitis
- Interstitial nephritis
- Pseudomembranous colitis.

Drug interactions
Pharmacokinetic
- Oral contraceptives—reduced efficacy.

Pharmacodynamic
- None known.

⚗ Dose
Standard doses are described here. Refer to local guidelines for specific advice.
- 250–500mg PO QDS, at least 30min before food.
- 250–1g IV injection or infusion QDS.

🤞 Dose adjustments

Elderly
* No dose adjustment necessary.

Hepatic/renal impairment
* No specific guidance is available for use in hepatic impairment. Use the lowest effective dose.
* Patients in severe renal impairment (CrCl <10mL/min) may need dose adjustments. The manufacturer suggests a reduction in dose or extension of the dose interval should be considered. Standard adult doses should be tolerated; only the high doses for severe infections may need reducing.

Additional information

* Once reconstituted, the *oral solution* must be discarded after 14 days.
* To reconstitute the *injection*, add 5mL WFI to 250mg vial, 10mL WFI to 500mg vial, or 15–20mL WFI to 1g vial.
* Administer IV *injection* over 3–4min; administer IV *infusion* in 50–100mL NaCl 0.9% (or glucose 5%) over 30–60min.

⟡ Pharmacology

Flucloxacillin is a β-lactam antibiotic active against Gram-positive bacteria. It is bactericidal in that it interferes with the synthesis of the bacterial cell wall. As a result, the cell wall is weakened and the bacterium swells, then ruptures. Flucloxacillin is stable against hydrolysis by a variety of beta-lactamases.

Fluconazole

Diflucan® (POM)
Capsule: 50mg (7); 150mg (1); 200mg (7).
Suspension: 50mg/5mL (35mL); 200mg/5mL (35mL) (both supplied as powder for reconstitution with 24mL water).

Generic (POM)
Capsule: 50mg (7); 150mg (1); 200mg (7).
Note: capsules may be sold in pharmacies for genital candidiasis in those aged 16–60 years of age at a max. dose of 150mg.

Indications
- Mucosal candidiasis (including oropharyngeal and oesophageal).
- Genital candidiasis.
- For other fungal infections, seek local microbiological advice.

Contraindications and precautions
- Patients may develop abnormal LFTs during fluconazole therapy. Fluconazole should be discontinued if clinical signs or symptoms consistent with liver disease develop.
- Fluconazole is tenuously associated with prolongation of the QT interval and it should be used with caution in the following circumstances:
  - electrolyte disturbances, e.g. hypokalaemia
  - co-administration drugs that prolong the QT interval (see 🕮 Drug Interactions, p.14).

☺ Adverse effects

Common
- Abdominal pain
- Diarrhoea
- Elevated LFTs
- Headache
- Nausea
- Minor GI disturbances
- Rash
- Vomiting.

Uncommon
- Anaemia
- Cholestasis
- Constipation
- Dizziness
- Drowsiness
- Dry mouth
- Dysgeusia
- Fatigue
- Insomnia
- Jaundice
- Myalgia
- Pruritus
- Urticaria
- Vertigo.

Rare
- Blood dyscrasias (e.g. leucopenia, thrombocytopenia)
- Hepatitis
- Hypokalaemia
- QT prolongation
- Skin reactions (Stevens–Johnson syndrome has been reported)
- Tremor.

Drug interactions

Pharmacokinetic

- Fluconazole is a potent inhibitor of both CYP2C9 and CYP2C19; at higher doses (>200mg/day) it inhibits CYP3A4. Interactions are less likely to be clinically relevant with a single-dose course of treatment (e.g. 150mg for genital candidiasis). Co-administration with drugs that are metabolized by, or affect the activity (induction or inhibition—see 📖 inside back cover) of these pathways may lead to clinically relevant drug interactions and the prescriber should be aware that dosage adjustments may be necessary, particularly of drugs with a narrow therapeutic index.
- *Alfentanil*—metabolism may be inhibited (although more likely to occur when fluconazole doses >200mg daily).
- *Amitriptyline*—increased risk of adverse effects due to inhibition of metabolism; other factors may be necessary before this interaction becomes significant (e.g. co-administration of other interacting drugs).
- *Calcium channel blockers*—increased risk of adverse effects due to inhibition of CYP3A4; dose adjustments may be necessary.
- *Carbamazepine*—increase in adverse effects possible due to inhibition of CYP3A4.
- *Celecoxib*—increased plasma levels due to inhibition of CYP2C9; half celecoxib dose if combination necessary.
- *Citalopram*—serotonin syndrome has been reported with this combination (CYP2C19 inhibition).
- *Cyclophosphamide*—possible reduced effect due to a decrease in the formation of active metabolite via CYP2C9.
- *Fentanyl*—metabolism may be inhibited (although more likely to occur when fluconazole doses >200mg daily).
- *Midazolam*—increased sedative effects due to CYP3A4 inhibition (although more likely to occur when fluconazole doses >200mg daily).
- *Phenytoin*—increases the plasma concentrations of phenytoin; consider alternative treatment or closely monitor phenytoin plasma concentration.
- *Rifampicin*—reduces the plasma concentration of fluconazole.
- *Warfarin*—anticoagulant effect potentiated in dose-related manner; patient should be closely monitored and the warfarin dose adjusted accordingly.

Pharmacodynamic

- Fluconazole has been associated with prolongation of the QT interval. There is a potential risk that co-administration with other drugs that also prolong the QT interval (e.g. amiodarone, amitriptyline, erythromycin, quinine) may result in ventricular arrhythmias.

⚡ Dose

Mucosal candidiasis

- 50mg PO OD for 7–14 days.
- Dose may be increased as appropriate to 100mg PO OD in difficult cases.
- In oesophagitis, duration of treatment may need to be up to 30 days.

Genital candidiasis

- 150mg PO as a single dose.

℥ Dose adjustments

Elderly
- No dose adjustments necessary.

Hepatic/renal impairment
- Adjustments to single-dose therapy are not necessary.
- While fluconazole is excreted predominantly in the urine as unchanged drug, due consideration should be given to the inhibitory effects on CYP2C9 and CYP2C19 (and CYP3A4 at higher doses).
- In patients with impaired renal function, the normal dose should be used on day 1; subsequent doses are based on the degree of renal impairment as shown in Table 3.13.

Table 3.13 Fluconazole dose for patients with impaired renal function

Creatinine clearance (mL/L)	Percent of recommended dose
>50	100%
≤50 (no dialysis)	50%
Regular dialysis	100% after each dialysis

Additional information

- In general, the treatment of choice for oral candidiasis is *miconazole* or *nystatin*.
- The oral suspension is preferred formulation for the treatment of oral candidiasis
- Resistance to fluconazole is a problem and should be borne in mind in apparent cases of treatment failure
- Be aware of the potential for drug interactions with fluconazole.

⊕ Pharmacology

The mechanism of action of fluconazole is believed to be through an increase in the permeability of the cellular membrane. The resulting in damage leads to leakage of cellular contents and the prevention of uptake of essential molecules. Fluconazole is not greatly affected by enzyme induction/inhibition since the majority of a dose is excreted unchanged in the urine.

Flumazenil

Anexate® (POM)
Injection: 500 micrograms/5mL.

Generic (POM)
Injection: 500 micrograms/5mL.

Indications
● Reversal of sedative effects of benzodiazepines.

Contraindications and precautions
● Flumazenil is contraindicated in patients receiving a benzodiazepine for control of a potentially life-threatening condition (e.g. control of intracranial pressure or status epilepticus).
● Use with caution in epileptic patients receiving benzodiazepines as the abrupt cessation of effect may precipitate a seizure.
● Use with caution in patients with hepatic impairment (see 🕮 Dose adjustments).

☹ Adverse effects
The frequency is not defined, but reported adverse effects generally subside rapidly and include:
● Agitation/anxiety (if given too rapidly)
● Flushing
● Nausea
● Seizures (in patients with epilepsy or severe hepatic impairment)
● Vomiting.

Drug interactions
Pharmacokinetic
● None known.

Pharmacodynamic
● *Benzodiazepines*—reversal of effect.
● *Zolpidem/zopiclone*—reversal off effect.

♣ Dose
● 200 micrograms slow IV injection in 15 seconds.
● If desired level of consciousness is not obtained within 60 seconds, a further 100 micrograms IV should be given and repeated at 60-second intervals to a maximum dose of 1mg IV (or 2mg IV if in intensive care).
● Usual dose needed is 300–600 micrograms.

♣ Dose adjustments
Elderly
● No specific guidance available. Titrate dose to effect.

Hepatic/renal impairment
● No specific guidance is available for use in hepatic impairment. However, the manufacturer advises caution in hepatic impairment

due to the hepatic metabolism of flumazenil. In any event, the dose is titrated to effect.
- No dose adjustments are necessary in renal impairment.

Additional information
- If drowsiness recurs, an infusion of 100–400 micrograms per hour may be used. The rate of infusion is individually determined

◈ Pharmacology
Flumazenil antagonizes the actions of drugs that act via benzodiazepine receptors in the CNS.

Fluoxetine

Prozac® *(POM)*
Capsule: 20mg (30).
Liquid: 20mg/5mL (70mL).

Generic (POM)
Capsule: 20mg (30); 60mg (30).
Liquid: 20mg/5mL (70mL).

Indications

- Depression
- ¥Anxiety.[1]

Contraindications and precautions

- Do not use with an irreversible MAOI (including *rasagiline* and *selegiline*), or within 14 days of stopping one, or at least 24 hours after discontinuation of a reversible MAOI (e.g. moclobemide, linezolid). At least 5 weeks should elapse after discontinuing fluoxetine treatment before starting a MAOI. Note that in exceptional circumstances linezolid may be given with fluoxetine, but the patient must be closely monitored for symptoms of serotonin syndrome (see 📖 Box 1.10, p.18).
- Fluoxetine inhibits the metabolism of tamoxifen via CYP2D6 (reducing the concentration of the active metabolite, endoxifen). Wherever possible, avoid this combination.
- Depression is associated with an increased risk of suicidal thoughts, self-harm, and suicide which persists until remission. Note that that the risk of suicide may increase during initial treatment.
- Hyponatraemia should be considered in all patients who develop drowsiness, confusion, or convulsions while taking an antidepressant. Hyponatraemia has been associated with all types of antidepressants, although it is reportedly more common with SSRIs. Hyponatraemia/SIADH has been reported only very rarely with the use of mirtazapine.
- Use with caution in:
  - diabetes (alters glycaemic control)
  - elderly (greater risk of hyponatraemia)
  - epilepsy (lowers seizure threshold)
  - hepatic impairment (see 📖 Dose adjustments, p.221).
- May precipitate psychomotor restlessness, which usually appears during early treatment.
- Withdrawal symptoms can occur. Agitation, anxiety, asthenia (weakness), dizziness, headache, nausea/vomiting, sensory disturbances (e.g. paraesthesia), sleep disturbances (e.g. insomnia, intense dreams), and tremor are the most commonly reported reactions. They usually occur within the first few days of discontinuing treatment. Generally, these symptoms are self-limiting and usually resolve within 2 weeks, although some may persist for up to 3 months or longer. While it is advised that fluoxetine is gradually tapered over 1–2 weeks, it has a longer plasma half-life than other SSRIs and seems to be associated with a lower incidence of withdrawal symptoms; discontinuation without tapering can be considered. See 📖 Discontinuing and/or

switching antidepressants, p.45 for information about switching or stopping antidepressants.
- Fluoxetine may increase the risk of haemorrhage (see Drug interactions).
- It may modify reactions and patients should be advised not drive (or operate machinery) if affected. Refer to 📖 Drugs and driving, p.25.

☹ Adverse effects

Very common
- Diarrhoea
- Fatigue
- Headache
- Insomnia
- Nausea.

Common
- Abnormal dreams
- Anorexia
- Anxiety
- Appetite decreased
- Arthralgia
- Attention disorder
- Dizziness
- Drowsiness
- Dry mouth
- Dysgeusia
- Dyspepsia
- Hot flushes
- Hyperhidrosis
- Lethargy
- Palpitations
- Rash
- Restlessness
- Sexual dysfunction
- Sleep disorder
- Tremor
- Urticaria
- Visual disturbances
- Weight decrease
- Yawning.

Uncommon
- Alopecia
- Ataxia
- Dyskinesia
- Dysphagia
- Dyspnoea
- Dysuria
- Euphoria
- Hypotension
- Malaise
- Mydriaisis
- Myoclonus
- Psychomotor restlessness.

Rare
- Anaphylaxis
- Akathisia
- Hallucinations
- Pharyngitis
- Photosensitivity
- Urinary retention.

Unknown
- Abnormal LFTs
- Confusion
- Erythema multiforme
- Hepatitis
- Hyponatraemia/SIADH (a few case reports only)
- Myalgia
- Priapism
- Suicidal behaviour
- Serotonin syndrome
- Stevens–Johnson syndrome.

Drug interactions

The long elimination half-lives (plasma concentrations detectable for up to 5–6 weeks after withdrawal) of both fluoxetine and its metabolite, norfluoxetine, should be borne in mind when considering pharmacokinetic and/or pharmacodynamic drug interactions.

Pharmacokinetic

- Fluoxetine is a strong inhibitor of CYP2D6 and moderately inhibits CYP1A2 and CYP2C19. It is a substrate of CYP2C9 and CYP2D6. Co-administration with drugs that are metabolized by, or affect the activity (induction or inhibition—see 📖 inside back cover) of these pathways may lead to clinically relevant drug interactions and the prescriber should be aware that dosage adjustments may be necessary, particularly of drugs with a narrow therapeutic index.
- *Carbamazepine*—potential risk of carbamazepine toxicity possibly due to CYP2C19 inhibition. Possible reduction in effect of fluoxetine due to CYP2C9 induction.
- *Codeine*—reduced analgesic benefit due to CYP2D6 inhibition.
- *Fluconazole*—risk of fluoxetine toxicity due to inhibition of CYP2C9.
- *Haloperidol*—increased risk of adverse effects from both drugs due to CYP2D6 inhibition.
- *Risperidone*—increased risk of adverse effects due to CYP2D6 inhibition.
- *Phenytoin*—risk of phenytoin toxicity.
- *Tamoxifen*—possible reduced efficacy of tamoxifen; avoid combination.
- *Tramadol*—reduced analgesic benefit due to CYP2D6 inhibition.
- *TCAs*—metabolism may be inhibited by fluoxetine.

Pharmacodynamic

- Risk of serotonin syndrome (see 📖 Box 1.10, p.18) with:
  - MAOIs
  - Rasagiline
  - Selegiline
  - Serotonergic drugs—e.g. duloxetine, methadone, mirtazapine, TCAs, tramadol, and trazodone.
- *Anticoagulants*—potential increased risk of bleeding.
- *Antidiabetics*—increased risk of hypoglycaemia.
- *Carbamazepine*—increased risk of hyponatraemia.
- *Cyproheptadine*—may inhibit the effects of fluoxetine.
- *Diuretics*—increased risk of hyponatraemia.
- *NSAIDs*—increased risk of GI bleeding.

₃ Dose

Depression

- Initial dose 20mg PO OD, increased if necessary after 3–4 weeks of initiation of treatment and subsequently as judged clinically appropriate to a maximum of 60mg PO OD.

¥ *Anxiety*

- Initial dose 10mg PO OD. After 1 week, the dose can be increased to 20mg PO OD if necessary. The dose can be increased after several weeks if no clinical improvement is observed. The maximum dose is 60mg PO OD.

₃ Dose adjustments

Elderly

- No specific dose reductions are necessary, but the elderly may tolerate lower doses better. Generally, 40mg PO OD should not be exceeded.

Hepatic/renal impairment
- In significant liver impairment, a lower dose or alternate day dosing is recommended.
- A dose reduction is considered unnecessary in patients with impaired renal function.

Additional information
- Fluoxetine and norfluoxetine have long half-lives that may minimize the risk of withdrawal symptoms after sudden cessation of treatment. Gradual reduction of the dose is generally unnecessary. If, however, withdrawal symptoms are apparent, resuming the previous dose and instigating a more gradual withdrawal is advised.
- Fluoxetine should be administered as a single dose during or between meals. If adverse effects are troublesome, the dose can be divided. If insomnia is a particular problem, give the dose in the morning.
- The oral liquid formulations contain sucrose.

⊸ Pharmacology
Fluoxetine is a selective inhibitor of serotonin reuptake. It has almost no affinity for adrenergic, dopaminergic, histaminergic, muscarinic, or serotonergic receptors. Fluoxetine is well absorbed from the GI tract after oral administration. It is extensively metabolized by the polymorphic enzymes CYP2D6 and CYP2C8/9, with minor metabolic pathways involving several other isoenzymes (including CYP3A4). Fluoxetine also significantly inhibits CYP2D6, as well as moderately inhibiting CYP1A2 and CYP2C19. There is one active metabolite, norfluoxetine, which contributes to the overall pharmacodynamic profile of fluoxetine.

The elimination half-life of fluoxetine is 4–6 days and for norfluoxetine 4–16 days. These long half-lives are responsible for persistence of the drug for 5–6 weeks after discontinuation. Excretion is mainly (about 60%) via the kidney.

Flutamide

Generic (POM)
Tablet: 250mg (84).

Indications

- Advanced prostate cancer.

Contraindications and precautions

- Use with caution in hepatic impairment—flutamide is associated with hepatic toxicity.
- Must not be used in patients with serum transaminase levels exceeding 2–3 times the upper limit of normal.
- LFTs should be checked monthly for first 4 months of treatment and periodically thereafter.
- Patient should be advised to seek medical attention at the first sign or symptom of liver impairment (e.g. pruritus, dark urine, jaundice).
- Avoid excessive alcohol consumption.
- Avoid combination with CYP1A2 inhibitors (see 📖 Drug interactions).

☺ Adverse effects

Very common
- Galactorrhoea
- Gynaecomastia

Common
- Diarrhoea
- Drowsiness
- Increased appetite
- Insomnia
- Nausea
- Vomiting.

Rare
- Anxiety
- Depression
- Dizziness
- Lymphoedema
- Oedema
- Visual disturbance.

Drug interactions

Pharmacokinetic
- Is metabolized by CYP1A2 to an active metabolite. Co-administration with drugs that are metabolized by, or affect the activity (induction or inhibition—see 📖 inside back cover) of this pathway may lead to clinically relevant drug interactions and the prescriber should be aware that dosage adjustments may be necessary, particularly of drugs with a narrow therapeutic index.
- *Theophylline*—cases of theophylline toxicity reported.

Pharmacodynamic
- None known.

💊 Dose

- 250mg PO TDS.

₰ Dose adjustments

Elderly

- No dose adjustments are necessary.

Hepatic/renal impairment

- No specific guidance is available for use in hepatic impairment. The manufacturer advises flutamide should only be administered after careful assessment of the individual benefits and risks.
- No specific guidance is available for use in renal impairment. The manufacturer does not make a recommendation for dose adjustments. It is highly protein bound and unlikely to be removed by dialysis.

Additional information

- Although tablets may be crushed and dispersed in water prior to administration, it is not recommended to be performed due to the risk of exposure.

⊕ Pharmacology

Flutamide is a non-steroidal anti-androgen that blocks the action of androgens of adrenal and testicular origin which stimulate the growth of normal and malignant prostatic tissue. It is completely absorbed following oral administration and is highly protein bound. Flutamide is extensively metabolized by CYP1A2 to an active metabolite. The metabolites are eliminated via the kidneys and bile.

Furosemide

Lasix® (POM)
Injection: 20mg/2mL (10).

Generic (POM)
Tablet: 20mg (8); 40mg (28); 500mg (28).
Oral solution (sugar-free): 20mg/5mL (150mL); 40mg/5mL (150mL); 50mg/5mL (150mL).
Injection: 20mg/2mL; 50mg/5mL; 250mg/25mL.

Indications

- Management of oedema associated with CHF, cirrhosis of the liver, or renal disease.
- Resistant hypertension.
- ✤Malignant ascites.[1,2]

Contraindications and precautions

- Refer to 📖 Use of drugs in end-of-life care, p.53 for end-of-life care issues.
- Furosemide is contraindicated for use in the following conditions:
  - anuria
  - dehydration
  - drug-induced renal failure
  - hypersensitivity to sulphonamides
  - hypovolaemia
  - severe hypokalaemia or hyponatraemia.
- The manufacturers of risperidone advise against concurrent use with furosemide due to increased risk of mortality.
- Use with caution in the following:
  - bladder outflow obstruction (risk of urinary retention)
  - diabetes (may cause hyperglycaemia)
  - gout
  - hepatorenal syndrome
  - hypotension
  - nephrotic syndrome (the effect of furosemide may be reduced and its ototoxicity potentiated)
  - patients at risk of electrolyte imbalance
  - prostatic hypertrophy (risk of urinary retention)
  - Oral solutions may contain up to 10% v/v of alcohol.

☺ Adverse effects

The frequency is not defined, but reported adverse effects include:

- Arrhythmias
- Confusion
- Diarrhoea
- Dizziness
- Electrolyte disturbances (e.g. hyponatraemia, hypokalaemia, hypomagnesaemia, hypocalcaemia)
- Headache
- Hyperglycaemia (less common than with thiazides)
- Hyperuricaemia (and gout)
- Hypotension
- Muscle cramps
- Muscle weakness
- Nausea
- Tetany
- Thirst
- Vomiting.

Other reported, rare adverse effects include:
- Aplastic anaemia
- Bone marrow depression
- Hypersensitivity manifested as skin reactions, dermatitis
- Pancreatitis
- Paraesthesia
- Tinnitus and deafness (especially associated with over-rapid IV injection/infusion).

Drug interactions
Pharmacokinetic
- *Phenytoin*—effect of furosemide reduced, possibly through an unknown effect on absorption.
- *Sucralfate*—reduced absorption of furosemide; not be taken within 2 hours of each other.

Pharmacodynamic
- *ACEIs*—increased risk of hypotension.
- *Aminoglycosides*—furosemide may increase nephrotoxicity.
- *Antihypertensives*—increased risk of hypotension.
- *Antipsychotics*—increased risk of hypotension with certain antipsychotics.
- *β_2-agonists*—increased risk of hypokalaemia.
- *Baclofen*—increased risk of hypotension.
- *Bisphosphonates*—risk of hypocalcaemia and dehydration.
- *Corticosteroids*—increased risk of hypokalaemia; diuretic effect reduced.
- *Digoxin*—hypokalaemia increases toxicity.
- *NSAIDs*—reduced diuretic effect; risk of renal impairment increased.
- *Reboxetine*—increased risk of hypokalaemia.
- *Theophylline*—increased risk of hypokalaemia.

Unknown
- *Risperidone*—increased risk of death in elderly patients with dementia.

⚕ Dose
Oral
- Oral doses should be administered in the morning to avoid nocturnal diuresis.
Oedema
- Initial dose 40mg PO OM. Typical maintenance doses range from 20–40mg PO OD. In resistant cases, this may be increased to 80–120mg PO OM. Higher doses may be required.
- ¥Alternatively, 20–40mg SL OM (using tablet formulation) may be used

Resistant hypertension
- 40–80mg PO OM. Higher doses may be required.

¥ Ascites
- Use only in combination with spironolactone (see 🕮 Spironolactone, p.500).
- Initial dose 40mg PO OM. Typical maintenance dose 20–40mg PO OM. In resistant cases, this may be increased to 160mg PO OM, or higher in refractory cases.

Parenteral

IV furosemide must be injected or infused slowly; a rate of 4mg/min must not be exceeded.

Oedema

- By IM or slow IV injection 20–50mg increased if necessary in steps of 20mg, not more frequently than every 2 hours. Doses above 50mg should be administered via slow IV infusion. Maximum 1.5g daily.
- ⚥Alternatively, 20–140mg via CSCI over 24 hours can be used for management of end-stage CHF.

⚥ Dose adjustments

Elderly

- No specific guidance is available, but the dose should be titrated until the required response is achieved.

Hepatic/renal impairment

- Patients with hepatic impairment are more at risk of encephalopathy due to hypokalaemia so other diuretics may be more appropriate
- Patients with renal impairment may require higher doses (furosemide must be excreted in order to exert its effect).

Additional information

- Diuresis normally starts within 1 hour of oral administration and is regarded as complete after 6 hours.
- The kidney appears to develop tolerance to furosemide for 6 hours post-diuresis. It should therefore be given as a single daily dose in the morning *unless* the patient has an indwelling urinary catheter, when it can be given twice daily (12 hours apart).
- Furosemide injection has an alkaline pH, so is unlikely to be compatible with many drugs. It is advisable to use a separate CSCI. However, furosemide is compatible with dexamethasone via CSCI.

⚥ Pharmacology

Furosemide is a loop diuretic, which acts by inhibiting reabsorption of sodium and chloride in the ascending limb of the loop of Henle leading to an increased excretion of water and sodium. Its mechanism of action involves the inhibition of a Na/K/Cl co-transport system. Potassium secretion from the distal convoluted tubule is also increased due to the exchange of potassium for sodium. Furosemide also increases the excretion of bicarbonate, calcium, hydrogen, magnesium, and phosphate.

References

1. Smith EM, Jayson GC. The current and future management of malignant ascites. *Clin Oncol* 2003; **15**(2):59–72.
2. Moore KP, Aithal GP. Guidelines on the management of ascites in cirrhosis. *Gut* 2006; **55**(Suppl 6):vi1–12.

Gabapentin

Neurontin® (POM)
Capsule: 100mg (100); 300mg (100); 400mg (100).
Tablet (scored): 600mg (100); 800mg (100).

Generic (POM)
Capsule: 100mg (100); 300mg (100); 400mg (100).
Tablet: 600mg (100); 800mg (100).
Oral suspension/solution: 250mg/5mL (see 📖 Additional information, p.231 for supply issues).

Indications

- Monotherapy and adjunctive treatment of partial seizures with or without secondary generalization
- Peripheral neuropathic pain
- *Hiccups[1]
- *Insomnia[2]
- *Malignant bone pain (see 📖 Additional information, p.231)[3]
- *Pruritus[4]
- *Restless leg syndrome[5]
- *Sweats.[6]

Contraindications and precautions

- Avoid sudden withdrawal. Independent of indication, discontinue gradually over at least 1 week in order to avoid adverse effects such as nausea, vomiting, flu syndrome, anxiety, and insomnia. These withdrawal effects have been reported even after short-term use.
- Caution in elderly and renal impairment—dosage adjustments may be necessary (see 📖 Dose adjustments, p.230).
- Use with caution in patients with CHF.
- Diabetic patients may need to adjust hypoglycaemic treatment as weight gain occurs.
- Severe, life-threatening, systemic hypersensitivity reactions such as Drug rash with eosinophilia and systemic symptoms (DRESS) have been reported with gabapentin. The patient should be advised to report early manifestations of hypersensitivity, such as fever or lymphadenopathy (with or without a rash) immediately.
- If affected by drowsiness and dizziness, patients should be warned about driving. Refer to 📖 Drugs and driving, p.25.

☺ Adverse effects

Very common

- Ataxia
- Dizziness
- Drowsiness
- Fatigue
- Pyrexia
- Viral infection.

Common

- Abdominal pain
- Abnormal thoughts
- Amnesia
- Anorexia
- Arthralgia
- Confusion
- Constipation
- Cough

- Depression
- Diarrhoea
- Dry mouth
- Dyspepsia
- Dyspnoea
- Erectile dysfunction
- Flatulence
- Gingivitis
- Headache
- Hostility
- Impotence
- Increased appetite

- Infection (chest, ear, UTI)
- Insomnia
- Leucopenia
- Nausea/vomiting
- Oedema (facial, peripheral)
- Pruritus
- Tremor
- Vertigo
- Vomiting
- Visual disturbances
- Weight gain.

Unknown

- Acute pancreatitis
- Acute renal failure
- Angio-oedema
- Breast hypertrophy
- Dyskinesia
- Dystonia
- Hallucinations
- Hypersensitivity reactions
  (e.g. fever, hepatitis,
  lymphadenopathy, rash)

- Jaundice
- Pancreatitis
- Stevens–Johnson syndrome
- Thrombocytopenia
- Tinnitus.

Drug interactions

Pharmacokinetic

- Avoid taking *antacid* medication within 2 hours of gabapentin (may reduce bioavailability by 20% or more).
- *Morphine* and *other opioids* may increase the absorption of gabapentin.
- The clinical significance of these interactions is unknown but the prescriber should be aware of the potential for interactions and that dosage adjustments may be necessary.

Pharmacodynamic

- *CNS depressants*—increased risk of CNS adverse effects.
- *Opioids*—possible opioid-sparing effect, necessitating opioid dose review.

⚕ Dose

Pain/epilepsy

- The licensed schedule is shown in Table 3.14. This may be poorly tolerated by elderly patients or those with cancer, and for these patients, a more cautious titration is suggested. Whichever strategy is adopted, adverse effects are more common around the time of dose escalation but usually resolve in a few weeks. The slower titration may be preferred in the elderly or cancer population, although it may take longer appreciate the therapeutic benefit.

¥ Hiccups

- Initial dose 100mg PO TDS and increase as necessary up to 600mg PO TDS. Treatment should be reviewed once hiccups have resolved.

¥ Insomnia

- Initial dose 100mg PO ON. Increase as necessary, or as tolerated, up to a usual maximum of 600mg PO ON.

¥ *Pruritus*
- Titrate as for pain (see Table 3.14) to a daily maximum of 1800mg.

¥ *Restless legs syndrome*
- Initial dose 300mg PO BD, increasing by 300mg BD as necessary every 2 weeks, to a maximum of 1200mg PO BD.
- A more cautious approach may be warranted in patients taking opioids or other CNS depressants (e.g. initial dose of 100mg PO ON).

¥ *Sweats*
- Titrate as for pain (see Table 3.14) to a maximum of 900mg daily.

Table 3.14 Licensed and suggested dose schedules for gabapentin

	Licensed dose		Suggested dose
Day 1	300mg PO ON	**Day 1**	100mg PO ON
Day 2	300mg PO BD	**Day 2**	100mg PO BD
Day 3	300mg PO TDS	**Day 3**	100mg PO TDS
Increase by 300mg PO OD according to response up to a maximum of 1200mg PO TDS		Increase by 100mg PO TDS every 2 days as needed to a maximum of 1200mg PO TDS	

Dose adjustments

Elderly
- May require a more cautious titration as described earlier, or may need a dose reduction due to renal impairment.

Renal impairment
- Dose adjustments are necessary for patients in renal failure or undergoing haemodialysis, as shown in Table 3.15. Adjust the starting dose as necessary.
- For patients undergoing haemodialysis:
  - anuric patients—initial loading dose of 300–400mg, then 200–300mg of gabapentin following each 4 hours of haemodialysis. On dialysis-free days, there should be no treatment with gabapentin
  - renally impaired patients—dose as per Table 3.15, based on creatinine clearance. An additional 200–300mg dose following each 4-hour haemodialysis treatment is recommended.

Table 3.15 Dose adjustments of pregabalin according to renal impairment

Creatinine clearance (mL/min)	Maximum dose
≥80	1200mg PO TDS
50–79	600mg PO TDS
30–49	300mg PO TDS
15–29	300mg PO OD
<15	300mg PO ALT DIE–OD

Additional information

- Gabapentin oral suspension/solution is available as a special order from various suppliers (e.g. Martindale Pharma 01277 266600; Rosemont Pharmaceuticals Ltd 0800 919 312).
- In the absence of a suspension, gabapentin capsules can be opened and the contents dispersed in water or fruit juice immediately prior to use.
- Neuropathic pain should improve within 1 week.
- There may be a reduction in anxiety within a few weeks, although the effect is not as pronounced as pregabalin.
- Some patients may respond to a BD regimen.
- With high doses, increasing the dosing frequency can improve tolerance and possibly effect due to the saturable nature of absorption.
- There may be an improvement is sleep, but the effect does not appear as pronounced as pregabalin.
- Malignant bone pain has been shown to be multifactorial in origin, with both inflammatory and neuropathic features.

♦ Pharmacology

Gabapentin was originally developed as an agonist of the $GABA_A$ receptor, but it is actually devoid of GABA effects. The analgesic benefit of gabapentin is due to its affinity for the $\alpha 2\delta$ subunit of N and P/Q voltage-dependent calcium channels. Gabapentin binds to the $\alpha 2\delta$ subunit, effectively closing the channel and preventing the release of neurotransmitters and modulators. Gabapentin is readily absorbed after oral administration, although the mechanism of absorption is saturable within the normal dosing range. Therefore increasing the dose does not proportionally increase the amount absorbed. Gabapentin is largely excreted unchanged in the urine, so dose adjustment is needed in renal impairment.

References

1. Porzio G, Aielli F, Verna L, et al. Gabapentin in the treatment of hiccups in patients with advanced cancer: a 5-year experience. Clin Neuropharmacol 2010; 33(4):179–80.
2. Lo HS, Yang CM, Lo HG, et al. Treatment effects of gabapentin for primary insomnia. Clin Neuropharmacol 2010; 33(2):84–90.
3. Caraceni A, Zecca E, Martini C, et al. Gabapentin for breakthrough pain due to bone metastases. Palliat Med 2008; 22(4):392–3.
4. Vila T, Gommer J, Scates AC. Role of gabapentin in the treatment of uremic pruritus. Ann Pharmacother 2008; 42(7):1080–4.
5. Happe S, Sauter C, Klösch G, et al. Gabapentin versus ropinirole in the treatment of idiopathic restless legs syndrome. Neuropsychobiology 2003; 48(2):82–6.
6. Porzio G, Aielli F, Verna L, et al. Gabapentin in the treatment of severe sweating experienced by advanced cancer patients. Support Care Cancer 2006; 14(4):389–91.

Gliclazide

Standard release
Diamicron® (POM)
Tablet (scored): 80mg (60).

Generic (POM)
Tablet: 40mg (28); 80mg (28).

Modified release
Diamicron® MR (POM)
Tablet: 30mg (28; 56).

Generic (POM)
Tablet: 30mg (28; 56).

Indications
• Type 2 diabetes mellitus.

Contraindications and precautions
• Gliclazide is contraindicated for use in the following:
  • concurrent use of miconazole (see 📖 Drug interactions)
  • diabetic ketoacidosis
  • diabetic pre-coma and coma
  • hypersensitivity to sulphonylurea or sulphonamides
  • severe hepatic impairment (see 📖 Dose adjustments, p.233)
  • severe renal impairment (see 📖 Dose adjustments, p.233)
  • type 1 diabetes.
• Use with caution in patients with hepatic and/or renal impairment (see 📖 Dose adjustments, p.233).
• The risk of hypoglycaemia increases with:
  • adrenal insufficiency
  • hepatic impairment
  • hypopituitarism
  • renal impairment.
• Patients must have a regular carbohydrate intake, avoid skipping meals and ensure a balance between physical exercise and carbohydrate intake.
• Patients should be aware of the symptoms of hypoglycaemia and be careful about driving and the use of machinery.

☺ Adverse effects
The frequency is not defined, but reported adverse effects include:
• Diarrhoea
• Dizziness
• Headache
• Hepatitis
• Hypoglycaemia (especially if meals skipped; dose dependent)
• Hyponatraemia
• Jaundice
• Nausea
• Nervousness
• Transient visual disturbances
• Vomiting.

Drug interactions
Pharmacokinetic
• The metabolism of gliclazide appears to be mediated mainly via CYP2C9. Co-administration with drugs that are metabolized by, or

affect the activity (induction or inhibition—see 📖 inside back cover) of this pathway may lead to clinically relevant drug interactions and the prescriber should be aware that dosage adjustments may be necessary, particularly of drugs with a narrow therapeutic index.

- *Miconazole*—contraindicated for use (enhanced hypoglycaemic effect, presumably CYP2C9 inhibition).

Pharmacodynamic

- *ACEIs*—increased risk of hypoglycaemia.
- *β_2-agonists*—hypoglycaemic effect may be antagonized.
- *Corticosteroids*—hypoglycaemic effect antagonized.
- *Diuretics*—hypoglycaemic effect may be antagonized.
- *Fluoxetine*—increased risk of hypoglycaemia.
- *Warfarin*—increased anticoagulant effect.

₷ Dose

Standard release

- Initial dose, 40–80mg PO OD. Dose can be increased as necessary up to 160mg as a single daily dose, with breakfast. Higher doses must be administered in divided doses. Maximum dose 320mg daily.

Modified release

- Initial dose 30mg PO OD with breakfast. Dose can be adjusted according to response every 4 weeks, or after 2 weeks if no decrease in blood glucose. Maximum dose 120mg daily.

Note: *Diamicron*® MR 30mg may be considered to be approximately equivalent in therapeutic effect to standard formulation *Diamicron*® 80mg.

₷ Dose adjustments

Elderly

- Usual adult doses can be used. Dose should be titrated to effect.

Hepatic/renal impairment

- Care should be exercised in patients with hepatic and/or renal impairment and a smaller initial dose should be used with careful patient monitoring. Dose should be titrated to effect.
- Patients with mild to moderate renal impairment may use the usual dosing regimen for *Diamicron*® MR with careful patient monitoring.
- In severe hepatic and renal impairment, insulin therapy should be used.

Additional information

- Standard release tablets can be crushed and dispersed in water immediately prior to use.

☼ Pharmacology

Gliclazide is a sulphonylurea which stimulates β-cells of the islet of Langerhans in the pancreas to release insulin. It also enhances peripheral insulin sensitivity. It restores the first peak of insulin secretion in response to glucose and increases the second phase of insulin secretion. The metabolism of many sulphonylureas is catalysed by CYP2C9. While this has not been categorically shown for gliclazide, drug interactions would suggest this is the case.

Glimepiride

Amaryl® (POM)
Tablet (scored): 1mg (30); 2mg (30); 3mg (30); 4mg (30).

Generic (POM)
Tablet: 1mg (30); 2mg (30); 3mg (30); 4mg (30).

Indications
- Type 2 diabetes mellitus.

Contraindications and precautions
- Glimepiride is contraindicated for use in the following:
  - diabetic ketoacidosis
  - diabetic pre-coma and coma
  - hypersensitivity to sulphonylurea or sulphonamides
  - severe hepatic impairment (see 📖 Dose adjustments, p.235)
  - severe renal impairment (see 📖 Dose adjustments, p.235)
  - type 1 diabetes.
- Use with caution in patients with:
  - concomitant use of CYP2C9 inducers/inhibitors (see 📖 Drug interactions, p.235)
  - G6PD deficiency
  - hepatic and/or renal impairment (see 📖 Dose adjustments, p.235).
- The risk of hypoglycaemia increases with:
  - adrenal insufficiency
  - hepatic impairment
  - hypopituitarism
  - renal impairment.
- Patients must have a regular carbohydrate intake, avoid skipping meals, and ensure a balance between physical exercise and carbohydrate intake.
- The manufacturer recommends regular hepatic and haematological monitoring (especially leucocytes and thrombocytes) during treatment.
- Patients should be aware of the symptoms of hypoglycaemia and be careful about driving and the use of machinery.

☺ Adverse effects
Rare
- Blood dyscrasias (e.g. thrombocytopenia, agranulocytosis, haemolytic anaemia)
- Hypoglycaemia (especially if meals skipped; dose dependent).

Very rare
- Abdominal pain
- Cholestatic jaundice
- Diarrhoea
- Hypersensitivity reaction (with associated dyspnoea, hypotension)
- Hyponatraemia
- Nausea
- Vomiting.

Unknown
- Pruritus
- Rash
- Transient visual disturbances.

Drug interactions

Pharmacokinetic
- Glimepiride is a substrate of CYP2C9. Co-administration with drugs that are metabolized by, or affect the activity (induction or inhibition—see 📖 inside back cover) of this pathway may lead to clinically relevant drug interactions and the prescriber should be aware that dosage adjustments may be necessary, particularly of drugs with a narrow therapeutic index.
- *Fluconazole*—increases plasma concentration of glimepiride.

Pharmacodynamic
- *ACEIs*—increased risk of hypoglycaemia.
- *β_2-agonists*—hypoglycaemic effect may be antagonized.
- *Corticosteroids*—hypoglycaemic effect antagonized.
- *Diuretics*—hypoglycaemic effect may be antagonized.
- *Fluoxetine*—increased risk of hypoglycaemia.
- *Warfarin*—increased anticoagulant effect.

🥄 Dose
- Initial dose 1mg PO OD taken shortly before or during the first main meal. The dose can be increased by 1mg daily every 1–2 weeks to a usual maximum of 4mg PO OD. A dose of 6mg PO OD can be used in exceptional cases.

🥄 Dose adjustments
Elderly
- Usual adult doses can be used and the dose should be titrated to effect.

Hepatic/renal impairment
- Care should be exercised in patients with hepatic and/or renal impairment. Dose should be titrated to effect.
- Glimepiride should be avoided in patients with severe hepatic and/or renal impairment and insulin treatment should be initiated.

Additional information
- Tablets can be crushed and dispersed in water immediately prior to administration if necessary.

⟜ Pharmacology
Glimepiride is a sulphonylurea which stimulates β-cells of the islet of Langerhans in the pancreas to release insulin. It also enhances peripheral insulin sensitivity. It restores the first peak of insulin secretion in response to glucose and increases the second phase of insulin secretion. The metabolism of glimepiride is catalysed by CYP2C9.

Glipizide

Minodiab® (POM)
Tablet: 5mg (28).

Generic (POM)
Tablet: 5mg (56).

Indications
• Type 2 diabetes mellitus.

Contraindications and precautions
• Glipizide is contraindicated for use in the following:
  • concurrent use of miconazole (see 🕮 Drug interactions)
  • diabetic ketoacidosis
  • diabetic pre-coma and coma
  • hypersensitivity to sulphonylurea or sulphonamides
  • severe hepatic impairment (see 🕮 Dose adjustments, p.237)
  • severe renal impairment (see 🕮 Dose adjustments, p.237)
  • type 1 diabetes.
• Use with caution in patients with hepatic and/or renal impairment (see
  🕮 Dose adjustments, p.237).
• The risk of hypoglycaemia increases with:
  • adrenal insufficiency
  • hepatic impairment
  • hypopituitarism
  • renal impairment.
• Patients must have a regular carbohydrate intake, avoid skipping meals,
  and ensure a balance between physical exercise and carbohydrate intake.
• Patients should be aware of the symptoms of hypoglycaemia and be
  careful about driving and the use of machinery.

☺ Adverse effects
The frequency is not defined, but reported adverse effects include:
• Cholestatic jaundice
• Diarrhoea
• Dizziness
• Drowsiness
• Headache
• Hypoglycaemia (especially if meals skipped; dose dependent)
• Hyponatraemia
• Nausea
• Nervousness
• Transient visual disturbances
• Vomiting.

Drug interactions
Pharmacokinetic
• Glipizide is a substrate of CYP2C9. Co-administration with drugs that
  are metabolized by, or affect the activity (induction or inhibition—see

📖 inside back cover) of this pathway may lead to clinically relevant drug interactions and the prescriber should be aware that dosage adjustments may be necessary, particularly of drugs with a narrow therapeutic index.
- *Miconazole*—contraindicated for use (enhanced hypoglycaemic effect, presumably CYP2C9 inhibition).

Pharmacodynamic
- *ACEIs*—increased risk of hypoglycaemia.
- *β_2-agonists*—hypoglycaemic effect may be antagonized.
- *Corticosteroids*—hypoglycaemic effect antagonized.
- *Diuretics*—hypoglycaemic effect may be antagonized.
- *Fluoxetine*—increased risk of hypoglycaemia.
- *Warfarin*—increased anticoagulant effect.

Dose
- Initial dose 2.5–5mg PO OD, taken before breakfast or lunch. The dose can be increased as necessary by 2.5–5mg PO OD over several days. The maximum recommended single dose is 15mg PO daily; doses above 15mg should be divided. The maximum daily dose is 20mg.

Dose adjustments
Elderly
- Usual adult doses can be used, although the elderly are more susceptible to adverse effects. The initial dose should be 2.5mg PO OD and should be titrated to effect.

Hepatic/renal impairment
- Care should be exercised in patients with hepatic and/or renal impairment and a smaller initial dose should be used with careful patient monitoring. Dose should be titrated to effect.
- Glipizide should be avoided in patients with severe hepatic and/or renal impairment and insulin treatment should be initiated.

Additional information
- Tablets can be crushed and dispersed in water immediately prior to administration if necessary.

Pharmacology
Glipizide is a sulphonylurea which stimulates β-cells of the islet of Langerhans in the pancreas to release insulin. It also enhances peripheral insulin sensitivity. It restores the first peak of insulin secretion in response to glucose and increases the second phase of insulin secretion. The metabolism of many sulphonylureas is catalysed by CYP2C9.

Glyceryl trinitrate

Rectogesic® (POM)
Rectal ointment: glyceryl trinitrate 0.4% (30g).

Unlicensed Special (POM)
Rectal ointment: glyceryl trinitrate 0.2% (20g).
See 📖 Additional information, p.240 for supply issues.

Generic (P)
Sublingual tablet: 300 micrograms (100); 500 micrograms (100); 600 micrograms (100)
Note: tablets should be stored in the original container and discarded 8 weeks from opening.
Aerosol spray: 400 micrograms/metered dose (200).
Transdermal patch: 5mg/24 hours (28); 10mg/24 hours (28); 15mg/24 hours (28).
Various proprietary formulations are available (see current *BNF*).

Indications
- Anal fissure
- Angina (*not discussed*)
- Smooth muscle spasm pain (e.g. anus, oesophagus, rectum).¥

Contraindications and precautions
- Contraindicated for use in the following:
  - aortic and/or mitral stenosis
  - closed-angle glaucoma
  - concomitant use with phosphodiesterase inhibitors (e.g. sildenafil, tadalafil, or vardenafil)
  - constrictive pericarditis
  - extreme bradycardia
  - G6PD-deficiency
  - hypertrophic obstructive cardiomyopathy
  - hypotensive shock
  - migraine or recurrent headache
  - severe anaemia
  - severe hypotension (systolic BP <90mmHg)
- Use with caution in the patients with:
  - hypothermia
  - hypothyroidism
  - malnutrition
  - recent history of myocardial infarction
  - severe hepatic impairment
  - severe renal impairment
  - susceptibility to angle-closure glaucoma.
- Note that transdermal patches that contain metal must be removed before an MRI (to avoid burns).

- Tolerance can rapidly develop with long-acting or transdermal nitrates with consequential loss of effect. This can be prevented by adopting a 'nitrate free' period of 4–8 hours each day.
- Dry mouth may reduce the effectiveness of transmucosal GTN.
- Can exacerbate the hypotensive effects of other drugs (see 📖 Drug interactions).
- GTN may cause dizziness, light-headedness, and blurred vision especially on first use. Patients should be advised not drive (or operate machinery) if affected.

😬 Adverse effects

Very common
- Headache (throbbing).

Common
- Dizziness
- Facial flushing
- Nausea
- Weakness.

Uncommon
- Diarrhoea (rectal formulation)
- Anal discomfort (rectal formulation)
- Vomiting (rectal formulation)
- Rectal bleeding (rectal formulation)
- Oral discomfort e.g. stinging, burning (oral formulations).

Rare
- Tachycardia.

Drug interactions

Pharmacokinetic
- None known.

Pharmacodynamic
- *Alcohol*—potentiates the hypotensive effect of GTN.
- *Heparin*—the anticoagulant effect may be reduced by GTN; dose adjustment may be necessary.
- The risk of hypotension is increased if GTN is taken concurrently with the following drugs:
  - β-blockers
  - calcium antagonists
  - diuretics
  - haloperidol
  - levomepromazine
  - opioids
  - phosphodiesterase inhibitors (e.g. sildenafil, tadalafil, or vardenafil)
  - TCAs.

💊 Dose

Anal fissure
- Apply a small amount (approximately 2.5cm) intra-anally BD until the pain improves or for a maximum of 8 weeks.

¥ *Oesophageal spasm*
- 400–500 micrograms SL 5–15min before food.
- If the tablet is used, it can be removed once the pain has subsided.

¥ *Rectal pain*
- Apply a small amount (~2.5cm) PR BD; do not use for more than 8 weeks.

♪ Dose adjustments
Elderly
- No dose adjustment necessary.

Liver/renal impairment
- No specific guidance available. Manufacturers advise caution in patients with severe hepatic and/or renal impairment.

Additional information
- The rectal ointment should be applied using a finger covering, such as cling film.
- Rectal ointment 0.2% is an unlicensed special and is available from Queens Medical Centre, Nottingham (0115 875 4521)

♦ Pharmacology
GTN is converted to nitric oxide (NO) *in vivo* which causes a cascade of intracellular events resulting in the subsequent release of calcium ions and relaxation of smooth muscle cells.

Glycopyrronium

Robinul® (POM)
Injection: 200 micrograms/mL (10 × 1mL; 10 × 3mL).
Powder: 3g.

Generic (POM)
Injection: 200 micrograms/mL (10 × 1mL; 10 × 3mL).

Unlicensed (POM)
Tablet (scored): 1mg; 2mg.
Oral solution: various strengths (prepared from injection, powder or tablets).
See 📖 Additional information, p.242 for supply issues.

Indications
- *Hypersalivation[1]
- *Nausea and vomiting (associated with bowel obstruction)[2]
- *Smooth muscle spasm (e.g. bowel colic)[2]
- *Terminal secretions,[3]

Contraindications and precautions
- Refer to 📖 Use of drugs in end-of-life care, p.53 for end-of-life care issues.
- No absolute contraindications. However, it has potent peripheral anticholinergic activity and can predispose to tachycardia.
- Use with caution in patients with:
  - bladder outflow obstruction
  - cardiac arrhythmias
  - CHF
  - coronary artery disease
  - hypertension
  - myasthenia gravis (particularly larger doses)
  - narrow angle glaucoma
  - paralytic ileus
  - pyrexia (reduces sweating)
  - renal impairment (see 📖 Dosage adjustment, p.242)
  - thyrotoxicosis.
- Glycopyrronium may modify reactions and patients should be advised not drive (or operate machinery) if affected.

☺ Adverse effects
The frequency is not defined, but reported adverse effects include
- Confusion
- Difficulty in micturition
- Dizziness
- Drowsiness
- Dry mouth
- Inhibition of sweating
- Palpitations
- Tachycardia
- Visual disturbances.

Drug interactions

Pharmacokinetic
- Undergoes minimal hepatic metabolism; mostly excreted unchanged by the kidneys.
- No recognized pharmacokinetic interactions.

Pharmacodynamic
- β_2 *agonists*—increased risk of tachycardia.
- *Cyclizine*—increased risk of anticholinergic adverse effects.
- *Domperidone*—may inhibit prokinetic effect.
- *Metoclopramide*—may inhibit prokinetic effect.
- *Nefopam*—increased risk of anticholinergic adverse effects.
- *TCAs*—increased risk of anticholinergic adverse effects.

Dose

¥ *Hypersalivation*
- Initial dose 200 micrograms PO TDS and increase every 2–3 days as necessary up to 1mg PO TDS. Higher doses have been used (e.g. 2mg PO TDS).

¥ *Nausea and vomiting/smooth muscle spasm/terminal secretions*
- Initial dose 200microgram SC PRN, or 600micrograms via CSCI over 24 hours.
- Dose can be increased to a maximum of 2.4mg via CSCI over 24 hours.

Dose adjustments

Elderly
- No specific guidance available. Use the lowest effective dose as the elderly may be more susceptible to the adverse effects.

Hepatic/renal impairment
- No specific guidance available. However, glycopyrronium accumulates in renal impairment, so dosage adjustments will be necessary.

Additional information
- Glycopyrronium tablets can be imported as unlicensed products via IDIS (Tel: 01932 824 000; ⌂ http://www.idispharma.com).
- Glycopyrronium oral solution can 1mg/5mL can be ordered as a special from the pharmacy manufacturing unit at Huddersfield (Tel: 01484 355388).
- Alternatively, an oral solution can be prepared in several ways. For immediate use, the contents of the ampoule can be administered orally or via a percutaneous endoscopic gastrostomy (using a filter needle). The tablets can also be dispersed in water prior to administration. Alternatively, a 1mg/10mL oral solution can be prepared from the powder (this can be stored in a refrigerator for 7 days).
- The stability of glycopyrronium is affected above pH 6 as ester hydrolysis can occur. There are incompatibility issues with dexamethasone, dimenhydrinate and phenobarbital.

- Via CSCI, glycopyrronium is reportedly compatible with alfentanil, clonazepam, diamorphine, haloperidol, hydromorphone, levomepromazine, metoclopramide, midazolam, octreotide, ondansetron, oxycodone, promethazine, ranitidine, and tramadol.
- There may be concentration-dependent compatibility issues with cyclizine (but less so than with hyoscine butylbromide-cyclizine)

◈ Pharmacology

Glycopyrronium is a quaternary ammonium antimuscarinic that inhibits the peripheral actions of acetylcholine (e.g. smooth muscle, cardiac muscle, AV node, exocrine glands). At higher doses, it may also block nicotinic receptors. Due to the polarity of the quaternary compound, it does not readily cross the blood–brain barrier and is unlikely to produce symptoms such as sedation, or paradoxical agitation (see 📖 Hyoscine hydrobromide, p.256). However, it does not have a direct anti-emetic action like hyoscine hydrobromide. Glycopyrronium is mainly excreted unchanged by the kidneys and lower doses may be required in renal impairment.

References

1. Arbouw MEL, Movig KLL, Koopmann M, et al. Glycopyrrolate for sialorrhea in Parkinson disease: a randomized, double-blind, crossover trial. Neurology 2010; 74(15):1203–7.
2. Davis MP, Furste A. Glycopyrrolate: a useful drug in the palliation of mechanical bowel obstruction. J Pain Symptom Manage 1999; 18(3):153–4.
3. Hugel H, Ellershaw J, Gambles M. Respiratory tract secretions in the dying patient: a comparison between glycopyrronium and hyoscine hydrobromide. J Pall Med 2006; 9(2):279–84.

Granisetron

Kytril® (POM)
Tablet: 1mg (10); 2mg (5).

Generic (POM)
Injection: 1mg/mL (5).

Indications

- Nausea and vomiting (induced by chemotherapy or radiotherapy)
- ¥Nausea and vomiting (e.g. drug-induced, cancer-related, refractory).[1]

Contraindications and precautions

- Refer to 📖 Use of drugs in end-of-life care, p.53 for end-of-life care issues.
- Since granisetron increases large bowel transit time, use with caution in patients with signs of sub-acute bowel obstruction.
- Use with caution in patients with:
  - cardiac rhythm or conduction disturbances
  - concurrent use of anti-arrhythmic agents or beta-adrenergic blocking agents (see 📖 Drug interactions)
  - significant electrolyte disturbances.
- Granisetron may modify reactions and patients should be advised not drive (or operate machinery) if affected. Refer to 📖 Drugs and driving, p.25.

☺ Adverse effects

Very common
- Headache.

Common
- Agitation
- Anorexia
- Anxiety
- Constipation
- Dizziness
- Hypertension
- Insomnia
- Somnolence
- Taste disorder
- Weakness.

Uncommon
- Abnormal vision
- Skin rashes.

Rare
- Abnormal LFTs (raised transaminases)
- Arrhythmias
- Dystonia and dyskinesia.

Drug interactions

Pharmacokinetic
- Is metabolized by CYP3A4. Co-administration with drugs that are metabolized by, or affect the activity (induction or inhibition—see 📖 inside back cover) of this pathway may lead to clinically relevant drug interactions and the prescriber should be aware that dosage adjustments may be necessary, particularly of drugs with a narrow therapeutic index.
- *Carbamazepine* and *phenytoin* can reduce granisetron serum concentrations and reduce the effect.
- *Paracetamol*—possible reduced analgesic benefit.

- *Tramadol*—reduced analgesic benefit.
- The effect of grapefruit juice on the absorption of granisetron is unknown.

Pharmacodynamic
- Granisetron may cause prolongation of the QT interval. There is a potential risk that co-administration with other drugs that also prolong the QT interval (e.g. *amiodarone, erythromycin, haloperidol, quinine*) may result in ventricular arrhythmias.
- Granisetron increases bowel transit time. This effect can be enhanced by drugs such as *opioids, TCAs, anticholinergics*.
- *Domperidone/metoclopramide*—granisetron reduces the prokinetic effect.
- *SSRIs*—risk of serotonin syndrome.

Dose
Nausea and vomiting
- 1mg PO BD or 2mg PO OD. *Higher doses have been used (up to 9mg PO daily in divided doses).
- Alternatively, the parenteral route may be used:
  - 1mg IV/SC* BD, increased to 3mg IV/SC* TDS if necessary
  - *1–3mg via CSCI over 24 hours, increased to a max. of 9mg daily.

Dose adjustments
Elderly
- No dosage adjustments are necessary.

Hepatic/renal impairment
- No dosage adjustments are necessary in liver or renal impairment. Nonetheless, since hepatic metabolism is important for the elimination of granisetron, the lowest effective dose should be used in patients with hepatic impairment.

Additional information
- 5-HT$_3$ antagonists differ in chemical structure, pharmacokinetics, and pharmacodynamics. There may be individual variation in response and it may be worth considering an alternative 5-HT$_3$ antagonist if response to granisetron is not as expected.
- Treatment with granisetron should be used regularly for 3 days and then response assessed. Avoid using on a PRN basis.
- The compatibility of granisetron with other drugs via CSCI is unknown, although it is expected to be similar to ondansetron.

Pharmacology
Granisetron is a selective 5-HT$_3$ receptor antagonist, blocking serotonin peripherally on vagal nerve terminals and centrally in the CTZ. It is a particularly useful in the treatment of nausea/vomiting associated with serotonin release (e.g. damage to enterochromaffin cells due to bowel injury, chemotherapy or radiotherapy). It has little or no affinity for other serotonin receptors (including 5-HT$_2$), dopamine D$_2$ receptors, α_1 -, α_2 -, or β-adrenoreceptors and histamine H$_1$ receptors.

Reference
1. Buchanan D, Muirhead K. Intractable nausea and vomiting successfully related with granisetron 5-hydroxytryptamine type 3 receptor antagonists in Palliative Medicine. *Palliat Med* 2007; **21**(8):725–6.

Haloperidol

Serenace® (POM)
Capsule: 500 micrograms (30).
Tablet: 1.5mg (30); 5mg (30); 10mg (30).
Oral liquid: 2mg/mL (500mL, *sugar-free*).

Haldol® (POM)
Tablet (scored): 5mg (20); 10mg (20).
Oral liquid: 2mg/mL (100mL, *sugar-free*).
Injection: 5mg/mL (1mL).

Dozic® (POM)
Oral liquid: 1mg/mL (100mL, *sugar-free*).

Generic (POM)
Tablet: 500 micrograms (28); 1.5mg (28); 5mg (28); 10mg (28); 20mg (28).

Indications
- Psychosis
- Intractable hiccup
- Restlessness and agitation in the elderly
- ⁺Delirium[1]
- ⁺Nausea and vomiting.[2]

Contraindications and precautions
- Refer to 🕮 Use of drugs in end-of-life care, p.53.

- Elderly patients with dementia-related psychosis treated with antipsychotic drugs are at an increased risk of mortality. Citalopram, sertraline, or trazodone may be more appropriate choices.
- Do not administer adrenaline with haloperidol as severe hypotension and tachycardia may result.

- Avoid in the following circumstances:
  - lesions of the basal ganglia
  - Parkinson's disease
  - recent acute myocardial infarction.
- Avoid in patients with dementia unless patient at immediate risk of harm or severely distressed (increased mortality reported).
- Haloperidol should be used with caution in the following circumstances:
  - co-administration of CYP2D6 and/or CYP3A4 inhibitors (see 🕮 Drug interactions, p.247)
  - diabetes (risk of hyperglycaemia in elderly)
  - elderly (see 🕮 Dose adjustments, p.249)
  - epilepsy
  - hepatic/renal impairment (see 🕮 Dose adjustments, p.249)
  - Lewy body dementia
  - poor metabolizers of CYP2D6 (if aware).
- Electrolyte disturbances must be corrected (e.g. hypokalaemia) due to the risk of QT prolongation.

- Antipsychotic drugs may increase the risk of VTE; assess risks before and during treatment.
- Rapid discontinuation may lead to a rebound worsening of symptoms. Withdraw gradually whenever possible.
- Haloperidol may modify reactions and patients should be advised not drive (or operate machinery) if affected. Refer to 📖 Drugs and driving, p.25.

☹ Adverse effects

Very common
- Agitation
- Headache

- Hyperkinesia
- Insomnia.

Common
- Akathisia
- Constipation
- Depression
- Dizziness
- Drowsiness
- Dry mouth
- Dystonia
- Nausea/vomiting
- Oculogyric crisis

- Postural hypotension
- Rash
- Sexual dysfunction (male)
- Tardive dyskinesia
- Tremor
- Urinary retention
- Visual disturbance
- Weight changes.

Uncommon
- Agitation
- Dyspnoea
- Cogwheel rigidity
- Confusion
- Hepatitis
- Jaundice

- Parkinsonism
- Photosensitivity
- Pruritus
- Sexual dysfunction (female)
- Tachycardia
- Urticaria.

Rare
- Bronchospasm
- Hyperprolactinaemia

- Neuroleptic malignant syndrome
- Prolonged QT interval.

Unknown
- Gynaecomastia
- Hypoglycaemia

- SIADH.

Drug interactions

Pharmacokinetic
- Haloperidol is metabolized by CYP2D6 and CYP3A4, with a minor pathway involving CYP1A2. It is an inhibitor of CYP2D6. Co-administration with drugs that are metabolized by, or affect the activity (induction or inhibition—see 📖 inside back cover) of these pathways may lead to clinically relevant drug interactions and the prescriber should be aware that dosage adjustments may be necessary, particularly of drugs with a narrow therapeutic index.
- *Carbamazepine*—increases the metabolism of haloperidol through CYP3A4 induction. Other CYP3A4 inducers may have the same effect.

The haloperidol dose may therefore need to be increased, according to the patient's response.

- *Fluoxetine*—increased risk of haloperidol adverse effects through inhibition of CYP2D6.
- *Paroxetine*—increased risk of adverse effects from both drugs due to inhibition of CYP2D6.
- *Venlafaxine*—increased risk of haloperidol adverse effects through inhibition of CYP2D6.
- Avoid grapefruit juice as it may increase the bioavailability of haloperidol through inhibition of intestinal CYP3A4.

Pharmacodynamic

- Haloperidol can cause dose-related prolongation of the QT interval. There is a potential risk that co-administration with other drugs that also prolong the QT interval (e.g. *amiodarone, erythromycin, quinine*) may result in ventricular arrhythmias.
- *Adrenaline*—avoid as α-adrenergic effects blocked with consequential paradoxical hypotension and tachycardia.
- *Anti-epileptics*—may need to be increased to take account of the lowered seizure threshold.
- *Antihypertensives*—increased risk of hypotension.
- *CNS depressants*—additive sedative effect.
- *Levodopa and dopamine agonists* —effect antagonized by haloperidol.
- *Levomepromazine*—may be an additive hypotensive effect; increased risk of extrapyramidal symptoms.
- *Metoclopramide*—increased risk of extrapyramidal symptoms.
- *Opioids*—may be an additive hypotensive effect.
- *Trazodone*—may be an additive hypotensive effect.

⟐ Dose

When prescribing haloperidol, the subcutaneous dose should be lower than the corresponding oral dose (which undergoes significant first-pass metabolism). There should be a separate prescription for each route ensuring that the same dose cannot be given PO or by SC/CSCI. A ratio of 3:2 is suggested (i.e. 3mg PO = 2mg SC)

Psychosis

- Initial dose 1.5mg PO BD–TDS. If severe, 3mg PO BD–TDS.
- Increase as necessary to a maximum of 30mg PO daily. Usual maintenance dose is 5–10mg PO daily.
- May be prescribed on a PRN basis (e.g. 1.5mg PO PRN, max. BD–TDS).
- *Alternatively, 3–5mg SC OD, or via CSCI. Can increase to usual max. 10mg SC daily, or via CSCI.
- *May be prescribed on a PRN basis (e.g. 0.5–1.5mg SC PRN max. TDS).

Intractable hiccup

- Initial dose 1.5mg PO TDS and adjust to response.
- Usual maintenance dose 1.5–3mg PO ON.
- May be prescribed on a PRN basis (e.g. 1.5mg PO PRN, max. BD–TDS)
- *Alternatively, 1.5–3mg SC OD, or via CSCI, and adjust to response.
- *May be prescribed on a PRN basis (e.g. 0.5–1.5mg SC PRN max. TDS).

Restlessness and agitation in the elderly

- Initial dose 1.5–3mg PO BD-TDS titrated as required to achieve maintenance dose (range 1.5–30mg PO daily)
- May be prescribed on a PRN basis (e.g. 1.5mg PO PRN, max. BD–TDS).
- ¥Alternatively, 1.5–3mg SC OD, or via CSCI. Can increase to usual max. 10mg SC daily, or via CSCI.
- ¥May be prescribed on a PRN basis (e.g. 0.5–1.5mg SC PRN max. TDS).

Delirium

- Initial dose 1.5–3mg PO OD–TDS titrated as required to achieve the maintenance dose (range 1.5–30mg daily).
- May be prescribed on a PRN basis (e.g. 1.5mg PO PRN, max. BD–TDS)
- Alternatively 1.5–3mg SC OD, or via CSCI. Increase to usual max. 10mg SC daily, or via CSCI.

Nausea and vomiting

- Initial dose 1.5–3mg SC OD, or via CSCI. Increase to usual max. of 10mg SC daily, or via CSCI.
- Oral route not usually appropriate, but 1.5–3mg PO ON–BD can be used. Can be increased to 5mg PO ON–BD as necessary.

Dose adjustments

Elderly

- Wherever possible, lower doses should be used. Elderly are more susceptible to adverse effects, particularly the anticholinergic effects; there may be an increased risk for cognitive decline and dementia.

Hepatic/renal impairment

- Wherever possible, lower doses should be used. Patients may be more susceptible to adverse effects.

Additional information

- Injection must not be administered IV.
- Haloperidol via CSCI is compatible with alfentanil, cyclizine, diamorphine, fentanyl, glycopyrronium, hydromorphone, ketamine, metoclopramide, midazolam, oxycodone, and tramadol.

Pharmacology

The pharmacology of haloperidol is complex and has not as yet been fully elucidated. It is a butyrophenone antipsychotic agent which selectively acts via dopamine D_2 receptors. It also has some effects at α_1-adrenoreceptors, muscarinic, H_1 and $5\text{-}HT_2$ receptors. The metabolism of haloperidol is complex, with a variety of metabolites being formed (including active metabolites). It is extensively metabolized by CYP2D6 and (at higher doses) by CYP3A4, with a minor pathway involving CYP1A2.

References

1. Attard A, Ranjith G, Taylor D. Delirium and its treatment. *CNS Drugs* 2008; **22**(8):631–44.
2. Hardy JR, O'Shea A, White C, Gilshenan K et al. The efficacy of haloperidol in the management of nausea and vomiting in patients with cancer. *J Pain Symptom Manage* 2010; **40**(1):111–16.

Hydromorphone

Standard release
Palladone® (CD2 POM)
Capsule: 1.3mg (orange/clear—56); 2.6mg (red/clear—56).

Unlicensed (CD2 POM)
Injection: 10mg/mL; 20mg/mL; 50mg/mL.
See 📖 Additional information, p.252 for supply issues.

Modified release
Palladone SR® (CD2 POM)
Capsule: 2mg (yellow/clear—56); 4mg (pale blue/clear—56); 8mg (pink/clear—56); 16mg (brown/clear—56); 24mg (dark blue/clear—56).

- Hydromorphone is a Schedule 2 CD. Refer to 📖 Legal categories of medicines, p.21 for further information.

Indications
- Severe cancer pain.

Contraindications and precautions
- Refer to 📖 Use of drugs in end-of-life care, p.53 for end-of-life care issues.
- If the dose of an opioid is titrated correctly, it is generally accepted that there are no absolute contraindications to the use of such drugs in palliative care, although there may be circumstances where one opioid is favoured over another (e.g. renal impairment, constipation). Nonetheless, hydromorphone is contraindicated for use in patients with
  - acute abdomen
  - concurrent administration of MAOIs or within 2 weeks of discontinuation of their use
  - head injury
  - hepatic impairment (see 📖 Dose adjustments, p.252)
  - paralytic ileus
  - raised intracranial pressure.
- Use with caution in following instances:
  - acute alcoholism
  - Addison's disease (adrenocortical insufficiency)
  - delirium tremens
  - diseases of the biliary tract
  - elderly patients
  - hepatic impairment (see 📖 Dose adjustments, p.252)
  - history of alcohol and drug abuse
  - hypotension
  - hypothyroidism
  - hypovolaemia
  - inflammatory bowel disorders
  - pancreatitis
  - prostatic hypertrophy
  - raised intracranial pressure
  - renal impairment
  - severe pulmonary disease
  - toxic psychosis.

• Hydromorphone may modify reactions and patients should be advised not drive (or operate machinery) if affected. Refer to 📖 Drugs and driving, p.25.

Adverse effects

Strong opioids tend to cause similar adverse effects, albeit to varying degrees.

The frequency is not defined, but commonly reported adverse effects include:

- Anorexia
- Biliary pain
- Confusion
- Constipation
- Drowsiness
- Dry mouth
- Dyspepsia
- Exacerbation of pancreatitis
- Euphoria
- Insomnia
- Headache
- Hyperhidrosis

- Myoclonus
- Nausea
- Pruritus
- Sexual dysfunction (e.g. amenorrhea, decreased libido, erectile dysfunction)
- Urinary retention
- Vertigo
- Visual disturbance
- Vomiting
- Weakness.

The following can occur with excessive dose:

- Agitation
- Exacerbation of pain
- Hallucinations
- Miosis

- Paraesthesia
- Respiratory depression
- Restlessness.

Drug interactions

Pharmacokinetic

- CYP3A4 and CYP2C9 appear to have a minor role in the metabolism of hydromorphone. Major route of metabolism is via glucuronidation. To date, no clinically significant pharmacokinetic interactions have been reported.

Pharmacodynamic

- *Antihypertensives*—increased risk of hypotension.
- *CNS depressants*—risk of excessive sedation.
- *Haloperidol*—may be an additive hypotensive effect.
- *Ketamine*—there is a potential opioid-sparing effect with ketamine and the dose of hydromorphone may need reducing.
- *Levomepromazine*—may be an additive hypotensive effect.

Dose

The initial dose of hydromorphone depends upon the patient's previous opioid requirements. Refer to 📖 Management of pain: opioid substitution, p.32 for information regarding opioid dose equivalences. Refer to 📖 Management of pain: breakthrough pain, p.35 for guidance relating to BTcP.

Oral

Standard release

- For opioid naïve patients, initial dose is 1.3mg PO every 4–6 hours and PRN. The dose is then increased as necessary until a stable dose is attained. The patient should then be converted to a m/r formulation.

Modified release
- Patients should ideally be titrated using *Palladone®* before commencing *Palladone SR®*.
- If necessary, for opioid naïve patients, initial dose is 2mg PO BD. The dose can then be titrated as necessary.

¥ *Subcutaneous*
- Initial dose in opioid naïve patients is 1–2mg via CSCI over 24 hours and increase as necessary.

₰ Dose adjustments
Elderly
- No specific guidance available, although lower starting doses in opioid naïve patients may be preferable. Dose requirements should be individually titrated.

Hepatic/renal impairment
- The manufacturer contraindicates the use of hydromorphone in patients with hepatic impairment. Nonetheless, hydromorphone is used in this group of patients and the dose should be titrated carefully to the patients need.
- No specific guidance is available for patients with renal impairment and dose requirements should be individually titrated. Alternatively, a different opioid may be more appropriate (e.g. oxycodone or fentanyl).
- By CSCI, hydromorphone is reportedly compatible with cyclizine, glycopyrronium, haloperidol, hyoscine hydrobromide, ketorolac, levomepromazine, metoclopramide, midazolam, octreotide, ondansetron, and phenobarbital.
- Hydromorphone shows concentration-dependent compatibility with dexamethasone

Additional information
- The capsules can be swallowed whole or opened and their contents sprinkled on to cold soft food.
- The unlicensed injection is available from Martindale Pharma (Tel: 01277 266 600).

⊙ Pharmacology
Hydromorphone is a synthetic analogue of morphine with analgesic activity at μ-opioid receptors. Oral bioavailability is variable, with a PO:IV equianalgesic ratio of between 2:1 and 5:1. Hydromorphone is extensively metabolized via glucuronidation, with >95% of the dose metabolized to hydromorphone-3-glucuronide. Accumulation of the main metabolite occurs in renal impairment and has led to the development of adverse effects, such as nausea and delirium.

Hyoscine butylbromide

Buscopan® (POM)
Tablet: 10mg (56).
Injection: 20mg/mL (10).
Note: hyoscine butylbromide tablets can be sold to the public provided a single dose ≤20mg, the daily dose ≤80mg, and pack contains ≤240mg.

Indications
- Spasm of the genito-urinary tract or GI tract (tablet)
- Irritable bowel syndrome (tablet)
- *Nausea and vomiting (associated with bowel obstruction)[1,2]
- *Smooth muscle spasm (e.g. bowel colic)[1,2]
- *Terminal secretions.[3]

Contraindications and precautions
- Refer to 📖 Use of drugs in end-of-life care, p.53 for end-of-life care issues.
- Note that for the management of terminal secretions, contraindications should be individually assessed.
- Manufacturer states that hyoscine butylbromide should be avoided in patients with
  - mechanical stenoses in the region of the GI tract
  - megacolon
  - myasthenia gravis
  - narrow-angle glaucoma
  - paralytic ileus
  - prostatic enlargement with urinary retention
  - tachycardia.
- It possesses anticholinergic properties so it should be used with caution in the following:
  - bladder outflow obstruction
  - cardiac arrhythmias
  - CHF
  - coronary artery disease
  - diarrhoea (may be masking intestinal obstruction)
  - elderly (more susceptible to adverse effects)
  - GI reflux disease
  - hypertension
  - hyperthyroidism
  - pyrexia (reduces sweating)
  - renal impairment (see 📖 Dosage adjustment, p.254)
  - ulcerative colitis.
- Hyoscine butylbromide may modify reactions and patients should be advised not drive (or operate machinery) if affected. Refer to 📖 Drugs and driving, p.25.

☺ Adverse effects
The frequency is not defined, but reported adverse effects include:
- Confusion

- Difficulty in micturition
- Dizziness
- Drowsiness
- Dry mouth
- Inhibition of sweating.
- Palpitations
- Tachycardia
- Visual disturbances.

Drug interactions

Pharmacokinetic

- No recognized pharmacokinetic interactions.

Pharmacodynamic

- *β_2 agonists*—increased risk of tachycardia.
- *Cyclizine*—increased risk of anticholinergic adverse effects.
- *Domperidone*—may inhibit prokinetic effect.
- *Metoclopramide*—may inhibit prokinetic effect.
- *Nefopam*—increased risk of anticholinergic adverse effects.
- *TCAs*—increased risk of anticholinergic adverse effects.

⚕ Dose

Spasm of the genito-urinary tract or GI tract

- 20mg PO QDS.
- ¥Alternatively, 10–20mg SC and 60mg via CSCI.

Irritable bowel syndrome

- Initial dose 10mg PO TDS, increasing as necessary to 20mg PO QDS.

¥ Nausea and vomiting/smooth muscle spasm/sweating/terminal secretions

- Initial dose 20mg SC, or 60mg via CSCI over 24 hours.
- Dose can be increased as necessary to a usual maximum of 120mg.
- Higher doses (e.g. 300mg) have been reported, although treatment should be reviewed if 120mg is unsatisfactory.

⚕ Dose adjustments

Elderly

- No specific guidance available. Use the lowest effective dose as the elderly may be more susceptible to the adverse effects.

Hepatic/renal impairment

- No specific guidance available. Use the lowest effective dose.

Additional information

- Tablets may be crushed prior to administration if necessary.
- It is poorly absorbed orally, so the usefulness of this route of administration is questionable, apart from possible benefit in bowel colic.
- Via CSCI, hyoscine butylbromide is reportedly compatibility with alfentanil, clonazepam, diamorphine, fentanyl, levomepromazine, metoclopramide, midazolam, octreotide, ondansetron, oxycodone, ranitidine, and tramadol.

* There may be concentration-dependent incompatibility with cyclizine and haloperidol.

Pharmacology

Hyoscine butylbromide is a quaternary ammonium antimuscarinic that inhibits the peripheral actions of acetylcholine. Following both oral and parenteral administration, hyoscine butylbromide concentrates in the tissue of the GI tract, liver, and kidneys. Although oral bioavailability is poor, the drug produces its effect because of its high tissue affinity. It is a quaternary ammonium compound so it does not usually pass the blood–brain barrier, thus it is devoid of central activity such as drowsiness or a direct anti-emetic effect.

References

. Tytgat GN. Hyoscine butylbromide—a review on its parenteral use in acute abdominal spasm and as an aid in abdominal diagnostic and therapeutic procedures. *Curr Med Res Opin* 2008; **24**(11):3159–73.

. Ripamonti CI, Easson AM, Gerdes H. Management of malignant bowel obstruction. *Eur J Cancer* 2008; **44**(8):1105–15.

. Wildiers H, Dhaenekint C, Demeulenaere P, et al. Atropine, hyoscine butylbromide, or scopolamine are equally effective for the treatment of death rattle in terminal care. *J Pain Symptom Manage* 2009; **38**(1):124–33.

Hyoscine hydrobromide

Kwells® (P)
Tablet: 150 micrograms (12); 300 micrograms (12).

Joy-rides® (P).
Tablet: 150 micrograms.

Scopoderm TTS® (POM)
Transdermal patch: 1.5mg (releasing 1mg over 72 hours).

Generic (POM)
Injection: 400 micrograms/mL (10); 600 micrograms/mL (10).

Indications
- Motion sickness (oral/transdermal)
- ✱End stage Parkinson's disease[1]
- ✱Hypersalivation[2]
- ✱Nausea and vomiting[3,4]
- ✱Smooth muscle spasm (e.g. bowel colic)[4]
- ✱Terminal secretions.[5]

Contraindications and precautions
- Refer to 📖 Use of drugs in end-of-life care, p.53 for end-of-life care issues.
- Note that for the management of terminal secretions, contraindications and precautions should be individually assessed.
- Contraindicated for use in patients with narrow-angle glaucoma.
- The manufacturers state use with caution in the following circumstances:
  - bladder outflow obstruction
  - cardiac arrhythmias
  - CHF
  - diarrhoea (may be masking intestinal obstruction)
  - Down's syndrome
  - elderly patients (see 📖 Dose adjustments, p.258)
  - epilepsy
  - GI reflux disease
  - hepatic impairment
  - hyperthyroidism
  - intestinal obstruction
  - myasthenia gravis
  - paralytic ileus
  - prostatic enlargement
  - pyrexia (reduces sweating)
  - renal impairment.
  - ulcerative colitis.
- Idiosyncratic reactions may occur with ordinary therapeutic doses of hyoscine (e.g. agitation, hallucinations).
- Care should be taken after removal of the transdermal patch as adverse effects may persist for up to 24 hours or longer.

Remove transdermal patch prior to MRI due to risk of burns.
• Hyoscine hydrobromide may modify reactions and patients should be advised not drive (or operate machinery) if affected. Refer to 📖 Drugs and driving, p.25.
Subtle deficits in attention, memory, and reasoning may occur with therapeutic dosages of anticholinergic drugs without signs of obvious toxicity. These deficits have often been mistaken for symptoms of early dementia in elderly patients.

Adverse effects
The frequency is not defined, but reported adverse effects include:
• Agitation (paradoxical)
• Amnesia
• Bradycardia (tachycardia with excessive dose)
• Confusion
• Difficulty in micturition
• Dizziness
• Drowsiness
• Dry mouth
• Hallucinations
• Inhibition of sweating (risk of hyperthermia in hot weather, or pyrexia)
• Seizures
• Visual disturbances (e.g. blurred vision).

Drug interactions
Pharmacokinetic
• No recognized pharmacokinetic interactions.

Pharmacodynamic
• *Donepezil*—effect may be antagonized.
  β_2 *agonists*—increased risk of tachycardia.
  Cyclizine—increased risk of anticholinergic adverse effects.
  Domperidone—may inhibit prokinetic effect.
  Galantamine—effect may be antagonized.
  Metoclopramide—may inhibit prokinetic effect.
• *Nefopam*—increased risk of anticholinergic adverse effects.
  Rivastigmine—effect may be antagonized.
• *TCAs*—increased risk of anticholinergic adverse effects.

Dose
End-stage Parkinson's disease
• Initial dose 1.2mg via CSCI over 24 hours and adjust empirically.

Hypersalivation
• 1mg every 72 hours via transdermal patch. 2 patches may be used if necessary
• Alternatively, 300 micrograms PO up to TDS can be tried.
• It may be more appropriate to use alternative treatments (e.g. glycopyrronium, propantheline).

Nausea and vomiting/smooth muscle spasm
Other options are usually used for these indications (e.g. hyoscine butylbromide).

- 1mg every 72 hours via transdermal patch. 2 patches may be used if necessary.
- Alternatively, 300 micrograms PO up to TDS can be tried.
- Via CSCI, initially 400 micrograms over 24 hours increased as necessary up to 1.2mg.

¥ *Terminal secretions*

- Initial dose 400 micrograms SC injection, followed by 1.2mg via CSCI over 24 hours.
- If necessary, the dose can be increased to 2.4mg over 24 hours.

Dose adjustments
Elderly

- No specific guidance available. Use the lowest effective dose as the elderly may be more susceptible to the adverse effects, particularly the anticholinergic effects. The patient may be at an increased risk for cognitive decline and dementia.

Hepatic/renal impairment

- No specific guidance available. Use the lowest effective dose.

Additional information

- Via CSCI, hyoscine hydrobromide is reportedly compatible with alfentanil, clonazepam, cyclizine, dexamethasone, diamorphine, fentanyl, haloperidol, hydromorphone, levomepromazine, metoclopramide, midazolam, morphine hydrochloride, morphine sulphate, morphine tartrate, octreotide, ondansetron, oxycodone, promethazine, and ranitidine.

Pharmacology

Hyoscine is an anticholinergic drug which blocks the action of acetylcholine at post-ganglionic parasympathetic sites including smooth muscle, secretary glands and CNS sites. It effectively reduces secretions (bowel, salivary and bronchial), has a direct anti-emetic effect (unlike glycopyrronium and hyoscine butylbromide) and reduces sweating. It may cause amnesia and unlike glycopyrronium, it is more likely to cause bradycardia rather than tachycardia. It is extensively metabolized, although the exact details are unknown.

References

1. Pérez LM, Farriols C, Puente V, et al. The use of subcutaneous scopolamine as a palliative treatment in Parkinson's disease. *Palliat Med* 2011; **25**(1):92–3.
2. Mato A, Limeres J, Tomás I, et al. Management of drooling in disabled patients with scopolamine patches. *Br J Clin Pharmacol* 2010; **69**(6):684–8.
3. LeGrand SB, Walsh D. Scopolamine for cancer-related nausea and vomiting. *J Pain Symptom Manage* 2010; **40**(1):136-141.
4. Ripamonti CI, Easson AM, Gerdes H. Management of malignant bowel obstruction. *Eur J Cancer* 2008; **44**(8):1105–15.
5. Wildiers H, Dhaenekint C, Demeulenaere P, et al. Atropine, hyoscine butylbromide, or scopolamine are equally effective for the treatment of death rattle in terminal care. *J Pain Symptom Manage* 2009; **38**(1):124–33.

Ibandronic acid (ibandronate)

Bondronat® *(POM)*
Tablet: 50mg (28).
Injection (concentrate): 2mg/2mL vial; 6mg/6mL vial.

Bonviva® *(POM)*
(Licensed for the treatment of osteoporosis in postmenopausal women at increased risk of fracture and not discussed further.)

Generic (POM)
Tablet: 50mg (28).

Indications

- Prevention of skeletal events in patients with breast cancer and bone metastases.
- Treatment of tumour-induced hypercalcaemia (*injection only*).

Contraindications and precautions

- Ibandronic acid is contraindicated in the following situations:
  - abnormalities of the oesophagus which delay oesophageal emptying such as stricture or achalasia (*tablet*)
  - inability to stand or sit upright for at least 60min (*tablet*)
  - hypocalcaemia.
- Use with caution in patients with renal impairment (see 📖 Dose adjustments, p.261).
- Assess the need for calcium and vitamin D supplements in patients receiving ibandronic acid other than for hypercalcaemia.
- Consider dental examination before initiating therapy due to the possibility of inducing osteonecrosis of the jaw (see 📖 Adverse effects)
- Oral bisphosphonates may cause local irritation of the upper GI mucosa. Use with caution in patients with upper GI problems (e.g. Barrett's oesophagus, dysphagia, gastritis, duodenitis or peptic ulcers). Patients should not lie down for 60min after taking.

Adverse effects

Osteonecrosis of the jaw has been discovered to be a potential complication of bisphosphonate therapy. It has been reported in cancer patients, many who had a pre-existing local infection or recent extraction. Cancer patients are more likely to be at risk of osteonecrosis as a result of their disease, cancer therapies, and blood dyscrasias. Dental examination is recommended for patients undergoing repeated infusions of ibandronic acid (and other bisphosphonates) and dental surgery should be avoided during this treatment period as healing may be delayed.

Severe and occasionally incapacitating bone, joint, and/or muscle pain has been reported with bisphosphonate use. Time to onset varies from one day to several months after initiation of treatment, but symptoms should improve upon discontinuation. Some patients will develop the same symptoms upon subsequent treatment with ibandronic acid or another bisphosphonate.

Atypical femoral fractures have been reported with bisphosphonate therapy. Although a rare occurrence, during bisphosphonate treatment patients should be advised to report any new thigh, hip, or groin pain.

Adverse effects are for the oral route, unless otherwise described.

Very common
- Pyrexia (*parenteral*).

Common
- Abdominal pain
- Arthralgia (*parenteral* —at doses >4mg)
- Asthenia (*oral and parenteral*)
- Bone pain (*parenteral*—usually transient)
- Cataract (*parenteral*—at doses >4mg)
- Diarrhoea (*parenteral*—at doses >4mg)
- Dizziness (*parenteral*—at doses >4mg)
- Dyspepsia
- Headache (*parenteral*—at doses >4mg)
- Hypocalcaemia (*oral and parenteral*)
- Influenza-like symptoms (*parenteral*—at doses >4mg)
- Myalgia (*parenteral*—at doses >4mg)
- Nausea
- Oedema (*parenteral*—at doses >4mg)
- Oesophagitis
- Osteoarthritis (*parenteral*—at doses >4mg)
- Pharyngitis (*parenteral*—at doses >4mg)

Uncommon
- Anaemia
- Anxiety (*parenteral*—at doses >4mg)
- Chest pain
- Cystitis (*parenteral*—at doses >4mg)
- Dry mouth
- Duodenal ulcer
- Dysgeusia
- Dysphagia
- Gastritis
- Gastrointestinal haemorrhage
- Hypophosphataemia (*parenteral*—at doses >4mg)
- Influenza-like symptoms (*parenteral*)
- Injection site pain (*parenteral*—at doses >4mg)
- Mouth ulceration ((*parenteral*—at doses >4mg)
- Myalgia (*parenteral*)
- Paraesthesia
- Parathyroid disorder
- Pruritus

Rare
- Femoral fracture (*oral and parenteral*)
- Ocular inflammation (*oral and parenteral*)

Very rare
- Bronchospasm (*parenteral*)
- Osteonecrosis of the jaw (*oral and parenteral*).

Unknown
- Atrial fibrillation.

Drug interactions
Pharmacokinetic
- None known.

Pharmacodynamic
- *Aminoglycosides*—may have additive hypocalcaemic effect.
- NSAIDs—may increase risk of GI irritation.

Dose
Tumour-induced hypercalcaemia
- Corrected serum calcium <3.0mmol/L, 2mg by IV infusion as a single dose.
- Corrected serum calcium >3.0mmol/L, 4mg by IV infusion as a single dose.
- Dilute appropriate dose in 100mL NaCl 0.9% or glucose 5% and give over 15min (for patients with CrCl >50mL/min).

Prevention of skeletal events
- 50mg PO OD.
- Alternatively, 6mg by IV infusion every 3–4 weeks. Administer in 100mL NaCl 0.9% or glucose 5% over 15min (for patients with CrCl >50mL/min).

Dose adjustments
Elderly
- No dose adjustments are necessary.

Hepatic/renal impairment
- No dose adjustments are necessary for patients with hepatic impairment.
- Ibandronic acid is renally excreted; the manufacturer does not make a specific recommendation for dose adjustment when prescribing for hypercalcaemia. However, adjustments must be made when treating skeletal events:
  - eGFR 30–50mL/min, reduce dose to 4mg and infuse over at least 1 hour in 500mL of NaCl 0.9% or glucose 5%.
  - eGFR <30mL/min, reduce dose to 2mg and infuse over at least 1 hour in 500mL NaCl 0.9% or glucose 5%.

Additional information
- Corrected serum calcium = actual serum calcium+[(40 − serum albumin g/L) × 0.02].
- In the treatment of hypercalcaemia, serum calcium levels should not be measured until 5–7 days post dose. Calcium levels start to fall after 48 hours, with a median time to normalization of 4–7 days and normalization in 80% of patients within 7 days. Seek specialist advice should the corrected serum calcium concentration not return to

normal after 7–10 days; a second dose of ibandronic acid can be given 7–10 days after the initial dose in such patients.
- The onset of treatment effect for skeletal related events is 2–3 months.
- Relief from bone pain may occur within 14 days, although it may be up to 3 months before maximum effect is seen.

⊹ Pharmacology

Ibandronic acid is a bisphosphonate that inhibits osteoclast activity, which in turn reduces bone resorption and turnover. It is excreted unchanged by the kidney.

Ibuprofen

Standard release

Brufen® (POM)
Tablet: 200mg (100); 400mg (100); 600mg (100).
Effervescent granules: 600mg (20) (contains 9mmol Na$^+$ per sachet).
Syrup: 100mg/5mL (500mL).

Generic (POM)
Tablet: 200mg; 400mg; 600mg (various pack sizes)
Oral suspension: 100mg/5mL (100mL; 150mL; 500mL) (*sugar-free versions are available—specify on prescription*)

Modified release

Brufen Retard® (POM)
Tablet: 800mg (56).

Fenbid Spansule® (POM)
Capsule: 300mg (120).

Note: ibuprofen is available OTC in a variety of formulations (e.g. tablets, caplets, capsules, creams, gels) and strengths.

Indications
- Mild to moderate pain
- Inflammatory conditions (e.g. rheumatoid and other musculoskeletal disorders)
- Fever
- ✱Pain associated with cancer.[1]

Contraindications and precautions
- Contraindicated for use in patients with:
  - a history of, or active, peptic ulceration
  - hypersensitivity reactions to ibuprofen, aspirin or other NSAIDs
  - severe heart failure.
- Use the minimum effective dose for the shortest duration necessary in order to reduce the risk of cardiac and GI events.
- Elderly patients are more at risk of developing adverse effects.
- Use with caution in the following circumstances:
  - concurrent use of diuretics, corticosteroids, and NSAIDs (see ☐ Drug interactions, p.264)
  - CHF and/or left ventricular dysfunction
  - diabetes mellitus
  - established ischaemic heart disease, peripheral arterial disease, and/or cerebrovascular disease need careful consideration due to the increased risk of thrombotic events (especially at doses >1200mg/day)
  - hepatic impairment
  - hyperlipidaemia
  - hypertension (particularly uncontrolled)
  - recovery from surgery

- renal impairment
- smoking.
- Patients taking long-term therapy need regular monitoring of renal and liver function.
- Abnormal LFTs can occur; discontinue NSAID if this persists.
- Ibuprofen may prevent the development of signs and symptoms of inflammation/infection (e.g. fever).
- Consider co-prescription of misoprostol or a PPI if:
  - long-term NSAID therapy
  - concurrent use of drugs that increase the risk of GI toxicity (see 📖 Drug Interactions, p.264)
- Refer to 📖 Selection of NSAID, p.29 for further information, including selection.

☻ Adverse effects

The frequency is not defined, but reported adverse effects include:
- Abdominal pain
- Cardiac failure
- Diarrhoea
- Dyspepsia
- Fatigue
- GI haemorrhage
- Headache
- Hypersensitivity reactions (e.g. anaphylaxis, asthma, dyspnoea, pruritus, rash, severe skin reactions)
- Hypertension
- Jaundice
- Melaena
- Nausea
- Oedema
- Peptic ulcer
- Renal failure
- Vomiting.

Drug interactions

Pharmacokinetic
- Ibuprofen is a minor substrate of CYP2C8/9 and CYP2C19; it is also an inhibitor of CYP2C8/9. Co-administration with drugs that are metabolized by, or affect the activity (induction or inhibition—see 📖 inside back cover) of these pathways may lead to clinically relevant drug interactions and the prescriber should be aware that dosage adjustments may be necessary, particularly of drugs with a narrow therapeutic index.
- *Methotrexate*—reduced excretion of methotrexate.
- *Warfarin*—possible increased risk of bleeding through inhibition of warfarin metabolism (5–11% of Caucasians have a variant of CYP2C9, requiring lower maintenance doses of warfarin. Combination with ibuprofen may further reduce warfarin metabolism).

Pharmacodynamic
- *Anticoagulants*—increased risk of bleeding.
- *Antihypertensives*—reduced hypotensive effect.
- *Antiplatelet drugs*—increased risk of bleeding.

- *Corticosteroids*—increased risk of GI toxicity.
- *Ciclosporin*—increased risk of nephrotoxicity.
- *Diuretics*—reduced diuretic effect; nephrotoxicity of ibuprofen may be increased.
- *SSRIs*—increased risk of GI bleeding.

Dose

To be taken with or after food.

Standard release

- Initial dose 400mg PO TDS, increasing if necessary to a maximum of 800mg PO TDS.

Modified release

Brufen Retard ®

- Initial dose 2 tablets (1600mg) PO OD, preferably in the early evening.
- Can be increased to 3 tablets (2400mg) PO daily in 2 divided doses.

Fenbid Spansule ®

- Initial dose 2 capsules (600mg) PO BD
- Can be increased in severe cases to 3 capsules (900mg) PO BD

Dose adjustments

Elderly

- No special dosage modifications are required, but check hepatic/renal impairment as listed.

Hepatic/renal impairment

- No specific dosage modifications are available. However, NSAIDs should be used cautiously in patients with liver and/or renal impairment due to the increased risks of adverse effects. The lowest effective dose should be used for the shortest time permissible and regular monitoring of liver and/or renal function is advisable.

Additional information

- Ibuprofen at doses <1200mg/day appears not to increase the risk of thrombotic events.
- It is considered to be the safest NSAID in terms of GI toxicity, especially at doses <1200mg/day.

Pharmacology

Ibuprofen is a NSAID that possesses anti-inflammatory, analgesic and antipyretic activity. Its mode of action, like that of other NSAIDs, is not completely understood, but may be related to inhibition of COX-1 and COX-2. Ibuprofen is well-absorbed orally and is rapidly metabolized and eliminated in the urine.

Reference

1. McNicol ED, Strassels S, Goudas L, *et al.* NSAIDS or paracetamol, alone or combined with opioids, for cancer pain. *Cochrane Database Syst Rev* 2005; **2**: CD005180.

Imatinib

Glivec® (POM)
Tablet: 100mg (*scored*—60); 400mg (30).

Indications

- Acute lymphoblastic leukaemia
- Advanced hypereosinophilic syndrome and chronic eosinophilic leukaemia
- Chronic myeloid leukaemia (accelerated and chronic phase; blast crisis)
- Dermatofibrosarcoma protuberans
- Gastrointestinal stromal tumours (GISTs)
- Myelodysplastic/myeloproliferative diseases.

Contraindications and precautions

- Use cautiously in the following:
  - cardiac disease (risk of fluid retention and subsequent cardiac failure)
  - concomitant use with drugs that inhibit CYP3A4 (see 🕮 Drug interactions, p.267)
  - diabetes (can cause hyperglycaemia)
  - elderly
  - gout (can cause hyperuricaemia)
  - hepatic impairment (see 🕮 Dose adjustments, p.268)
  - renal impairment (see 🕮 Dose adjustments, p.268).
- Patients should ideally not use high doses of paracetamol with imatinib since glucuronidation may be affected.
- Imatinib may cause dizziness and fatigue. Patients should be advised not drive (or operate machinery) if affected. Refer to 🕮 Drugs and driving, p.25.

☺ Adverse effects

Very common

- Abdominal pain
- Anaemia
- Arthralgia
- Bone pain
- Dermatitis/eczema/rash
- Diarrhoea
- Dyspepsia
- Fatigue
- Fluid retention
- Headache
- Muscle spasm and cramps
- Myalgia
- Nausea
- Neutropenia
- Periorbital oedema
- Thrombocytopenia
- Vomiting
- Weight increase (likely fluid retention).

Common

- Anorexia
- Blurred vision
- Conjunctival haemorrhage
- Conjunctivitis
- Constipation
- Cough
- Dizziness
- Dry eye
- Dry mouth
- Dyspnoea
- Epistaxis
- Eyelid oedema
- Febrile neutropenia
- Flatulence

- Flushing
- Gastritis
- Gastro-oesophageal reflux
- Hypoaesthesia
- Insomnia
- Lacrimation increased
- Night sweats
- Pancytopenia

- Paraesthesia
- Photosensitivity reaction
- Pruritus
- Pyrexia
- Raised LFTs
- Taste disturbance
- Weight loss.

Uncommon

- Acute renal failure
- Gastric ulcer
- Gout/hyperuricaemia
- Haematuria
- Hepatitis
- Hypercalcaemia
- Hyperglycaemia

- Hypertension
- Hypokalaemia
- Jaundice
- Oesophagitis
- Pleural effusion
- Sexual dysfunction
- Stomatitis.

Drug interactions

Pharmacokinetic

- Imatinib is metabolized by CYP3A4; it is also an inhibitor of CYP3A4 and possibly CYP2C9. Co-administration with drugs that are metabolized by, or affect the activity (induction or inhibition—see 📖 inside back cover) of this pathway may lead to clinically relevant drug interactions and the prescriber should be aware that dosage adjustments may be necessary, particularly of drugs with a narrow therapeutic index.
- *Paracetamol*—glucuronidation inhibited by imatinib; potential paracetamol toxicity with prolonged use.
- *Warfarin* —manufacturer advises use of LMWH with imatinib.
- Avoid grapefruit juice as it may increase the bioavailability of imatinib through inhibition of intestinal CYP3A4.

Pharmacodynamic

- None known.

💊 Dose

Acute lymphoblastic leukaemia

- 600mg PO OD.

Advanced hypereosinophilic syndrome and chronic eosinophilic leukaemia

- 600mg PO OD, increased if necessary to max. dose of 400mg PO BD.

Chronic myeloid leukaemia (CML)

- Accelerated phase—600mg PO OD, increased if necessary to max. dose 400mg PO BD.
- Blast crisis—600mg PO OD, increased if necessary to max. dose 400mg PO BD.
- Chronic phase—400mg PO OD, increased if necessary to max. dose 400mg PO BD.

Dermatofibrosarcoma protuberans

- 400mg PO BD.

GISTs
- 400mg PO OD.

Myelodysplastic/myeloproliferative diseases
- 400mg PO OD.

🖐 Dose adjustments for adverse reactions

- If severe non-haematological adverse effects occur, imatinib should be discontinued until the event has resolved. Imatinib can be re-introduced as appropriate at a reduced dose:
  - 400mg PO OD reduce dose to 300mg PO OD
  - 600mg PO OD reduce dose to 400mg PO OD
  - 400mg PO BD reduce dose to 600mg PO OD
- Refer to the SPC if haematological adverse effects occur.

🖐 Dose adjustments

Elderly
- No dose adjustments are necessary.

Hepatic/renal impairment
- Imatinib is significantly metabolized by the liver. Patients with mild, moderate, or severe liver impairment should be given the minimum recommended dose of 400mg PO OD. The dose can be reduced if not tolerated.
- For patients with renal impairment (CrCl <60mL/min) or those on dialysis, the recommended maximum starting dose is 400mg PO OD.

Additional information

- Tablets should be taken with a meal and a large glass of water to minimize the risk of GI irritation.
- If necessary, tablets may be dispersed in water or apple juice (~50mL for a 100mg tablet, and 200mL for a 400mg) tablet immediately prior to administration.

⊘ Pharmacology

Imatinib is a Bcr-Abl tyrosine kinase inhibitor which is the product of the Philadelphia chromosome in CML. It induces apoptosis in Bcr-Abl positive cell lines as well as in fresh leukemic cells in Philadelphia chromosome positive CML. It also inhibits other tyrosine kinases and inhibits proliferation and induces apoptosis in gastrointestinal stromal tumour (GIST) cells. It is well absorbed after oral administration, with a bioavailability of 98% and is highly protein bound. It is extensively metabolized, mainly by CYP3A4, to a compound with similar activity. Imatinib and its metabolites are not excreted via the kidney to a significant extent.

Insulin: biphasic insulin aspart

NovoMix® 30 (POM)

Biphasic insulin aspart (recombinant human insulin analogue), 30% insulin aspart, 70% insulin aspart protamine, 100 units/mL.

Injection: 5 × 3mL *Penfill®* cartridge for *Novopen®* device.

Injection: 5 × 3mL prefilled disposable *FlexPen®* injection devices; (range 1–60 units, allowing 1-unit dosage adjustment).

Indications

- Diabetes mellitus.

Contraindications and precautions

- Refer to 📖 Use of drugs in end-of-life care, p.53 for end-of-life care issues.
- *NovoMix®* 30 has a faster onset of action than biphasic human insulin and should generally be given within 10min of a meal or snack containing carbohydrates.
- It must only be administered by SC injection.
  Use with caution in the following:
  - elderly patients (see 📖 Dose adjustments, p.270)
  - renal impairment (see 📖 Dose adjustments, p.270)
  - severe hepatic impairment (see 📖 Dose adjustments, p.270)
  - systemic illness (dose increase may be necessary).
- The risk of reduced warning symptoms of hypoglycaemia is increased in the following circumstances:
  - after transfer from animal insulin to human insulin
  - autonomic neuropathy is present
  - concurrent treatment with particular drugs (see 📖 Drug interactions, p.270)
  - elderly
  - gradual onset of hypoglycaemia
  - long history of diabetes
  - markedly improved glycaemic control
  - psychiatric illness.

☺ Adverse effects

Very common

- Hypoglycaemia (also depends on other factors).

Uncommon

- Injection site reactions (generally minor, e.g. redness, pain, itching, or inflammation)
- Lipodystrophy
- Oedema (may cause sodium retention; usually transitory during initiation)
- Peripheral neuropathy
- Retinopathy (usually temporary deterioration associated with abrupt improvement in glycaemic control)
- Urticaria
- Visual disturbances (usually temporary due to marked glycaemic control and associated altered lens properties).

Drug interactions

Pharmacokinetic

- None recognized.

Pharmacodynamic

- *ACEIs*—increased risk of hypoglycaemia.
- *Antipsychotics* —glucose metabolism can be affected; dose adjustments may be necessary.
- *β2-agonists*—hypoglycaemic effect may be antagonized.
- *Corticosteroids*—hypoglycaemic effect antagonized.
- *Diuretics*—hypoglycaemic effect may be antagonized.
- *Fluoxetine*—increased risk of hypoglycaemia.
- *Octreotide*—can affect glucose metabolism; dose adjustments may be necessary.

Dose

- Biphasic insulin aspart is usually given OD–BD.
- In patients with type 1 diabetes the individual insulin requirement is usually between 0.5–1.0 units/kg/day. Nonetheless, dose according to requirements.
- In patients with type II diabetes, biphasic insulin aspart can be combined with oral antidiabetic drugs. The usual starting dose is 6 units at breakfast and 6 units with the evening meal. It can also be initiated as 12 units with the evening meal. Doses above 30 units once daily should be divided into 2 equal doses.
- If BD dosing results in recurrent daytime hypoglycaemic episodes, the morning dose can be split into morning and lunchtime doses (i.e. TDS regimen).

Dose adjustments

Elderly

- In the elderly, progressive deterioration of renal function may lead to a steady decrease in insulin requirements.

Hepatic/renal impairment

- In patients with severe hepatic impairment, insulin requirements may be diminished due to reduced capacity for gluconeogenesis and reduced insulin metabolism.
- In patients with renal impairment, insulin requirements may be diminished due to reduced insulin metabolism.

Additional information

- During the early stages of palliative care diabetes should be managed conventionally.
- As disease progresses and prognosis becomes short term, the importance of treatment shifts to preventing symptomatic hyperglycaemia and hypoglycaemia. Fasting blood glucose should be maintained between 8–15mmol/L.
- As the patient deteriorates and oral intake declines, consider halving the dose of insulin.
- During use, do not refrigerate and do not store above 25°C.

❖ Pharmacology

Biphasic insulin aspart is a suspension of human insulin aspart complexed with protamine sulphate, combined with insulin aspart. The net effect is a formulation with an immediate effect, followed by a more sustained action. Onset of action is within 10–20min, with a maximum effect within 1–4 hours; the duration of effect is up to 24 hours.

Insulin: biphasic insulin lispro

Humalog® Mix25 (POM)

Biphasic insulin lispro (recombinant human insulin analogue), 25% insulin lispro, 75% insulin lispro protamine, 100 units/mL.
Injection: 1000 units/10mL vial.
Injection: 5 × 3mL cartridge for *Autopen® Classic* or *HumaPen®* devices.
Injection: 5 × 3mL prefilled disposable *KwikPen®* injection devices; range 1–60 units, allowing 1-unit dosage adjustment.

Humalog® Mix50 (POM)

Biphasic insulin lispro (recombinant human insulin analogue), 50% insulin lispro, 50% insulin lispro protamine, 100 units/mL.
Injection: 5 × 3mL cartridge for *Autopen® Classic* or *HumaPen®* devices.
Injection: 5 × 3mL prefilled disposable *KwikPen®* injection devices; range 1–60 units, allowing 1unit dosage adjustment.

Indications

- Diabetes mellitus.

Contraindications and precautions

- Refer to 📖 Use of drugs in end-of-life care, p.53 for end-of-life care issues.
- Biphasic insulin lispro has a faster onset of action than biphasic human insulin and should generally be given within 15min of a meal or snack containing carbohydrates.
- It must only be administered by SC injection.
- Use with caution in the following:
  - elderly patients (see 📖 Dose adjustments, p.273)
  - renal impairment (see 📖 Dose adjustments, p.273)
  - severe hepatic impairment (see 📖 Dose adjustments, p.273)
  - systemic illness (dose increase may be necessary)
- The risk of reduced warning symptoms of hypoglycaemia is increased in the following circumstances:
  - after transfer from animal insulin to human insulin
  - autonomic neuropathy is present
  - concurrent treatment with particular drugs (see 📖 Drug interactions, p.273)
  - elderly
  - gradual onset of hypoglycaemia
  - long history of diabetes
  - markedly improved glycaemic control
  - psychiatric illness.

😐 Adverse effects

The frequency is not specifically defined, but in common with other insulin products, adverse effects include:
- Hypoglycaemia (also depends on other factors)
- Injection site reactions (generally minor, e.g. redness, pain, itching, or inflammation)
- Lipodystrophy

- Oedema (may cause sodium retention; usually transitory during initiation)
- Peripheral neuropathy
- Retinopathy (usually temporary deterioration associated with abrupt improvement in glycaemic control)
- Urticaria
- Visual disturbances (usually temporary due to marked glycaemic control and associated altered lens properties).

Drug interactions

Pharmacokinetic
- None recognized.

Pharmacodynamic
- *ACEIs*—increased risk of hypoglycaemia.
- *Antipsychotics*—glucose metabolism can be affected; dose adjustments may be necessary.
- *β₂-agonists*—hypoglycaemic effect may be antagonized.
- *Corticosteroids*—hypoglycaemic effect antagonized.
- *Diuretics*—hypoglycaemic effect may be antagonized.
- *Fluoxetine*—increased risk of hypoglycaemia.
- *Octreotide*—can affect glucose metabolism; dose adjustments may be necessary.

Dose
- Biphasic insulin lispro is usually given within 15min of meals.
- The dose is individually determined.

Dose adjustments
Elderly
- In the elderly, progressive deterioration of renal function may lead to a steady decrease in insulin requirements.

Hepatic/renal impairment
- In patients with severe hepatic impairment, insulin requirements may be diminished due to reduced capacity for gluconeogenesis and reduced insulin metabolism.
- In patients with renal impairment, insulin requirements may be diminished due to reduced insulin metabolism.

Additional information
- During the early stages of palliative care diabetes should be managed conventionally.
- As disease progresses and prognosis becomes short term, the importance of treatment shifts to preventing symptomatic hyperglycaemia and hypoglycaemia. Fasting blood glucose should be maintained between 8–15mmol/L.
- As the patient deteriorates and oral intake declines, consider halving the dose of insulin.
- During use, do not refrigerate and do not store above 25°C.

⊅ **Pharmacology**

Biphasic insulin lispro is a suspension of insulin lispro complexed with protamine sulphate, combined with insulin lispro. The net effect is a formulation with an immediate effect, followed by a more sustained action. Onset of action is within 15min, with a maximum effect within 1–4 hours; the duration of effect is up to 24 hours.

Insulin: biphasic isophane insulin

Humulin M3® (POM)
Biphasic isophane insulin (human, prb), 30% soluble, 70% isophane, 100 units/mL.
Injection: 10mL vial.
Injection: 5 × 3mL cartridge for most *Autopen® Classic* or *HumaPen®* devices.
Injection: 5 × 3mL prefilled disposable *KwikPen®* injection devices (range 1–60 units, allowing 1-unit dosage adjustment).

Insuman® Comb 15 (POM)
Biphasic isophane insulin (human, crb), 15% soluble, 85% isophane, 100 units/mL.
Injection: 5 × 3mL cartridge for *ClikSTAR®*, *OptiPen® Pro 1*, and *Autopen®* 24 injection devices.
Injection: 5 × 3mL prefilled disposable *OptiSet®* injection devices; range 2–40 units, allowing 2-unit dosage adjustment.

Insuman® Comb 25 (POM)
Biphasic isophane insulin (human, crb), 25% soluble, 75% isophane, 100 units/mL.
Injection: 5mL vial.
Injection: 5 × 3mL cartridge for *ClikSTAR®*, *OptiPen® Pro 1*, and *Autopen®* 24 injection devices.
Injection: 5 × 3mL prefilled disposable *SoloStar®* injection devices; range 1–80 units, allowing 1-unit dosage adjustment.

Insuman® Comb 50 (POM)
Biphasic isophane insulin (human, crb), 50% soluble, 50% isophane, 100 units/mL.
Injection: 5 × 3mL cartridge for *ClikSTAR®*, *OptiPen® Pro 1*, and *Autopen®* 24 injection devices.
Injection: 5 × 3mL prefilled disposable *OptiSet®* injection devices; range 2–40 units, allowing 2-unit dosage adjustment.

Hypurin® Porcine 30/70 Mix (POM)
Biphasic isophane insulin (porcine, highly purified), 30% soluble, 70% isophane, 100 units/mL.
Injection: 10mL vial.
Injection: 5 × 3mL cartridge for *Autopen® Classic* device.

Indications
- Diabetes mellitus.

Contraindications and precautions
- Refer to 📖 Use of drugs in end-of-life care, p.53 for end-of-life care issues.
- An injection should be followed within 30min by a meal or snack containing carbohydrates.
- It must only be administered by SC injection.

- Use with caution in the following:
  - elderly patients (see 📖 Dose adjustments, p.277)
  - renal impairment (see 📖 Dose adjustments, p.277)
  - severe hepatic impairment (see 📖 Dose adjustments, p.277)
  - systemic illness (dose increase may be necessary).
- The risk of reduced warning symptoms of hypoglycaemia is increased in the following circumstances:
  - after transfer from animal insulin to human insulin
  - autonomic neuropathy is present
  - concurrent treatment with particular drugs (see 📖 Drug interactions)
  - elderly
  - gradual onset of hypoglycaemia
  - long history of diabetes
  - markedly improved glycaemic control
  - psychiatric illness.

☺ Adverse effects

Very common
- Hypoglycaemia (also depends on other factors).

Uncommon
- Injection site reactions (generally minor, e.g. redness, pain, itching, or inflammation)
- Lipodystrophy
- Oedema (may cause sodium retention; usually transitory during initiation)
- Peripheral neuropathy
- Retinopathy (usually temporary deterioration associated with abrupt improvement in glycaemic control)
- Urticaria.

Very rare
- Visual disturbances (usually temporary due to marked glycaemic control and associated altered lens properties).

Drug interactions

Pharmacokinetic
- None recognized.

Pharmacodynamic
- *ACEIs*—increased risk of hypoglycaemia.
- *Antipsychotics*—glucose metabolism can be affected; dose adjustments may be necessary.
- *β_2-agonists*—hypoglycaemic effect may be antagonized.
- *Corticosteroids*—hypoglycaemic effect antagonized.
- *Diuretics*—hypoglycaemic effect may be antagonized.
- *Fluoxetine*—increased risk of hypoglycaemia.
- *Octreotide*—can affect glucose metabolism; dose adjustments may be necessary.

♣ Dose

- Biphasic isophane insulin is usually given OD–BD. As a suitable starting dose would be 10 units SC OD and titrate according to requirements.

Dose adjustments

Elderly

- In the elderly, progressive deterioration of renal function may lead to a steady decrease in insulin requirements.

Hepatic/renal impairment

- In patients with severe hepatic impairment, insulin requirements may be diminished due to reduced capacity for gluconeogenesis and reduced insulin metabolism.
- In patients with renal impairment, insulin requirements may be diminished due to reduced insulin metabolism.

Additional information

- During the early stages of palliative care diabetes should be managed conventionally.
- As disease progresses and prognosis becomes short term, the importance of treatment shifts to preventing symptomatic hyperglycaemia and hypoglycaemia. Fasting blood glucose should be maintained between 8–15mmol/L.
- As the patient deteriorates and oral intake declines, consider halving the dose of insulin.
- During use, do not refrigerate and do not store above 25°C.

Pharmacology

Biphasic isophane insulin is a suspension of either porcine or human insulin complexed with protamine sulphate, combined with soluble insulin. The net effect is a formulation with an immediate effect, followed by a more sustained action. Onset of action is within 30min, with a maximum effect within 2–8 hours; the duration of effect is up to 24 hours.

Insulin: insulin aspart

NovoRapid® (POM)
Insulin aspart (recombinant human insulin analogue), 100 units/mL.
Injection: 10mL vial.
Injection: 5 × 3mL *Penfill®* cartridge for *Novopen®* devices.
Injection: 5 × 3mL prefilled disposable *FlexPen®* injection devices; range 1–60 units, allowing 1unit dosage adjustment.

Indications
• Diabetes mellitus.

Contraindications and precautions
• Refer to 📖 Use of drugs in end-of-life care, p.53 for end-of-life care issues.
• *NovoRapid®* has a faster onset of action than soluble human insulin and should generally be given within 10min of a meal or snack containing carbohydrates.
• Use with caution in the following:
  • elderly patients (see 📖 Dose adjustments, p.279)
  • renal impairment (see 📖 Dose adjustments, p.279)
  • severe hepatic impairment (see 📖 Dose adjustments, p.279)
  • systemic illness (dose increase may be necessary).
• The risk of reduced warning symptoms of hypoglycaemia is increased in the following circumstances:
  • after transfer from animal insulin to human insulin
  • autonomic neuropathy is present
  • concurrent treatment with particular drugs (see 📖 Drug interactions, p.279)
  • elderly
  • gradual onset of hypoglycaemia
  • long history of diabetes
  • markedly improved glycaemic control
  • psychiatric illness

☺ Adverse effects
Very common
• Hypoglycaemia.

Uncommon
• Injection site reactions (generally minor, e.g. redness, pain, itching, or inflammation)
• Lipodystrophy
• Oedema (may cause sodium retention; usually transitory during initiation)
• Peripheral neuropathy
• Retinopathy (usually temporary deterioration associated with abrupt improvement in glycaemic control)
• Urticaria
• Visual disturbances (usually temporary due to marked glycaemic control and associated altered lens properties).

Drug interactions

Pharmacokinetic

• None recognized.

Pharmacodynamic

• *ACEIs*—increased risk of hypoglycaemia.
• *Antipsychotics*—glucose metabolism can be affected; dose adjustments may be necessary.
• *β_2-agonists*—hypoglycaemic effect may be antagonized.
• *Corticosteroids*—hypoglycaemic effect antagonized.
• *Diuretics*—hypoglycaemic effect may be antagonized.
• *Fluoxetine*—increased risk of hypoglycaemia.
• *Octreotide*—can affect glucose metabolism; dose adjustments may be necessary.

⚗ Dose

• Dosing must be individualized. As a rule, if blood glucose >15mmol/L and patient symptomatic, give up to 5 units SC. Recheck after an hour; if it has remained above 15mmol/L treat with the same dose only if symptomatic.

⚗ Dose adjustments

Elderly

• In the elderly, progressive deterioration of renal function may lead to a steady decrease in insulin requirements.

Hepatic/renal impairment

• In patients with severe hepatic impairment, insulin requirements may be diminished due to reduced capacity for gluconeogenesis and reduced insulin metabolism.
• In patients with renal impairment, insulin requirements may be diminished due to reduced insulin metabolism.

Additional information

• During the early stages of palliative care diabetes should be managed conventionally.
• As disease progresses and prognosis becomes short term, the importance of treatment shifts to preventing symptomatic hyperglycaemia and hypoglycaemia. Fasting blood glucose should be maintained between 8–15mmol/L.
• As the patient deteriorates and oral intake declines, consider halving the dose of insulin.

⟿ Pharmacology

Insulin aspart is a fast-acting insulin. Onset of action is within 10–20min, with a maximum effect within 1–4 hours; the duration of effect is up to 3–5 hours.

Insulin: insulin detemir

Levemir® (POM)
Insulin detemir (recombinant human insulin analogue) 100 units/mL.
Injection: 5 × 3mL cartridge for *NovoPen®* device.
Injection: 5 × 3mL prefilled disposable *FlexPen®* injection devices; range 1–60 units, allowing 1-unit dosage adjustment.
Injection: 5 × 3mL prefilled disposable *InnoLet®* injection devices; range 1–50 units, allowing 1-unit dosage adjustment.

Indications
• Diabetes mellitus.

Contraindications and precautions
• Refer to 📖 Use of drugs in end-of-life care, p.53 for end-of-life care issues.
• Insulin detemir is not the insulin of choice for the treatment of diabetic ketoacidosis.
• It must only be administered by SC injection.
• Use with caution in the following:
  • elderly patients (see 📖 Dose adjustments, p.281)
  • renal impairment (see 📖 Dose adjustments, p.281)
  • severe hepatic impairment (see 📖 Dose adjustments, p.281)
  • systemic illness (dose increase may be necessary).
• The risk of reduced warning symptoms of hypoglycaemia is increased in the following circumstances:
  • after transfer from animal insulin to human insulin
  • autonomic neuropathy is present
  • concurrent treatment with particular drugs (see 📖 Drug interactions, p.281)
  • elderly
  • gradual onset of hypoglycaemia
  • long history of diabetes
  • markedly improved glycaemic control
  • psychiatric illness.

☺ Adverse effects

Common
• Hypoglycaemia (also depends on other factors)
• Injection site reactions (generally minor, e.g. redness, pain, itching, or inflammation).

Uncommon
• Lipodystrophy
• Oedema (may cause sodium retention; usually transitory during initiation)
• Retinopathy (usually temporary deterioration associated with abrupt improvement in glycaemic control)
• Visual disturbances (usually temporary due to marked glycaemic control and associated altered lens properties).

Rare
• Peripheral neuropathy
• Urticaria.

Drug interactions
Pharmacokinetic
- None recognized.

Pharmacodynamic
- *ACEIs*—increased risk of hypoglycaemia.
- *Antipsychotics*—glucose metabolism can be affected; dose adjustments may be necessary.
- *β_2-agonists*—hypoglycaemic effect may be antagonized.
- *Corticosteroids*—hypoglycaemic effect antagonized.
- *Diuretics*—hypoglycaemic effect may be antagonized.
- *Fluoxetine*—increased risk of hypoglycaemia.
- *Octreotide*—can affect glucose metabolism; dose adjustments may be necessary.

Dose
- Initial dose 10 units SC OD (or 0.1–0.2 units/kg SC OD) at any time but at the same time each day.
- The dosage and timing of dose of insulin detemir should be individually adjusted. Some patients may require BD dosing.

Dose adjustments
Elderly
- In the elderly, progressive deterioration of renal function may lead to a steady decrease in insulin requirements.

Hepatic/renal impairment
- In patients with severe hepatic impairment, insulin requirements may be diminished due to reduced capacity for gluconeogenesis and reduced insulin metabolism.
- In patients with renal impairment, insulin requirements may be diminished due to reduced insulin metabolism.

Additional information
- During the early stages of palliative care diabetes should be managed conventionally.
- As disease progresses and prognosis becomes short term, the importance of treatment shifts to preventing symptomatic hyperglycaemia and hypoglycaemia. Fasting blood glucose should be maintained between 8–15mmol/L.
- As the patient deteriorates and oral intake declines, consider halving the dose of insulin. A dose of insulin determir 10 units SC ON will provide a basal insulin level and can be used if the patient is not eating.
- During use, do not refrigerate and do not store above 25°C.

Pharmacology
Insulin detemir is a long-acting human insulin analogue. It has a duration of action of 24 hours that closely resembles the basal insulin secretion of the normal pancreatic β-cells. In patients with type I diabetes, a fast-acting insulin taken with food will also be needed in order to reduce post-prandial glucose elevations.

Insulin: insulin glargine

Lantus® (POM)

Insulin glargine, 100 units/mL.
Injection: 10mL vial.
Injection: 5 × 3mL cartridge for ClikSTAR®, OptiPen® Pro 1, and Autopen® 24 injection devices.
Injection: 5 × 3mL OptiClik® cartridge for OptiClik® injection device.
Injection: 5 × 3mL prefilled disposable OptiSet® injection devices; (range 2–40 units, allowing 2-unit dosage adjustment).
Injection: 5 × 3mL prefilled disposable SoloStar® injection devices (range 1–80 units, allowing 1-unit dosage adjustment).

Indications

- Diabetes mellitus.

Contraindications and precautions

- Refer to 📖 Use of drugs in end-of-life care, p.53 for end-of-life care issues.
- Insulin glargine is not the insulin of choice for the treatment of diabetic ketoacidosis.
- It must only be administered by SC injection.
- Use with caution in the following:
  - elderly patients (see 📖 Dose adjustments, p.283)
  - renal impairment (see 📖 Dose adjustments, p.283)
  - severe hepatic impairment (see 📖 Dose adjustments, p.283)
  - systemic illness (dose increase may be necessary).
- The risk of reduced warning symptoms of hypoglycaemia is increased in the following circumstances:
  - after transfer from animal insulin to human insulin
  - autonomic neuropathy is present
  - concurrent treatment with particular drugs (see 📖 Drug interactions)
  - elderly
  - gradual onset of hypoglycaemia
  - long history of diabetes
  - markedly improved glycaemic control
  - psychiatric illness.

☺ Adverse effects

Very common

- Hypoglycaemia (also depends on other factors).

Common

- Injection site reactions (generally minor, e.g. redness, pain, itching, or inflammation)
- Lipohypertrophy.

Rare

- Oedema (may cause sodium retention)

- Retinopathy (usually temporary deterioration associated with abrupt improvement in glycaemic control)
- Visual disturbances (usually temporary due to marked glycaemic control and associated altered lens properties).

Drug interactions

Pharmacokinetic
- None recognized.

Pharmacodynamic
- *ACEIs*—increased risk of hypoglycaemia.
- *Antipsychotics*—glucose metabolism can be affected; dose adjustments may be necessary.
- *β_2-agonists*—hypoglycaemic effect may be antagonized.
- *Corticosteroids*—hypoglycaemic effect antagonized.
- *Diuretics*—hypoglycaemic effect may be antagonized.
- *Fluoxetine*—increased risk of hypoglycaemia.
- *Octreotide*—can affect glucose metabolism; dose adjustments may be necessary.

Dose

- Glargine should be administered OD at any time but at the same time each day.
- The dosage and timing of dose of insulin glargine should be individually adjusted. For type 2 diabetic patients, it can be given at the same time as oral hypoglycaemics.

Dose adjustments

Elderly
- In the elderly, progressive deterioration of renal function may lead to a steady decrease in insulin requirements.

Hepatic/renal impairment
- In patients with severe hepatic impairment, insulin requirements may be diminished due to reduced capacity for gluconeogenesis and reduced insulin metabolism.
- In patients with renal impairment, insulin requirements may be diminished due to reduced insulin metabolism.

Additional information

- NICE (May 2008) has recommended that, if insulin is required in patients with type 2 diabetes, insulin glargine may be considered if:
  - assistance with injecting insulin is needed, or
  - recurrent symptomatic hypoglycaemia, or
  - twice daily insulin injections necessary in addition to oral antidiabetic drugs.
- During the early stages of palliative care diabetes should be managed conventionally.
- As disease progresses and prognosis becomes short term, the importance of treatment shifts to preventing symptomatic hyperglycaemia and hypoglycaemia. Fasting blood glucose should be maintained between 8–15mmol/L.

- As the patient deteriorates and oral intake declines, consider halving the dose of insulin. A dose of insulin glargine 10 units SC ON will provide a basal insulin level and can be used if the patient is not eating.
- During use, do not refrigerate and do not store above 25°C.

⊸ Pharmacology

Insulin glargine is a long-acting human insulin analogue. It has a duration of action of 24 hours that closely resembles the basal insulin secretion of the normal pancreatic β-cells. In patients with type 1 diabetes, a fast-acting insulin taken with food will also be needed in order to reduce post-prandial glucose elevations.

Insulin: insulin lispro

Humalog® (POM)

Insulin lispro (recombinant human insulin analogue), 100 units/mL.
Injection: 10mL vial.
Injection: 5 × 3mL cartridge for Autopen® Classic or HumaPen® devices.
Injection: 5 × 3mL prefilled disposable KwikPen® injection devices; range
1–60 units, allowing 1unit dosage adjustment.

Indications
- Diabetes mellitus.

Contraindications and precautions
- Refer to 📖 Use of drugs in end-of-life care, p.53 for end-of-life care
  issues.
- Insulin lispro has a faster onset of action than soluble human insulin and
  should generally be given within 15min of a meal or snack containing
  carbohydrates.
- Use with caution in the following:
  - elderly patients (see 📖 Dose adjustments, p.286)
  - renal impairment (see 📖 Dose adjustments, p.286)
  - severe hepatic impairment (see 📖 Dose adjustments, p.286)
  - systemic illness (dose increase may be necessary).
- The risk of reduced warning symptoms of hypoglycaemia is increased in
  the following circumstances:
  - after transfer from animal insulin to human insulin
  - autonomic neuropathy is present
  - concurrent treatment with particular drugs (see 📖 Drug
    interactions, p.286)
  - elderly
  - gradual onset of hypoglycaemia
  - long history of diabetes
  - markedly improved glycaemic control
  - psychiatric illness.

☺ Adverse effects
The frequency is not specifically defined, but in common with other insulin
products, adverse effects include:
- Hypoglycaemia (also depends on other factors)
- Injection site reactions (generally minor, e.g. redness, pain, itching, or
  inflammation)
- Lipodystrophy
- Oedema (may cause sodium retention; usually transitory during initiation)
- Peripheral neuropathy
- Retinopathy (usually temporary deterioration associated with abrupt
  improvement in glycaemic control)
- Urticaria
- Visual disturbances (usually temporary due to marked glycaemic
  control and associated altered lens properties).

Drug interactions

Pharmacokinetic
- None recognized.

Pharmacodynamic
- *ACEIs*—increased risk of hypoglycaemia.
- *Antipsychotics*—glucose metabolism can be affected; dose adjustments may be necessary.
- *β_2-agonists*—hypoglycaemic effect may be antagonized.
- *Corticosteroids*—hypoglycaemic effect antagonized.
- *Diuretics*—hypoglycaemic effect may be antagonized.
- *Fluoxetine*—increased risk of hypoglycaemia.
- *Octreotide*—can affect glucose metabolism; dose adjustments may be necessary.

Dose
- Dosing must be individualized. As a rule, if blood glucose >15 mol/L and patient symptomatic, give up to 5 units SC. Recheck after an hour; if it has remained above 15mmol/L treat with the same dose only if symptomatic.

Dose adjustments

Elderly
- In the elderly, progressive deterioration of renal function may lead to a steady decrease in insulin requirements.

Hepatic/renal impairment
- In patients with severe hepatic impairment, insulin requirements may be diminished due to reduced capacity for gluconeogenesis and reduced insulin metabolism.
- In patients with renal impairment, insulin requirements may be diminished due to reduced insulin metabolism.

Additional information
- During the early stages of palliative care diabetes should be managed conventionally.
- As disease progresses and prognosis becomes short term, the importance of treatment shifts to preventing symptomatic hyperglycaemia and hypoglycaemia. Fasting blood glucose should be maintained between 8–15mmol/L.
- As the patient deteriorates and oral intake declines, consider halving the dose of insulin.

Pharmacology
Insulin lispro is a fast-acting insulin. Onset of action is within 15min, with a maximum effect within 1–2 hours; the duration of effect is up to 2–5 hours.

Insulin: isophane insulin

Humulin I® (POM)
Isophane insulin (human, prb), 100 units/mL.
Injection: 10mL vial.
Injection: 5 × 3mL cartridge for Autopen® Classic or HumaPen® devices.
Injection: 5 × 3mL prefilled disposable Humulin I KwikPen® injection devices; range 1–60 units, allowing 1-unit dosage adjustment.

Insulatard® (POM)
Isophane insulin (human, pyr), 100 units/mL.
Injection: Insulatard® (10mL vial).
Injection: 5 × 3mL Penfill® cartridge for Novopen® device.
Injection: 5 × 3mL prefilled disposable InnoLet® injection devices; range 1–50 units, allowing 1-unit dosage adjustment.

Insuman® Basal (POM)
Isophane insulin (human, crb) 100 units/mL.
Injection: 5mL vial.
Injection: 5 × 3mL cartridge for ClikSTAR®, OptiPen® Pro 1, and Autopen® 24 injection devices.
Injection: 5 × 3mL prefilled disposable Basal Solostar® injection devices; range 1–80 units, allowing 1-unit dosage adjustment.

Hypurin® Bovine Isophane (POM)
Isophane insulin (bovine, highly purified) 100 units/mL.
Injection: 10mL vial.
Injection: 5 × 3mL cartridge for Autopen® Classic device.

Hypurin® Porcine Isophane (POM)
Isophane insulin (porcine, highly purified) 100 units/mL.
Injection: 10mL vial.
Injection: 5 × 3mL cartridge for Autopen® Classic device.

Indications
- Diabetes mellitus.

Contraindications and precautions
- Refer to 📖 Use of drugs in end-of-life care, p.53 for end-of-life care issues.
- It must only be administered by SC injection.
- Use with caution in the following:
  - elderly patients (see 📖 Dose adjustments, p.288)
  - renal impairment (see 📖 Dose adjustments, p.288)
  - severe hepatic impairment (see 📖 Dose adjustments, p.288)
  - systemic illness (dose increase may be necessary).
- The risk of reduced warning symptoms of hypoglycaemia is increased in the following circumstances:
  - after transfer from animal insulin to human insulin
  - autonomic neuropathy is present

- concurrent treatment with particular drugs (see 📖 Drug interactions)
- elderly
- gradual onset of hypoglycaemia
- long history of diabetes
- markedly improved glycaemic control
- psychiatric illness.

☺ Adverse effects

Very common
- Hypoglycaemia (also depends on other factors).

Uncommon
- Injection site reactions (generally minor, e.g. redness, pain, itching, or inflammation)
- Lipodystrophy
- Oedema (may cause sodium retention; usually transitory during initiation)
- Peripheral neuropathy
- Retinopathy (usually temporary deterioration associated with abrupt improvement in glycaemic control)
- Urticaria.

Very rare
- Visual disturbances (usually temporary due to marked glycaemic control and associated altered lens properties).

Drug interactions

Pharmacokinetic
- None recognized.

Pharmacodynamic
- *ACEIs*—increased risk of hypoglycaemia.
- *Antipsychotics*—glucose metabolism can be affected; dose adjustments may be necessary.
- *β_2-agonists*—hypoglycaemic effect may be antagonized.
- *Corticosteroids*—hypoglycaemic effect antagonized.
- *Diuretics*—hypoglycaemic effect may be antagonized.
- *Fluoxetine*—increased risk of hypoglycaemia.
- *Octreotide*—can affect glucose metabolism; dose adjustments may be necessary.

⚗ Dose

- Suitable initial dose 10 units SC OD and titrate according to response.
- Some patients may require BD dosing.
- Can be combined with fast-acting insulin.

⚗ Dose adjustments

Elderly
- In the elderly, progressive deterioration of renal function may lead to a steady decrease in insulin requirements.

Hepatic/renal impairment

* In patients with severe hepatic impairment, insulin requirements may be diminished due to reduced capacity for gluconeogenesis and reduced insulin metabolism.
  In patients with renal impairment, insulin requirements may be diminished due to reduced insulin metabolism.

Additional information

* During the early stages of palliative care diabetes should be managed conventionally.
* As disease progresses and prognosis becomes short term, the importance of treatment shifts to preventing symptomatic hyperglycaemia and hypoglycaemia. Fasting blood glucose should be maintained between 8–15mmol/L.
* As the patient deteriorates and oral intake declines, consider halving the dose of insulin. A dose of isophane insulin 10 units SC ON will provide a basal insulin level and can be used if the patient is not eating.
* During use, do not refrigerate and do not store above 25°C.

⤳ Pharmacology

Isophane insulin is a suspension of either porcine or human insulin complexed with protamine sulphate. Onset of action is within 90min, with a maximum effect within 4–12 hours; the duration of effect is up to 24 hours.

Insulin: soluble

Actrapid® (POM)
Soluble insulin (human, pyr) 100 units/mL.
Injection: 10mL vial.

Humulin S® (POM)
Soluble insulin (human, prb), 100 units/mL.
Injection: 10mL vial.
Injection: 5 × 3mL cartridge for Autopen® Classic or HumaPen® device.

Insuman® Rapid (POM)
Soluble insulin (human, crb) 100 units/mL.
Injection: 5 × 3mL cartridge for ClikSTAR®, OptiPen® Pro 1, and Autopen® 24 injection devices.
Injection: 5 × 3mL prefilled disposable Rapid OptiSet® injection devices range 2–40 units, allowing 2-unit dosage adjustment.

Hypurin® Bovine Neutral (POM)
Soluble insulin (bovine, highly purified) 100 units/mL.
Injection: 10mL vial.
Injection: 5 × 3mL cartridge for Autopen® Classic device.

Hypurin® Porcine Neutral (POM)
Soluble insulin (porcine, highly purified) 100 units/mL.
Injection: 10mL vial.
Injection: 5 × 3mL cartridge for Autopen® Classic device.

Indications
- Diabetes mellitus.

Contraindications and precautions
- Refer to 📖 Use of drugs in end-of-life care, p.53 for end-of-life care issues.
- An injection should be followed within 30min by a meal or snack containing carbohydrates.
- Use with caution in the following:
  - elderly patients (see 📖 Dose adjustments, p.291)
  - renal impairment (see 📖 Dose adjustments, p.291)
  - severe hepatic impairment (see 📖 Dose adjustments, p.291)
  - systemic illness (dose increase may be necessary).
- The risk of reduced warning symptoms of hypoglycaemia is increased in the following circumstances:
  - after transfer from animal insulin to human insulin
  - autonomic neuropathy is present
  - concurrent treatment with particular drugs (see 📖 Drug interactions, p.291)
  - elderly
  - gradual onset of hypoglycaemia
  - long history of diabetes
  - markedly improved glycaemic control
  - psychiatric illness.

Adverse effects

Very common
- Hypoglycaemia (also depends on other factors).

Uncommon
- Injection site reactions (generally minor, e.g. redness, pain, itching, or inflammation)
- Lipodystrophy
- Oedema (may cause sodium retention; usually transitory during initiation)
- Peripheral neuropathy
- Retinopathy (usually temporary deterioration associated with abrupt improvement in glycaemic control)
- Urticaria.

Very rare
- Visual disturbances (usually temporary due to marked glycaemic control and associated altered lens properties).

Drug interactions

Pharmacokinetic
- None recognized.

Pharmacodynamic
- *ACEIs*—increased risk of hypoglycaemia.
- *Antipsychotics*—glucose metabolism can be affected; dose adjustments may be necessary.
- *β_2-agonists*—hypoglycaemic effect may be antagonized.
- *Corticosteroids*—hypoglycaemic effect antagonized.
- *Diuretics*—hypoglycaemic effect may be antagonized.
- *Fluoxetine*—increased risk of hypoglycaemia.
- *Octreotide*—can affect glucose metabolism; dose adjustments may be necessary.

Dose

Dosing must be individualized. As a rule, if blood glucose >15mmol/L and patient symptomatic, give up to 5 units SC. Recheck after an hour; if it has remained above 15mmol/L treat with the same dose only if symptomatic.

Dose adjustments

Elderly
- In the elderly, progressive deterioration of renal function may lead to a steady decrease in insulin requirements.

Hepatic/renal impairment
- In patients with severe hepatic impairment, insulin requirements may be diminished due to reduced capacity for gluconeogenesis and reduced insulin metabolism.
- In patients with renal impairment, insulin requirements may be diminished due to reduced insulin metabolism.

Additional information
- During the early stages of palliative care diabetes should be managed conventionally.
- As disease progresses and prognosis becomes short term, the importance of treatment shifts to preventing symptomatic hyperglycaemia and hypoglycaemia. Fasting blood glucose should be maintained between 8–15mmol/L.
- As the patient deteriorates and oral intake declines, consider halving the dose of insulin.
- During use, do not refrigerate and do not store above 25°C.

❖ Pharmacology
Soluble insulin is fast acting. Onset of action is within 30min with the maximum effect within 1–3 hours; the duration of effect is ~7–8 hours.

Ipratropium bromide

Atrovent® (POM)

Dry powder for inhalation (Aerocaps® capsules for use with Aerohaler®):
40 micrograms (100).
Aerosol inhalation: 20 micrograms/metered dose (200-dose unit).
Nebulizer solution: 250 micrograms/mL unit-dose vials (20; 60); 500 micrograms/2mL unit-dose vials (20; 60).

Ipratropium Steri-Neb® (POM)

Nebulizer solution: 250 micrograms/mL unit-dose vials (20); 500 micrograms/2mL unit-dose vials (20).

Respontin® (POM)

Nebulizer solution: 250 micrograms/mL unit-dose vials (20); 500 micrograms/2mL unit-dose vials (20).

Generic (POM)

Nebulizer solution: 250 micrograms/mL unit-dose vials (20); 500 micrograms/2mL unit-dose vials (20).

Indications

• Reversible airways obstruction.

Contraindications and precautions

Ipratropium bromide should be used with caution in patients with:
  • angle-closure glaucoma
  • bladder outflow obstruction
  • cystic fibrosis (may cause GI motility disturbances)
  • prostatic hyperplasia.
• Should eye pain, blurred vision or visual halos develop, treatment with miotic drops should be initiated and specialist advice sought immediately.

Adverse effects

Common
• Bronchoconstriction
• Constipation
• Cough
• Dizziness
• Dry mouth
• Headache.

Uncommon
• Angle-closure glaucoma
• Tachycardia
• Visual disturbances.

Rare
• Ocular pain
• Urinary retention.

Drug interactions

Pharmacokinetic
- None of clinical significance noted.

Pharmacodynamic
- *Anticholinergics*—concurrent use with ipratropium may increase risk of adverse events.

,ʒ Dose

Dry powder inhalation
- 40 micrograms TDS–QDS (may be doubled in less responsive patients).
- Note 1 *Aerocap*® = 2 puffs of *Atrovent*® metered aerosol inhalation.

Aerosol inhalation
- 20–40 micrograms TDS–QDS (may be doubled in less responsive patients).

Nebulized solution
- 250–500 micrograms TDS–QDS.
- Higher doses (>2g daily) may be given if necessary under medical supervision.

,ʒ Dose adjustments

Elderly
- Usual adult doses can be used. Note, though, that the elderly are more susceptible to adverse effects.

Hepatic/renal impairment
- No specific dose reductions stated.

Additional information

- The bronchodilatory effect may not occur for up to 30min (unlike β_2 agonists).
- If nebulized ipratropium therapy is initiated, ensure any ipratropium (or tiotropium) inhaler device is withdrawn.
- If dilution of the unit dose vials is necessary, use only sterile sodium chloride 0.9%.

⟩ Pharmacology

Ipratropium bromide is an anticholinergic agent. It blocks muscarinic cholinergic receptors, without specificity for subtypes. Following inhalation, up to 30% of the dose is deposited in the lungs, with the majority of the dose being swallowed. The GI absorption is negligible. Ipratropium is metabolized to inactive compounds and 40% of the dose is excreted by the kidneys unchanged.

Itraconazole

Sporanox® (POM)
Capsule: 100mg (4; 15; 28).
Oral liquid: 10mg/mL (150mL).

Generic (POM)
Capsule: 100mg (15).

Indications

- Seek local microbiological advice before using.
- Oral and/or oesophageal candidiasis in HIV-positive or other immunocompromised patients.
- Systemic fungal conditions when first-line systemic antifungal therapy is inappropriate or has proved ineffective.

Contraindications and precautions

- Co-administration of the following drugs is contraindicated:
  - CYP3A4 metabolized substrates that can prolong the QT-interval (e.g. quinidine)
  - CYP3A4 metabolized HMG-CoA reductase inhibitors (e.g. atorvastatin, simvastatin)
  - midazolam (oral)—see 📖 Drug interactions, p.296.
- Itraconazole must not be administered to patients with CHF, or a history of CHF, except for the treatment of life-threatening or other serious infections.
- Use with caution in patients with risk factors for CHF, including:
  - concurrent use of calcium channel blockers (see 📖 Drug interactions, p.296)
  - COPD
  - high doses (of itraconazole) and prolonged treatment course
  - ischemic or valvular disease
  - renal impairment.
- Hepatotoxicity has been reported. Warn the patient about the importance of reporting signs of hepatitis such as abdominal pain, anorexia, dark urine, fatigue, nausea, and vomiting. Treatment should be stopped immediately and LFTs performed.
- Use with caution in patients with pre-existing liver disease; LFTs must be monitored closely if treatment is initiated.
- Absorption of itraconazole from capsules (*not oral liquid*) is reduced if gastric pH is raised (see 📖 Drug interactions, p.296).
- Itraconazole is an inhibitor of CYP3A4. Many drugs metabolized by CYP3A4 can be affected. Similarly, CYP3A4 inducers may significantly reduce the effect of itraconazole (see 📖 Drug interactions, p.296).

⊕ Adverse effects

Common

- Abdominal pain
- Nausea
- Rash.

Uncommon

- Alopecia
- Constipation
- Diarrhoea
- Dizziness
- Dysgeusia
- Dyspepsia
- Flatulence
- Headache
- Hypersensitivity
- Menstrual disorder
- Oedema
- Paraesthesia (discontinue if peripheral neuropathy suspected)
- Pruritus
- Raised LFTs
- Urticaria
- Vomiting.

Rare

- Dyspnoea
- Leucopenia
- Pancreatitis
- Tinnitus (transient hearing loss reported)
- Visual disturbance.

Unknown

- Anaphylaxis
- Arthralgia
- CHF (discontinue)
- Erectile dysfunction
- Hepatitis (discontinue)
- Hypokalaemia
- Hypertriglyceridaemia
- Myalgia
- Neutropenia
- Peripheral neuropathy (discontinue)
- Pulmonary oedema
- Severe skin reactions (e.g. Stevens–Johnson syndrome, toxic epidermal necrolysis)
- Thrombocytopenia
- Urinary incontinence.

Drug interactions

Pharmacokinetic

- The absorption of itraconazole is pH dependent. Drugs that raise gastric pH can reduce oral bioavailability and result in sub-therapeutic plasma concentrations (e.g. *antacids, lansoprazole, omeprazole, ranitidine*).
- Itraconazole is a substrate of CYP3A4; it is also strong inhibitor of CYP3A4 and P-gp. Co-administration with drugs that are metabolized by, or affect the activity (induction or inhibition—see 📖 inside back cover) of this pathway may lead to clinically relevant drug interactions and the prescriber should be aware that dosage adjustments may be necessary, particularly of drugs with a narrow therapeutic index.
- Several interactions are listed here, but refer to 📖 inside back cover for a list of drugs that may potentially be affected.
- *Alfentanil*—increased risk of alfentanil toxicity; dose reduction may be necessary.
- *Carbamazepine*—risk of carbamazepine toxicity (avoid combination or monitor closely); risk of itraconazole therapeutic failure.
- *Ciclosporin*—risk of ciclosporin toxicity.
- *Clarithromycin*—risk of itraconazole toxicity.
- *Dexamethasone*—increased effect; dose reduction may be necessary.
- *Digoxin*—dose reduction may be necessary (P-gp inhibition).
- *Erythromycin*—risk of itraconazole toxicity.
- *Fentanyl*—increased risk of fentanyl toxicity; dose reduction may be necessary.

- *Midazolam*—increased risk of midazolam toxicity—use lower initial doses; dose adjustments may be necessary if itraconazole is added or discontinued (*NB oral midazolam is contraindicated due to risk of toxicity*).
- *Phenytoin*—risk of itraconazole therapeutic failure.
  Reboxetine—risk of reboxetine toxicity.
- *Theophylline*—risk of theophylline toxicity; dose reduction may be necessary.
- *Warfarin*—risk of raised INR.
- *Zopiclone*—increased plasma concentration and effects of zopiclone.

Pharmacodynamic
  Calcium channel blockers—increased risk of CHF due to negative inotropic effects

Dose
Standard doses are described here. Refer to local guidelines for specific advice.

Oral/oesophageal candidiasis
  Oral solution is preferred.
  10–20mL (100–200mg) PO BD for 14 days. Use the solution as a mouthwash and swallow. Ensure the patient does not rinse the mouth afterwards.

Dose adjustments
Elderly
- The manufacturers state that itraconazole should not be used in the elderly unless the potential benefit outweighs the potential risks.

Hepatic/renal impairment
- No specific guidance is available for patients with hepatic impairment. The manufacturers state that since itraconazole is predominantly metabolized by the liver, it should be used with caution and a dose adjustment may be considered.
- No specific guidance is available for patients with renal impairment. The oral bioavailability may be reduced in patients with renal impairment and a dose adjustment may be considered

Additional information
- The oral solution should be taken without food and patients must be advised avoid eating for at least 1 hour after intake.
- The capsules must be taken with food for maximal absorption.
  Be aware of the potential for drug interactions with itraconazole.

Pharmacology
Itraconazole is rapidly absorbed after oral administration and is extensively metabolized by the liver via CYP3A4 into several metabolites. Plasma concentrations of hydroxy-itraconazole, an active metabolite with similar antifungal activity to itraconazole, are about double those of itraconazole. Metabolism is saturable. <0.05% of a dose is excreted unchanged by the kidneys. The majority of a dose is excreted as inactive metabolites in the urine and faeces.

Ketamine

Ketalar® (CD4a POM)

Injection: 10mg/mL (20mL vial); 50mg/mL (10mL vial); 100mg/mL (10mL vial).
See 📖 Additional information, p.000 for supply issues.

Unlicensed Special (CD4a POM)

Oral solution: 50mg/5mL (available in a variety of volumes and flavours)
See 📖 Additional information, p.300 for supply issues.

Indications

- ⁺Refractory chronic pain.[1,2]

Contraindications and precautions

- Refer to 📖 Use of drugs in end-of-life care, p.53 for end-of-life care issues.
- Contraindicated for use in patients with intracranial hypertension, or where a rise in blood pressure may pose a serious hazard.
- Continuous use of ketamine has been reported to cause urinary tract symptoms, such as urinary frequency, incontinence, and haemorrhagic cystitis. This is believed to occur with continuous and prolonged use (e.g. >5 months), although there are case reports of earlier development. If symptoms develop in the absence of a UTI, a urologist should be consulted. If ketamine is considered to be the cause, it should be withdrawn gradually. In most cases symptoms improve after discontinuation, although there are reports of irreversible renal impairment.
- Avoid in acute porphyria.
- Use with caution in patients with hypertension, epilepsy, cardiac failure, ischaemic heart disease, or previous CVAs.
- Dose adjustments may be necessary in the elderly and liver impairment (see 📖 Dose adjustments, p.300).
- It is advisable to reduce any concurrent opioid dose by 30–50% prior to commencing ketamine.
- Ketamine may cause drowsiness and dizziness. Patients should be advised not drive (or operate machinery) if affected. Refer to 📖 Drugs and driving, p.25.
- Avoid grapefruit juice with oral ketamine.

☺ Adverse effects

Given the manner in which ketamine is used in palliative care, the incidence of adverse effects is difficult to judge. Anxious patients may be more at risk. adverse effects from oral use tend to be less intense. The following have been reported:

- Confusion
- Cystitis (may be haemorrhagic)
- Dizziness

Excessive salivation
Euphoria
Hallucinations
Hypertension
Pain and inflammation around injection site
Sedation
Vivid dreams.

Drug interactions

Pharmacokinetic

Ketamine is metabolized by CYP2B6, CYP2C9, and CYP3A4.
Co-administration with drugs that are metabolized by, or affect the activity (induction or inhibition—see 📖 inside back cover) of these pathways may lead to clinically relevant drug interactions and the prescriber should be aware that dosage adjustments may be necessary, particularly of drugs with a narrow therapeutic index.

Note that norketamine (see 📖 Pharmacology, p.301) is produced by the action of CYP3A4 and use of drugs that inhibit or induce this isoenzyme may affect analgesia.

The effect of grapefruit juice on the first-pass metabolism of oral ketamine is unknown.

Pharmacodynamic

CNS depressants—risk of excessive sedation.
Opioids—dose of opioid should be reviewed when ketamine is introduced; there is likely to be an opioid-sparing effect necessitating a dose reduction.

Dose

Burst ketamine

Treatment is given short-term, via CSCI, usually for no longer than 5 days. Initial dose 100mg over 24 hours via CSCI. The dose is increased by 200mg every 24 hours as necessary, to a maximum of 500mg over 24 hours. Treatment is discontinued after 3 days of the effective dose (i.e. day 3 at 100mg, day 4 at 300mg or day 5 at 500mg).

Burst ketamine has been shown to relieve pain in up to 50% of patients with intractable pain for at least 2 weeks; some patients may remain free for several months. Treatment has been repeated at 4–8-weekly intervals.

By CSCI

Initial dose 50–100mg over 24 hours, with 25mg SC PRN (suggested QDS maximum). Dose can be increased by 50–100mg every 24 hours until benefit achieved. Doses above 600mg over 24 hours should be under specialist guidance only.

Oral

Initial dose 10–25mg PO TDS–QDS and PRN (suggested QDS maximum). Increase in steps of 10–25mg TDS–QDS, to a maximum dose of 100mg PO QDS. Higher doses have been used under specialist guidance (e.g. up to 200mg PO QDS).

- Consider gradual withdrawal of ketamine over 1–2 weeks once analgesia is achieved.
- If pain recurs, consider a further course of treatment.

⚕ Dose adjustments

Elderly

- No information is available. Nonetheless, it is advisable to initiate treatment with doses at the low end of the ranges quoted.

Hepatic/renal impairment

- Ketamine is hepatically metabolized. Although no information exists, it is advisable to initiate treatment with doses at the low end of the ranges quoted.
- No dose adjustments should be necessary in renal impairment.

Additional information

Supply issues

Ketamine vials

- Ketamine injection is easily available in hospitals and the community. In the community, the patient should present the prescription to the pharmacist is the usual way. The community pharmacist can then place an order through Alliance Healthcare, or directly with Pfizer (Tel: 01304 645262).
- Supply should be made within 3 days of the request. The patient should be advised to request a prescription from the GP at least 5 days before the supply is needed.

Ketamine oral solution 50mg/5mL

- This unlicensed product is available as a special order from various suppliers, e.g. Martindale Pharma (0800 137627).
- There are a variety of flavours (e.g. aniseed, peppermint) and volumes available. The flavour should be specified on the prescription; if not, determine the patient's preference.
- It can take up to 7 days for delivery. The patient should be advised to request a prescription from the GP at least 10 days before the supply is needed.

Extemporaneous preparation of ketamine oral solution

- The injection can be used directly from the vial, although flavouring will be needed to mask the taste (e.g. fruit juice, but *not* grapefruit).
- Alternatively, the injection can be transferred from the vial (e.g. 100mg/ mL vial) and diluted with a suitable vehicle (e.g. Raspberry Syrup BP or purified water) to a concentration of 50mg/5mL. If purified water is used, the patient should be advised to use a flavouring to mask the taste.
- The extemporaneous product has an expiry of 7 days and should be refrigerated.

CSCI issues

- The injection is irritant and infusions should be maximally diluted with sodium chloride 0.9%. Low-dose dexamethasone (0.5–1mg) can be added to the infusion to help prevent site reactions.
- Ketamine via CSCI is compatible with alfentanil, diamorphine, haloperidol, levomepromazine, midazolam, morphine sulphate, and oxycodone.

• Ketamine is considered to be incompatible with cyclizine, dexamethasone (higher doses) and phenobarbital.

Pharmacology

Ketamine has a variety of pharmacological actions, including interaction with N-methyl-D-aspartate (NMDA) receptors, opioids receptors, muscarinic receptors and Na^+ ion channels. The analgesic effect of ketamine that is seen at sub-anaesthetic doses is due to non-competitive antagonism of the NMDA receptor. Ketamine interacts with a specific binding site on the NMDA receptor complex, blocking the influx of Na^+ and Ca^{2+}. Binding of ketamine will only occur when the ion channel has been opened though neuronal excitation. The analgesic activity is believed to be due to the attenuation of the 'wind-up' phenomenon by reducing the excitability of the neuron.

Oral ketamine is poorly absorbed after oral administration and undergoes extensive first-pass metabolism to norketamine. CYP3A4 is the major isoenzyme responsible (both enteric and hepatic) while CYP2B6 and CYP2C9 have a minor role. On repeated administration, ketamine induces its own metabolism. Although the analgesic potencies of ketamine and norketamine are thought to be similar, the peak plasma concentration of norketamine produced after oral administration is greater than that by parenteral. With chronic use, norketamine may have a more influential analgesic effect. Consequently, on chronic dosing analgesia appears to be achieved with lower oral doses compared to parenteral. A recent review[3] however, raises doubts. Until definitive evidence is available, when converting from PO:SC for use in a CSCI, a conversion of 1:1 is suggested; when converting from SC:PO, a conversion of 3:1 is suggested. In both cases, there should be the provision for close monitoring and ability to alter the dose as necessary.

References

1. Soto E, Stewart DR, Mannes AJ, et al. Oral ketamine in the palliative care setting: A review of the literature and case report of a patient with neurofibromatosis type 1 and glomus tumor-associated complex regional pain syndrome. Am J Hosp Palliat Care 2011 Jul 29. (Epub ahead of print.)

2. Jackson K, Ashby M, Howell D, et al. The effectiveness and adverse effects profile of 'burst' ketamine in refractory cancer pain: The VCOG PM 1-00 study. J Palliat Care 2010; **26**(3): 176–83.

3. Benitez-Rosario MA, Salinas-Martin A, Gonzalez-Guillermo T, Feria M. A strategy for conversion from subcutaneous to oral ketamine in cancer pain patients: Effect of a 1:1 ratio. J Pain Symptom Manage 2011; **41**(6): 1098–1105.

Ketorolac

Toradol® (POM)
Tablet: 10mg (20).
Injection: 10mg/mL (5); 30mg/mL (5).

Indications

- Short-term management of moderate to severe acute postoperative pain.
- *Short-term management of cancer pain.[1]

Contraindications and precautions

- Refer to 📖 Use of drugs in end-of-life care, p.53 for end-of-life care issues.
- Contraindicated for use in patients with:
  - a history of, or active, peptic ulceration
  - hypersensitivity reactions to ibuprofen, aspirin, or other NSAIDs
  - moderate or severe renal impairment (serum creatinine >160micromol/L)
  - severe heart failure
  - suspected or confirmed cerebrovascular bleeding
  - haemorrhagic diatheses, including coagulation disorders
  - complete or partial syndrome of nasal polyps, angio-oedema, or bronchospasm
  - hypovolaemia from any cause or dehydration
  - concurrent treatment with aspirin, other NSAIDs including COX-2 inhibitors, anticoagulants including low dose heparin, pentoxifylline, probenecid, or lithium (see 📖 Drug interactions, p.303).
- Use the minimum effective dose for the shortest duration necessary in order to reduce the risk of cardiac and GI events.
- Elderly patients are more at risk of developing adverse effects.
- Patients with uncontrolled hypertension, CHF, established ischaemic heart disease, peripheral arterial disease, and/or cerebrovascular disease need careful consideration due to the increased risk of thrombotic events.
- Similar consideration should be made before initiating longer-term treatment of patients with risk factors for cardiovascular events (e.g. hypertension, hyperlipidaemia, diabetes mellitus, and smoking).
- Caution should be exercised in patients with a history of cardiac failure left ventricular dysfunction, or hypertension. Deterioration may occur due to fluid retention.
- In patients with renal, cardiac or hepatic impairment, caution is required since the use of NSAIDs may result in deterioration of renal function.
- Refer to 📖 Selection of NSAID, p.29 for further information, including selection.
- Ketorolac may modify reactions and patients should be advised not drive (or operate machinery) if affected. Refer to 📖 Drugs and driving, p.25.

ⓘ Adverse effects

The frequency is not defined, but reported adverse effects include:

- Abdominal pain
- Acute renal failure
- Coagulopathy
- Diarrhoea
- Dizziness
- Drowsiness
- Dyspepsia
- Flatulence
- GI haemorrhage

- Headache
- Hypertension
- Oedema
- Pain at injection site (less so for CSCI)
- Rash
- Stomatitis
- Vomiting.

Drug interactions

Pharmacokinetic

Lithium—increased risk of lithium toxicity due to reduced renal clearance.
Methotrexate—reduced excretion of methotrexate.

Pharmacodynamic

Anticoagulants—increased risk of bleeding (concurrent use contraindicated).
Antihypertensives—reduced hypotensive effect.
Antiplatelet drugs—increased risk of bleeding (concurrent use contraindicated).
Corticosteroids—increased risk of GI toxicity.
Ciclosporin—increased risk of nephrotoxicity.
Diuretics—reduced diuretic effect; nephrotoxicity of ketorolac may be increased.
Rosiglitazone—increased risk of oedema.
SSRIs—increased risk of GI bleeding.

ⓘ Dose

Gastroprotective treatment must be prescribed concurrently if appropriate. Consider misoprostol or a PPI. Alternatively, ranitidine via CSCI can be considered.

Cancer pain

Initial dose 10–30mg SC TDS PRN. Alternatively, 60mg OD via CSCI, increasing to 90mg if necessary.

ⓘ Dose adjustments

Elderly

The elderly are at an increased risk of adverse effects due to an increased plasma half-life and reduced plasma clearance of ketorolac. Initial dose 30mg OD via CSCI, increasing by 15mg/day increments to a maximum recommended dose of 60mg/day.

Hepatic/renal impairment

In liver impairment, no specific dose recommendations are available. However, the lowest dose possible should be used for the shortest duration possible.

- Ketorolac must not be used in patients with moderate to severe renal impairment. In patients with mild renal impairment, the dose used should not exceed 60mg/day.

Additional information

- Ensure concurrent opioid requirements are reviewed; since ketorolac is such a potent analgesic, it may have opioid-sparing effects.
- The risk of clinically serious GI bleeding is dose-dependent. This is particularly true in elderly patients who receive an average daily dose >60mg/day of ketorolac.
- Ketorolac via CSCI should be diluted with NaCl 0.9% and administered a separate infusion, unless compatibility data are available. There is a risk of incompatibility with many drugs given via CSCI since ketorolac has an alkaline pH. However, it is compatible with diamorphine and oxycodone.
- Ketorolac may precipitate in solutions with a low pH and is reportedly incompatible with cyclizine, haloperidol, morphine, and promethazine. There are mixed reports of incompatibility with hydromorphone. Glycopyrronium is likely to be incompatible due to the alkaline pH of ketorolac.

⋏ Pharmacology

Ketorolac exhibits anti-inflammatory, analgesic, and antipyretic activity although the analgesic effect appears to be the predominant action The mechanism of action of ketorolac, like that of other NSAIDs, is no completely understood but may be related to inhibition of COX-1 an COX-2. The major metabolic pathway is glucuronic acid conjugation an about 90% of a dose is excreted in urine as unchanged drug metabolites.

Reference

1. Hughes A, Wilcock A, Corcoran R. Ketorolac: continuous subcutaneous infusion for cancer pain. *J Pain Symptom Manage* 1997; **13**(6):315–16.

Lactulose

Generic (P)
Solution: 3.1–3.7g/5mL (300mL; 500mL).
Sachets: 10 g/15mL oral solution per sachet.

Indications

- Treatment of constipation.
- Treatment of hepatic encephalopathy.

Contraindications and precautions

- Contraindicated for use in:
  • galactosaemia
  • intestinal obstruction.
- Use with caution in patients with lactose intolerance.

☺ Adverse effects

Very common
- Abdominal pain
- Flatulence (should improve after a few days treatment).

Common
- Diarrhoea
- Nausea
- Vomiting.

Drug interactions

Pharmacokinetic
- None known.

Pharmacodynamic
- *Anticholinergics*—antagonizes the laxative effect.
- *Cyclizine*—antagonizes the laxative effect.
- *Opioids*—antagonizes the laxative effect.
- *5-HT₃ antagonists*—antagonizes the laxative effect.
- *TCAs*—antagonizes the laxative effect.

⚖ Dose

Constipation
- Initial dose 15mL PO BD, adjusted to the patient's needs.

Hepatic encephalopathy
- Initial dose 30–50mL PO TDS, adjusted to produce 2–3 soft stools each day.

⚖ Dose adjustments

Elderly
- No dose adjustment necessary.

Hepatic/renal impairment
- No dose adjustment necessary.

Additional information

• Can take up to 48 hours for the laxative effect to work.

⟐ Pharmacology

Lactulose is a synthetic sugar consisting of fructose and galactose. In the colon, it is broken down primarily to lactic acid by the action colonic bacteria. This results in an increase in osmotic pressure and slight reduction of colonic pH which cause an increase in stool water content and softens the stool. In the treatment of hepatic encephalopathy, it is thought that the low pH reduces the absorption of ammonium ions and other toxic nitrogenous compounds.

Lansoprazole

Zoton Fastabs® (POM)
Orodispersible tablet: 15mg (28); 30mg (7; 14; 28).

Generic (POM)
Capsule (enclosing e/c granules): 15mg (28); 30mg (28).

Indications

- Treatment of benign gastric and duodenal ulcer.
- Treatment and prophylaxis of gastro-oesophageal reflux disease.
- Treatment and prophylaxis of NSAID associated benign gastric and duodenal ulcers requiring continual therapy.

Contraindications and precautions

- Do not administer with atazanavir or erlotinib.
- Treatment with lansoprazole may lead to a slightly increased risk of developing GI infections (e.g. *Clostridium difficile*). Therefore, avoid unnecessary use or high doses.
- *Zoton Fastabs*® contain aspartame—avoid in phenylketonuria.
- Lansoprazole may modify reactions and patients should be advised not drive (or operate machinery) if affected.
- Rebound acid hypersecretion may occur on discontinuation of the patient has received >8 weeks' treatment.
- PPIs are associated with a range of electrolyte disturbances, such as hyponatraemia and hypomagnesaemia (and associated hypocalcaemia and hypokalaemia). Suspect the PPI should unexplainable symptoms present (e.g. confusion, delirium, generalized weakness, nausea). The effect on sodium metabolism is unclear, possibly involving ADH. PPIs may reduce active magnesium absorption in the small intestine by affecting function of a transient receptor protein channel.

⚕ Adverse effects

Common

- Abnormal LFTs
- Diarrhoea
- Dry mouth
- Fatigue
- Flatulence
- Headache
- Nausea/vomiting
- Rash.

Uncommon

- Arthralgia
- Blood dyscrasias
- Myalgia
- Oedema.

Rare

- Confusion
- Gynaecomastia
- Hepatitis
- Insomnia
- Pancreatitis
- Taste disturbances.

Very rare

- Stevens–Johnson syndrome.

Drug interactions

Pharmacokinetic

- Lansoprazole is metabolized mainly by CYP2C19 with a minor role involving CYP3A4. It also has a moderate inhibitory effect on CYP2C19 and can induce CYP1A2. Co-administration with drugs that are metabolized by, or affect the activity (induction or inhibition—see 📖 inside back cover) of these pathways may lead to clinically relevant drug interactions and the prescriber should be aware that dosage adjustments may be necessary, particularly of drugs with a narrow therapeutic index.
- P-gp is inhibited by lansoprazole, but the clinical significance is presently unknown.
- Drugs with pH dependent absorption can be affected:
  - *atazanavir*—avoid combination due to substantially reduced absorption
  - *digoxin*—increased plasma concentrations possible
  - *erlotinib*—avoid combination as bioavailability of erlotinib can be significantly reduced
  - *ferrous sulphate*—reduced absorption likely to result in treatment failure; some recommend co-administration of ascorbic acid (e.g. 100mg) at the same as ferrous sulphate to improve absorption
  - *ketoconazole/itraconazole*—risk of sub-therapeutic plasma concentrations
  - *metronidazole suspension* —ranitidine may reduce/prevent the absorption of metronidazole.
- *Antacids*—should be given at least 1 hour before lansoprazole (reduced bioavailability).
- *Clopidogrel*—antiplatelet action may be reduced (avoid combination).
- *Theophylline*—lansoprazole can reduce the plasma concentration (CYP1A2 induction).

Pharmacodynamic

- No clinically significant interactions noted.

💊 Dose

Treatment of peptic ulcer disease

- 30mg PO OD for 2–4 weeks.
- Gastric ulcer treatment may need to continue for 4–8 weeks.

Reflux oesophagitis

- Treatment: 30mg PO OD for 4–8 weeks.
- Prophylaxis: 15–30mg PO OD as necessary.

NSAID associated benign gastric and duodenal ulcers:

- Treatment: 30mg PO OD for 4 weeks, continuing to 8 weeks if not fully healed. 30mg PO BD can be considered.
- Prophylaxis: 15–30mg PO OD.

NB There is little evidence to recommend routine prescribing of lansoprazole 30mg PO OD for dyspeptic symptoms. If 30mg PO OD fails to control such symptoms, treatment should be combined with antacids (given at least 1 hour before lansoprazole) such as Gaviscon®.

Dose adjustments

Elderly
- 30mg PO OD should not usually be exceeded unless there are compelling clinical reasons.

Hepatic/renal impairment
- A 50% dose reduction is recommended in moderate–severe hepatic impairment.
- No dose adjustment is necessary in renal impairment.

Additional information

- Lansoprazole capsules may be opened and emptied into a glass of orange juice or apple juice, mixed, and swallowed immediately. The glass should be rinsed with additional juice to assure complete delivery of the dose.
- The intact e/c granules should not be chewed or crushed.
- *Zoton Fastabs®* may block NG tubes. Lansoprazole capsules cannot be used to form a suspension suitable to put through an NG tube. Use *Losec® MUPS®* (see 📖 Omeprazole, p.400) if PPI therapy is required.
- Symptoms can be relieved following the first dose.

Pharmacology

Lansoprazole is a gastric PPI, reducing the release of H^+ from parietal cells by inhibiting H^+/K^+-ATPase. It is rapidly inactivated by gastric acid; hence oral formulations are enteric coated. Oral bioavailability is high (~90%) but administration with food can reduce this. It is extensively metabolized, mainly by CYP2C19 although an alternative pathway involves CYP3A4. Note that CYP2C19 poor metabolizers (or patients taking CYP2C19 inhibitors) can have significantly higher plasma concentrations, leading to unexpected results. Metabolites are virtually inactive and are eliminated by both renal and biliary excretion.

Letrozole

Femara® (POM)
Tablet: 2.5mg (14; 28).

Generic (POM)
Tablet: 2.5mg (14; 28)

Indications

- Treatment (primary or adjuvant) of postmenopausal women with hormone receptor-positive invasive early breast cancer.

Contraindications and precautions

- Letrozole is contraindicated for use in patients with:
  - severe hepatic impairment
  - unknown or negative receptor status.
- It should be used with caution in patients with severe renal impairment (CrCl <10mL/min).
- May cause reduction in bone mineral density; treatment for osteoporosis may be required.
- Fatigue and dizziness have been reported with letrozole. Caution should be observed when driving or operating machinery while such symptoms persist. Refer to 📖 Drugs and driving, p.25.

☺ Adverse effects

Very common
- Arthralgia
- Hot flushes.

Common
- Alopecia
- Anorexia
- Bone fractures
- Bone pain
- Constipation
- Depression
- Diarrhoea
- Dizziness
- Dyspepsia
- Fatigue
- Headache
- Myalgia
- Osteoporosis
- Nausea
- Peripheral oedema
- Raised serum cholesterol
- Sweating
- Vomiting.

Uncommon
- Anxiety
- Drowsiness
- Dyspnoea
- Hypertension
- Ischemic cardiac events
- Leucopenia
- Tumour pain
- UTI
- Vaginal bleeding/discharge
- Visual disturbances.

Drug interactions

Pharmacokinetic
- Letrozole is metabolized by CYP2A6 and CYP3A4; it inhibits CYP2A6 and also moderately affects CYP2C19. Co-administration with drugs that are metabolized by, or affect the activity (induction or inhibition—see 📖 inside back cover) of these pathways may lead to

clinically relevant drug interactions and the prescriber should be aware
that dosage adjustments may be necessary, particularly of drugs with a
narrow therapeutic index.
* Letrozole is unlikely to be a cause of many drug interactions since
CYP2A6 does not have a major role in drug metabolism. At usual
doses, letrozole is unlikely to affect CYP2C19 substrates.

Pharmacodynamic
* None known.

Dose
* 2.5mg PO OD.

Dose adjustments

Elderly
* No dose adjustments are necessary for elderly patients.

Hepatic/renal impairment
* No dose adjustments are necessary for patients with mild–moderate
hepatic impairment or mild–moderate renal impairment (CrCl ≥10mL/
min).
* Letrozole is contraindicated for use in severe hepatic impairment and
should be used with caution in severe renal impairment (due to lack of
data).

Additional information
* Letrozole should be continued for 5 years or until tumour relapse
occurs.

Pharmacology
Letrozole is a non-steroidal aromatase inhibitor. It is believed to work
by significantly lowering serum oestradiol concentrations through inhibition of aromatase (converts adrenal androstenedione to oestrone, which
is precursor of oestradiol). Many breast cancers have oestrogen receptors
and growth of these tumours can be stimulated by oestrogens.

Levetiracetam

Keppra® (POM)
Tablet: 250mg (60); 500mg (60); 750mg (60); 1000mg (60).
Oral solution (sugar-free): 100mg/mL (150mL; 300mL).
Concentrate for IV infusion: 500mg/5mL.

Generic (POM)
Tablet: 250mg (60); 500mg (60); 750mg (60); 1000mg (60).
Oral solution (sugar-free): 100mg/mL (150mL; 300mL).

Indications
- Treatment of partial onset seizures with or without secondary generalization (in patients from 16 years old).
- Adjunctive therapy of myoclonic seizures in patients with juvenile myoclonic epilepsy and primary generalized tonic–clonic seizures

Contraindications and precautions
- As with all anti-epileptics, avoid abrupt withdrawal. The manufacturer advises in adults and adolescents weighing more than 50kg, no more than 500mg decreases BD every 2–4 weeks.
- Refer to 🕮 Use of drugs in end-of-life care, p.53 for end-of-life care issues.
- Use with caution in patients with hepatic or renal impairment (see 🕮 Dose adjustments, p.313).
- Patients should be monitored for signs of suicidal ideation since anti-epileptic drugs have been associated with this behaviour.
- Levetiracetam may modify reactions and patients should be advised not drive (or operate machinery) if affected. Refer to 🕮 Drugs and driving, p.25.

☺ Adverse effects
Very common
- Headache
- Nasopharyngitis
- Sedation.

Common
- Abdominal pain
- Anorexia
- Cough
- Depression
- Diarrhoea
- Dizziness
- Dyspepsia
- Fatigue
- Insomnia
- Nausea/vomiting
- Nervousness/irritability
- Rash
- Tremor
- Vertigo.

Uncommon
- Abnormal LFTs
- Agitation
- Alopecia (reversible on discontinuation)
- Ataxia
- Diplopia
- Hallucination
- Leucopenia

- Memory impairment (e.g. amnesia)
- Myalgia
- Paraesthesia
- Pruritus

- Suicidal ideation
- Thrombocytopenia
- Weight changes (gain or loss reported).

Rare

- Dyskinesia
- Erythema multiforme
- Hepatitis
- Infection
- Pancreatitis

- Pancytopenia
- Personality disorder
- Stevens–Johnson syndrome
- Toxic epidermal necrolysis.

Drug interactions

Pharmacokinetic

- Levetiracetam, unlike other anti-epileptics, has a low potential for pharmacokinetic drug interactions since drug-metabolizing systems are unaffected.
- Drugs excreted by renal tubular secretion (e.g. amiloride, cefalexin, digoxin, morphine, quinine) have the potential to interact with levetiracetam, increasing plasma concentrations. The clinical significance is presently unknown.
- Drugs which affect renal function have the potential to interact with levetiracetam. If such drugs are co-administered, regular monitoring of renal function is advisable. Such drugs include:
  • ACEIs
  • NSAIDs.

Pharmacodynamic

- *Antipsychotics*—seizure threshold lowered.
- *Antidepressants*—seizure threshold lowered.
- *CNS depressants*—risk of excessive sedation.
- *Tramadol*—seizure threshold lowered.

♂ Dose

Note that the IV route can be substituted for PO at the same dose. There is, however, no experience with administration of IV levetiracetam for >4 days.

Monotherapy

- Initial dose 250mg PO OD, increased after 1–2 weeks to 250mg PO BD. Dose can be increased as necessary in steps of 250mg PO BD every 2 weeks to a maximum of 1500mg PO BD.

Adjunctive treatment

- Initial dose 500mg PO BD (or 250mg PO BD for patients <50kg). Dose can be increased as necessary in steps of 500mg PO BD every 2–4 weeks, to a maximum of 1500mg PO BD.

♂ Dose adjustments

Elderly

- Dose adjustments may be necessary, based on renal function (see Table 3.16).

Hepatic/renal impairment
- Dose adjustments are unnecessary in patients with mild to moderate hepatic impairment. In patients with severe hepatic impairment, however, a dose reduction is recommended because creatinine clearance may be unreliable; in patients with creatinine clearance <60mL/min/1.73m^2 a 50% reduction of the daily maintenance dose is recommended.
- Dose adjustments are necessary for patients with renal impairment or undergoing dialysis (refer to Table 3.16).

Table 3.16 Dose adjustments based on renal function

Creatinine clearance (mL/min/1.73m^2)	Dose
>80	500–1500mg PO/IV BD
50–79	500–1000mg PO/IV BD
30–49	250–750mg PO/IV BD
<30	250–500mg PO/IV BD
End-stage renal disease patient undergoing haemodialysis	500–1000mg PO/IV OD*

* For patients >50kg with end stage renal disease undergoing haemodialysis, a loading dose of 750mg is recommended on the first day of treatment. Following dialysis, a 250–500mg supplemental dose is recommended. Refer to the SPC for dose adjustments in patients <50kg.

Additional information
- The oral solution may be diluted prior to administration if needed.
- The concentrate for IV infusion must be diluted in at least 100mL of suitable diluent (e.g. NaCl 0.9% or glucose 5%) and administered over 15min.

⟴ Pharmacology

The exact mechanism of action of levetiracetam is presently unknown. It is believed that the anti-epileptic activity relates to its binding to synaptic vesicle protein (SV2A), a protein important for normal neurotransmission. After oral administration, levetiracetam is rapidly and almost completely absorbed. It does not inhibit or induce drug metabolism to any significant degree and its main metabolic pathway does not involve cytochrome P450 isoenzymes. Levetiracetam is excreted by the kidneys as either the unchanged drug (66%) or as an inactive metabolite formed by hydrolysis (24%).

Levomepromazine

Nozinan® (POM)
Tablet (scored): 25mg (84)
Injection: 25mg/mL (10)

Levinan® (POM)
(Unlicensed product—see 📖 Additional information, p.317.)
Tablet (scored): 6mg (30).

Unlicensed Special (POM)
Oral solution: Available in a variety of concentrations, volumes and
flavours—see 📖 Additional information (p.317).

Indications
- Psychosis (*injection unlicensed).
- Terminal agitation.
- Nausea/vomiting (*tablets unlicensed).

Contraindications and precautions
- Refer to 📖 Use of drugs in end-of-life care, p.53 for end-of-life care issues.
- There are no absolute contraindications to the use of
  levomepromazine in terminal care.
- Avoid using in patients with dementia unless patient at immediate risk
  of harm or severely distressed (increased mortality reported).
- Antipsychotic drugs may increase the risk of VTE; assess risks before
  and during treatment.
- Levomepromazine should be used with caution in patients with:
  - concurrent antihypertensive medication (see 📖 Drug interactions,
    p.316)
  - diabetes mellitus (risk of hyperglycaemia in elderly)
  - epilepsy
  - liver dysfunction
  - Parkinson's disease
  - postural hypotension.
- Electrolyte disturbances must be corrected (e.g. hypokalaemia) due to
  the risk of QT prolongation.
- Levomepromazine should be used with caution in ambulant patients
  over 50 years of age due to the risk of a hypotensive reaction.
- Levomepromazine may modify reactions and patients should be
  advised not drive (or operate machinery) if affected. Refer to 📖 Drugs
  and driving, p.25.
- Subtle deficits in attention, memory, and reasoning may occur with
  therapeutic dosages of anticholinergic drugs without signs of obvious
  toxicity. These deficits have often been mistaken for symptoms of early
  dementia in elderly patients.

☺ Adverse effects
The frequency is not defined, but commonly reported adverse effects include:
- Drowsiness
- Dry mouth and other anticholinergic symptoms
- Postural hypotension (especially the elderly)
- Weakness.

Drug interactions

Pharmacokinetic

- Levomepromazine is an inhibitor of CYP2D6. Co-administration with drugs that are metabolized by, or affect the activity (induction or inhibition—see 📖 inside back cover) of this pathway may lead to clinically relevant drug interactions and the prescriber should be aware that dosage adjustments may be necessary, particularly of drugs with a narrow therapeutic index. Although metabolized by the liver, involvement of specific pathways is unclear.

Pharmacodynamic

- Levomepromazine can cause dose-related prolongation of the QT interval. There is a potential risk that co-administration with other drugs that also prolong the QT interval (e.g. *amiodarone, erythromycin, haloperidol, quinine*) may result in ventricular arrhythmias.
- *Anticholinergics*—increased risk of adverse effects.
- *Anti-epileptics*—dose may need to be increased to take account of the lowered seizure threshold.
- *Antihypertensives*—increased risk of hypotension.
- *CNS depressants*—additive sedative effect.
- *Haloperidol*—may be an additive hypotensive effect; increased risk of extrapyramidal symptoms.
- *Levodopa and dopamine agonists*—effect antagonized by levomepromazine.
- *Metoclopramide*—increased risk of extrapyramidal symptoms.
- *Opioids*—may be an additive hypotensive effect.
- *Trazodone*—may be an additive hypotensive effect.

⚗ Dose

When prescribing levomepromazine, the subcutaneous dose should be lower than the corresponding oral dose (which undergoes significant first-pass metabolism). There should be a separate prescription for each route ensuring that the same dose cannot be given PO or by SC/CSCI.

Psychosis

- Initial dose 25–50mg PO daily in 2–3 divided doses. Larger doses can be given at bedtime. Doses can be increased as necessary to the most effective level compatible with sedation and other adverse effects.
- ✴Alternatively, by 12.5–25mg SC OD or via CSCI. Can increase as necessary up to a max. of 200mg daily via CSCI.

Terminal agitation

- Initial dose 12.5–25mg SC✴ OD or via CSCI. The dose can be increased as necessary up to a max. of 200mg daily via CSCI, although higher doses may be necessary.

Nausea and vomiting

- ✴6–12mg PO PRN or OD to a max. of 50mg daily. Regular daily doses are generally administered at bedtime.
- ✴Alternatively, 6.25–12.5mg SC PRN or via CSCI to a max. of 25mg daily.

✒ Dose adjustments

Elderly

- No specific adjustments required. However, patients over the age of 50 years may be more susceptible to adverse effects, such as postural hypotension and anticholinergic effects (with an increased risk for cognitive decline and dementia). Wherever possible, the lowest effective dose should be used

Hepatic/renal impairment

- Wherever possible, lower doses should be used. Patients may be more susceptible to adverse effects.

Additional information

- Tablets can be dispersed in water immediately prior to administration if necessary.
- The injection may change colour if placed in direct sunlight (e.g. deep purple) and is incompatible with alkaline solutions (e.g. dexamethasone).
- In order to reduce the risk of site reactions, levomepromazine via CSCI should be diluted with sodium chloride 0.9%.
- Levomepromazine via CSCI has been shown to be compatible with alfentanil, clonazepam, cyclizine, diamorphine, dihydrocodeine, fentanyl, glycopyrronium, haloperidol, hyoscine butylbromide, hyoscine hydrobromide, ketamine, methadone, metoclopramide, midazolam, octreotide, ondansetron, oxycodone, and tramadol.
- *Levinan*® tablets are presently an unlicensed product and are available on a named-patient basis only. Contact Archimedes Pharma UK Ltd on (0118) 931 5060 for further information. The tablets are generally less expensive than the oral suspension.
- Levomepromazine oral suspension is available as a special order from various suppliers.

⟳ Pharmacology

Levomepromazine is an antipsychotic drug that shares similar properties with chlorpromazine. It is an antagonist at dopamine D_2-receptors, serotonin $5-HT_2$-receptors, α_1-adrenergic receptors, histamine H_1-receptors, and acetylcholine muscarinic receptors. Consequently it has a wide spectrum of adverse effects.

Lidocaine

Versatis® (POM)
Medicated plaster: 5% w/w lidocaine (700mg); 10cm × 14cm (30).

Indications

- Symptomatic relief of neuropathic pain associated with post-herpetic neuralgia
- *Post-thoracotomy pain[1,2]
- *Post-mastectomy pain[2]
- *There is developing experience that suggests that topical lidocaine may be useful in other localized neuropathies and musculoskeletal pain.[3]

Contraindications and precautions

- Contraindicated in patients with known hypersensitivity to lidocaine or other local anaesthetics of the amide type, e.g. bupivacaine.
- Do not apply to inflamed or broken skin.
- Although only 3 ± 2% of the total applied dose is systemically available, lidocaine plasters should be used with caution in patients with severe cardiac impairment, severe renal impairment or severe hepatic impairment.

☻ Adverse effects

Very common
- Administration site reactions (e.g. erythema, rash, pruritus).

Uncommon
- Site injury (e.g. skin lesion).

Very rare
- Anaphylaxis.

Drug interactions

Pharmacokinetic
- None have been reported. Given the low systemic absorption, it is unlikely that lidocaine plasters will be involved in pharmacokinetic interactions.

Pharmacodynamic
- Although none have been reported, lidocaine plasters may have an opioid-sparing effect, so regular review of analgesia requirements should be performed.

⌁ Dose

- Apply up to 3 plasters over the affected area(s) for 12 hours, followed by a 12-hour plaster-free period.
- The plasters may be cut to size, before removal of the backing material.
- Response to treatment can occur with application of the first plaster, but it may take up to 4 weeks for a response to occur. Treatment outcome should be re-assessed after 2–4 weeks.
- *Patches may be kept *in situ* for up to 18 hours if necessary.

♪ Dose adjustments

Elderly
- No adjustments necessary.

Hepatic/renal impairment
- No adjustments are necessary, but the manufacturer recommends the plasters should be used with caution.

Additional information

- Do not refrigerate or freeze the plasters.
- Hair in the area that the plaster is to be applied should be cut with scissors prior to application. The area must not be shaved.
- After 12 hours, 650mg lidocaine remains in the plaster, so it must be disposed of carefully by folding the adhesive sides in half.

◑ Pharmacology

Lidocaine prevents the generation and conduction of nerve impulses by blocking Na^+ channels. As a general rule, small nerve fibres are more susceptible to the action of lidocaine than large fibres. C and Aδ fibres, that mediate pain and temperature, are blocked before larger fibres that mediate, for example, touch and pressure (Aβ). Lidocaine binds more tightly and rapidly to open channels and it appears to preferentially inhibit abnormal excessive activity at ectopic foci with increased Na^+ channel density. These conditions are present after peripheral nerve injury and in nociceptors sensitized by inflammatory modulators. The release characteristics of the lidocaine plaster are such that only very low concentrations penetrate the skin. Spontaneous ectopic discharges are suppressed by lidocaine applied topically and normal function is unaffected i.e. the lidocaine plaster produces analgesia rather than anaesthesia.

References

1. Devers A, Galer BS. Topical lidocaine patch relieves a variety of neuropathic pain conditions: an open-label study. *Clin J Pain* 2000; **16**(3):205–8.
2. Hans G, Joukes E, Verhulst J, *et al.* Management of neuropathic pain after surgical and non-surgical trauma with lidocaine 5% patches: study of 40 consecutive cases. *Curr Med Res Opin* 2009; **25**(11):2737–43.
3. Morlion B. Pharmacotherapy of low back pain: targeting nociceptive and neuropathic pain components. *Curr Med Res Opin* 2011; **27**(1):11–33.

Loperamide

Imodium® *(POM)*
Capsule: 2mg (30).
Syrup: 1mg/5mL (100mL).

Generic (POM)
Capsule: 2mg (30).
Tablet: 2mg (30).
Note: loperamide can be sold OTC provided it is licensed and labelled for the treatment of acute diarrhoea and the maximum daily dose does not exceed 12mg, maximum pack size of 6 doses (*GSL*)

Imodium® *Instants (GSL).*
Orodispersible tablet: 2mg (6).
Note: this product is licensed for the acute treatment of diarrhoea, with a maximum daily dose of 12mg.

Indications
- Acute diarrhoea
- Chronic diarrhoea (*POM* only).

Contraindications and precautions
- Contraindicated for use in:
  - abdominal distension
  - acute ulcerative colitis
  - antibiotic-associated colitis
  - ileus
  - toxic megacolon.
- Use with caution in patients with hepatic impairment (risk of CNS toxicity)
- Avoid use of *Imodium®* *Instants* in patients with phenylketonuria—orodispersible tablets contain aspartame, a source of phenylalanine.
- Patients with diarrhoea treated with loperamide may experience dizziness or drowsiness and should not drive (or operate machinery) if affected. Refer to 🕮 Drugs and driving, p.25.

☺ Adverse effects
Common
- Constipation
- Dizziness
- Flatulence
- Headache
- Nausea.

Uncommon
- Abdominal pain
- Drowsiness
- Dry mouth
- Dyspepsia
- Rash.

Rare
- Abdominal bloating
- Erythema multiforme
- Fatigue
- Miosis
- Paralytic ileus
- Pruritus
- Stevens–Johnson syndrome
- Toxic epidermal necrolysis
- Urticaria.

Drug interactions

Pharmacokinetic

- Loperamide is almost completely metabolized by CYP2C8 and CYP3A4. It is also a substrate of P-gp. Co-administration with drugs that are metabolized by, or affect the activity (induction or inhibition— see 📖 inside back cover) of these pathways may lead to clinically relevant drug interactions and the prescriber should be aware that dosage adjustments may be necessary.
- The effect of grapefruit juice on the bioavailability of loperamide is unknown.
- Co-administration with P-gp inhibitors (e.g. lansoprazole, quinidine) may result in raised plasma levels. Although a drug interaction is unlikely to occur at therapeutic doses, the prescriber should be aware of the potential for interactions and that dose adjustments may be necessary.

Pharmacodynamic

- *Anticholinergic drugs*—additive constipating effects.
- *Erythromycin*—antagonism of anti-diarrhoeal effect.
- *Domperidone*—antagonism of anti-diarrhoeal effect.
- *Metoclopramide*—antagonism of anti-diarrhoeal effect.
- *Octreotide*—enhanced constipating effect.

💰 Dose

Acute diarrhoea

- Initial dose 4mg PO, followed by 2mg PO after each loose stool. Max. 16mg PO daily (*POM*) or 12mg PO daily (*GSL*).

Chronic diarrhoea

- Initial dose 4-8mg PO daily in divided doses, adjusted to response. Max. dose 16mg PO daily in 2 or more divided doses. *Higher doses may be necessary.

💰 Dose adjustments

Elderly

- No dose adjustment is necessary

Hepatic/renal impairment

- No specific guidance is available for patients with hepatic impairment. However, the manufacturer advises caution given the extensive hepatic metabolism.
- No dose adjustment is necessary in renal impairment

⊙ Pharmacology

Loperamide is an opioid receptor agonist and acts on μ-opioid receptors in the bowel. It works specifically by reducing peristalsis and increasing intestinal transit time. Loperamide is well absorbed orally and is extensively metabolized by CYP2C8 and CYP3A4.

Lorazepam

Generic (CD4a POM)
Tablet: 1mg (28); 2.5mg (28). Note that not all generic formulations are scored, so the prescriber should specify if a scored tablet is required.
Injection: 4mg/mL (midazolam generally preferred).

Indications
- Anxiety
- Insomnia
- Status epilepticus (injection)
- ⱽDyspnoea (*second-line*).[1]

Contraindications and precautions
- Is contraindicated for use in patients with
  - acute pulmonary insufficiency
  - myasthenia gravis
  - severe hepatic insufficiency
  - sleep apnoea syndrome.
- Use with caution if there is a history of drug or alcohol abuse.
- Lorazepam should be used with caution in patients with chronic respiratory disease, renal impairment or moderate hepatic impairment.
- Dose reductions may be necessary in the elderly (see 📖 Dose adjustments, p.323).
- Avoid abrupt withdrawal, even if short duration treatment. Prolonged use of benzodiazepines may result in the development of dependence with subsequent withdrawal symptoms on cessation of use, e.g. agitation, anxiety, confusion, headaches, restlessness, sleep disturbances, sweating, and tremor. The risk of dependence increases with dose and duration of treatment. Gradual withdrawal is advised.
- Lorazepam may modify reactions and patients should be advised not drive (or operate machinery) if affected. Refer to 📖 Drugs and driving, p.25.

☺ Adverse effects
The frequency is not defined, but reported adverse effects include:
- Anterograde amnesia
- Ataxia
- Confusion
- Depression
- Dizziness
- Drowsiness
- Fatigue
- Hallucinations
- Headache
- Muscle weakness
- Nightmares
- Paradoxical events such as agitation, irritability, and restlessness
- Sexual dysfunction
- Sleep disturbance
- Visual disturbances.

Drug interactions

Pharmacokinetic

- Given the fact that metabolism of lorazepam does not involve the cytochrome P450 system, pharmacokinetic interactions are likely to be minimal in comparison to the other benzodiazepines.

Pharmacodynamic

- Alcohol—may precipitate seizures.
- Antidepressants—reduced seizure threshold.
- Antipsychotics—reduced seizure threshold.
- CNS depressants—additive sedative effect.

Dose

Anxiety

- Initial dose 0.5–1mg SL stat¥ or 0.5mg PO BD. Dose can be increased as necessary to 4mg daily.
- Alternatively, 0.5mg SL PRN, to a max. of 4mg daily.¥

Insomnia

- 1–2mg PO before bedtime.

Status epilepticus

- 4mg IV stat.
- The injection may be diluted 1:1 with sodium chloride 0.9% or WFI immediately before administration.

¥ Dyspnoea

- 0.5mg SL PRN, to a max. of 4mg daily.

Dose adjustments

Elderly

- No specific guidance is available. Use the lowest effective dose.

Hepatic/renal impairment

- No specific guidance is available. The dose of lorazepam must be carefully adjusted to individual requirements.

Additional information

- Although the injection has been administered via CSCI, it generally not recommended and midazolam or clonazepam are preferred choices.
- Tablets can be crushed and dispersed in water if necessary. A low volume of water can be used (e.g. ≤2mL).

Pharmacology

Potentiates action of GABA, resulting in increased neuronal inhibition and CNS depression, especially in limbic system and reticular formation. Metabolism of lorazepam is through direct glucuronide conjugation, avoiding the cytochrome P450 system.

Reference

1. Simon ST, Higginson IJ, Booth S, et al. Benzodiazepines for the relief of breathlessness in advanced malignant and non-malignant diseases in adults. Cochrane Database Syst Rev 2010; 1:CD007354.

Macrogol 3350

Laxido® (P)
Oral powder: macrogol '3350', 13.125g, sodium bicarbonate 178.5mg, sodium chloride 350.7mg, potassium chloride 46.6mg/sachet (20; 30); *sugar-free* product is available.

Movicol® (P)
Oral powder: macrogol '3350', 13.125g, sodium bicarbonate 178.5mg, sodium chloride 350.7mg, potassium chloride 46.6mg/sachet (20; 30; 50).
Liquid (sugar-free; orange flavour): each 25mL contains macrogol '3350', 13.125g, sodium bicarbonate 178.5mg, sodium chloride 350.7mg, potassium chloride 46.6mg (500mL).

Movicol Half®
Oral powder: macrogol '3350', 6.563g, sodium bicarbonate 89.3mg, sodium chloride 175.4mg, potassium chloride 23.3mg/sachet (20; 30).

Indications

- Constipation
- Faecal impaction.

Contraindications and precautions

- Contraindicated for use in the following conditions:
  - Crohn's disease
  - ileus
  - intestinal perforation or obstruction
  - toxic megacolon
  - ulcerative colitis.
- Patients with cardiovascular disease should not take more than 2 sachets in any 1 hour.

☻ Adverse effects

The frequency is not defined, but reported adverse effects include:
- Abdominal distension
- Abdominal pain
- Allergic reaction (e.g. dyspnoea, pruritus, urticaria)
- Anal discomfort
- Borborygmi
- Diarrhoea
- Electrolyte disturbances
- Flatulence
- Headache
- Nausea
- Peripheral oedema
- Vomiting.

Drug interactions

Pharmacokinetic
- No known pharmacokinetic interactions.

Pharmacodynamic
- *Anticholinergics*—antagonizes the laxative effect.
- *Cyclizine*—antagonizes the laxative effect.
- *Opioids*—antagonizes the laxative effect.
- *5-HT$_3$ antagonists*—antagonizes the laxative effect.
- *TCAs*—antagonizes the laxative effect.

Dose

The contents of each sachet should be dissolved in 125mL of water. If *Movicol*® liquid is used, 25mL should be measured out using the dosing cup provided. This should be diluted in 100mL of water.

Constipation
- Usual dose 1 sachet/25mL *Movicol*® liquid OD–TDS.
- *The dose can be increased if necessary up to 2 sachets TDS.

Faecal impaction
- 8 sachets, to be taken within a 6-hour period.
- Patients with cardiovascular disease should not take more than 2 sachets in 1 hour.
- The dose can be repeated on days 2 and 3 if necessary.

Dose adjustments

Elderly
- No dose adjustment necessary.

Hepatic/renal impairment
- No specific dose adjustments are recommended by the manufacturers. However, given the electrolyte content, caution is advised in patients with significant renal impairment.

Additional information

- *Movicol*® liquid contains 45.6mg of benzyl alcohol in each diluted dose of 125mL. The acceptable daily intake (ADI) of benzyl alcohol is 5mg/kg body weight. The maximum daily dose (25mL diluted in 100mL of water OD–TDS) should not be exceeded.
- After dilution of *Movicol*® liquid, the solution should be used within 24 hours.
- After reconstitution of sachets, the solution should be kept in a refrigerator and discarded if unused after 6 hours.
- An effect should be seen within 1–3 days.

Pharmacology

Macrogol 3350 is a polymer that produces an osmotic laxative effect.

Magnesium hydroxide

Generic (GSL)
Oral suspension: magnesium hydroxide BP, containing 415mg per 5mL (100mL; 200mL).

Indications
• Constipation.

Contraindications and precautions
• Contraindicated in acute GI conditions (e.g. acute inflammatory bowel diseases, abdominal pain of unknown origin, intestinal obstruction).
• Use with caution in patients with:
  • renal impairment—risk of hypermagnesaemia
  • severe dehydration
  • severe hepatic impairment (see ☐ Dose adjustment, p.327).

☻ Adverse effects
The frequency is not stated, but adverse effects include:
• Diarrhoea
• Symptoms of hypermagnesaemia (e.g. nausea, vomiting, confusion, drowsiness).

Drug interactions
Pharmacokinetic
• Magnesium hydroxide should not be given within at least 1 hour of the following drugs/formulations:
  • *bisacodyl*—may remove the enteric coat and increase the risk of dyspepsia
  • *demeclocycline*—reduced absorption
  • *digoxin*—possible reduced absorption
  • *enteric-coated formulations*
  • *ferrous sulphate*—possible reduced absorption
  • *gabapentin*—reduced absorption
  • *lansoprazole*—reduced absorption
  • *paroxetine*—reduced absorption of suspension
  • *rabeprazole*—reduced absorption.

Pharmacodynamic
• *Anticholinergics*—antagonizes the laxative effect.
• *Cyclizine*—antagonizes the laxative effect.
• *Opioids*—antagonizes the laxative effect; risk of respiratory depression (associated with hypermagnesaemia).
• *5-HT$_3$ antagonists*—antagonizes the laxative effect.
• *TCAs*—antagonizes the laxative effect.

⚬ Dose
Antacid
• 5–10mL PO as necessary, to a maximum of 60mL daily.

Laxative
- 30–45mL PO at bedtime. May be taken with water if necessary.
- Occasionally used at a dose of 10–20mL BD.

⚕ Dose adjustments
Elderly
- No specific dose adjustments recommended by the manufacturer.

Hepatic/renal impairment
- No specific dose adjustments recommended by the manufacturer for patients with hepatic impairment. Nonetheless, use with caution in patients with severe hepatic impairment due the possible risk of subsequent renal impairment.
- Magnesium can accumulate in patients with renal impairment. Use lower doses or choose an alternative.

Additional information
- Laxative effect can work within 1–6 hours, so administration times may need to be adjusted. Dose may need to be adjusted if co-administered with a stimulant laxative.

⟐ Pharmacology
Magnesium hydroxide has an indirect laxative effect caused by water retention in the intestinal lumen.

Magnesium-L-aspartate

Magnaspartate® (GSL)
Oral powder: 6.5g (10mmol Mg^{2+})/sachet (10).

Indications
- Hypomagnesaemia.

Contraindications and precautions
- Contraindicated in severe renal impairment.
- Use with caution in patients with:
  - diabetes (sucrose content of product)
  - mild-moderate renal impairment—risk of hypermagnesaemia
  - severe dehydration
  - severe hepatic impairment (see 📖 Dose adjustment).

☺ Adverse effects
The frequency is not stated, but adverse effects include:
- Diarrhoea
- Symptoms of hypermagnesaemia (e.g. nausea, vomiting, confusion, drowsiness).

Drug interactions
Pharmacokinetic
- None known.

Pharmacodynamic
- Opioids—risk of respiratory depression (associated with hypermagnesaemia).

₰ Dose
- Initial dose 10mmol (1 sachet) PO OD in 200mL water, increasing 10mmol PO BD and above as necessary dependent on serum magnesium. High doses will lead to the development of diarrhoea.

₰ Dose adjustments
Elderly
- No specific dose adjustments recommended by the manufacturer.

Hepatic/renal impairment
- No specific dose adjustments recommended by the manufacturer.
- It should be used with caution in patients with severe hepatic impairment due to the possible risk of subsequent renal impairment.
- Magnesium can accumulate in patients with renal impairment. Use lower doses or choose an alternative.

Additional information
- Low serum Mg^{2+} can cause secondary low serum Ca^{2+}, Na^+, and K^+.
- Compared with oral magnesium supplements, Magnaspartate® has excellent bioavailability.
- Magnaspartate® is available from KoRa Healthcare (Tel: 0114 299 4979).

Pharmacology

Magnaspartate® is a food supplement used in the management of magnesium deficiency. Magnesium is an essential electrolyte and is involved in many enzyme systems. The largest body stores are found in bone. Magnesium salts are generally poorly absorbed orally, with the exception of Magnaspartate®, necessitating replacement therapy for symptomatic hypomagnesaemia by the IV route. Magnesium is excreted renally and can accumulate in renal impairment.

Magnesium sulphate

Generic (POM)
Magnesium sulphate 50%.
Injection (amp): 1g/2mL; 2g/4mL; 2.5g/5mL; 5g/10mL.
NB: 50% = 500mg/mL = 2mmol/mL.

Indications
- Symptomatic hypomagnesaemia.

Contraindications and precautions
- Contraindicated in severe renal impairment.
- Use with caution in patients with:
  - mild-moderate renal impairment —risk of hypermagnesaemia
  - severe dehydration
  - severe hepatic impairment (see 📖 Dose adjustment).

☺ Adverse effects
The frequency is not stated, but adverse effects include:
- Diarrhoea
- Symptoms of hypermagnesaemia (e.g. nausea, vomiting, confusion, drowsiness).

Drug interactions
Pharmacokinetic
- None known.

Pharmacodynamic
- *Opioids*—risk of respiratory depression (associated with hypermagnesaemia).

🎴 Dose
- Up to 160mmol Mg^{2+} via IV infusion over up to 5 days may be required to replace the deficiency.
- Serum Mg^{2+} should be measured throughout treatment.
- There are several suggested methods of replacement therapy:
  - a) 35mmol to 50mmol (8.75g to 12.5g magnesium sulphate, or 17.5mL to 25mL of 50% solution) diluted in 1L of NaCl 0.9% or glucose 5% via an infusion pump over 12–24 hours. Subsequent daily doses can be reviewed as per serum Mg^{2+}.
  - b) 20mmol (5g magnesium sulphate, or 10mL of 50% solution) diluted in 1L of NaCl 0.9% or glucose 5% via an infusion pump over 3 hours. Subsequent daily doses can be reviewed as per serum Mg^{2+}.

🎴 Dose adjustments
Elderly
- No specific dose adjustments recommended by the manufacturer.

Hepatic/renal impairment
- No specific dose adjustments recommended by the manufacturer.

- It should be used with caution in patients with severe hepatic impairment due the possible risk of subsequent renal impairment.
- Magnesium can accumulate in patients with renal impairment. Use lower doses or choose an alternative.

Additional information

- To reduce venous irritation, IV infusion dilution to a concentration up to 200mg/mL (or 0.8mmol/mL) is recommended.
- The administration rate should not exceed 150mg/min (0.6mmol/min) in order to avoid excessive renal losses.
- Low serum Mg^{2+} can cause secondary low serum Ca^{2+}, Na^+, and K^+.

⟡ Pharmacology

Magnesium is an essential electrolyte and is involved in many enzyme systems. The largest body stores are found in bone. Magnesium salts are generally poorly absorbed orally, with the exception of Magnaspartate®, necessitating replacement therapy by the IV route. Magnesium is excreted renally and can accumulate in renal impairment.

Medroxyprogesterone

Provera® (POM)
Tablet (scored): 2.5mg (30); 5mg (10); 10mg (10; 90); 100mg (60; 100); 200mg (30); 400mg (30).

Climanor® (POM)
Tablet: 5mg (28).

Indications

- Endometrial carcinoma
- Renal cell carcinoma
- Carcinoma of breast in postmenopausal women
- ¥Anorexia and cachexia[1]
- ¥Sweating (associated with castration in men and women).[2,3]

Contraindications and precautions

- Medroxyprogesterone is contraindicated in patients with:
  - acute porphyria
  - angina
  - atrial fibrillation
  - cerebral infarction
  - DVT
  - endocarditis
  - heart failure
  - hypercalcaemia associated with bone metastases
  - impaired liver function or active liver disease
  - PE
  - thromboembolic ischaemic attack
  - thrombophlebitis
  - undiagnosed vaginal bleeding.
- May cause hypercalcaemia in patients with breast cancer and bone metastases.
- Unexpected vaginal bleeding during treatment should be investigated.
- Treatment with medroxyprogesterone can cause Cushingoid symptoms.
- Discontinue treatment if the following develop:
  - jaundice or deterioration in liver function
  - significant increase in blood pressure
  - new onset of migraine-type headache
  - sudden change in vision
- Use with caution in patients with:
  - continuous treatment with relatively large doses continuously (monitor for signs hypertension, sodium retention, oedema)
  - depression
  - diabetes
  - epilepsy
  - hyperlipidaemia
  - hypertension
  - migraine
  - renal impairment.

• Patients may experience dizziness or drowsiness with medroxyprogesterone and should not drive (or operate machinery) if affected. Refer to 📖 Drugs and driving, p.25.

☹ Adverse effects

The frequency is not defined, but reported adverse effects include:

• CHF
• Depression
• Dizziness
• Drowsiness
• Headache
• Hypercalcaemia
• Hypertension
• Increased appetite
• Insomnia
• Malaise
• Menstrual irregularities
• Nervousness
• Oedema
• Reduced libido
• Thromboembolic disorders (e.g. PE, retinal thrombosis)
• Weight gain.

Drug interactions

Pharmacokinetic

• Medroxyprogesterone is a substrate of CYP3A4. Despite this, the clearance of medroxyprogesterone is believed to be approximately equal to hepatic blood flow. Therefore, medroxyprogesterone would not be expected to be affected by drugs that alter hepatic enzyme activity.
• Nonetheless, co-administration with drugs that are metabolized by, or affect the activity (induction or inhibition—see 📖 inside back cover) of this pathway may lead to clinically relevant drug interactions and the prescriber should be aware that dosage adjustments may be necessary, particularly of drugs with a narrow therapeutic index.
• Avoid excessive amounts of grapefruit juice as it may increase the bioavailability of medroxyprogesterone through inhibition of intestinal CYP3A4.

Pharmacodynamic

• *NSAIDs*—increased risk of fluid retention.
• *Warfarin*—possible effect on bleeding times; INR should be monitored.

⅃ Dose

Endometrial and renal cell carcinoma

• 200—600mg PO daily.

Breast carcinoma

• 400–1500mg PO daily.

¥ Anorexia and cachexia

• Initial dose 400mg PO OM. Increase as necessary to a maximum of 1000mg PO daily (e.g. 500mg PO BD).

¥ *Sweating*
- 20mg PO OD for at least 4 weeks, then reduce to lowest possible dose that continues to relieve symptoms

♪ Dose adjustments

Elderly
- No dose adjustments are necessary.

Hepatic/renal impairment
- Although specific guidance is unavailable, the lowest effective dose should be used. Medroxyprogesterone is contraindicated in severe impaired liver function.
- Although specific guidance is unavailable, the lowest effective dose should be used. Medroxyprogesterone should be used with caution in patients with renal impairment

Additional information
- As with corticosteroids and megestrol, the increase in body mass is likely to be due to retention of fluid or increase in body fat.
- Medroxyprogesterone has a catabolic effect on skeletal muscle which could further weaken the patient.

⊕ Pharmacology
Medroxyprogesterone is a synthetic progestin and has the same physiologic effects as natural progesterone. It has a similar effect as megestrol.

References

1. Madeddu C, Macciò A, Panzone F, et al. Medroxyprogesterone acetate in the management of cancer cachexia. *Expert Opin Pharmacother* 2009; **10**(8):1359–66.
2. Irani J, Salomon L, Oba R, et al. Efficacy of venlafaxine, medroxyprogesterone acetate, and cyproterone acetate for the treatment of vasomotor hot flushes in men taking gonadotropin-releasing hormone analogues for prostate cancer: a double-blind, randomised trial. *Lancet Oncol* 2010; **11**(2):147–54.
3. Prior JC, Nielsen JD, Hitchcock CL, et al. Medroxyprogesterone and conjugated oestrogen are equivalent for hot flushes: A 1-year randomized double-blind trial following premenopausal ovariectomy. *Clin Sci* 2007; **112**(10):517–25.

Megestrol

Megace® (POM)
Tablet (scored): 160mg (30).

Generic (POM)
Oral suspension: 40mg/5mL (150mL) (see 📖 Additional information, p.336 for supply issues).

Indications
- Breast cancer
- ⁺Anorexia and cachexia[1]
- ⁺Sweating (associated with castration in men and women).[2]

Contraindications and precautions
- Use with caution in patients with:
  - history of thrombophlebitis
  - severe impaired liver function.
- Glucose intolerance and Cushing's syndrome have been reported with the use of megestrol. The possibility of adrenal suppression should be considered in all patients taking or withdrawing from chronic megestrol treatment. Glucocorticoid replacement treatment may be necessary.
- Two case reports have associated its use in patients with prostate cancer with worsening disease.

☺ Adverse effects
The frequency is not defined, but commonly reported adverse effects include:
- Breakthrough uterine bleeding
- Headache
- Increased appetite and food intake
- Oedema
- Nausea
- Vomiting
- Weight gain.

Other reported adverse effects include:
- Alopecia
- Carpal tunnel syndrome
- Cushingoid facies
- Dyspnoea
- Heart failure
- Hot flushes
- Hyperglycaemia
- Hypertension
- Mood changes
- PE
- Thrombophlebitis
- Tumour flare (with or without hypercalcaemia).

Drug interactions
Pharmacokinetic
- None stated.

Pharmacodynamic
- None stated.

ᴊ Dose

Breast cancer
- 160mg PO OD.

Endometrial cancer
- 40–320mg PO daily, in 2 or more divided doses.

¥ Anorexia and cachexia
- Initial dose 160mg PO OD, increased as necessary up to 800mg daily in two or more divided doses. Treatment should be continued for at least 6 weeks.

¥ Sweating
- 20–40mg PO OM for at least 4 weeks.

ᴊ Dose adjustments

Elderly
- No dose adjustment is necessary.

Hepatic/renal impairment
- Undergoes complete hepatic metabolism. Although specific guidance is unavailable, the lowest effective dose should be used. Megestrol is contraindicated in severe impaired liver function.
- Doses adjustments are not necessary in renal impairment.

Additional information

- Although an oral suspension is available as a special order (e.g. Martindale Pharma—01277 266600), tablets can be crushed and dispersed in water immediately prior to administration.
- As with corticosteroids and medroxyprogesterone, the increase in body mass is likely to be due to retention of fluid or increase in body fat.
- Megestrol has a catabolic effect on skeletal muscle which could further weaken the patient.

⟿ Pharmacology

Megestrol is a synthetic progestin and has the same physiological effects as natural progesterone. It interferes with the oestrogen cycle and it suppresses luteinizing hormone release from the pituitary. It has a slight but significant glucocorticoid effect and a very slight mineralocorticoid effect. The precise mechanism of the effect on anorexic and cachexia is unknown. Megestrol has direct cytotoxic effects on breast cancer cells in tissue culture and may also have a direct effect on the endometrium.

References

1. Berenstein G, Ortiz Z. Megestrol acetate for treatment of anorexia-cachexia syndrome. *Cochrane Database Syst Rev* 2005; **2**: CD004310.
2. Quella SK, Loprinzi CL, Sloan JA, *et al.* Long term use of megestrol acetate by cancer survivors for the treatment of hot flashes. *Cancer* 1998; **82**(9):1784–8.

Metformin

Standard release

Glucophage® (POM)
Tablet: 500mg (84); 850mg (56).
Powder for oral solution: 500mg (30); 1000mg (30).
Generic (POM)
Tablet: 500mg (28; 84); 850mg (56).
Oral solution: 500mg/5mL (100mL, sugar-free).

Modified release

Glucophage SR® (POM)
Tablet: 500mg (28; 56); 750mg (28; 56); 1000mg (56).

Generic (POM)
Tablet: 500mg (28; 56).

Indications

* Type 2 diabetes (particularly in overweight patients) not controlled by
  diet or exercise.

Contraindications and precautions

* Do not use metformin in conditions that may increase the risk of
  developing lactic acidosis:
  * liver impairment
  * renal impairment where creatinine clearance is <60mL/min
  * severe CHF
  * severe COPD.
* *Glucophage®* powder for oral solution contains aspartame. Avoid in
  patients with phenylketonuria.
* Metformin must be discontinued prior to and not restarted until
  48 hours post administration of iodinated contrast agent.
* Discontinue metformin 48 hours prior to elective surgery requiring a
  general anaesthetic. Restart not less than 48 hours afterwards.

☺ Adverse effects

Very common
These tend to be GI in nature and can be reduced with slow titration; they
usually resolve spontaneously.
* Diarrhoea
* Loss of appetite
* Nausea/vomiting.

Common
* Metallic taste.

Very rare
* Lactic acidosis.

Unknown
- Metformin has been associated with vitamin B_{12} deficiency which is more likely to occur after more than 3 years of use.

NB Hypoglycaemia should not occur with metformin at normal doses.

Drug interactions

Pharmacokinetic
- Drugs excreted by renal tubular secretion (e.g. *amiloride*, *cefalexin*, *digoxin*, *morphine*, *quinine*) have the potential to interact with metformin, increasing plasma concentrations. The clinical significance is unknown and until further information is available, the following is suggested:
  - if metformin is co-administered with these drugs, a slow and cautious titration is advisable
  - if these drugs are prescribed for a patient already using metformin, it is advisable to review the metformin dose (lower doses may be required).
- Drugs which affect renal function have the potential to interact with metformin. If such drugs are co-administered, regular monitoring of renal function is advisable. Such drugs include:
  - ACEIs
  - NSAIDs
  - Iodinated contrast agent (see 📖 Contraindications and precautions, p.337).

Pharmacodynamic
- Drugs that may precipitate hyperglycaemia may interfere with blood glucose control, e.g.:
  - Corticosteroids
  - Diuretics
  - Nifedipine.
- ACEIs can cause hypoglycaemia by an unknown mechanism. Severe symptomatic cases have been reported when used in combination with antidiabetic drugs.
- Alcohol (increased risk of lactic acidosis with acute intoxication).

💊 Dose

Standard release
- Initial dose 500mg PO BD, with or after meals and allow 1–2 weeks before increasing the dose. A slower titration improves GI tolerance.
- Dose increases of 500mg PO OD can be made at 1–2-weekly intervals to a max. dose of 3g daily, in 2–3 divided doses, with or after meals.

Modified release
- Initial dose 500mg PO OD with evening meal.
- Dose can be increased every 1–2 weeks by 500mg OD, to a max. of 2g OD with evening meal (or 1g BD, with meals, to improve blood glucose control).
- If blood glucose control is not achieved, change to standard release formulations or review treatment.

5 Dose adjustments

Elderly

* Renal function must be assessed. Must not be used if creatinine clearance is <60mL/min.

Hepatic/renal impairment

* Avoid in hepatic impairment due to increased risk of lactic acidosis.
* Must not be used if creatinine clearance is <60mL/min.

Additional information

* Metformin is occasionally combined with insulin to improve blood glucose control. Dose metformin as previously described.
* In the absence of the oral solution, metformin tablets can be crushed and dispersed in water immediately prior to administration. The suspension can be flushed through an NG tube.

Pharmacology

Metformin is a biguanide that delays the intestinal absorption of glucose, reduces hepatic glucose production (inhibits glycogenolysis and gluconeogenesis), and increases peripheral glucose uptake and utilization in muscle. It lowers basal and postprandial plasma glucose concentrations, but does not stimulate insulin secretion (minimal risk of hypoglycaemia). The pharmacodynamics of metformin may rely upon a type of transport protein (see Pharmacogenetics, p.11) the organic cation transporter (OCT). OCT1 is involved in the uptake of metformin by hepatocytes, while OCT2 is involved in renal excretion. Unexpected responses to metformin may be due to genetic polymorphisms (see Pharmacogenetics, p.11) in OCT1 and OCT2 genes, or by drug interactions. Metformin is excreted unchanged in the urine.

Methadone

Generic (CD2 POM)
Tablet: 5mg (50).
Injection: 10mg/mL; 20mg/2mL; 35mg/3.5mL; 50mg/5mL; 50mg/2mL; 50mg/mL.
Oral solution: 1mg/mL (various volumes); 5mg/mL (various volumes)
Note: some generic formulations are sugar-free.
Oral concentrate: 10mg/mL (*blue*, 150mL); 20mg/mL (*brown*, 150mL)
Note: prescriptions should only be dispensed after appropriate dilution with Methadose® Diluent.
Linctus: 2mg/5Ml.

- Methadone is a Schedule 2 CD. Refer to 📖 Legal categories of medicines, p.21 for further information.

Indications
- Moderate to severe pain
- Treatment of opioid dependence
- Cough (linctus).

Contraindications and precautions
- If the dose of an opioid is titrated correctly, it is generally accepted that there are no absolute contraindications to the use of such drugs in palliative care, although there may be circumstances where one opioid is favoured over another (e.g. renal impairment, constipation). Nonetheless, manufacturers state that methadone is contraindicated for use in patients with:
  - concurrent administration of MAOIs or within 2 weeks of discontinuation of their use
  - head injury
  - obstructive airways disease (may cause histamine release)
  - paralytic ileus
  - respiratory depression.
- Use with caution in the following instances:
  - Addison's disease (adrenocortical insufficiency)
  - asthma (may cause histamine release)
  - cardiac disease (methadone may increase QT interval)
  - concurrent administration of drugs that:
    —have a potential for QT prolongation
    —are CYP3A4 and CYP2B6 inhibitors (see 📖 Drug interactions, p.341)
  - diseases of the biliary tract
  - epilepsy (morphine may lower seizure threshold)
  - hepatic impairment
  - hypotension
  - hypothyroidism
  - inflammatory bowel disorders

- myasthenia gravis
- prostatic hypertrophy
- raised intracranial pressure
- renal impairment (if *sodium bicarbonate* is co-prescribed—see 📖 Drug interactions).
- Electrolyte disturbances must be corrected (e.g. hypokalaemia) due to the risk of QT prolongation. ECG monitoring is recommended for doses above 100mg daily (unlikely in palliative care).
- Methadone may modify reactions and patients should be advised not drive (or operate machinery) if affected. Refer to 📖 Drugs and driving, p.25.

☺ Adverse effects

Strong opioids tend to cause similar adverse effects, albeit to varying degrees. The frequency is not defined, but reported adverse effects include:

- Anorexia
- Biliary pain
- Confusion
- Constipation
- Drowsiness
- Dry mouth
- Dyspepsia
- Exacerbation of pancreatitis
- Euphoria
- Insomnia
- Headache
- Hyperhidrosis

- Myoclonus
- Nausea
- Pruritus
- Sexual dysfunction (e.g. amenorrhea, decreased libido, erectile dysfunction)
- Urinary retention
- Vertigo
- Visual disturbance
- Vomiting
- Weakness.

The following can occur with excessive dose:

- Agitation
- Exacerbation of pain
- Hallucinations
- Miosis

- Paraesthesia
- Respiratory depression
- Restlessness.

Drug interactions

Pharmacokinetic

- Methadone is metabolized by CYP3A4 and CYP2B6. To a lesser extent, CYP1A2 and CYP2D6 are involved. Methadone weakly inhibits CYP2D6. Co-administration with drugs that are metabolized by, or affect the activity (induction or inhibition—see 📖 inside back cover) of these pathways may lead to clinically relevant drug interactions and the prescriber should be aware that dosage adjustments may be necessary, particularly of drugs with a narrow therapeutic index.
- *Amiodarone*—may increase plasma concentration of methadone.
- *Carbamazepine*—reduces effect of methadone.
- *Ciprofloxacin*—may increase plasma concentration of methadone.
- *Clopidogrel*—may increase plasma concentration of methadone.
- *Erythromycin*—may increase plasma concentrations of methadone.
- *Fluconazole*—may increase plasma concentration of methadone.
- *Fluoxetine*—may increase plasma concentration of methadone.
- *Paroxetine*—may increase plasma concentration of methadone.

- *Phenobarbital*—reduces effect of methadone.
- *Sertraline*—may increase plasma concentration of methadone.
- *Sodium bicarbonate*—increases plasma concentration of methadone due to reduced renal excretion.
- Avoid grapefruit juice as it may increase the bioavailability of methadone through inhibition of intestinal CYP3A4.

Pharmacodynamic

- Methadone can cause dose-related prolongation of the QT interval. There is a potential risk that co-administration with other drugs that also prolong the QT interval (e.g. *amiodarone*, *erythromycin*, *quinine*) may result in ventricular arrhythmias.
- *Antihypertensives*—increased risk of hypotension.
- *CNS depressants*—risk of excessive sedation.
- *Haloperidol*—may be an additive hypotensive effect and additive QT effect.
- *Ketamine*—there is a potential opioid-sparing effect with ketamine and the dose of methadone may need reducing.
- *Levomepromazine*—may be an additive hypotensive effect and additive QT effect.

♨ Dose

Oral

- Initial dose depends upon the patient's previous opioid requirements.
- Methadone is rarely initiated in opioid naïve patients and such use is not mentioned here.
- If converting from oral hydromorphone or oxycodone, convert the total daily dose to morphine (refer to 🕮 Management of pain: opioid substitution, p.32 for information regarding opioid dose equivalences).
- The following method is suggested when switching from oral morphine. It involves a 5 day titration phase using an initial *loading dose*, followed by administration of a *fixed dose* of methadone 3-hourly PO PRN.
- The loading dose is calculated as 1/10 of the previous total daily morphine dose, to a **maximum of 30mg**.
- The fixed dose is calculated as 1/30 of the previous total daily morphine dose.
- For example:
  - 120mg PO BD morphine—*loading dose* of PO methadone = 24mg
  - 120mg PO BD morphine—*fixed dose* of PO methadone = 8mg.

Procedure

a) Stop morphine abruptly (or hydromorphone/oxycodone).
b) If switching from 12 hourly modified-release morphine (or other oral opioid):
  - in pain—give the *loading dose* of methadone 6 hours after the last dose
  - pain free—give the *loading dose* of methadone 12 hours after last dose.

c) If switching from 24 hourly modified-release morphine:
- in pain—give the *loading dose* of methadone 12 hours after last dose
- pain free—give the *loading dose* of methadone 24 hours after the last dose.

d) If switching from transdermal fentanyl:
- in pain—give the *loading dose* of methadone 12 hours after the patch removal
- pain free—give the *loading dose* of methadone 24 hours after patch removal.

e) Administer the *fixed dose* 3 hourly PRN for 5 days.

f) On day 6, review the amount of methadone used in the preceding 48 hours (i.e. days 4 and 5). Divide this by **4** to arrive at a 12 hourly maintenance dose. Rescue doses are 1/6 of the total daily maintenance dose. For example:
- 64mg methadone in 48 hours; maintenance dose = 16mg BD
- Suggested rescue dose = 5mg PRN.

g) If more than **2** PRN doses are given in a 24-hour period, the maintenance dose should be increased weekly.

h) If the patient experiences pain within 3 hours of the last PRN methadone dose, give a rescue dose as per the previously taken opioid (dose between 50–100%).

Subcutaneous
- Methadone can be administered via SC injection, or ¥CSCI, but it is never initiated this way. To convert from oral to subcutaneous methadone, halve the oral dose, although some patients may require a fairly rapid dose escalation as for some the ratio approaches 1:1.
- The SC injection can be painful and the CSCI is preferred.

Dose adjustments

Elderly
- No specific guidance is available; dose requirements should be individually titrated.

Hepatic/renal impairment
- No specific guidance is available, although in patients with hepatic impairment, the plasma concentration is expected to be increased. In view of its hepatic metabolism, caution is advised when giving methadone to patients with hepatic impairment. Dose requirements should be individually titrated.
- No specific guidance is available for patients with renal impairment. The manufacturers suggest in moderate or severe renal impairment dose reductions may be necessary. Dose requirements should be individually titrated.

Additional information
- It is probably safer to manage conversions in an in-patient unit where a patient can be observed closely for toxic effect.

- Concentrated methadone oral solution is intended for dilution for the treatment of addiction but can be a useful preparation if high oral doses are required for pain. If being used in this way, it may be more convenient to dilute each dose individually.
- To reduce the incidence of CSCI site reactions, ensure the infusion is diluted maximally with NaCl 0.9%. The addition of 1mg dexamethasone may improve tolerability, although check for compatibility. Changing to a 12-hourly infusion with site rotation may also help.
- By CSCI, methadone is stated to be compatible with dexamethasone, haloperidol, hyoscine butylbromide, ketorolac, levomepromazine, metoclopramide, and midazolam.

❖ Pharmacology

Methadone is less sedating than morphine and as it exerts opioid and NMDA activity, it may be more useful than other opioids for the management of neuropathic pain. Its metabolism is not linear and it has a long half-life so accumulation can occur. The half-life of a single injected dose is 6–8 hours but for a single oral dose it is 12–18 hours. However, as the drug is lipid soluble, it accumulates and its half-life on repeated doses can extend to between 12–48 hours. For this reason and because of great interindividual variations in metabolism it must be introduced carefully and gradually starting with low doses and gradually increasing the dosing interval to the usual 12-hourly regimen.

Methylnaltrexone

Relistor® (POM)

Injection: 12mg (0.6mL ampoule); 20mg/mL pre-filled syringe (7 × 1mL).

Indications

- Treatment of opioid-induced constipation in advanced illness patients who are receiving palliative care when response to usual laxative therapy has not been sufficient.

Contraindications and precautions

- Must not be used in patients with known or suspected mechanical bowel obstruction, or acute surgical abdomen.
- Should not be used for treatment of patients with constipation not related to opioid use.
- Administer with caution to patients with:
  - colostomy
  - peritoneal catheter
  - active diverticular disease
  - faecal impaction.
- A bowel movement can occur within 30–60min of administration. Patients should be made aware and be in close proximity to toilet facilities.
- Treatment should not be continued beyond 4 months
- Methylnaltrexone should be added to usual laxative treatment, not replace it.
- Not recommended in patients with severe hepatic impairment or with end-stage renal impairment requiring dialysis (see 📖 Dose adjustments, p.346).

☺ Adverse effects

Very common

- Abdominal pain
- Nausea
- Flatulence
- Diarrhoea.

Common

- Dizziness
- Injection site reactions (e.g. stinging, burning, pain, redness, oedema).

Drug interactions

Pharmacokinetic

- Methylnaltrexone is a weak inhibitor of CYP2D6. It is unlikely to cause clinically significant interactions.
- Drugs excreted by renal tubular secretion (e.g. amiloride, digoxin, morphine, quinine) have the potential to interact with methylnaltrexone, increasing plasma concentrations. The clinical significance is unknown.

Pharmacodynamic

- While none have currently been observed, there is the theoretical risk that peripheral opioid analgesia will be antagonized.

Dose

Given by subcutaneous injection:
- 38–61kg, 8mg (0.4mL).
- 62–114kg, 12mg (0.6mL).
- Patients whose weight falls outside of the ranges quoted should be dosed at 0.15mg/kg.
- The recommended administration schedule is 1 single dose every other day. Doses may also be given with longer intervals, as per clinical need. Patients may receive 2 consecutive doses 24 hours apart, only when there has been no response (bowel movement) to the dose on the preceding day.

Dose adjustments

Elderly
- No dose adjustments are necessary based on age alone.

Hepatic/renal impairment
- No dose adjustments are necessary for patients with mild to moderate hepatic impairment. No data exist for use in patients with severe hepatic impairment and caution is advised.
- If CrCl <30mL/min, the dose should be reduced to:
  - 8mg (0.4 mL) for weight 62–114kg
  - 0.075mg/kg for those whose weight falls outside of the 62–114kg range.
- No information is currently available for patients with end-stage renal failure undergoing dialysis.

Additional information

- Initial response to treatment can produce abdominal pain, cramping, or colic. If severe, it can be managed by administration of an opioid or anticholinergic agent (e.g. morphine, glycopyrronium).
- Areas for injection include upper legs, abdomen, and upper arms.
- Rotate injection site.
- Avoid areas where skin is tender, bruised, red, or hard. Scars or stretch marks should also be avoided.

Pharmacology

Methylnaltrexone is a peripherally-acting selective μ-opioid receptor antagonist. It does not penetrate the blood–brain barrier to any significant extent because of its chemical structure. Opioid derived analgesia is not affected by treatment with methylnaltrexone.

Following subcutaneous administration, methylnaltrexone is rapidly absorbed with peak concentrations achieved within 30min. It does not affect the cytochrome P450 system to any significant degree, although it is a weak inhibitor of CYP2D6. Methylnaltrexone is primarily eliminated as the unchanged drug; approximately half of the dose is excreted in the urine.

Methylphenidate

Ritalin® *(CD2 POM)*
Tablet (scored): 10mg (30).

Generic (CD2 POM)
Tablet: 5mg (30); 10mg (30); 20mg (30).

- Methylphenidate is a Schedule 2 CD. Refer to 📖 Legal categories of medicines, p.21 for further information.

Indications
- ¥Depression[1]
- ¥Opioid-related fatigue.[1,2]

Contraindications and precautions
- Methylphenidate is contraindicated for use in patients with:
  - agitation
  - arrhythmia
  - glaucoma
  - hyperthyroidism
  - marked anxiety,
  - motor tics, tics in siblings, or a family history or diagnosis of Tourette's syndrome
  - severe angina pectoris
  - thyrotoxicosis.
- It should be avoided in patients with severe hypertension.
- Use with caution in patients with:
  - epilepsy (withdraw treatment if seizures occur)
  - hepatic impairment
  - pre-existing hypertension, heart failure, recent myocardial infarction.
- Avoid concurrent use with an irreversible MAOI, or within 14 days of stopping one. In exceptional cases, concurrent use of the reversible MAOI *linezolid* may occur but the patient must be closely monitored (see 📖 Drug interactions, p.348).
- If affected by drowsiness and dizziness, patients should be warned about driving. Refer to 📖 Drugs and driving, p.25.

Adverse effects
Very common
- Headache
- Insomnia (give last dose no later than 2pm)
- Nervousness.

Common
- Abdominal pain
- Aggression
- Agitation
- Alopecia

- Anorexia
- Anxiety
- Arrhythmias
- Arthralgia
- Cough
- Diarrhoea
- Dizziness
- Drowsiness
- Dry mouth
- Dyskinesia
- Fever

- Hypertension
- Nasopharyngitis
- Nausea and vomiting (usually occurs during initiation; may improve if administered with food)
- Pruritus
- Rash
- Tachycardia
- Urticaria.

Uncommon
- Altered LFTs
- Blurred vision
- Hallucinations
- Haematuria
- Hypersensitivity reactions (e.g. dyspnoea, rash)

- Myalgia
- Suicidal ideation
- Tremor.

Rare
- Angina
- Gynaecomastia

- Hyperhidrosis.

Very rare
- Muscle cramps

- Seizures.

Unknown
- Serotonin syndrome.

Drug interactions
Pharmacokinetic
- It undergoes fairly significant first-pass metabolism and the carboxylesterase CES1A1 is involved. The cytochrome system may also be involved as methylphenidate appears to be a major substrate of CYP2D6 and a weak inhibitor of CYP2D6.
- The clinical significance of co-administration with inhibitors of CYP2D6 (see 📖 inside back cover) is unknown. The prescriber should be aware of the potential for interactions and that dose adjustments may be necessary.
- *Carbamazepine*—may reduce plasma concentration of methylphenidate.
- May inhibit the metabolism of *TCAs*, *SSRIs*, and *warfarin*. Caution is advised if methylphenidate is co-administered with other drugs that are predominantly metabolized by CYP2D6 as a degree of competitive inhibition may develop. The prescriber should be aware of the potential for interactions and that dose adjustments may be necessary.

Pharmacodynamic
- *Anti-epileptics*—methylphenidate may antagonize the effects of anti-epileptics.
- *Antihypertensives*—effect may be reduced by methylphenidate.
- *Antidepressants*—may increase the risk of serotonin syndrome; note SSRIs have been combined successfully with methylphenidate to augment antidepressant action.

Haloperidol—reverses the wakefulness effect of methylphenidate (other dopamine antagonists may do the same).
Linezolid—risk of hypertension; in exceptional circumstances linezolid may be given with methylphenidate, but the patient must be closely monitored.
MAOI—avoid concurrent use; risk of serotonin syndrome and may lead to increase in blood pressure.

Dose
Blood pressure should be monitored at appropriate intervals in all patients taking methylphenidate.

Depression and fatigue
Initial dose 2.5mg PO OM. Increase dose by 2.5mg every 2–3 days as tolerated. Doses above 2.5mg are usually divided, with the final dose being no later than 2pm. Usual maximum dose is 20mg PO daily.

Dose adjustments
Elderly
Manufacturer states no evidence in this cohort of patients and should be avoided. No specific information available. Use the lowest effective dose.

Hepatic/renal impairment
There are no specific instructions for dose reduction in hepatic impairment. However, given the fact that methylphenidate is extensively metabolized, if the drug has to be used, the patient should be closely monitored and the lowest effective dose should be prescribed.
There are no specific instructions for dose adjustment in renal impairment. However, since methylphenidate undergoes significant first-pass metabolism (to relatively inactive compounds) renal impairment is unlikely to have a great effect. Nonetheless, caution is advised and the lowest effective dose should be prescribed.

Additional information
Methylphenidate can be cautiously combined with SSRIs in the treatment of resistant depression. It should be introduced slowly and the patient should be closely monitored.

Pharmacology
Methylphenidate is a mild CNS stimulant with more prominent effects on mental than on motor activities. Its mode of action in man is not completely understood but it appears to blocks the reuptake mechanism of dopaminergic neurons and has a similar action to amphetamines.

References
Sood A, Barton DL, Loprinzi CL. Use of methylphenidate in patients with cancer. *Am J Hosp Palliat Care* 2006; **23**(1):35–40.
Portela MA, Rubiales AS, Centeno C. The use of psychostimulants in cancer patients. *Curr Opin Support Palliat Care* 2011; **5**(2):164–8.

Metoclopramide

Standard release

Maxolon® (POM)
Tablet (scored): 10mg (84).
Syrup (sugar-free): 5mg/5mL (200mL).
Paediatric liquid (sugar-free): 1mg/mL (15mL).
Injection: 10mg/2mL (10).

Generic (POM)
Tablet (scored): 10mg (84).
Syrup (sugar-free): 5mg/5mL (200mL).
Injection: 10mg/2mL (10).

Modified release

Maxolon SR® (POM)
Capsule: 15mg (56).

Indications

- Nausea and vomiting
- Dyspepsia
- Reflux.

Contraindications and precautions

- Refer to 📖 Use of drugs in end-of-life care, p.53 for end-of-life care issues.
- Contraindicated in patients with:
  - GI obstruction, perforation, or haemorrhage
  - phaeochromocytoma.
- Avoid within 3 days of GI surgery.
- Use with caution in patients with:
  - acute porphyria
  - concurrent use of serotonergic drugs (e.g. SSRIs) and antipsychotics (see 📖 Drug interactions, p.351)
  - epilepsy (frequency and severity of seizures may increase)
  - severe renal and hepatic insufficiency (see 📖 Dose adjustments, p.351)
  - Parkinson's disease.
- The elderly and young adults <20 years of age (especially female) are more susceptible to adverse effects.
- Metoclopramide may modify reactions and patients should be advised not drive (or operate machinery) if affected. Refer to 📖 Drugs and driving, p.25.

☹ Adverse effects

The frequency is not defined, but reported adverse effects include:
- Breast tenderness
- Confusion
- Depression
- Diarrhoea
- Drowsiness

- Extrapyramidal symptoms
- Galactorrhoea
- Gynaecomastia
- Headache
- Impotence
- Insomnia
- Neuroleptic malignant syndrome (rare)
- Restlessness.

Drug interactions

Pharmacokinetic

- *Carbamazepine* —possible risk of neurotoxicity due to increased speed of absorption.
- *Paracetamol* —potential increase in onset of analgesia.

Pharmacodynamic

- *Anticholinergics* —may antagonize the prokinetic effect.
- *Antipsychotics* —increased risk of extrapyramidal effects.
- *Cyclizine* —may antagonize the prokinetic effect.
- *Levodopa and dopamine agonists* —effect antagonized by metoclopramide.
- *Opioids*—antagonize the prokinetic effect.
- *Serotonergic drugs*—caution is advisable if metoclopramide is co-administered with serotonergic drugs (e.g. *methadone, methylphenidate, mirtazapine, oxycodone, SSRIs, TCAs, trazodone, venlafaxine*) due to the risk of serotonin syndrome (see 📖 Box 1.10, p.18).
- *5-HT$_3$ antagonists*—antagonize the prokinetic effect.
- *TCAs*—may antagonize the prokinetic effect.

💊 Dose

- Initial dose, 10mg PO TDS PRN. This can be increased to 20mg PO TDS.¥
- *Maxolon SR®* is given 15mg PO BD.
- Alternatively, 30mg via CSCI¥ over 24 hours. The dose can be increased to a maximum of 120mg daily.¥

💊 Dose adjustments

Elderly

- The elderly are more susceptible to adverse effects. Therapy should be initiated at a reduced dose and the maintained at the lowest effective dose.

Hepatic/renal impairment

- The manufacturer recommends that in patients with hepatic or renal impairment, therapy should be initiated at a reduced dose and the maintained at the lowest effective dose. Metoclopramide is metabolized in the liver and the predominant route of elimination of metoclopramide and its metabolites is via the kidney.

Additional information

- Metoclopramide via CSCI is reportedly compatible with alfentanil, dexamethasone, diamorphine, dimenhydrinate (not in UK), fentanyl, glycopyrronium, granisetron, hydromorphone, levomepromazine, methadone, midazolam, morphine, octreotide, ondansetron, and tramadol.

⌖ Pharmacology

Metoclopramide is primarily a D_2 antagonist. It also has serotonergic properties, being a 5-HT_3 antagonist and 5-HT_4 agonist. The antiemetic action of metoclopramide is results from its antagonist activity at D_2 receptors in the CTZ, making it a suitable choice for drug-induced causes of nausea vomiting. At higher doses, the 5-HT_3 antagonist activity may also contribute to the antiemetic effect. D_2 antagonism in the GI tract enhances the response to acetylcholine, thereby indirectly increasing GI motility and accelerating gastric emptying. The 5-HT_4 agonist effect also has a direct stimulatory effect on the bowel and both properties contribute to the prokinetic effect (which will in turn contribute to the antiemetic effect). The D_2 antagonism can lead to increases in prolactin secretion, with consequences such as galactorrhoea, gynaecomastia, and irregular periods.

Metoclopramide is rapidly and almost completely absorbed from the GI tract after oral doses, although conditions such as vomiting or impaired gastric motility may reduce absorption. It is a minor substrate of CYP2D6 and CYP1A2. About 20% of the dose is excreted unchanged and plasma concentrations can increase in renal impairment.

Metronidazole

Flagyl® (POM)
Tablet: 200mg (21); 400mg (14).
Suppository: 500mg (10); 1g (10).
Injection: 500mg/100mL.

Flagyl S® (POM)
Oral suspension: 200mg/5mL (100mL).

Metrogel® (POM)
Gel: metronidazole 0.75% (40g).

Metrotop® (POM)
Gel: metronidazole 0.8% (15g).

Generic (POM)
Tablet: 200mg (21); 400mg (21); 500mg (21).
Oral suspension: 200mg/5mL (100mL).
Injection: 100mg/20mL; 500mg/100mL.

Indications
- Refer to local guidelines
- Anaerobic infections
- *Helicobacter pylori* eradication
- Malodorous fungating tumours (topical)
- *Pseudomembranous colitis.[1]

Contraindications and precautions
- Avoid in acute porphyria.
- Use with caution in hepatic impairment (see 🕮 Dose adjustments, p.354).
- If treatment exceeds 10 days, the manufacturer recommends laboratory monitoring.
- Use the infusion with caution in patients on a low sodium diet.

☺ Adverse effects
The frequency is not defined, but reported adverse effects include:
- Abnormal LFTs
- Anorexia
- Arthralgia
- Ataxia
- Blood dyscrasias (e.g. agranulocytosis, neutropenia, thrombocytopenia)
- Cholestatic hepatitis
- Dark urine (due to metronidazole metabolite)
- Diarrhoea
- Dizziness
- Drowsiness
- Furred tongue
- Headache
- Mucositis

- Myalgia
- Nausea
- Pancreatitis
- Skin rashes
- Transient visual disorders
- Unpleasant taste.
- Vomiting.

Drug interactions

Pharmacokinetic
- Metronidazole is a substrate of CYP3A4 and CYP2C9. It inhibits CYP2C9. Co-administration with drugs that are metabolized by, or affect the activity (induction or inhibition—see 🕮 inside back cover) of these pathways may lead to clinically relevant drug interactions and the prescriber should be aware that dosage adjustments may be necessary, particularly of drugs with a narrow therapeutic index.
- *Warfarin*—risk of raised INR.
- *Alcohol*—concurrent use can give rise to the disulfiram reaction (includes that present in medication).

Pharmacodynamic
- None known.

⚗ Dose

Standard doses are described here. Refer to local guidelines for specific advice.

Anaerobic infections
- Initial dose 400mg PO TDS, or 1g PR TDS for 3 days, then 1g PR BD.
- Alternatively, if rectal administration is inappropriate, 500mg by IV infusion TDS.
- In most cases, a course of 7–10 days should be sufficient.

Malodorous fungating tumour
- Apply gel to clean wound OD–BD and cover with non-adherent dressing.
- ¥Alternatively, apply 200mg crushed tablet (in suitable vehicle).

¥ *Pseudomembranous colitis*
- 400mg PO TDS for 7–10 days
- IV therapy may be appropriate for the first 48 hours, after which effectiveness is reduced due to reduced penetration into the bowel lumen.

⚗ Dose adjustments

Elderly
- No dose adjustments are necessary.

Hepatic/renal impairment
- In patients with severe hepatic impairment, the manufacturer advises that the daily dose should be reduced to one-third and be administered once daily.
- No dose adjustments are necessary in patients with renal impairment.

Additional information

» Metronidazole suspension should not be used in patients with an *in situ* feeding tube, or in those receiving a PPI. The suspension contains the metronidazole benzoate salt and the absorption of this is significantly reduced in the presence of food. In addition, it requires the action of stomach acids to convert it to the active metronidazole base.

» If necessary, tablets can be crushed and added to water to form a suspension.

» Administer the *IV infusion* over 20min (i.e. 5mL/min).

Pharmacology

Metronidazole is a nitroimidazole antibiotic with specific activity against anaerobic bacteria and some protozoa. Metronidazole diffuses into the organism where it is converted to its active form which then disrupts the helical structure of DNA, inhibiting bacterial nucleic acid synthesis and resulting in bacterial cell death. Metronidazole is well absorbed and penetrates well into body tissues. It is extensively metabolized by CYP3A4 and CYP2C9 and any unchanged drug along with metabolites are excreted renally.

Reference

. Nelson RL, Kelsey P, Leeman H, et al. Antibiotic treatment for Clostridium difficile-associated diarrhea in adults. *Cochrane Database Syst Rev* 2011; **9**:CD004610.

Miconazole

Daktarin® (POM)
Oral gel (sugar-free): 24mg/mL (15g; 80g).
Note: the 15g tube (P) can be sold to the public.

Indications

- Treatment and prevention of fungal infections of the oropharynx and GI tract, and of super infections due to Gram-positive bacteria.

Contraindications and precautions

- Contraindicated for use in patients with liver dysfunction.
- Miconazole is an inhibitor of CYP2C9 and CYP3A4. Concurrent administration with the following drugs should be avoided (see 📖 Drug interactions):
  - midazolam (oral)
  - reboxetine
  - simvastatin
  - sulfonylureas (e.g. gliclazide, glipizide).
- Use with caution in patients taking the following drugs:
  - carbamazepine
  - phenytoin
  - warfarin.

😣 Adverse effects

Common
- Dry mouth
- Nausea
- Oral discomfort
- Regurgitation
- Vomiting.

Uncommon
- Dysgeusia.

Unknown
- Diarrhoea (most likely with long-term treatment)
- Hepatitis
- Rash
- Stevens–Johnson syndrome
- Stomatitis
- Tongue discoloration
- Toxic epidermal necrolysis
- Urticaria.

Drug interactions

Pharmacokinetic
- Miconazole is a substrate of CYP3A4; it is an inhibitor of CYP2C9, CYP2D6, and CYP3A4.
- Co-administration with drugs that are metabolized by, or affect the activity (induction or inhibition—see 📖 inside back cover) of these

pathways may lead to clinically relevant drug interactions and the prescriber should be aware that dosage adjustments may be necessary, particularly of drugs with a narrow therapeutic index.

Alfentanil—may enhance effect of alfentanil.

Carbamazepine—plasma concentration of carbamazepine may be increased.

Celecoxib—plasma concentration of celecoxib may be increased.

Midazolam—may enhance effect of midazolam; risk of toxicity with oral midazolam.

Phenytoin—increases the plasma concentrations of phenytoin; consider alternative treatment or closely monitor phenytoin plasma concentration.

Reboxetine—risk of reboxetine toxicity; avoid combination.

Simvastatin—risk of myopathy; avoid combination.

Sulfonylureas—risk of hypoglycaemia; avoid combination.

Warfarin—anticoagulant effect may be enhanced.

Pharmacodynamic

None known.

Dose

5–10mL of PO QDS after food for up to 2 days after symptoms have resolved. Retain oral gel around lesion(s) for as long as possible before swallowing.

Dose adjustments

Elderly

Normal doses can be used.

Hepatic/renal impairment

The manufacturer contraindicates the use of miconazole in patients with liver dysfunction.

Dose adjustments are unnecessary in patients with renal impairment.

Additional information

Recommended first-line treatment for oral candidiasis.

Patients with dentures should remove them before using miconazole and clean them before re-insertion. Overnight, dentures should be removed at night and brushed with the gel.

Pharmacology

Miconazole is a broad-spectrum antifungal agent with antibacterial against certain Gram-positive bacteria. It produces an antifungal effect by inhibition of ergosterol biosynthesis in the cell membrane, changing the barrier function. Oral bioavailability of miconazole is low due to poor systemic absorption, with the majority of absorbed miconazole being metabolized and <1% of a dose excreted unchanged in the urine.

Midazolam

Hypnovel® (CD3 POM)
Injection: 10mg/5mL (10); 10mg/2mL (10).

Buccolam® (CD3 POM)
Oromucosal solution: Prefiiled syringes in packages of 4 containing: 2.5m (yellow); 5mg (blue); 7.5mg (purple); 10mg (orange)

Generic (CD3 POM)
Injection: 2mg/2mL; 5mg/5mL; 50mg/50mL; 10mg/5mL; 10mg/2m 50mg/10mL.

Unlicensed Special (CD3 POM)
Oral liquid: 2.5mg/mL (100mL).
Buccal liquid: 50mg/5mL; 250mg/25mL.

- Note: midazolam is a Schedule 3 CD. Refer to 📖 Legal categories of medicines, p.21 for further information.

Indications
- ¥Dyspnoea[1,2]
- ¥Epilepsy[1]
- ¥Major haemorrhage[3]
- ¥Myoclonus[1]
- ¥Status epilepticus[4,5]
- ¥Terminal agitation or anxiety.[1,6,7]

Contraindications and precautions
- Refer to 📖 Use of drugs in end-of-life care, p.53 for end-of-life care issues.
- Must not be used in patients with severe respiratory failure or acute respiratory depression.
- The manufacturers of itraconazole and miconazole oral gel contraindicate co-administration with oral midazolam due to a potential CYP3A4 interaction (see 📖 Drug interactions, p.359).
- Use with caution in patients with:
  - myasthenia gravis
  - chronic renal failure
  - impaired hepatic function
  - impaired cardiac function
  - chronic respiratory insufficiency.
- Prolonged treatment with midazolam can lead to the development of physical dependence. Abrupt cessation of treatment may precipitate withdrawal symptoms, such as anxiety, confusion, convulsions, hallucinations, headaches, insomnia, and restlessness. Note such changes can occur after the introduction of a CYP3A4 inducer (see 📖 Drug interactions, p.359).
- Midazolam may modify reactions and, if appropriate, patients should be advised not drive (or operate machinery) if affected. Refer to 📖 Drug and driving, p.25.

Adverse effects

The frequency is not defined, but reported adverse effects include:

- Amnesia
- Anterograde amnesia
- Confusion
- Drowsiness
- Hiccups
- Nausea
- Vomiting.

Drug interactions

Pharmacokinetic

Midazolam is a major substrate of CYP3A4. Co-administration with drugs that are metabolized by, or affect the activity (induction or inhibition—see 📖 inside back cover) of this pathway may lead to clinically relevant drug interactions and the prescriber should be aware that dosage adjustments may be necessary, particularly of drugs with a narrow therapeutic index.

Interactions with CYP3A4 inhibitors or inducers will be more pronounced for oral administration (compared to parenteral, buccal, or intranasal) because midazolam undergoes significant first-pass metabolism.

Alfentanil—may inhibit the metabolism of midazolam via competitive inhibition.

Carbamazepine—reduces the plasma concentrations of midazolam (CYP3A4 induction); the dose of midazolam may need to be titrated accordingly if carbamazepine is added or discontinued.

Clarithromycin—increased risk of midazolam toxicity, use lower initial doses; dose adjustments may be necessary if clarithromycin is added or discontinued.

Diltiazem—increased risk of midazolam toxicity, use lower initial doses; dose adjustments may be necessary if diltiazem is added or discontinued.

Erythromycin—increased risk of midazolam toxicity, use lower initial doses; dose adjustments may be necessary if erythromycin is added or discontinued.

Fentanyl—may inhibit the metabolism of midazolam via competitive inhibition

Fluconazole—may inhibit the metabolism of midazolam (although more likely to occur when fluconazole doses >200mg daily).

Grapefruit juice—significantly increases the effect of midazolam administered orally; avoid concurrent use.

Itraconazole—may significantly increase the effect of *oral* midazolam; manufacturer of itraconazole contraindicates concurrent use

Miconazole—may significantly increase the effect of *oral* midazolam; manufacturer of miconazole oral gel contraindicates concurrent use.

Pharmacodynamic

- *Alcohol*—may precipitate seizures and significantly increases sedative effect of midazolam.
- *Antidepressants*—reduced seizure threshold.
- *Antipsychotics*—reduced seizure threshold.
  CNS depressants—additive sedative effect.

Dose

¥ Dyspnoea

- Dose should be titrated and adjusted to individual requirements.
- Typical initial dose is 2.5–5mg SC PRN, or 10mg via CSCI.
- Dose can be increased as necessary to 5–10mg SC PRN, or 60mg via CSCI.
- Midazolam can be used as an adjunct to morphine for breathlessness

¥ Epilepsy/myoclonus

- Dose should be titrated and adjusted to individual requirements.
- Typical initial dose is 10mg SC PRN, or 10–20mg via CSCI increasing to 30–60mg via CSCI.
- If the patient has not settled with 60mg midazolam via CSCI, an alternative treatment such as phenobarbital should be considered.

¥ Hiccup

- Typical dose 10–60mg via CSCI.
- Note that midazolam is also implicated as a cause of hiccup.

¥ Major haemorrhage

- 5–10mg IV/IM/intranasal titrated to the patient's requirements to a maximum dose of 30mg per episode.
- Avoid the SC route due to poor and erratic absorption.

¥ Status epilepticus

- The intranasal route can be appropriate for the treatment of seizures and the dose is determined by weight:
  - <50kg 5mg intranasal midazolam
  - >50kg 10mg intranasal midazolam.
- The buccal route can be used as an alternative to the intranasal route if there is excessive head movement due to seizures.
  - 10mg buccal midazolam (Note—Buccolam® is presently not licensed for use in adults)
- Doses of intranasal or buccal midazolam may be repeated after 10min if necessary. Further doses should not be given without further medical assessment.

¥ Terminal agitation or anxiety

- Typical dose 2.5–10mg SC PRN, or 10–60mg via CSCI. The dose should be titrated and adjusted to individual requirements.
- If the patient has not settled at 60mg via CSCI, addition of an antipsychotic such as *levomepromazine* should be considered.

Dose adjustments

Elderly

- No specific guidance is available, but the dose should be carefully adjusted to individual requirements.

Hepatic/renal impairment

- No specific guidance is available, but in liver impairment empirical dose reductions may be necessary.
- In patients with CrCl <10mL/min, a dose reduction should be considered due to an increased risk of sedation as accumulation of an active metabolite can occur.

Additional information

A buccal liquid is available from Special Products Ltd (Tel: 01932 690325).

Although the injection can be administered buccally, the volume may be too much for some patients.

The injection may also be administered intranasally¥ (see 📖 Dose, p.360) using a mucosal atomization device (MAD). This is available from Wolfe-Tory Medical (see ℜ http://www.wolfetory.com/nasal.php for further information regarding supply).

Midazolam precipitates in solutions containing bicarbonate and it is likely to be unstable in solutions of alkaline pH (e.g. dexamethasone, dimenhydrinate, ranitidine)

Midazolam via CSCI is reportedly compatible with alfentanil, cyclizine, diamorphine, fentanyl, glycopyrronium, haloperidol, hydromorphone, hyoscine butylbromide, hyoscine hydrobromide, levomepromazine, metoclopramide, morphine (hydrochloride, sulphate, tartrate), midazolam, promethazine, octreotide, and oxycodone.

⊕ Pharmacology

Midazolam is a short-acting benzodiazepine whose exact mechanism of action is unknown, but is believed to involve enhancement of GABA-ergic transmission in the CNS. It is extensively metabolized by CYP3A4 and has an active metabolite (α-hydroxymidazolam glucuronide).

References

. Gremaud G, Zulian GB. Indications and limitations of intravenous and subcutaneous midazolam in a palliative care center. *Journal Pain Symptom Manage* 1998; **15**(6):331–3.
. Navigante AH, Castro MA, Cerchietti LC. Morphine versus midazolam as upfront therapy to control dyspnea perception in cancer patients while its underlying cause is sought or treated. *J Pain Symptom Manage* 2010; **39**(5):820–30.
. Harris DG, Noble SI. Management of terminal hemorrhage in patients with advanced cancer: a systematic literature review. *J Pain Symptom Manage* 2009; **38**(6):913–27.
. de Haan GJ, van der Geest P, Doelman G, *et al.* A comparison of midazolam nasal spray and diazepam rectal solution for the residential treatment of seizure exacerbations. *Epilepsia* 2010; **51**(3):478–82.
. Shorvon S. The treatment of status epilepticus. *Curr Opin Neurol* 2011; **24**(2):165–70.
. Kehl KA. Treatment of terminal restlessness: a review of the evidence. *J Pain Palliat Care Pharmacother* 2004; **18**(1):5–30.
. Mercadante S, Intravaia G, Villari P, *et al.* Controlled sedation for refractory symptoms in dying patients. *J Pain Symptom Manage* 2009; **37**(5):771–9.

Mirtazapine

Zispin SolTab® (POM)
Orodispersible tablet: 15mg (30), 30mg (30), 45mg (30).

Generic (POM)
Tablet: 15mg (28), 30mg (28), 45mg (28).
Orodispersible tablet: 15mg (30); 30mg (30); 45mg (30).
Oral solution: 15mg/mL (66ml bottle).

Indications
- Depression
- ¥Appetite[1]
- ¥Insomnia[2]
- ¥Nausea/vomiting (see 📖 Additional information, p.364)[3]
- ¥Pruritus.[4]

Contraindications and precautions
- Do not use with an MAOI, or within 14 days of stopping one; avoid concomitant use with linezolid or moclobemide.
- Use cautiously in patients receiving *rasagiline* or *selegiline* (see 📖 Additional information, p.364).
- Use with caution in epilepsy (lowers seizure threshold).
- Depression is associated with an increased risk of suicidal thoughts, self-harm, and suicide which persists until remission. Note that that the risk of suicide may increase during initial treatment.
- Hyponatraemia should be considered in all patients who develop drowsiness, confusion, or convulsions while taking an antidepressant. Hyponatraemia has been associated with all types of antidepressants, although it is reportedly more common with SSRIs.
- May precipitate psychomotor restlessness, which usually appears during early treatment.
- Avoid abrupt withdrawal as symptoms such as dizziness, agitation, anxiety, headache, nausea, and vomiting can occur. Mirtazapine should be withdrawn gradually over several weeks whenever possible. See 📖 Discontinuing and/or switching antidepressants, p.45 for information about switching or stopping antidepressants.
- Avoid in patients with phenylketonuria—orodispersible tablets contain aspartame, a source of phenylalanine.
- Mirtazapine may modify reactions and patients should be advised not drive (or operate machinery) if affected. Refer to 📖 Drugs and driving p.25.
- Warn the patient about the importance of reporting signs of infection such as sore throat and fever during initial treatment (risk of agranulocytosis).

☺ Adverse effects
Very common
- Drowsiness (paradoxically improves as dose increases)
- Dry mouth

Increased appetite
Weight gain (≥ 7% bodyweight).

Common

Abnormal dreams
Anxiety (may worsen during initial treatment)
Back pain
Confusion
Dizziness
Insomnia (may occur during initial treatment)
Lethargy
Myalgia
Peripheral oedema
Postural hypotension
Tremor
Weakness.

Uncommon

Hallucinations
Mania
Psychomotor restlessness
Restless legs.

Rare

Myoclonus.

Unknown

Bone marrow depression (usually appears after 4–6 weeks of
treatment)
Convulsions
Hyponatraemia
Serotonin syndrome
Stevens–Johnson syndrome
Suicidal ideation (can also occur shortly after discontinuation)
Toxic epidermal necrolysis.

Drug interactions

Pharmacokinetic

Mirtazapine is metabolized by CYP1A2, CYP2D6 and CYP3A4.
Co-administration with drugs that are metabolized by, or affect the
activity (induction or inhibition—see 📖 inside back cover) of these
pathways may lead to clinically relevant drug interactions and the
prescriber should be aware that dosage adjustments may be necessary,
particularly of drugs with a narrow therapeutic index.
Carbamazepine and *phenytoin* can reduce mirtazapine levels by at least
50%.
Dose adjustments may be necessary upon smoking cessation.
The effect of grapefruit juice on the absorption of mirtazapine is
unknown.

Pharmacodynamic

• Risk of serotonin syndrome (see 📖 Box 1.10, p.18) with:
  • MAOIs

- Rasagiline
- Selegiline
- Serotonergic drugs—e.g. duloxetine, methadone, SSRIs, TCAs, tramadol, and trazodone.
- *CNS depressants*—risk of excessive sedation.
- *Tramadol*—increased risk of seizures (and serotonin syndrome); may reduce effect of tramadol by blocking 5-HT$_3$ receptor mediated analgesia.

Dose

Depression

- Initial dose 15mg PO ON.
- Adjust dose as clinically appropriate; review within 2–4 weeks and increase dose to a maximum of 45mg/day, as a single dose at bedtime, or as 2 divided doses.

¥ Appetite/insomnia/nausea/vomiting

- Initial dose 7.5–15mg PO ON. Review dose within 1 week and increase as necessary to a maximum dose of 45mg/day, as a single dose at bedtime, or as 2 divided doses.
- Patient may show improved response to a BD dosing schedule.

¥ Pruritus

- Initial dose 7.5–15mg PO ON. Higher doses may be of no further benefit.

Dose adjustments

Elderly

- Initial dose as previously described.
- 7.5mg dose may actually be more sedative.
- Adjust dose as clinically appropriate.

Hepatic/renal impairment

- Clearance is reduced in moderate—severe renal or hepatic impairment.
- Specific dose recommendations not warranted—adjust as clinically appropriate.
- Prescriber must be aware that plasma levels may be raised in these patients.

Additional information

- Relief of insomnia and anxiety can start shortly after initiation of dosing but in general, it begins to exert an antidepressant effect after 1–2 weeks of treatment.
- Presently, Clinical Knowledge Summaries (NHS Evidence) states that mirtazapine and trazodone may be used with caution in patients receiving *rasagiline* or *selegiline*.[5]
- Mirtazapine, by virtue of its pharmacology, should have useful anti-emetic activity. While there are no clinical studies to prove this, clinical experience would suggest that it can be helpful.
- Weight gain more likely in women and unlikely to see benefit after 6 weeks of treatment.

- Mirtazapine is more likely than SSRIs to cause dry mouth and drowsiness.
- Orodispersible tablets may block feeding tubes; in such instances, the oral solution should be used.
- The degree of buccal or sublingual absorption from the orodispersible tablet is presently unknown.

Pharmacology

Mirtazapine is an antidepressant that is believed to produce its effect through a presynaptic α_2-adrenoreceptor antagonism, increasing central noradrenergic and serotonergic neurotransmission. It is also an antagonist at 5-HT$_2$, 5-HT$_3$, and H$_1$ receptors which explains its anti-emetic activity. Mirtazapine actually has similar binding affinity for the 5-HT$_3$ receptor as the 5-HT$_3$ antagonists. It is rapidly absorbed after oral administration, with a bioavailability of ~50%. Mirtazapine is extensively metabolized (via CYP1A2, CYP2D6, and CYP3A4) and eliminated via the urine and faeces. At low doses, the H$_1$ antagonistic effect generally predominates, leading to sedation during initial treatment, which improves as the dose escalates.

References

1. Riechelmann RP, Burman D, Tannock IF, et al. Phase II trial of mirtazapine for cancer-related cachexia and anorexia. *Am J Hosp Palliat Care* 2010; **27**(2):106–10.
2. Cankurtaran ES, Ozalp E, Soygur H, et al. Mirtazapine improves sleep and lowers anxiety and depression in cancer patients: superiority over imipramine. *Support Care Cancer* 2008; **16**(11):1291–8.
3. Kast RE, Foley KF. Cancer chemotherapy and cachexia: mirtazapine and olanzapine are 5-HT3 antagonists with good antinausea effects. *Eur J Cancer Care* 2007; **16**(4):351–4.
4. Davis MP, Frandsen JL, Walsh D, et al. Mirtazapine for pruritus. *J Pain Symptom Manage* 2003; **25**(3):288–91.
5. NHS Evidence Clinical Knowledge Summaries (2011). *Parkinson's disease —Management. Which drugs should be used in the treatment of depression in people with Parkinson's disease?* Available from: M http://www.cks.nhs.uk/parkinsons_disease/management/detailed_answers/confirmed_parkinsons_disease_primary_care/managing_non_motor_symptoms_and_complications/depression/drug_treatment_of_depression#-380720. Accessed 3 November 2011

Misoprostol

Cytotec® (POM)
Tablet (scored): 200 micrograms (60).
With diclofenac (📖 Diclofenac, p.159).

Arthrotec® 50 (POM)
Tablet: diclofenac sodium 50mg, misoprostol 200 micrograms (60).

Arthrotec® 75 (POM)
Tablet: diclofenac sodium 75mg, misoprostol 200 micrograms (60).
With naproxen (📖 Naproxen, p.381).

Napratec OP® Combination Pack (POM)
Tablets: naproxen 500mg + misoprostol 200 micrograms (56).

Indications
- Healing of duodenal and gastric ulcers including those induced by NSAIDs.
- Prophylaxis of NSAID-induced ulcers.

Contraindications and precautions
- Contraindicated for use in pregnancy (causes uterine contractions). Additionally, women of child-bearing potential must use effective contraception.
- Misoprostol should be used with caution in conditions where hypotension may precipitate severe complications, e.g. cerebrovascular disease, coronary artery disease.

☺ Adverse effects
The frequency is not defined, but reported adverse effects include:
- Abdominal pain
- Diarrhoea (occasionally severe, necessitating discontinuation)
- Dizziness
- Flatulence
- Intermenstrual bleeding
- Nausea and vomiting
- Uterine contractions
- Vaginal bleeding (both pre- and postmenstrual women).

Drug interactions
Pharmacokinetic
- No clinically significant interactions noted.

Pharmacodynamic
- No clinically significant interactions noted.

⚗ Dose
Healing of duodenal and gastric ulcers
- Initial dose 200 micrograms PO QDS or 400 micrograms PO BD with food.

• *Patients may not tolerate this dose initially and a more gradual dose titration may be warranted.
• If necessary, the dose may be increased further to a maximum of 400mg PO OD, or 200mg PO BD.

Prophylaxis of NSAID-induced ulcers
• 200 micrograms PO BD–QDS.
• *Patients may not tolerate this dose initially and a more gradual dose titration may be warranted

Dose adjustments

Elderly
• No dose adjustments are necessary based on age alone.

Hepatic/renal impairment
• No dose adjustments are necessary in patients with liver or renal impairment.

Additional information

• Diarrhoea is often a dose-limiting adverse effect. It can be minimized by using single doses ≤ 200 micrograms with food and by avoiding the use of magnesium-containing antacids.
• Misoprostol has been used to treat intractable constipation.
• Although the tablets can be crushed and dispersed in water prior to administration, this is generally not recommended due to the effect it may have on woman of child-bearing potential.

Pharmacology

Misoprostol is a prostaglandin E1 (PGE1) analogue which acts by binding to the prostaglandin receptor on parietal cells. The resulting cytoprotective actions include:
• Enhanced mucosal blood flow as a result of direct vasodilatation.
• Inhibiting gastric acid secretion.
• Reducing the volume and proteolytic activity of gastric secretions.
• Increasing bicarbonate and mucus secretion.

Modafinil

Provigil® *(POM)*
Tablet: 100mg (30 per pack), 200mg (30 per pack).

Indications

- ¥Cancer-related fatigue.[1,2]

Contraindications and precautions

- Modafinil is contraindicated for use in patients with uncontrolled moderate to severe hypertension, or arrhythmia.

- Serious skin rashes have been reported with the use of modafinil occurring within 1–5 weeks after treatment initiation. Treatment should be withdrawn immediately and not restarted.
- Use with caution in patients with a history of psychosis, mania, depression, or substance/alcohol abuse. If psychiatric symptoms develop, modafinil should be withdrawn immediately and not restarted.
- Modafinil is associated with cardiovascular adverse effects. The manufacturer and MHRA recommend that a baseline ECG should be performed before treatment initiation. Avoid in patients with left ventricular hypertrophy or cor pulmonale.

- Anxiety may worsen with modafinil. Patients with major anxiety should only receive modafinil under specialist supervision.
- Use with caution in patients with renal impairment (see 📖 Dose adjustments, p.369).
- Modafinil may modify reactions and patients should be advised not drive (or operate machinery) if affected. Refer to 📖 Drugs and driving, p.25.

☻ Adverse effects

Very common

- Headache (up to 21% of patients may be affected).

Common

- Abdominal pain
- Abnormal LFTs
- Anxiety
- Asthenia
- Blurred vision
- Confusion
- Depression
- Diarrhoea
- Dizziness
- Drowsiness
- Dry mouth
- Dyspepsia
- Insomnia
- Nausea
- Nervousness
- Paraesthesia
- Reduced appetite
- Tachycardia.

Uncommon

- Amnesia
- Arrhythmia
- Cough
- Diabetes mellitus
- Dysgeusia
- Dyskinesia
- Dysphagia
- Hypertension/hypotension

- Migraine
- Myalgia
- Peripheral oedema
- Rhinitis
- Sweating
- Thirst
- Tremor
- Vomiting.

Unknown

- Serious skin reactions, e.g. Stevens–Johnson (usually within first 5 weeks of treatment).
- Psychosis, mania, and hallucinations have been reported.

Drug interactions

Pharmacokinetic

- Modafinil is metabolized by CYP3A4 and is also a strong inhibitor of CYP2C19. It is a weak inhibitor of CYP2C9 and weak inducer of CYP3A4 and CYP2B6. Co-administration with drugs that are metabolized by, or affect the activity (induction or inhibition—see 📖 inside back cover) of these pathways may lead to clinically relevant drug interactions and the prescriber should be aware that dosage adjustments may be necessary, particularly of drugs with a narrow therapeutic index.
- In patients CYP2D6 deficient (or taking inhibiting drugs), the metabolism of SSRIs and TCAs via CYP2C19 becomes more important. Consequently, lower doses of the antidepressants may be necessary in patients co-administered modafinil.

Pharmacodynamic

- None of significance noted.

Dose

- 100mg PO OM initially, increasing to 200mg PO OM if necessary after 7 days.

Dose adjustments

Elderly

- Usual adult dosing described previously can be used.

Hepatic/renal impairment

- The manufacturer recommends using half the usual adult dose in patients with severe hepatic impairment.
- The manufacturer states there is inadequate experience to determine the safety and efficacy of modafinil in patients with renal impairment. Severe renal failure (CrCl up to 20mL/min) does not significantly affect the pharmacokinetics of modafinil; however, exposure to the inactive metabolite, modafinil acid, can increase up to 9-fold.

Additional information

- An effect should be seen within 2 hours of dosing although it may take several days to achieve optimal clinical response. If no effect is seen after 7–10 days, discontinue.
- Monitor blood pressure and heart rate in hypertensive patients.
- Patients who complain of headaches may find that taking with or after food may ameliorate the symptom.
- Tablets are dispersible in water. If necessary, the tablets can be crushed and dispersed in water prior to use. The resulting solution can be flushed down a feeding tube.

⟡ Pharmacology

The mechanism of action is unknown but its therapeutic effects are similar to methylphenidate. Unlike the amphetamine, the effect of modafinil does not appear to be related to dopamine and drugs such as haloperidol do not reduce its effect.

References

1. Portela MA, Rubiales AS, Centeno C. The use of psychostimulants in cancer patients. *Curr Opin Support Palliat Care* 2011; **5**(2):164–8.
2. Blackhall L, Petroni G, Shu J, et al. A pilot study evaluating the safety and efficacy of modafinil for cancer-related fatigue. *J Palliat Med* 2009; **12**(5):433–9.

Morphine

It is not possible to ensure the interchangeability of different makes of modified-release oral morphine preparations in individual patients. Therefore, it is recommended that patients should remain on the same product once treatment has been stabilized. Inclusion of the brand name on the prescription is suggested.

Standard oral release

Oramorph® Oral solution (CD5 POM)
Solution: 10mg/5mL (100mL; 300mL; 500mL).
Note: discard 90 days after opening.

Oramorph® Concentrated oral solution (CD2 POM)
Solution (sugar-free): 20mg/mL (30mL; 120mL).
Note: discard 120 days after opening.

Sevredol® (CD2 POM)
Tablet (scored): 10mg (blue, 56); 20mg (pink, 56); 50mg (pale green, 56).

Generic (POM)
Solution: 10mg/5mL (100mL).

Standard release rectal products

Generic (CD2 POM)
Suppository: 10mg (12); 15mg (12); 20mg (12); 30mg (12).
Note: products contain morphine sulphate or hydrochloride. Prescription must state the morphine salt to be dispensed.

Parenteral products

Generic (CD2 POM)
Injection: 10mg/mL; 15mg/mL; 20mg/mL; 30mg/mL all in 1mL and 2mL amps.

12-hourly modified release

Morphgesic® (CD2 POM)
Tablet: 10mg (buff, 60); 30mg (violet, 60); 60mg (orange, 60); 100mg (grey, 60).

MST Continus® (CD2 POM)
Tablet: 5mg (white, 60); 10mg (brown—60); 15mg (green, 60); 30mg (purple, 60); 60mg (orange, 60); 100mg (grey, 60); 200mg (teal green, 60).
Suspension (granules): 20mg (30); 30mg (30); 60mg (30); 100mg (30); 200mg (30).

Zomorph® (CD2 POM)
Capsule: 10mg (yellow/clear, 60); 30mg (pink/clear, 60); 60mg (orange/clear, 60); 100mg (white/clear, 60); 200mg (clear, 60).

24-hourly modified release

MXL® (CD2 POM)
Capsule: 30mg (light blue, 28); 60mg (brown, 28); 90mg (pink, 28); 120mg (green, 28); 150mg (blue, 28); 200mg (red-brown, 28)

- Note: morphine is a Schedule 2 CD. Refer to Legal categories of medicines, p.21 for further information.

Indications

- Relief of severe pain
- ¥Relief of moderate pain
- ¥Painful skin lesions (topical)[1,2]
- ¥Mucositis (topical)[1,2]
- ¥Cough[3]
- ¥Dyspnoea.[4]

Contraindications and precautions

- If the dose of an opioid is titrated correctly, it is generally accepted that there are no absolute contraindications to the use of such drugs in palliative care, although there may be circumstances where one opioid is favoured over another (e.g. renal impairment, constipation). Nonetheless, manufacturers state that morphine is contraindicated for use in patients with:
  - acute abdomen
  - acute diarrhoeal conditions associated with antibiotic-induced pseudomembranous colitis
  - acute hepatic disease
  - concurrent administration of MAOIs or within 2 weeks of discontinuation of their use. *NB initial low doses, careful titration and close monitoring may permit safe combination.*
  - delayed gastric emptying
  - head injury
  - obstructive airways disease (morphine may release histamine)
  - paralytic ileus
  - phaeochromocytoma (due to the risk of pressor response to histamine release)
  - respiratory depression.
- Use with caution in the following instances:
  - Addison's disease (adrenocortical insufficiency)
  - asthma (morphine may release histamine)
  - constipation
  - delirium tremens
  - diseases of the biliary tract
  - elderly patients
  - epilepsy (morphine may lower seizure threshold)
  - hepatic impairment
  - history of alcohol and drug abuse
  - hypotension associated with hypovolaemia (morphine may result in severe hypotension)
  - hypothyroidism
  - inflammatory bowel disorders
  - pancreatitis

- prostatic hypertrophy
- raised intracranial pressure
- significantly impaired hepatic and renal function.
- Refer to 📖 Use of drugs in end-of-life care, p.53 for end-of-life care issues.
- Morphine may modify reactions and patients should be advised not drive (or operate machinery) if affected.

☺ Adverse effects

Strong opioids tend to cause similar adverse effects, albeit to varying degrees. The frequency is not defined, but reported adverse effects include:

- Anorexia
- Biliary pain
- Confusion
- Constipation
- Drowsiness
- Dry mouth
- Dyspepsia
- Exacerbation of pancreatitis
- Euphoria
- Insomnia
- Headache
- Hyperhidrosis

- Myoclonus
- Nausea
- Pruritus
- Sexual dysfunction (e.g. amenorrhea, decreased libido, erectile dysfunction)
- Urinary retention
- Vertigo
- Visual disturbance
- Vomiting
- Weakness.

The following can occur with excessive dose:

- Agitation
- Exacerbation of pain
- Hallucinations
- Miosis

- Paraesthesia
- Respiratory depression
- Restlessness.

Drug interactions

Pharmacokinetic

- Morphine is metabolized mainly by glucuronidation, via UGT enzymes, particularly UGT2B7. Drugs that affect the activity of these (e.g. *diclofenac*) could influence the response to morphine, although the clinical significance is presently unknown. A minor pathway involves CYP2D6.
- Morphine is a substrate of P-gp. Inhibitors of P-gp may enhance the effect of morphine. *Itraconazole* has been shown to increase plasma concentrations of morphine.

Pharmacodynamic

- *Antihypertensives*—increased risk of hypotension.
- *CNS depressants*—risk of excessive sedation.
- *Haloperidol*—may be an additive hypotensive effect.
- *Ketamine*—there is a potential opioid-sparing effect with ketamine and the dose of morphine may need reducing.
- *Levomepromazine*—may be an additive hypotensive effect.

⚚ Dose

Pain

The initial dose of morphine depends upon the patient's previous opioid requirements. Refer to 📖 Management of pain: opioid substitution, p.32 for information regarding opioid dose equivalences. Refer to 📖 Management of pain: breakthrough pain, p.35 for guidance relating to BTcP.

Oral

Standard release:
- For opioid naïve patients, initial dose is 5–10mg PO every 4-6 hours and PRN. The dose is then increased as necessary until a stable dose is attained. The patient should then be converted to a modified-release formulation.
- ¥Lower initial doses (e.g. 2.5mg PO every 4-6 hours and PRN) can be used for opioid naïve patients to treat moderate pain (i.e. instead of using codeine)

Modified release:
- For opioid naïve patients, initial dose is 5–10mg PO BD. The dose can then be titrated as necessary.
- MXL® can be introduced once a total daily dose of 30mg is reached.

Subcutaneous

- Initial dose in opioid naïve patients is 5mg SC 4-hourly PRN. Alternatively, 10mg via CSCI over 24 hours and increase as necessary.
- The maximum dose per injection site that should be given by SC bolus injection is 60mg (=2mL).

Rectal

- Initial dose 15–30mg PR every 4 hours, adjusted according to response.

¥ Painful skin lesions

- Often use 0.1% or 0.125% w/w gels initially. These can be prepared immediately prior to administration by adding 10mg morphine injection to 8g Intrasite® gel (making a 0.125% w/w gel). Higher strength gels, typically up to 0.5%, can be made if necessary.
- Initial dose: 5–10mg morphine in Intrasite® gel to affected area at dressing changes (up to twice daily).
- Use within 1 hour of preparation and discard any remaining product.

¥ Mucositis

- Often use 0.1% w/v initially. Preparations should be prepared immediately prior to administration by adding 10mg morphine injection to 10mL of a suitable carrier (e.g. Gelclair®, Oral Balance Gel®).
- Higher strength preparations, up to 0.5% w/v can be used if required.
- Initial dose: 10mg to the affected area BD–TDS.
- Use within 1 hour of preparation and discard any remaining product.

¥ Dyspnoea

Oral

Standard release:
- For opioid naïve patients, initial dose is 2.5–5mg PO PRN. A regular prescription every 4 hours, plus PRN may be necessary.

- In patients established on opioids, a dose that is equivalent to 25% of the current PRN rescue analgesic dose may be effective. This can be increased up to 100% of the rescue dose in a graduated fashion.

Subcutaneous
- For opioid naïve patients, initial dose is 1.25–2.5mg SC PRN. If patients require >2 doses daily, use of a CSCI should be considered.
- In patients established on opioids, a dose that is equivalent to 25% of the current PRN rescue analgesic dose may be effective. This can be increased up to 100% of the rescue dose in a graduated fashion.

¥ Cough
Standard release
- Initial dose 5mg PO every 4 hours, and increase as necessary.

♣ Dose adjustments
Elderly
- No specific guidance is available, although lower starting doses in opioid naïve patients may be preferable (e.g. for severe pain, 2.5–5mg PO 4 hourly and PRN). Dose requirements should be individually titrated.

Hepatic/renal impairment
- No specific guidance is available, although in patients with hepatic impairment, the plasma concentration is expected to be increased. In view of its hepatic metabolism, caution is advised when giving morphine to patients with hepatic impairment. Lower starting doses in opioid naïve patients may be preferable and dose requirements should be individually titrated.
- No specific guidance is available for patients with renal impairment. However, in view of the fact that the active metabolite morphine-6-glucuronide is renally excreted, lower starting doses in opioid naïve patients may be preferable and dose requirements should be individually titrated. Alternatively, a different opioid may be more appropriate (e.g. oxycodone or fentanyl).

Additional information
- *Oramorph*® oral solution 10mg/5ml contains alcohol 10% v/v. It may cause stinging in patients with mucositis.
- *MXL*® and *Zomorph*® capsules should be swallowed whole, or the capsules can be opened and the contents sprinkled on soft food.
- Morphine sulphate via CSCI is stated to be compatible with clonazepam, cyclizine, dexamethasone, glycopyrronium, haloperidol, hyoscine butylbromide, hyoscine hydrobromide, ketamine, ketorolac, levomepromazine, metoclopramide, midazolam, octreotide, ondansetron, and ranitidine. Refer to Dickman A, Schneider J. *The Syringe Driver* (3rd edn). Oxford: Oxford University Press, 2011, for further information.

♦ Pharmacology
Morphine is a strong opioid that interacts predominantly with the μ-opioid receptor. Following oral administration, morphine undergoes

extensive first-pass metabolism, with bioavailability is ~30%, but can range from 10–65%. The major pathway for morphine metabolism is glucuronidation, catalysed by UDP glucuronyltransferase, in the liver and GI tract to produce morphine-3-glucuronide (M3G) and morphine-6-glucuronide (M6G). The latter metabolite is considered to significantly contribute to the analgesic effect of morphine, while M3G is devoid of analgesic action and may even antagonize the action of morphine. It is likely that enterohepatic circulation of metabolites probably occurs. ~90% of the dose is excreted renally within 24 hours.

References

1. Tran QN, Fancher T. Achieving analgesia for painful ulcers using topically applied morphine gel. *J Support Oncol* 2007; **5**(6):289–93.
2. LeBon B, Zeppetella G, Higginson IJ. Effectiveness of topical administration of opioids in palliative care: a systematic review. *J Pain Symptom Manage* 2009; **37**(5):913–17.
3. Wee B, Browning J, Adams A, et al. Management of chronic cough in patients receiving palliative care: review of evidence and recommendations by a task group of the Association for Palliative Medicine of Great Britain and Ireland. *Palliat Med* 2011 Oct 12. (Epub ahead of print.)
4. Viola R, Kiteley C, Lloyd NS, et al. The management of dyspnea in cancer patients: a systematic review. *Support Care Cancer* 2008; **16**(4):329–37.

Nabumetone

Relifex® (POM)
Tablet: 500mg (56).
Suspension (sugar-free): 500mg/5mL (300mL).

Generic (POM)
Tablet: 500mg (56).

Indications

- Pain and inflammation associated with osteoarthritis and rheumatoid arthritis.
- *Pain associated with cancer.[1]

Contraindications and precautions

- Contraindicated for use in patients with:
  - a history of, or active, peptic ulceration
  - hypersensitivity reactions to ibuprofen, aspirin, or other NSAIDs
  - severe heart, hepatic, or renal failure.
- Certain NSAIDs are associated with an increased risk of thrombotic events. There are presently insufficient data to exclude such a risk for nabumetone.
- Use the minimum effective dose for the shortest duration necessary in order to reduce the risk of cardiac and GI events.
- Elderly patients are more at risk of developing adverse effects.
- Use with caution in the following circumstances:
  - concurrent use of diuretics, corticosteroids, and NSAIDs (see 📖 Drug interactions, p.378)
  - CHF and/or left ventricular dysfunction
  - diabetes mellitus
  - established ischaemic heart disease, peripheral arterial disease, and/ or cerebrovascular disease need careful consideration due to the increased risk of thrombotic events
  - hepatic impairment
  - hyperlipidaemia
  - hypertension (particularly uncontrolled)
  - recovery from surgery
  - renal impairment
  - smoking.
- Patients taking long-term therapy need regular monitoring of renal and liver function.
- Abnormal LFTs can occur; discontinue NSAID if this persists.
- Nabumetone may prevent the development of signs and symptoms of inflammation/infection (e.g. fever).
- Nabumetone is believed to have an improved GI tolerability compared to other NSAIDs. Nonetheless, consider co-prescription of misoprostol or a PPI if:
  - long-term NSAID therapy
  - concurrent use of drugs that increase the risk of GI toxicity (see 📖 Drug interactions, p.378)

- Refer to 📖 Selection of a NSAID, p.29 for further information, including selection.
- Nabumetone may modify reactions and patients should be advised not drive (or operate machinery) if affected.

😊 Adverse effects

Common

- Abdominal pain
- Constipation
- Diarrhoea
- Dyspepsia
- Flatulence
- Gastritis

- Nausea
- Oedema
- Pruritus
- Rash
- Tinnitus.

Uncommon

- Altered LFTs
- Confusion
- Dizziness
- Dry mouth
- Dyspnoea
- Fatigue
- GI ulceration, bleeding or perforation
- Headache
- Haematemesis
- Insomnia

- Melaena
- Myopathy
- Nervousness
- Paraesthesia
- Photosensitivity
- Somnolence
- Stomatitis
- Sweating
- Urticaria
- Visual disturbances
- Vomiting.

Drug interactions

Pharmacokinetic

- Nabumetone is metabolized to the active metabolite, 6-methoxy-2-naphthylacetic acid (6-MNA). In vitro studies suggest CYP1A2 is involved. Metabolism if 6-MNA is believed to involve CYP2C9. Although there are presently no recognized clinically significant drug interactions, the prescriber should be aware that co-administration of CYP1A2 inhibitors or CYP2C9 inducers may reduce the effect of nabumetone. Co-administration of CYP1A2 inducers or CYP2C9 inhibitors may necessitate dosage adjustment.
- Dose adjustments may be necessary upon smoking cessation.
- *Methotrexate*—reduced excretion of methotrexate.

Pharmacodynamic

- *Anticoagulants*—increased risk of bleeding.
- *Antihypertensives*—reduced hypotensive effect.
- *Antiplatelet drugs*—increased risk of bleeding.
- *Corticosteroids*—increased risk of GI toxicity.
- *Ciclosporin*—increased risk of nephrotoxicity.
- *Diuretics*—reduced diuretic effect; nephrotoxicity of nabumetone may be increased.
- *Rosiglitazone*—increased risk of oedema.
- *SSRIs*—increased risk of GI bleeding.

Dose

The dose should be taken preferably with or after food.

¥ Cancer pain

- Initial dose 1g PO ON. Dose can be increased if necessary to 500mg PO OM and 1g PO ON, followed by a further increase to 1g PO BD. Use the lowest effective dose and for the shortest duration possible.

Dose adjustments

Elderly

- Initial dose 500mg PO ON, increased to a maximum of 1g PO ON. Use the lowest effective dose and for the shortest duration possible.

Hepatic/renal impairment

- Since the formation of the active metabolite depends on biotransformation in the liver, plasma concentrations could be decreased in patients with severe hepatic impairment; therefore, the manufacturer states that the drug should be used cautiously in such patients.
- Modification of nabumetone dose generally is not necessary in patients with mild renal impairment (CrCl of 50mL/min or greater).
- In patients with severe renal impairment (creatinine clearance <30mL/min), the initial dose should not exceed 500mg PO OD. After careful monitoring of renal function, dose may be increased, if needed, to a maximum dose of 1g PO daily.

⊙ Pharmacology

Nabumetone is a prodrug and has little pharmacologic activity until it undergoes oxidation in the liver to form an active metabolite, 6-MNA that is structurally similar to naproxen. 6-MNA is a relatively selective COX-2 inhibitor.

Reference

1. McNicol ED, Strassels S, Goudas L, et al. NSAIDS or paracetamol, alone or combined with opioids, for cancer pain. Cochrane Database Syst Rev 2005; 2:CD005180.

Naloxone

Generic (POM)
Injection (ampoule): 400 micrograms/mL.
Injection (pre-filled syringe): 2mg/2mL.

Indications

- Treatment of opioid overdose (use only if respiratory rate is <8 breaths/min, or <10–12 breaths/min and patient difficult to rouse and cyanosed).

Contraindications and precautions

- No absolute contraindication when used for life-threatening respiratory depression.
- Do not use to treat opioid-induced drowsiness.

☺ Adverse effects

The frequency is not defined, but reported adverse effects include:

- Cardiac arrest
- Hypertension
- Nausea
- Reversal of opioid analgesia
- Seizures
- Sweating
- Tachycardia
- Vomiting.

Drug interactions

Pharmacokinetic

- None known.

Pharmacodynamic

- *Opioids*—antagonism of effects.

♣ Dose

- Initial dose 0.4–2mg IV injection, repeated every 2–3min if necessary to a maximum of 10mg.
- The SC or IM route can be used (same dose) if the IV access is unavailable.
- The duration of action of some opioids, or modified release formulations, may exceed that of naloxone. In such situations, an IV infusion of naloxone will provide sustained antagonism of the opioid and avert the need for repeated injections.

♣ Dose adjustments

Elderly

- No specific guidance is available. The dose should be titrated to effect.

Hepatic/renal impairment

- No specific guidance is available. The dose should be titrated to effect. The manufacturer advises caution and close monitoring of the patient.

Additional information

- To prepare an IV infusion for the reversal of opioid overdose, add 2mg naloxone to 500mL NaCl 0.9% or glucose 5%. The rate of administration should be titrated in accordance with the patient's response.
- Naloxone has an onset of action of 1–2min by IV injection and 2—5min by SC/IM injection.

⟐ Pharmacology

Naloxone is an opioid antagonist, with strong affinity for the μ-opioid receptor. It competes with and displaces opioids at receptor sites.

Naproxen

Naprosyn® (POM)
Tablet (scored): 250mg (56); 500mg (56).

Naprosyn EC® (POM)
Tablet (e/c): 250mg (56); 375mg (56); 500mg (56).

Synflex® (POM)
Tablet: 275mg (60) (NB Synflex is naproxen sodium; 275mg naproxen sodium = 250mg naproxen).

Generic (POM)
Tablet: 250mg (28); 500mg (28).
Tablet (e/c): 250mg (56); 375mg (56); 500mg (56).
With misoprostol (📖 Misoprostol, p.366).

Napratec OP® (POM)
Tablet: naproxen 500mg, misoprostol 200 micrograms (56).

Indications

- Pain and inflammation in musculoskeletal disorders
- ⁜Pain associated with cancer.[1]

Contraindications and precautions

- Contraindicated for use in patients with:
  - a history of, or active, peptic ulceration
  - hypersensitivity reactions to ibuprofen, aspirin or other NSAIDs
  - severe heart, hepatic or renal failure.
- To date, naproxen has not shown an increased risk of thrombotic events as have many other NSAIDs. It has been suggested that naproxen possesses significant antiplatelet activity when administered regularly, twice daily.
- Use the minimum effective dose for the shortest duration necessary in order to reduce the risk of cardiac and GI events.
- Elderly patients are more at risk of developing adverse effects.
- Use with caution in the following circumstances:
  - concurrent use of diuretics, corticosteroids, and NSAIDs (see 📖 Drug interactions, p.382)
  - CHF and/or left ventricular dysfunction
  - diabetes mellitus
  - established ischaemic heart disease, peripheral arterial disease, and/or cerebrovascular disease need careful consideration due to the increased risk of thrombotic events
  - hepatic impairment
  - hyperlipidaemia
  - hypertension (particularly uncontrolled)
  - recovery from surgery
  - renal impairment
  - smoking
- Patients taking long-term therapy need regular monitoring of renal and liver function.

- Abnormal LFTs can occur; discontinue NSAID if this persists.
- Naproxen may prevent the development of signs and symptoms of inflammation/infection (e.g. fever).
- Consider co-prescription of misoprostol or a PPI if:
  - long-term NSAID therapy
  - concurrent use of drugs that increase the risk of GI toxicity (see 📖 Drug interactions)
- Refer to 📖 Selection of a NSAID, p.29 for further information, including selection.
- Naproxen may modify reactions and patients should be advised not drive (or operate machinery) if affected.

☻ Adverse effects

The frequency is not defined, but reported adverse effects include:

- Abdominal pain
- CHF
- Constipation
- Diarrhoea
- Dyspepsia
- Dyspnoea
- Fatigue
- Flatulence
- Gastrointestinal haemorrhage
- Headache
- Hypersensitivity reactions (e.g. anaphylaxis, asthma, dyspnoea, pruritus, rash, severe skin reactions)
- Hypertension
- Jaundice
- Melaena
- Nausea
- Oedema
- Peptic ulcer
- Renal failure
- Stomatitis
- Tinnitus
- Vomiting.

Drug interactions

Pharmacokinetic

- Is a minor substrate of CYP1A2 and CYP2C8/9 and is unlikely to be affected by enzyme inhibitors.
- *Methotrexate*—reduced excretion of methotrexate.
- *Warfarin*—possible increased risk of bleeding through inhibition of warfarin metabolism (5–11% of Caucasians have a variant of CYP2C9, requiring lower maintenance doses of warfarin. Combination with naproxen may further reduce warfarin metabolism).

Pharmacodynamic

- *Anticoagulants*—increased risk of bleeding.
- *Antihypertensives*—reduced hypotensive effect.
- *Antiplatelet drugs*—increased risk of bleeding.
- *Corticosteroids*—increased risk of GI toxicity.
- *Ciclosporin*—increased risk of nephrotoxicity.
- *Diuretics*—reduced diuretic effect; nephrotoxicity of naproxen may be increased.
- *Rosiglitazone*—increased risk of oedema.
- *SSRIs*—increased risk of GI bleeding.

⚖ Dose

Naprosyn EC® should be swallowed whole, while the other products should be taken with or after food.

- Initial dose 500–1000mg PO daily in 1–2 divided doses.
- Maximum daily dose is 1250mg PO daily, which can be taken in 2–3 divided doses.
- For *Naprotec*® the usual dose is 1 tablet PO BD.

Dose adjustments

Elderly
- Use the lowest effective dose and for the shortest duration possible.

Hepatic/renal impairment
- In liver impairment, no specific dose recommendations are available. However, the lowest dose possible should be used for the shortest duration possible.
- Naproxen should be used with extreme caution in renal impairment. Close monitoring of renal function is recommended. Naproxen is contraindicated for use in patients with a CrCl <30mL/min.

Additional information

- If *Naprotec*® is used, ensure a PPI is not co-prescribed.

Pharmacology

Naproxen is a NSAID with analgesic, anti-inflammatory, and antipyretic properties. The sodium salt of naproxen is more rapidly absorbed. The mechanism of action of naproxen, like that of other NSAIDs, is not completely understood but may be related to inhibition of COX-1 and COX-2. Naproxen and naproxen sodium are rapidly and completely absorbed after oral administration. It is highly protein bound and extensively metabolized in the liver (involving CYP1A2 and CYP2C8/9); the metabolites are excreted renally.

Reference

1. McNicol ED, Strassels S, Goudas L, et al. NSAIDS or paracetamol, alone or combined with opioids, for cancer pain. *Cochrane Database Syst Rev* 2005; **2**:CD005180.

Nifedipine

Standard release
Adalat® (POM)
Capsule: 5mg (90); 10mg (90).

Generic (POM)
Capsule: 5mg (84); 10mg (84).

Modified release
Different versions of modified-release preparations may not have the same clinical effect; prescribers should specify the brand to be dispensed.

Adalat LA® (POM)
Tablet: 20mg (28); 30mg (28); 60mg (28).

Adalat Retard® (POM)
Tablet: 10mg (56); 20mg (56).

A variety of other products are available and include Adipine® MR, Adipine® XL, Coracten SR®, Coracten XL®, Fortipine LA, Hypolar® Retard 20, Nifedipress® MR, Tensipine MR®, and Valni XL®; consult the BNF for more information.

Indications
- Prophylaxis of chronic stable angina
- Hypertension (*modified-release only*)
- Raynaud's phenomenon (*standard-release only*)
- ⃰Smooth muscle spasm pain (e.g. tenesmus)[1]
- ⃰Intractable hiccup.[2]

Contraindications and precautions
- Contraindicated for use in:
  - clinically significant aortic stenosis
  - during or within 4 weeks of a myocardial infarction
  - unstable angina.
- Standard-release formulations cause a dose-dependent increase in the risk of cardiovascular complications (e.g. myocardial infarction); only use if no other treatment suitable.
- Once daily modified release formulations are contraindicated for use in inflammatory bowel disease or Crohn's disease.
- Use with caution in patients with:
  - concurrent administration of CYP3A4 inducers or inhibitors (see 📖 Drug interactions, p.386)
  - concurrent administration of other antihypertensive drugs (see 📖 Drug interactions, p.386)
  - diabetes (can impair glucose tolerance)
  - hepatic impairment
  - low systolic blood pressure (<90mmHg).

☺ Adverse effects

Common
- Constipation
- Headache
- Oedema
- Vasodilatation.

Uncommon
- Anxiety
- Dizziness
- Dry mouth
- Dyspepsia
- Migraine
- Nausea
- Sexual dysfunction
- Sleep disorder
- Tremor
- Vertigo
- Visual disturbances.

Drug interactions

Pharmacokinetic
- Nifedipine is metabolized mainly by CYP3A4; it is an inhibitor of CYP1A2. Co-administration with drugs that are metabolized by, or affect the activity (induction or inhibition—see 📖 inside back cover) of these pathways may lead to clinically relevant drug interactions and the prescriber should be aware that dosage adjustments may be necessary, particularly of drugs with a narrow therapeutic index.
- *Erythromycin*—increased effect of nifedipine.
- *Rifampicin*—significant reduction in effect of nifedipine.
- Avoid grapefruit juice as it may increase the bioavailability of nifedipine through inhibition of intestinal CYP3A4.

Pharmacodynamic
- *Alcohol*—potentiates the hypotensive effect of nifedipine.
- The risk of hypotension is increased if nifedipine is taken concurrently with the following drugs:
  - β-blockers
  - diuretics
  - haloperidol
  - levomepromazine
  - opioids
  - phosphodiesterase inhibitors (e.g. sildenafil, tadalafil, or vardenafil)
  - TCAs.

⚕ Dose

¥ Smooth muscle spasm pain/¥ intractable hiccup:
Standard release
- Initial dose 5mg PO TDS with food (or 30min before food in oesophageal spasm); increase dose as necessary to maximum 20mg PO TDS.

Modified release
- Initial dose 20mg PO OD, or 10mg PO BD; increase dose as necessary to maximum 60mg PO daily.

Dose adjustments
Elderly
- No specific guidance is available; use the lowest effective dose.

Liver/renal impairment
- No specific guidance is available for patients with hepatic impairment. Manufacturers advise caution, given the hepatic metabolism. Use the lowest effective dose.
- Patients with renal impairment are unlikely to need dose adjustments.

Pharmacology
Nifedipine is a dihydropyridine calcium-channel antagonist. It inhibits the entry of calcium through cell membranes by blocking channels. The decrease in intracellular calcium inhibits the contractile processes of smooth muscle cells, thereby attenuating spasm.

References
1. McLoughlin R, McQuillan R. Using nifedipine to treat tenesmus. *Pall Med* 1997; **11**(5):419–20.
2. Quigley C. Nifedipine for hiccups. *J Pain Symptom Manage* 1997; **13**(6):313.

Nitrofurantoin

Standard release

Macrodantin® (POM)
Capsule: 50mg (30); 100mg (30).

Furadantin® (POM)
Tablet (scored): 50mg; 100mg.

Generic (POM)
Tablet: 50mg; 100mg.
Oral suspension: 25mg/5mL (300mL).

Modified release

Macrobid® (POM)
Capsule: 100mg (14).

Indications

* Refer to local guidelines.
* Prophylaxis against and treatment of acute or recurrent uncomplicated lower UTIs.

Contraindications and precautions

* Avoid in patients with:
  * acute porphyria
  * CrCl <60mL/min (ineffective as inadequate urine concentrations achieved)
  * G6PD deficiency.
* Due to the risk of peripheral neuropathy, use with caution in patients with:
  * anaemia,
  * diabetes mellitus (may also get false positive for glucose in urinary tests)
  * electrolyte imbalance
  * folate deficiency
  * vitamin B deficiency.
* Use with caution in the following conditions as adverse pulmonary and hepatic effects can be masked:
  * allergic diathesis
  * hepatic impairment
  * neurological disorders
  * pulmonary disease.
* Monitor lung and hepatic function if long-term therapy, especially in the elderly.
* Nitrofurantoin may modify reactions and patients should be advised not drive (or operate machinery) if affected.

☺ Adverse effects

The frequency is not defined, but reported adverse effects include:
* Acute pulmonary reactions (can occur within the 1st week).
* Allergic skin reactions
* Anorexia

- Blood dyscrasias (e.g. agranulocytosis, leucopenia, haemolytic anaemia, thrombocytopenia)
- Cholestatic jaundice
- Chronic pulmonary reactions
- Diarrhoea
- Dizziness
- Drowsiness
- Erythema multiforme
- Headache
- Hepatitis
- Nausea (reduce dose)
- Peripheral neuropathy
- Vomiting
- Weakness.

Drug interactions

Pharmacokinetic

- *Magnesium trisilicate*—reduced absorption of nitrofurantoin.
- *Probenecid*—reduced renal excretion (reduced effect) and increased plasma concentrations.

Pharmacodynamic

- *Quinolones*—increased risk of adverse effects.

⚖ Dose

Standard doses are described here. Refer to local guidelines for specific advice.

Standard release

- Prophylaxis: 50–100mg PO ON.
- Treatment: 50–100mg PO QDS for 7 days.

Modified release

- Treatment: 100mg PO BD for 7 days.

⚖ Dose adjustments

Elderly

- No dose adjustment necessary.

Hepatic/renal impairment

- No specific guidance is available for use in hepatic impairment, but refer to 📖 Contraindications and precautions, p.387.
- Nitrofurantoin should not be used in patients with CrCl <60mL/min.

Additional information

- Patients should be warned that urine may be coloured yellow, orange, or brown.

⊙ Pharmacology

Nitrofurantoin is a broad-spectrum, bactericidal antibacterial agent active against many Gram-negative and some Gram-positive bacteria. It inhibits bacterial acetyl-coenzyme A, interfering with the carbohydrate metabolism. Nitrofurantoin may also disrupt bacterial cell wall formation. ~20–25% of the total single dose of nitrofurantoin is excreted unchanged.

Nortriptyline

Allegron® (POM)
Tablet: 10mg (100); 25mg (*scored;* 100).

Indications
- Depression
- Nocturnal enuresis (*not discussed*)
- *Neuropathic pain.[1]

Contraindications and precautions
- Do not use with an irreversible MAOI (including *rasagiline* and *selegiline*), or within 14 days of stopping one, or at least 24 hours after discontinuation of a reversible MAOI (e.g. *moclobemide, linezolid*). Note that in exceptional circumstances linezolid may be given with nortriptyline, but the patient must be closely monitored for symptoms of serotonin syndrome (see 📖 Box 1.10, p.18; 📖 Drug interactions, p.390)
- Nortriptyline is contraindicated for use in the following:
  - arrhythmias
  - mania
  - porphyria
  - recent myocardial infarction
  - severe liver disease.
- Nortriptyline should be used with caution in patients with:
  - cardiovascular disorders
  - epilepsy
  - hepatic impairment
  - hyperthyroid patients or those receiving thyroid medication (enhances response to antidepressant)
  - narrow-angle glaucoma
  - prostatic hypertrophy
  - urinary retention.
- Elderly patients are more susceptible to adverse effects, especially agitation, confusion, and postural hypotension (see 📖 Dose adjustments, p.391).
- Depression is associated with an increased risk of suicidal thoughts, self-harm, and suicide which persists until remission. Note that that the risk of suicide may increase during initial treatment.
- Hyponatraemia should be considered in all patients who develop drowsiness, confusion, or convulsions while taking an antidepressant. Hyponatraemia has been associated with all types of antidepressants, although it is reportedly more common with SSRIs.
- Avoid abrupt withdrawal as symptoms such as insomnia, irritability, and excessive perspiration can occur. Although generally mild, they can be severe in some patients. Withdrawal symptoms usually occur within the first few days of discontinuing treatment and they usually resolve within 2 weeks, though they can persist in some patients for up to 3 months or longer. See 📖 Discontinuing and/ or switching antidepressants, p.45 for information about switching

or stopping antidepressants. If withdrawal symptoms emerge during discontinuation, raise the dose to stop symptoms and then restart withdrawal much more gradually.
- Nortriptyline may modify reactions and patients should be advised not drive (or operate machinery) if affected.
- Subtle deficits in attention, memory, and reasoning may occur with therapeutic dosages of anticholinergic drugs without signs of obvious toxicity. These deficits have often been mistaken for symptoms of early dementia in elderly patients.

☺ Adverse effects
The frequency is not defined, but reported adverse effects include:
- Abnormal LFTs
- Arrhythmias
- Blurred vision
- Confusion (particularly elderly)
- Constipation
- Convulsions
- Delirium (particularly elderly)
- Difficulty with micturition
- Dizziness
- Dry mouth
- Galactorrhoea
- Gynaecomastia
- Hallucinations
- Headache
- Hypomania or mania
- Hyponatraemia
- Increased appetite and weight gain
- Movement disorders
- Nausea
- Postural hypotension
- Sedation
- Sexual dysfunction
- Stomatitis
- Sweating
- Tachycardia
- Taste disturbances
- Tinnitus
- Tremor.

Drug interactions
Pharmacokinetic
- Nortriptyline is a substrate of CYP1A2, CYP2C19, and CYP2D6 (major). In patients lacking CYP2D6, the pathways involving CYP1A2 and CYP2C19 become of greater significance. Co-administration with drugs that are metabolized by, or affect the activity (induction or inhibition—see 📖 inside back cover) of these pathways may lead to clinically relevant drug interactions and the prescriber should be aware that dosage adjustments may be necessary, particularly of drugs with a narrow therapeutic index.
- *Fluoxetine*—has been shown to increase the plasma concentrations of nortriptyline (via CYP2D6 inhibition).

Pharmacodynamic
- Risk of serotonin syndrome (see 📖 Box 1.10, p.18) with:
  - MAOIs
  - Rasagiline
  - Selegiline
  - Serotonergic drugs—e.g. duloxetine, methadone, mirtazapine, SSRIs, tramadol, trazodone, and venlafaxine.
- *Anticholinergics*—increased risk of adverse effects.
- *Anti-epileptics*—nortriptyline antagonizes the effect.
- *Antihypertensives*—possible increased risk of hypotension.
- *CNS depressants*—additive sedative effect.

- *Domperidone*—may inhibit prokinetic effect.
- *Metoclopramide*—may inhibit prokinetic effect.
- *Nefopam*—increased risk of anticholinergic adverse effects.
- *SSRIs*—increased risk of seizures (and serotonin syndrome).
- *Tramadol*—increased risk of seizures (and serotonin syndrome).

Dose

Depression

- 10–25mg PO ON, increasing as necessary to a usual dose of 75–100mg daily in 3–4 divided doses, or as a single dose (e.g. at bedtime).

¥ Neuropathic pain

- 10–25mg PO ON, increasing as necessary to a maximum of 50mg PO daily in divided doses, or as a single dose (e.g. at bedtime). Higher doses may be used under specialist supervision.
- The manufacturer advises monitoring of plasma nortriptyline concentrations if a dose above 100mg daily is prescribed (optimum range of 50–150ng/mL), although the practical value is uncertain.

Dose adjustments

Elderly

- Elderly patients are particularly susceptible to adverse anticholinergic effects, with an increased risk for cognitive decline and dementia. No specific dose reductions are recommended by manufacturers. However, it is suggested that elderly patients are initiated on the lower end of the usual range i.e. for pain, 10mg ON and the dose increased as necessary and as tolerated.

Hepatic/renal impairment

- There are no specific instructions for dose reduction in hepatic impairment. It is contraindicated for use in severe liver disease. If the drug has to be used, the patient should be closely monitored and the lowest effective dose should be prescribed.
- There are no specific instructions for dose adjustment in renal impairment. The lowest effective dose should be prescribed.

Additional information

- Nortriptyline may have a better adverse effect profile than amitriptyline, including a reduced likelihood of prolongation of the interval.
- May have immediate benefits in treating insomnia or anxiety; anti-depressant action may be delayed 2–4 weeks.

Pharmacology

Nortriptyline is the primary active metabolite of amitriptyline. Both drugs block the reuptake of noradrenaline and serotonin. The interference with the reuptake of noradrenaline and serotonin is believed to explain the mechanism of the antidepressant and analgesic activity of nortriptyline.

Reference

1. Saarto T, Wiffen PJ. Antidepressants for neuropathic pain. *Cochrane Database Syst Rev* 2007; **4**:CD005454.

Nystatin

Nystan® (POM)
Oral suspension: 100,000 units/mL (30mL).

Indications
• Candidal infections of the oral cavity, oesophagus.

Contraindications and precautions
• None stated.

☺ Adverse effects
Frequency is not stated, but reported adverse effects include:
• Diarrhoea (more likely with high doses)
• Hypersensitivity
• Nausea
• Oral irritation
• Vomiting.

Drug interactions
Pharmacokinetic
• None known.

Pharmacodynamic
• *Chlorhexidine*—nystatin inactivated by chlorhexidine; separate administration by at least 1 hour.

♣ Dose
• Initial dose 1mL PO QDS, rinsed around the mouth for 1min before swallowing.
• If necessary, dose can be increased to 5mL PO QDS.
• Patients with dentures should remove them before using nystatin and clean them before re-insertion. Overnight, dentures should be soaked in an appropriate antiseptic solution (and rinsed before reinsertion).

♣ Dose adjustments
Elderly
• Dose adjustments are unnecessary.

Hepatic/renal impairment
• Dose adjustments are unnecessary.

♻ Pharmacology
Nystatin is a polyene antifungal drug active against a wide range of yeasts and yeast-like fungi, including *Candida albicans*. Nystatin acts by binding to the cell membrane causing a change in membrane permeability and the subsequent leakage of intracellular components. *Candida albicans* (the organism responsible for the majority of oral candidiasis) does not develop resistance to nystatin. Other species of *Candida* can become quite resistant during treatment, resulting in cross-resistance to amphotericin. This resistance is lost once nystatin is discontinued.

Absorption of nystatin from the GI tract is negligible; excessive doses tend only to produce GI adverse effects such as diarrhoea, nausea, and vomiting.

Octreotide

Sandostatin® *(POM)*
Injection: 50 micrograms/mL (5); 100 micrograms/mL (5); 1mg/5mL (multi-dose vial); 500 micrograms/mL (5).

Generic (POM)
Injection: 50 micrograms/mL (5); 100 micrograms/mL (5); 1mg/5mL (multi-dose vial); 500 micrograms/mL (5).

Indications
- Relief of symptoms associated with functional gastroenteropancreatic (GEP) endocrine tumours (e.g. carcinoid, VIPomas, glucagonomas).
- Anti-secretory effect:
  - ⚥Large volume vomiting associated with bowel obstruction[1]
  - ⚥Excessive diarrhoea[1]
  - ⚥Bronchorrhoea[2]
  - ⚥Ascites[1]
  - ⚥Rectal discharge.[1]

Contraindications and precautions
- Refer to 📖 Use of drugs in end-of-life care, p.53 for end-of-life care issues.
- Abrupt withdrawal of subcutaneous octreotide is associated with biliary colic and pancreatitis
- Octreotide reduces gall bladder motility and there is a risk of gallstone development.
- Use with caution in patients with
  - type 1 diabetes (insulin and oral hypoglycaemic doses may need reducing)
  - type 2 diabetes (dose adjustment may be needed)
  - hepatic impairment (e.g. cirrhosis—dose reduction may be necessary)
- Monitor thyroid function if on long-term treatment.

☺ Adverse effects
Common
- Abdominal pain
- Constipation
- Diarrhoea
- Flatulence
- Local injection site pain, swelling and irritation.

Uncommon
- Hair loss
- Cholecystitis.

Rare
- Abdominal bloating
- Gallstones
- Nausea
- Steatorrhoea
- Vomiting.

Drug interactions

Pharmacokinetic

- Through suppression of growth hormone, octreotide may reduce the metabolic clearance of drugs metabolized by the cytochrome P450 system. The prescriber should be aware that drugs mainly metabolized by CYP3A4 and with a narrow therapeutic index may need dose adjustments.
- Octreotide can reduce the absorption of *ciclosporin,* potentially resulting in reduced plasma levels and possible treatment failure.

Pharmacodynamic

- *Anticholinergics*—additive antisecretory effect.

Dose

GEP tumours

- Initial dose 50 micrograms SC OD–BD. Increase according to response to a maximum of 200 micrograms TDS. To reduce pain on administration, ensure the ampoule is warmed to room temperature beforehand.
- *Alternatively, 100 micrograms daily via CSCI. Increase as necessary to 600 micrograms daily.
- Discontinue after 1 week if no improvement.

*Antisecretory effect

- Initial dose 200–500 micrograms daily via CSCI. Dose can be increased to a usual maximum of 600 micrograms daily. Higher doses (e.g. 1mg) have been used successfully.
- Alternatively, 50–100 micrograms SC TDS, increased as necessary to 200 micrograms SC TDS. To reduce pain on administration, ensure the ampoule is warmed to room temperature beforehand.

Dose adjustments

Elderly

- Normal doses can be used.

Hepatic/renal impairment

- Manufacturer advises that a dose reduction may be necessary in patients with hepatic impairment.
- No dose adjustments are necessary for patients with renal impairment.

Additional information

- Octreotide via CSCI is reportedly compatible with alfentanil, clonazepam, cyclizine, diamorphine, glycopyrronium, haloperidol, hydromorphone, hyoscine butylbromide, hyoscine hydrobromide, levomepromazine, metoclopramide, midazolam, morphine, ondansetron, oxycodone, and ranitidine.
- Combination with an anticholinergic drug such as glycopyrronium may have an additive antisecretory effect.

✧ Pharmacology
Octreotide is a somatostatin analogue that has multitude of inhibitory actions (e.g. reduction of insulin and glucagon secretion; reduction of pancreatic and intestinal secretions of water and sodium, in addition to stimulating absorption of water and electrolytes).

References
1. Prommer EE. Established and potential therapeutic applications of octreotide in palliative care. *Support Care Cancer* 2008; **16**(10):1117–23.
2. Hudson E, Lester JF, Attanoos RL, *et al.* Successful treatment of bronchorrhea with octreotide in a patient with adenocarcinoma of the lung. *J Pain Symptom Manage* 2006; **32**(3):200–2.

Olanzapine

Zyprexa® (POM)
Tablet: 2.5mg (28); 5mg (28); 7.5mg (56); 10mg (28); 15mg (28); 20mg (28).

Zyprexa Velotab® (POM)
Orodispersible tablet: 5mg (28); 10mg (28); 15mg (28); 20mg (28).

Generic (POM)
Tablet: 2.5mg (28); 5mg (28); 7.5mg (56); 10mg (28); 15mg (28); 20mg (28).
Orodispersible tablet: 5mg (28); 10mg (28); 15mg (28); 20mg (28).

Indications

- Psychosis
- ✹Nausea and vomiting[1]
- ✹Delirium[2]
- ✹Terminal agitation refractory to conventional treatment.[2]

Contraindications and precautions

Warning

- Olanzapine should not be used to treat behavioural symptoms of dementia. Elderly patients with dementia-related psychosis treated with olanzapine are at an increased risk of CVA and mortality. Citalopram, sertraline or trazodone may be more appropriate choices.
- The risks associated with CVA (e.g. diabetes, hypertension, smoking) should be assessed before commencing treatment with olanzapine.

- Antipsychotic drugs may increase the risk of VTE; assess risks before and during treatment.
- Use with caution in:
  - diabetes (risk of hyperglycaemia in elderly)
  - epilepsy (seizure threshold may be lowered)
  - hepatic/renal impairment (see 📖 Dose adjustments, p.398)
  - Parkinson's disease (olanzapine may worsen Parkinsonian symptomatology and cause hallucinations)
- Electrolyte disturbances must be corrected (e.g. hypokalaemia) due to the risk of QT prolongation.
- Must not be used in patients with known risk for narrow-angle glaucoma.
- Phenylketonuria—*Zyprexa Velotab*® contains aspartame, a source of phenylalanine.
- Avoid sudden discontinuation as this may lead to the development of acute withdrawal symptoms (e.g. sweating, insomnia, tremor, anxiety, nausea, and vomiting).
- Sudden cessation of smoking may lead to the development of adverse effects, such as Parkinsonism.
- Olanzapine may modify reactions and patients should be advised not drive (or operate machinery) if affected.

● Subtle deficits in attention, memory, and reasoning may occur with therapeutic dosages of anticholinergic drugs without signs of obvious toxicity. These deficits have often been mistaken for symptoms of early dementia in elderly patients.

☹ Adverse effects

Very common
● Drowsiness
● Weight gain (≥7% of baseline body weight with short-term treatment; with long-term exposure, defined as >48 weeks, weight gain may be ≥25% of baseline body weight).

Common
● Constipation
● Dizziness
● Dry mouth
● Fatigue
● Increased appetite
● Increased cholesterol and triglyceride plasma concentrations
● Orthostatic hypotension
● Weakness
● Weight gain (≥15% of baseline body weight with short-term treatment).

Uncommon
● Alopecia
● Bradycardia
● Neutropenia
● QT prolongation
● Thromboembolism.

Unknown
● Diabetes (development or exacerbation of)
● Neuroleptic malignant syndrome
● Pancreatitis
● Restless legs syndrome
● Seizures
● Thrombocytopenia
● Withdrawal symptoms upon sudden discontinuation.

Drug interactions

Pharmacokinetic
● Is metabolized mainly by glucuronidation, but CYP1A2 is involved to a lesser degree. CYP2D6 has a minor role.
● Co-administration with drugs that are metabolized by, or affect the activity (induction or inhibition—see 📖 inside back cover) of CYP1A2 may lead to clinically relevant drug interactions and the prescriber should be aware that dosage adjustments may be necessary, particularly of drugs with a narrow therapeutic index. Co-administration of CYP2D6 inhibitors is unlikely to be of any clinical significance.
● Smoking may lead to faster metabolism of olanzapine. Dose adjustments may be necessary upon smoking cessation—see 📖 Box 1.9, p.16.

Pharmacodynamic
- Olanzapine can cause dose-related prolongation of the QT interval. There is a potential risk that co-administration with other drugs that also prolong the QT interval (e.g. *amiodarone, erythromycin, haloperidol, quinine*) may result in ventricular arrhythmias.
- *Antihypertensives*—increased risk of hypotension.
- *CNS depressants*—additive sedative effect.
- *Haloperidol*—increased risk of extrapyramidal reactions.
- *Levodopa* and *dopamine agonists*—effect antagonized by olanzapine.
- *Levomepromazine*—increased risk of extrapyramidal reactions.
- *Metoclopramide*—increased risk of extrapyramidal reactions.

Dose

The dose is usually administered in early evening.

Psychosis
- Initial dose 10mg PO OD, adjusted on the basis of individual clinical response within the range 5–20mg/day.

¥ Nausea and vomiting
- Initial dose 2.5mg PO ON, increased as necessary to a max. of 10mg PO ON

¥ Delirium
- Initial dose 2.5mg PO ON, increased as necessary to a max. of 10mg PO ON

Dose adjustments

Elderly
- Note that the elderly are more susceptible to the anticholinergic adverse effects which may increase the risk for cognitive decline and dementia.
- For psychosis, initial dose 5mg daily.
- For delirium, nausea, and vomiting increase dose gradually to improve tolerance.

Hepatic/renal impairment
- For psychosis, initial dose 5mg daily (in both cases).
- For delirium, nausea, and vomiting increase dose gradually to improve tolerance.

Additional information
- The Velotab® may be placed on the tongue and allowed to dissolve or dispersed in water, orange juice, apple juice, milk, or coffee.
- Therapeutic doses of olanzapine can precipitate an acute confusional state in vulnerable individuals. This may be related to the anticholinergic effects of olanzapine.

- Risk factors for a poor response to olanzapine in cancer patients with delirium include:
  - age >70 years
  - history of dementia
  - CNS metastases.
- Of the antipsychotics, quetiapine is believed to have a low risk of extrapyramidal symptoms. Nonetheless, it should be avoided in patients with Parkinson's disease. Should delirium or agitation develop in a patient with Parkinson's disease, the following is suggested:
  - trazodone ± benzodiazepine
  - dose reduction and/or discontinuation of anti-parkinsonian medications (anticholinergics initially, then dopamine agonists)
  - low-dose quetiapine in difficult cases.

Pharmacology

Olanzapine is an atypical antipsychotic agent which antagonizes a wide range of receptors in producing its therapeutic effects, including $5HT_{2A/2C}$, D_1, D_2, D_3, and D_4. It also antagonizes additional receptors that explain the range of effects that are produced; these include $5HT_3$, muscarinic, α_1-adrenergic, and H_1 receptors. Olanzapine is well absorbed after oral administration, reaching peak plasma concentrations within 5–8 hours. It is mainly metabolized in the liver by glucuronidation, although some oxidation via CYP1A2 does occur. CYP2D6 also has a minor role in the metabolism of olanzapine. The main metabolite of olanzapine is inactive.

References

1. Licup N. Olanzapine for nausea and vomiting. *Am J Hosp Palliat Care* 2010; **27**(6):432–4.
2. Elsayem A, Bush SH, Munsell MF, *et al.* Subcutaneous olanzapine for hyperactive or mixed delirium in patients with advanced cancer: a preliminary study. *J Pain Symptom Manage* 2010; **40**(5):774–82.

Omeprazole

Losec® (POM)
Capsule: 10mg (28); 20mg (28); 40mg (7).
IV Infusion: 40mg.
IV Injection: 40mg.

Losec® MUPS® (POM)
Dispersible tablet: 10mg (28); 20mg (28); 40mg (7).

Generic (POM)
Capsule: 10mg (28); 20mg (28); 40 mg (28).
Tablet: 10mg (28); 20mg (28); 40mg (7;28).
Dispersible tablet: 10mg (28); 20mg (28); 40mg (7).
IV Infusion: 40mg.
Note: omeprazole 10mg tablets can be sold over the counter for the short-term relief of reflux-like symptoms (e.g. heartburn) in adults >18 years max. daily dose 20mg PO for max. 4 weeks, and a pack size of 28 tablets.

Indications
- Treatment of duodenal and benign gastric ulcers.
- Treatment of oesophageal reflux disease.
- Treatment and prophylaxis of NSAID-associated peptic ulcer disease.
- Dyspepsia.

Contraindications and precautions
- Do not administer with atazanavir or erlotinib.
- Treatment with omeprazole may lead to a slightly increased risk of developing GI infections (e.g. *Clostridium difficile*). Therefore, avoid unnecessary use or high doses.
- Omeprazole may modify reactions and patients should be advised not drive (or operate machinery) if affected.
- Rebound acid hypersecretion may occur on discontinuation of the patient has received >8 weeks of treatment.
- PPIs are associated with a range of electrolyte disturbances, such as hyponatraemia and hypomagnesaemia (and associated hypocalcaemia and hypokalaemia). Suspect the PPI should unexplainable symptoms present (e.g. confusion, delirium, generalized weakness, nausea). The effect on sodium metabolism is unclear, possibly involving ADH. PPIs may reduce active magnesium absorption in the small intestine by affecting function of a transient receptor protein channel.

☺ Adverse effects
Common
- Abdominal pain
- Constipation
- Diarrhoea
- Flatulence
- Headache
- Nausea/vomiting.

Uncommon
- Dermatitis
- Dizziness
- Drowsiness
- Insomnia
- Light headedness
- Paraesthesia

- Pruritus
- Raised liver enzymes
- Rash

- Urticaria
- Vertigo.

Rare

- Aggression
- Agitation
- Confusion
- Depression
- Dry mouth
- Electrolyte disturbances
  (e.g. hypomagnesaemia,

  hyponatraemia,
  hypocalcaemia)
- Gynaecomastia
- Hallucinations
- Hepatitis
- Muscular weakness
- Stomatitis.

Drug interactions

Pharmacokinetic

- Omeprazole is a major substrate of CYP2C19; it is a minor substrate of CYP2C8/9, CYP2D6, and CYP3A4. It is a strong inhibitor of CYP2C19, moderate inhibitor of CYP2C8/9, and weak inhibitor of CYP2D6 and CYP3A4. Omeprazole is also a substrate and inhibitor of P-gp. Co-administration with drugs that are metabolized by, or affect the activity (induction or inhibition—see 📖 inside back cover) of these pathways may lead to clinically relevant drug interactions and the prescriber should be aware that dosage adjustments may be necessary, particularly of drugs with a narrow therapeutic index.
- Drugs with pH dependent absorption can be affected:
  - *Atazanavir*—avoid combination due to substantially reduced absorption.
  - *Digoxin*—increased plasma concentrations possible.
  - *Erlotinib*—avoid combination as bioavailability of erlotinib can be significantly reduced.
  - *Ferrous sulphate*—reduced absorption likely to result in treatment failure; some recommend co-administration of ascorbic acid (e.g. 100mg) at the same as ferrous sulphate to improve absorption.
  - *Ketoconazole/Itraconazole*—risk of sub-therapeutic plasma concentrations.
  - *Metronidazole suspension*—ranitidine may reduce/prevent the absorption of metronidazole.
- *Citalopram*—omeprazole can increase the plasma concentration of citalopram through inhibition of CYP2C19.
- *Clopidogrel*—antiplatelet action may be reduced (avoid combination).
- *Diazepam*—plasma concentrations of diazepam can be increased through inhibition of CYP2C19.
- *Phenytoin*—risk of phenytoin toxicity with higher omeprazole doses (>40mg/day).
- *Warfarin*—possible increase in INR.

Pharmacodynamic

- No clinically significant interactions noted.

🔊 Dose

Duodenal and benign gastric ulcers

- Initial dose 20mg PO OD for 4 weeks in duodenal ulceration or 8 weeks in gastric ulceration.

- In severe or recurrent cases the dose may be increased to 40mg PO OD
- Maintenance treatment for recurrent duodenal ulcer is recommended at a dose of 20mg PO OD.
- Alternatively, in patients unable to tolerate oral therapy, 40mg IV or IV infusion OD for up to 5 days.

Oesophageal reflux disease
- Initial dose 20mg PO OD for 4–12 weeks. For refractory disease, 40mg PO OD has been given for 8 weeks.
- Maintenance 10mg PO OD, increasing to 20mg PO OD if necessary.
- Alternatively, in patients unable to tolerate oral therapy, 40mg IV or IV infusion OD for up to 5 days.

Treatment of NSAID-associated peptic ulcer disease
- Initial dose 20mg PO OD, continued for 4–8 weeks.
- Alternatively, in patients unable to tolerate oral therapy, 40mg IV injection or IV infusion OD for up to 5 days.

Prophylaxis of NSAID-associated peptic ulcer disease
- 20mg PO OD.

Dyspepsia
- 10–20mg PO OD for 2–4 weeks depending on the severity and persistence of symptoms.

Dose adjustments
Elderly
- Dose adjustments are not necessary in the elderly.

Hepatic/renal impairment
- In liver impairment, the dose should not exceed 20mg PO OD.
- Dose adjustments are not required for patients with renal impairment.

Additional information
- Losec® MUPS® tablets can be dispersed in 10mL of water prior to administration. Alternatively, fruit juice (e.g. apple, orange) can be used. The mixture should be stirred before drinking and it is recommended that half a glass of water is taken afterwards.
- The content of Losec® capsules can be swallowed directly with half a glass of water, or may be suspended in 10mL of water prior to administration. Alternatively, fruit juice can be used. The mixture should be stirred before drinking and it is recommended that half a glass of water is taken afterwards.
- Omeprazole IV injection is to be given slowly over a period of 5min.
- Omeprazole IV infusion should be administered in either 100mL NaCl 0.9% or 100ml glucose 5% over 20–30min.

Pharmacology
Omeprazole is a PPI that suppresses gastric acid secretion in a dose-related manner by specific inhibition of the H^+/K^+-ATPase in the gastric parietal cell. Oral bioavailability is low (~40%). It is extensively metabolized, mainly by CYP2C19 although several alternative pathways are involved (e.g. CYP2C8/9, CYP2D6, and CYP3A4). Note that CYP2C19 poor metabolizers (or patients taking CYP2C19 inhibitors) can have significantly higher plasma concentrations, leading to unexpected results.

Ondansetron

Zofran® (POM)
Tablet: 4mg (30); 8mg (10).
Syrup (sugar-free): 4mg/5mL (50mL).
Injection: 4mg/2mL (5); 8mg/4mL (5).
Suppository: 16mg (1).

Zofran Melt® (POM)
Oral lyophilisate: 4mg (10); 8mg (10).

Generic (POM)
Tablet: 4mg; 8mg.
Injection: 4mg/2mL; 8mg/4mL.

Indications
Nausea and vomiting (postoperative, induced by chemotherapy or radiotherapy).
¥Nausea and vomiting (e.g. drug-induced, cancer-related, refractory).[1]
¥Pruritus (e.g. cholestatic, uraemic, opioid-induced).[2]

Contraindications and precautions
Refer to 📖 Use of drugs in end-of-life care, p.53 for end-of-life care issues.
Since ondansetron increases large-bowel transit time, use with caution in patients with signs of sub-acute bowel obstruction.
Use with caution in patients with:
- cardiac rhythm or conduction disturbances (e.g. QT-interval prolongation)
- concurrent use of anti-arrhythmic agents or β-adrenergic blocking agents (see 📖 Drug interactions, p.404)
- hepatic impairment (see 📖 Dose adjustments, p.404)
- significant electrolyte disturbances.

⚠ Adverse effects
Very common
- Headache.

Common
- Constipation
- Flushing.

Uncommon
- Abnormal LFTs
- Arrhythmias
- Extrapyramidal symptoms
- Hiccups
- Seizures.

Rare
- Anaphylaxis.

Drug interactions
Pharmacokinetic
- Is metabolized by a variety of cytochromes (e.g. CYP1A2, CYP2D6), but is a major substrate of CYP3A4. Co-administration with drugs that are metabolized by, or affect the activity (see 🕮 inside back cover) of these pathways may lead to clinically relevant drug interactions and the prescriber should be aware that dosage adjustments may be necessary, particularly of drugs with a narrow therapeutic index. Note that co-administration of an enzyme inhibitor is unlikely to be clinically significant due to metabolism via multiple pathways.
- *Carbamazepine* and *phenytoin* can reduce ondansetron levels and reduce the effect.
- The clinical significance of co-administration with other CYP3A4 inducers, or inhibitors (see 🕮 inside back cover) is unknown. The prescriber should be aware of the potential for interactions and that dose adjustments may be necessary.
- *Paracetamol*—possible reduced analgesic benefit.
- *Tramadol*—reduced analgesic benefit.
- The effect of grapefruit juice on the absorption of ondansetron is unknown.

Pharmacodynamic
- Ondansetron can cause prolongation of the QT interval. There is a potential risk that co-administration with other drugs that also prolong the QT interval (e.g. *amiodarone, erythromycin, haloperidol, quinine*) may result in ventricular arrhythmias.
- Ondansetron increases bowel transit time. This effect can be enhanced by drugs such as *opioids, TCAs, anticholinergics*.
- *Domperidone/metoclopramide*—ondansetron reduces the prokinetic effect.
- *SSRIs*—risk of serotonin syndrome.

💊 Dose
¥ *Nausea and vomiting (e.g. drug-induced, cancer-related, refractory)*
- Initial dose 4–8mg PO/SC BD–TDS.
- Alternatively, 8–16mg via CSCI daily. The dose can be increased if necessary to a max. of 32mg daily.
- Alternatively, 16mg PR OD.

¥ *Pruritus*
- Initial dose 4mg PO/SC BD, increasing if necessary to 8mg PO/SC TDS. Treatment may be continued via CSCI if necessary.

💊 Dose adjustments
Elderly
- Adult doses can be used.

Hepatic/renal impairment
- In moderate or severe impairment hepatic impairment, the manufacturer advises that a total daily dose of 8mg should not be exceeded (no dose adjustment necessary for *granisetron*)
- No dose adjustments are necessary for patients with renal impairment.

Additional information

- 5-HT$_3$ antagonists differ in chemical structure, pharmacokinetics, and pharmacodynamics. There may be individual variation in response and it may be worth considering an alternative 5-HT$_3$ antagonist if response to ondansetron is not as expected.
- Treatment with ondansetron should be used regularly for 3 days and then response assessed. Avoid using on a PRN basis.
- Response in pruritus is highly variable.
- Ondansetron via CSCI is compatible with alfentanil, dexamethasone, diamorphine, fentanyl, glycopyrronium, metoclopramide, midazolam, morphine, octreotide, and oxycodone.

Pharmacology

Ondansetron is a selective 5-HT$_3$ receptor antagonist, blocking serotonin peripherally on vagal nerve terminals and centrally in the CTZ. It is a particularly useful in the treatment of nausea/vomiting associated with serotonin release (e.g. damage to enterochromaffin cells due to bowel injury, chemotherapy, or radiotherapy).

References

1. Currow DC, Coughlan M, Fardell B, et al. Use of ondansetron in palliative medicine. *J Pain Symptom Manage* 1997; **13**(5):302–7.
2. Jones EA. Pruritus and fatigue associated with liver disease: is there a role for ondansetron? *Expert Opin Pharmacother* 2008; **9**(4):645–51.

Oxybutynin

Standard release
Cystrin® (POM)
Tablet: 3mg (56); 5mg (*scored*; 84).

Ditropan® (POM)
Tablet (scored): 2.5mg (84); 5mg (84).
Elixir: 2.5mg/5mL (150mL).

Modified release
Lyrinel® XL (POM)
Tablet: 5mg (30); 10mg (30).

Kentera® (POM)
Transdermal patch: 3.9mg/24 hours (applied for 72–96 hours).

Indications
• Urinary incontinence
• Urinary frequency.

Contraindications and precautions
• Oxybutynin is contraindicated for use in patients with:
  • myasthenia gravis
  • narrow-angle glaucoma
  • porphyria
  • severe ulcerative colitis
  • toxic megacolon
  • urinary retention.
• It should be used with caution in the following:
  • cardiac arrhythmia
  • CHF
  • dementia
  • elderly (see 📖 Dose adjustments, p.408)
  • GI reflux disease
  • hepatic impairment
  • hypertension
  • hyperthyroidism
  • prostatic hypertrophy
  • pyrexia (reduces sweating)
  • renal impairment.
• Oxybutynin may modify reactions and patients should be advised not drive (or operate machinery) if affected.
• Subtle deficits in attention, memory, and reasoning may occur with therapeutic dosages of anticholinergic drugs without signs of obvious toxicity. These deficits have often been mistaken for symptoms of early dementia in elderly patients.

☺ Adverse effects
Very common
• Application site reaction (patch)
• Dry mouth.

Common

- Asthenia
- Confusion
- Constipation
- Cough
- Depression
- Diarrhoea (overflow)
- Dizziness
- Drowsiness
- Dry skin
- Dyspepsia
- Fatigue
- Flatulence

- Headache
- Hypertension
- Insomnia
- Nausea
- Peripheral oedema
- Pharyngitis
- Sinusitis
- Urinary retention
- UTI
- Visual disturbances
- Vomiting
- Weakness.

Uncommon

- Anorexia
- Anxiety
- Conjunctivitis
- Dehydration
- Dysphagia
- Dyspnoea

- Hyperglycaemia
- Migraine
- Mouth ulceration
- Rhinitis
- Paraesthesia
- Vertigo.

Rare

- Appetite increase
- Arrhythmia
- Leucopenia

- Pyrexia
- Thrombocytopenia
- Tremor.

Unknown

- Convulsions
- Erectile dysfunction

- Hallucinations
- Memory impairment.

Drug interactions

Pharmacokinetic

- Is metabolized by CYP3A4. Co-administration with drugs that are metabolized by, or affect the activity (induction or inhibition—see 📖 inside back cover) of this pathway may lead to clinically relevant drug interactions and the prescriber should be aware that dosage adjustments may be necessary, particularly of drugs with a narrow therapeutic index.
- The effect of grapefruit juice on the bioavailability oxybutynin is unknown.

Pharmacodynamic

- *Donepezil*—effect may be antagonized.
- *β_2 agonists*—increased risk of tachycardia.
- *Cyclizine*—increased risk of anticholinergic adverse effects.
- *Domperidone*—may inhibit prokinetic effect.
- *Galantamine*—effect may be antagonized.
- *Metoclopramide*—may inhibit prokinetic effect.
- *Nefopam*—increased risk of anticholinergic adverse effects.
- *Rivastigmine*—effect may be antagonized.
- *TCAs*—increased risk of anticholinergic adverse effects.

Dose
Standard release
- Initial dose 5mg PO BD. Can be increased as necessary up to a maximum of 5mg PO QDS.

Modified release
- Patients may be transferred from the standard-release product.
- Initial dose 5mg PO OD. The dose can be increased after at least one week to 10mg PO OD. The dose can be further increased, at weekly intervals, to a maximum of 20mg PO OD.
- Alternatively, a 3.9mg transdermal patch can be applied twice weekly (every 3–4 days). The patch should be applied to dry, intact skin on the abdomen, hip, or buttock. A new application site should be used for each new patch and the same site should not be used within 7 days.

Dose adjustments
Elderly
- For the standard-release formulations, manufacturers recommend lower initial doses (e.g. 2.5mg PO BD) as elderly patients are more susceptible to adverse effects. In particular, the elderly may have an increased risk for cognitive decline and dementia.

Liver/renal impairment
- No specific guidance available. Use the lowest effective dose.

Additional information
- Plasma concentration of oxybutynin declines within 1–2 hours after removal of the transdermal patch.
- For *Lyrinel*® XL, the tablet membrane may pass through the GI tract unchanged.
- Standard release tablets can be dispersed in water immediately prior to use if necessary (elixir would be preferable).

Pharmacology
Oxybutynin is an anticholinergic drug that competitively antagonizes acetylcholine at post-ganglionic sites including smooth muscle, secretary glands and CNS sites. It is extensively metabolized by the liver, primarily by CYP3A4 there is an active metabolite that has similar actions to oxybutynin.

Oxycodone

Standard release

OxyNorm® (CD2 POM)

Capsule: 5mg (*orange/beige*, 56); 10mg (*white/beige*, 56); 20mg (*pink/beige*, 56).
Oral solution (sugar-free; alcohol-free): 5mg/5mL (250mL); 10mg/mL (120mL).
Injection: 10mg/mL (5); 20mg/2mL (5); 50mg/mL (5).

Generic (CD2 POM)

Oral solution: (sugar-free; alcohol-free): 5mg/5mL (250mL); 10mg/mL (120mL).
Injection: 10mg/mL (5); 20mg/2mL (5).

Modified release

OxyContin® (CD2 POM)

Tablet: 5mg (*blue*, 28); 10mg (*white*, 56); 15mg (*grey*, 56); 20mg (*pink*, 56);
30mg (*brown*, 56); 40mg (*yellow*, 56); 60mg (*red*, 56); 80mg (*green*, 56);
120mg (*purple*, 56).

Targinact® (CD2 POM)

Tablet: oxycodone 5mg/naloxone 2.5mg (28;) oxycodone 10mg/naloxone
5mg (56); oxycodone 20mg/naloxone 10mg (56); oxycodone 40mg/
naloxone 20mg (56).

- Note: oxycodone is a Schedule 2 CD. Refer to 📖 Legal categories of
  medicines, p.21 for further information.

Indications

- Moderate to severe pain in patients with cancer.
- Severe pain requiring the use of a strong opioid (*Targinact®*).
  Post-operative pain (*not Targinact®* not discussed).
- ★Dyspnoea.[1]
- Refer to 📖 Use of drugs in end-of-life care, p.53 for end-of-life care
  issues.

Contraindications and precautions

- If the dose of an opioid is titrated correctly, it is generally accepted
  that there are no absolute contraindications to the use of such
  drugs in palliative care, although there may be circumstances
  where one opioid is favoured over another (e.g. renal impairment,
  constipation). Nonetheless, the manufacturer states that oxycodone is
  contraindicated for use in patients with:
  - acute abdomen
  - chronic bronchial asthma
  - chronic constipation
  - chronic obstructive airways disease
  - concurrent administration of MAOIs or within 2 weeks of
    discontinuation of their use
  - cor pulmonale

- delayed gastric emptying
- head injury
- hypercarbia
- moderate to severe hepatic impairment
- non-opioid induced paralytic ileus
- respiratory depression
- severe renal impairment (CrCl <10mL/min).
- Use with caution in following instances:
  - acute alcoholism
  - Addison's disease (adrenocortical insufficiency)
  - delirium tremens
  - diseases of the biliary tract
  - elderly patients
  - hepatic impairment (see 📖 Dose adjustments, p.412)
  - history of alcohol and drug abuse
  - hypotension
  - hypothyroidism
  - hypovolaemia
  - inflammatory bowel disorders
  - pancreatitis
  - prostatic hypertrophy
  - raised intracranial pressure
  - renal impairment
  - severe pulmonary disease
  - toxic psychosis.
- Oxycodone may modify reactions and patients should be advised not drive (or operate machinery) if affected.

☺ Adverse effects

- Strong opioids tend to cause similar Adverse effects, albeit to varying degrees. See also 📖 Morphine, p.371.

Very common

- Constipation (*not Targinact®*)
- Dizziness
- Drowsiness
- Fatigue
- Nausea
- Pruritus
- Somnolence
- Vomiting.

Common

- Abnormal thoughts
- Anxiety
- Confusion
- Dry mouth
- Dyspepsia (give with food if problematic)
- Headache
- Postural hypotension
- Rash
- Restlessness
- Sedation
- Sweating
- Tremor
- Weakness
- Yawning.

Uncommon

- Biliary spasm
- Dyspnoea
- Hiccups
- Insomnia
- Miosis
- Stomatitis (*Targinact®*)
- Vasodilatation
- Vertigo.

Rare
- Convulsions (particularly in patients with epilepsy) (*Targinact®*)
- Weight increase (*Targinact®*).

Unknown
- Long-term use may result in symptoms related to an increase of plasma prolactin concentrations and reduced plasma concentrations of cortisol and testosterone (e.g. amenorrhea, decreased libido, erectile dysfunction).

Drug interactions

Pharmacokinetic
- Is a major substrate of CYP3A4; is a minor substrate of CYP2D6. Co-administration with drugs that are metabolized by, or affect the activity (induction or inhibition—see 📖 inside back cover) of these pathways may lead to clinically relevant drug interactions and the prescriber should be aware that dosage adjustments may be necessary, particularly of drugs with a narrow therapeutic index.
- The clinical significance of co-administration with CYP3A4 inhibitors (see 📖 inside back cover) is unknown. Clinical reports are lacking; in theory this interaction may lead to an increased risk of toxicity due to possible increases in the plasma concentration of oxycodone and an increase in metabolism by CYP2D6 to the active metabolite, oxymorphone. Dose adjustments may be necessary.
- Co-administration of both CYP3A4 and CYP2D6 inhibitors can substantially increase the effect of oxycodone.
- *Miconazole*—has been shown to increase the exposure to oral oxycodone.
- Avoid excessive amounts of grapefruit juice as it may increase the bioavailability of oxycodone through inhibition of intestinal CYP3A4.

Pharmacodynamic
- *Alcohol*—may enhance the pharmacodynamic effects of oxycodone.
- *Antihypertensives*—increased risk of hypotension.
- *CNS depressants*—risk of excessive sedation.
- *Haloperidol*—may be an additive hypotensive effect.
- *Ketamine*—there is a potential opioid-sparing effect with ketamine and the dose of oxycodone may need reducing.
- *Levomepromazine*—may be an additive hypotensive effect.
- *MAOIs and linezolid*—avoid concurrent use (see 📖 Morphine, p.371).
- *SSRIs*—serotonin syndrome has been reported with oxycodone and various SSRIs.

💊 Dose

Pain
The initial dose of oxycodone depends upon the patient's previous opioid requirements. Refer to 📖 Management of pain: opioid substitution, p.32 for information regarding opioid dose equivalences. Refer to 📖 Management of pain: breakthrough pain, p.35 for guidance relating to BTcP.

Oral

Standard release:
- For opioid naïve patients, initial dose is 2.5–5mg PO every 4–6 hours and PRN. The dose is then increased as necessary until a stable dose is attained. The patient should then be converted to a modified-release formulation.

Modified release:
- For opioid naïve patients, initial dose is 5–10mg PO BD. The dose can then be titrated as necessary.

Targinact®:
- For opioid naïve patients, initial dose is 10mg/5mg of oxycodone/naloxone PO BD. This can be increased to 20mg/10mg PO BD if needed.
- *The dose can be increased further as necessary, although higher doses are presently unlicensed.

Subcutaneous
- Initial dose in opioid naïve patients is 2.5mg SC 4-hourly PRN. Alternatively, 5–10mg via CSCI over 24 hours and increase as necessary.

¥ Dyspnoea
Oral—standard release
- For opioid naïve patients, initial dose is 2.5mg PO PRN. A regular prescription every 4 hours, plus PRN may be necessary.
- In patients established on opioids, a dose that is equivalent to 25% of the current PRN rescue analgesic dose may be effective. This can be increased up to 100% of the rescue dose in a graduated fashion.

Subcutaneous
- For opioid naïve patients, initial dose is 1.25–2.5mg SC PRN. If patients require >2 doses daily, use of a CSCI should be considered.
- In patients established on opioids, a dose that is equivalent to 25% of the current PRN rescue analgesic dose may be effective. This can be increased up to 100% of the rescue dose in a graduated fashion.

⚬ Dose adjustments
Elderly
- No specific guidance available, although lower starting doses in opioid naïve patients may be preferable. Dose requirements should be individually titrated.

Hepatic/renal impairment
- In patients with mild hepatic impairment, the plasma concentration is expected to be increased. Lower doses may be needed and the starting dose is suggested to be 2.5mg PO every 6 hours and titrate to pain relief. The manufacturer contraindicates the use of oxycodone in patients with moderate to severe hepatic impairment. Nonetheless, oxycodone is used in this group of patients and the dose should be titrated carefully to the patient's need.

In patients with mild to moderate renal impairment, the plasma concentration of oxycodone is likely to be increased. The initial dose is suggested to be 2.5mg PO every 6 hours and titrate to pain relief. The use of oxycodone in patients with severe renal impairment is contraindicated. Nonetheless, oxycodone is used in this group of patients and the dose should be titrated carefully to the patient's need.

If patients with hepatic and/or renal impairment are switched to oxycodone, doses representing a 33–50% reduction of usual equianalgesic doses may be needed.

In patients established on oxycodone, with subsequent development of hepatic or renal impairment, an empirical dose reduction may be required.

Additional information

OxyNorm® 10mg/mL oral solution may be mixed with a soft drink to improve taste.

OxyNorm® 5mg/5mL and 10mg/mL oral solutions do not contain alcohol as an excipient.

Ultrarapid metabolizers of CYP2D6 may be at risk of toxicity due to the potential increase in formation of the active metabolite oxymorphone.

Oxycodone via CSCI is stated to be compatible with clonazepam, dexamethasone, glycopyrronium, haloperidol, hyoscine butylbromide, hyoscine hydrobromide, ketamine, ketorolac, levomepromazine, metoclopramide, midazolam, octreotide, ondansetron, and ranitidine. There is a concentration-dependent compatibility issue with cyclizine; unlike diamorphine, the exact concentrations have not yet been identified. Refer to Dickman A, Schneider J. *The Syringe Driver* (3rd edn). Oxford: Oxford University Press, 2011, for further information.

⊕ Pharmacology

Oxycodone is a strong opioid with similar properties to morphine and acts primarily via μ-opioid receptors, although it is also stated to have affinity for δ- and κ-opioid receptors (the clinical significance of this has yet to be realized). Following oral administration, oxycodone is well absorbed with a bioavailability of up to 87%. It is metabolized principally to the inactive metabolite noroxycodone by CYP3A4. A minor metabolic pathway involves CYP2D6, with the active metabolite oxymorphone being produced. In general, the contribution of oxymorphone to the overall analgesic benefit of oxycodone is minimal since it is generally present in the plasma at low concentrations. However, ultrarapid CYP2D6 metabolizers or patients receiving CYP3A4 inhibitors can respond to oxycodone at lower than expected doses. ~10% of oxycodone is excreted unchanged, which can accumulate in patients with renal impairment.

Reference

. Viola R, Kiteley C, Lloyd NS, *et al.* The management of dyspnea in cancer patients: a systematic review. *Support Care Cancer* 2008; **16**(4):329–37.

Pamidronate disodium

Aredia Dry Powder® (POM)
Injection (powder for reconstitution): 15mg; 30mg; 90mg.

Generic (POM)
Injection (concentrate solution):
- 3mg/mL: 5mL vial (15mg); 10mL vial (30mg); 20mL vial (60mg); 30mL vial (90mg)
- 6mg/mL: 10mL vial (60mg)
- 9mg/mL: 10mL vial (90mg)
- 15mg/mL: 1mL amp (15mg); 2mL amp (30mg); 4mL amp (60mg); 6mL amp (90mg).

Indications
- Tumour-induced hypercalcaemia.
- Bone pain and osteolytic lesions due to metastases associated with breast cancer or multiple myeloma.
- Paget's disease of bone (*not discussed*).

Contraindications and precautions
- Pamidronate must be given as an infusion as described earlier and not as a bolus injection.
- Assess renal function and electrolytes (e.g. calcium, magnesium) before each dose and ensure adequate hydration (especially hypercalcaemia)
- Use with caution in the following circumstances:
  - cardiac disease (risk of fluid overload)
  - elderly
  - patients who have undergone thyroid surgery (risk of hypocalcaemia if hypoparathyroidism)
  - renal impairment (see 🕮 Dose adjustments, p.416)
  - severe hepatic impairment (see 🕮 Dose adjustments, p.416)
- Assess the need for calcium and vitamin D supplements in patients receiving pamidronate other than for hypercalcaemia.
- Consider dental examination before initiating therapy due to the possibility of inducing osteonecrosis of the jaw (see 🕮 Adverse effects).

☺ Adverse effects

- Osteonecrosis of the jaw is a potential complication of bisphosphonate therapy. It has been reported in cancer patients, many who had a pre-existing local infection or recent extraction. Cancer patients are more likely to be at risk of osteonecrosis as a result of their disease, cancer therapies, and blood dyscrasias. Dental examination is recommended for patients undergoing repeated infusions of pamidronate (and other bisphosphonates) and dental surgery should be avoided during this treatment period as healing may be delayed.
- Severe and occasionally incapacitating bone, joint, and/or muscle pain has been reported with bisphosphonate use. Time to onset

varies from 1 day to several months after initiation of treatment, but symptoms should improve upon discontinuation. Some patients will develop the same symptoms upon subsequent treatment with pamidronate or another bisphosphonate.
• Atypical femoral fractures have been reported with bisphosphonate therapy. Although a rare occurrence, during bisphosphonate treatment patients should be advised to report any new thigh, hip or groin pain.

Very common
• Fever (within 48 hours of treatment; sometimes with rigor, fatigue, and flushes)
• Hypocalcaemia
• Hypophosphataemia.

Common
• Abdominal pain
• Anaemia
• Arthralgia
• Conjunctivitis
• Constipation
• Diarrhoea
• Drowsiness
• Headache
• Hypertension
• Hypokalaemia
• Hypomagnesaemia
• Insomnia
• Infusion site reactions
• Nausea
• Rash
• Transient bone pain
• Thrombocytopenia
• Vomiting.

Uncommon
• Acute renal failure
• Agitation
• Dizziness
• Dyspepsia
• Hypotension
• Muscle cramps
• Osteonecrosis of the jaw
• Pruritis
• Seizures
• Uveitis.

Unknown
• Atrial fibrillation.

Drug interactions

Pharmacokinetic
• None known.

Pharmacodynamic
• *Aminoglycosides*—may have additive hypocalcaemic effect.
• *Diuretics*—increased risk of renal impairment.
• *NSAIDs*—increased risk of renal impairment.
• *Thalidomide*—increased risk of renal impairment (in treatment of multiple myeloma).

Dose

Tumour-induced hypercalcaemia
• Ensure patients are well hydrated prior to and following administration of pamidronate.

- The dose of pamidronate depends on the patient's initial serum calcium levels. The dose is usually infused as a single dose (see Table 3.17).
- Must be given as an IV infusion at a rate not exceeding 1mg/min.

Table 3.17 Pamidoronate dosage

Initial serum calcium (mmol/L)	Recommended dose (mg)
Up to 3.0	15–30
3.0–3.5	30–60
3.5–4.0	60–90
>4.0	90

Osteolytic lesions and bone pain
- 90mg by IV infusion at a rate not exceeding 1mg/min every 4 weeks

Dose adjustments
Elderly
- Usual adult doses can be used.

Hepatic/renal impairment
- Dose adjustment is unnecessary in patients with mild to moderate hepatic impairment. The manufacturer advises caution in patients with severe hepatic impairment due to lack of data.
- For the treatment of osteolytic lesions, if renal function deteriorates, treatment should be withheld until renal function returns to within 10% of the baseline value.
- For the treatment of hypercalcaemia, dose adjustment is unnecessary in patients with mild–moderate renal impairment (CrCl >30mL/min). In severe renal impairment the infusion rate should not exceed 90mg/4 hours

Additional information
- To reconstitute Aredia Dry Powder® the powder in the vials should be first dissolved in sterile water for injection i.e. 15mg in 5mL, 30mg and 90mg in 10mL.
- The concentrate solution should be diluted to a maximum concentration of 60mg/250mL with infusion fluid (NaCl 0.9% or glucose 5%). One manufacturer (Medac) permits a maximum concentration of 90mg/250mL.
- Corrected serum calcium = actual serum calcium+[(40—serum albumin g/L) × 0.02].
- In the treatment of hypercalcaemia, serum calcium levels should not be measured until 5–7 days post dose. Calcium levels start to fall after 48 hours, with a median time to normalization of 3–7 days and normalization in 70% of patients within 7 days. Seek specialist advice should the corrected serum Ca^{2+} concentration not return to normal after 7–10 days; a second dose of pamidronate can be given 7–10 days after the initial dose in such patients.

The onset of treatment effect for skeletal related events is 2–3 months. Relief from bone pain may occur within 14 days, although it may be up to 3 months before maximum effect is seen.

Pharmacology

Pamidronate disodium is an inhibitor of osteoclastic bone resorption. It has been shown to exert its activity by binding strongly to hydroxyapatite crystals, inhibiting their formation and dissolution, and suppressing the accession of osteoclast precursors onto the bone. Additionally, and to a greater extent, as the drug binds to bone mineral, this reduces the resorption of osteoclastic bone. It is almost exclusively excreted unchanged by the kidney.

Pantoprazole

Protium® (POM)
Injection: 40mg.

Pantoloc Control® (P)
Tablet: 20mg (14).

Generic (POM)
Tablet: 20mg (28); 40mg (28)
Injection: 40mg
Note: pantoprazole 20mg tablets can be sold over the counter for the short-term treatment of reflux symptoms (e.g. heartburn) in adults over 18 years; max. daily dose 20mg PO for max. 4 weeks (P)

Indications
- Treatment of gastric and duodenal ulcer.
- Treatment of moderate and severe reflux oesophagitis.
- Treatment of mild reflux disease and associated symptoms.
- Long-term treatment and prevention of relapse in reflux oesophagitis.
- Prophylaxis of NSAID-associated peptic ulcer disease

Contraindications and precautions
- Do not administer with atazanavir or erlotinib.
- Treatment with omeprazole may lead to a slightly increased risk of developing GI infections (e.g. *Clostridium difficile*). Therefore, avoid unnecessary use or high doses.
- The manufacturer recommends monitoring of LFTs in patients on long-term treatment.
- Rebound acid hypersecretion may occur on discontinuation of the patient has received >8 weeks of treatment.
- PPIs are associated with a range of electrolyte disturbances, such as hyponatraemia and hypomagnesaemia (and associated hypocalcaemia and hypokalaemia). Suspect the PPI should unexplainable symptoms present (e.g. confusion, delirium, generalized weakness, nausea). The effect on sodium metabolism is unclear, possibly involving ADH. PPIs may reduce active magnesium absorption in the small intestine by affecting function of a transient receptor protein channel.

☹ Adverse effects
Uncommon

- Altered LFTs
- Constipation
- Diarrhoea
- Dizziness
- Dry mouth
- Fatigue

- Flatulence
- Headache
- Nausea/vomiting
- Pruritus
- Sleep disorders
- Upper abdominal pain.

Rare

- Arthralgia
- Depression
- Gynaecomastia
- Hypersensitivity

- Myalgia
- Peripheral oedema
- Visual disturbances.

Unknown

Confusion
Hallucinations
Hepatitis

- Hyponatraemia
- Interstitial nephritis
- Stevens–Johnson syndrome.

Drug interactions

Pharmacokinetic

- Pantoprazole is metabolized by CYP2C19; a minor pathway involves CYP3A4. It is a moderate inhibitor of CYP2C8/9. Co-administration with drugs that are metabolized by, or affect the activity (induction or inhibition—see 📖 inside back cover) of these pathways may lead to clinically relevant drug interactions and the prescriber should be aware that dosage adjustments may be necessary, particularly of drugs with a narrow therapeutic index.
- Drugs with pH dependent absorption can be affected:
  - *Atazanavir*—avoid combination due to substantially reduced absorption.
  - *Digoxin*—increased plasma concentrations possible.
  - *Erlotinib*—avoid combination as bioavailability of erlotinib can be significantly reduced.
  - *Ferrous sulphate*—reduced absorption likely to result in treatment failure; some recommend co-administration of ascorbic acid (e.g. 100mg) at the same as ferrous sulphate to improve absorption.
  - *Ketoconazole/Itraconazole*—risk of sub-therapeutic plasma concentrations.
  - *Metronidazole suspension*—ranitidine may reduce/prevent the absorption of metronidazole.
- *Azole antifungals*—PPIs may decrease the absorption of itraconazole and ketoconazole

Pharmacodynamic

- No clinically significant interactions noted.

💊 Dose

Treatment of duodenal ulcer and gastric ulcer

- 40mg PO OM for 2–4 weeks (duodenal) or 4–8 weeks (gastric).
- Alternatively, 40mg IV OD until oral treatment is possible.

Treatment of moderate and severe reflux oesophagitis

- 40mg PO OM for 4–8 weeks.
- Alternatively, 40mg IV OD until oral treatment is possible.

Treatment of mild reflux disease and associated symptoms

- 20mg PO OM for 2–8 weeks. After this time, patients can be controlled with 20mg PO OD PRN, switching to regular treatment if necessary.

Long-term treatment and prevention of relapse in reflux oesophagitis

- 20–40mg PO OM

Prophylaxis of NSAID-associated peptic ulcer disease

- 20mg PO OM.

⚖ Dose adjustments

Elderly
- No dose adjustments are necessary.

Hepatic/renal impairment
- In patients with severe liver impairment, 20mg OM should not be exceeded and regular LFTs should be performed.
- No dose adjustments are necessary in renal impairment.

Additional information
- Tablets should not be chewed or crushed, but should be swallowed whole.

⟐ Pharmacology
Pantoprazole is a gastric PPI, reducing the release of H^+ from parietal cells by inhibiting H^+/K^+-ATPase. It is rapidly inactivated by gastric acid; hence oral formulations are enteric coated. It is extensively metabolized, mainly by CYP2C19 although an alternative pathway involves CYP3A4. Note that CYP2C19 poor metabolizers (or patients taking CYP2C19 inhibitors) can have significantly higher plasma concentrations, leading to unexpected results. Metabolites are virtually inactive and are eliminated mainly by both renal excretion, with a small percentage eliminated in faeces.

Paracetamol

Perfalgan® (POM)
Intravenous infusion: 500mg/50mL; 1g/100mL.

Generic (POM)*
Tablet: 500mg (16; 32; 100).
Caplet: 500mg (16; 32; 100).
Soluble tablet: 500mg (60).
Oral suspension: 250mg/5mL (100mL); 500mg/5mL (300mL).
Note: sugar-free suspensions are available.
Suppository: 60mg, 125mg, 250mg, 500mg.

Combination products

See codeine (📖 Codeine, p.128), dihydrocodeine (📖 Dihydrocodeine, p.165) and tramadol (📖 Tramadol, p.528).

The legal status of paracetamol depends upon pack size: 16 (*GSL*), 32 (*P*), >100 (*POM*).

Indications

Mild to moderate pain
Pyrexia.

Contraindications and precautions

Paracetamol is contraindicated for use in severe hepatic impairment.
It should be used with caution in patients with:
- alcohol dependence
- concurrent use of enzyme-inducing drugs (see 📖 Drug interactions)
- hepatic impairment
- renal impairment
- state of malnutrition (low reserves of hepatic glutathione).

⚠ Adverse effects

Rare
Abnormal LFTs
Hypotension (on infusion).

Very rare
Blood dyscrasias.

Drug interactions

Pharmacokinetic
Carbamazepine—increased risk of paracetamol toxicity (especially in overdose).
Colestyramine—absorption of paracetamol is reduced (avoid co-administration by 2 hours).
Imatinib—glucuronidation inhibited by imatinib; potential paracetamol toxicity with prolonged use.

- *Metoclopramide*—increased rate of absorption of paracetamol.
- *Warfarin*—monitor with long-term paracetamol therapy as INR may be raised.

Pharmacodynamic
- None known.

˷ Dose

For pain and fever
- 0.5–1g PO or PR up to every 4–6 hours. Max. dose 4g in 24 hours.
- Alternatively, if necessary, by IV infusion:
  - for adult >50kg, give 1g every 4–6 hours; max. dose 4g in 24 hours
  - for adult <50kg, give 15mg/kg every 4–6 hours, max. 60mg/kg in 24 hours.

˷ Dose adjustments

Elderly
- No dose adjustments are necessary.

Hepatic/renal impairment
- Dose reductions may be necessary in liver impairment; avoid if severe impairment.
- For patients with severe renal impairment (CrCl <30mL/min), the dose interval of *Perfalgan*® should be increased to 6 hours.

Additional information
- Liver damage can occur with small increases of the dose above the 4g recommendation and so it is especially important to ensure that patients are not taking proprietary preparations as well as prescribed paracetamol or combinations products.

˸ Pharmacology
The precise analgesic action of paracetamol is unknown but it has generally been accepted that paracetamol exerts its analgesic effect by inhibition of prostaglandin synthesis within the CNS. Recent studies have suggested that the metabolites, N-acetyl-p-benzoquinoneimine and p-benzoquinone produce the antinociceptive effect of paracetamol by activating spinal TRPA1 receptors. When used regularly it is an effective and useful analgesic and it can be a useful adjunct at any step on the WHO analgesic ladder.

Paracetamol is quickly absorbed after oral administration with a bioavailability of around 60%. After rectal administration, its bioavailability is considerably lower and absorption is often delayed and erratic. It is largely metabolized by conjugation reactions in the liver, but a minor route of paracetamol metabolism involves CYP1A2 and CYP2E1 which forms a reactive intermediate, N-acetyl-p-benzoquinimine (NAPQI). Usually, NAPQI is inactivated by conjugation with glutathione in the liver. However, following ingestion of a large amount of paracetamol the hepatic stores of glutathione become depleted so more NAPQI is available to cause hepatic damage and cellular death. Toxicity may occur following ingestion of approximately twice the normal daily dose (i.e. 14–1 paracetamol 500mg tablets in an adult). Drugs that induce CYP1A2 and CYP2E1 may increase the risk of paracetamol toxicity.

aroxetine

eroxat® *(POM)*
ablet (scored): 10mg (28); 20mg (30); 30mg (30).
ral suspension (sugar-free): 10mg/5mL (150mL).

eneric (POM)
ablet: 20mg (30); 30mg (30).

ndications
Anxiety
Depression
Panic
¥Pruritus.[1]

Contraindications and precautions
Do not use with an irreversible MAOI, or within 14 days of stopping one, or at least 24 hours after discontinuation of a reversible MAOI (e.g. moclobemide, linezolid). Note that in exceptional circumstances linezolid may be given with paroxetine, but the patient must be closely monitored for symptoms of serotonin syndrome (see 📖 Box 1.10, p.18).

Depression is associated with an increased risk of suicidal thoughts, self-harm, and suicide which persists until remission. Note that that the risk of suicide may increase during initial treatment.

Hyponatraemia should be considered in all patients who develop drowsiness, confusion, or convulsions while taking an antidepressant. Hyponatraemia has been associated with all types of antidepressant, although it is reportedly more common with SSRIs.

Co-administration with tamoxifen has been shown to reduce the plasma levels of the potent anti-oestrogen endoxifen. The precise clinical significance of this interaction is presently unknown, but the MHRA has recently advised co-administration of CYP2D6 inhibitors should be avoided (see 📖 Drug interactions, p.424).

Use with caution in:
• diabetes (alters glycaemic control)
• elderly (greater risk of hyponatraemia)
• epilepsy (lowers seizure threshold)
• hepatic/renal impairment (see 📖 Dose adjustments, p.425)
• glaucoma (may cause mydriasis).

May precipitate psychomotor restlessness, which usually appears during early treatment.

Avoid abrupt withdrawal as symptoms such as agitation, anxiety, confusion, diarrhoea, dizziness, emotional instability, nausea, and sleep disturbances (including intense dreams) can occur. Although generally mild, they can be severe in some patients. Withdrawal symptoms usually occur within the first few days of discontinuing treatment and they usually resolve within 2 weeks, though they can persist in some patients for up to 3 months or longer. See 📖 Discontinuing and/ or switching antidepressants, p.45 for information about switching or stopping antidepressants.

- Paroxetine may increase the risk of haemorrhage (see 📖 Drug interactions).
- The oral suspension contains parabens, sunset yellow, and sorbitol which may cause allergic reactions in susceptible patients.
- It may modify reactions and patients should be advised not drive (or operate machinery) if affected.
- Subtle deficits in attention, memory, and reasoning may occur with therapeutic dosages of anticholinergic drugs without signs of obvious toxicity. These deficits have often been mistaken for symptoms of early dementia in elderly patients.

☺ Adverse effects

Very common
- Nausea
- Sexual dysfunction.

Common
- Agitation
- Appetite reduced
- Diarrhoea
- Dizziness
- Drowsiness
- Dry mouth (may be more common than with other SSRIs)
- Headache
- Insomnia
- Sweating
- Tremor
- Weakness
- Weight gain
- Yawning.

Uncommon
- Abnormal bleeding (e.g. bruising)
- Confusion
- Extrapyramidal symptoms
- Hallucinations
- Mydriasis.

Rare
- Anxiety (mainly during initial treatment)
- Hyponatraemia
- Seizures.

Very rare
- SIADH.

Drug interactions

Pharmacokinetic
- Paroxetine is a potent CYP2D6 inhibitor and a moderate CYB2B6 inhibitor; it is also a substrate of CYP2D6 and inhibits its own metabolism. Co-administration with drugs that are metabolized by, or affect the activity (induction or inhibition—see 📖 inside back cover) of these pathways may lead to clinically relevant drug interactions and the prescriber should be aware that dosage adjustments may be necessary, particularly of drugs with a narrow therapeutic index.
- *Codeine*—reduced analgesic benefit.
- *Haloperidol*—increased risk of adverse effects from both drugs due to inhibition of CYP2D6. The clinical significance of co-administration with other inhibitors of CYP2D6 (see 📖 inside back cover) is unknown, but plasma concentrations of paroxetine may increase. The prescriber

should be aware of the potential for interactions and that dose adjustments may be necessary.

Risperidone—metabolism inhibited by paroxetine; increased risk of adverse effects.

Tamoxifen—avoid combination, due to possible reduced efficacy of tamoxifen.

Tramadol—reduced analgesic benefit.

TCAs—metabolism may be inhibited by paroxetine.

Drugs that affect gastric pH (e.g. PPIs, H_2-antagonists, antacids) can reduce the absorption of the oral suspension. Dose increases may be necessary if swapping from the tablet formulation.

Pharmacodynamic

• Risk of serotonin syndrome (see 📖 Box 1.10, p.18) with:
  • MAOIs
  • Rasagiline
  • Selegiline
  • Serotonergic drugs—e.g. duloxetine, methadone, mirtazapine, TCAs, tramadol, and trazodone.
• *Anticoagulants*—potential increased risk of bleeding.
• *Carbamazepine*—increased risk of hyponatraemia.
• *Cyproheptadine*—may inhibit the effects of paroxetine.
• *Diuretics*—increased risk of hyponatraemia.
• *NSAIDs*—increased risk of GI bleeding.

💊 Dose

It is recommended that doses are taken with or after food.

Anxiety/depression

• Initial dose 20mg PO OM, increased gradually up to a maximum of 50mg PO OM in 10mg increments according to the patient's response.

Panic

• Initial dose 10mg PO OM, increased to a usual maximum of 40mg PO OM in 10mg increments according to the patient's response. Further dose increases up to 60mg PO OM may be required.

≠ Pruritus

• Initial dose 5mg PO OM, increased to a maximum of 20mg PO OM. Doses of up to 40mg PO OM have been suggested. Any beneficial effect may be short lived.

💊 Dose adjustments

Elderly

• Normal initial doses can be used, but the maximum dose should not exceed 40mg PO daily.

Hepatic/renal impairment

• Increased plasma concentrations of paroxetine occur in patients with hepatic impairment or those with severe renal impairment (CrCl <30mL/min). Wherever possible, doses at the lower end of the range should be used. Patients may be more susceptible to adverse effects.

Additional information

- Remember that up to 10% of the Caucasian population are classified as CYP2D6 poor metabolizers which will have implications for treatment.
- If withdrawal symptoms emerge during discontinuation, increase the dose to prevent symptoms and then start to withdrawal more slowly.
- Withdrawal symptoms may be more likely with paroxetine than other SSRIs.
- Symptoms of anxiety or panic may worsen on initial therapy. This can be minimized by using lower starting doses.

⟐ Pharmacology

Paroxetine is a potent and highly selective inhibitor of neuronal serotonin reuptake, with only very weak effects on noradrenaline and dopamine neuronal reuptake. It has a weak affinity for muscarinic receptors, but little affinity for α_1, α_2, D_2, 5-HT$_1$, 5-HT$_2$, and H$_1$ receptors. Paroxetine is metabolized by primarily by CYP2D6 to virtually inactive metabolites which are excreted by the kidneys; it is a potent inhibitor of CYP2D6 and a moderate inhibitor of CYP2B6.

Reference

1. Patel T, Yosipovitch G. Therapy of pruritus. *Expert Opin Pharmacother* 2011; **11**(10):1673–82.

Phenobarbital

Generic (CD3 POM)
Tablet: 15mg (28); 30mg (28); 60mg (28).
Elixir: 15mg/5mL (some products contain alcohol).
Injection (as phenobarbital sodium): 200mg/mL (10).

- Phenobarbital is a Schedule 3 CD. Refer to 📖 Legal categories of medicines, p.21 for further information.

Indications
- Epilepsy (not absence seizures)
- Status epilepticus,
- *Terminal agitation (in patients who have failed to be controlled by usual interventions).[1]

Contraindications and precautions
- Refer to 📖 Use of drugs in end-of-life care, p.53 for end-of-life care issues.
- Avoid phenobarbital in the following circumstances:
  - acute intermittent porphyria
  - severe respiratory depression
  - severe hepatic/renal impairment.
- Suicidal ideation and behaviour have been reported with anti-epileptics.
- Use with caution in:
  - children
  - elderly
  - hepatic impairment (avoid if severe)
  - hypothyroidism (increased metabolism of levothyroxine)
  - renal impairment (avoid if severe)
  - respiratory depression (avoid if severe).
- Avoid sudden withdrawal (may precipitate seizures).
- Phenobarbital may modify reactions and patients should be advised not drive (or operate machinery) if affected.
- Phenobarbital sodium injection is strongly alkaline and *must* be diluted with 10 times its own volume of WFI before administration via IV injection or CSCI.

😔 Adverse effects
The frequency is not defined, but reported adverse effects include:
- Ataxia
- Cholestasis
- Confusion
- Drowsiness
- Hepatitis
- Hyperkinesia and behavioural disturbances in children

- Lethargy
- Local necrosis following SC injection (avoid)
- Megaloblastic anaemia (due to folate deficiency)
- Memory and cognitive impairment (especially in the elderly)
- Nystagmus
- Osteomalacia (with long-term treatment)
- Paradoxical excitement
- Respiratory depression
- Restlessness.

Drug interactions

Pharmacokinetic

- Phenobarbital is metabolized by CYP2C19. It is also a strong inducer of CYP1A2, CYP2B6, CYP2C8/9, CYP2C19, CYP3A4, and UGT enzymes. Co-administration with drugs that are metabolized by, or affect the activity (induction or inhibition—see 🕮 inside back cover) of these pathways may lead to clinically relevant drug interactions and the prescriber should be aware that dosage adjustments may be necessary, particularly of drugs with a narrow therapeutic index.
- Affects many drugs through enzyme induction. Refer to 🕮 inside back cover for potential list of affected drugs, although the clinical significance is unknown.
- *Alfentanil*—risk of reduced analgesic benefit.
- *Celecoxib*—effect of celecoxib may be reduced.
- *Clonazepam*—effect of clonazepam may be reduced.
- *Codeine*—possible altered analgesic effect (due to CYP3A4/UGT induction).
- *Corticosteroids*—effect of corticosteroids reduced; higher doses necessary (possibly double or more).
- *Haloperidol*—effect of haloperidol reduced.
- *Fentanyl*—risk of reduced analgesic benefit.
- *Levothyroxine*—increased metabolism may precipitate hypothyroidism.
- *Mirtazapine*—effect of mirtazapine may be reduced.
- *Modafinil*—effect of modafinil may be reduced; may enhance effect of phenobarbital.
- *Oxycodone*—possible risk of reduced analgesic benefit.
- *Paracetamol*—may increase the risk of hepatoxicity of paracetamol.
- *Tramadol*—reduced analgesic benefit.

Pharmacodynamic

- *Antipsychotics*—seizure threshold lowered.
- *Antidepressants*—seizure threshold lowered.
- *CNS depressants*—risk of excessive sedation.
- *MAOIs*—avoid concurrent use.
- *Tramadol*—seizure threshold lowered.

💊 Dose

Epilepsy

- 60–180mg PO ON.
- ¥Alternatively, 200–400mg (11–22mL after dilution with 10 times own volume) via CSCI over 24 hours. If necessary, give stat dose of 100mg

by IV injection (ensure dilution with 10 times own volume, i.e. dilute 0.5mL with 5mL WFI).

Status epilepticus

● 10mg/kg by IV injection at a rate of not more than 100mg/min. Ensure dilution with 10 times own volume with WFI.

⚕ *Terminal agitation*

● Initial dose 100–200mg IM (undiluted) or IV (diluted with 10 times own volume) injection. Continue treatment with 200–600mg (11–33mL after dilution with 10 times own volume) via CSCI over 24 hours. Higher doses may be used but the volume of infusion will necessitate 12-hourly infusions.

⚖ Dose adjustments

Elderly

● No specific dose adjustments are suggested. Use the lowest dose possible and monitor the patient closely since the elderly are more susceptible to adverse effects.

Hepatic/renal impairment

● Phenobarbital is contraindicated for use in severe hepatic or renal impairment. In mild to moderate impairment, no guidance is available; use the lowest effective dose and monitor for adverse effects.

Additional information

● Phenobarbital sodium injection is incompatible with most drugs via CSCI. Unless compatibility information is available, it should be administered via a separate CSCI.
● The CSCI may be diluted with either WFI or NaCl 0.9%. Dilution with NaCl 0.9% may improve site tolerance.
● Therapeutic plasma concentration range: 15–40mg/L, or 65–170micromol/L.

⊹ Pharmacology

Phenobarbital is sedative anti-epileptic which acts on GABA$_A$ receptors, increasing synaptic inhibition by modulation of chloride currents through receptor channels. It may also affect calcium channels. It is extensively hepatically metabolized, principally by CYP2C19 and it is a potent inducer of CYP1A2, CYP2B6, CYP2C9, CYP2C19, CYP3A4, and UGT enzymes. Many drugs are affected (see 📖 Drug interactions, p.428).

Reference

1. Stirling LC, Kurowska A, Tookman A. The use of phenobarbitone in the management of agitation and seizures at the end of life. *J Pain Symptom Manage* 1999; **17**(5):363–8.

Phenytoin

Epanutin® (POM)
Capsule: 25mg (28); 50mg (28); 100mg (84); 300mg (28).
Note: contains phenytoin sodium (see 📖 Additional information, p.432).
Chewable tablet (Infatab®, scored): 50mg (112).
Note: contains phenytoin.
Suspension: 30mg/5mL (500mL).
Note: contains phenytoin.
Injection: 250mg/5mL.

Generic (POM)
Tablet: 100mg (28).
Note: contains phenytoin sodium (see 📖 Additional information, p.432).
Injection: 250mg/5mL.

Indications
- Generalized tonic–clonic and partial seizures.
- Trigeminal neuralgia (although carbamazepine preferred).
- Status epilepticus (*injection*).

Contraindications and precautions
- Use with caution in:
  - elderly (see 📖 Dose adjustments, p.432)
  - Han Chinese and Thai population (patient should be screened for HLA-B*1502 before initiating treatment due to association with risk of developing Stevens–Johnson syndrome)
  - liver impairment (see 📖 Dose adjustments, p.432)
  - porphyria.
- Patients should be monitored for signs of suicidal ideation since anti-epileptic drugs have been associated with this behaviour.
- Avoid abrupt withdrawal, unless clearly indicated, as seizures may be precipitated. Refer to 📖 Use of drugs in end-of-life care, p.53 for end-of-life care issues.
- Phenytoin can cause rare, serious skin adverse events. Ensure patients and/or their carers can recognize signs of skin rash and blisters, fever, or other signs of hypersensitivity such as itching and advise they seek immediate medical attention if symptoms develop.
- It may modify reactions and patients should be advised not drive (or operate machinery) if affected.
- Phenytoin can affect bone mineral metabolism. Consider vitamin D supplementation in patients on long-term treatment and at risk of developing complications, e.g. immobilized patients, low dietary intake of calcium.

☺ Adverse effects
The frequency is not defined, but reported adverse effects include:

- Ataxia
- Blood dyscrasias (including megaloblastic anaemia, thrombocytopenia and aplastic anamia)
- Confusion
- Drowsiness
- Dysgeusia
- Gingival hyperplasia
- Headaches

- Hepatitis (discontinue immediately)
- Hirsutism
- Hypertrichosis
- Insomnia
- Myoclonus/tremor
- Nausea
- Nystagmus
- Osteomalacia

- Paraesthesia
- Rash (morbilliform most common)
- Slurred speech
- Stevens–Johnson syndrome
- Thrombocytopenia
- Toxic epidermal necrolysis
- Vertigo
- Vomiting.

Drug interactions

Pharmacokinetic

- Phenytoin is a substrate primarily of CYP2C9 and CY2C19. It is also a strong inducer of CYP1A2, CYP2B6, CYP2C9, CYP2C19, CYP3A4, and UGT enzymes. Co-administration with drugs that are metabolized by, or affect the activity (induction or inhibition—see 📖 inside back cover) of these pathways may lead to clinically relevant drug interactions and the prescriber should be aware that dosage adjustments may be necessary, particularly of drugs with a narrow therapeutic index. Phenytoin may lower the plasma concentration, diminish or even abolish the activity of many drugs through enzyme induction. Several interactions are listed here, but refer to 📖 inside back cover for a list of drugs that may potentially be affected.
- *Alfentanil*—risk of reduced analgesic benefit.
- *Celecoxib*—effect of celecoxib may be reduced.
- *Clonazepam*—effect of clonazepam may be reduced.
- *Codeine*—possible altered analgesic effect (due to CYP3A4/UGT induction).
- *Dexamethasone*—effect of dexamethasone likely to be reduced —a dose doubling may be necessary; phenytoin plasma concentrations may also be affected (increased or decreased).
- *Fentanyl*—risk of reduced analgesic benefit.
- *Fluconazole*—increases the plasma concentrations of phenytoin; consider alternative treatment or closely monitor phenytoin plasma concentration.
- *Fluoxetine*—risk of phenytoin toxicity.
- *Haloperidol*—effect of haloperidol reduced.
- *Levothyroxine*—increased metabolism may precipitate hypothyroidism.
- *Metoclopramide*—theoretical risk of neurotoxicity due to possible increased rate of absorption of carbamazepine.
- *Miconazole*—increases the plasma concentrations of phenytoin; consider alternative treatment or closely monitor phenytoin plasma concentration.
- *Mirtazapine*—effect of mirtazapine may be reduced.
- *Modafinil*—effect of modafinil may be reduced.
- *Omeprazole*—risk of phenytoin toxicity with large doses of omeprazole (>40mg/day).
- *Oxycodone*—possible risk of reduced analgesic benefit.
- *Paracetamol*—may increase the risk of hepatotoxicity of paracetamol.
- *Tramadol*—reduced analgesic effect.
- *Trazodone*—risk of phenytoin toxicity (mechanism unknown).

Pharmacodynamic
- *Antipsychotics*—seizure threshold lowered.
- *Antidepressants*—seizure threshold lowered.
- *CNS depressants*—risk of excessive sedation.
- *MAOIs*—avoid concurrent use.
- *Tramadol*—seizure threshold lowered.

⁙ Dose
- Initial dose 150–300mg (3–4mg/kg) PO daily as a single dose or in 2 divided doses. The dose can be increased gradually, with plasma concentrations being closely monitored. Usual maximum dose 500mg PO daily, although higher doses may be necessary (according to plasma concentrations).

⁙ Dose adjustments
Elderly
- Dose can be titrated to effect as per usual adult doses.

Hepatic/renal impairment
- Lower doses may be necessary in patients with hepatic impairment since phenytoin is highly protein bound and undergoes extensive hepatic metabolism. Adjust according to plasma concentration.
- Dose adjustments are unlikely to be required in patients with renal impairment. Although uraemia may affect protein binding, for any given dose, the free fraction of phenytoin is unlikely to change such that patients may respond at lower than expected plasma concentrations.

Additional information
- Note that 100mg phenytoin sodium is equivalent to 92mg phenytoin, although these values are not necessarily biologically equivalent. In situations where it is necessary to change from one formulation to another, plasma concentration monitoring is advised.
- Therapeutic plasma concentration range: 10–20mg/L (40–80 micromoles/L). Plasma samples are taken immediately prior to next dose (at steady state).

⊸ Pharmacology
Phenytoin is an anti-epileptic drug that is believed to stabilize the seizure threshold. Its mechanism of action is unknown, but it is believed to interfere with sodium and calcium transport across cell membranes and to enhance GABA-mediated inhibition. After oral administration, it is well absorbed and is highly protein bound. It is metabolized by CYP2C9 and CY2C19, but this metabolism is saturable at concentrations that can occur clinically, hence the need for monitoring of plasma concentrations. It is a potent inducer of CYP1A2, CYP2B6, CYP2C9, CYP2C19, CYP3A4, and UGT enzymes. Many drugs are affected (see 📖 Drug interactions, p.431).

Pramipexole

Standard release

Mirapexin® (POM)

Tablet: 88 micrograms (30); 180 micrograms (*scored*—30; 100); 350 micrograms (*scored*—30; 100); 700 micrograms (*scored*—30; 100)

Generic (POM)

Tablet: 88 micrograms (30); 180 micrograms (30; 100); 350 micrograms (30; 100); 700 micrograms (30; 100).

Prolonged release

Mirapexin® (POM)

Tablet: 0.26mg (30); 0.52mg (30); 1.05mg (30); 2.1mg (30); 3.15mg (30).

Indications

- Parkinson's disease
- Restless legs syndrome (up to 540 micrograms daily) (only standard release formulations).

Contraindications and precautions

- Use with caution in patients with:
  - psychotic disorders (antagonism between drugs)
  - renal impairment
  - severe cardiovascular disease (risk of hypotension—monitor BP during initiation)
- Dopamine receptor agonists can cause excessive daytime sleepiness and sudden onset of sleep.
- Behavioural symptoms of impulse control disorders and compulsions such as binge eating and compulsive shopping can occur. Dose reduction/tapered discontinuation should be considered.
- Due to the risk of visual disturbances, ophthalmological monitoring is recommended at regular intervals.
- Pramipexole must not be suddenly discontinued due to the risk of neuroleptic malignant syndrome. This only applies to Parkinson's disease as the dose for RLS does not exceed 0.54mg daily (although rebound symptoms can develop). The recommended withdrawal schedule is as follows.
- Standard release:
  - taper dose at a rate of 0.54mg daily until the dose has been reduced to 0.54mg
  - reduce the dose thereafter by 0.264mg per day.
- Modified release:
  - taper dose at a rate of 0.52mg daily until the daily dose has been reduced to 0.52mg
  - reduce the dose thereafter by 0.26mg per day.
- Pramipexole may modify reactions and patients should be advised not drive (or operate machinery) if affected.

☺ Adverse effects

Adverse effects are generally dose-related. As such, they are more likely to be experienced by patients receiving pramipexole for Parkinson's disease than for restless legs syndrome.

Very common
- Dizziness
- Drowsiness
- Dyskinesia
- Hypotension
- Nausea.

Common
- Abnormal dreams
- Amnesia
- Confusion
- Constipation
- Fatigue
- Hallucinations
- Headache
- Insomnia
- Peripheral oedema
- Restlessness
- Vomiting
- Visual disturbance.

Uncommon
- Compulsive shopping
- Delusion
- Hypersexuality
- Paranoia
- Pathological gambling.

Drug interactions

Pharmacokinetic
- Pramipexole is mainly eliminated unchanged by the kidneys.
- Drugs that are secreted by the cationic transport system (e.g. *diltiazem, quinine, ranitidine, verapamil*) have the potential to interact with pramipexole, increasing plasma concentrations. The clinical significance is unknown and until further information is available, the following is suggested:
  - if pramipexole is co-administered with these drugs, a slow and cautious titration is advisable.
  - if these drugs are prescribed for a patient already using pramipexole, it is advisable to review the pramipexole dose (lower doses may be required).
- Drugs which affect renal function have the potential to interact with pramipexole. If such drugs are co-administered, regular monitoring of renal function is advisable. Such drugs include:
  - ACEIs
  - NSAIDs

Pharmacodynamic
- *Alcohol*—additive sedative effect.
- *CNS depressants*—additive sedative effect.
- *Dopamine antagonists (e.g. antipsychotics, metoclopramide)*—may decrease the efficiency of pramipexole due to dopamine antagonism.

⚚ Dose

Parkinson's disease
Standard release
- Initial dose 88 micrograms PO TDS. The dose can be doubled every 5–7 days if necessary and tolerated to 350 micrograms PO TDS.

- The dose can be further increased if necessary by 180 micrograms PO TDS at weekly intervals to a maximum of 3.3mg daily in 3 divided doses (i.e. 3 × 350 micrograms TDS).

Modified release
- Initial dose 0.26mg PO OD. The dose can be doubled every 5–7 days if necessary and tolerated to 1.05mg PO OD. If a further dose increase is necessary the daily dose should be increased by 0.52mg at weekly intervals up to a maximum dose of 3.15mg PO OD.

Restless legs syndrome
- Initial dose 88 micrograms PO 2–3 hours before bedtime.
- The dose can be doubled every 4–7 days if necessary to 350 micrograms PO daily
- The dose can be further increased after 4–7 days to a maximum of 540 micrograms PO daily

Dose adjustments
Elderly
- No specific guidance available. Dose requirements should be individually titrated.

Hepatic/renal impairment
- Dose adjustment in patients with hepatic impairment is not required.
- The elimination of pramipexole is dependent on renal function. The manufacturer gives advice on dosing that is dependent on condition being treated:
- Parkinson's disease:
  • Patients with a CrCl >50mL/min require no reduction in dose.
- Standard release:
  • for a CrCl 20–50mL/min, initial dose should be 88mmicrograms PO BD. A maximum daily dose of 1.57mg PO OD should not be exceeded
  • if CrCl <20mL/min, the recommended dose is 88mmicrograms PO OD. A maximum daily dose of 1.1mg PO OD should not be exceeded
  • if renal function deteriorates during treatment, reduce the dose by the same percentage as the decline in creatinine clearance.
- Prolonged release:
  • for a CrCl 30–50mL/min, initial dose 0.26mg PO ALT DIE, increasing to 0.26mg PO OD after 7 days. If necessary, the dose may be further increased by 0.26mg at weekly intervals up to a maximum dose of 1.57mg PO OD
  • for a CrCl <30mL/min, treatment with prolonged release tablets is not recommended and the use of the standard release formulation should be considered.
- For restless legs syndrome:
  • patients with a CrCl >20mL/min require no reduction in dose
  • for patients with a CrCl <20mL/min, a dose reduction will be necessary, although the initial dose cannot practically be reduced.

Additional information

- Pramipexole is given orally as the dihydrochloride monohydrate (DHCM) salt but doses are described in terms of the base. Dose equivalents are as follows:
  - pramipexole base 88 micrograms = pramipexole DHCM 125 micrograms
  - pramipexole base 180 micrograms = pramipexole DHCM 350 micrograms
  - pramipexole base 350 micrograms = pramipexole DHCM 500 micrograms
  - pramipexole base 700 micrograms = pramipexole DHCM 1mg.
- Tablets can be crushed and mixed with water immediately prior to administration if necessary

⊕ Pharmacology

Pramipexole is a dopamine agonist that binds with high selectivity and specificity to dopamine receptors of which it has a preferential affinity for D_3 receptors. The mechanism of action of pramipexole as treatment for Parkinson's disease or restless legs syndrome is unknown, although in the former case it is believed to be related to its ability to stimulate dopamine receptors in the striatum. Pramipexole completely absorbed after oral administration. It is metabolized to a small extent, with the majority of the dose being renally excreted.

Prednisolone

Generic (POM)
Tablet: 1mg (28); 5mg (28); 25mg (56).
Tablet (enteric coated): 2.5mg (28; 30); 5mg (30).
Soluble tablet: 5mg (30).

Indications

Suppression of inflammatory and allergic disorders.
Also inflammatory bowel disease, asthma, immunosuppression,
rheumatic disease, adjunct to chemotherapy.

Contraindications and precautions

The use of dexamethasone is contraindicated in systemic infection
unless specific anti-infective therapy is employed.
Patients without a definite history of chickenpox should be advised to
avoid close personal contact with chickenpox or herpes zoster.
Caution is advised when considering the use of systemic
corticosteroids in patients with the following conditions:
- concurrent use of NSAIDs (see 📖 Drug interactions, p.439)
- CHF
- diabetes mellitus (risk of hyperglycaemia—close monitoring of
  blood glucose recommended)
- epilepsy (see 📖 Drug interactions, p.439)
- glaucoma
- hypertension
- hypokalaemia (correct before starting dexamethasone)
- liver or renal impairment (see 📖 Dose adjustments, p.440)
- osteoporosis (see BNF for bisphosphonate guidance)
- peptic ulceration
- psychotic illness (symptoms can emerge within a few days or weeks
  of starting the treatment).

Prednisolone withdrawal

In patients who have received more than physiological doses of systemic
corticosteroids (i.e. >7.5mg prednisolone) for >3 weeks, withdrawal
should be gradual in order to avoid acute adrenal insufficiency. Abrupt
withdrawal of doses of up to 40mg daily of prednisolone for 3 weeks
is unlikely to lead to clinically relevant HPA-axis suppression in the
majority of patients. In the following cases, withdrawal may need to be
more gradual:
- Patients who have had repeated courses of systemic corticosteroids,
  particularly if taken for >3 weeks.
- Patients receiving doses of systemic corticosteroid >40mg daily of
  prednisolone.
- Patients repeatedly taking doses in the evening.

There is no evidence as to the best way to withdraw corticosteroids
and it is often performed with close monitoring of the patient's condition. The dose may initially be reduced rapidly (e.g. by halving the dose

daily) to physiological doses (approximately 7.5mg prednisolone) and then more slowly (e.g. 1mg per week for 1–2 weeks).

A 'withdrawal syndrome' may also occur including fever, myalgia, arthralgia, rhinitis, conjunctivitis, painful itchy skin nodules, and loss of weight.

In dying patients, once the decision is made to withdraw corticosteroids, they can be discontinued abruptly. Patients with brain tumours may require additional analgesia as raised intracranial pressure can develop and may manifest as worsening headache, or terminal restlessness.

☹ Adverse effects

The frequency is not defined. Adverse effects are generally predictable and related to dose, timing of administration and the duration of treatment. They include:

- Endocrine:
  - hirsutism
  - hyperglycaemia
  - hyperlipidaemia
  - weight gain.
- Fluid and electrolyte disturbances:
  - CHF
  - hypertension
  - hypokalaemia
  - sodium and water retention.
- Gastrointestinal:
  - acute pancreatitis
  - dyspepsia peptic ulceration with perforation
  - haemorrhage.
- Musculoskeletal:
  - aseptic necrosis of femoral head
  - avascular necrosis
  - loss of muscle mass
  - osteoporosis
  - proximal myopathy
  - tendon rupture.
- Neurological:
  - aggravation of epilepsy
  - anxiety
  - confusion
  - depression
  - insomnia
  - mood elevation
  - psychotic reactions.
- Other:
  - glaucoma
  - impaired wound healing
  - increased susceptibility and severity of infections (signs can be masked)
  - sweating.

Corticosteroid-induced osteoporosis

- Patients aged over 65 years and with prior or current exposure to oral corticosteroids are at an increased risk of osteoporosis and bone fracture. Treatment with corticosteroids for periods as short as 3 months may result in increased risk. 3 or more courses of corticosteroids taken in the previous 12 months are considered to be equivalent to at least 3 months of continuous treatment.
- Prophylactic treatment (e.g. bisphosphonate, calcium and vitamin D supplements, hormone replacement therapy) should be considered for all patients who may take an oral corticosteroid for 3 months or longer.

Drug interactions

Pharmacokinetic

- Prednisolone is a substrate of CYP3A4. Co-administration with drugs that are metabolized by, or affect the activity (induction or inhibition— see 📖 inside back cover) of this pathway may lead to clinically relevant drug interactions and the prescriber should be aware that dosage adjustments may be necessary, particularly of drugs with a narrow therapeutic index.
- Note that low activity of CYP3A4 (e.g. through inhibition) can contribute to the development of osteonecrosis of the femoral head.
- *Carbamazepine*—effect of prednisolone likely to be reduced; consider doubling the prednisolone dose and monitor the response.
- *Colestyramine*—may decrease the absorption of prednisolone.
- *Erythromycin*—may increase the effects of prednisolone through inhibition of CYP3A4.
- *Phenytoin*—effect of prednisolone likely to be reduced; consider doubling the prednisolone dose and monitor the response.
- Avoid excessive amounts of grapefruit juice as it may increase the bioavailability of prednisolone through inhibition of intestinal CYP3A4.

Pharmacodynamic

- *Anticoagulants*—increased risk of bleeding.
- *Antihypertensives*—effect antagonized by prednisolone.
- *Ciclosporin*—additive immunosuppressive effect; convulsions reported with combination.
- *Diuretics*—effect antagonized by prednisolone; increased risk of hypokalaemia and hyperglycaemia.
- *Hypoglycaemic drugs*—effect antagonized by prednisolone.
- *NSAIDs*—increased risk of GI toxicity.
- *SSRIs*—increased risk of bleeding.

💊 Dose

- Initial dose up to 10–20mg PO OD (severe disease up to 60mg PO daily) preferably in the morning.
- With acute conditions, the dose can usually be reduced after a few days but also may need to be continued for several weeks or months, tapering to the lowest effective dose.

- Maintenance dose usually between 2.5 and 15mg PO OD.
- Specifically for pulmonary fibrosis, an initial dose of 0.5mg/kg/day, tapering over 3 months to 10–20mg/day maintenance dose.

⚖ Dose adjustments

Elderly

- No specific dose adjustments are necessary. Use the lowest dose for the shortest duration possible since the elderly are more susceptible to adverse effects.

Liver/renal impairment

- No specific guidance available. The lowest effective dose should be used for the shortest duration possible.

Additional information

- Prednisolone is less commonly used in palliative care than dexamethasone as it has a slightly higher mineralocorticoid activity.
- Consider oral hygiene with prednisolone use. The patient may develop oral thrush and may need a course of nystatin.
- Oral anti-inflammatory corticosteroid equivalences are:
  - dexamethasone 750 micrograms = hydrocortisone 20mg = prednisolone 5mg.

⟐ Pharmacology

Prednisolone is a synthetic corticosteroid used as a replacement or adjunctive therapy in a wide range of inflammatory or allergic conditions. It is rapidly and almost completely absorbed after oral administration. Prednisolone is metabolized primarily in the liver by CYP3A4 to inactive metabolites which, together with small amounts of unchanged drug, are excreted renally.

Pregabalin

Lyrica® (POM)
Capsule: 25mg (56; 84), 50mg (84), 75mg (56), 100mg (84), 150mg (56),
Oral solution: 20mg/mL (473mL) 200mg (84), 225mg (56), 300mg (56).

Indications
- Central and peripheral neuropathic pain
- Generalized anxiety disorder
- Adjunctive therapy for partial seizures
- ¥Malignant bone pain[1]
- ¥Restless legs syndrome[2]
- ¥Sleep improvement[3]
- ¥Sweats[4]
- ¥Uraemic pruritus.[5]

Contraindications and precautions
- Avoid sudden withdrawal. Discontinue gradually over at least 1 week in order to avoid adverse effects such as nausea, vomiting, flu syndrome, anxiety, and insomnia. These withdrawal effects have been reported even after short-term use.
- Suicidal ideation and behaviour have been reported with anti-epileptics.
- Caution in renal impairment—dose adjustments may be necessary (see 📖 Dose adjustments, p.443).
- Use with caution in patients with CHF.
- Diabetic patients may need to adjust hypoglycaemic treatment as weight gain occurs.
- If affected by drowsiness and dizziness, patients should be warned about driving.

☺ Adverse effects
Very common
- Dizziness
- Drowsiness.

Common
- Blurred vision
- Confusion
- Constipation
- Dry mouth
- Erectile dysfunction
- Fatigue
- Headache
- Impaired memory
- Increase in appetite
- Paraesthesia
- Peripheral oedema
- Tremor
- Vomiting
- Weight gain (effect may plateau after 3–4 months).

Uncommon
- Agitation
- Hallucinations
- Myoclonus
- Panic
- Sweating.

Unknown
- CHF
- Diarrhoea
- Gynaecomastia
- Loss of vision.

Drug interactions

Pharmacokinetic
- No clinically significant pharmacokinetic drug interactions.

Pharmacodynamic
- Opioids (possible opioid-sparing affect, necessitating opioid dose review).
- CNS depressants (increased risk of CNS adverse effects).

♪ Dose

All formulations of pregabalin are priced equally. Avoid using multiple capsules to fulfil a dose. Pregabalin is licensed for both BD and TDS dosing. There may be reasons for selecting a TDS regimen, but prescribers are encouraged to use BD dosing initially.

Pain
- The licensed schedule is shown in Table 3.18. This may be poorly tolerated by elderly patients or those with cancer, and for these patients, a more cautious titration is suggested. Whichever strategy is adopted, adverse effects are more common around the time of dose escalation but usually resolve in a few weeks. The slower titration may be preferred in the elderly or cancer population, although it may take longer appreciate the therapeutic benefit

Table 3.18 Licensed and suggested dose schedules for pregabalin

	Licensed dose		Suggested dose
Day 1	75mg PO BD	**Day 1**	25mg PO ON
Days 3–7	150mg PO BD	**Day 2**	25mg PO BD
Days 10–14	300mg PO BD	**Days 6–7**	75mg PO BD

Increase dose according to response. Max. dose 600mg/day

Increase dose by 25mg BD every 2 days as needed to a max. of 600mg daily

Epilepsy
- Initial dose 75mg PO BD, increased if necessary to 150mg PO BD after 7 days. The dose can be increased further to a maximum of 300mg PO BD after an additional 7 days. The dose titration may need to be individualized if poorly tolerated.

Anxiety
- Initial dose 75mg PO BD, increased as necessary after 7 days in steps of 150mg daily, to a maximum of 300mg PO BD.

¥ Sleep/¥ restless legs syndrome
- Usual initial dose 150mg PO ON, increased by 150mg at weekly intervals to a dose of 450mg PO ON. For restless legs syndrome, if daytime symptoms are still present at this point, an additional 75–150mg PO OD (e.g. 2pm) can be taken.
- A more cautious approach may be warranted in patients taking opioids or other CNS depressants (e.g. initial dose of 50mg PO ON).

✂ *Chronic pruritus/¥ sweats*
• Titrate the dose as shown on 📖 inside back cover to a usual maximum of 150mg PO BD.

⚡ Dose adjustments

Elderly
• May require a more cautious titration as described in Table 3.18, or may need a dose reduction due to renal impairment (see Table 3.19).

Hepatic/renal impairment
• Dose adjustments are necessary for patients with renal impairment or undergoing haemodialysis (refer to Table 3.19).
• A supplementary dose should be given immediately following every 4-hour haemodialysis treatment.

Table 3.19 Dose adjustments of pregabalin according to renal impairment

Creatinine clearance (mL/min)	Maximum dose
≥60	300mg PO BD
≥30–<60	150mg PO BD
≥15–<30	75mg PO BD or 150mg PO OD
<15	75mg PO OD

Additional information
• Neuropathic pain and anxiety can improve within a week.
• Pregabalin readily dissolves in water. If necessary, the capsules may be opened and mixed with water prior to use. The solution may have a bitter taste; there are no problems flushing the solution down an enteral feeding tube.

⊙ Pharmacology
Pregabalin is an anti-epileptic which reduces the release of neurotransmitters through an interaction with the $\alpha2\delta$ subunit of voltage-dependent calcium channels. Its bioavailability is >90% which, unlike gabapentin, is independent of dose. Pregabalin is excreted by the kidneys, with 98% of an administered dose being excreted unchanged in urine, so dose adjustment is required in renal impairment (see 📖 Dose adjustment).

References
1. Middlemiss T, Laird BJA, Fallon MT. Mechanisms of cancer-induced bone pain. *Clin Oncol* 2011; **23**(6):387–92.
2. Garcia-Borreguero D, Larrosa O, Williams AM, *et al.* Treatment of restless legs syndrome with pregabalin: a double-blind, placebo-controlled study. *Neurology* 2010; **74**(23):1897–904.
3. Manas A, Ciria JP, Fernandez MC, *et al.* Post hoc analysis of pregabalin vs. non-pregabalin treatment in patients with cancer-related neuropathic pain: better pain relief, sleep and physical health. *Clin Transl Oncol* 2011; **13**(9):656–63.
4. Loprinzi CL, Qin R, Balcueva EP, *et al.* Phase III, randomized, double-blind, placebo-controlled evaluation of pregabalin for alleviating hot flashes, N07C1. *J Clin Oncol* 2010; **28**(4):641–7.
5. Aperis G, Paliouras C, Zervos A, *et al.* The use of pregabalin in the treatment of uraemic pruritus in haemodialysis patients. *J Ren Care* 2010; **36**(4):180–5.

Prochlorperazine

Stemetil® (POM)
Tablet: 5mg (28).
Syrup: 5mg/5mL (100mL).
Injection: 12.5mg/mL (not for subcutaneous use).

Buccastem® (POM)
Tablet (buccal): 3mg (10).

Generic (POM)
Tablet: 5mg (28).
Injection: 12.5mg/mL (not for subcutaneous use).

Indications
- Anxiety
- Nausea and vomiting
- Schizophrenia/psychosis.

Contraindications and precautions
- Avoid use in patients with:
  - agranulocytosis
  - cardiac failure
  - dementia (unless patient at immediate risk of harm or severely distressed; increased mortality reported)
  - hepatic dysfunction (see 📖 Dose adjustments, p.446)
  - hypothyroidism
  - myasthenia gravis
  - narrow-angle glaucoma
  - Parkinson's disease
  - phaeochromocytoma
  - prostate hypertrophy
  - renal dysfunction (see 📖 Dose adjustments, p.446).
- Antipsychotic drugs may increase the risk of VTE; assess risks before and during treatment.
- Use with caution in:
  - diabetes mellitus (hyperglycaemia or intolerance to glucose has been reported)
  - elderly—risk of hyperthermia and hypothermia in hot and cold weather respectively; risk of postural hypotension (see 📖 Dose adjustments, p.446).
  - epilepsy (lowers seizure threshold).
- Electrolyte disturbances must be corrected (e.g. hypokalaemia) due to the risk of QT prolongation.
- Warn the patient about:
  - the importance of reporting signs of infection such as sore throat and fever during initial treatment (risk of agranulocytosis)
  - reducing exposure to direct sunlight (or UV lamps) due to the risk of photosensitization (usually with higher doses)
  - prochlorperazine may modify reactions and patients should be advised not drive (or operate machinery) if affected; refer to 📖 Drugs and driving, p.25.

- Subtle deficits in attention, memory, and reasoning may occur with therapeutic dosages of anticholinergic drugs without signs of obvious toxicity. These deficits have often been mistaken for symptoms of early dementia in elderly patients.

☹ Adverse effects

The frequency is not defined, but reported adverse effects include:

- Agitation
- Akathisia (restlessness; may occur with antiemetic doses)
- Blurred vision
- Constipation
- Dry mouth
- Galactorrhoea
- Gynaecomastia
- Impotence
- Insomnia
- Neuroleptic malignant syndrome
- Parkinsonian symptoms
- Postural hypotension
- Tardive dyskinesia (involuntary movements of face, jaw, or tongue; may be irreversible even after withdrawal)
- Thermoregulation problems (hyper- or hypothermia)
- Urinary retention
- Visual disturbances.

Drug interactions

Pharmacokinetic

- Prochlorperazine is believed to be metabolized by CYP2C19, CYP2D6, and CYP3A4.
- Co-administration with drugs that are metabolized by, or affect the activity (induction or inhibition—see ▢ inside back cover) of these pathways may lead to clinically relevant drug interactions and the prescriber should be aware that dosage adjustments may be necessary.

Pharmacodynamic

- Prochlorperazine can cause dose-related prolongation of the QT interval. There is a potential risk that co-administration with other drugs that also prolong the QT interval (e.g. *amiodarone, erythromycin, haloperidol, quinine*) may result in ventricular arrhythmias.
- *Anticholinergics*—increased risk of adverse effects.
- *Anti-epileptics*—dose may need to be increased to take account of the lowered seizure threshold.
- *Antihypertensives*—increased risk of hypotension.
- *CNS depressants*—additive sedative effect.
- *Haloperidol*—may be an additive hypotensive effect; increased risk of extrapyramidal symptoms.
- *Levodopa* and *dopamine agonists*—effect antagonized by prochlorperazine.
- *Metoclopramide*—increased risk of extrapyramidal symptoms.
- *Opioids*—may be an additive hypotensive effect.
- *Trazodone*—may be an additive hypotensive effect.

₰ Dose

Anxiety
- Initial dose 15–20mg PO daily in divided doses (e.g. 5mg TDS or 10mg BD). Increase to a maximum of 40mg PO daily in divided doses.

Nausea and vomiting
- 5–10mg PO BD or TDS. Alternatively, 12.5mg by deep IM injection followed by oral medication 6 hours later, if necessary.
- *Buccastem®*: 3–6mg BD placed in the buccal cavity.

Psychosis
- Initial dose 12.5mg PO BD for 7 days, increasing as necessary by 12.5mg PO daily at 4–7-days intervals. Usual effective daily dosage is 75–100mg (in divided doses). After some weeks at the effective dosage, an attempt should be made at dose reduction. Daily doses of 25–50mg have been shown to be effective.

₰ Dose adjustments

Elderly
- A lower initial dose is recommended due to the increased susceptibility to adverse effects, particularly postural hypotension and drug-induced Parkinsonism after prolonged use.

Hepatic/renal impairment
- Manufacturer advises prochlorperazine should be avoided in patients with hepatic and/or renal dysfunction. Nonetheless, if prochlorperazine must be prescribed, lower doses should be used. Patients may be more susceptible to adverse effects due to accumulation of the drug and/or metabolite(s).

Additional information

Prochlorperazine injection must not be administered subcutaneously.

⟿ Pharmacology

Prochlorperazine is a piperazine phenothiazine drug related to chlorpromazine. The mechanism of action of prochlorperazine has not been fully determined, but its anti-emetic effect is believed to be mainly due to D_2 antagonism, but it also displays some ACh and H_1 receptor antagonism, although in the latter case it appears to occur on chronic dosing. Prochloperazine also blocks α_1-adrenoceptors. It has a low and variable bioavailability due to extensive first-pass metabolism. It is believed to be metabolized by several cytochromes, including CYP2C19, CYP2D6, and CYP3A4.

Propantheline

Pro-Banthine® *(POM)*
Tablet: 15mg (112).

Indications
- Smooth muscle spasm (e.g. bladder, bowel)
- Sweating
- Urinary frequency.

Contraindications and precautions
- Propantheline is contraindicated in patients with:
  - hiatus hernia associated with reflux oesophagitis
  - myasthenia gravis
  - narrow-angle glaucoma
  - obstructive diseases of the GI or urinary tract
  - paralytic ileus
  - prostatic enlargement
  - pyloric stenosis
  - severe ulcerative colitis
  - toxic megacolon.
- It should be used with caution in the following:
  - cardiac arrhythmias
  - CHF
  - coronary heart disease
  - dementia
  - Down's syndrome
  - elderly (see 🕮 Dose adjustments, p.448)
  - gastrointestinal reflux disease
  - hepatic impairment
  - hypertension
  - hyperthyroidism
  - pyrexia (reduces sweating)
  - renal impairment
  - ulcerative colitis.
- Propantheline may modify reactions and patients should be advised not drive (or operate machinery) if affected. Refer to 🕮 Drugs and driving, p.25.
- Subtle deficits in attention, memory, and reasoning may occur with therapeutic dosages of anticholinergic drugs without signs of obvious toxicity. These deficits have often been mistaken for symptoms of early dementia in elderly patients.

☺ Adverse effects
The frequency is not defined, but reported adverse effects include:
- Confusion
- Difficulty in micturition
- Dizziness
- Drowsiness
- Dry mouth

- Inhibition of sweating
- Palpitations
- Tachycardia
- Visual disturbances.

Drug interactions

Pharmacokinetic

- Propantheline may reduce gastric emptying and therefore affect the absorption of concomitant drugs.

Pharmacodynamic

- *Donepezil*—effect may be antagonized.
- *β₂ agonists*—increased risk of tachycardia.
- *Cyclizine*—increased risk of anticholinergic adverse effects.
- *Domperidone*—may inhibit prokinetic effect.
- *Galantamine*—effect may be antagonized.
- *Metoclopramide*—may inhibit prokinetic effect.
- *Nefopam*—increased risk of anticholinergic adverse effects.
- *Rivastigmine*—effect may be antagonized.
- *TCAs*—increased risk of anticholinergic adverse effects.

Dose

- Tablets should be taken at least 1 hour before food.
- Initial dose 15mg PO BD–TDS, increased if necessary up to max. of 30mg PO QDS

Dose adjustments

Elderly

- No specific guidance available. Use the lowest effective dose as the elderly may be more susceptible to the adverse effects. In particular, there is an increased risk for cognitive decline and dementia.

Hepatic/renal impairment

- No specific guidance available. Use the lowest effective dose.

Additional information

- Tablet may be dispersed in water immediately prior to administration if necessary.

Pharmacology

Propantheline is a quaternary ammonium anticholinergic drug which blocks the action of acetylcholine at post-ganglionic sites including smooth muscle, secretary glands, and CNS sites. It inhibits peristalsis, reduces gastric acid secretion, and also decreases pharyngeal, tracheal, and bronchial secretions. Propantheline is poorly absorbed from the bowel, partly due to the polar nature of the molecule, and partly due to extensive first-pass metabolism in the small intestine prior to absorption.

Propranolol

Standard release

Generic (POM)
Tablet: 10mg (28); 40mg (28); 80mg (56); 160mg (56)
Oral solution: 5mg/5 mL (150mL); 10mg/5mL (150mL); 40mg/5mL (150mL); 50mg/5mL (150mL)

Modified release

Half-Inderal LA® (POM)
Capsule: 80mg (28).

Inderal LA® (POM)
Capsule: 160mg (28).

A variety of other products are available and include Bedranol SR®, Beta Prograne®/Half Beta Prograne®, Slo-Pro®; consult the *BNF* for more information.

Indications

Propranolol has a variety of indications (refer to the SPC for further details); those listed here reflect indications likely to be encountered in the palliative care setting
- Anxiety
- Portal hypertension
- *Sweats.

Contraindications and precautions

- Contraindicated for use in:
  - asthma
  - bradycardia (heart rate <45–50 beats/min)
  - hypotension
  - metabolic acidosis
  - untreated phaeochromocytoma.
- Use with caution in patients with:
  - chronic obstructive airways disease
  - concurrent administration of diltiazem or verapamil (see 📖 Drug interactions, p.450)
  - concurrent administration of other antihypertensive drugs (see 📖 Drug interactions, p.450)
  - diabetes (can impair glucose tolerance)
  - hepatic impairment (see 📖 Dose adjustments, p.451)
  - low systolic blood pressure (<90mmHg)
  - overt heart failure (may be used in patients whose signs of failure have been controlled)
  - renal impairment (see 📖 Dose adjustments, p.451).
- Do not withdraw abruptly, especially in patients with ischaemic heart disease.
- Propranolol may cause a more severe reaction to known allergens.

☺ Adverse effects

Common

- Bradycardia
- Cold extremities
- Fatigue
- Raynaud's phenomenon
- Sleep disturbances (e.g. nightmares).

Uncommon

- Diarrhoea
- Nausea
- Vomiting.

Rare

- Bronchospasm
- Confusion
- Deterioration of heart failure
- Dry eyes
- Hallucinations
- Rare
- Paraesthesia
- Postural hypotension
- Psychoses.

Drug interactions

Pharmacokinetic

- Propranolol is metabolized by several pathways, specifically CYP2D6, CYP1A2 and CYP2C19; concomitant use of drugs that are substrates of, or affect the activity (induction or inhibition—see 📖 inside back cover) of one or more of these pathways may lead to clinically relevant drug interactions. Propranolol is also a substrate of P-gp, although the clinical relevance is unknown.
- Smoking induces the hepatic metabolism of propranolol; sudden cessation may lead to the development of adverse effects.

Pharmacodynamic

- *Antihyperstensives*—increased risk of hypotension.
- *Clonidine*—propranolol may exacerbate the rebound hypertension that can occur on withdrawal of clonidine; if both are co-administered, withdraw propranolol several days before discontinuing clonidine
- *Digoxin*—increased risk of bradycardia.
- *Diltiazem*—increased risk of hypotension and AV block.
- *Haloperidol*—potential increased risk of hypotension.
- *Insulin/oral antidiabetic drugs*—symptoms of hypoglycaemia may be masked.
- *Levomepromazine* —potential increased risk of postural hypotension.
- *NSAIDs*—may reduce hypotensive effect of bisoprolol.
- *Verapamil*—increased risk of hypotension and AV block.

🜊 Dose

Anxiety
Standard release
- Initial dose 40mg PO OD, increased to 40mg PO TDS if necessary.

Modified release
- Initial dose 80mg PO OD, increased to 160mg PO OD if necessary.

Portal hypertension
Standard release
- Initial dose 40mg PO BD, increased to 80mg PO BD if necessary depending on heart rate response. The dose can be increased incrementally to a maximum dose of 160mg PO BD.

Modified release
- Initial dose 80mg PO OD, increased to 160mg PO OD if necessary depending on heart rate response. The dose can be increased further in 80mg increments to a maximum dose of 320mg PO OD.

¥ Sweats
- There is little evidence to support the use of propranolol for sweating associated with cancer. Nonetheless, an initial dose of 10mg PO BD, increasing as tolerated to a maximum of 40mg PO TDS (as for anxiety) may be tried.

🜊 Dose adjustments

Elderly
- No specific guidance is available; use the lowest effective dose.

Liver/renal impairment
- No specific guidance is available for patients with hepatic impairment. Manufacturers advise caution, given the hepatic metabolism, and suggest patients with severe liver disease should be started on a lower initial dose (e.g. 10–20mg PO OD) and titrate to the lowest effective dose. For this reason, modified release formulations should only be used once the dose has been successfully titrated.
- No specific guidance is available for patients with renal impairment. Use lower initial doses and titrate according to response.

⊙ Pharmacology

Propranolol is a non-selective, beta-adrenergic receptor-blocking agent and is available as a racemic mixture of two enantiomers, R(+) and S(−). The majority of the pharmacological action is due to the S(−)-enantiomer. Propranolol is highly lipophilic and undergoes extensive first-pass metabolism in the liver, via CYP2D6, CYP1A2 and CYP2C19, as well as direct glucuronidation; it is also a substrate of P-gp. Most metabolites are eliminated in urine.

Quetiapine

Standard release

Seroquel® (POM)
Tablet: 25mg (60); 100mg (60); 150mg (60); 200mg (60); 300mg (60).

Generic (POM)

Tablet: 25mg (60); 100mg (60); 150mg (60); 200mg (60); 300mg (60)
Oral suspension: 12.5mg/5mL (150mL) (see ☐ Additional information, p.456 for supply issues).

Modified release

Seroquel® XL (POM)
Tablet: 50mg (60); 150mg (60); 200mg (60); 300mg (60); 400mg (60).

Generic (POM)

Tablet: 50mg (60); 200mg (60); 300mg (60); 400mg (60).

Indications

- Schizophrenia
- Bipolar disorder (manic/depressive episodes)
- Refractory depression (*Seroquel® XL*)
- *Delirium (particularly nocturnal confusion, or 'sun downing').*[1]

Contraindications and precautions

- Concomitant administration of cytochrome CYP3A4 inhibitors (e.g. clarithromycin, erythromycin) is contraindicated (see ☐ Drug interactions, p.454).
- Avoid grapefruit juice as it may increase the bioavailability of quetiapine through inhibition of intestinal CYP3A4.
- Quetiapine should be used with caution in the following circumstances:
  - cardiovascular disease (quetiapine may induce postural hypotension—see ☐ Drug interactions, p.454; ☐ Dose adjustments, p.455)
  - cerebrovascular disease (risk of cerebrovascular events with antipsychotics)
  - diabetes mellitus (risk of hyperglycaemia and weight gain)
  - hepatic impairment (see ☐ Dose adjustments, p.455)
  - history of drug induced neutropenia (discontinue in patients with a neutrophil count <1.0 × 10^9/L).
- Use adrenaline with caution as severe hypotension and tachycardia may result.
- Electrolyte disturbances must be corrected (e.g. hypokalaemia) due to the risk of QT prolongation.
- Antipsychotic drugs may increase the risk of VTE; assess risks before and during treatment.
- Gradual withdrawal over a period of at least 1–2 weeks is recommended in order to avoid withdrawal symptoms such as diarrhoea, dizziness, headache, insomnia, irritability, nausea, and vomiting. The incidence of these symptoms significantly reduces after 7 days. Refer to ☐ Use of drugs in end-of-life care, p.53 for end-of-life care issues.
- Depression is associated with an increased risk of suicidal thoughts, self-harm, and suicide which persists until remission. Note that that the risk of suicide may increase during initial treatment.

- Elderly people with dementia who are treated with antipsychotics are at a small increased risk of death compared with those who are not treated.
- It may modify reactions and patients should be advised not drive (or operate machinery) if affected. Refer to 📖 Drugs and driving, p.25.

😣 Adverse effects

Very common
- Dizziness
- Drowsiness (onset usually within the first 3 days of treatment)
- Dry mouth
- Haemoglobin lowered
- Headache
- Lipid metabolism affected (elevated low-density lipoprotein cholesterol and triglycerides; decreased high-density lipoprotein cholesterol)
- Weight gain (at least >7% increase; occurs within first few weeks of treatment)
- Withdrawal symptoms (on discontinuation).

Common
- Abnormal dreams
- ALT/AST elevated (asymptomatic)
- Appetite increased
- Asthenia
- Blurred vision
- Constipation
- Dysarthria
- Dyspepsia
- Extrapyramidal symptoms
- Hyperglycaemia
- Hyperprolactinaemia
- Irritability
- Leucopenia
- Peripheral oedema
- Postural hypotension
- Pyrexia
- Rhinitis
- Syncope (especially during the initial dose-titration period; α_1 antagonism)
- T_4 (free and total) concentration reduced
- Tachycardia.

Uncommon
- Dysphagia
- GGT elevated
- Hyponatraemia
- QT prolongation
- Restless leg syndrome
- Seizure
- Sexual dysfunction
- Tardive dyskinesia
- Thrombocytopenia.

Rare
- Galactorrhoea
- Hepatitis
- Neuroleptic malignant syndrome
- Priapism
- Venous thromboembolism.

Very rare
- Diabetes mellitus
- Rhabdomyolysis
- SIADH
- Stevens–Johnson syndrome.

Unknown
- Neutropenia.

Drug interactions

Pharmacokinetic
- Quetiapine is metabolized by CYP3A4. Co-administration with drugs that are metabolized by, or affect the activity (induction or inhibition—see 📖 inside back cover) of this pathway may lead to clinically relevant drug interactions and the prescriber should be aware that dosage adjustments may be necessary, particularly of drugs with a narrow therapeutic index.
- *Carbamazepine*—decreases quetiapine plasma concentrations.
- *Clarithromycin*—potential to increase quetiapine plasma concentrations.
- *Erythromycin*—potential to increase quetiapine plasma concentrations.
- *Fluconazole*—potential to increase quetiapine plasma concentrations (although more likely to occur when fluconazole doses >200mg daily).
- *Grapefruit juice*—potential to increase quetiapine plasma concentrations.
- *Phenytoin*—decreases quetiapine plasma concentrations.
- *Rifampicin*—decreases quetiapine plasma concentrations.

Pharmacodynamic
- Quetiapine has been associated with prolongation of the QT interval. There is a potential risk that co-administration with other drugs that also prolong the QT interval (e.g. *amiodarone, amitriptyline, haloperidol, quinine*) may result in ventricular arrhythmias.
- *Adrenaline*—α-adrenergic effects may be blocked with consequential paradoxical hypotension and tachycardia.
- *Antihypertensives*—increased risk of hypotension.
- *CNS depressants*—additive sedative effect.
- *Haloperidol*—increased risk of extrapyramidal reactions.
- *Levodopa* and *dopamine agonists*—effect antagonized by quetiapine.
- *Levomepromazine*—increased risk of extrapyramidal reactions.
- *Metoclopramide*—increased risk of extrapyramidal reactions.

Dose

Standard release
Schizophrenia
- Initial dose 25mg PO BD on day 1, then 50mg PO BD on day 2, then 100mg PO BD on day 3, then 150mg PO BD on day 4. Further dose

adjustments should be titrated according to response, to a maximum dose of 375mg PO BD. Usual range is 150–225mg PO BD.

Bipolar disorder (mania)
- Initial dose 50mg PO BD on day 1, then 100mg PO BD on day 2, then 150mg PO BD on day 3, then 200mg PO BD on day 4. Further dose adjustments should be titrated according to response, to a maximum of 400mg PO BD. Daily dose increments should not be greater than 200mg. Once the acute episode has resolved, the lowest effective dose may be used for maintenance therapy.

Bipolar disorder (depression)
- Initial dose 50mg PO ON on day 1, then 100mg PO ON on day 2, then 200mg PO ON on day 3, then 300mg PO ON on day 4. Further dose adjustments may be necessary in only a few patients; the maximum dose is 600mg PO ON. Once the acute episode has resolved, the lowest effective dose may be used for maintenance therapy.

¥Delirium
- Suggested initial dose is 12.5–25mg PO ON, increasing as necessary up to 50mg PO BD. Higher doses may be needed, but risk of adverse effects will increase.

Modified release
Schizophrenia
- Initial dose 300mg PO OD on day 1, then 600mg PO OD on day 2. Adjust dose according to response.

Bipolar disorder (mania)
- Initial dose 300mg PO OD on day 1, then 600mg PO OD on day 2. Adjust dose according to response.

Bipolar disorder (depression)
- Initial dose 50mg PO ON on day 1, then 100mg PO ON on day 2, then 200mg PO ON on day 3, then 300mg PO ON on day 4. Further dose adjustments should be titrated according to response, to a maximum dose of 600mg PO ON; usual maintenance dose is 300mg PO ON.

Refractory depression (adjunctive treatment)
- 50mg PO ON for 2 days, then 150mg PO ON for 2 days. Further dose adjustments should be titrated according to response, to a maximum dose of 300mg PO ON.

₰ Dose adjustments
Elderly
- Quetiapine can induce postural hypotension during initiation, more commonly in the elderly. A dose reduction and more gradual titration are recommended should this occur. *Seroquel*® should be started at 25mg PO ON, with a slower rate of titration of 25–50mg daily. Note the lower starting dose suggested for ¥delirium.
- For refractory depression, the initial dose of *Seroquel*® XL should be 50mg PO ON for 3 days, increasing if necessary to 100mg PO ON for at least 4 days before further adjusting the dose in 50mg increments

every 4 days, according to response. Note that the usual maximum dose of 300mg PO ON should not be attained until at least day 22.
- For all other indications, *Seroquel*® XL should be started at 50mg PO OD. The dose can be increased in increments of 50mg daily to an effective dose, depending on the clinical response.

Hepatic/renal impairment
- Use with caution in patients with hepatic impairment. An initial dose of 25mg PO daily is recommended by the manufacturer, with further daily increases in increments of 25–50mg until an effective dose is attained.
- Dose adjustments are unnecessary in renal impairment.

Additional information
- Quetiapine oral suspension/solution is available as a special order product from Martindale Pharma (01277 266600).
- Patients taking divided doses of *Seroquel*® can be switched to *Seroquel*® XL at the equivalent total daily dose taken once daily. Note that dose titration may be required.
- Of the antipsychotics, quetiapine is believed to have a low risk of extrapyramidal symptoms. Nonetheless, it should be avoided in patients with Parkinson's disease. Should delirium or agitation develop in a patient with Parkinson's disease, the following is suggested:
  - trazodone ± benzodiazepine
  - dose reduction and/or discontinuation of anti-parkinsonian medications (anticholinergics initially, then dopamine agonists)
  - low-dose quetiapine in difficult cases.

⟳ Pharmacology
Quetiapine is an atypical antipsychotic agent. Quetiapine and an active metabolite, norquetiapine, act as antagonists at $5\text{-}HT_2$ and D_1/D_2 receptors. The higher selectivity for $5\text{-}HT_2$ relative to dopamine D_2 receptors is believed to contribute to the antipsychotic effect, yet with a low risk of extrapyramidal symptoms compared to typical antipsychotics. Quetiapine is well absorbed following oral administration and extensively metabolized by CYP3A4 to norquetiapine (which is also extensively metabolized by CYP3A4). <5% of a dose is excreted as unchanged drug.

Reference
1. Caraceni A, Simonetti F. Palliating delirium in patients with cancer. *Lancet Oncol* 2009; **10**(2):164–72.

Quinine sulphate

Generic (POM)
Tablet: 200mg (28); 300mg (28).
Suspension: varying strengths are available from Specials manufacturers.

Indications

* Nocturnal leg cramps that cause regular disruption of sleep.
* Falciparum malaria (not discussed).

Contraindications and precautions

* Quinine is contraindicated for use in patients with:
  * G6PD deficiency (use not justified for the treatment of leg cramps)
  * haemoglobinuria
  * myasthenia gravis
  * optic neuritis
  * tinnitus.
* In 2010, the MHRA advised that quinine should only be considered when:
  * cramps are very painful or frequent and regularly disrupt sleep
  * other treatable causes of cramp have been excluded
  * non-pharmacological measures have been unsuccessful (e.g. passive stretching exercises).
* Discontinue if there is no benefit after an initial trial of 4 weeks.
* Electrolyte disturbances must be corrected (e.g. hypokalaemia) due to the risk of QT prolongation.
* Avoid combination with CYP3A4 inhibitors (see 🕮 Drug interactions).
* Quinine should be used with caution in patients with:
  * atrial fibrillation
  * cardiac conduction defects
  * heart block.

☻ Adverse effects

The frequency is not defined, but reported adverse effects include:
* Cinchonism (related to dose and duration of therapy)
* Confusion
* Diarrhoea
* Hypersensitivity (e.g. angio-oedema)
* Nausea
* QT prolongation
* Severe headache
* Tinnitus
* Visual disturbances (e.g. blurred vision, night blindness, diplopia)
* Vomiting.

Quinine is extremely toxic in overdose. Urgent advice must be sought if overdose is suspected.

Drug interactions

Pharmacokinetic
* Quinine is a substrate of CYP3A4. It is an inhibitor of CYP2D6 and CYP2C8/9. Co-administration with drugs that are metabolized by, or

affect the activity (induction or inhibition—see 🕮 inside back cover) of these pathways may lead to clinically relevant drug interactions and the prescriber should be aware that dosage adjustments may be necessary, particularly of drugs with a narrow therapeutic index.

- *Clarithromycin*—avoid combination; may increase plasma concentration of quinine.
- *Digoxin*—plasma concentration of digoxin can rise by >50% (reduce digoxin dose and monitor levels).
- *Erythromycin*—avoid combination; may increase plasma concentration of quinine.
- *Warfarin*—INR may increase due to inhibition of CYP2C8/9.
- Grapefruit juice is not believed to significantly affect quinine. Nonetheless, avoid excessive intake.

Pharmacodynamic

- Quinine can cause dose-related prolongation of the QT interval. There is a potential risk that co-administration with other drugs that also prolong the QT interval (e.g. amiodarone, erythromycin, haloperidol) may result in an increased risk of developing ventricular arrhythmias.

₰ Dose

Take evening dose with a snack or milk to reduce GI irritation. The tablets must be swallowed whole.

Nocturnal leg cramps

- 200–300mg PO ON.

₰ Dose adjustments

Elderly

- No specific guidance is available. Use the lowest effective dose.

Hepatic/renal impairment

- No specific guidance is available for either hepatic or renal impairment. Since reduced clearance may occur in hepatic impairment, the patient should be monitored for signs of excessive dose. Renal clearance accounts for <20% of total clearance, but accumulation may occur as renal function deteriorates.

Additional information

- Treatment should be interrupted at intervals of approximately 3 months to assess the need for further treatment.
- Due to the irritant nature of quinine, the tablet should not be crushed.

⟿ Pharmacology

Quinine is believed to affect calcium distribution within muscle fibres and also decrease the excitability of the motor end-plate region. It is well absorbed orally (80%) and undergoes extensive hepatic metabolism, with the major metabolic pathway thought to involve glucuronidation, although CYP3A4 is also involved.

Rabeprazole

Pariet® *(POM)*
Tablet: 10mg (28); 20mg (28)

Indications

- Treatment of benign gastric and duodenal ulcer.
- Treatment and maintenance of gastro-oesophageal reflux disease.
- Treatment and prophylaxis of NSAID associated peptic ulcer disease.¥

Contraindications and precautions

- Treatment with rabeprazole may lead to a slightly increased risk of developing GI infections (e.g. *Clostridium difficile*). Therefore, avoid unnecessary use or high doses.
- Do not administer with atazanavir or erlotinib.
- Use with caution in patients with severe hepatic dysfunction (see 📖 Dose adjustments, p.460).
- Rabeprazole may modify reactions and patients should be advised not drive (or operate machinery) if affected.
- Rebound acid hypersecretion may occur on discontinuation of the patient has received >8 weeks of treatment.
- PPIs are associated with a range of electrolyte disturbances, such as hyponatraemia and hypomagnesaemia (and associated hypocalcaemia and hypokalaemia). Suspect the PPI should unexplainable symptoms present (e.g. confusion, delirium, generalized weakness, nausea). The effect on sodium metabolism is unclear, possibly involving ADH. PPIs may reduce active magnesium absorption in the small intestine by affecting function of a transient receptor protein channel.

☺ Adverse effects

Common
- Abdominal pain
- Cough
- Diarrhoea
- Dizziness
- Flatulence
- Headache
- Influenza like illness
- Insomnia
- Weakness.

Uncommon
- Abnormal LFTs
- Arthralgia
- Drowsiness
- Dry mouth
- Myalgia
- Rash.

Rare
- Blood dyscrasias
- Depression
- Hepatitis
- Jaundice
- Pruritus
- Visual disturbance
- Weight gain.

Unknown
- Confusion
- Gynaecomastia
- Hyponatraemia
- Oedema.

Drug interactions

Pharmacokinetic

- Rabeprazole is metabolized by CYP2C19 and CYP3A4; it has a weak-moderate inhibitory effect on CYP2C19. Co-administration with drugs that are metabolized by, or affect the activity (induction or inhibition—see 📖 inside back cover) of these pathways may lead to clinically relevant drug interactions and the prescriber should be aware that dosage adjustments may be necessary, particularly of drugs with a narrow therapeutic index.
- Drugs with pH dependent absorption can be affected:
  - *Atazanavir*—avoid combination due to substantially reduced absorption.
  - *Digoxin*—increased plasma concentrations possible.
  - *Erlotinib*—avoid combination as bioavailability of erlotinib can be significantly reduced.
  - *Ferrous sulphate*—reduced absorption likely to result in treatment failure; some recommend co-administration of ascorbic acid (e.g. 100mg) at the same as ferrous sulphate to improve absorption.
  - *Ketoconazole/Itraconazole*—risk of sub-therapeutic plasma concentrations.
  - *Metronidazole suspension*—ranitidine may reduce/prevent the absorption of metronidazole.
- *Antacids*—should be given at least 1 hour before rabeprazole (reduced bioavailability).
- *Azole antifungals*—PPIs may decrease the absorption of itraconazole and ketoconazole.
- *Clopidogrel*—antiplatelet action may be reduced.

Pharmacodynamic

- No clinically significant interactions noted.

₃ Dose

Treatment of benign gastric and duodenal ulcer

- 20mg PO OM for 4–8 weeks.

Treatment of gastro-oesophageal reflux disease

- 20mg PO OM for 4–8 weeks.

Maintenance of gastro-oesophageal reflux disease

- 10–20mg PO OM.

¥ Treatment and prophylaxis of NSAID associated peptic ulcer disease

- 20mg PO OM.

₃ Dose adjustments

Elderly

- No dose adjustments are necessary.

Hepatic/renal impairment

- No dose adjustments are necessary for patients with liver or renal impairment.

Additional information
* Tablets should not be chewed or crushed, but should be swallowed whole.

◈ Pharmacology

Rabeprazole a gastric PPI, reducing the release of H^+ from parietal cells by inhibiting H^+/K^+-ATPase. It is rapidly inactivated by gastric acid; hence oral formulations are enteric coated. It is extensively metabolized by CYP2C19 and CYP3A4 and the metabolites are excreted principally in the urine. Note that CYP2C19 poor metabolizers (or patients taking CYP2C19 inhibitors) can have significantly higher plasma concentrations, leading to unexpected results.

Ranitidine

Zantac® (POM)
Tablet: 150mg (60); 300mg (30).
Syrup (sugar-free): 75mg/5mL (300mL).
Injection: 50mg/2mL (5).

Generic (POM)
Tablet: 150mg (60); 300mg (30).
Effervescent tablet: 150mg (60); 300mg (30).
Oral solution: 75mg/5mL (300mL).

Note: ranitidine can be sold in pharmacies the short-term symptomatic relief of heartburn, dyspepsia, and hyperacidity, and for the prevention of these symptoms when associated with consumption of food or drink in those aged >16 years at a maximum single dose of 75mg and a maximum daily dose of 300mg.

Indications
- Treatment of duodenal and benign gastric ulcer.
- Prevention of NSAID associated duodenal ulcers.
- Oesophageal reflux disease.
- Chronic episodic dyspepsia.
- Symptomatic relief in gastro-oesophageal reflux disease.
- Zollinger–Ellison syndrome.
- *Prevention of NSAID associated gastric ulcers.

Contraindications and precautions
- Use with caution in patients with renal impairment (see 🕮 Dose adjustments, p.464).
- Ranitidine should be avoided in patients with a history of acute porphyria.
- The elderly may be at a greater risk of developing community acquired pneumonia when prescribed ranitidine.
- *Zantac*® effervescent tablets contain aspartame—avoid in phenylketonuria (check individual generic products).
- Refer to 🕮 Use of drugs in end-of-life care, p.53 for end-of-life care issues.

☻ Adverse effects
Common
- Diarrhoea
- Dizziness
- Headache.

Uncommon
- Hypersensitivity reactions
- Reversible blurred vision
- Skin rash.

Rare
- Depression.

Unknown
- Acute interstitial nephritis
- Acute pancreatitis
- Alopecia
- Arthralgia
- Bradycardia
- Confusion
- Gynaecomastia
- Galactorrhoea
- Hallucinations
- Hepatitis
- Jaundice
- Leucopenia
- Thrombocytopenia.

Drug interactions

Pharmacokinetic

It is a minor substrate of CYP1A2, CYP2C19 and CYP2D6. It is unlikely to be involved in cytochrome related interactions.

Drugs with pH dependent absorption can be affected:

- *Atazanavir*—avoid combination due to substantially reduced absorption.
- *Digoxin*—increased plasma concentrations possible.
- *Erlotinib*—avoid combination as bioavailability of erlotinib can be significantly reduced.
- *Ferrous sulphate*—reduced absorption likely to result in treatment failure; some recommend co-administration of ascorbic acid (e.g. 100mg) at the same as ferrous sulphate to improve absorption.
- *Ketoconazole/Itraconazole*—risk of sub-therapeutic plasma concentrations.
- *Metronidazole suspension*—ranitidine may reduce/prevent the absorption of metronidazole.

Pharmacodynamic
- No clinically significant interactions noted.

℥ Dose

Treatment of duodenal ulcer and benign gastric ulcer:
- 150mg PO BD or 300mg PO ON for at least 4 weeks.
- A further 4 week course may be necessary; 8 weeks' treatment may be required for ulcers associated with NSAIDs.

Prevention of NSAID associated duodenal ulcers
- 300mg PO BD.
- ¥Alternatively, 150–300mg via CSCI over 24 hours.

Oesophageal reflux disease
- 150mg PO BD or 300mg PO ON for 8–12 weeks.
- Dose can be increased to 150mg PO QDS in severe cases.
- ¥Alternatively, 150–300mg via CSCI over 24 hours.

Chronic episodic dyspepsia
- 150mg PO BD for up to 6 weeks.
- ¥Alternatively, 150–300mg via CSCI over 24 hours.

Gastro-oesophageal reflux disease
- 150mg PO BD for 2 weeks.
- ¥Alternatively, 150–300mg via CSCI over 24 hours.

Zollinger–Ellison syndrome
- 150mg PO TDS, increased as necessary up to a maximum of 6g PO daily in divided doses.

¥ Prevention of NSAID associated gastric ulcers
- 300mg PO BD.
- Alternatively, 150–300mg via CSCI over 24 hours.

₰ Dose adjustments
Elderly
- No dose adjustments are necessary. However, given the risk of developing community acquired pneumonia, ranitidine should be used at the lowest dose and for the shortest duration possible.

Hepatic/renal impairment
- For liver impairment, no specific guidance is available. However, ranitidine is excreted via the kidneys mainly as the free drug, so dose adjustments are unlikely.
- In patients with CrCl clearance <50mL/min, the daily dose of ranitidine should be 150mg PO ON. This can be increased to 150mg PO BD if necessary and reviewed after 4–8 weeks.

Additional information
- Ranitidine is generally considered a second-line option gastro-protective agent; the PPIs remain the first choice. However, in certain circumstances, such as intolerable adverse effects, ranitidine may be preferred.
- By CSCI, ranitidine is compatible with cyclizine, diamorphine, glycopyrronium, haloperidol, hyoscine butylbromide, hyoscine hydrobromide, ketorolac, octreotide, and oxycodone. It is incompatible with levomepromazine, midazolam and phenobarbital.

⊸ Pharmacology
Ranitidine is a non-imidazole histamine H_2 receptor antagonist that blocks the action of histamine on parietal cells in the stomach, thereby decreasing gastric acid secretion.

Rasagiline

Azilect® *(POM)*
Tablet: 1mg (28).

Indications

- Early treatment of Parkinson's disease as monotherapy; adjunct to co-beneldopa or co-careldopa in later Parkinson's disease.

Contraindications and precautions

- The manufacturer advises at least 14 days must elapse between discontinuation of rasagiline and initiation of treatment with MAOIs or pethidine.
- Do not use in patients with severe hepatic impairment, but can be used with caution in patients with mild hepatic impairment (see 📖 Dose adjustments, p.466).
- Due to the risk of CNS toxicity (e.g. serotonin syndrome), co-administration of the following drugs should be used with caution or avoided (see 📖 Drug interactions, p.466; 📖 Additional information, p.466):
  - SSRIs (e.g. citalopram, escitalopram, fluoxetine, fluvoxamine, paroxetine, sertraline)
  - TCAs (e.g. amitriptyline, nortriptyline)
  - duloxetine
  - mirtazapine
  - trazodone
  - venlafaxine.
- All patients receiving rasagiline should have their ability to continue driving or operating complex machines evaluated.

☺ Adverse effects

Very common
- Dyskinesia
- Headache.

Common
- Abdominal pain
- Abnormal dreams
- Angina
- Appetite reduced
- Conjunctivitis
- Constipation
- Depression
- Dermatitis
- Dry mouth
- Fever
- Flatulence
- Hallucinations
- Influenza-like symptoms
- Leucopoenia
- Malaise
- Musculoskeletal pain
- Rhinitis
- Skin carcinoma
- Urinary urgency
- Vertigo
- Weight loss.

Uncommon
- CVA
- Confusion
- Myocardial infarction.

Drug interactions

Pharmacokinetic

- Rasagiline is a substrate of CYP1A2 and UGTs. Co-administration with drugs that are metabolized by, or affect the activity (induction or inhibition—see 🕮 inside back cover) of these pathways may lead to clinically relevant drug interactions and the prescriber should be aware that dosage adjustments may be necessary.
- *Ciprofloxacin*—plasma concentration of rasagiline may be significantly increased, with increased risk of hypertensive crisis and other adverse reactions associated with non-selective inhibition of MAO.
- Dose adjustments may be necessary upon smoking cessation.

Pharmacodynamic

- Risk of serotonin syndrome (see 🕮 Box 1.10, p.18) with:
  - SSRIs
  - TCAs
  - Serotonergic drugs—e.g. duloxetine, methadone, mirtazapine, tramadol, trazodone and venlafaxine (but see 🕮 Additional information).
- *MAOI* —risk of hypertensive crisis.
- *Sympathomimetics*—includes topical nasal decongestants; avoid combination due to risk of hypertensive crisis and other adverse effects.

💊 Dose

- 1mg PO OD with or without levodopa (as co-beneldopa or co-careldopa).

💊 Dose adjustments

Elderly

- Dosage adjustments are unnecessary.

Hepatic/renal impairment

- Rasagiline is contraindicated for use in patients with severe hepatic impairment and should be avoided in patients with moderate impairment. If used in patients with mild hepatic impairment, the manufacturer recommends caution during initiation. Should mild impairment progress to moderate impairment during treatment, rasagiline must be stopped.
- Dosage adjustments are not required for patients with mild-moderate renal impairment. No specific guidance is available for use in severe renal impairment.

Additional information

- Presently, Clinical Knowledge Summaries (NHS Evidence) states that mirtazapine and trazodone may be used with caution in patients receiving rasagiline.[1] Manufacturers of citalopram state that it can be used cautiously in combination with MAOIs (including *selegiline*) at doses ≤ 10mg/day.

Pharmacology

Rasagiline is a potent, irreversible MAO-B selective inhibitor. It is believed to increase levels of free dopamine in the striatum, leading to an increase in dopaminergic activity. This in turn is believed to mediate rasagiline's therapeutic effects. It is rapidly absorbed, with an oral bioavailability of ~40%. It is extensively hepatically metabolized via CYP1A2 and direct glucuronidation.

Reference

1. NHS Evidence Clinical Knowledge Summaries (2011). *Parkinson's disease – Management. Which drugs should be used in the treatment of depression in people with Parkinson's disease?* Available from: ℘ http://www.cks.nhs.uk/parkinsons_disease/management/detailed_answers/ confirmed_parkinsons_disease_primary_care/managing_non_motor_symptoms_ and_complications/depression/drug_treatment_of_depression#-380720. Accessed 3 November 2011.

Reboxetine

Edronax® *(POM)*
Tablet (scored): 4mg (60).

Indications
• Major depression.

Contraindications and precautions
• Do not use with an MAOI (including *rasagiline* and *selegiline*), or within 14 days of stopping one; avoid concomitant use with linezolid or moclobemide. At least 1 week should elapse after stopping reboxetine therapy before starting an MAOI.
• Use with caution in patients with epilepsy due to the risk of seizures.
• Clinical experience with reboxetine in patients affected by co-morbidity is limited. Close supervision should be applied in patients with current evidence of:
  • cardiac disease
  • glaucoma
  • prostatic hypertrophy
  • urinary retention.
• Concurrent use with CYP3A4 inhibitors should be avoided (see 📖 Drug interactions, p.469).
• Depression is associated with an increased risk of suicidal thoughts, self-harm, and suicide which persists until remission. Note that that the risk of suicide may increase during initial treatment.
• Use with caution in the elderly as experience is limited.
• Avoid abrupt withdrawal, although there does not appear to be a withdrawal syndrome.

☺ Adverse effects
Very common
• Insomnia
• Dry mouth
• Constipation
• Sweating.

Common
• Vertigo
• Tachycardia
• Palpitation
• Vasodilation
• Postural hypotension
• Loss of appetite
• Urinary hesitancy (treat with α_1-antagonist, such as tamsulosin)
• UTIs
• Sexual dysfunction (including ejaculatory and testicular pain, impotence).

Unknown
• Aggression
• Agitation
• Allergic dermatitis/rash
• Anxiety
• Cold extremities
• Hallucination
• Hypertension
• Hypokalaemia
• Irritability
• Nausea
• Paraesthesia
• Suicidal ideation
• Vomiting.

Drug interactions

Pharmacokinetic

Reboxetine is metabolized by CYP3A4. It may have weak inhibitory actions on CYP2D6 and CYP3A4, but at concentrations which exceed those in clinical use. Reboxetine has a narrow therapeutic index and reduction of elimination through CYP3A4 inhibition is a concern.

Co-administration with drugs that inhibit CYP3A4 should be avoided as clinically significant effects may occur.

Co-administration with CYP3A4 inducers (see 📖 inside back cover) may reduce the efficacy of reboxetine.

Avoid excessive amounts of grapefruit juice as this may increase the bioavailability of reboxetine through inhibition of intestinal CYP3A4.

Pharmacodynamic

Diuretics—increased risk of hypokalaemia

MAOIs—risk of CNS toxicity (see 📖 Contraindications and precautions, p.468)

Tramadol—increased risk of seizures

🔔 Dose

4mg PO BD increased if necessary after 3–4 weeks to 10mg PO daily in divided doses; maximum dose 12mg PO daily.

🔔 Dose adjustments

Elderly

Manufacturer does not recommend use in the elderly due to insufficient data.

Hepatic/renal impairment

Initial dose in patients with liver or renal impairment should be 2mg PO BD, which can be increased as necessary and as tolerated, but not to exceed 12mg PO daily.

Additional information

If necessary, the tablets can be crushed and dispersed in water prior to use.

Onset of therapeutic action is usually not immediate, but often delayed 2–4 weeks.

Although some adverse effects may appear anticholinergic, reboxetine does not directly antagonize cholinergic receptors. These effects are due in some degree to α_1-receptor activation, causing acetylcholine release.

May have beneficial analgesic effects when combined with an opioid.

⯈ Pharmacology

Reboxetine is a selective noradrenaline reuptake inhibitor (NaRI). It has a weak effect on serotonin reuptake but no effect on dopamine reuptake. Reboxetine has no significant affinity for muscarinic receptors. It is predominantly metabolized by CYP3A4, with ~10% of the dose excreted unchanged in urine.

Repaglinide

Prandin® *(POM)*
Tablet: 500 micrograms (30; 90); 1mg (30; 90); 2mg (90).

Generic (POM)
Tablet: 500 micrograms (30; 90); 1mg (30; 90); 2mg (90).

Indications

- Type 2 diabetes mellitus (as monotherapy or in combination with metformin when metformin alone inadequate).

Contraindications and precautions

- Is contraindicated for use in patients with:
  - concurrent use of gemfibrozil (see 📖 Drug interactions)
  - ketoacidosis
  - severe hepatic impairment.
- Repaglinide should be used with caution or be avoided in patients receiving drugs which affect CYP2C8.
- Use with caution in:
  - debilitated or malnourished patients (lower initial doses recommended)
  - renal impairment (increased insulin sensitivity).

😣 Adverse effects

Common

- Abdominal pain
- Diarrhoea
- Hypoglycaemia.

Rare

- Constipation
- Visual disturbances
- Vomiting.

Drug interactions

Pharmacokinetic

- Is mainly metabolized by CYP2C8. A minor pathway involves CYP3A4 (which becomes important if CYP2C8 is inhibited). Co-administration with drugs that are metabolized by, or affect the activity (induction or inhibition—see 📖 inside back cover) of these pathways may lead to clinically relevant drug interactions and the prescriber should be aware that dosage adjustments may be necessary, particularly of drugs with a narrow therapeutic index. Repaglinide is also a substrate for active hepatic uptake via organic anion transporting (OAT) protein. Certain drugs may interfere with this process.
- *Ciclosporin*—increases the effect of repaglinide, possibly through inhibition of OAT.
- *Gemfibrozil*—combination contraindicated (CYP2C8 inhibition).

Pharmacodynamic

- *Metformin* —increased risk of hypoglycaemia.

Drugs that may precipitate hyperglycaemia may interfere with blood glucose control, e.g.:
- corticosteroids
- diuretics
- nifedipine.

Dose
- Initial dose 500 micrograms PO within 30min of main meals; starting dose is recommended to be 1mg if transferring from another oral hypoglycaemic.
- Patients who skip a meal (or add an extra meal) should be instructed to skip (or add) a dose for that meal.
  The dose is titrated individually according to response at intervals of 1–2 weeks.
- Up to 4mg may be given as a single dose; maximum dose 16mg PO daily.

Dose adjustments
Elderly
- No specific guidance is available. Use the lowest effective dose.

Hepatic/renal impairment
- No specific guidance is available for use in mild-moderate hepatic impairment; use the lowest effective dose. Repaglinide is contraindicated for use in patients with severe hepatic impairment. Repaglinide is mainly excreted via hepatic metabolism, so renal impairment is unlikely to cause problems. Nonetheless, the manufacturer advises caution in renal impairment due to an increase in insulin sensitivity.

Additional information
- Tablets can be crushed and mixed with water immediately prior to administration if necessary

Pharmacology
Repaglinide closes ATP-dependent potassium channels in the β-cell membrane. This depolarizes the β-cell that leads to an opening of the calcium channels. The resulting increased calcium influx induces insulin secretion. The net effect is an acute lowering of blood glucose. Note that repaglinide requires functioning β-cells to work. It is rapidly absorbed orally and virtually completely metabolized to inactive compounds. The majority of the dose is excreted in bile.

Rifampicin

Rifadin® (POM)
Capsule: 150mg (100); 300mg (100).
Syrup: 100mg/5mL (120mL).
Infusion: 600mg vial (**not for subcutaneous use**).

Rimactane® (POM)
Capsule: 150mg (60); 300mg (60).

Generic (POM)
Capsule: 150mg (100); 300mg (100).

Indications
- Refer to local guidelines.
- Broad-spectrum antibiotic indicated for the treatment of infections caused by susceptible organisms.
- ¥Opioid-induced pruritus.[1]

Contraindications and precautions
- Rifampicin is contraindicated for use in patients:
  - with jaundice
  - co-prescribed saquinavir/ritonavir (increased risk of hepatotoxicity).
- Rifampicin is a potent enzyme inducer. Many drugs metabolized by the cytochrome P450 system will be affected, with the exception of CYP2D6 substrates (see 📖 Drug interactions, p.473).
- Use with caution in:
  - acute porphyria
  - elderly patients
  - hepatic impairment (see 📖 Dose adjustments, p.473)
  - renal impairment (if dose>600mg/day) (see 📖 Dose adjustments, p.473).
- Warn the patient about the importance of reporting signs of liver impairment, such as persistent nausea, vomiting, malaise or jaundice. Additionally, warn the patient that rifampicin may colour urine, sweat, tears and sputum red. Contact lenses can be permanently stained.

☺ Adverse effects
The frequency is not defined, but reported adverse effects include:
- Abdominal discomfort
- Acute renal failure (discontinue treatment)
- Anorexia
- Diarrhoea
- Haemolytic anaemia (discontinue treatment)
- Headache
- Hepatitis
- Influenza-like syndrome (e.g. bone pain, chills, dizziness, fever)
- Jaundice
- Muscle weakness
- Myopathy
- Nausea

- Oedema
- Pseudomembranous colitis
- Raised liver enzymes
- Thrombocytopenia (discontinue treatment)
- Vomiting.

Drug interactions

Pharmacokinetic

- Rifampicin is metabolized by CYP2C8/9 and CYP3A4; it is also a strong inducer of CYP1A2, CYP2B6, CYP2C8/9, CYP2C19, CYP2E1, and CYP3A4. Rifampicin may also induce Phase II metabolism, such as glucuronidation. Co-administration with drugs that are metabolized by, or affect the activity (induction or inhibition—see 📖 inside back cover) of these pathways may lead to clinically relevant drug interactions and the prescriber should be aware that dosage adjustments may be necessary, particularly of drugs with a narrow therapeutic index. Rifampicin may lower the plasma concentration, diminish, or even abolish the activity of many drugs through enzyme induction. Several interactions are listed below, but refer to 📖 inside back cover for a list of drugs that may potentially be affected.
- *Celecoxib*—effect of celecoxib may be reduced.
- *Clonazepam*—effect of clonazepam may be reduced.
- *Corticosteroids*—effect of corticosteroids reduced; higher doses necessary (possibly double or more).
- *Fentanyl*—risk of reduced analgesic benefit.
- *Fluconazole*—possible loss of activity of fluconazole.
- *Haloperidol*—effect of haloperidol reduced.
- *Levothyroxine*—increased metabolism may precipitate hypothyroidism.
- *Mirtazapine*—effect of mirtazapine may be reduced.
- *Modafinil*—effect of modafinil may be reduced.
- *Morphine*—possible risk of reduced analgesia.
- *Oxycodone*—possible risk of reduced analgesia.
- *Paracetamol*—may increase the risk of hepatoxicity of paracetamol.
- *Tapentadol*—possible risk of reduced analgesia.
- *Tramadol*—reduced analgesic effect.

Pharmacodynamic

- None known.

💊 Dose

- Dose depends on indication/infection. Refer to local guidelines.
- Typically 0.6–1.2g PO/IV infusion daily, in 2–4 divided doses
- For opioid-induced pruritus[¥], a dose of 150mg PO OD–150mg PO BD can be used.

💊 Dose adjustments

Elderly

- Unless there is evidence of hepatic and/or renal impairment, no dosage adjustments are necessary.

Hepatic/renal impairment
- Patients with liver impairment should only be given rifampicin if benefits outweigh risks. Lower doses should be used and LFTs (especially serum glutamic pyruvic transaminase (SGPT) and serum glutamic oxaloacetic transaminase (SGOT)) should be performed prior to therapy, weekly for 2 weeks, then every 2 weeks for the next 6 weeks. If signs of hepatocellular damage occur, rifampicin should be discontinued. A daily dose of 8mg/kg should not be exceeded in patients with liver impairment.
- Rifampicin should be used with caution in renal impairment if the daily dose exceeds 600mg.

Additional information
- To reconstitute the injection, use the solvent provided then dilute with 500mL infusion fluid (glucose 5% or NaCl 0.9%); give over 2–3 hours.

⊕ Pharmacology
Rifampicin is a bactericidal antibiotic with a broad-spectrum of activity against most Gram-positive and Gram-negative organisms (including *Pseudomonas aeruginosa*). It is believed to work through inhibition of bacterial DNA-dependent RNA polymerase activity. Rifampicin is distributed widely in body tissues. It is metabolized in the liver and eliminated mainly in bile; enterohepatic circulation occurs. <30% of a dose is renally excreted, with approximately half of this being unchanged drug.

Reference
1. Kremer AE, Beuers U, Oude-Elferink RP, *et al.* Pathogenesis and treatment of pruritus in cholestasis. *Drugs* 2008; **68**(15):2163–82.

Risperidone

Risperdal® (POM)
Tablet (scored): 500 micrograms (20); 1mg (20, 60); 2mg (60); 3mg (60);
4mg (60); 6mg (28).
Liquid: 1mg/mL (100mL).

Generic (POM)
Tablet: 500 micrograms (20); 1mg (20, 60); 2mg (60); 3mg (60); 4mg (60);
6mg (28).
Orodispersible tablet: 500 micrograms (28); 1mg (28); 2mg (28), 3mg (28);
4mg (28).
Liquid: 1mg/mL (100mL).

Risperdal Quicklet® (POM)
Orodispersible tablet: 500 micrograms (28); 1mg (28); 2mg (28), 3mg (28);
4mg (28).

Indications

Psychosis.
Short-term treatment (up to 6 weeks) of persistent aggression in patients
with moderate to severe Alzheimer's dementia (with risk of harm).
¥Delirium.[1]
¥Anti-emetic (refractory nausea and vomiting).[2]
¥Major depression.[3]

Contraindications and precautions

Warning

- Risperidone should not be used to treat behavioural symptoms of
  dementia. Elderly patients with dementia-related psychosis treated
  with risperidone are at an increased risk of CVA and mortality.
  Citalopram, sertraline or trazodone may be more appropriate choices.
- For persistent aggression in patients with moderate to severe
  Alzheimer's dementia, risperidone may be used for short-term
  treatment only (max. 6 weeks), under specialist advice. The risks
  associated with CVA (e.g. diabetes, hypertension, smoking) should be
  assessed before commencing treatment with risperidone.
- Avoid combination of risperidone and furosemide. Treatment with
  this combination is associated with a higher mortality than with either
  drug alone.

Avoid in acute porphyria.
Antipsychotic drugs may increase the risk of VTE; assess risks before
and during treatment.
Use with caution in:
- diabetes (risk of hyperglycaemia in elderly; significant weight gain
  reported)
- epilepsy (seizure threshold may be lowered, although risk is
  relatively small)
- hepatic/renal impairment (see ⬚ Dose adjustment, p.477)
- Parkinson's disease (risperidone may interfere with treatment)
- phenylketonuria—*Risperdal Quicklet®* contains aspartame, a source
  of phenylalanine.

- Postural hypotension may occur during initiation.
- Avoid sudden withdraw treatment as this may lead to recurrence of symptoms, or rarely, acute withdrawal symptoms, such as nausea, vomiting and sweating.
- Electrolyte disturbances must be corrected (e.g. hypokalaemia) due to risk of QT prolongation.
- Risperidone may modify reactions and patients should be advised not drive (or operate machinery) if affected.

☺ Adverse effects

Very common

- Extrapyramidal symptoms (dose dependent)
- Headache
- Insomnia.

Common

- Agitation
- Anxiety
- Appetite changes (increase or decrease)
- Arthralgia
- Asthenia
- Blurred vision
- Chest pain
- Constipation
- Cough
- Diarrhoea
- Dizziness
- Drowsiness
- Dry mouth
- Dyspepsia
- Dyspnoea

- Dystonia
- Enuresis
- Epistaxis
- Fatigue
- Hyperprolactinaemia
- Infection (e.g. influenza, upper respiratory tract infection, UTI)
- Nausea/vomiting
- Peripheral oedema
- Pyrexia
- Rash
- Rhinitis
- Tachycardia
- Tremor
- Weight gain (may be >5% gain).

Uncommon

- Anaemia
- Conjunctivitis
- Dysphagia
- Hyperglycaemia

- Hypotension
- Sexual dysfunction
- Thrombocytopenia
- Wheezing.

Drug interactions

Pharmacokinetic

- Risperidone is metabolized mainly by CYP2D6; a minor pathway involves CYP3A4. Co-administration with drugs that are metabolized by, or affect the activity (induction or inhibition—see 🕮 inside back cover) of these pathways may lead to clinically relevant drug interactions and the prescriber should be aware that dosage adjustments may be necessary, particularly of drugs with a narrow therapeutic index.
- *Carbamazepine* significantly reduces the plasma concentrations of both risperidone and the active metabolite (CYP3A4 induction). The dose o risperidone may need to be titrated accordingly when carbamazepine i added or discontinued.

harmacodynamic

Risperidone can cause dose-related prolongation of the QT interval. There is a potential risk that co-administration with other drugs that also prolong the QT interval (e.g. *amiodarone, erythromycin, quinine*) may result in ventricular arrhythmias.

Anti-epileptics—may need to be increased to take account of the lowered seizure threshold.

CNS depressants—additive sedative effect.

Levodopa and *dopamine agonists*—effect antagonized by risperidone.

Levomepromazine—increased risk of extrapyramidal symptoms.

Metoclopramide—increased risk of extrapyramidal symptoms.

Unknown

Furosemide—increased risk of death in elderly patients with dementia.

Dose

Psychosis

Initial dose 1mg PO BD, increasing on the second day to 2mg PO BD. Some patients may benefit from a slower dose increase (see Elderly, p.477). Dose can be increased further to a usual max. of 3mg PO BD. Higher doses are possible, but should be used under expert supervision.

Delirium

Initial dose 500 micrograms PO BD, increased as necessary by 500 micrograms PO daily to a usual maximum of 1mg PO BD. Unusual to require higher doses.

Refractory nausea and vomiting

Initial dose 500 micrograms PO ON. Usual maximum of 1mg PO ON.

Major depression

Initial dose 1mg PO ON, increased to 1mg PO BD or 2mg PO ON if necessary after 1–2 weeks. To be used in conjunction with standard antidepressant monotherapy.

Dose adjustments

Elderly

For psychosis and delirium, an initial dose of 0.5mg PO BD is suggested. Increase by 0.5mg PO once–twice daily to a maximum of 2mg PO BD.

For major depression, or refractory nausea and vomiting, an initial dose of 0.25–0.5mg PO ON is suggested. No more than 1mg PO ON should be necessary.

Hepatic/renal impairment

The manufacturer advises caution in this group of patients since data are lacking. For all indications, starting and consecutive dosing should be halved, and dose titration should be slower for patients with hepatic or renal impairment.

Additional information

Weight gain generally occurs during the first 6–12 months of treatment.

- The liquid may be mixed with water, black coffee, or orange juice prior to administration. Orodispersible tablets will begin disintegrating within seconds after placing on the tongue.
- If necessary, risperidone tablets can be crushed and dispersed in water immediately prior to use. The resulting suspension will easily pass through an NG tube.
- Risk of extrapyramidal effects with risperidone is lower than with haloperidol.
- Risperidone may be a useful antiemetic for refractory nausea and vomiting (D_2 and 5-HT$_2$ antagonist)

◈ Pharmacology

Risperidone is a benzisoxazole antipsychotic which acts as a 5-HT$_2$ and D_2 receptor antagonist. The serotonin antagonism is believed to improve negative symptoms of psychoses and reduce the incidence of extrapyramidal adverse effects. Risperidone is also an antagonist at α_1, α_2, and H receptors, with no activity at muscarinic receptors. It is rapidly and well absorbed orally and extensively metabolized by CYP2D6 to the active metabolite, 9-hydroxyrisperidone. A minor metabolic pathway involves CYP3A4, but significant induction can reduce the effectiveness of risperidone (see 📖 Drug interactions, p.476). Since risperidone metabolism involves CYP2D6, the effect of drug inhibition and polymorphism must be considered if unexpected results are observed.

References

1. Caraceni A, Simonetti F. Palliating delirium in patients with cancer. *Lancet Oncol* 2009; **10**(2):164–72.
2. Okamoto Y, Tsuneto S, Matsuda Y, *et al.* A retrospective chart review of the antiemetic effectiveness of risperidone in refractory opioid-induced nausea and vomiting in advanced cancer patients. *J Pain Symptom Manage* 2007; **34**(2):217–22.
3. Owenby RK, Brown LT, Brown JN. Use of risperidone as augmentation treatment for major depressive disorder. *Ann Pharmacother* 2011; **45**(1):95–100.

Rivastigmine

Exelon® (POM)
Capsule: 1.5mg (28; 56); 3mg (28; 56); 4.5mg (28; 56); 6mg (28; 56).
Oral solution: 2mg/mL (120mL).
Transdermal patch: 4.6mg/24 hours (30); 9.5mg/24 hours (30).

Generic (POM)
Capsule: 1.5mg; 3mg; 4.5mg; 6mg.
Oral solution: 2mg/mL (120mL).

Indications
- Mild to moderate dementia in Alzheimer's disease.
- Mild to moderate Parkinson's disease dementia (PDD)
  Note: although licensed for Parkinson's disease dementia, rivastigmine may exacerbate or induce extrapyramidal symptoms.

Contraindications and precautions
- Use with caution in patients with:
  - asthma
  - COPD
  - hepatic impairment (see 📖 Dose adjustments, p.480)
  - Parkinson's disease
  - renal impairment (see 📖 Dose adjustments, p.480)
  - supraventricular conduction abnormalities (may cause bradycardia)
  - susceptibility to peptic ulcers (increase in gastric acid secretion)
- Adverse effects are dose related. If treatment is interrupted for several days (e.g. due to vomiting), the dose must be re-titrated to avoid the development of adverse effects.
- During therapy, the patient's weight should be monitored (rivastigmine is associated with weight loss)
- All patients receiving rivastigmine should have their ability to continue driving or operating complex machines evaluated.

⊘ Adverse effects
Very common
- Anorexia
- Diarrhoea
- Dizziness
- Nausea
- Tremor (PDD)
- Vomiting.

Common
- Abdominal pain
- Agitation
- Anxiety
- Application site skin reactions (patch)
- Asthenia
- Confusion
- Dehydration (PDD)
- Delirium (patch)
- Drowsiness
- Dyspepsia
- Exacerbation of Parkinson's disease (PDD)
- Fatigue
- Headache
- Insomnia (PDD)
- Pyrexia (patch)
- Rash (patch)
- Restlessness
- Salivary hypersecretion (PDD)

- Sweats
- Tremor

- UTI (patch).

Uncommon

- Cardiac disorders
  (e.g. AF, bradycardia)
- Depression

- Dystonia (PDD)
- Syncope
- Raised LFTs.

Rare

- Angina
- Gastric and duodenal ulcers

- Seizures.

Very rare

- Gastrointestinal haemorrhage
- Hallucinations

- Hypertension
- Pancreatitis.

Drug interactions

Pharmacokinetic

- None known. Rivastigmine does not undergo hepatic metabolism via the CYP450 system.

Pharmacodynamic

- *Anticholinergics*—may antagonize the effects.

Dose

Oral

- Initial dose 1.5mg PO BD. The dose can be increased by 1.5mg PO BD every 2 weeks according to response. The maximum dose is 6mg PO BD.
- *Note:* if treatment is interrupted for more than several days, rivastigmine should be re-commenced at 1.5mg PO BD and re-titrated.

Transdermal

- Initial dose 4.6mg/24 hours patch. Removing the patch after 24 hours and siting the replacement on a different area of skin.
- The dose can be increased to 9.5mg/24 hours after at least 4 weeks.
- *Note:* if treatment is interrupted for more than several days, rivastigmine should be re-commenced at 4.6mg/24 hours and re-titrated.

Dose adjustments

Elderly

- No dose adjustments are necessary.

Hepatic/renal impairment

- Although plasma concentrations have been shown to increase, no dose adjustments are necessary in patients with renal or mild to moderate hepatic impairment; the dose, however, must be carefully titrated to effect.
- The manufacturer states that there is no increased exposure to rivastigmine in patients with severe renal impairment.
- Rivastigmine can be used in patients with severe hepatic impairment, but close monitoring of treatment is required.

Additional information

Transdermal administration of rivastigmine is less likely to cause GI disturbances.

If changing from oral to transdermal therapy:
- 3–6mg PO daily, initial transdermal dose is 4.6mg/24 hours (then titrate as previously described)
- 9–12mg PO daily initial transdermal dose is 9.5mg/24 hours.

The first patch should be applied on the day following the last oral dose.

Patches should be applied to clean, dry, non-hairy, non-irritated skin on the back, upper arm, or chest. The same area should be avoided for at least 14 days.

Pharmacology

Rivastigmine is an anticholinesterase inhibitor. It is rapidly and extensively metabolized primarily via cholinesterase-mediated hydrolysis.

Ropinirole

Standard release

Adartrel® (POM)
Tablet: 250 micrograms (12); 500 micrograms (28; 84); 2mg (28; 84).

Requip® (POM)
Tablet: 1mg (84); 2mg (84); 5mg (84).
Tablet (starter pack): 250 micrograms (42), 500 micrograms (42), 1mg (21)
Tablet (follow-on pack): 500 micrograms (42), 1mg (42), 2mg (63).

Generic (POM)
Tablet: 250 micrograms (12); 500 micrograms (28; 84); 2mg (28; 84); 5m
(84).

Modified release

Requip® XL (POM)
Tablet: 2mg (28); 4mg (28); 8mg (28).

Indications
- Restless legs syndrome (*Adartrel®*).
- Parkinson's disease (*Requip®* and *Requip® XL*).

Contraindications and precautions
- Manufacturer states that ropinirole should not be used in patients with severe hepatic impairment, or severe renal impairment (CrCl <30mL/min).
- Ropinirole should be used with caution in patients with:
  - cardiovascular disease (risk of arrhythmias and hypotension—monitor BP during initiation)
  - hepatic impairment
  - major psychotic disorders (antagonism between drugs)
  - renal impairment.
- Paradoxical worsening of restless legs syndrome symptoms can occur; dose adjustment or discontinuation should be considered.
- Dopamine receptor agonists can cause excessive daytime sleepiness and sudden onset of sleep.
- Behavioural symptoms of impulse control disorders and compulsions such as binge eating and compulsive shopping can occur. Dose reduction/tapered discontinuation should be considered.
- Ropinirole may modify reactions and patients should be advised not drive (or operate machinery) if affected.

☹ Adverse effects

Very common
- Dyskinesia
- Drowsiness

- Nausea.

Common
- Abdominal pain
- Confusion

- Constipation
- Dizziness

Dyspepsia
Fatigue
Hallucinations
Hypotension

- Nervousness
- Peripheral oedema
- Vomiting.

Incommon

Delirium
Delusion
Hypersexuality

- Paranoia
- Pathological gambling.

Drug interactions

Pharmacokinetic

Ropinirole is a substrate of CYP1A2; it may inhibit CYP2D6.
Co-administration with drugs that are metabolized by, or affect the activity (induction or inhibition—see 📖 inside back cover) of these pathways may lead to clinically relevant drug interactions and the prescriber should be aware that dosage adjustments may be necessary, particularly of drugs with a narrow therapeutic index.
Ciprofloxacin—increased plasma concentrations of ropinirole.
Smoking may increase the clearance of ropinirole. If a patient starts or stops smoking, dose adjustments may be necessary.

Pharmacodynamic

Alcohol—additive sedative effect.
CNS depressants—additive sedative effect.
Dopamine antagonists (e.g. *antipsychotics, metoclopramide*)—may decrease the efficiency of ropinirole due to dopamine antagonism.

💊 Dose

Parkinson's disease

Standard release

Initial dose 250 micrograms PO TDS. The dose can be increased by increments of 750 micrograms at weekly intervals to 1mg PO TDS. Further dose increases can be made in increments of up to 3mg per week.
Usual dose range is 9–16mg PO in 3 divided doses; maximum dose 24mg PO daily.

Modified release

To be used in patients with stable Parkinson's disease, transferring from a standard-release formulation.
Initial dose is based on the previous total daily dose of a standard release formulation. If patients are taking a different total daily dose of ropinirole immediate release tablets to those available as modified release, they should be switched to the nearest available dose.
If control of symptoms is not achieved or maintained:
- in patients receiving <8mg PO OD, increase in steps of 2mg at intervals of at least 1 week to 8mg PO OD according to response
- in patients receiving >8mg PO OD, increase in steps of 2mg at intervals of at least 2 weeks according to response to a maximum of 24mg PO OD

Restless legs syndrome
- Initial dose 250 micrograms PO ON for 2 days, increased if tolerated to 500 micrograms PO ON for 5 days. The dose can be increased if necessary to 1mg PO ON for 7 days. Further dose increases of 500 micrograms per week over a 2-week period to a dose of 2mg PO OD can be made if needed. The maximum daily dose of 4mg is achieved by increasing the dose by 500 micrograms per week over a 2-week period to 3mg PO OD, followed by an additional 1mg PO OD thereafter.

⚓ Dose adjustments

Elderly
- No specific guidance available. The manufacturers state that dose increases should be gradual and titrated against the symptomatic response.

Liver/renal impairment
- Use with caution in moderate hepatic impairment, but avoid in patients with severe hepatic impairment.
- Doses adjustment is unnecessary in patients with mild-moderate renal impairment (CrCl 30–50mL/min). Ropinirole is contraindicated for use in patients with severe renal impairment (CrCl <30mL/min) not receiving haemodialysis. For patients with end-stage renal disease receiving haemodialysis, recommended doses are as follows:
  - initial dose of *standard release* ropinirole is 0.25mg PO TDS
  - initial dose of *Requip® XL* is 2mg PO OD
- Further dose escalations should be based on tolerability and efficacy. The recommended maximum dose is 18mg/day in patients receiving regular haemodialysis. Supplemental doses after haemodialysis are not required.

Additional information
- In the management of restless legs syndrome, should treatment be interrupted for more than a few days, ropinirole should be re-initiated by dose titration as described previously.
- For patients experiencing intolerable adverse effects, down-titration followed by more gradual up-titration has been shown to be beneficial
- Standard release tablets can be dispersed in water immediately prior to administration if necessary.

⊙ Pharmacology
Ropinirole is a dopamine D_2 and D_3 receptor agonist. The mechanism of action of ropinirole as treatment for Parkinson's disease or restless legs syndrome is unknown, although in the former case it is believed to be related to its ability to stimulate dopamine receptors in the striatum. Ropinirole is completely absorbed after oral administration. It is extensively metabolized by CYP1A2 to inactive metabolites that are mainly excreted in the urine.

Salbutamol

Airomir® (POM)
Aerosol inhalation: 100 micrograms/metered dose (200-dose unit).
Autohaler: 100 micrograms/metered dose (200-dose breath-actuated unit).

Asmasal Clickhaler® (POM)
Dry powder for inhalation: 95 micrograms/metered dose (200-dose unit).

Salamol Easi-Breathe® (POM)
Aerosol inhalation: 100 micrograms/metered dose (200-dose breath-actuated unit).

Salbulin Novolizer® (POM)
Dry powder for inhalation: 100 micrograms/metered dose (200-refillable dose).

Ventolin® (POM)
Dry powder for inhalation: 200 micrograms/blister (60 doses via Accuhaler®).
Aerosol inhalation: 100 micrograms/metered dose (200-dose unit).
Nebulizer solution: 2.5mg/2.5mL (20 unit dose vials); 5mg/5mL (20-unit dose vials).
Respirator solution: 5mg/mL (20mL multidose bottle).

Generic (POM)
Aerosol inhalation: 100 micrograms/metered dose (200-dose unit).
Dry powder for inhalation: 100 micrograms/metered dose (200-dose unit).
Inhalation powder (Cyclocaps® capsules for use with Cyclohaler®): 200 micrograms (120); 400 micrograms (120).
Nebulizer solution: 2.5mg/2.5mL (20 unit dose vials); 5mg/5mL (20 unit dose vials).

Indications
- Asthma and other conditions associated with reversible airways obstruction.
- Consider nebulizer treatment for patients with persistent symptoms, despite regular inhaler therapy.

Contraindications and precautions
- Potentially serious hypokalaemia may result from β_2-agonist treatment. Caution is required if salbutamol is used in combination with theophylline and its derivatives, corticosteroids, and diuretics.
- Use with caution in patients with:
  - arrhythmias
  - cardiovascular disease
  - diabetes (may need to monitor blood glucose more frequently)
  - hypertension
  - hyperthyroidism
  - susceptibility to QT-interval prolongation

☺ Adverse effects

Common
- Tremor
- Headache
- Tachycardia.

Uncommon
- Mouth and throat irritation
- Muscle cramps.

Rare
- Hypokalaemia.

Drug interactions

Pharmacokinetic
- It is metabolized by CYP3A4, but there are no clinically significant pharmacokinetic interactions.

Pharmacodynamic
- *Corticosteroids*—increased risk of hypokalaemia.
- *Diuretics*—increased risk of hypokalaemia.
- *Non-selective β-blockers (e.g. propranolol)* antagonize effect of salbutamol—avoid concurrent use.
- *Theophylline*—risk of hypokalaemia.

⚗ Dose

Dry powder inhalation
- 200–400 micrograms PRN up to QDS.

Aerosol inhalation
- 100–200 micrograms PRN up to QDS.

Nebulized solution
- 2.5–5mg PRN up to QDS.
- Can be given more frequently in severe cases (max. dose 40mg daily), but monitor for adverse effects.

⚗ Dose adjustments

Elderly
- Usual adult doses can be used. Note, though, that the elderly are more susceptible to adverse effects.

Hepatic/renal impairment
- No specific dose reductions stated.

Additional information

- If dilution of the nebules is necessary, use only sterile sodium chloride 0.9%.
- Angina may be precipitated in susceptible patients with high doses of nebulized salbutamol.
- The patient should be reminded to clean the aerosol inhaler at least once a week by to prevent blockages.

Pharmacology

Salbutamol is a selective β_2-adrenoceptor agonist that produces a cascade of intracellular events terminating in smooth muscle relaxation. Following inhalation, up to 20% of the dose is deposited in the lungs, with the majority of the dose being swallowed (which undergoes significant first-pass metabolism).

Salmeterol

Serevent® (POM)

Dry powder for inhalation: 50 micrograms/blister (60 doses via Accuhaler® or 4 × 15 dose via Diskhaler®).
Aerosol inhalation: 25 micrograms/metered dose (120-dose unit).

Neovent® (POM)

Aerosol inhalation: 25 micrograms/metered dose (120-dose unit).
Note: this formulation contains soya lecithin, so it is contraindicated for use in patients with soya and/or peanut allergies.

Compound formulations

Seretide® 100, 250, and 500 Accuhaler® (POM)

Dry powder for inhalation, containing salmeterol 50 micrograms/blister and increasing doses of fluticasone (100, 250, and 500 micrograms/blister) (60 blisters per Accuhaler®).

Seretide® 50, 125, and 250 Evohaler® (POM)

Aerosol inhalation, containing salmeterol 25 micrograms/metered dose and increasing doses of fluticasone (50, 125, and 250 micrograms/metered dose) (120-dose unit).

Indications

- Add-on treatment of reversible airways obstruction.
- COPD.
- Prevention of exercise-induced asthma.

Contraindications and precautions

- Potentially serious hypokalaemia may result from β_2-agonist treatment. Caution is required if salbutamol is used in combination with theophylline and its derivatives, corticosteroids, and diuretics.
- Use with caution in patients with:
  - arrhythmias
  - cardiovascular disease
  - diabetes (may need to monitor blood glucose more frequently)
  - hypertension
  - hyperthyroidism
  - susceptibility to QT-interval prolongation.
- Use with caution in patients receiving CYP3A4 inhibitors (see 📖 Drug interactions, p.489).
- Salmeterol should not be used for relief of acute exacerbations of breathlessness.

😐 Adverse effects

Common

- Headache
- Muscle cramps
- Palpitations
- Tremor.

Uncommon

- Nervousness
- Tachycardia.

Rare

- Dizziness
- Hypokalaemia.

Drug interactions

Pharmacokinetic

- Is metabolized by CYP3A4. Despite very low systemic levels, there is a potential for drug interactions. Co-administration with drugs that are metabolized by, or affect the activity (induction or inhibition—see 📖 inside back cover) of this pathway may lead to clinically relevant drug interactions and the prescriber should be aware that dosage adjustments may be necessary, particularly of drugs with a narrow therapeutic index.
- *Erythromycin*—interaction is unlikely to be clinically significant. Caution if additional CYP3A4 inhibitors are prescribed.
- *Ketoconazole*—avoid combination; risk of salmeterol toxicity.

Pharmacodynamic

- *Corticosteroids*—increased risk of hypokalaemia.
- *Diuretics*—increased risk of hypokalaemia.
- *Non-selective β-blockers (e.g. propranolol)* antagonize effect of salbutamol—avoid concurrent use.
- *Theophylline*—risk of hypokalaemia.

🥄 Dose

Serevent®

- Usual dose 50 micrograms BD.
- In severe cases, dose can be increased to 100 micrograms BD.

Seretide®

- Usual dose 50 micrograms salmeterol/100 micrograms fluticasone BD (via *Accuhaler®*) *or* 25 micrograms salmeterol/50 micrograms fluticasone BD (via *Evohaler®*).
- Dose can be increased as necessary to maximum 50 micrograms salmeterol/500 micrograms fluticasone BD (via *Accuhaler®*) *or* 25 micrograms salmeterol/250 micrograms fluticasone BD (via *Evohaler®*).

🥄 Dose adjustments

Elderly

- Usual adult doses can be used. Note, though, that the elderly are more susceptible to adverse effects.

Hepatic/renal impairment

- No specific dose reductions stated for patients with hepatic impairment.
- Manufacturer states dose adjustments are unnecessary in patients with renal impairment.

Additional information

- The patient should be reminded to clean the aerosol inhaler at least once a week by to prevent blockages.
- Review need for steroid card with *Seretide®* preparations.

⟡ Pharmacology

Salmeterol is a selective long-acting β₂-adrenoceptor agonist with a duration of action lasts ~12 hours.

Senna (sennosides)

Senokot® (P)
Tablet: 7.5mg (60).
Syrup (sugar-free): 7.5mg/5mL (500mL).

Generic (P)
Tablet: 7.5mg (60).
Note: senna is available as a GSL medicine provided the maximum dose does not exceed 15mg.

Indications
• Management of constipation.

Contraindications and precautions
• Contraindicated in intestinal obstruction.
• Avoid in patients with abdominal pain of unknown origin.

☺ Adverse effects
• May cause abdominal cramps.

Drug interactions
Pharmacokinetic
• No known pharmacokinetic interactions.

Pharmacodynamic
• *Anticholinergics*—antagonizes the laxative effect.
• *Cyclizine*—antagonizes the laxative effect.
• *Opioids*—antagonizes the laxative effect.
• *5-HT₃ antagonists*—antagonizes the laxative effect.
• *TCAs*—antagonizes the laxative effect.

Dose
• Initial dose 7.5–15mg PO ON, usually in combination with a stool softener.
• Higher doses may well be necessary for patients receiving opioids.
  The licensed maximum dose is 30mg PO ON, but as much as 60mg in divided doses may be necessary.

Dose adjustments
Elderly
• No specific dose adjustments recommended by the manufacturer.

Hepatic/renal impairment
• No specific dose adjustments recommended by the manufacturer.

Additional information
• Laxative effect usually evident within 8–12 hours.

⟐ Pharmacology
Sennosides are inactive glycosides that pass through to the large intestine, where they are hydrolyzed by bacteria to the active anthraquinone fraction. This stimulates peristalsis via the submucosal and myenteric nerve plexuses. Very little reaches the systemic circulation.

Sertraline

Lustral® *(POM)*
Tablet (scored): 50mg (28); 100mg (28).

Generic (POM)
Tablet: 50mg (28); 100mg (28).

Indications

- Depression (including anxiety)
- Obsessive–compulsive disorder
- ¥Cholestatic pruritus[1]
- ¥Delirium/agitation (including that associated with dementia).[2]

Contraindications and precautions

- Contraindicated for use in patients with significant hepatic impairment.
- Do not use with an irreversible MAOI (including *rasagiline* and *selegiline*), or within 14 days of stopping one, or at least 24 hours after discontinuation of a reversible MAOI (e.g. moclobemide, linezolid). At least 7 days should elapse after discontinuing sertraline before starting a MAOI or reversible MAOI. Note that in exceptional circumstances linezolid may be given with sertraline, but the patient must be closely monitored for symptoms of serotonin syndrome (see 📖 Box 1.9, p.16).
- Depression is associated with an increased risk of suicidal thoughts, self-harm, and suicide which persists until remission. Note that that the risk of suicide may increase during initial treatment.
- Hyponatraemia should be considered in all patients who develop drowsiness, confusion, or convulsions while taking an antidepressant. Hyponatraemia has been associated with all types of antidepressants, although it is reportedly more common with SSRIs.
- Use with caution in
  - diabetes (alters glycaemic control)
  - elderly (greater risk of hyponatraemia)
  - epilepsy (lowers seizure threshold)
  - hepatic/renal impairment (see 📖 Dose adjustments, p.493).
- Avoid abrupt withdrawal as symptoms such as anxiety, dizziness, headache, nausea, and paraesthesia can occur. Although generally mild, they can be severe in some patients. Withdrawal symptoms usually occur within the first few days of discontinuing treatment and they usually resolve within 2 weeks, though they can persist in some patients for up to 3 months or longer. See 📖 Discontinuing and/or switching antidepressants, p.45 for information about switching or stopping antidepressants.
- Sertraline may increase the risk of haemorrhage (see 📖 Drug interactions, p.493).
- It may modify reactions and patients should be advised not drive (or operate machinery) if affected.

😣 Adverse effects

Very common
- Diarrhoea
- Dizziness
- Drowsiness
- Dry mouth
- Fatigue
- Headache
- Insomnia
- Nausea
- Sexual dysfunction (male).

Common
- Abdominal pain
- Agitation
- Anorexia
- Anxiety
- Appetite increased
- Attention disorder
- Chest pain
- Dysgeusia
- Dyspepsia
- Flatulence
- Hot flushes
- Hyperhidrosis
- Myalgia
- Nightmares
- Palpitations
- Paraesthesia
- Pharyngitis
- Rash
- Tinnitus
- Tremor
- Visual disturbances
- Yawning.

Uncommon
- Alopecia
- Amnesia
- Apathy
- Bronchospasm
- Convulsion
- Dry skin
- Dysphagia
- Dyspnoea
- Epistaxis
- Euphoria
- Hallucination
- Hypersalivation
- Hypertension
- Malaise
- Migraine
- Nocturia
- Oesophagitis
- Osteoarthritis
- Rhinitis
- Sexual dysfunction (female)
- Speech disorder
- Thirst
- Upper respiratory tract infection
- Urinary retention
- Urticaria
- Weakness.

Rare
- Abnormal liver function
- Diplopia
- Gastroenteritis
- Glaucoma
- Hiccups
- Hypoglycaemia
- Lymphadenopathy
- Malaena
- Mouth ulceration
- Mydriasis
- Myocardial infarction
- Paranoia
- Peripheral ischaemia
- Psychotic disorder
- Sleep walking
- Suicidal ideation
- Urinary incontinence.

Unknown
- Abnormal bleeding
- Arthralgia
- Gynaecomastia
- Hepatitis
- Movement disorders
- Pancreatitis
- Psychomotor restlessness
- Serotonin syndrome
- SIADH
- Stevens–Johnson syndrome.

Drug interactions

Pharmacokinetic

- Is a moderate inhibitor of CYP2B6, CYP2C19, CYP2D6 and CYP3A4. Sertraline is a major substrate of CYP2C19 and CYP2D6 and a minor substrate of CYP3A4. Co-administration with drugs that are metabolized by, or affect the activity (induction or inhibition—see 📖 inside back cover) of these pathways may lead to clinically relevant drug interactions and the prescriber should be aware that dosage adjustments may be necessary, particularly of drugs with a narrow therapeutic index.
- Despite being a minor substrate of CYP3A4, the manufacturer advises avoidance of *grapefruit juice*.

Pharmacodynamic

- Risk of serotonin syndrome (see 📖 Box 1.10, p.18) with:
  - MAOIs
  - Rasagiline
  - Selegiline
  - Serotonergic drugs—e.g. duloxetine, methadone, mirtazapine, TCAs, tramadol, and trazodone.
- *Anticoagulants*—potential increased risk of bleeding.
- *Carbamazepine*—increased risk of hyponatraemia.
- *Cyproheptadine*—may inhibit the effects of sertraline.
- *Diuretics*—increased risk of hyponatraemia.
- *NSAIDs*—increased risk of GI bleeding.

℞ Dose

Anxiety/depression

- Initial dose 50mg PO OD, increased if necessary to 200mg PO OD. Usual maintenance dose is 50mg PO OD.

Obsessive–compulsive disorder

- Initial dose 50mg PO OD, increased if necessary to 200mg PO OD. Usual maintenance dose is 50mg PO OD.

¥ Cholestatic pruritus

- Initial dose: 50mg PO OD, increased as necessary after 7 days to a usual maintenance of 75–100mg PO OD. Note that the effect may be short-lived.

¥ Delirium/agitation

- Initial dose 25–50mg PO OD, increased if necessary to 200mg PO OD.

℞ Dose adjustments

Elderly

- The usual adult dose can be recommended.

Hepatic/renal impairment

- Sertraline is extensively metabolized and it is contraindicated for use in patients with significant hepatic impairment.
- The manufacturer states that a lower or less frequent dose of sertraline should be used in patients with hepatic impairment.
- In renal impairment, wherever possible, doses at the lower end of the range should be used.

Additional information
- Tablets can be dispersed in water prior to administration if necessary. They do not disperse easily, however.
- Up to 10% of the Caucasian population are classified as CYP2D6 poor metabolizers which may have implications for treatment.
- If withdrawal symptoms emerge during discontinuation, increase the dose to prevent symptoms and then start to withdrawal more slowly.
- Symptoms of anxiety or panic may worsen on initial therapy. This can be minimized by using lower starting doses.
- The SSRIs sertraline and citalopram may be of use in the management of agitation and psychosis in patients with dementia.

⟡ Pharmacology
Sertraline is a potent and specific inhibitor of neuronal serotonin uptake but has little affinity for adrenergic, benzodiazepine, dopaminergic, GABA, histaminergic, muscarinic, or serotonergic receptors. At clinical doses, sertraline does impair reuptake of serotonin into platelets. Sertraline and its major metabolite are extensively metabolized and the resultant metabolites excreted in faeces and urine in equal amounts. Only a very small amount of unchanged sertraline is excreted in the urine.

References
1. Mayo MJ, Handem I, Saldana S, *et al*. Sertraline as a first-line treatment for cholestatic pruritus. *Hepatology* 2007; **45**(3):666–74.
2. Seitz DP, Adunuri N, Gill SS, *et al*. Antidepressants for agitation and psychosis in dementia. *Cochrane Database Syst Rev* 2011; **2**:CD008191.

Sevelamer

Renagel® (POM)
Tablet: 800mg sevelamer hydrochloride (180).

Renvela® (POM)
Tablet: 800mg sevelamer carbonate (180).
Powder (for oral suspension): 2.4g/sachet sevelamer carbonate (60).

Indications

* Hyperphosphataemia in adult patients receiving haemodialysis or peritoneal dialysis.

Contraindications and precautions

* Contraindicated for use in patients with bowel obstruction.

☺ Adverse effects

Very common

* Constipation
* Nausea
* Vomiting.

Common

* Abdominal pain
* Diarrhoea
* Dyspepsia
* Flatulence.

Unknown

* Bowel obstruction
* Ileus.

Drug interactions

Pharmacokinetic

* Sevelamer should not be given with the following drugs:
  * *ciclosporin*—reduced absorption
  * *ciprofloxacin* —reduced oral absorption by up to 50%
  * *mycophenolate* —reduced absorption
  * *tacrolimus* —reduced absorption.

Pharmacodynamic

* None known.

♪ Dose

* Initial dose 800mg–1.6g PO TDS with meals, then adjusted according to plasma-phosphate concentration.
* Usual range 2.4–12g PO daily in 3 divided doses.

♪ Dose adjustments

Elderly

* No specific dose adjustments recommended by the manufacturer.

Hepatic/renal impairment

* No specific dose adjustments recommended by the manufacturer.

♦ Pharmacology

Sevelamer is a phosphate binding drug used to prevent hyperphosphataemia in patients with chronic renal failure. It is taken with meals and binds to dietary phosphate thereby preventing its absorption.

Sodium valproate

Different preparations may vary in bioavailability. Therefore, it is recommended that patients should remain on the same product once treatment has been stabilized. Inclusion of the brand name on the prescription is suggested.

Standard release
Epilim® (POM)
Crushable tablet: 100mg (100).
Tablet: 200mg (100); 500mg (100).
Liquid (sugar-free): 200mg/5mL (300mL).
Syrup: 200mg/5mL (300mL).
Injection (powder): 400mg vial (with 4mL WFI for reconstitution).

Generic (POM)
Crushable tablet: 100mg (100).
Tablet: 200mg (100); 500mg (100).
Liquid (sugar-free): 200mg/5mL (300mL).
Injection: 300mg/3mL.
Includes branded-generics.

Modified release
Epilim Chrono® (POM)
Tablet: 200mg (100); 300mg (100); 500mg (100).

Epilim Chronosphere® (POM)
Granules: 50mg (30); 100mg (30); 250mg (30); 500mg (30); 750mg (30); 1000mg (30).

Episenta® (POM)
Capsules: 150mg (100); 300mg (100).
Granules: 500mg (100); 1000mg (100).

Indications
• Generalized tonic–clonic and partial seizures.

Contraindications and precautions
• Sodium valproate is contraindicated for use in patients with:
  • acute hepatic disease
  • past history or family history of liver dysfunction (especially drug-related) porphyria.
• Liver dysfunction is a rare complication of sodium valproate treatment and generally becomes apparent within the first 6 months of treatment, often in patients receiving multiple anti-epileptic drugs. Liver function should be measured before starting sodium valproate and then periodically during the first 6 months of therapy. A short-lived increase in liver enzymes is commonly seen, particularly during early treatment.
• Those particularly at risk are children <3 years and patients with metabolic or degenerative disorders, organic brain disease, or severe seizure disorders associated with mental retardation. Patients and/or

carers should be asked to contact their doctor should the following non-specific symptoms occur with sudden onset:
- abdominal pain
- anorexia
- drowsiness
- lethargy
- malaise
- oedema
- vomiting
- weakness.
- Should there be any concerns, however, the patient should be reassessed and additional LFTs (including prothrombin time) should be monitored until it returns to normal. Treatment must be discontinued if liver dysfunction is confirmed.
- Pancreatitis is a rarely reported adverse effect, but it has led to fatalities. Patients with nausea, vomiting and/or acute abdominal pain should contact their doctor.
- Haematological disorders can occur with sodium valproate, thrombocytopenia being stated as a frequent occurrence. Full blood count and INR are recommended before starting treatment and before surgery, or in case of spontaneous bruising or bleeding.
- Use with caution in hepatic and renal impairment (see 📖 Dose adjustments, p.499).
- Sodium valproate may give false positive results in testing for ketones in urine.
- Patients should be warned about the weight gain that commonly occurs with sodium valproate.
- Discontinuation should normally be done gradually and under the supervision of a specialist.
- Patients should be monitored for signs of suicidal ideation since anti-epileptic drugs have been associated with this behaviour.

😕 Adverse effects

The frequency is not defined in the usual way, but a selection of reported adverse effects are listed here.

Frequent/common
- Altered liver enzymes (usually during early treatment; short-lived, but see 📖 Contraindications and precautions, p.496)
- Diarrhoea
- GI disorders (e.g. diarrhoea, nausea; usually at the start of treatment, but improve after a few days; consider taking with or after food, or use an enteric coated formulation)
- Transient hair loss (may grow back more curly)
- Hyperammonaemia
- Thrombocytopenia
- Weight gain.

Occasional/rare
- Blood dyscrasias (e.g. anaemia, leucopenia)
- Confusion
- Hearing loss

- Hyperactivity
- Lethargy
- Rash

- Sedation
- Severe liver damage
- Vasculitis.

Very rare

- Encephalopathy
- Enuresis
- Extrapyramidal symptoms (reversible on discontinuation e.g. Parkinson's disease, dementia, postural tremor)
- Fanconi's syndrome
- Gynaecomastia
- Hirsutism

- Hyponatraemia
- Menstrual disorders
- Pancreatitis (risk reduces with increasing age)
- Peripheral oedema
- Reduced bone mineral density
- SIADH
- Systemic lupus erythematosus
- Toxic epidermal necrolysis.

Drug interaction

Pharmacokinetic

- Sodium valproate is metabolized by glucuronidation via UGTs, mitochondrial oxidation, and a minimal input from CYP2A6, CYP2B6, and CYP2C9. Sodium valproate has been shown to inhibit UGTs.
- Drugs that affect UGTs would be expected to affect serum concentrations of sodium valproate.
- *Carbamazepine*—valproate may potentiate the toxic effects of carbamazepine; plasma concentrations may need monitoring during early combined treatment; valproate plasma concentrations may be reduced.
- *Carbapenems*—reduction in plasma concentrations of valproate have been observed, occasionally resulting in seizures.
- *Erythromycin*—plasma concentrations of valproate may be increased due to reduced metabolism.
- *Phenobarbital*—increased plasma concentrations due to inhibition of metabolism by valproate (reduced glucuronidation); valproate plasma concentrations may be reduced.
- *Phenytoin*—risk of phenytoin toxicity due to displacement from protein binding sites; valproate plasma concentrations may be reduced.
- *Rifampicin*—risk of reduction in plasma concentrations of valproate.
- *Warfarin*—risk of increased INR due to displacement from protein binding sites.

Pharmacodynamic

- *Antipsychotics*—seizure threshold lowered; valproate may potentiate effects (and increase risk of adverse effects).
- *Antidepressants*—seizure threshold lowered; valproate may potentiate effects (and increase risk of adverse effects).
- *CNS depressants*—risk of excessive sedation.
- *MAOIs*—valproate may potentiate the effect.
- *Tramadol*—seizure threshold lowered.

Dose

Oral

- Initial dose 600mg PO OD or 300mg PO BD. Dose can be increased by 200mg daily every 3 days as necessary, to a maximum of 2.5g daily

Parenteral

Note: there are 2 injectable products available. Refer to 📖 Additional information for further details.

- Initial dose, 10mg/kg (usual range 400–800mg) by IV injection over 3–5min, followed by 10mg/kg in 2–4 divided doses by IV injection (over 3–5min) or IV infusion. Increase by 150–300mg at 3-day intervals until control is achieved; maximum dose 2500mg daily.
- If replacing oral treatment, give the established PO dose in 2–4 divided doses by IV injection (over 3–5min) or IV infusion; alternatively, administer as a continuous IV infusion. Maximum dose 2500mg daily.

🥄 Dose adjustments

Elderly

- No specific guidance available. Dose should be determined by seizure control.

Hepatic/renal impairment

- Valproate is contraindicated for use in patients with acute hepatic impairment. If possible, use should be avoided in patients with hepatic impairment due to the risk of hepatotoxicity. The SPC states sodium valproate and salicylates should not be used concomitantly since they share the same metabolic pathway.
- Patients with renal impairment may need a dose reduction. Treatment should be adjusted according to clinical response as plasma concentrations may be misleading (see 📖 Additional information).

Additional information

- To reconstitute *Epilim*® for injection, use the solvent provided; dissolve and extract the appropriate dose. Note that due to displacement, *the concentration of reconstituted sodium valproate is 95mg/mL.*
- *Episenta*® for injection is already in solution.
- Administer the IV infusion over 60min in at least 50mL of glucose 5% *or* NaCl 0.9%.
- Despite a tenuous relationship between plasma concentration and clinical response, there is a usually accepted therapeutic range of 50–100mg/L. There is a risk of toxicity with plasma concentrations above this level. If a satisfactory response is not obtained, plasma levels should be measured to determine whether or not they are within the therapeutic range.

🔆 Pharmacology

The exact mechanism of action of sodium valproate is presently unknown. It is believed that the action involves potentiation of the inhibitory action of GABA through mechanisms that affect the metabolism or synthesis of GABA. Sodium valproate is well absorbed from the GI tract and undergoes extensive metabolism, mainly via glucuronidation and mitochondrial ß-oxidation. A minor metabolic pathway involves cytochrome P450 isozymes, namely CYP2A6, CYP2B6 and CYP2C9. <3% of a dose is excreted unchanged.

Spironolactone

Aldactone® (POM)
Tablet: 25mg (100); 50mg (100); 100mg (28).

Generic (POM)
Tablet: 25mg (28); 50mg (28); 100mg (28).

Unlicensed Special (POM)
Oral suspension (sugar-free): 5mg/5mL, 10mg/5mL, 25mg/5mL, 50mg/5mL, 100mg/5mL
See 📖 Additional information, p.501 for supply issues.

Indications
- Congestive cardiac failure (NYHA class III or IV disease).
- Ascites associated with cirrhosis or malignancy.
- Nephrotic syndrome.
- Primary aldosteronism.

Contraindications and precautions
- Is contraindicated in patients with:
  - acute renal insufficiency
  - Addison's disease
  - anuria
  - hyperkalaemia, or whose baseline serum K^+ is >5mmol/L
  - severe renal impairment (e.g. serum creatinine is >220micromol/L).
- Monitor U&E status regularly. May cause hyperkalaemia, hyponatraemia, and a reversible hyperchloraemic metabolic acidosis.
- Spironolactone may modify reactions and patients should be advised not to drive (or operate machinery) if affected.

☺ Adverse effects
The frequency is not defined, but reported adverse effects include:

- Confusion
- Dizziness
- Drowsiness
- Gynaecomastia (related to dose and duration of therapy; is usually reversible)
- Headache
- Hyperkalaemia
- Hyponatraemia
- Nausea
- Sexual dysfunction.

Drug interactions
Pharmacokinetic
- Spironolactone may inhibit CYP2C8. Co-administration with drugs that are metabolized by, or affect the activity (induction or inhibition—see 📖 inside back cover) of this pathway may lead to clinically relevant drug interactions and the prescriber should be aware that dosage adjustments may be necessary, particularly of drugs with a narrow therapeutic index.
- *Digoxin*—half-life of digoxin is increased by spironolactone (plasma concentration increased <30%).

Pharmacodynamic

- *ACEIs*—increased risk of hyperkalaemia and additive hypotensive effect.
- *Angiotensin II antagonists*—increased risk of hyperkalaemia and additive hypotensive effect.
- *Potassium-sparing diuretics*—increased risk of hyperkalaemia and additive hypotensive effect.
- *Potassium supplements*—increased risk of hyperkalaemia.
- *NSAIDs*—may attenuate the natriuretic efficacy of diuretics due to inhibition of intrarenal synthesis of prostaglandins.

Dose

It is recommended that doses are taken with or after food. Renal function should be closely monitored during treatment. There is a lag of 3–5 days between initiation of spironolactone and the onset of the natriuretic effect.

Congestive cardiac failure

- Spironolactone should only be used in moderate–severe heart failure on the recommendation of specialist advice. There is no evidence that spironolactone is particularly effective in mild heart failure.
- Initial dose 25mg PO OM, increased if necessary to 50mg PO OM. Higher doses are indicated, but are not recommended.
- If K^+ rises to 5.5mmol/L or creatinine rises to >220micromol/L reduce dose to 25mg PO on alternate days.
- If K^+ is ≥6.0mmol/L or creatinine ≥310micromol/L, stop spironolactone immediately and seek specialist advice.
- Check U&Es at 1, 4, 8, and 12 weeks; 6, 9, and 12 months; 6-monthly thereafter.

Ascites

- Initial dose 100mg PO OM. Increase as necessary, in 100mg increments every 3–5 days, to a maximum of 400mg PO daily (in divided doses to reduce the risk of nausea).
- Stop spironolactone immediately if Na^+ <120mmol/L, or K^+ is ≥6.0mmol/L or creatinine ≥310micromol/L, and seek specialist advice.
- Consider adding furosemide (see 📖 Furosemide, p.225) if not achieving the desired effect.

Dose adjustments

Elderly

- No specific guidance available. Dose requirements should be individually titrated.

Hepatic/renal impairment

- No specific guidance available. Dose requirements should be individually titrated. Severe hepatic and renal impairment may affect metabolism and excretion.

Additional information

- Spironolactone can interfere with digoxin assays.
- Excessive liquorice intake could reduce the effectiveness of spironolactone.

- An oral suspension is available from Rosemont Pharmaceuticals Ltd as an unlicensed special (Tel: 0113 244 1999).
- Tablets may be dispersed in water immediately prior to use if necessary.
- Advise patients not to self-medicate with NSAIDs.
- As with all diuretics, if vomiting or diarrhoea develops, the patient should stop taking spironolactone and speak to a doctor.

⊙ Pharmacology

Spironolactone is a specific antagonist of aldosterone, acting primarily at aldosterone-dependent sodium–potassium pumps in the distal convoluted renal tubule. It causes increased sodium and water to be excretion, while preserving potassium. Spironolactone has a gradual onset of action that may take up to a week before effects are seen. Spironolactone is rapidly metabolized, possibly to at least 2 active metabolites, which are mainly eliminated renally.

Sucralfate

Antepsin® *(POM)*
Tablet (scored): 1g (50).
Suspension: 1g/5mL (250mL).

Indications
- Treatment of duodenal and gastric ulcer.
- Chronic gastritis.
- Prophylaxis of GI haemorrhage from stress ulceration.
- *Surface bleeding.

Contraindications and precautions
- Use with caution in patients with renal impairment (see 🕮 Dose adjustments, p.504).
- Sucralfate may modify reactions and patients should be advised not drive (or operate machinery) if affected.
- Bezoars (insoluble mass in the intestine) have been reported, especially in the seriously ill or those receiving enteral feeds.

☺ Adverse effects
The frequency is not defined, but reported adverse effects include:
- Back pain
- Bezoar formation (see 🕮 Contraindications and precautions)
- Constipation
- Diarrhoea
- Dizziness
- Drowsiness
- Dry mouth
- Flatulence
- Gastric discomfort
- Headache
- Indigestion
- Nausea/vomiting
- Rash.

Drug interactions
Pharmacokinetic
- Sucralfate can affect the absorption of several drugs (see list); administration should be separated by 2 hours:
  - ciprofloxacin
  - digoxin
  - furosemide
  - ketoconazole
  - levothyroxine
  - phenytoin
  - ranitidine
  - tetracycline
  - theophylline
  - warfarin.
- Other drugs may be affected; if there are unexpected outcomes, consider separating administration by 2 hours.
- Sucralfate and enteral feeds by NG tube should be separated by 1 hour in order to prevent bezoar formation.

Pharmacodynamic
- No known pharmacodynamic interactions.

♣ Dose

Treatment of duodenal and gastric ulcer and chronic gastritis

- 2g PO BD (on rising and at bedtime) or 1g PO QDS 1 hour before meals and at bedtime.
- Should be taken for 4–6 weeks or, in resistant cases, up to 12 weeks.
- Dose can be increased if necessary to a maximum of 8g daily.

Stress ulceration

- Usual dose 1g PO 6 times a day; can be increased to a maximum of 8g PO daily.

¥ Surface bleeding

- 1–2g PO BD (as suspension) rinsed around mouth for oral bleeding.
- 2g (crushed tablets) in suitable agent (e.g. *Intrasite*® gel) for bleeding wounds (other alternatives may be preferred, e.g. adrenaline, tranexamic acid).

♣ Dose adjustments

Elderly

- No specific adjustments are required, but the lowest effective dose should be used.

Hepatic/renal impairment

- No specific guidance is available for patients with hepatic impairment. Use the lowest effective dose.
- The manufacturer recommends sucralfate should be used with extreme caution and only for short-term treatment in patients with severe renal impairment. This is unlikely to apply to topical use (surface bleeding).

Additional information

- Tablets can be crushed and dispersed in water if necessary.

⟐ Pharmacology

Sucralfate is a complex of sucrose and aluminium sulphate. In solutions with a low pH (e.g. gastric acid) it forms a thick paste that has a strong negative charge. It then binds to exposed positively-charged proteins located within or around ulcers forming a physical barrier, protecting the ulcer from further direct injury. Sucralfate is poorly absorbed from the GI tract. Any amounts that are absorbed are excreted primarily in the urine.

Reference

1. Masuelli L, Tumino G, Turriziani M, et al. Topical use of sucralfate in epithelial wound healing: clinical evidences and molecular mechanisms of action. *Recent Pat Inflamm Allergy Drug Discov* 2010; **4**(1):25–36.

Tamoxifen

Generic (POM)
Tablet: 10mg (30); 20mg (30).
Oral solution: 10mg/5mL (150mL).

Indications
- Breast cancer
- Anovulatory infertility.

Contraindications and precautions
- Tamoxifen is linked to an increased risk of endometrial changes including hyperplasia, polyps, cancer, and uterine sarcoma. Any patient with unexpected or abnormal gynaecological symptoms, especially vaginal bleeding, should be investigated.
- There is a 2–3 times increase in risk of VTE in patients taking tamoxifen. Long-term anticoagulant prophylaxis may be necessary for some patients who have multiple risk factors for VTE.
- Increased bone pain, tumour pain, and local disease flare are sometimes associated with a good tumour response shortly after starting tamoxifen, and generally subside rapidly.
- Avoid combination with CYP2D6 inhibitors because these may interact with tamoxifen resulting in a poorer clinical outcome (see 📖 Drug interactions).

☺ Adverse effects
The frequency is not defined, but reported adverse effects include:
- Alopecia
- Fluid retention
- Headache
- Hot flushes
- Hypercalcaemia (may occur on initiation of therapy)
- Light-headedness
- Liver enzyme changes
- Mood changes (e.g. depression)
- Nausea
- Pruritus vulvae
- Tumour flare (e.g. bone pain)
- Vaginal bleeding
- Vaginal discharge.

Drug interactions
Pharmacokinetic
- Tamoxifen is a major substrate of CYP2C8/9, CYP2D6, and CYP3A4. Co-administration with drugs that are metabolized by, or affect the activity (induction or inhibition—see 📖 inside back cover) of these pathways may lead to clinically relevant drug interactions and the prescriber should be aware that dosage adjustments may be necessary, particularly of drugs with a narrow therapeutic index.

- Co-administration with certain CYP2D6 inhibitors (e.g. *paroxetine*) has been shown to reduce the plasma levels of the potent anti-oestrogen endoxifen. The precise clinical significance of this interaction is presently unknown, but the MHRA has recently advised co-administration of CYP2D6 inhibitors should be avoided. Patients who are CYP2D6 poor metabolizers may possibly have poorer than expected outcomes with tamoxifen.

Pharmacodynamic
- *Warfarin*—increased anticoagulant sensitivity. Mechanism unknown.

⚬ Dose
Breast cancer
- 20mg PO OD. No evidence exists for superiority of higher doses.

⚬ Dose adjustments
Elderly
- Usual adult doses can be used.

Hepatic/renal impairment
- No specific guidance is available for use in liver impairment. In view of the extensive metabolism of tamoxifen, the patient may be more susceptible to adverse effects and/or treatment failure.
- No dose adjustments are necessary for patients with renal impairment.

⚬ Pharmacology
Tamoxifen is a non-steroidal anti-oestrogen that has both oestrogen antagonist and agonist activity. It acts as an antagonist on breast tissue and as an agonist in the endometrium, bone, and lipids. The precise mechanism of action is unknown, but the effect of tamoxifen is mediated by its metabolites, 4-hydroxytamoxifen and endoxifen. The formation of these active metabolites is catalysed by CYP2D6. It is also metabolized by several other cytochrome P450 isoenzymes (CYP2C8/9 and CYP3A4).

Tamsulosin

Modified release

Flomaxtra® XL (POM)
Tablet: 400 micrograms (30).

Generic (POM)
Capsule: 400 micrograms (30).
Note: tamsulosin hydrochloride 400microgram capsules (*Flomax Relief®* MR) can be sold over the counter for the treatment of functional symptoms of benign prostatic hyperplasia in men aged 45–75 years for up to 6 weeks before clinical assessment by a doctor.

Indications

- Benign prostatic hyperplasia.

Contraindications and precautions

- Contraindicated for use in patients with:
  - postural hypotension
  - severe hepatic impairment.
- Use with caution in patients with severe renal impairment.

☺ Adverse effects

Common

- Dizziness
- Headache
- Sexual dysfunction
- Weakness.

Uncommon

- Constipation
- Diarrhoea
- Nausea
- Palpitations
- Rhinitis
- Vomiting.

Unknown

- Blurred vision
- Drowsiness
- Dry mouth
- Intraoperative floppy iris syndrome (caution before cataract surgery)
- Oedema.

Drug interactions

Pharmacokinetic

- Tamsulosin is a substrate of CYP2D6 and CYP3A4. Co-administration with drugs that are metabolized by, or affect the activity (induction or inhibition—see 📖 inside back cover) of these pathways may lead to clinically relevant drug interactions and the prescriber should be aware

that dosage adjustments may be necessary, particularly of drugs with a narrow therapeutic index.
- Avoid excessive amounts of grapefruit juice as it may increase the bioavailability of tamsulosin through inhibition of intestinal CYP3A4.

Pharmacodynamic
- The following drugs can potentially increase the risk of postural hypotension:
  - diuretics
  - levomepromazine
  - sildenafil
  - tadalafil.

Dose
- 400 micrograms PO OD.

Dose adjustments
Elderly
- Dose adjustments are unnecessary.

Hepatic/renal impairment
- No specific guidance is available for patients with hepatic impairment. Given that tamsulosin is extensively metabolized, the patient should be closely monitored.
- The manufacturer recommends that patients with severe renal impairment (CrCl <10mL/min) should be treated with caution.

Pharmacology
Tamsulosin is a selective antagonist of α_{1A}-adrenoceptors, which results in relaxation of the smooth muscle of the prostate and bladder neck. Tamsulosin is extensively metabolized by CYP2D6 and CYP3A4, but the complete pharmacokinetic profile has not been established.

Tapentadol

Standard release
Palexia® (CD2 POM)
Tablet: 50mg (28; 56); 75mg (28; 56).

Modified release
Palexia SR® (CD2 POM)
Tablet: 50mg (28; 56); 100mg (28; 56); 150mg (56); 200mg (56); 250mg (56).

Note: tapentadol is a Schedule 2 CD. Refer to Legal categories of medicines, p.21 for further information.

Indications
- Management of severe chronic pain (*Palexia SR®*).
- Relief of moderate to severe acute pain (*Palexia®*).

Contraindications and precautions
- Tapentadol is contraindicated for use in:
  - acute intoxication of CNS depressants, including alcohol
  - acute or severe asthma
  - hypercapnia (e.g. patients with raised intracranial pressure)
  - paralytic ileus
  - respiratory depression.
- Do not use with a MAOI, or within 14 days of stopping one.
- Use with caution in:
  - biliary disease/acute pancreatitis (may cause spasm of sphincter of Oddi)
  - brain tumour
  - epilepsy
  - head injury
  - hepatic impairment (see Dose adjustments, p.511)
  - renal impairment (see Dose adjustments, p.511).
- Although no specific or significant issues have been identified upon abrupt withdrawal, the manufacturer recommends that the dose is gradually tapered upon discontinuation.
- Tapentadol may modify reactions and patients should be advised not drive (or operate machinery) if affected.

☺ Adverse effects
Very common
- Constipation
- Dizziness
- Drowsiness
- Headache
- Nausea.

Common
- Anxiety
- Attention disturbances
- Diarrhoea
- Dyspepsia
- Dyspnoea

- Fatigue
- Hyperhidrosis
- Nervousness
- Oedema
- Restlessness
- Reduced appetite
- Tremor
- Vomiting
- Weakness.

Uncommon
- Agitation
- Balance disorder
- Dysarthria
- Euphoria
- Hypoaesthesia
- Hypotension
- Loss of weight
- Paraesthesia
- Perception disturbances
- Sexual dysfunction
- Urticaria
- Visual disturbance
- Withdrawal syndrome (see 📖 Additional information, p.511).

Rare
- Convulsion
- Impaired gastric emptying
- Respiratory depression

Drug interactions
Pharmacokinetic
- Tapentadol is primarily metabolized by UGT (UGT1A6, UGT1A9, and UGT2B7 isoforms); minor amounts (15%) are metabolized by CYP2C9, CYP2C19, and CYP2D6.
- *Phenobarbital*—possible risk of reduced analgesia.
- *Rifampicin*—possible risk of reduced analgesia.

Pharmacodynamic
- *Antihypertensives*—increased risk of hypotension.
- *CNS depressants*—risk of excessive sedation.
- *Haloperidol*—may be an additive hypotensive effect.
- *Ketamine*—there is a potential opioid-sparing effect with ketamine and the dose of tapentadol may need reducing.
- *Levomepromazine*—may be an additive hypotensive effect.
- *MAOIs and linezolid*—avoid concurrent use.
- *SSRIs*—serotonin syndrome has been reported in isolated cases with tapentadol and serotonergic drugs such as SSRIs.

💊 Dose
The initial dose of tapentadol depends upon the patient's previous opioid requirements. Refer to 📖 Additional information, p.511.

Standard release
- Initial dose is 50mg PO every 4–6 hours. The dose is then increased as necessary until a stable dose is attained. Doses >600mg daily are presently not recommended.

Modified release
- For opioid naïve patients, initial dose is 50mg PO BD. The dose can then be titrated as necessary in increments of 50mg BD every 3 days. Doses >250mg BD are presently not recommended.

Dose adjustments

Elderly
- Dose adjustments are unnecessary.

Hepatic/renal impairment
- Patients with mild hepatic impairment do not need any dosage adjustments. In patients with moderate hepatic impairment, an initial dose of *Palexia SR*® 50mg PO OD, or *Palexia*® 50mg PO 8 hourly is recommended with further dose increases as necessary.
- In patients with mild or moderate renal impairment a dosage adjustment is not required.
- There is no data for administration in patients with severe hepatic or renal impairment.

Additional information

- Tapentadol has a 50-fold lower binding affinity to the μ-opioid receptor than morphine, yet the analgesic potency of tapentadol is only 2.5 times lower than that of morphine.
- When converting from morphine or oxycodone (or others) to tapentadol, although analgesic benefit has been demonstrated, the patient should be warned that there is a risk of an opioid withdrawal syndrome, due to the lower affinity for the μ-opioid receptor.
- Tapentadol 100mg PO is considered to produce similar analgesia to morphine 40mg PO and oxycodone 20mg PO.
- Refer to Ⅲ Management of pain: opioid substitution, p.32 for further information regarding opioid dose equivalences.
- *Palexia SR*® must be swallowed whole, not divided or chewed.
- For neuropathic pain, a response should be seen within 4 weeks.

✧ Pharmacology
Tapentadol is the first of a new class of drug, called MOR-NRI (μ-opioid receptor agonist, noradrenaline reuptake inhibitor). It is a novel analgesic that combines 2 mechanisms of action. Unlike tramadol, tapentadol does not require metabolic activation, there is no relevant serotonin activity and it exists only as a single enantiomer. The 2 distinct pharmacological profiles may explain the efficacy demonstrated in nociceptive and neuro-pathic pains. Tapentadol is extensively metabolized via glucuronidation, with some minor metabolic routes involving CYP2C9, CYP2C19, and CYP2D6. <3% is excreted renally as unchanged drug.

Temazepam

Generic (CD3 POM)
Tablet: 10mg (28); 20mg (28).
Oral solution: 10mg/5mL (300mL).
Sugar-free formulations are available.
Note: discard 3 months after opening.

- Note: temazepam is a Schedule 3 CD. Refer to ☐ Legal categories of medicines, p.21 for further information.

Indications
- Short-term treatment of sleep disturbances.

Contraindications and precautions
- Temazepam is contraindicated for use in patients with the following conditions:
  - acute narrow-angle glaucoma
  - mild anxiety states
  - myasthenia gravis
  - phobic or obsessional state
  - severe hepatic insufficiency
  - severe respiratory insufficiency
  - sleep apnoea syndrome.
- Temazepam should not be used alone in the treatment of depression or anxiety associated with depression due to the risk of precipitation of suicide.
- Use with caution if there is a history of drug or alcohol abuse.
- Dose reductions may be necessary in the elderly (see ☐ Dose adjustment, p.513).
- Avoid abrupt withdrawal, even if short-duration treatment. The risk of dependence increases with dose and duration of treatment. Prolonged use of benzodiazepines may result in the development of dependence with subsequent withdrawal symptoms on cessation of use, e.g. agitation, anxiety, confusion, headaches, restlessness, sleep disturbances (e.g. broken sleep with vivid dreams; may persist for several weeks after withdrawal), sweating, and tremor. Gradual withdrawal is advised.
- The oral solution contains 10% v/v ethanol.
- Temazepam may modify reactions and patients should be advised not drive (or operate machinery) if affected.

☺ Adverse effects
The frequency is not defined, but reported adverse effects include:
- Anterograde amnesia
- Ataxia
- Confusion
- Depression
- Dizziness
- Drowsiness
- Fatigue
- Hallucinations

- Headache
- Muscle weakness
- Nightmares
- Paradoxical events such as agitation, irritability and restlessness
- Respiratory depression
- Sexual dysfunction
- Sleep disturbance
- Visual disturbances.

Drug interactions

Pharmacokinetic
- Is a minor substrate of CYP2C19 and is unlikely to be affected by inducers/inhibitors.
- Pharmacokinetic interactions are likely to be minimal in comparison to the other benzodiazepines.

Pharmacodynamic
- *Alcohol*—may precipitate seizures.
- *Antidepressants*—reduced seizure threshold.
- *Antipsychotics*—reduced seizure threshold.
- *Baclofen*—increased risk of sedation.
- *CNS depressants*—additive sedative effect.

Dose
- 10–20mg PO ON. This can be increased to 30–40mg PO ON as necessary.

Dose adjustments

Elderly
- Half the usual adult dose is suggested.

Hepatic/renal impairment
- No specific guidance is available. The dose of temazepam must be carefully adjusted to individual requirements.

Additional information
- Tablets may be crushed and dispersed in water immediately prior to administration if necessary.

Pharmacology

Temazepam potentiates the action of GABA, resulting in increased neuronal inhibition and CNS depression, especially in limbic system and reticular formation. It is well absorbed and undergoes extensive hepatic metabolism through conjugation. Enterohepatic recirculation is anticipated.

Thalidomide

Thalidomide Celgene® (POM)
Capsule: 50mg (28).

Indications
- Multiple myeloma
- *Cancer cachexia[1]
- *Paraneoplastic sweating[2]
- *Management of tumour-related gastric bleeding.[3]

Contraindications and precautions
- Must not be used in the following circumstances:
  - pregnant women
  - women of childbearing potential unless all the conditions of the Thalidomide Celgene Pregnancy Prevention Programme are met (see manufacturer's SPC).
- The conditions of the Thalidomide Celgene Pregnancy Prevention Programme (see manufacturer's SPC) must be fulfilled for all male and female patients.
- For women of childbearing potential, prescriptions for thalidomide should not exceed 4 weeks. Dispensing should occur within 7 days of the date of issue. For other patients, supply should be limited to 12 weeks.
- Thromboembolism and peripheral neuropathy have been reported to occur with thalidomide. Use cautiously with drugs that may increase the risk of thromboembolism or peripheral neuropathy (see 🕮 Drug interactions, p.515).

- Patients prescribed thalidomide are at an increased risk of arterial and VTE (including cerebrovascular events, DVT, myocardial infarction, and PE). Thromboprophylaxis should be administered for at least the first 5 months of treatment especially in patients with additional thrombotic risk factors (e.g. LMWH, warfarin). Thalidomide must be discontinued if the patient experiences a thromboembolic event. Once the patient is stabilized on appropriate anticoagulant treatment, thalidomide can be re-started. The anticoagulant must be continued throughout the course of thalidomide treatment.
- Peripheral neuropathy can present with the following symptoms:
  - abnormal co-ordination
  - dysaesthesia
  - paraesthesia
  - weakness.
- Patients presenting with these symptoms should be assessed according the manufacturer's SPC. Treatment may be withheld or discontinued.

- Unused capsules should be returned to a pharmacy.
- Thalidomide may modify reactions and patients should be advised not to drive (or operate machinery) if affected.

☺ Adverse effects

Very common

- Anaemia
- Constipation
- Dizziness
- Drowsiness
- Dysaesthesia
- Leucopenia
- Lymphopenia

- Neutropenia
- Paraesthesia
- Peripheral neuropathy
- Peripheral oedema
- Thrombocytopenia
- Tremor.

Common

- Bradycardia
- Cardiac failure
- Confusion
- DVT
- Depression
- Dry mouth
- Dyspnoea

- Malaise
- Nausea/vomiting
- Pneumonia
- PE
- Pyrexia
- Toxic skin eruptions
- Weakness.

Drug interactions

Pharmacokinetic

- Thalidomide does not appear to be metabolized by the liver. Clinically significant pharmacokinetic drug interactions have not been reported.

Pharmacodynamic

- *Anti-arrhythmics*—increased risk of bradycardia.
- *Bisphosphonates*—increased risk of renal impairment (in treatment of multiple myeloma).
- *CNS depressants*—risk of excessive sedation.
- *Dexamethasone*—may increase the risk of toxic skin reactions, immunosuppression, and thromboembolic events.
- *Epoetins*—increased risk of thromboembolic events.
- *NSAIDs*—theoretical increased risk of thromboembolic events.

⚖ Dose

Multiple myeloma

- 200mg PO ON for 6-week cycle. Patient can receive a maximum of 12 cycles.

¥ Cancer cachexia

- 50–100mg PO ON. Further dose increases up to 200mg PO ON may be considered.

¥ Paraneoplastic sweating

- 50–100mg PO ON. Further dose increases up to 200mg PO ON may be considered.

¥ Management of tumour-related gastric bleeding

- 100–300mg PO ON
- Used in combination with other agents such as sucralfate and PPIs.

🎭 Dose adjustments

Elderly

• No dose adjustments are necessary.

Hepatic/renal impairment

• There are no specific instructions for dose adjustment in liver or renal impairment. The lowest effective dose should be prescribed and the patient should be closely monitored.

Additional information

• The capsule must not be broken/opened; it must be swallowed whole.

⟳ Pharmacology

Thalidomide is an immunomodulatory agent that also has anti-inflammatory and anti-angiogenic properties. The mechanism of action of thalidomide is not completely understood, although it has been shown to inhibit the synthesis of tumour necrosis factor (TNF)-α and modulates the effects of other cytokines. The exact metabolic pathway of thalidomide is unknown, but it is believed not to involve the cytochrome P450 system, but undergoes non-enzymatic hydrolysis in plasma.

References

1. Davis M, Lasheen W, Walsh D, *et al.* A Phase II Dose Titration Study of Thalidomide for Cancer-Associated Anorexia. *J Pain Symptom Manage* 2012; **43**(1):78–86.
2. Deaner PB. The use of thalidomide in the management of severe sweating in patients with advanced malignancy: trial report. *Palliat Med* 2000; **14**(5):429–31.
3. Lambert K, Ward J. The use of thalidomide in the management of bleeding from a gastric cancer. *Palliat Med* 2009; **23**(5):473–5.

Theophylline

It is not possible to ensure the interchangeability of different makes of modified release. Therefore, it is recommended that patients should remain on the same product once treatment has been stabilized. Inclusion of the brand name on the prescription is suggested.

Standard release
Unlicensed Special (P)
Liquid: 60mg/5mL (300mL).

Modified release
Nuelin SA® (P)
Tablet: 175mg (60); 250mg (scored, 60).

Slo-Phyllin® (P)
Capsule: 60mg (56); 125mg (56); 250mg (56).

Uniphyllin® (P)
Tablet (scored): 200mg (56); 300mg (56); 400mg (56).

Aminophylline
Modified release
Phyllocontin Continus® (P)
Tablet: 225mg (56); 350mg (56).

Indications
- Prophylaxis and treatment of reversible bronchospasm.

Contraindications and precautions
- Contraindicated for use in patients with porphyria.
- Potentially serious hypokalaemia may result from theophylline treatment, particularly if used in combination with β_2-agonists, corticosteroids, and diuretics.
- Use with caution in the following circumstances:
  - acute febrile illness
  - cardiac arrhythmias
  - chronic alcoholism
  - CHF (increased half-life)
  - elderly (increased half-life)
  - hepatic impairment (increased half-life)
  - hyperthyroidism
  - peptic ulcer
  - severe hypertension.

☺ Adverse effects
The frequency is not defined, but reported adverse effects include:
- Abdominal discomfort
- Diarrhoea
- Gastric irritation

- Headache
- Hypotension
- Insomnia
- Nausea/vomiting
- Palpitations.

Drug interactions

Pharmacokinetic

- Is a major substrate of CYP1A2 and CYP2E1; it is also metabolized by CYP3A4 and xanthine oxidase to a lesser extent. Co-administration with drugs that are metabolized by, or affect the activity (induction or inhibition—see 📖 inside back cover) of these pathways may lead to clinically relevant drug interactions and the prescriber should be aware that dosage adjustments may be necessary, particularly of drugs with a narrow therapeutic index.
- Theophylline may be affected by many drugs; several interactions are listed here, but refer to 📖 inside back cover for a list of drugs that may potentially affect theophylline.
- *Allopurinol*—may increase the plasma concentration of theophylline.
- *Amiodarone*—may increase the plasma concentration of theophylline.
- *Carbamazepine*—reduces the plasma concentration of theophylline.
- *Ciprofloxacin*—can increase the plasma concentration of theophylline.
- *Erythromycin*—can increase the plasma concentration of theophylline.
- *Phenobarbital*—reduces the plasma concentration of theophylline.
- *Phenytoin*—reduces the plasma concentration of theophylline.
- *Rifampicin*—reduces the plasma concentration of theophylline.
- Note that smoking and chronic alcohol consumption increase the clearance of theophylline (induce CYP1A2/CYP2E1). If a patient stops smoking, ensure the dose of theophylline is closely monitored. See 📖 Box 1.9, p.16.

Pharmacodynamic

- *β_2-agonists*—increased risk of hypokalaemia.
- *Corticosteroids*—increased risk of hypokalaemia.
- *Diuretics*—increased risk of hypokalaemia.

💊 Dose

Standard release

- Usually initiate treatment with m/r formulation and use liquid for patients with difficulty swallowing. Administer TDS. When converting to liquid, monitor plasma concentrations.

Modified release

Nuelin SA®

- Initial dose 175mg PO BD. The dose is adjusted according to plasma concentrations.

Slo-Phyllin®

- Initial dose 250mg PO BD. The dose is adjusted according to plasma concentrations.

Uniphyllin®
- Initial dose 200mg PO BD. The dose is adjusted according to plasma concentrations.

Phyllocontin Continus®
- Initial dose 225mg PO BD. The dose is adjusted according to plasma concentrations.

🕭 Dose adjustments

Elderly
- The lowest initial doses should be prescribed, with dose adjustments occurring based on plasma concentrations.

Hepatic/renal impairment
- Theophylline is hepatically metabolized. Although no information exists, it is advisable to initiate treatment with low doses with close monitoring of plasma concentrations.
- No dose adjustments should be necessary in renal impairment.

Additional information
- Plasma-theophylline concentration for optimum response is 10–20mg/L (55–110micromol/L). Samples should be taken 4–6 hours after a dose and at least 5 days after starting treatment. There is a narrow margin between therapeutic and toxic dose.
- Unlicensed liquid formulation is available from a variety of manufacturers.

✦ Pharmacology

Theophylline is a xanthine derivative that is chemically similar to caffeine. It competitively inhibits type III and type IV phosphodiesterase (PDE) and also binds to the adenosine A_2B receptor, blocking adenosine mediated bronchoconstriction.

It is rapidly and completely absorbed after oral administration; it is extensively metabolized by the liver via CYP1A2 and CYP2E1 in processes that are capacity limited.

Tinzaparin

Innohep® (POM)

Injection (single-dose syringe for SC use): tinzaparin sodium 10,000 units/mL, 2500 units (0.25mL syringe); 3500 units (0.35mL syringe); 4500 units (0.45mL syringe).
Injection (single-dose syringe for SC use): tinzaparin sodium 20,000 units/mL, 10,000 units (0.5mL syringe); 14,000 units (0.7mL syringe), 18,000 units (0.9mL syringe).
Injection (vial): tinzaparin sodium 20,000 units/2mL.
Injection (vial): tinzaparin sodium 40,000 units/2mL.

Indications
- Treatment and prophylaxis of DVT and PE.
- Other indications apply but are not normally relevant in palliative care.

Contraindications and precautions
- Tinzaparin is contraindicated for use in patients with:
  - active gastric or duodenal ulceration
  - acute bacterial endocarditis
  - current or history of heparin-induced thrombocytopenia
  - recent haemorrhagic stroke
  - severe liver insufficiency
  - spinal anaesthesia
  - uncontrolled severe hypertension.
- Use with caution in patients with an increased risk of bleeding complications:
  - brain tumours (increased risk of intracranial bleeding)
  - concurrent use of anticoagulant/antiplatelet agents/NSAIDs (see 📖 Drug interactions, p.521)
  - diabetes mellitus (increased risk of hyperkalaemia and metabolic acidosis)
  - renal impairment (see 📖 Dose adjustments, p.522)
  - retinopathy (hypertensive or diabetic)
  - surgery
  - trauma.
- A baseline platelet count should be taken prior to initiating treatment and monitored closely during the first 3 weeks (e.g. every 2–4 days) and regularly thereafter.
- Advice should be sought from anaesthetic colleagues if considering an epidural intervention in a patient receiving tinzaparin due to the risk of spinal haematoma.
- LMWH can inhibit aldosterone secretion, which can cause hyperkalaemia. Patients with pre-existing renal impairment are more at risk. Potassium should be measured in patients at risk prior to starting a LMWH and monitored regularly thereafter, especially if treatment is prolonged beyond 7 days.
- *Prophylactic doses of tinzaparin are not sufficient to prevent valve thrombosis in patients with prosthetic heart valves.*
- Not for IM use.

☺ Adverse effects

Very common
- Anaemia
- Haemorrhage.

Common
- Injection site reactions (local irritation, pain, bruising).

Uncommon
- Allergic reactions (injection also contains metabisulphate)
- Headache
- Pruritus
- Raised liver transaminases (improve upon cessation)
- Rash
- Thrombocytopenia
- Urticaria.

Rare
- Skin necrosis.

Unknown
- Angio-oedema
- Epidural or spinal haematoma
- Heparin-induced thrombocytopenia
- Hyperkalaemia
- Hypoaldosteronism
- Osteoporosis with long-term treatment
- Priapism
- Prosthetic cardiac valve thrombosis (see 📖 Contraindications and precautions, p.520)
- Raised GGT
- Stevens–Johnson syndrome
- Toxic epidermal necrolysis.

Drug interactions

Pharmacokinetic
- None recognized.

Pharmacodynamic
- Drugs with anticoagulant or antiplatelet effect may enhance the effect of tinzaparin:
  - aspirin
  - clopidogrel
  - dipyridamole
  - NSAIDs.
- *ACEIs*—increased risk of hyperkalaemia.
- *Amiloride*—increased risk of hyperkalaemia.
- *Antihistamines*—possibly reduce anticoagulant effect.
- *Ascorbic acid*—possibly reduces anticoagulant effect.
- *Corticosteroids*—increased risk of GI bleeding.
- *Spironolactone*—increased risk of hyperkalaemia.
- *SSRIs*—increased risk of bleeding.

⚗️ Dose

Treatment of DVT and PE
- Usual dose 175 units/kg SC OD.
- Patients usually start oral anticoagulation at the same time and continue both until the INR is within the target range. This generally takes 6 days. However, cancer patients unsuitable for oral anticoagulation may require long-term treatment with a LMWH. Treatment is occasionally continued indefinitely.

Prophylaxis of DVT and PE
- For medical prophylaxis (including immobile cancer patients), 4500 units SC OD. The duration of treatment depends upon the risk factors identified (e.g. immobile in-patients may be considered for treatment from admission until discharge). Graduated compression stockings should be considered if LMWH is contraindicated.
- For surgical prophylaxis:
  - low–moderate risk—3500 units 2 hours before procedure and each day for 7–10 days or longer (until mobilized)
  - high risk —4500 units 12 hours before procedure, or 50 units/kg 2 hours before procedure and each day for 7–10 days or longer (until mobilized).

⚗️ Dose adjustments

Elderly
- Usual adult doses recommended.

Hepatic/renal impairment
- No specific guidance is available for patients with hepatic impairment. The manufacturer advices caution due to an increased risk of bleeding.
- No specific dosage adjustments are available for patients with renal impairment. However, monitoring of anti-factor Xa activity is suggested for patients with severe renal impairment (CrCl <30mL/min). The manufacturer states that no dose reduction should be necessary in patients with creatinine clearance levels as low as 20mL/min.

Additional information
- The 20,000-unit/2mL vial should be discarded 14 days after first use.
- The risk of heparin-induced thrombocytopenia is low with LMWH but may occur after 5–10 days. If there is a 50% reduction of the platelet count, LMWH should be stopped.

⟶ Pharmacology
Tinzaparin is a LMWH which acts mainly through its potentiation of the inhibition of Factor Xa and thrombin by antithrombin. It is eliminated primarily via the kidneys, hence the need for close monitoring in renal impairment. Local protocols may help to indicate when treatment of palliative care patients with tinzaparin is appropriate.

Tiotropium

Spiriva® (POM)
Inhalation powder: hard capsule (for use with HandiHaler® device):
18 micrograms (30).

Spiriva Respimat® (POM)
Solution for inhalation: 2.5 micrograms/metered dose (60-dose unit).

Indications

- Maintenance treatment of COPD.

Contraindications and precautions

- Tiotropium should be used with caution in patients with:
  - angle-closure glaucoma
  - bladder outflow obstruction
  - prostatic hyperplasia
  - renal impairment (see 🕮 Dose adjustments, p.524).
- Should eye pain, blurred vision, or visual halos develop, treatment
  should be discontinued and specialist advice sought immediately.

☺ Adverse effects

Common
- Dry mouth.

Uncommon
- Bronchospasm
- Cough
- Dizziness
- Headache
- Oral candidiasis
- Taste disorder.

Rare
- Visual disturbances.

Unknown
- Dental caries
- Glaucoma
- Sinusitis.

Drug interactions

Pharmacokinetic
- Although it is metabolized by CYP2D6 and CYP3A4, no interactions of
  clinical significance have been noted

Pharmacodynamic
- *Anticholinergics*—concurrent use with ipratropium may increase risk of
  adverse events.

⚬ Dose

Dry powder inhalation
- 18 micrograms OD. This dose should not be exceeded.

Solution for inhalation
• 5 micrograms OD. This dose should not be exceeded.

♣ Dose adjustments
Elderly
• No dose adjustment is necessary.

Hepatic/renal impairment
• No dose reduction is necessary in patients with hepatic impairment.
• Tiotropium may accumulate in patients with renal impairment. In patients with moderate to severe renal impairment (CrCl ≤50mL/min), tiotropium should be used only if the expected benefit outweighs the potential risk. There is no information for severe renal impairment.

Additional information
• The bronchodilatory effect may not occur for up to 2 hours. Tiotropium must not be used for acute episodes of breathlessness.
• If nebulized ipratropium therapy is initiated, ensure tiotropium is withdrawn.

♦ Pharmacology
Tiotropium bromide is a long-acting, specific, muscarinic receptor antagonist acting mainly on M3 muscarinic receptors located in the airways to produce smooth muscle relaxation. Following inhalation, a small proportion of the dose is deposited in the lungs, with the majority of the dose being swallowed. The GI absorption is negligible. Ipratropium is metabolized to inactive compounds, although the majority of the dose is excreted by the kidneys unchanged.

Tolterodine

Standard release
Detrusitol® (POM)
Tablet: 1mg (56); 2mg (56).

Modified release
Detrusitol® XL (POM)
Capsule: 4mg (28).

Indications
• Urinary frequency
• Urinary incontinence.

Contraindications and precautions
• Tolterodine is contraindicated for use in patients with:
  • myasthenia gravis
  • narrow-angle glaucoma
  • severe ulcerative colitis
  • toxic megacolon
  • urinary retention.
• Concomitant use with other drugs known to prolong QT interval and/
  or inhibit CYP3A4 should be avoided (see 📖 Drug interactions,
  p.526).
• It should be used with caution in the following:
  • autonomic neuropathy
  • cardiac arrhythmia
  • CHF
  • elderly (see 📖 Dose adjustments, p.527)
  • gastrointestinal reflux disease
  • hepatic impairment
  • hiatus hernia
  • history of QT-interval prolongation
  • hyperthyroidism
  • prostatic hypertrophy
  • pyrexia (reduces sweating)
  • renal impairment.
• Tolterodine may modify reactions and patients should be advised not
  drive (or operate machinery) if affected.
• Subtle deficits in attention, memory, and reasoning may occur with
  therapeutic dosages of anticholinergic drugs without signs of obvious
  toxicity. These deficits have often been mistaken for symptoms of early
  dementia in elderly patients.

☺ Adverse effects
Very common
• Dry mouth
• Headache.

Common
- Bronchitis
- Constipation
- Diarrhoea (overflow)
- Dizziness
- Drowsiness
- Dyspepsia
- Fatigue
- Palpitations
- Paraesthesia
- Urinary retention
- Visual disturbances
- Vertigo.

Uncommon
- Gastro-oesophageal reflux
- Memory impairment
- Tachycardia.

Unknown
- Confusion
- Hallucinations.

Drug interactions

Pharmacokinetic
- Tolterodine is metabolized by CYP3A4 and CYP2D6.
  Co-administration with drugs that are metabolized by, or affect the activity (induction or inhibition—see 📖 inside back cover) of these pathways may lead to clinically relevant drug interactions and the prescriber should be aware that dosage adjustments may be necessary, particularly of drugs with a narrow therapeutic index.
- Co-administration with CYP3A4 inhibitors (see 📖 inside back cover) can cause increased pharmacological effect due to increased serum concentrations of the parent drug and active metabolite. This is likely to be of importance in poor CYP2D6 metabolizers, or those co-prescribed both CYP3A4 and CYP2D6 inhibitors.
- The effect of grapefruit juice on the bioavailability tolterodine is unknown.

Pharmacodynamic
- *Donepezil*—effect may be antagonized.
- *β_2 agonists*—increased risk of tachycardia.
- *Cyclizine*—increased risk of anticholinergic adverse effects.
- *Domperidone*—may inhibit prokinetic effect.
- *Galantamine*—effect may be antagonized.
- *Metoclopramide*—may inhibit prokinetic effect.
- *Nefopam*—increased risk of anticholinergic adverse effects.
- *Rivastigmine*—effect may be antagonized.
- *TCAs*—increased risk of anticholinergic adverse effects.

♪ Dose

Standard release

- Initial dose 2mg PO BD; if adverse effects troublesome, reduce dose to 1mg PO BD.

Modified release

- Initial dose 4mg PO OD; revert to st
andard release should adverse effects become troublesome

♪ Dose adjustments

Elderly

- No dose adjustments are necessary.

Hepatic/renal impairment

- The manufacturer recommends that a dose of 1mg PO BD be used initially for patients with hepatic impairment or renal impairment (GFR <30mL/min). The modified release formulation is not appropriate for use in these patients.

Additional information

- Standard-release tablet can be crushed and dispersed in water immediately prior to administration if necessary.
- A response to treatment should be seen within 4 weeks.

⊙ Pharmacology

Tolterodine is a competitive muscarinic receptor antagonist with selectivity for the bladder. It is metabolized by both CYP3A4 and CYP2D6; metabolism by CYP2D6 produces a metabolite with activity similar to the parent drug which must be borne in mind should a CYP3A4 inhibitor be administered concurrently (see 📖 Drug interactions, p.526).

Tramadol

Standard release (POM)

Zamadol®
Capsule: 50mg (100).
Orodispersible tablet: 50mg (60).
Injection: 50mg/mL (2mL ampoule).

Zydol®
Capsule: 50mg (30; 100).
Soluble tablet: 50mg (20; 100).
Injection: 50mg/mL (2mL ampoule).

Generic
Capsule: 50mg (30; 100).
Oral drops: tramadol 100mg/mL (10mL).
Injection: 50mg/mL (2mL ampoule).

Modified release (POM)

12-hour release tablet formulation: 100mg (60); 150mg (60); 200mg (60).
Brands: Larapam®; Mabron®; Marol®; Zeridame SR®; Zydol SR®
12-hour release capsule formulation: 50mg (60); 100mg (60); 150mg (60); 200mg (60).
Brands: Maxitram SR®; Zamadol SR®
24-hour release tablet formulations:
Tradorec XL®: 100mg (30); 200mg (30); 300mg (30)
Zamadol 24hr®: 150mg (28); 200mg (28); 300mg (28); 400mg (28)
Zydol XL®: 150mg (28); 200mg (28); 300mg (28); 400mg (28).

Combination with paracetamol

Tramacet® (POM)
Tablet: tramadol 37.5mg, paracetamol 325mg (60).

Indications

- Moderate to severe pain.

Contraindications and precautions

- Do not use with an MAOI, or within 14 days of stopping one.
- Not be used in epilepsy not adequately controlled by treatment.
- Use with caution in patients with:
  - concurrent use of serotonergic drugs, e.g. SSRIs, TCAs (see 📖 Drug interactions, p.529)
  - epilepsy
  - head injury,
  - increased intracranial pressure,
  - porphyria
  - severe impairment of hepatic and renal function (see 📖 Dose adjustments, p.530)
- A withdrawal syndrome may occur with abrupt discontinuation; symptoms include anxiety, diarrhoea, hallucinations, nausea, pain, sweating, and tremor.

- Phenylketonuria—*Zamadol*® orodispersible tablets contain aspartame, a source of phenylalanine.
- Ultrarapid metabolizers of CYP2D6 may produce higher plasma concentrations of the active metabolite. Even at usual doses, ultrarapid metabolizers may experience symptoms of overdose, such as extreme sleepiness, confusion or shallow breathing.
- Tramadol may modify reactions and patients should be advised not drive (or operate machinery) if affected.

- The literature suggests an equianalgesic ratio for PO tramadol:PO morphine of 5:1. In practice, a 10:1 conversion is recommended because the opioid analgesia derived from tramadol in the clinical situation is unknown due to the dependence upon CYP2D6 activity (see 📖 Pharmacology, p.531).
- The prescriber has 2 options when faced with the need to commence a more potent opioid:
  - stop tramadol and either titrate the strong opioid using standard release formulations (e.g. morphine 5–10mg PO 4 hourly PRN), or convert to a m/r formulation (using a ratio of PO tramadol:PO morphine of 10:1, e.g. tramadol 200mg PO BD to *Zomorph*® 20mg PO BD)
  - gradual cross-tapering, e.g. reduce tramadol dose while introducing standard-release morphine 2.5–5mg 4-hourly PRN.

😔 Adverse effects

Very common
- Dizziness
- Nausea.

Common
- Vomiting
- Constipation
- Diarrhoea
- Dry mouth
- Sweating.

Uncommon
- Pruritus
- Rash.

Rare
- Withdrawal reactions (anxiety, diarrhoea, hallucinations, nausea, pain, sweating, and tremor).

Drug interactions

Pharmacokinetic
- Tramadol is metabolized to the opioid +M1 (see 📖 Pharmacology, p.531) by CYP2D6; additional metabolism of tramadol to inactive metabolites occurs via CYP3A4.
- Co-administration with CYP2D6 inhibitors may alter the analgesic effect of tramadol:
  - *paroxetine* has been shown to reduce the analgesic benefit of tramadol
  - the efficacy of tramadol may be altered by other CYP2D6 inhibitors, such as *duloxetine, fluoxetine, haloperidol,* and *levomepromazine*. The clinical implications of co-administration with these drugs are unknown; the prescriber should be aware of the potential for altered response.

- *Carbamazepine* reduces the analgesic benefit of tramadol through induction of CYP3A4.
- The clinical significance of co-administration of inhibitors of CYP3A4 (see 🔲 inside back cover) is presently unknown. The prescriber should be aware of the potential for interactions (increased opioid effect).
- *Warfarin*—possible risk of increased INR in susceptible patients

Pharmacodynamic

- Risk of serotonin syndrome (see 🔲 Box 1.10, p.18) with:
  - MAOIs
  - Rasagiline
  - Selegiline
  - Serotonergic drugs—e.g. duloxetine, methadone, mirtazapine, SSRIs, TCAs, trazodone, and venlafaxine.
- *Antipsychotics*—increased risk of seizures.
- *CNS depressants*—risk of excessive sedation.
- *Mirtazapine*—increased risk of seizures (and serotonin syndrome); may reduce effect of tramadol by blocking 5-HT$_3$ receptor mediated analgesia.
- *Ondansetron*—reduces effect of tramadol by blocking 5-HT$_3$ receptor mediated analgesia.
- *TCAs*—increased risk of seizures (and serotonin syndrome).

🔳 Dose

Note: 20 oral drops can be considered equivalent in therapeutic effect to 50mg s/r tramadol.

Oral

- Slow titration with m/r formulations has been shown to improve tolerability. S/r formulations are generally not as well tolerated.

Modified release

- Initial dose 100mg daily (50mg m/r PO BD or 100mg m/r PO OD) increasing to 200mg daily (100mg m/r PO BD or 200mg m/r PO OD) several days later, with further dose increases up to a maximum of 400mg PO daily.

Standard release

- Initial dose 50mg PO followed by doses of 50–100mg PO not more frequently than 4-hourly, titrating the dose according to pain severity. Maximum dose 400mg PO daily.

Tramacet®

- Initial dose 2 tablets. Additional doses can be taken as needed, not less than 6 hours apart. Total daily dose must not exceed 8 tablets.

Subcutaneous

- Rarely administered via CSCI in the UK.
- *Initial dose 100mg via CSCI, diluted with NaCl 0.9%, or WFI.

🔳 Dose adjustments

Elderly

- Dose as for adults; slow titration advised.
- Patients >75 years may need a dose reduction.

Hepatic/renal impairment

- In severe hepatic impairment, avoid the m/r formulation; the dose interval (of the s/r) should be increased to 12-hourly.
- If CrCl is <30mL/min, avoid the m/r formulation; the dose interval (of the standard formulation) should be increased to 12-hourly.
- Avoid in patients with a CrCl of <10mL/min.
- Patients undergoing haemofiltration or haemodialysis will not require post-dialysis because tramadol is removed very slowly.

Additional information

- Combination of tramadol with strong opioids has suggested a synergistic effect, such that lower doses of the more potent opioid could be used.
- *Zamadol SR*® capsules can be opened and the pellets added to jam or yoghurt. Alternatively, the pellets can be deposited on to a spoon. The spoon and pellets should be taken into the mouth, followed by a drink of water to rinse the mouth of all pellets. The pellets must not be chewed or crushed.
- The oral drops should be diluted with water before administration, independent of meals.
- *Tramacet*® may be useful for patients taking concurrent antidepressants in order to reduce the incidence of adverse effects.
- Tramadol via CSCI is compatible with dexamethasone, glycopyrronium, haloperidol, hyoscine butylbromide, levomepromazine, metoclopramide, and midazolam.
- CYP2D6 poor metabolizers cannot produce (+) M1, while ultrametabolizers may produce excessive amounts. Drug interactions can affect the metabolism of (±) tramadol via enzyme inhibition (CYP2D6) or induction (CYP3A4 only). The clinical consequences of genotype and drug interaction depend upon the type of pain being treated as the monoaminergic and opioid effects both independently produce analgesia. Genetic variations lead to the possibility of a modified adverse effect profile and varied analgesic response with tramadol.

⊙ Pharmacology

Tramadol is a centrally acting analgesic with a unique and complex pharmacology. Analgesia is produced by a synergistic interaction between 2 distinct pharmacological effects. Tramadol has a μ-opioid effect and it also activates descending antinociceptive pathways in the spinal cord via inhibition of reuptake of serotonin and noradrenaline and via pre-synaptic release of serotonin.

Tramadol is available commercially as a racemate, consisting of enantiomers (+) tramadol and (−) tramadol that have different pharmacological actions. Opioid and serotonergic actions are associated with (+) tramadol, whereas noradrenaline reuptake inhibition is associated with (−) tramadol. The only pharmacologically active metabolite (+) O-desmethyltramadol (or (+) M1) is produced by the polymorphic cytochrome CYP2D6. The opioid effect of (±) tramadol is mostly due to (+) M1. Additional metabolism of (±) tramadol and (+) M1 is catalysed by CYP3A4 and CYP2B6.

Tranexamic acid

Cyklokapron® (POM)
Tablet (scored): 500mg (60).
Injection: 500mg/5mL.

Generic (POM)
Tablet (scored): 500mg (60).

Indications
- Short-term use for haemorrhage or risk of haemorrhage in increased fibrinolysis or fibrinogenolysis.
- Local fibrinolysis (e.g. associated with prostatectomy, bladder surgery, menorrhagia, epistaxis).
- *¥*Surface bleeding (topical application).[1]

Contraindications and precautions
- Contraindications and precautions should be individually assessed when used for topical use.
- Tranexamic acid is contraindicated for use in patients with:
  - active thromboembolic disease
  - history of venous or arterial thrombosis
  - severe renal failure (risk of accumulation).
- Use with caution in the following:
  - disseminated intravascular coagulation
  - massive haematuria (risk of ureteric obstruction)
  - past history of thromboembolic disease
  - renal impairment.
- If appropriate, patients on long term treatment should have regular eye examinations and LFTs. Patients who develop visual disturbances should be withdrawn from treatment.

☺ Adverse effects
Rare
- Allergic skin reactions
- Colour vision disturbances
- Retinal/artery occlusion
- Thromboembolic events.

Very rare
- Arterial or venous thrombosis
- Diarrhoea
- Hypersensitivity reactions
- Nausea
- Vomiting.

Drug interactions
Pharmacokinetic
- None recognized.

Pharmacodynamic
- Will counteract the effect of fibrinolytic drugs.

♂ Dose
Local fibrinolysis
- Dose is quoted as 15–25mg/kg bodyweight PO BD–TDS e.g. 1g PO TDS. Can be increased as necessary to 1.5g PO TDS. Consider reducing the dose after 7 days once bleeding has stopped.

¥ Topical
- 0.5–1g (using injection, or crushed tablets if warranted) directly into wound via suitable dressing and apply pressure. Review after 10–20min.

♂ Dose adjustments
Elderly
- Usual adult doses recommended.

Hepatic/renal impairment
- No specific guidance is available for patients with hepatic impairment. Use the lowest effective dose.
- For patients with a SeCr of 120–249micromol/L, oral dose should not exceed 15mg/kg BD. For patients with a SeCr of 250–500micromol/L, oral dose should not exceed 15mg/kg OD. The drug is contraindicated in patients with severe renal impairment.

Additional information
- Tablets can be dispersed in water immediately prior to use if necessary.

♦ Pharmacology
Tranexamic acid is an antifibrinolytic drug that competitively inhibits the activation of plasminogen to plasmin.

Reference
1. Coker N, Higgins DJ. Tranexamic acid applied topically to achieve haemostasis. *Anaesthesia.* 2000; **55**(6):600–1.

Trazodone

Molipaxin® (POM)
Capsule: 50mg (84), 100mg (56).
Tablet: 150mg (28).
Liquid: 50mg/5mL (120mL bottle).

Generic (POM)
Capsule: 50mg (84), 100mg (56).
Tablet: 150mg (28).

Indications
- Depression
- Anxiety
- ¥Delirium/agitation (including that associated with dementia) [1]
- ¥Insomnia.[2]

Contraindications and precautions
- Avoid use with *MAOIs*, or within 14 days of stopping one; avoid concomitant use with *linezolid* or *moclobemide*.
- Use cautiously in patients receiving *rasagiline* or *selegiline* (see 📖 Additional information, p.536).
- Avoid sudden discontinuation, although no specific withdrawal syndrome has been reported.
- Careful dosing and regular monitoring is recommended in patients with:
  - cardiac disease
  - epilepsy
  - hypothyroidism
  - severe hepatic or renal impairment (see 📖 Dose adjustments, p.536).
- Closely monitor the patient if drugs known to affect CYP3A4 are co-administered (see 📖 Drug interactions, p.535).
- Hyponatraemia should be considered in all patients who develop drowsiness, confusion, or convulsions while taking an antidepressant. Hyponatraemia has been associated with all types of antidepressants, although it is reportedly more common with SSRIs.
- Depression is associated with an increased risk of suicidal thoughts, self-harm, and suicide which persists until remission. Note that that the risk of suicide may increase during initial treatment.
- Trazodone may modify reactions and patients should be advised not drive (or operate machinery) if affected.
- See 📖 Discontinuing and/or switching antidepressants, p.45 for information about switching or stopping antidepressants.

☺ Adverse effects
Very common
- Blurred vision
- Dizziness

- Dry mouth
- Headache
- Nausea
- Sedation.

Common
- Confusion
- Constipation
- Diarrhoea
- Fatigue
- Oedema
- Postural hypotension
- Tremor.

Uncommon
- Agitation
- Rash
- Restlessness.

Rare
- Hyponatraemia
- Pianism.

Drug interactions

Pharmacokinetic
- Trazodone is significantly metabolized by CYP3A4; additional metabolism occurs via CYP2D6. It is a weak CYP2D6 inhibitor. Co-administration with drugs that are metabolized by, or affect the activity (induction or inhibition—see 🕮 inside back cover) of these pathways may lead to clinically relevant drug interactions and the prescriber should be aware that dosage adjustments may be necessary, particularly of drugs with a narrow therapeutic index.
- *Carbamazepine*—may reduce effect of trazodone due to CYP3A4 induction. The clinical significance of co-administration with other inducers of CYP3A4 (see 🕮 inside back cover) is unknown. Increased doses of trazodone may be required.
- *Phenytoin*—possible risk of increased phenytoin toxicity (mechanism unknown).
- Avoid grapefruit juice as it may increase the bioavailability of trazodone through inhibition of intestinal CYP3A4.

Pharmacodynamic
- Risk of serotonin syndrome (see 🕮 Box 1.10, p.18) with:
  - MAOIs including linezolid
  - Rasagiline
  - Selegiline
  - Serotonergic drugs—e.g. duloxetine, methadone, mirtazapine, SSRIs, TCAs, tramadol, and venlafaxine.
- *CNS depressants*—risk of excessive sedation.

♪ Dose

Depression
- Initial dose 150mg PO ON, increasing as necessary to a usual max. of 300mg PO ON (or 150mg PO BD).

Anxiety
- Initial dose 75mg PO ON, increasing as necessary to 300mg PO ON (or 150mg PO BD).

¥ *Agitation/delirium*
- Initial dose 25–50mg PO ON, increasing as necessary to a max. of 300mg PO ON.

¥ *Insomnia*
- Initial dose 25–50mg PO ON, increasing as necessary to a usual max. of 100mg PO ON. Some patients may require higher doses.

♪ Dose adjustments

Elderly
- Age-related changes in hepatic metabolism can produce significantly higher plasma concentrations of trazodone. Dose reductions are necessary:
  - depression: 100mg PO ON or 50mg PO BD initially and increase as necessary to a maximum of 300mg PO daily
  - anxiety: 25–50mg PO ON and increase as necessary to a maximum of 300mg PO daily
  - insomnia: as for anxiety
  - agitation/delirium: as for anxiety.

Hepatic/renal impairment
- Trazodone is extensively metabolized by the liver and has been associated with hepatotoxicity. The manufacturer recommends caution when prescribing for patients with hepatic impairment. Periodic liver monitoring is suggested.
- No dose adjustments are necessary in mild–moderate renal impairment. The manufacturer advises caution when used in patients with severe renal impairment.

Additional information

- Onset of action for insomnia can be within 1–3 hours of the initial dose. Onset of action for depression usually occurs within 2–4 weeks.
- The sedative effect of trazodone may persist the following morning, particularly if the dose is too high.
- Adverse effects may be minimized by taking the dose with or after a meal.
- Presently, Clinical Knowledge Summaries (NHS Evidence) states that mirtazapine and trazodone may be used with caution in patients receiving *rasagiline* or *selegiline*.[3]
- Although there is a paucity of evidence, trazodone is occasionally used as the drug of choice to treat behavioural symptoms of delirium associated with Parkinson's disease (although

see 📖 Drug interactions, p.14). Should delirium or agitation develop in a patient with Parkinson's disease, the following is suggested:

• trazodone ± benzodiazepine
• dose reduction and/or discontinuation of anti-parkinsonian medications (anticholinergics initially, then dopamine agonists)
• low-dose quetiapine in difficult cases.

➔ Pharmacology

Trazodone blocks post-synaptic 5-HT$_{2A}$ and 5-HT$_{2C}$ receptors. At high doses, it selectively inhibits pre-synaptic serotonin re-uptake. Trazodone also antagonizes H$_1$- and α$_1$-adrenergic receptors. It has no effect on muscarinic receptors. It is well absorbed by mouth and food delays, but enhances, the amount absorbed. Trazodone is metabolized by CYP3A4 to an active metabolite, which is further metabolized by CYP2D6 to an inactive compound. Elimination is almost exclusively by urinary excretion of metabolites.

References

1. Seitz DP, Adunuri N, Gill SS, Gruneir A et al. Antidepressants for agitation and psychosis in dementia. *Cochrane Database Syst Rev* 2011; **2**:CD008191.
2. Mittur A. Trazodone: properties and utility in multiple disorders. *Expert Rev Clin Pharmacol* (2011); **4**(2):181–96.
3. NHS Evidence Clinical Knowledge Summaries (2011). Parkinson's disease —Management. Which drugs should be used in the treatment of depression in people with Parkinson's disease? Available from: M http://www.cks.nhs.uk/parkinsons_disease/management/detailed_ answers/confirmed_parkinsons_disease_primary_care/managing_non_motor_symptoms_ and_complications/depression/drug_treatment_of_depression#-380720. Accessed 3 November 2011.

Trimethoprim

Generic (POM)
Tablet: 100mg (28); 200mg (28).
Oral suspension: 50mg/5mL (100mL).

Indications
- Refer to local guidelines.
- Treatment of infections caused by trimethoprim-sensitive organisms including UTIs and respiratory tract infections.
- Long term prophylaxis of UTIs.

Contraindications and precautions
- Trimethoprim is contraindicated for use in:
  - blood dyscrasias
  - severe renal impairment (if blood levels cannot be measured —see 📖 Dose adjustments, p.539).
- Use with caution in the following:
  - elderly patients (see 📖 Dose adjustments, p.539)
  - folate deficiency
  - renal impairment (see 📖 Dose adjustments, p.539).
- With long-term treatment, patients and carers should be told how to recognize signs of blood disorders (e.g. fever, sore throat, rash, mouth ulcers, purpura, bruising or bleeding) and to seek immediate medical attention if they develop.

☺ Adverse effects
The frequency is not defined, but reported adverse effects include:
- Blood dyscrasias (depression of haematopoiesis)
- Hyperkalaemia
- Nausea
- Photosensitivity
- Pruritus
- Skin rashes
- Severe skin sensitivity reactions (e.g. erythema multiforme, toxic epidermal necrolysis)
- Vomiting.

Drug interactions
Pharmacokinetic
- Trimethoprim is a substrate of CYP2C8; it is an inhibitor of CYP2C8 and may affect CYP2C9.
- *Rifampicin*—may reduce the effect of trimethoprim.
- *Warfarin*—possible increase in INR.
- The clinical significance of co-administration with substrates of CYP2C8 (see 📖 inside back cover) is unknown. Caution is advised if trimethoprim is co-administered with drugs that are predominantly metabolized by CYP2C8. The prescriber should be aware of the potential for interactions and that dose adjustments may be necessary, particularly of drugs with a narrow therapeutic index.

Pharmacodynamic
- *ACEIs*—risk of hyperkalaemia.
- *Amiloride*—risk of hyperkalaemia.
- Co-administration with bone marrow depressants (e.g. *methotrexate*) may increase the risk of bone marrow aplasia.

Dose
Standard doses are described here. Refer to local guidelines for specific advice.
- Treatment: 200mg PO BD.
- Prophylaxis: 100mg PO ON.

Dose adjustments
Elderly
- No specific guidance, but the manufacturer states that the elderly may be more susceptible to the haematopoietic effects and a lower dose may be advisable.

Hepatic/renal impairment
- No specific guidance is available for hepatic impairment.
- Up to 60% of a dose is excreted unchanged. If CrCl 15–30mL/min, use half the normal dose after 3 days
- If CrCl <15mL/min, use half normal dose (monitor plasma-trimethoprim concentration if CrCl <10mL/min).

Additional information
- If necessary, tablets can be dispersed in water immediately prior to administration.

Pharmacology
Trimethoprim is a broad-spectrum antibiotic effective *in vitro* against a wide range of Gram-positive and aerobic Gram-negative organisms. Trimethoprim is a dihydrofolate reductase inhibitor which affects folic acid metabolism and interferes with an essential component of bacterial development. It is rapidly and almost completely absorbed after oral administration. Hepatic metabolism occurs via CYP2C8, although 40–60% of a dose is excreted unchanged in the urine within 24 hours.

Venlafaxine

Normal release
Generic (POM)
Tablet: 37.5mg (56); 75mg (56).

Modified release
Efexor XL® (POM)
Capsule: 75mg (28); 150mg (28).

Generic (POM)
Capsule: 75mg (30); 150mg (30).
Tablet: 37.5mg (30); 75mg (30); 150mg (30); 225mg (30).

Indications
- Major depressive episodes
- Generalized anxiety disorder
- Generalized social anxiety disorder
- ¥Sweats.[1,2]

Contraindications and precautions
- Venlafaxine is contraindicated for use in patients with:
  - conditions associated with high risk of cardiac arrhythmia
  - uncontrolled hypertension.
- Do not use with an irreversible MAOI (including *rasagiline* and *selegiline*), or within 14 days of stopping one; at least 7 days should be allowed after stopping venlafaxine before starting a irreversible MAOI. Note that in exceptional circumstances *linezolid* may be given with venlafaxine, but the patient must be closely monitored for symptoms of serotonin syndrome for several weeks (see 📖 Box 1.10, p.18).
- Use with caution in the following:
  - concomitant use of drugs that increase risk of bleeding (see 📖 Drug interactions, p.541)
  - diabetes (may alter glycaemic control)
  - elderly (greater risk of hyponatraemia)
  - epilepsy (lowers seizure threshold)
  - glaucoma (may cause mydriasis)
  - heart disease (monitor blood pressure);
  - hepatic and renal impairment (see 📖 Dose adjustments, p.542)
  - history of bleeding disorders.
- Depression is associated with an increased risk of suicidal thoughts, self-harm, and suicide which persists until remission. Note that that the risk of suicide may increase during initial treatment.
- May precipitate psychomotor restlessness, which usually appears during early treatment. The use of venlafaxine should be reviewed.
- Hyponatraemia should be considered in all patients who develop drowsiness, confusion, or convulsions while taking an antidepressant. Hyponatraemia has been associated with all types of antidepressants, although it is reportedly more common with SSRIs.

- Abrupt discontinuation should be avoided due to the risk of withdrawal reactions, e.g. agitation, anxiety, diarrhoea, dizziness, fatigue, headache, hyperhidrosis, nausea and/or vomiting, sensory disturbances (including paraesthesia), sleep disturbances and tremor. When stopping treatment, the dose should be reduced gradually over at least 1–2 weeks. See 📖 Discontinuing and/or switching antidepressants, p.45 for information about switching or stopping anti-depressants.
- Venlafaxine may modify reactions and patients should be advised not drive (or operate machinery) if affected.

☺ Adverse effects

Very common

- Constipation
- Dizziness
- Drowsiness
- Dry mouth
- Headache
- Hyperhidrosis (including night sweats)

- Insomnia
- Nausea (common at initiation; less likely with m/r products)
- Nervousness
- Sexual dysfunction
- Weakness.

Common

- Abdominal pain
- Abnormal dreams
- Agitation
- Anorexia
- Anxiety
- Appetite decreased
- Arthralgia
- Confusion
- Diarrhoea
- Dyspepsia
- Dyspnoea
- Hypertension

- Hypertonia
- Myalgia
- Palpitation
- Paraesthesia
- Pruritus
- Pyrexia
- Serum cholesterol increased
- Tremor
- Vasodilatation
- Visual disturbances
- Vomiting
- Yawning.

Uncommon

- Arrhythmias
- Hallucinations
- Myoclonus

- Photosensitivity
- Postural hypotension
- SIADH/hyponatraemia.

Rare

- Serotonin syndrome.

Drug interactions

Pharmacokinetic

- Venlafaxine is metabolized mainly by CYP2D6. Also metabolized by CYP3A4 which is important in CYP2D6 poor metabolizers. It is a weak inhibitor of CYP2D6. Co-administration with drugs that are metabolized by, or affect the activity (induction or inhibition—see 📖 inside back cover) of these pathways may lead to clinically relevant drug interactions and the prescriber should be aware that dosage adjustments may be necessary, particularly of drugs with a narrow therapeutic index.

- *Haloperidol*—increased risk of haloperidol adverse effects through inhibition of CYP2D6.
- The clinical significance of co-administration with inhibitors of CYP2D6 (see 📖 inside back cover) is unknown, but plasma concentrations of venlafaxine may increase. The prescriber should be aware of the potential for interactions and that dose adjustments may be necessary.
- Avoid grapefruit juice as it may increase the bioavailability of haloperidol through inhibition of intestinal CYP3A4.

Pharmacodynamic

- Risk of serotonin syndrome (see 📖 Box 1.10, p.18) with:
  - MAOIs including linezolid
  - Rasagiline
  - Selegiline
  - Serotonergic drugs—e.g. methadone, mirtazapine, SSRIs, TCAs, tramadol, and trazodone.
- *Anticoagulants*—potential increased risk of bleeding.
- *CNS depressants*—additive sedative effect.
- *Cyproheptadine*—may inhibit the effects of duloxetine.
- *Diuretics*—increased risk of hyponatraemia.
- *NSAIDs*—increased risk of GI bleeding.
- *SSRIs*—increased risk of seizures (and serotonin syndrome).
- *Tramadol*—increased risk of seizures (and serotonin syndrome).

⚡ Dose

Depression

- Initial dose 37.5mg PO BD increased if necessary after at least 3–4 weeks to 75mg PO BD. Dose may be increased further on specialist advice if necessary in steps of up to 75mg every 2–3 days to a max. 375mg PO daily.
- Alternatively, 75mg m/r PO OD, increased if necessary after at least 2 weeks to 150mg m/r PO OD. Dose can be increased to a max. of 225mg PO OD.

Generalized anxiety disorder

- 75mg m/r PO OD. Discontinue if no response after 8 weeks (withdraw over 1–2 weeks).

Generalized social anxiety disorder

- 75mg m/r PO OD. Discontinue if no response after 12 weeks (withdraw over 1–2 weeks).

¥ Sweats

- Initial dose 37.5mg PO OD. If necessary, increase after 7 days to 37.5mg PO BD (or 75mg m/r PO OD). Review treatment after 2 weeks and discontinue if no improvement (withdraw over 1–2 weeks). Higher doses have been suggested, but should be used with caution.

⚡ Dose adjustments

Elderly

- No dose adjustment is necessary but, wherever possible, lower doses should be used. Elderly are more susceptible to adverse effects.

Hepatic/renal impairment
- In patients with moderate hepatic impairment, the dose should be reduced by 50%. Avoid in severe hepatic impairment since no information is available.
  - In patients with moderate renal impairment (GFR 10–30mL/min), the dose should be reduced by 50%. Avoid in severe renal impairment (GFR <10mL/min) since no information is available.

Additional information
- Antidepressant therapeutic response is usually seen after 2–4 weeks of treatment.
- Withdrawal effects can be seen as early as a few hours after missing a dose. Ensure patients adhere to the dosing schedule.
- Venlafaxine may be preferable to gabapentin in the treatment of hot flushes associated with breast cancer.

◈ Pharmacology
Venlafaxine is a serotonin noradrenaline reuptake inhibitor (SNRI). Like duloxetine, it inhibits the reuptake of both serotonin and noradrenaline, with a weaker action on the reuptake of dopamine. It has no action at muscarinic, H_1 or α_1-adrenergic receptors. It is metabolized to its active metabolite, O-desmethylvenlafaxine (ODV), by CYP2D6. The clinical significance of inhibition of CYP2D6, or use in poor metabolizers, is unknown. An additional pathway involves CYP3A4.

References
1. Irani J, Salomon L, Oba R, et al. Efficacy of venlafaxine, medroxyprogesterone acetate, and cyproterone acetate for the treatment of vasomotor hot flushes in men taking gonadotropin-releasing hormone analogues for prostate cancer: a double-blind, randomised trial. *Lancet Oncol* 2010; **11**(2):147–54.
2. Bordeleau L, Pritchard KI, Loprinzi CL, et al. Multicenter, randomized, cross-over clinical trial of venlafaxine versus gabapentin for the management of hot flashes in breast cancer survivors. *J Clin Oncol* 2010; **28**(35):5147–52.

Warfarin

Generic (POM)
Tablet: 0.5mg (*white*, 28); 1mg (*brown*, 28); 3mg (*blue*, 28); 5mg (*pink*, 28).

Indications

- Prophylaxis of systemic embolism in patients with rheumatic heart disease and atrial fibrillation.
- Prophylaxis after insertion of prosthetic heart valves.
- Prophylaxis and treatment of venous thrombosis and pulmonary embolism.
- Transient attacks of cerebral ischaemia.

Contraindications and precautions

- Warfarin is contraindicated for use in the following circumstances:
  - bacterial endocarditis
  - haemophilia
  - peptic ulcer
  - recent surgery (within 24 hours)
  - severe hepatic impairment (use LMWH)
  - severe renal impairment
  - uncontrolled hypertension.
- INR must be measured daily or on alternate days initially and then at longer intervals depending on response but usually every 12 weeks
- For instructions on the management of bleeding—see the current edition of the *BNF*.
- Use with caution in:
  - elderly patients
  - renal impairment
  - hepatic impairment (LMWH may be preferred).

☺ Adverse effects

The frequency is not defined, but reported adverse effects include:

- Alopecia
- Diarrhoea
- Hepatic dysfunction
- Hypersensitivity
- Jaundice
- Skin necrosis
- Skin rashes
- Purple toes syndrome
- Unexplained drop in haematocrit.

If the following occur, the manufacturer advises that warfarin must be discontinued:

- Epistaxis
- Fever
- Haemothorax
- Nausea
- Pancreatitis
- Purpura
- Vomiting.

Drug interactions

There are many potential drug interactions with warfarin but as the INR is regularly monitored, it is more important to take account of the introduction or discontinuation of concurrent medication. The following list contains only those interactions most likely to be relevant in palliative care. Changes in medical conditions, especially liver involvement and marked changes in diet are also a potential source of changes in warfarin levels.

Pharmacokinetic

- Warfarin is a substrate of CYP1A2, CYP2C9, and CYP2C19. Several interactions are listed here, but refer to 📖 inside back cover for a list of drugs that may potentially affect warfarin.
- The following can enhance the effect of warfarin:
  - Alcohol (acute use)
  - Amiodarone (may take up to 2 weeks to develop)
  - Cephalosporins
  - Ciprofloxacin
  - Cranberry juice
  - Erythromycin
  - Fluconazole
  - Metronidazole
  - Miconazole
  - Mirtazapine
  - Omeprazole
  - Penicillins
  - Trimethoprim.
- The following can reduce the effect of warfarin:
  - Alcohol (chronic use)
  - Carbamazepine
  - Menadiol (vitamin K)
  - Phenobarbital
  - St John's wort
  - Sucralfate.

Pharmacodynamic

- The following drugs increase the risk of bleeding:
  - Aspirin
  - Corticosteroids
  - NSAIDs
  - SSRIs.
- *Azathioprine*—anticoagulant effect may be inhibited.

💊 Dose

- Refer to local guidelines.

Rapid anticoagulation

- 10mg PO on day 1 then subsequent doses based on INR.

Less urgent cases
- Lower loading doses can be introduced over a period of 3–4 weeks.
- The daily dose is usually between 3–9mg

₰ Dose adjustments
Elderly
- No dose reductions necessary. Titrate the dose individually.

Hepatic/renal impairment
- Avoid in severe liver disease, especially if INR is already raised. LMWH may be preferred. In moderate hepatic impairment, more frequent monitoring will be required.
- Avoid in severe renal impairment; LMWH may be preferred.

Additional information
- The use of warfarin in palliative care needs to be balanced with the burden of monitoring and drug interactions. The use of LMWH is often preferred.
- As other pre-existing conditions in may have an effect on INR, monitoring may be needed more frequently than in otherwise healthy patients who are at risk of or requiring treatment for thrombosis
- Recommended ranges of therapeutic anticoagulation are the following:
  - INR 2–2.5: prophylaxis of DVT including surgery in high risk patients
  - INR 2–3: prophylaxis in hip surgery and fractured femur operations, treatment of DVT, PE; prevention of VTE in myocardial infarction, transient ischaemic attacks, mitral stenosis with embolism, tissue prosthetic heart valves
  - INR 3–4.5: recurrent DVT and PE, mechanical prosthetic heart valves, arterial disease including myocardial infarction

⊕ Pharmacology
Warfarin is one of the coumarin anticoagulants, which act by antagonising the effects of vitamin K. The anticoagulant effects do not develop fully until 48–72 hours after dose initiation so heparins should be given in addition during that period. Warfarin is metabolized by CYP2C9 and to a lesser extent by CYP1A2 and CYP2C19. As with other drugs with a narrow therapeutic margin, particular care must be taken when drug regimes are altered. An additional complication is the effect of genetic polymorphism with warfarin metabolism, although monitoring can normalize for this.

Zoledronic acid

Zometa® (POM)
concentrate for IV infusion: 4mg/5mL.
solution for IV infusion: 4mg/100mL.

Indications

Treatment of tumour-induced hypercalcaemia (corrected calcium >3.0mmol/L).
Prevention of skeletal related events in patients with advanced malignancies involving bone.
Bone pain.¥

Contraindications and precautions

Avoid in patients with:
- severe hepatic impairment (limited data available)
- renal impairment (see 📖 Dose adjustments, p.548)
- cardiac disease (avoid fluid overload)

Assess renal function and electrolytes (e.g. calcium, magnesium) before each dose and ensure adequate hydration (especially hypercalcaemia) —dehydration increases risk of renal failure.
Consider dental treatment prior to treatment due to the risk of osteonecrosis of the jaw.

Adverse effects

Osteonecrosis of the jaw is a potential complication of bisphosphonate therapy. It has been reported in cancer patients, many who had a pre-existing local infection or recent extraction. Cancer patients are more likely to be at risk of osteonecrosis as a result of their disease, cancer therapies and blood dyscrasias. Dental examination is recommended for patients undergoing repeated infusions of zoledronic acid (and other bisphosphonates) and dental surgery should be avoided during this treatment period as healing may be delayed.

Severe and occasionally incapacitating bone, joint, and/or muscle pain has been reported with bisphosphonate use. Time to onset varies from one day to several months after initiation of treatment, but symptoms should improve upon discontinuation. Some patients will develop the same symptoms upon subsequent treatment with zoledronic acid or another bisphosphonate.

Atypical femoral fractures have been reported with bisphosphonate therapy. Although a rare occurrence, during bisphosphonate treatment patients should be advised to report any new thigh, hip or groin pain.

Very common
- Hypophosphataemia.

Common
- Anaemia
- Anorexia
- Arthralgia
- Bone pain
- Conjunctivitis
- Fever

- Flu-like syndrome (including fatigue, rigors, malaise and flushing)
- Headache
- Hypocalcaemia (more severe if patient vitamin D deficient)

- Myalgia
- Nausea/vomiting
- Renal impairment (reported after a single 4mg dose).

Uncommon

- Abdominal pain
- Acute renal failure
- Bronchoconstriction
- Constipation
- Cough
- Diarrhoea
- Dry mouth
- Dyspepsia
- Dyspnoea

- Haematuria
- Hypokalaemia
- Hypomagnesaemia
- Leucopenia
- Muscle cramps
- Osteonecrosis of the jaw
- Stomatitis
- Thrombocytopenia.

Rare

- Hyperkalaemia
- Hypernatraemia.

Unknown

- Atrial fibrillation.

Drug interactions

Pharmacokinetic

- None known.

Pharmacodynamic

- *Aminoglycosides*—may have additive hypocalcaemic effect.
- *Diuretics*—increased risk of renal impairment.
- *NSAIDs*—increased risk of renal impairment.
- *Thalidomide*—increased risk of renal impairment (in treatment of multiple myeloma).

⚗ Dose

The concentrate must be diluted with 100mL NaCl 0.9% or glucose 5% and given in no less than a 15min IV infusion.

Treatment of tumour-induced hypercalcaemia

- Ensure patients are well hydrated prior to and following administration of zoledronic acid.
- 4mg by IV infusion as a single dose.

Prevention of skeletal related events

- 4mg by IV infusion every 3–4 weeks.
- Note that calcium 500mg and vitamin D 400 units should also be taken daily

¥ Bone pain

- 4mg by IV infusion every 3–4 weeks.
- Note that calcium 500mg and vitamin D 400 units should also be taken daily

⚗ Dose adjustments

Elderly

- No dose adjustments are necessary.

Hepatic/renal impairment

The manufacturer advises caution in severe hepatic impairment due to the lack of data in this population.

Zoledronic acid is not metabolized but is excreted unchanged via the kidney. For this reason, dose adjustments are necessary in patients with renal impairment:

Hypercalcaemia:

- avoid if SeCr is >400micromol/L unless benefits outweigh the risks—seek specialist advice (ibandronate may be preferred)
- no dose adjustment is necessary if SeCr <400micromol/L

Prevention of skeletal related events and bone pain (Table 3.20).

Table 3.20 Zoledronic acid dosage for prevention of skeletal-related events and bone pain

Baseline CrCl (mL/min)	Recommended dose (in 100ml NaCl 0.9% or glucose 5% over 15min via IV infusion)	Volume of concentrate	Volume of solution for infusion to remove (replace with NaCl 0.9% or glucose 5%)
>60	4.0mg	5mL	–
50–60	3.5mg	4.4mL	12mL
40–49	3.3mg	4.1mL	18mL
30–39	3.0mg	3.8mL	25mL
<30	Not recommended in severe renal impairment		

Additional information

- Corrected serum calcium = actual serum calcium+[(40 − serum albumin g/L) × 0.02].
- In the treatment of hypercalcaemia, serum calcium levels should not be measured until 5–7 days post dose. Calcium levels start to fall after 48 hours, with a median time to normalization of 4 days and normalization in 90% of patients within 7 days. Seek specialist advice should the corrected serum Ca^{2+} concentration not return to normal after 7–10 days; a second dose of zoledronic acid can be given 7–10 days after the initial dose in such patients.
- Zoledronic acid provides a longer duration of effect before relapse compared to pamidronate (4 weeks vs. 2.5 weeks).
- The onset of treatment effect for skeletal related events is 2–3 months.
- Relief from bone pain may occur within 14 days, although it may be up to 3 months before maximum effect is seen.

Pharmacology

Zoledronic acid is a bisphosphonate that inhibits osteoclast activity, which in turn reduces bone resorption and turnover. It is excreted unchanged by the kidney.

Reference

. Lipton A. Treatment of bone metastases and bone pain with bisphosphonates. *Support Cancer Ther* 2007; **4**(2):92–100.

Zolpidem

Stilnoct® (CD4a POM)
Tablet: 5mg (28); 10mg (28).

Generic (CD4a POM)
Tablet: 5mg (28); 10mg (28).

Indications
● Short-term treatment of insomnia.

Contraindications and precautions
● Zolpidem is contraindicated for use in patients with:
  • myasthenia gravis
  • obstructive sleep apnoea
  • respiratory failure
  • severe hepatic insufficiency.
● Use with caution in patients with hepatic impairment (see 🕮 Dose adjustments, p.551).
● Lower initial doses should be used in the elderly (see 🕮 Dose adjustments, p.551).
● Sleep walking and other associated behaviours have been reported with zolpidem and are usually related to concomitant use of alcohol and other CNS-depressants, or doses above that recommended.
● Zolpidem treatment can lead to the development of physical and psychological dependence. The risk of dependence increases with dose and duration. Patients with a history of alcohol and or drug abuse also have an increased risk. Withdrawal symptoms that can occur after prolonged treatment include anxiety, hallucinations, insomnia, mood changes, restlessness, sweating, and tremor.
● Zolpidem may modify reactions and patients should be advised not drive (or operate machinery) if affected.

☺ Adverse effects
Common

● Agitation
● Anterograde amnesia
● Diarrhoea
● Dizziness
● Drowsiness

● Exacerbated insomnia
● Fatigue
● Hallucination
● Headache
● Nightmare.

Uncommon

● Confusional state
● Diplopia

● Irritability.

Unknown

● Aggression
● Anger

● Delusion
● Depression

Muscular weakness
Psychosis
Raised LFTs

- Rash
- Restlessness
- Sleep walking.

Drug interactions

Pharmacokinetic

Is metabolized by mainly by CYP3A4 with a minor pathway involving CYP1A2. Drug interactions via cytochrome inhibition may be additive. Co-administration with drugs that are metabolized by, or affect the activity (induction or inhibition—see 📖 inside back cover) of these pathways may lead to clinically relevant drug interactions and the prescriber should be aware that dosage adjustments may be necessary, particularly of drugs with a narrow therapeutic index.
The effect of grapefruit juice on the bioavailability zolpidem is unknown.

Pharmacodynamic

CNS depressants—additive sedative effect.
Sertraline—appears to be an interaction that causes excessive drowsiness and hallucinations.

💊 Dose

10mg PO ON.

💊 Dose adjustments

Elderly

Initial dose 5mg PO ON. The dose may be increased to 10mg PO ON if necessary.

Hepatic/renal impairment

Initial dose in hepatic impairment is 5mg PO ON. The dose can be cautiously increased to 10mg PO ON if necessary. Note that zolpidem is contraindicated for patients with severe hepatic impairment.
- No specific guidance is available for patients with renal impairment.

Additional information

- The tablets can be crushed and dispersed in water immediately before use.

⊘ Pharmacology

Zolpidem is a short-acting non-benzodiazepine hypnotic drug that initiates and sustains sleep without affecting total REM sleep. It interacts preferentially with the GABA receptor via the ω_1 receptor subtype which leads to the sedative effects seen but also the lack of muscle relaxant effects. It is extensively metabolized by CYP3A4, with additional metabolism involving CYP1A2. All metabolites are inactive and are eliminated in the urine and faeces.

Zopiclone

Zimovane LS® (POM)
Tablet: 3.75mg (28).

Zimovane® (POM)
Tablet (scored): 7.5mg (28).

Generic (POM)
Tablet: 3.75mg (28); 7.5mg (28).

Indications
- Short-term treatment of insomnia.

Contraindications and precautions
- Zopiclone is contraindicated for use in patients with:
  - myasthenia gravis
  - respiratory failure
  - severe sleep apnoea syndrome
  - severe hepatic insufficiency.
- Use with caution in patients with hepatic and/or renal impairment (see 📖 Dose adjustments, p.553).
- Lower initial doses should be used in the elderly (see 📖 Dose adjustments, p.553).
- Zopiclone treatment can lead to the development of physical and psychological dependence. The risk of dependence increases with dose and duration. Patients with a history of alcohol and or drug abuse also have an increased risk.
- If treatment is limited to 4 weeks or less, discontinuation of therapy should not cause a withdrawal reaction. However, some patients may benefit from a tapered reduction. Withdrawal symptoms that can occur after prolonged treatment include anxiety, hallucinations, insomnia, mood changes, restlessness, sweating and tremor.
- Sleep walking and other associated behaviours have been reported with zopiclone and are usually related to concomitant use of alcohol and other CNS-depressants, or doses above the recommended.
- Zopiclone may modify reactions and patients should be advised not drive (or operate machinery) if affected.

☺ Adverse effects
The frequency is not defined, but reported adverse effects include:
- Aggressiveness
- Anterograde amnesia
- Bitter or metallic after-taste
- Confusion
- Depressed mood
- Dizziness
- Drowsiness
- Dry mouth
- Hallucinations
- Headache
- Irritability
- Nausea and vomiting
- Sleep walking.

Drug interactions

Pharmacokinetic

Zopiclone is metabolized by CYP3A4 (both metabolites formed) and CYP2C8/9 (to the inactive metabolite). Co-administration with drugs that are metabolized by, or affect the activity (induction or inhibition—see 🔲 inside back cover) of these pathways may lead to clinically relevant drug interactions and the prescriber should be aware that dosage adjustments may be necessary, particularly of drugs with a narrow therapeutic index.

* *Erythromycin*—increases plasma concentration and effects of zopiclone. The effect of grapefruit juice on the bioavailability zopiclone is unknown.

Pharmacodynamic

* *CNS depressants*—additive sedative effect.

💊 Dose

* 7.5mg PO ON.

💊 Dose adjustments

Elderly

* Initial dose 3.75mg PO ON. The dose may be increased to 7.5mg PO ON if necessary.

Hepatic/renal impairment

* Initial dose in hepatic impairment is 3.75mg PO ON. The dose can be cautiously increased to 7.5mg PO ON if necessary. Note that zopiclone is contraindicated for patients with severe hepatic impairment.
* Initial dose in renal impairment is 3.75mg PO ON. The dose can be increased to 7.5mg PO ON if necessary.

Additional information

The tablets can be crushed and dispersed in water immediately before use.

🔆 Pharmacology

Zopiclone is a non-benzodiazepine hypnotic agent that initiates and sustains sleep without affecting total REM sleep. It is unlikely to produce a hangover effect. Its pharmacological properties include hypnotic, sedative, anxiolytic, anticonvulsant and muscle-relaxant actions (at higher doses). Zopiclone binds with high affinity to the benzodiazepine receptor, although it is believed to act at a different site to the benzodiazepines. Zopiclone is extensively metabolized to two major metabolites, one active (N-oxide zopiclone) and one inactive (N-desmethyl zopiclone). It is a substrate of CYP3A4 and CYP2C8/9. Both metabolites are excreted via the kidneys.

Index

Cytochrome P450 table

Substrates

CYP1A2	CYP2B6	CYP2C8	CYP2C9	CYP2C19	CYP2D6	CYP2E1	CYP3A4
Amitriptyline	Diclofenac	Diclofenac	Amitriptyline	Amitriptyline	Amitriptyline	Domperidone	Alfentanil
Domperidone	Ketamine	Ibuprofen	Celecoxib	Citalopram	Codeine	Paracetamol	Amitriptyline
Duloxetine	Methadone	Naproxen	Diclofenac	Clopidogrel	Duloxetine	Theophylline	Carbamazepine
Flutamide		Omeprazole	Fluoxetine	Diazepam	Fluoxetine		Citalopram
Haloperidol		Repaglinide	Gliclazide	Diclofenac	Haloperidol		Clonazepam
Mirtazapine		Rosiglitazone	Glimepiride	Esomeprazole	Methylphenidate		Dexamethasone
Naproxen		Tamoxifen	Glipizide	Ibuprofen	Metoclopramide		Diazepam
Olanzapine			Ibuprofen	Lansoprazole	Mirtazapine		Domperidone
Ondansetron			Ketamine	Naproxen	Omeprazole		Esomeprazole
Paracetamol			Metronidazole	Omeprazole	Ondansetron		Etoricoxib
Ropinirole			Naproxen	Pantoprazole	Oxycodone		Exemestane
Theophylline			Omeprazole	Phenobarbital	Paroxetine		Fentanyl
Warfarin			Tamoxifen	Rabeprazole	Promethazine		Finasteride
			Warfarin	Sertraline	Risperidone		Granisetron
				Warfarin	Sertraline		Haloperidol
					Tamoxifen		Ketamine
					Tramadol		Medroxyprogesterone
					Trazodone		Methadone
					Venlafaxine		Methylphenidate
							Metronidazole
							Midazolam
							Mirtazapine
							Modafinil
							Omeprazole
							Ondansetron
							Oxycodone
							Pantoprazole
							Quinine
							Rabeprazole
							Reboxetine
							Risperidone
							Sertraline
							Simvastatin
							Tamoxifen
							Trazodone
							Venlafaxine
							Zopiclone

This table serves as a simple guide to identifying potential cytochrome P450 drug interactions, particularly if unexpected outcomes are experienced. Important points to consider include: drug interactions can depend on genetic factors, there may be competitive inhibition if concurrent drugs are metabolized by the same isoenzyme, interactions can be dose dependent, and time to interaction can be difficult to predict.